Introduction to Cisco Networking Technologies

Cisco Authorized Certification Study Guide for CCNA™ Exams 640-801 and 640-821

WestNet Learning Certification Series

WestNet's Signature Series Courseware

Textbook **Online Course** **Student Resources**

Visit the course companion web site at:

http://www.westnetlearning.com/gateway/srs.asp

You will find **Web Based Support**, **Online Course Links**, and **Practice Quizzes**.

CREDITS

Author and Development Editor: Tawnya K. Sawyer
Editorial Director: Marilee E. Aust
Managing Editor: Mara G. Gaiser
Technical Reviewers: Michael Woznicki, Dave Watts
Book Design and Composition: D. Kari Luraas
Illustrator: Lynn Siefken
Copy Editor: Judith Goode
Senior Copy Editor: Michelle Hanson
Technical Proofreader and Glossary Editor: Larry Beckett
Assistant Copy Editors: Charles Barnitz, Kenneth Chartrand
Proofreader: Betty Reed
Indexer: Amy Casey
Cover Design: David Jones

ISBN: 1-58676-146-3 (softcover)
Printed in the United States of America

Sawyer, Tawnya K.
CCNA, Introduction to Cisco Networking Technologies
800 pp., includes illustrations and index

1. Internetworking Review 2. IP Protocol Suite 3. IP Addressing and Subnetting 4. Router IOS
5. Managing and Troubleshooting the Network

VPS51.2

For instructor-led training, self-paced courses, turn-key curricula solutions, or more information contact:

WestNet Learning (dba: WestNet Inc.)
5420 Ward Road, Suite 150, Arvada, CO 80002 USA
E-mail: Info@westnetlearning.com

To access the WestNet student resource site, go to
http://www.westnetlearning.com/student

WESTNET LEARNING

Cisco® Authorized
•• COURSEWARE ••

Contents at a Glance

Contents

Figures

Preface

Introduction to Cisco Networking Technologies (CCNA INTRO) is the first volume in a two-book certification study guide that prepares students to take and pass the Cisco Certified Network Associate (CCNA) exam. This first volume provides materials and test questions that help prepare students for the exam 640-821 (INTRO). To successfully take the 640-801 exam (INTRO and ICND), students must study both this volume, as well as the second volume, *Interconnecting Cisco Networking Devices (CCNA ICND)*.

In the process of preparing students for the CCNA certification exam, *Introduction to Cisco Networking Technologies* imparts a well-rounded knowledge of Cisco's Router and Switch IOS, while reinforcing many network fundamentals. After laying a foundation of networking concepts, this certification study guide discusses higher-level topics and provides hands-on activities that provide the skills necessary to administer a network in a working environment.

Another useful—as well as targeted—component of this study program is the online, media-rich CCNA-INTRO course, which incorporates multimedia and interactivity to teach you the most essential CCNA certification information. You will only find an online course of this high caliber from WestNet Learning.

CCNA Certification Paths

The CCNA is one of the highest-ranking and honored certifications currently available in the information technology industry. It maintains this standing by being comprehensive and difficult to achieve. By successfully completing the CCNA, you validate your skills and knowledge and increase your marketability. You also lay the groundwork necessary for progressing through Cisco's professional path to the CCNP and CCIE certifications. The following table shows the WestNet study guides that will prepare you for CCNA certification exams.

CCNA Certification Paths

WestNet Course	Cisco Exam
EMERGING NETWORK PROFESSIONALS	
Introduction to Cisco Networking Technologies	Exam 640-821
Interconnecting Cisco Network Devices (ICND) 2.1	Exam 640-811
EXPERIENCED NETWORK PROFESSIONALS	
Interconnecting Cisco Network Devices (ICND) 2.1	Exam 640-801

For additional information on Cisco's certification programs, test requirements, or training centers, visit Cisco's Web site at **www.cisco.com** and select the Learning & Events link, and then the Career Certifications & Paths link.

Prerequisites

Because this is an introductory course, Cisco does not define any prerequisites. However, the CCNA exams cover topics that require a solid understanding of network fundamentals. To get the most out of this course and material, it is suggested that you prepare using the core curriculum of *Introduction to Networking, Introduction to Local Area Networks, Introduction to TCP/IP,* and *Introduction to Wide Area Networks,* offered by WestNet Learning. You may also find it helpful to develop additional knowledge in *Internetworking Devices, Protocol Analysis,* and *Network Design.* WestNet offers a variety of courses and books that complement the CCNA program and provide a thorough understanding of network fundamentals.

Who Should Study This Course?

If you are a networking professional who wants to obtain CCNA certification or re-certification, using this study guide can significantly increase your chances of passing the new CCNA exam(s). Candidates new to CCNA or to networking can use this comprehensive course to prepare for Cisco's intense exams, while this course can also serve as a simple refresher for experienced networking professionals who are pursuing re-certification and need to learn new exam information.

There are many compelling reasons for passing the CCNA exam. By successfully completing the CCNA, you validate your skills and knowledge and increase your "marketability" in comparison to your peers. Other reasons for obtaining CCNA certification are to:

- Increase your compensation and future earning potential
- Improve productivity
- Enhance professional credibility
- Improve your chances of finding employment

You will also lay the groundwork necessary for progressing through Cisco's certification professional path to the higher level CCNP and CCIE certifications.

Key Topics

- Computer hardware basics, binary and hexadecimal number systems, basic networking terminology, and internetworking concepts
- Major components of a network system, including clients and servers, network interface cards (NICs), internetworking devices, media, and topologies
- Functions, operations, and primary components of local area networks (LANs), wide area networks (WANs), metropolitan area networks (MANs), storage area networks (SANs), content networks (CNs), and virtual private networks (VPNs)
- Major network access methods
- Functions and operations of switching technologies
- Format and significance of each of the following components to a network system: IP addressing, classes, reserved address space, and subnetting

- Calculating valid subnetwork addresses and mask values so that user/network requirements are met when given an IP address scheme
- Purposes of networking addresses, routing protocols, and routed protocols
- Function, operation, and primary components of WAN technologies
- Function, operation, and primary components required to provide remote access services
- Configuration tools for establishing connectivity to the appropriate network device to complete the initial device configuration

CCNA Exam Information

The following sections will answer some questions you may have about taking the CCNA exam. For additional information on Cisco's certification programs, test requirements, or training centers, visit Cisco's Web site at **www.cisco.com** and select the Learning & Events link, and then the Career Certifications & Paths link.

CCNA Exam Objectives

The CCNA requires knowledge of Cisco router and Catalyst switch products used in the workgroup and network backbone environment. It also demands an understanding of many fundamental networking topics, such as the OSI model, the Internet Protocol (IP) suite, IP subnetting, Ethernet connectivity, and the ability to define and interconnect network devices.

The following table lists the objectives for CCNA exam 640-821 (INTRO) and the corresponding *CCNA INTRO* lessons in which they are covered.

Objectives for CCNA Exam 640-821 (INTRO) Objectives © 2003 Cisco Systems. Visit www.cisco.com for current information on CCNA certification.	**To meet this objective, study ALL of:**
Describe and install the hardware and software required to be able to communicate via a network.	Module 1, All Lessons
Demonstrate the mathematical skills required to work seamlessly with integer, decimal, binary, and hexadecimal numbers and simple binary logic.	Module 1, Lesson 1
Describe the role of a router in a WAN.	Module 1, Lesson 3
Compare and contrast collision and broadcast domains and describe the process of network segmentation.	Module 1, Lesson 3
Define and describe the structure and technologies of computer networks.	Module 2, Lessons 1 and 2
Identify the key characteristics of common wide area networking (WAN) configurations and technologies, and differentiate between these and common LAN technologies.	Module 2, Lesson 2
Describe the principles and practice of switching in an Ethernet network.	Module 2, Lesson 1
Explain how collisions are detected and handled in an Ethernet system.	Module 2, Lesson 1
Explain the fundamental concepts associated with the Ethernet media access technique.	Module 2, Lesson 1
Describe and install the hardware and software required to be able to communicate via a network.	Module 3, Lessons 1 and 2
Describe the physical, electrical, and mechanical properties and standards associated with optical, wireless, and copper media used in networks.	Module 3, Lesson 1
Describe the topologies and physical issues associated with cabling common LANs.	Module 3, Lesson 2

Objectives for CCNA Exam 640-821 (INTRO) Objectives © 2003 Cisco Systems. Visit www.cisco.com for current information on CCNA certification.	**To meet this objective, study ALL of:**
Describe and install the hardware and software required to be able to communicate via a network. Compare and contrast collision and broadcast domains, and describe the process of network segmentation. Describe the principles and practice of switching in an Ethernet network.	Module 4, Lessons 1 and 2 Module 4, Lesson 1 Module 4, Lesson 2
Describe how the protocols associated with TCP/IP allow host communication to occur. Describe the principles and practice of packet switching utilizing the Internet Protocol (IP). Describe the operation of the Internet Control Message Protocol (ICMP) and identify the reasons, types, and format of associated error and control message.	Module 5, All Lessons Module 5, Lesson 1 Module 5, Lesson 1
Determine IP addresses. Describe the concepts associated with routing, and the different methods and protocols used to achieve it. Describe how an IP address is associated with a device interface. Employ IP addressing techniques. Describe the principles and practice of packet switching utilizing the Internet Protocol (IP).	Module 6, Lesson 1 Module 6, Lessons 3 and 4 Module 6, Lesson 1 Module 6, Lessons 1 and 2 Module 6, Lessons 3 and 4
Identify the key characteristics of common wide area networking (WAN) configurations and technologies, and differentiate between these and common LAN technologies. Describe the role of a router in a WAN.	Module 7, All Lessons Module 7, Lesson 1

Objectives for CCNA Exam 640-821 (INTRO) Objectives © 2003 Cisco Systems. Visit www.cisco.com for current information on CCNA certification.	**To meet this objective, study ALL of:**
Perform an initial configuration on a router and save the resultant configuration file.	Module 8, Lesson 3
Assign IP addresses.	Module 8, Lessons 2 and 3
Describe and install the hardware and software required to be able to communicate via a network.	Module 8, All Lessons
Describe the purpose and fundamental operation of the internetwork operating system (IOS).	Module 8, Lesson 1
Use a subset of Cisco IOS commands to analyze and report network problems.	Module 9, All Lessons
Use embedded layer 3 through layer 7 protocols to establish, test, suspend, or disconnect connectivity to remote devices from the router console.	Module 9, Lesson 2
Manipulate system image and device configuration files.	Module 9, Lesson 4
Establish communication between a terminal device and the router IOS, and use IOS for system analysis.	Module 9, All Lessons
Use embedded Data Link Layer functionality to perform network neighbor discovery and analysis from the router.	Module 9, Lesson 1
Identify the major internal and external components of a router, and describe the associated functionality.	Module 9, Lesson 3
Identify and describe the stages of the router boot-up sequence.	Module 9, Lesson 3
Describe how the configuration register and boot system commands modify the router boot-up sequence.	Module 9, Lesson 3

Frequently Asked Questions

Q: Where do I register to take the CCNA certification exam?

A: You can register for your exam at **www.vue.com/cisco** or at **www.2test.com**.

Q: How can I find out what to expect when taking a Cisco Career Certifications exam at a testing center?

A: An Exam Interface Tutorial is provided for your review at **http://www.cisco.com/go/examtutorial**. It is recommended that you become familiar with the exam's functionality before test day so you are focused on the exam questions rather than how to correctly use the tools. Remember! Only authorized Cisco Learning Partners offer Cisco simulation training necessary to prepare you for the certification exams properly.

Q: The Course Simulation and Exam Interface Tutorial do not allow abbreviated commands; do Cisco certification exams allow abbreviated commands?

A: Yes, the router simulations in the Cisco certification exams will accept abbreviated commands that an actual Cisco router will understand. For example: `'Show running-config'` or `'Sh run'` and `'Router#show ip protocol'` or `'router#show ip prot'` would be acceptable. The exam commands must include the correct spacing, spelling and marks (#@!?).

Helpful Hints

Here are some helpful hints for the day of the exam:

- Obtain driving directions to the testing site.
- Arrive at the testing site at least 15 minutes prior to your scheduled exam time.
- Bring two forms of identification. (Both with your signature and one must be a Government Issued Photo ID.)
- All Cisco exams are closed book, no personal items will be allowed in the testing area. (No pagers, cellular phones, calculators, bags, dictionaries, books, or non-authorized paper.)
- You might receive a 15-minute survey prior to your exam. This survey is used to collect information regarding Cisco's testing audience and to improve the exam (This survey does not count as part of the exam testing time.)
- Before the start of the exam the system will provide the number of exam questions, the passing score for that particular exam, and the exam time.

- Cisco Career Certification exams do not allow skipping or marking a question to answer later. You must select the best answer, as you will not be able to return to the question once you have proceeded to the next question.
- All exams require the acceptance of the terms and conditions in the Cisco Systems Confidentiality Agreement. Candidates must acknowledge the Cisco Systems Confidentiality Agreement on-line at the authorized testing center prior to taking an exam.
- A text document may be provided explaining the types of exam questions prior to the exam start time. A free Exam Interface Tutorial is also provided for review at **www.cisco.com/go/examtutorial**. *It is recommended that you become familiar with the exam functionality before sitting an exam so you are focused on the exam questions rather than how to correctly use the tools. The tutorial will familiarize you with the software tools used in the Career Certification exams.*
- Please note that exams are proctored, timed, and delivered in a secure environment.
- When the exam is completed you will be asked to accept the terms and conditions of the Cisco Career Certifications Agreement. Signing this legal agreement is required to be officially certified and to receive your certificate.
- You will receive a score report, which includes a score breakout by exam section and the passing score for that given exam.
- Visit the Career Certifications Tracking System (**https://www.certmanager.net/cisco/login.aspx?ReturnUrl=%2fCisco%2fDefault.aspx**) 10 days after completing an exam to verify your current mailing address in order to ensure proper delivery of your certificate.
- Allow up to six weeks for delivery of the certificate and an additional two weeks for international shipments from the mail out date specified in the Career Certifications Tracking System.

WestNet's Blended Learning Solution for CCNA

WestNet has developed the most comprehensive CCNA certification preparation packages available today. You can choose from the following tools that comprise WestNet's blended learning solution for CCNA:

- Two complete certification study guides (*CCNA INTRO* and *CCNA ICND*, v.2.1)
- Two media-rich, Web-based courses with content-rich remediation (*CCNA INTRO* and *CCNA ICND*, v.2.1)
- Pathways certification prep assessments with learning plans
- E-Labs for structured lab exercises with live servers and routers

How Do I Use This Course?

This certification study guide is designed to prepare you to take CCNA exam 640-821 (INTRO), as well as instruct you in a significant amount of the topics covered on CCNA exam 640-801 (INTRO and ICND).

By reading the comprehensive material in this study guide, written by expert IT instructor Tawnya K. Sawyer, and by completing all the review questions, extended activities, and quizzes in each lesson of this book, you will be well on your way to obtaining CCNA certification.

The following sections describe the standard instructional hallmarks found in WestNet study guides. These features will help you obtain CCNA certification.

Figure Icons

Throughout this course, the following figure icons represent networking devices:

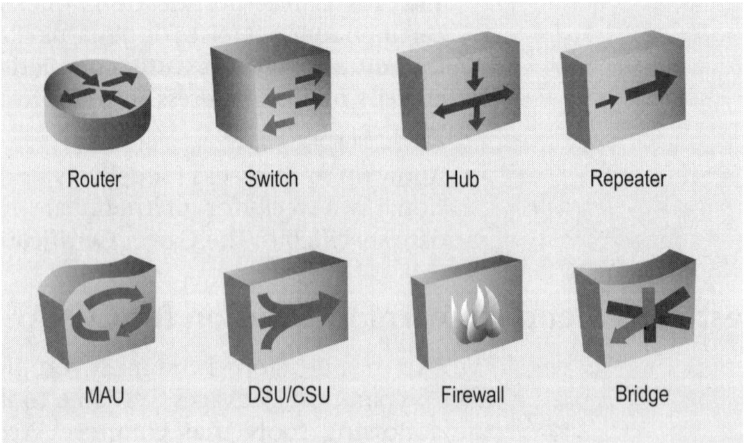

Real-World Scenarios

Several instructional features are included in this text to enhance the presentation of the materials so that you can easily understand the concepts and apply them. Throughout the book, emphasis is placed on applying real-world scenarios through review questions, extended activities, labs, and other exercises and examples.

Pedagogy

Learning objectives, module summaries, review questions, and extended activities are designed to function as integrated study tools. Learning objectives reflect what you should be able to accomplish after completing each module. Module summaries highlight the key concepts you should master. The review questions help guide critical thinking about those key concepts, and the extended activities provide you with opportunities to practice important techniques.

Key Terms

The information technology (IT) field includes many unique terms that are critical to creating a workable language when it is combined with the world of business. Definitions of key terms are provided in alphabetical order in a glossary at the end of the book.

Resources Available in Instructor-Led Settings

When this course is used in an academic or instructor-led setting, an Instructor's Resource Tool Kit accompanies it. The online-based kit includes an Instructor's Guide with the answers to review questions, extended activities, module quizzes, and the End-of-Course Exam. It also includes PowerPoint presentations organized by lesson, module, and course. WestNet Learning Technologies' cutting edge administrative tools offer unique, online Windows-based exam software. The Instructor's Resource site also includes sample syllabi, discussion topics, puzzles, cryptograms, and up-to-the-minute additions to the textbooks and supplemental course materials. The online course exam engine includes hundreds of lesson, module, and course questions. These questions can be accessed by individual students and are presented in randomized order, ensuring that students never get the same question in the same order. This feature allows instructors to create printed and online pretests, practice tests, and actual examinations.

Why Choose WestNet?

WestNet Learning offers comprehensive IT educational and certification programs and curricula to secondary schools, colleges and universities, as well as corporations, resellers, and individual participants around the globe. These programs provide participants with the tools necessary to further their technical knowledge and to obtain hands-on experience. This unique program, which is vendor neutral, helps prepare participants to pursue IT careers, earn secondary and post-secondary educational degrees, and/or obtain industry certification.

WestNet Learning's programs are currently provided to more than 1,000 institutions around the world. Its programs are offered internationally in more than a dozen countries and in five languages.

Introduction

Introduction to Cisco Networking Technologies (CCNA INTRO) is the first volume in a two part, Cisco-authorized study program that helps you prepare for the most current versions of Cisco's gateway certification exam: the Cisco Certified Network Associate (CCNA). *CCNA INTRO* prepares you for exam 640-821 and exam 640-801.

In addition to helping you master all the learning objectives for exams 640-801, 640-811, and 640-821, *CCNA INTRO* and *Interconnecting Cisco Network Devices (CCNA ICND)* cover the hands-on administration skills you need to walk into a job environment. You will learn to design, install, configure, and securely operate and maintain LAN and WAN services for small and medium networks (100 or fewer nodes), including the use of these and other technology components: IP, RIP, IGRP, EIGRP, OSPF, VLANs, Ethernet, Access Lists, dial-up connections, ISDN, and frame relay.

Although you are the only one who can guarantee your success, choosing a study program innovated by WestNet Learning is a wise first step toward serious CCNA exam preparation. Experienced networking insiders recognize WestNet Learning as one of the most effective and meticulous courseware developers in the IT industry.

Course Overview

The first volume of this certification study guide provides a foundational knowledge of many important areas in networking, technology, and computing. Mastering this information is essential to understanding connectivity, protocols, transmissions, and interoperability. Without this knowledge, more advanced topics in the second volume, *CCNA ICND*, will be difficult for you to comprehend and retain.

This study guide begins with an overview of computing that includes topics such as PC components, measurement terms, and the decimal, binary, and hexadecimal number conversion processes. Understanding decimal to binary conversions is important to successfully learning the subnetting steps covered later in the first volume. The next lesson covers network fundamentals, discussing important terminology used throughout the text and in the field. The highlight of this lesson is the Open Systems Interconnect (OSI) model, which is later compared to the IP suite. Lesson 3 discusses network devices by highlighting the important characteristics of repeaters, hubs, bridges, switches, routers, and layer 3 switches. The last lesson in Module 1 discusses the network topologies commonly used in local area networks (LANs). This lesson ends with a review of the mesh and cloud or service provider network topologies often found in wide area network (WAN) implementations.

The first lesson in Module 2 provides a more in depth discussion of LAN technologies. First it defines how the Data Link Layer is divided into the Media Access Control (MAC) and Logical Link Control (LLC) sublayers. The International Electrical and Electronic Engineer's (IEEE) specifications for Ethernet, Token, and FDDI are briefly reviewed. The rest of the lesson is dedicated to Ethernet technology because it is the most predominant and supported networking method. Lesson 2 reviews many important WAN terms, components, physical connectors, transmission rates and protocols. Finishing off Module 2 is a discussion of other network topology types including: campus area networks (CANs), metro area networks (MANs), storage area networks (SANs), content networks (CNs), and virtual private networks (VPNs). A brief discussion of intranets and extranets rounds out this informative module.

Module 3 delves into cable and wireless media types. Lesson 1 highlights the important points about unshielded twisted pair (UTP) and shielded twisted pair (STP), as well as the two types of coax cooper cable. It also discusses the properties of multimode and singlemode fiber optic cable. Then it reviews the various wireless options and details the IEEE 802.11 group of wireless transmission standards. Lesson 2 is focused on cabling a LAN with Electronic Industry Association/Telecommunications Industry Association EIA/TIA 568A/B standards for UTP cable. Emphasis is placed on determining when to use a straight-through, crossover or rollover cable, and how to establish a console connection. The final lesson describes how to cable a WAN.

Module 4 addresses switching fundamentals. Lesson 1 discusses LAN transmissions and how they share the available network bandwidth. The lesson introduces the essential terms collision domain and broadcast domain, which describe network access and device functionality. Bridging and switching is discussed in lesson 2. Although different in how they operate, both devices learn and store MAC address information to make filter and forward decisions. Also discussed are redundant network topologies, the potential for active loops, and how the Spanning Tree Protocol (STP) helps prevent issues. Finally, lesson 3 highlights VLANs, a method used to logically segment broadcast domains and allow for complete administrative control using layer 2 switches.

Module 5 focuses on the IP Protocol Suite (commonly referred to as TCP/IP). Lesson 1 provides an overview of Network Layer protocols, including the Internet Protocol (IP), Address Resolution Protocol (ARP), Reverse Address Resolution Protocol (RARP) and Internetwork Message Control Protocol (ICMP). Lesson 2 identifies the Transport Layer components: Transmission Control Protocol (TCP) for connection-oriented transmissions and User Datagram Protocol (UDP) for connectionless transmissions. Lesson 3 discusses a few of the upper layer applications used for e-mail, Web services, administration, and file transfers. After reviewing this module you will have a better understanding about the entire IP suite, not just TCP/IP.

Module 6 covers IP addressing, subnetting, and routing. The table used during the decimal to binary conversion process is also helpful for defining classes of addresses and performing the steps necessary for subnetting. Lesson 1 provides a detailed look at IP address classes A, B, C, and D. Also included in this lesson are updates about IPv6, a newer 128-bit IP addressing scheme, and Classless Internet Domain Routing (CIDR). Lesson 2 will give you practice performing the calculations involved in subnetting. The last two lessons in this module describe how the routing process occurs. Lesson 4 also details how the routing protocols are categorized both by their location (Interior Gateway Protocols – IGPs and Exterior Gateway Protocols – EGPs), and how they operate (Distance Vector vs. Link State). Finally, Module 6 ends with a brief review of RIP, IGRP, EIGRP, OSPF, and BGP.

Module 7 reviews WAN technologies commonly found in small to medium size networks. Lesson 1 discusses common telecommunications and WAN terminology. Lesson 2 identifies the characteristics of High-Level Data Link Control Protocol (HDLC), Point-to-Point Protocol (PPP), Integrated Services Digital Network (ISDN), frame relay, xDSL, Asynchronous Transfer Mode (ATM), and SONET. Lesson 3 discussed modem communications for analog services, as well as cable modem connections.

Module 8 finally gives students a chance to work with Cisco equipment and the command line interface. Lesson 1 opens with the features from the Internetwork Operating System (IOS) found on most Cisco switch and router devices. It also discusses the general bootup process, connecting to a device, and gaining access to the command line through user EXEC and then privileged EXEC modes. The information in Lesson 2 is specific to Catalyst switch startup, initial configuration, and basic commands. Lesson 3 prepares you to use the command line interface on a router by discussing the initial setup scripts, login process, help features, edit keys, and error messages. Lesson 4 shows you how to use configuration commands to set up IP address(es), a hostname, Ethernet and serial interfaces, passwords and other parameters. It also discusses a number of show commands used to verify and display information.

Module 9 describes how to manage a network with a number of different components. Lesson 1 discusses the Cisco proprietary protocol used to identify neighboring devices. Cisco Discovery Protocol (CDP) is topology and protocol independent and is an effective way to document network infrastructures. Lesson 2 highlights Telnet, which is used to provide remote console connections to a network device for administration purposes. Lesson 3 is an important topic about the router hardware components and the software defined configuration register. Lesson 4 instructs you to backup and restore IOS and configuration files using a TFTP server. Finally, Lesson 5 discusses some additional tools used to troubleshoot and help administration, such as ping, traceroute, and name resolutions services.

~Tawnya K. Sawyer, Author
CCNA INTRO and *CCNA ICND* Certification Study Guides

How to Contact the Author

You can send an e-mail to Tawnya K. Sawyer at:

tsawyer@westnetlearning.com

Module 1
Introduction to Networking

It is important to start by laying the foundation for the upcoming modules, rather than jumping into a discussion of configuring routers and switches. Thus, Lesson 1 defines the basics of computer hardware, network interface cards (NICs), and measurement terms. It also discusses the important topic of binary, decimal, and hexadecimal numbering conventions.

Lesson 2 begins with network terminology and defines the purpose and function of networks. It also reviews the Open Systems Interconnection (OSI) reference model. The OSI model is an industry-recognized standard that is taught in many courses. You may already be aware of each layer's responsibility and the protocols found there. It is helpful to review and even learn more details about this important reference.

The end of this lesson shows how each of the layers are used to build the frame for transmission. When the sender is adding headers to the information being sent, it is called encapsulation. On the receiving end, the headers are stripped away during decapsulation. The IP suite is compared to the OSI model, and a number of IP applications are discussed.

Lesson 3 discusses network devices. It begins with the functionality of Layer 1 devices—repeaters and hubs. The lesson moves on to Layer 2 devices—NICs, bridges, and switches; then on to Layer 3 devices—routers and multilayer switches. Each plays an important role in providing connectivity and data transmission. Lesson 3 includes other network devices that are found in LAN, WAN, and service provider networks.

Lesson 4 covers network topologies. It begins with a discussion of the difference between physical and logical topologies. It moves on to the historic bus and ring topologies. Star and star-ring topologies are also discussed as the more prominent LAN topology types. For WAN environments, mesh and service provider clouds are the two main options.

Lessons

1. Computing Basics
2. Networking Fundamentals
3. Network Devices
4. Network Topologies

Lesson 1—Computing Basics

This lesson tells you what you need to know to understand the basics of computers. It begins with an overview of the components commonly found in PCs and laptops. It goes on to discuss the characteristics of NICs. Before getting into extensive networking discussions, you will also learn the terms used to define transmission and storage measurements.

The remainder of this lesson focuses on the important topic of conversion between the different numbering schemes: decimal, binary, and hexadecimal. In all cases, the numbers are created with a single byte, also called an octet.

An octet or byte is 8 binary digits (bits), or eight 0s and 1s. When eight 0s and 1s are displayed, the number is represented in binary format. This is the format read by computer systems and used for transmitting information through a network.

Displaying in binary format can take a lot of space because each character is represented as 8 bits. Just imagine if you were viewing this book in 1s and 0s: you would think you were in the Matrix.

To condense this string of 0s and 1s, systems often represent the information in hexadecimal format. Hexadecimal notation is another numbering convention frequently used in the computer industry.

After learning the information in this lesson and working through the problems, you will understand how conversion works and be prepared to work the problems on an exam.

Objectives

At the end of this lesson you will be able to:

- Identify PC and laptop components
- Discuss the key features and functions of a NIC
- Define network transmission and storage measurement terms
- Convert decimal numbers to binary
- Convert binary numbers to decimal
- Convert to hexadecimal numbers

Key Point

More than one numbering scheme is used in the technology industry. It is important to recognize decimal, binary, and hexadecimal numbers and understand how to convert between them.

PC and Laptop Components

The following sections discuss the key components of personal computers (PCs) and laptop computers.

CPU

A central processing unit (CPU) is the brain of a computer. It executes the instructions in a computer program and directs the flow of information within the computer. At the heart of a CPU is a microprocessor (a highly complex integrated circuit chip), thus the terms "microprocessor" (also called "processor") and "CPU" are often used interchangeably. Two basic characteristics differentiate microprocessors:

- **Data bus size**—The size of the bus refers to the number of data bits a CPU can work on in a single instruction.
- **Clock speed**—The clock speed indicates how many instructions per second the processor can execute. Each "tick" of the clock is called a cycle, thus clock speed is measured in thousands of cycles per second. A single cycle per second is called 1 hertz (Hz), 1,000 Hz is 1 kilohertz (kHz), 1 million Hz is 1 megahertz (MHz), and 1 billion Hz is 1 gigahertz (GHz). Thus, a CPU that runs at 400,000,000 cycles per second is a 400-MHz processor.

For both characteristics, the higher the value, the more powerful the CPU. If two processors have the same bus size, the one with the higher clock speed will perform more work in the same time. If two CPUs have the same clock speed, the one with the larger data bus can process more data during each cycle.

The majority of all IBM-type PCs incorporate a single Intel architecture processor, such as Pentium. Apple PCs are based on a different processor from Motorola. The difference in these processor architectures is why these two types of computers have fundamentally different characteristics. Although Intel is the world's largest microprocessor manufacturer, it does not have the entire PC processor market. For example, Advanced Micro Devices (AMD) manufactures processors comparable to the Intel Pentium processor.

I/O

Input refers to data that enters a computer from the outside, such as keystrokes from a keyboard, mouse movements, or incoming data from another device on a network. Output is data a computer sends to the outside world, such as print jobs, alert beeps, images on the monitor screen, or outgoing data to be sent to another part of the network.

The input/output (I/O) of a computer is controlled by a program called the Basic Input/Output System (BIOS). This program contains the most basic instructions in the computer and is permanently written to an area of read-only memory (ROM), described later in this module.

I/O data travels over its own bus, which is a collection of wires that connect all internal computer components to the CPU, main memory, and each other. The I/O bus transmits incoming and outgoing data from one part of a computer to another.

The term "local bus" usually refers to a fast internal bus that connects devices directly to a CPU. An "expansion bus" connects expansion boards to the CPU and memory, as illustrated on the Computer I/O Bus Diagram.

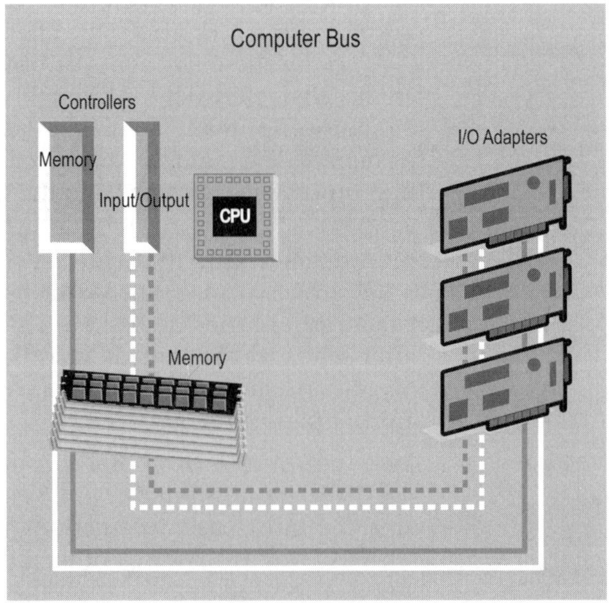

Computer I/O Bus

All buses consist of two parts: an address bus and a data bus. The data bus transfers the data, and the address bus transfers information about where the data should go. There are two basic types of I/O bus:

- A serial bus streams data, 1 bit at a time, as do cars on a one-lane road.
- A parallel bus is like a multilane highway that transmits many bits simultaneously, using multiple transmission channels or wires. The size of a parallel bus, called its width, is important because it determines how much data can be transmitted at one time. For example, a 16-bit bus transmits 16 bits of data simultaneously, and a 32-bit bus transmits 32 bits of data.

Every bus has a clock speed measured in MHz. A fast bus allows data to be transferred faster, making applications run faster. On PCs, the older 16-bit Industry Standard Architecture (ISA) expansion bus is being replaced by faster buses, such as the 32-bit

Peripheral Component Interconnect (PCI) bus. Newer PCs also include a local bus for data that requires especially fast transfer speeds, such as video data. The Bus Characteristics Table shows common bus technologies and their performance.

Bus Characteristics

Bus	Width (bits)	Speed (MHz)	Bandwidth (MB/sec)
8-bit ISA	8	8.33	8.3
16-bit ISA	16	8.33	16.6
Extended Industry Standard Architecture (EISA)	32	8.33	32
32-bit PCI	32	33	132
64-bit PCI	64	66	533.3
Universal Serial Bus (USB)	serial		1.2
FireWire	serial		80
USB 2.0	serial		12

The width of a bus describes the number of bits the bus can carry at one time. The term "bandwidth" describes the overall data-carrying capacity of a bus.

To find the bus bandwidth, multiply the bus width by the bus clock speed, then divide the result by the number of bits in a byte (8). The result is expressed in megabytes per second (Mbps), which means 1 million bytes per second.

For example, the bandwidth of the PCI bus is 32 bits * 33 MHz = 1,056,000 bits per second (bps). Divide this figure by 8 bits, and the resulting bandwidth is 132 Mbps.

Note: This is an instantaneous data burst rate figure; the average bandwidth is much lower.

Memory

A computer's memory holds data being worked on by the CPU; it is the computer's short-term storage. The term "memory" generally refers to random access memory (RAM), which comes in the form of integrated circuit chips that plug into the main circuit board (motherboard) of the computer.

The word "memory," often refers to the chips themselves. RAM is typically volatile, which means it needs a constant supply of electricity to hold data. If the power goes off, all data in RAM is lost.

The term "storage" is used to describe media that hold data for longer periods, even when the power goes off. Typically, computers use magnetic tapes or disks for long-term storage. However, in some cases, the concepts of memory and storage overlap.

Some computers can use hard disk storage to supplement RAM in a system called "virtual memory." Personal digital assistants (PDAs) and other small devices without a disk drive, often store data in programmable memory, described later in this lesson.

When you run a program, it is read from storage, such as a hard drive or compact disk read-only memory (CD-ROM) drive and put into memory for execution. After the program has completed or is no longer needed, it is typically removed from memory.

Every computer comes with a certain amount of RAM, and this supply can usually be increased by adding more memory chips. A computer that has 1 megabyte (MB) of RAM can hold approximately 1 million bytes of information. One byte can typically represent one letter of the alphabet or one numeral.

There are several different types of memory:

- **RAM**—RAM is the same as main memory. When used by itself, the term "RAM" refers to read and write memory; that is, you can both write data into RAM and read data from RAM. This is in contrast to ROM, which permits a user to read only data.

  Most RAM is volatile, which means it requires a steady flow of electricity to maintain its contents. As soon as the power is turned off, whatever data was in RAM is lost.

- **ROM**—Unlike RAM, ROM cannot be written to after it is first programmed. However, the data in ROM is nonvolatile; data is not lost if the power is turned off. Computers almost always contain a small amount of ROM that holds instructions for starting up the computer.

- **Programmable read-only memory (PROM)**—A PROM is a memory chip on which you can store a program. After the PROM has been programmed, you cannot wipe it clean and reprogram it.
- **Erasable programmable read-only memory (EPROM)**—An EPROM is a special type of PROM that can be erased by exposing it to ultraviolet light. An EPROM can be reprogrammed and reused after it has been erased. If a computer's BIOS program is stored in EPROM, the BIOS can be upgraded when necessary.
- **Electrically erasable programmable read-only memory (EEPROM)**—This type of PROM can be erased and reprogrammed by an electrical signal, without having to remove the chip from its device. This makes it possible for a device to use EEPROM to record changeable data.

  However, although the number of times an EEPROM can be reprogrammed is large, it is also limited. Thus, EEPROM is not useful for main working memory.
- **Flash ROM**—This type of EEPROM is faster to erase and reprogram because it operates on large blocks of memory; in contrast, an EEPROM can alter individual bytes. Thus, Flash ROM is commonly used in devices that must store settings and messages, such as cellular phones.

The Motherboard

The main component in a computer is the motherboard, also called the system board or the main board. It is the largest circuit board in the system and provides a foundation upon which the rest of the system is built.

The motherboard has the greatest impact on the performance and scalability of the system. It determines which and how many processors can be installed, how much memory the system can manage, and the number of peripheral devices that can be added.

Other components in the system are attached to the motherboard using expansion slots. Cards fit into the expansion slots to provide network access, video/graphics, music and sound, game ports, and many other components. Manufacturers can also hardwire these components directly to the motherboard, offering more available expansion slots for customers to use.

Storage Components

Storage is different from memory in that storage is a more permanent location for data that does not go away when the system is turned off. There are many different types of storage media available, depending upon the amount and mobility requirements. The following list describes common storage media options:

- **Floppy disk drive**—Drive used to read and write data. Now these are mostly high-density 3.5-inch diskettes for 1.5 Mb of storage capacity.
- **CD-ROM**—A read-only device that can be used to retrieve information stored on CDs.
- **CD-RW**—A CD drive that has both read and write capabilities. Using the right media, the CD can be written to more than once. Capacity is generally around 800 Mb.
- **Tape drives**—Different size tape drives used as backup media because they are not particularly fast access methods. Capacity is variable.
- **Jazz and zip drives**—Removable media that allow for high-density storage. The only drawback with these drives is that, unlike a floppy drive or CD-ROM, their disk drives are not commonly installed on PC systems.
- **Hard disks**—Used for high-capacity, long-term storage.

Other components worth mentioning that are also important parts of any PC or laptop include:

- **Expansion card**—A manufactured circuit board that plugs into an expansion slot in the motherboard. Each card provides a specific function such as high-resolution video and graphics, audio and music input or output, game ports, a NIC, modem capabilities, and many others.
- **Power supply**—Provides proper power voltages to all internal components. Does not shield power or protect the system from power surges or drops. An external power strip should be purchased for that purpose.
- **Video display**—A monitor's image, the type and quality of which are determined both by the monitor itself and by a circuit board called a "video adapter," "video card," or "graphics adapter." The monitor plugs into the video adapter or video port, which generates the signals that produce visible images.

Backplane Connections

The backplane connections are usually found on the back of the system, often the most inconvenient location. Many manufactures have begun to add some of these connections to the front of systems to enable users to easily connect such items as audio or video recording equipment and cameras. The majority of these connections are also available on laptops, although they may be on the back, either side, or on a docking station:

- **Video connection**—Used for connecting to a monitor, overhead display, or TV hookup.
- **Keyboard**—Uses either a small, round, IBM Personal System/2 (PS/2)-style connector or a larger, round IBM Advanced Technology (AT)-style connector.
- **Mouse**—Serial, bus, or universal serial bus (USB) mouse options have various different connector styles.
- **Power**—Used to plug in a power cord.
- **Serial port(s)**—Also called COM ports, they are used for mouse devices, keyboards, console connections to routers or switches, serial printers, and many other external peripherals. Bits are transmitted one at a time over a serial port.
- **Parallel port(s)**—Also called LPT ports, used mainly to connect printers. Parallel ports are also used to provide a security lock (called a "dongle") for certain software packages. Parallel ports send 8 bits simultaneously.
- **Universal Serial Bus (USB) port(s)**—Provide connections to printers, scanners, cameras, video and audio equipment, and much more. They are handy because they automatically recognize the device and do not require rebooting to gain access. Systems today have fewer standard serial and parallel ports and more USBs. USBs are put on the front of computers for easy connections.
- **Network interface card (NIC)**—May be in an expansion slot or built onto the motherboard. The NIC requires a specific cable type, a minimum of CAT 3 Unshielded Twisted Pair UTP cable with an RJ-45 connector. Note: 10/100 NICs donnott have to be connected with Cat5 (Cat 3 supports 10 Mpbs), but they should be.
- **Sound card**—Used to connect speakers and/or headphones.

- **Modem jack**—Internal modem connection through a telephone cable to the phone jack.
- **Firewire port**—Used for very high speed and quality digital transmissions of video, photos, and audio information.

Laptop Components

Laptops are just smaller, more compact versions of full-sized computers. The keyboard, monitor, and mouse have all been integrated into one handy package. Laptops do not always have the same number or type of ports as a standard PC. In addition, they cannot usually be opened like a PC case to install additional cards.

Instead, the key features most often used on laptops are built directly into the system. Common components include the NIC, modem, serial port, USB ports, monitor hookup, CD-ROM drive, sometimes a floppy drive, built-in speakers, headphone jack, and microphone jack.

Laptops usually have fixed harddrives, which have a preset capacity. They may have drive bays, which allow harddrives, and CD-ROM and floppy drives, to be interchanged as necessary. It is also common to see a CD-ROM, floppy, or tape drive hooked up externally through a special connection, the serial port, or a USB port. To keep size and weight to a minimum, many of the extras are left off the laptop. These components are included in a docking station, which the laptop fits into while at work or at a home office.

On the go, the laptop only has the essential elements. Docking stations give the user the option of a regular monitor, keyboard, and mouse. In addition, they often include network connectivity, which activates when the laptop is docked.

To expand a laptop, most have PCMCIA slots. The thick, credit-card-sized slots allow for additional functionality to be added, such as the expansion slots in a PC. PCMCIA cards can be purchased that provide wired network, wireless network, modem communications, and a host of other options.

Features and Functions of a NIC

Many types of plug-in expansion cards add features to a computer or other end device. The one you are most concerned about in this course is the NIC. Also called a network adapter, a NIC is an expansion board that physically connects a computer to a network.

A NIC fits into an expansion slot on a motherboard's bus. A network cable attaches to the NIC, allowing the computer to both transmit and receive the signals that represent data, as illustrated on the Connecting a NIC to the Network Diagram.

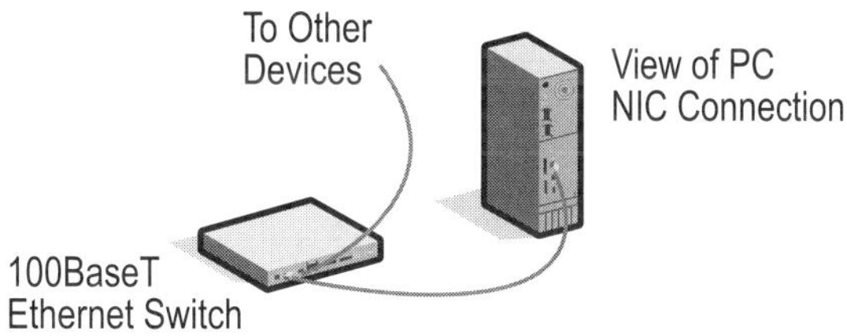

Connecting a NIC to the Network

The speed at which data can be transferred to and from a NIC is determined by many factors: the computer's bus, bandwidth and processor speed, design and quality of the NIC itself, the computer's operating system, and the type of network in use. Today, NICs are in more than just computers. A network interface can be built into a printer, a fax machine, a copier, and a phone.

Note: Normally, only one NIC is built into any of these devices.

With wireless transmissions, the traditional concept of a physical NIC with a physical connector and cable is changing. Many devices now have built-in wireless NICs that allow network access without physical connectivity. This is helpful when you use a laptop, mobile phone, or PDA that needs access without limitations.

Different Networks, Different NICs

Each type of NIC is designed for a particular type of transmission medium (wire, radio signals, or optical fiber) and network transmission method. (We will discuss all of these later in this course.) Thus, a computer would need one type of NIC to send electrical signals over a copper-wired network and a different NIC to send light pulses over a fiber optic system.

On a copper-wired network, a NIC varies the voltage level on the line in a precise pattern that represents data bits. On a fiber optic network, a NIC converts outgoing bits to flashes of light. On a wireless network, a NIC transmits bits by changing the pattern of a radio wave. In each case, the NIC also receives incoming signals as changing voltages, light flashes, or radio waves, and converts those signals into electrical bit patterns a computer can use.

Regardless of what physical medium a network uses, a NIC's job is to both generate and receive the signals that represent binary 1s and 0s. These signals must be precisely timed; thus, the timing circuitry in sending and receiving NICs must be coordinated. The resulting sequence of bits is called a "bit stream."

Each NIC is Unique

Each NIC contains a unique ID number that is burned in at the factory. A central organization of computer manufacturers coordinates the assignment of these numbers to ensure that each ID is used by only one NIC anywhere in the world. Thus, in addition to physically transmitting and receiving signals, a NIC also uniquely identifies each device.

The address of the NIC is called a Media Access Control (MAC) address. It is 48 bits long and is divided into two portions: a 3-byte vendor field and a 3-byte unique address. A MAC address is also called a physical address, NIC address, hardware address, burned-in address, vendor address, and Data Link Layer address. It is displayed in hexadecimal form as are the following two MAC addresses: 00:C0:9B:D7:10:62 and AB:92:44:D6:01:F7.

Each network node (computer, printer, or other device) must have a NIC to directly communicate with other nodes. However, if a resource, such as a printer, does not have a NIC, it can be indirectly connected to the network through a computer that does have a NIC. That computer can then "share" its resource with other network nodes. All traffic to that printer would then pass through the computer and not go to the printer directly.

Network Transmission and Storage Measurement Terms

Binary information is transmitted and processed 1 bit at a time. A bit is a single 0 or 1; 8 bits are combined to create a byte. A byte is also sometimes called an octet or character since 8 bits are required to create a letter, number, or other keyboard input.

The processor reviews the on and off electrical pulses to determine what service or function is necessary. Bits transmitted through a network are sent as electrical pulses across copper media, light pulses across fiber optical cable, and nondiscrete wave forms in wireless or analog transmissions.

Network transmission terms are used to identify the bandwidth of a link or the speed with which information is transferred across a connection. Transmissions are measured as amount per second.

Storage measurement terms are used when discussing storage capacity or memory; however, there is no time indicated with these measurements. The Network Transmission and Storage Management Terms Table lists the measurement term, the value it represents, and whether it is used for transmission or storage.

Network Transmission and Storage Management Terms

Measurement	Quantity	Usage
Bit	A single 0 or 1	Measurement
Byte	Eight bits in a byte	One character
Kilobits (Kb)	1,000 bits	Measurement
Kilobytes (KB or K)	1,000* bytes/character	Storage or memory
Kilobits per second (Kbps)	1,000 bits per second	Transmission
Megabits (Mb)	1,000,000 bits	Measurement
Megabytes (MB)—Meg	1,000,000** bytes	Storage or memory
Megabits per second (Mbps)	1,000,000 bits per second	Transmission
10 Mb or 10 Mbps or 10 meg	10,000,000 bits	Transmission
100 Mb or 100 Mbps or 100 meg	100,000,000 bits	Transmission
Gigabit (Gb)—1Gb	1,000,000,000 bits	Measurement term
Gigabytes (GB)—Gig	1,000,000,000 bytes	Storage
Gbps	1,000,000,000 bits per sec	Transmission
10 Gb or 10 Gbps or 10 gig	10,000,000,000 bits	Transmission
Terrabit	1,000,000,000,000 bits	Storage
Terrabyte	1,000,000,000,000 bytes	Storage
Hexabyte	1,000,000,000,000,000 bytes	Storage

* A kilobyte is exactly 1024 bytes, although it is most often discussed as shown.
** A megabyte is exactly 1,048,576 bytes, although it is most often rounded to a million bytes.

Three other measurement terms are also worth mentioning. Frequency is the state change of a wave form that is common for processor, electrical components, wireless transmissions, or analog communications. These measurements are often used to define the processing capabilities of a CPU, the rating of cable, or the range used for wireless communications:

- **Hertz (Hz)**—The frequency with which a signal state change occurs. Hz is one cycle change per second.
- **Megahertz (Mhz or MHz)**—Indicates that a cycle state change happens at 1,000,000 times per second. Megahertz was a common reference for processor speeds several years ago. It is also used to identify the non-licensed radio frequency band such as 915 Mhz.
- **Gigahertz (Ghz or GHZ)**—Indicates that a cycle state change happens at 1,000,000,000 times per second. Processor speeds today are defined in GHz. In addition, other unlicensed frequencies such as 2.4 and 5 GHz provide substantially more bandwidth than their predecessors.

It is interesting to note how far PC processors have come over the years. When first introduced, computer processors started at 4.77Hz. A year later, the 8-Hz processor was announced. Some computer programs at the time did not have the ability to use the higher processing capability and could not function. Therefore, many early computers had a "Turbo" button. This allowed the user to toggle between the higher and lower processor speeds as needed.

Through the 80s and 90s, microprocessor technology changed substantially. Processor speeds overcame many obstacles of size, heat, and accessibility. As of this writing, PC processors are manufactured at 2.6 GHz and higher.

Decimal-to-Binary Conversion

For the rest of this lesson to make sense, you need to have an understanding of decimal-to-binary conversions. Many textbooks, however, fail to mention binary numbers at all. A quick review of binary numbers and the conversion process follows.

A decimal number is made up of 8 bits or 1 byte, often called an "octet." A decimal number is one that we are accustomed to reading. For example, 5, 67, 102, 174, and 239 are all examples of decimal numbers. These numbers can also be represented in binary using only 0s and 1s, which are understood by a computer.

Because only two possible options exist, either a 0 or a 1, binary numbers are said to be Base 2. To make this easier, look at the eight bit positions and the numbers they represent, as shown in the Base 2 Table.

Base 2

Base 2	2^7	2^6	2^5	2^4	2^3	2^2	2^1	2^0
Decimal Value	128	64	32	16	8	4	2	1

Using this simple table, you can convert any decimal number to binary and vice versa. Remember that with all bits set to 1s, the highest possible number that can be created with only 8 bits is 255. Use the previous examples of 5, 67, 102, 174, and 239, and the following steps to convert these decimal numbers to binary. For example, these steps convert the decimal number 162 to binary:

1. Start with the highest or most significant bit, and identify the first number on the bottom row of the table that is smaller than or equal to the decimal number in question. For this example, the first number on the bottom row starting from the left that is smaller than 162 is the number 128.
   - If the number on the bottom row of the table is less than or equal to the decimal, place a 1 in that position, indicating that the value will be turned on.

     For this example, a 1 is placed under the 128, indicating that value must be used.
   - If the number in the table is greater than the decimal number, place a 0 in that position, indicating that the value will not be used.
2. If a position has a 1, subtract the decimal value from the original decimal number.

   For this example, the original number is 162 – 128 = 34
3. Moving to the right, repeat steps 1 and 2 with the last calculated decimal number.

   To finish the example, the next number in the table is 64. This is greater than 34. Thus, a 0 is placed in that position, indicating that the value will not be used. The next number in the table is 32, which is less than 34. Thus, a 1 is placed in that position, directly under 32. 34 – 32 = 2.

Looking on the bottom row, 0s can be placed under the values 16, 8, and 4 because they are not less than or equal to 2. Finally, a binary 1 is placed under the 2 and a 0 is placed under the 1 because the decimal number is completely converted.

Refer to the Converting from Decimal to Binary Table to see how this and other decimal numbers were converted by placing 1s in the correct positions and then doing the math.

Converting from Decimal to Binary

Base 2	2^7	2^6	2^5	2^4	2^3	2^2	2^1	2^0	
Value	128	64	32	16	8	4	2	1	
162	1	0	1	0	0	0	1	0	162-128=34 34-32=2 2-2=0
5	0	0	0	0	0	1	0	1	5-4=1 1-1=0
67	0	1	0	0	0	0	1	1	67-64=3 3-2=1 1-1=0
102	0	1	1	0	0	1	1	0	102-62=38 38-32=6 6-4=2 2-2=0
174	1	0	1	0	1	1	1	0	174-128=46 46-32=14 14-8=6 6-4=2 2-2=0
239	1	1	1	0	1	1	1	1	239-128=111 111-64=47 47-32=15 15-8=7 7-4=3 3-2=1 1-1=0

Binary-to-Decimal Conversion

Once you understand the decimal to binary conversation, binary to decimal is just a matter of adding, not subtracting. To convert from binary to decimal, place the binary bits in the appropriate position in the Base 2 table, starting from left to right, then add the corresponding value for each bit position as shown in the Converting from Binary to Decimal Table.

Converting from Binary to Decimal

Base 2	2^7	2^6	2^5	2^4	2^3	2^2	2^1	2^0	
Value	128	64	32	16	8	4	2	1	
01001111	0	1	0	0	1	1	1	1	64+8+4+2+1=79

Converting from Binary to Decimal (Continued)

01110101	0	1	1	1	0	1	0	1	64+32+16+4+1=117
10011011	1	0	0	1	1	0	1	1	128+16+8+2+1=155
10100001	1	0	1	0	0	0	0	1	128+32+1=161
11001010	1	1	0	0	1	0	1	0	128+64+8+2=202
11111111	1	1	1	1	1	1	1	1	128+64+32+16+8=4+2+1= 255

Converting to Hexadecimal

Humans have a hard time reading long strings of binary bits, thus the hexadecimal Base 16 numbering system is used to condense binary bits into a compact form for printing or analysis. Because it is a Base 16 system, it uses 16 different values: the numbers 0 through 9, plus the letters A through F. (A represents 10, B represents 11, and so forth.)

Eight bits are divided in half (four bits, called a "nibble") and they use only the least-significant portion of the Base 2 table introduced in the last section. This gives a maximum possible value of 15, binary 1111s, or hexadecimal F.

To give you a basis for how these numbering conventions compare, the Three Number Conventions Table outlines this relationship.

Three Number Conventions

Decimal	Binary	Hexadecimal
0	0000	0
1	0001	1
2	0010	2
3	0011	3
4	0100	4
5	0101	5
6	0110	6
7	0111	7
8	1000	8
9	1001	9

Three Number Conventions (Continued)

Decimal	Binary	Hexadecimal
10	1010	A
11	1011	B
12	1100	C
13	1101	D
14	1110	E
15	1111	F

Getting from zero to 15 is no problem, as long as you remember the letters A through F for numbers 10 through 15.

When the decimal number is over 15, more calculation is involved to determine the correct hex value. The steps for making the conversion are not difficult; it just takes a bit of practice like the conversions reviewed earlier.

The following steps outline the conversion process, which also uses the Base 2 table:

1. If the number is provided in decimal format, convert it to binary, placing the 0s and 1s in the correct positions in the Base 2 table.
2. Divide the table in half. Determine the decimal number of only the last 4 bits in the table by adding the values in each position where there is a 1. From memory or looking at the table, determine the associated hex number. This is the least significant value in the complete hex number.
3. Slide the first 4 bits all the way to the right and determine their decimal value based on the position of 1s in the table. From memory or looking at the table, determine the associated hex number. This is the most-significant value in the complete hex number.
4. Put the two numbers together to form a complete hexadecimal value.

Reading the steps may be confusing. Therefore, to understand the process better, you will convert the numbers 57, 108, and 219 using the Base 2 table:

1. Write 57 into the table, which gives the binary number 00111001.

Base 2	2^7	2^6	2^5	2^4	2^3	2^2	2^1	2^0
Value	128	64	32	16	8	4	2	1
57	0	0	1	1	1	0	0	1

2. After dividing the table in half, the decimal value of the last 4 bits (1001) is 9. This is the least-significant value in the hex number.

Base 2	2^7	2^6	2^5	2^4	2^3	2^2	2^1	2^0	
Value	128	64	32	16	8	4	2	1	
					1	0	0	1	8+1=9

3. Next, slide the first 4 bits of the original number over to the right in the table. The first 4 bits moved over to the right are 0011, which equals 2 + 1 = 3 in decimal.

Base 2	2^7	2^6	2^5	2^4	2^3	2^2	2^1	2^0	
Value	128	64	32	16	8	4	2	1	
					0	0	1	1	2+1=3

4. When you combine the two numbers, the correct hexadecimal value is revealed. Thus, 57 in decimal form is equal to 39 in hexadecimal form. To indicate hex, the number is sometimes displayed as 0x39.

Now for the other examples, 108 in decimal is what in hexadecimal?

1. Decimal value 108 written in binary is 01101100.

Base 2	2^7	2^6	2^5	2^4	2^3	2^2	2^1	2^0
Value	128	64	32	16	8	4	2	1
108	0	1	1	0	1	1	0	0

2. Divide the table in half, looking at only the numbers 1100, which equal 12. The Three Number Conventions table shows that a decimal 12 equals the letter C in hexadecimal. Therefore, C is the least significant value.
3. Slide the first four binary numbers 0110 into the last position and compute the decimal number 6.
4. Combining them converts decimal 108 into 0x6C.

For the last example of 219, work through the process one last time:

1. Decimal 219 written into the table is binary 11011011.

Base 2	2^7	2^6	2^5	2^4	2^3	2^2	2^1	2^0
Value	128	64	32	16	8	4	2	1
219	1	1	0	1	1	0	1	1

2. The last half, when you add 1011, is 11 in decimal form. The number 11 in hex form is B.
3. Slide the first half to the right to 1101 or 13. This means that the first number is hex D.
4. When combining the numbers together, the hex value for 219 is 0xDB.

The largest two-character hexadecimal number that can be created with all 1s is FF. This is because when you work through the process, the last 4 bits as all 1s (1111) would be 15, which equals F, and the first four bits are also 15, which again is F.

When sending a broadcast message at the Data Link Layer, the MAC address is displayed as FF:FF:FF:FF:FF:FF. All 1s are in all positions, similar to the Network Layer broadcast of 255.255.255.255, all ones in all positions. The main difference between Data Link and Network Layer broadcast messages is which devices (switch, router, firewall) operate on and filter them.

Review Questions

Answer the following questions using the Base 2 Table and other information in this lesson.

Base 2

Base 2	2^7	2^6	2^5	2^4	2^3	2^2	2^1	2^0
Value	128	64	32	16	8	4	2	1

1. Perform the following binary-to-decimal conversions:
   a. 11010010

   ____

   b. 00100101

   ____

   c. 00011111

   ____

   d. 11110000

   ____

   e. 10101010

   ____

   f. 11001100

   ____

   g. 00110011

   ____

   h. 10000111

   ____

2. Perform the following decimal-to-binary conversions:

   a. 187

   ____

   b. 24

   ____

   c. 169

   ____

   d. 82

   ____

   e. 231

   ____

   f. 96

   ____

   g. 124

   ____

   h. 248

   ____

Extended Activities

Answer the following questions using the Base 2 Table and other information in this lesson.

Base 2

Base 2	2^7	2^6	2^5	2^4	2^3	2^2	2^1	2^0
Value	128	64	32	16	8	4	2	1

1. What is the hexadecimal equivalent of the following decimal numbers?

   a. 2

   ____

   b. 64

   ____

   c. 169

   ____

   d. 222

   ____

   e. 19

   ____

2. What is the binary equivalent of the following hexadecimal numbers?

   a. A3

   ____

   b. FF

   ____

   c. 0A

   ____

   d. 01

   ____

   e. FF 89

   ____

3. What is the decimal equivalent of the following hexadecimal numbers?

   a. A3

   ____

   b. FF

   ____

   c. 0A

   ____

   d. 01

   ____

   e. FF 89

   ____

Lesson 2—Networking Fundamentals

This lesson starts out with an overview of terms that are commonly found in networking. It is not an all-inclusive list; however, many are used to describe how information is transmitted through a network. Next, the lesson discusses the types of computer networks and two common architectures: peer-to-peer and client/server.

The heart of this lesson is the OSI reference model. It was created by the International Standards Organization (ISO) and defines a neutral set of rules for data communication. Products that follow those rules can usually work together, even if they are made by different manufacturers.

The OSI model is an open standard. The term "open" means the standard's specifications are publicly available. It is not necessary to comply with the standard when developing and manufacturing hardware, software, and network components. However, most vendors understand the importance of interoperability.

The OSI model is made up of seven layers: Physical, Data Link, Network, Transport, Session, Presentation, and Application. This lesson provides a brief overview, including a description, the name of the protocol data unit, and the IP protocols, devices, and addresses associated with each layer.

When you understand the OSI model, it is much easier to see how information is encapsulated before transmission. Encapsulation is the process of adding headers and a trailer to the information for addressing, instructions and error detection. The IP suite and IP applications are also reviewed in this lesson because they closely relate to the layers of the OSI model.

Objectives

At the end of this lesson you will be able to:

- Define basic network terminology
- Compare peer-to-peer and client/server architectures
- Define the purpose of reference models
- Describe the layers and components of the OSI model
- Discuss encapsulation/decapsulation
- Compare the IP suite with the OSI model
- Describe the components of the IP suite

Key Point

The OSI and IP suite are two examples of layered reference models. The OSI model is a vendor-neutral open standard for interconnecting different systems. The IP suite is also an open standard protocol used for network and Internet communications.

Basic Network Terminology

Many terms used throughout this book are also commonly used by network administrators, designers, and others in the Information Technology (IT) industry to describe elements of their work. You should understand these terms before digging any deeper into this course. Some terms may be used generically and are often interchangeable—for example, the terms bandwidth, capacity, speed, and throughput. Although each one of these terms has a different meaning, they all discuss roughly the same things: the transmission characteristics of a network link.

This introduction is not a comprehensive list of all the terms. It is only a primer to start you off. For additional terms and definitions see the glossary at the back of this book.

Network Component Terms

- **Protocol and protocol suite**—A protocol is a set of rules or procedures that define a method of communication. A protocol suite is a group of protocols that work together to perform specific functions.
- **NIC**—A network interface card is used to make the connection from a device to the network. Although the name has the word card in it, many NICs are not cards at all. A card refers to the expansion card that is installed in a PC to provide network communications. However, a NIC can also be integrated onto the motherboard or be a PCMCIA component for a laptop.

  In addition, switches, bridges, routers, and hubs have many network interface connections, called "ports" that are not physical cards but part of the device. Each NIC has a physical Media Access Control (MAC) address that is burned in by the manufacturer to uniquely identify that device on the network.

- **Media**—The physical layer, wired or wireless connection used to transmit bits. Wired media include coax, shielded and unshielded twisted pair, and fiber optic cable. Wireless media include radio frequency, infrared, microwave, and satellite. Each media type has its own characteristics for representing and transmitting bits.
- **Network device or connectivity device**—A general term that represents the devices used to provide a connection to the network. Network devices include, but are not limited to, hubs, switches, bridges, routers, gateways, and others. These are the components that network administrators configure and manage.
- **End device, host, or node**—These are general terms that represents the devices typically accessed by a user. These devices are at the end of the cable segment, hence the name end device. A host is commonly considered a server that holds a database or repository of information that is retrieved from an end device. In today's terminology, a host is any device on the network that is assigned an IP address.

  The term node originally represented an end device connected to a particular network cable segment. Now the term is often interchanged with both end device and host. Regardless of the term used, end device, host, or node, these days they all represent PCs, servers, printers, network fax machines, scanner and document imagers, network copiers, IP telephones, and any other device that has a NIC and communicates on the network.
- **Hardware**—A term that describes anything built into the physical circuitry of the device. Hardware includes components such as the motherboard, or integrated circuit board, memory, disk storage, NIC, processor, and so forth.

Transmission Terms

- **Bandwidth, capacity, and available bandwidth**—Bandwidth is defined as the transmission capability of a network media. Bandwidth is often discussed in terms of capacity, meaning the maximum amount of information that can be sent through the network. Available bandwidth is the network capacity that is available to use for transmission. This is usually less than the capacity because of overhead and inefficiencies in network communications. These terms refer to a specific number in Kb, Mb, Gb, and so forth.

- **Speed and throughput**—Other terms often used interchangeably with those in the previous bulleted item. Whereas bandwidth and the other items concern a specific number of bits or bytes, speed and throughput concern how fast those bits and bytes are sent. Typically, this is measured in seconds—that is Kbps, Mbps, or Gbps. Speed represents the theoretical capacity of how fast a transmission can be performed. Rarely is that speed truly achieved. Throughput is a better representation because it defines the transmission time from sender to receiver.
- **Transmission**—A generic term for any information that is sent through the network. It can also be called data, message, packet, frame, or information, although these terms are more specific than transmission.

Unit of Information Terms

- **Information**—Upper-layer application data, voice, video, audio, and other multimedia communications that are sent through the network. Network engineers from a data background usually refer to all application information as data. This terminology is changing as different types of information are transmitted.
- **Message, packet, and frame**—A message is defined as the upper-layer information. It can also be used to mean the upper-layer information with a transport header. A packet is a message that has a Transport and Network Layer header. This term is commonly used to mean the majority of transmissions in the network, even though it is very specific. Router and layer 3 devices read the network layer address in a packet to make route selection decisions. A frame is a message that has a Transport, Network and Data Link Layer header and is used for transmissions at the Data Link Layer.
- **Cell**—The Data Link Layer transmission unit that is switched by Asynchronous Transfer Mode (ATM) and Switched Multimegabit Data Service (SMDS).

Operating Systems and Applications

- **Operating system**—The core code that is used by the device to provide specific functionality and services. The operating system is the foundation of the device's ability to operate, including processing requests for information and services and providing the resulting output, but not accepting input in the form of changes to the operating system's code.

- **Network operating system (NOS)**—An operating system that is designed for network communications on a server. A server is a system that is designated to provide services for requesting clients. A NOS has additional functionality over a standard operating system in that it allows multiple login access, multitasking, multiprocessing, multithreading, higher capacity storage and processing capabilities, more robust hardware and software, and so forth. Examples of a NOS include Novell, UNIX, Linux, Microsoft NT server, and the Microsoft 2000 server.
- **Cisco's Internetwork Operating System (IOS)**—The operating system used to provide the functionality for a Cisco device, such as a router or switch. The IOS provides device functionality, security, reliability, connectivity, and management capability. Cisco's IOS, like all operating system platforms, has evolved dramatically over the years and is constantly being updated to meet the demands of technology.
- **Command line interface (CLI)**—The foundation on which many operating systems are built. The CLI is a method of configuration and administration that uses specific, predefined codes and syntax, typed at the appropriate prompt, to perform a function. Cisco's CLI, Novell Netware, Linux, and UNIX all offer command line interfaces. A CLI relies on commands being entered using a keyboard.
- **Graphical user interface (GUI)**—The user-friendly graphical screens used for input and configuration. The options are already predefined in menus, drop-down lists, button bars, tool bars, tasklists, and so forth. A GUI relies on selections being made using a mouse or another pointer tool. Values and options are typed into the preset boxes; for example a device name, IP address, or default gateway address.
- **Software**—The generic term used to define any programmed code or anything that is logical processing versus hardware, which is physical processing. Software is also used to define the programs that are used for input/output by the end user.
- **Applications or programs**—The code that is written, packaged, and installed on a system to provide a specific end-user function. Word processing, e-mail, spreadsheets, and databases are commonly used applications.

Computer Networks

Networks are created to connect computers, servers, printers, and other network resources together. They developed out of the need of organizations to share files in a more sophisticated way than copying them to diskette for transfer. This need to share information took on new meaning as printers were added, then databases of information, e-mail services, bulletin boards, the Internet, and now all the multimedia communications as we know them.

Networks can be small, connecting two or more systems together. They can be simple, used for sharing files or a printer. Or a network can be a multimillion-dollar infrastructure of cable and wireless media, routers, switches, NICs, protocols, end-devices, operating systems, applications, peripherals, information storage, and so on.

When designing, implementing, or managing a network, the business needs of an organization must be accommodated. Therefore, networks are built around departmental functions, business locations, bandwidth and services, application access, protocols, and other key criteria. The business is broken down into major groups to help design and manage the special needs of each area. These groups are as follows:

- **Main office**—This is usually considered the local area network (LAN). It is composed of the main servers, users' PCs, and applications that are necessary for business operations. The network usually has a high bandwidth backbone designed for reliability. A large corporation may have many equally large LANs connected together throughout the country or across the world. In most cases, each one would function relatively independently of the other.

  Communication and information sharing between the LANs is through high-speed wide area network (WAN) lines leased from a telecommunications service provider. Another option would be to connect the network segments using private facilities; however, that is costly and difficult to install and manage. High-speed access to the Internet is often a requirement for the main office location as well.

- **Branch offices**—A branch office might be a subsidiary or smaller office location that connects to the main office. Branch offices often provide many of the services in the main location but are just a smaller version. A bank is a good example of this concept.

A bank has one or a few main large bank locations; then it has many, smaller branch offices located throughout the city or state. The branch offices have a connection to the main office for information exchange and communication. These may be WAN or metropolitan area network links (MANs).

- **Home office/small office**—Many companies find it advantageous for employees to work from home or from another location. Connections back to the main office for information sharing, network resources, and communications are important. Telecommuting, as this is called, can be done through a dial-up connection, or more commonly these days, through a virtual private network connection (VPN) using the Internet.
- **Virtual office/mobile office**—Employees who often travel away from the office or often work at home need access to corporate information, network resources, and communications. Network access may be necessary while traveling to customer or client sites, at a conference, from a hotel, in transit, or anywhere else not typically in a set location.

  Dialup modem connections have in the past been the connection of choice. More frequently, however, mobile employees are using VPN connections and Web access to e-mail and corporate information.

A final topic to discuss here is the architecture of computer networks. This is the method of access between end users and the resources they need. Network architectures fall loosely into two categories of access: peer-to-peer and client/server.

Peer-to-Peer Communication

When two processes have roughly the same power and can perform approximately the same services for each other, they are called "peer" processes. When systems communicate as peers, neither one controls the other.

A peer-to-peer computer network is created when a group of computers of roughly equal power and function are interconnected. This typically happens when a small office links the desktop computers of its employees. Each person's computer has a different set of applications and data, but the network connection allows various combinations of workers to share files, folders, applications, and printers. This type of relationship is illustrated on the Peer-to-Peer Communication Diagram.

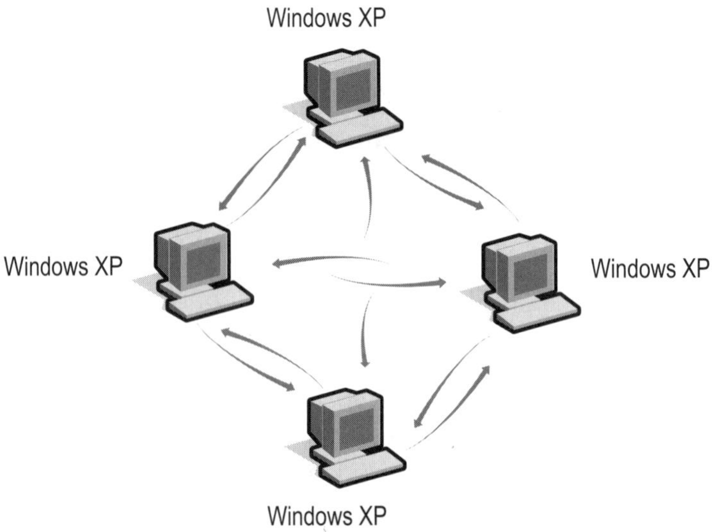

Peer-to-Peer Communication

No single computer sets the rules for these interactions. However, each computer's user can decide what resources to make available to other peer users.

Peer–to-peer network environments do not require a server, which means less equipment and little, if any, administration. However, this configuration also has the potential for security issues and poorer performance when resources are shared.

To create a peer-to-peer network, the following are required:

- Minimum two, maximum ten PCs
- NICs that use the same network topology and cable type
- A crossover cable if connecting two PCs directly together
- A hub or switch device if more than two PCs are connected
- Straight-through cables if PCs are connected to a hub or switch
- A common protocol for communication

Client/Server Communication

Another way that networks can cooperate is for one system to take the role of client and the other that of server. This arrangement is common on networks, which often set aside computers as file servers.

Everyone stores files on the common file server, which makes it easier to share data across an organization. This type of setup is shown on the Client/Server Communication Diagram.

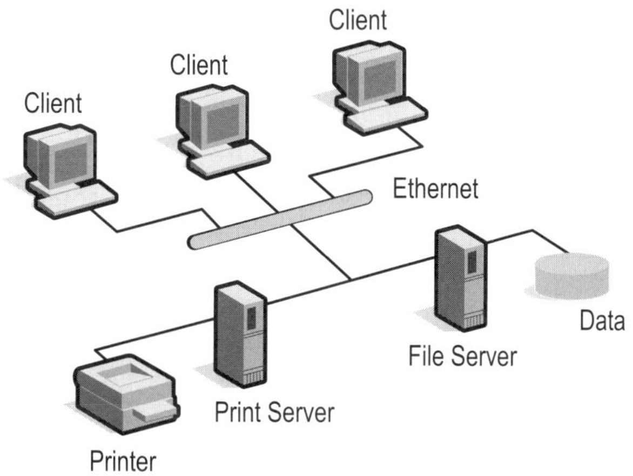

Client/Server Communication

Servers can also provide other types of resources. Examples are processing power, access to peripheral devices—printers, copiers and fax machines—or special applications such as databases, communication services, security, e-mail, and Web pages.

Clients and servers interact with each other by transmitting request/reply processes. The client process initiates an interaction by issuing a request to the server. The server process responds with a reply satisfying the request. This request/reply communication essentially divides a task into two parts and executes each part on a different system on the network.

For example, the task of creating a report can be divided into two parts. In the client part of the task, a worker uses a database application on the desktop to define what information a report should contain and the report definition gets sent as a request to the server. When the server receives the request, it retrieves the requested data, formats the report, and replies by sending the information back to the client.

Both client and server processes are dedicated to their respective tasks, and those roles never reverse. However, a single server can run multiple processes. Some of those processes can be requests from other servers acting in a client role. Thus, it is important to remember that "server" refers to a process, not necessarily a particular machine.

Client/server architecture has several advantages:

- **Distributed applications**—Applications can be distributed on the network based on their requirements for resources. For example, an application that provides computing-intensive services can be installed on a computer with very high processing capacity, whereas the user's client application runs on a workstation that provides high-end graphic display capabilities.
- **Resource sharing**—A server process typically can serve many clients, thus client/server architecture is a good way to share many types of resources across an organization.
- **Centralized administration**—This allows control over resource and file access, and prevents unauthorized use of network services. The server is also backed up regularly so that files and applications can be restored in the event of a hard drive failure or disaster situation.

Layered Reference Models

Throughout the technology industry, there are numerous reference models used to help implement and standardize communications between different systems. This becomes more and more necessary because a vast array of operating systems (OSs) and networking components are used in the business environment today.

Although a number of models in use help define networking standards, this book concentrates on the OSI reference model because it is the most widely acknowledged and used model in the industry. And this module details the OSI model to help you understand networking technology.

Reference models were developed to enable interconnection and communication between disparate systems. A layered approach provides the following benefits:

- Allows complicated and interrelated structures to be broken down into smaller, easy-to-understand components
- Allows vendors to create products that can communicate with different systems, support standardized Plug and Play interfaces, and provide compatibility in a multivendor environment

- Allows developers and designers to specialize in a specific layer, enabling a modular approach to application development
- Serves as a guideline for creating and implementing standards for hardware, software, networking, protocols, and so forth

The technology industry is overflowing with acronyms, protocols, methods, standards, and so forth. Models make these highly sophisticated and intricate processes easier to break down, learn, and understand. Models provide an important foundation for the entire technology industry and are a topic you will see on exams, regardless of the certification or vendor.

Layers and Components of the OSI Model

The OSI reference model was created by the International Standards Organization (ISO) to allow for intercommunication among all systems that have implemented this standard. As you may already know, the OSI model is based on seven layers. The bottom four layers facilitate system interconnectivity and data transfer, whereas the top three layers are concerned with application and user interaction.

Each of the layers is presented in the OSI Model Table. The table includes a brief description of the different layers, as well as associated protocol data units (PDUs), protocols, file types, connections, and devices.

OSI Model

Layer Name	Description	PDU	Protocol, File Type, or Connection	Devices
Application	User interface, file, print, e-mail, application services	Messages	Telnet, FTP, HTTP, SMTP, SNMP, DNS	
Presentation	Compression, representation, encryption/ decryption	Messages	ASCII, EBCDIC, JPEG, MIDI, GIF, PICT, MPEG, QuickTime	
Session	Session setup, data transfer, session release, multiple conversations	Messages	OS, NFS, SQL, RPC, X-Windows	

OSI Model (Continued)

Layer Name	Description	PDU	Protocol, File Type, or Connection	Devices
Transport	Reliable/unreliable delivery, end-to-end transport	Segments messages datagrams	TCP, UDP, SPX	Firewalls Layer 4 switches
Network	Route selection, logical addressing	Packets	IP, IPX	Routers, Layer 3 Switches, Firewalls
Data Link	Framing data, error detection, media access, physical address	Frames	Ethernet, Token Ring, PPP, ATM, HDLC, frame relay	Switches, Bridges, NICs
Physical	Send and receive bits, physical media	Bits	V.35, EIA/TIA-232, EIA/TIA 568A/B	Hubs, Repeaters, Modems, MUX

Application Layer

The Application Layer provides the **user interface** to programs available on a specific workstation. It also provides the program functionality such as file, database, and print sharing available through a network. Several protocols at this layer are key in identifying communication partners, such as electronic mail (e-mail) servers, Internet resources, or file transfer processes.

With the expansion of the World Wide Web (Web), businesses are going beyond the traditional network infrastructure and expanding their internetworking to include their partners, manufacturers, distributors, marketers, and customers. Programs at the Application Layer are major players in this arena because they have the ability to provide a common user interface.

Presentation Layer

The Presentation Layer receives data from the Application Layer and **represents** or codes it into a format that can be transmitted and read by the receiving system. It also provides **compression** and **encryption** services to make the best use of the available bandwidth and secure the data from eavesdropping, interception, or counterfeit information.

The reverse process takes place at the Presentation Layer on the receiving end, where the message is decompressed, decrypted, and translated to be used by the Application Layer of another system. This important layer provides communication capabilities between disparate systems for text files, video, graphics, and audio using the file formats listed in the OSI Model Table.

Session Layer

The Session Layer allows more than one conversation to take place without establishing a new connection. It also coordinates system communications by responding to service requests and organizes application data while keeping it separate from other data. The Session Layer provides simplex, half-duplex, and full-duplex modes to support this type of activity.

A number of protocols are used at this layer to provide client/server and remote access, as well as to create and receive service requests. These industry components include Structured Query Language (SQL), used to define information requests; Network File System (NFS), used to transport and store files on remote systems; and remote procedure call (RPC), used for redirection to server resources.

Transport Layer

A major function of the Transport Layer is to create a logical connection for end-to-end delivery of messages. A number of components allow this to happen, from segmenting the data received from the Session Layer, to controlling the flow of information across a network. The Transport Layer provides the following services:

- **Connection-oriented and connectionless services**—Connection-oriented protocols, such as Transmission Control Protocol (TCP) and Sequenced Packet Exchange (SPX), establish a connection, allow data transfer, and terminate the connection. These two protocols are considered reliable because they transmit acknowledgments, have flow control mechanisms, and offer some error correction. This is necessary for applications that cannot tolerate errors.

  With connection-oriented protocols, the Transport Layer is similar to making a telephone call. You start the conversation by saying "hello," then talking until all communication is complete, and end the session by saying "good-bye" and hanging up.

  In this example, the Transport Layer requests a connection, authorizes the communication, synchronizes and establishes a connection, transfers data, verifies and acknowledges the data, and then terminates the connection. The synchronize request, connection negotiation, and acknowledgment process is called a three-way handshake.

Connectionless protocols, such as User Datagram Protocol (UDP), are used when the error correction mechanisms inherent in connection-oriented protocols are not needed. They are also used when delay-sensitive transmissions, such as voice or video, make it preferable to lose a segment, rather than retransmit it.

- **Addressing, segmentation, and assembly**—Data at the Transport Layer is assigned a port number so it can be serviced by the process or application the data is destined for on the receiving system. Specific port numbers are assigned to Telnet, Domain Name System (DNS), File Transfer Protocol (FTP), Simple Mail Transfer Protocol (SMTP), and many other applications.

  In addition, messages received from the upper layers may also need to be broken down into smaller components or segmented to be sent across a network. The Transport Layer assigns each segment a sequence number so that the segment can be put in order by the destination device. The reassembly process by the receiving system is also a function of the Transport Layer.

- **Flow control and buffering**—These two components determine how much data will be transmitted at a given time. By managing congestion, flow control basically prevents data from being lost. Buffering allows datagrams that cannot be immediately serviced to be stored in memory until resources are available to process them.

  However, if the buffers overflow—meaning more data is coming in than being processed—newly arriving packets are discarded and data can be lost. To prevent this, flow control monitors the receiving system and signals a ready/not ready status, indicating its ability to receive and process more data.

- **Acknowledgments and windowing**—Finally, connection-oriented protocols use acknowledgments to ensure that all segments were received and not duplicated. If the sender does not receive an acknowledgment for a segment, the sender will retransmit it. The sending station must keep all segments in memory until it receives an acknowledgment in case it might have to resend one.

  However, there would be a lot of unnecessary traffic on the network if every segment had to be acknowledged before another is sent. Windowing allows a number of segments to be exchanged before an acknowledgment is received by the sender. Depending upon the communication protocol, the systems agree on the number that can be sent before the receiver transmits an acknowledgment.

Network Layer

The Network Layer of the OSI model is involved in getting packets from one location to another. It does this using logical source and destination addresses specific to the protocol used on the network. It then identifies the path that the packet will take through the network to reach its destination.

The two types of packets associated with the Network Layer are as follows:

- **Routable data packets**—These are the files, e-mail messages, Web pages, and control information transported between systems on a network. A header is added to the data packet, specifying the sender's and receiver's logical address in addition to protocol-specific information. Data packets are sent by means of a routable protocol, such as Internet Protocol (IP) or Internetwork Packet Exchange (IPX).
- **Route update or discovery packets**—These packets are sent between router devices to establish and maintain routing tables. The packets include information about each network, the path to reach a specific network, and a metric that defines the distance, or cost to get to each network. Route update information is sent by means of a routing protocol such as Routing Information Protocol (RIP), Interior Gateway Routing Protocol (IGRP), or Open Shortest Path First (OSPF).

The logical addresses used at the Network Layer identify both a specific end node and the network where it is located. It does this by implementing a hierarchical addressing scheme. This means that the address is broken down into a network piece (the network where the device is located) and a host piece (a specific device on the network).

A simple way to think of how logical addresses are used at the Network Layer is a telephone number, which includes the area code (for geographic location), the three digit prefix (for local region), and the last four digits (to uniquely identify a single individual).

Routers and other layer 3 devices play an integral part in making all this work. When a packet is received by a router, it looks at the destination's logical address to determine whether it is for a connected network; if so, it forwards the packet to the proper end node. If not, the router looks in its routing table for the destination network, then reframes the packet and sends it out of the appropriate exit interface. If the destination network is not in its router table, the router may forward the packet to a default gateway or simply drop the packet.

Data Link Layer

The Data Link Layer is responsible for defining how to get data onto the wire and transported over the physical media. It also defines the different logical network topologies and formats the packets received from the Network Layer into data frames to be sent to the Physical Layer. The Data Link Layer is divided into two Institute of Electrical and Electronics Engineers (IEEE) Ethernet sublayers. This discussion is based on Ethernet implementation at the Data Link Layer.

- **Logical Link Control (LLC) (802.2)**—The LLC sublayer is used to identify and properly encapsulate protocols by including a type code or a service access point (SAP) identifier in the header. This is used by upper layers to determine the correct protocol stack. For example, hexidecimal 06 associates the frame with IP, whereas hexidecimal E0 means the frame is destined for the IPX stack.

  Another type code used by some applications and proprietary protocols is Subnetwork Access Protocol (SNAP). This is identified using hexidecimal AA with the control field set to 3, and includes a vendor code and ethertype for the frame.

- **Media Access Control (MAC) (802.3)**—The MAC sublayer locates network devices using the burned-in address (BIA), also called the MAC address, that is assigned by a manufacturer. This 48-bit address uses the first six hexadecimal digits to identify the vendor, and the last six to uniquely identify each network node. Cisco's original vendor code is 0x00000C.

  The MAC sublayer also defines how information will be physically transmitted over various network topologies. It provides some sequencing and flow control, line discipline, and error notification (not correction).

Unlike the Network Layer, which is concerned with a logical address, the Data Link Layer is concerned with the device's physical address. Header and trailer information added to the frame includes the MAC addresses of the source and destination. Although the source is always a single node, the destination may be unicast (single node), multicast (a number of end stations), or broadcast (all nodes within the network segment).

Devices that function at the Data Link Layer are bridges and layer 2 switches, which read and forward frames based on data link information. They are faster than routers because they do not have to dissect as much of the frame or make routing decisions. The process that a switch/bridge uses to transport data is discussed later in this module.

The Data Link Layer includes other encapsulation types for both LANs and WANs, in addition to Ethernet. This means that the Data Link portion of the frame is replaced with header information and physical addresses appropriate for the encapsulation protocol. Other LAN encapsulation types include Token Ring, FDDI, and ATM, and are outside the scope of this text. WAN encapsulation types include: HDLC, PPP, SLIP, frame relay, and ATM, and are discussed in more detail in Module 7.

Physical Layer

At the bottom of the OSI model is the Physical Layer, which is most involved in specifying physical components of network connectivity. The Physical Layer is essential in sending and receiving bits (0s and 1s) across a network. It also specifies network topologies (star, ring, or bus), media types (bounded or unbounded), connector types (fiber optic, attachment unit interface [AUI], or RJ-45), and transmission distances for different cabling specifications (10Base2 = 185 meters, 10Base5 = 500 meters, and 10BaseT = 100 meters). In addition, the Physical Layer defines data rates, voltage levels, and signaling types.

Hubs, repeaters, modems, and the interface between the data terminal equipment/data communication equipment DTE/DCE are just a few of the components at the Physical Layer. Hubs create a physical star network structure, and repeat or regenerate each signal out of all active ports. Hubs are discussed further in Lesson 3.

Encapsulation Process

Encapsulation is the process of adding header information to data sent across a network. Each layer of the OSI model is involved in manipulating the message and adding information that is necessary to successfully transport and process the message on the receiving side.

The name given to the PDU also changes as it moves from one layer to the next. As a simple example, imagine someone sending an e-mail message. The information in that message will be sent across the network, so it must be properly encapsulated. The process is shown on the Encapsulation Diagram.

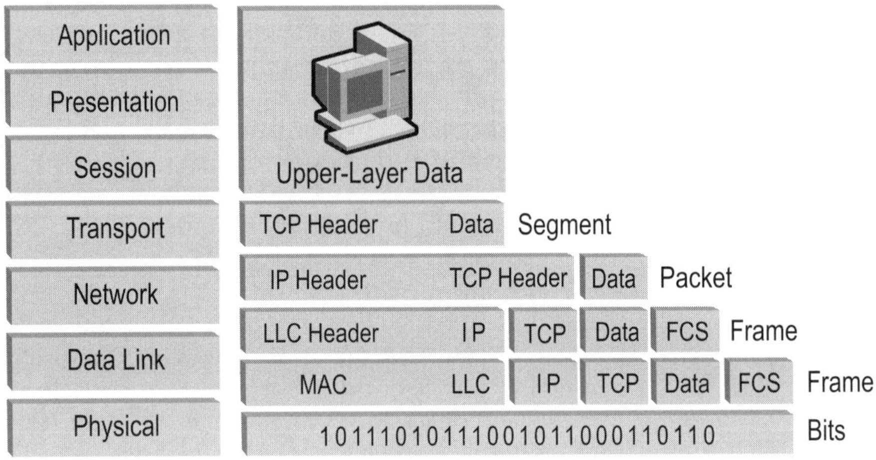

Encapsulation

The encapsulation process and corresponding OSI model layers are as follows:

- **Application Layer**—Body of the e-mail message is input by the user and sent by means of the e-mail application.
- **Presentation Layer**—The e-mail characters are represented; encryption and compression may be performed on the message.
- **Session Layer**—A service request is created for the server on which the e-mail system resides.
- **Transport Layer**—TCP header information, such as port number, is added and, if necessary, the data is broken into smaller pieces and sequence numbers are added. The PDU starts as a message, segment, or datagram.
- **Network Layer**—Source and destination IP addresses are added to the segment that is passed from the Transport Layer and renamed a packet.

- **Data Link Layer**—Header information is added for both the LLC and MAC sublayers. The LLC sublayer adds the source and destination SAP identifier or a SNAP type code. It also adds some control information, then passes the frame to the MAC sublayer.

  The MAC sublayer adds a preamble, as well as the physical source and destination addresses, and a length field for the number of bytes of data. These additions are followed by a frame check sequence (FCS) trailer used for error detection.
- **Physical Layer**—The entire frame, with information added from all the layers above, is received by the Physical Layer, which converts it to bits (0s and 1s) to be transported across the network.

During the encapsulation process, the original transmission gains a number of new headers. All the layers of header information are shown in the OSI Ethernet Frame Diagram.

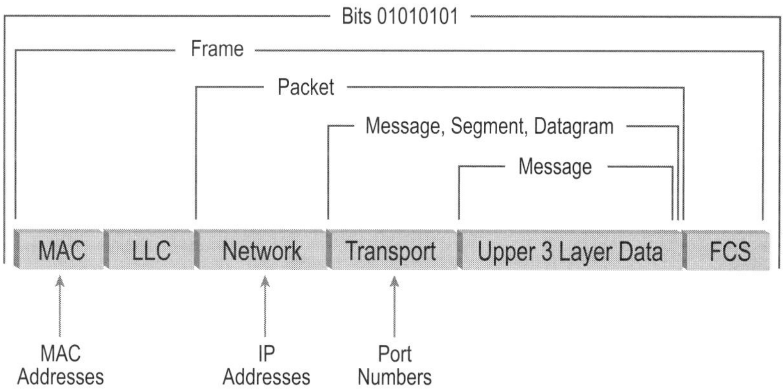

OSI Ethernet Frame

Notice from the diagram that as each layer adds its information, the resulting PDU name changes as follows:

- **Upper 3 layers**—The PDU is called a message.
- **Transport**—After the port numbers are added, the PDU can still be called a message. More specifically, it is a segment if TCP is used and a datagram if UDP is used.
- **Network**—When the IP addresses are added, the upper layer data with the transport and network headers is now called a packet.

- **Data Link**—The LLC identifies the network layer protocol and MAC addresses are added. Then the FCS is computed and appended to the end. The PDU is now called a frame.
- **Physical**—At this layer, there are no more addresses or header information to add. The frame is turned into bits that can be sent across the media. As 0s and 1s, these bits may take the form of electrical signals, light pulses, or radio waves.

Decapsulation Process

When the destination station receives the bits from the network, it goes through the process of decapsulation, as shown on the Decapsulation Diagram. Each layer reads the appropriate control information, strips off the header, then passes the data up to the next layer, using the header's instructions. In this way, each layer in the sending station communicates directly to the same layer in the receiving station.

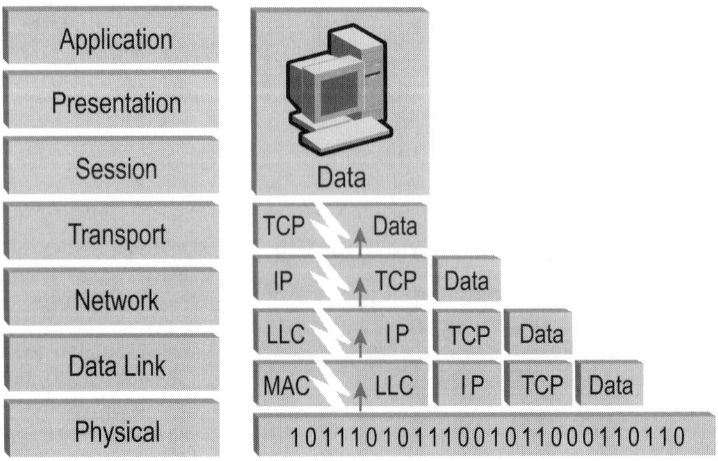

Decapsulation

Now review what happens in the OSI model layers when the e-mail message from the example is received at its final destination:

- **Physical Layer**—The 0s and 1s are received from the media.
- **Data Link Layer**—The receiving device was identified by the destination MAC address. A cyclic redundancy check (CRC) is performed and verified against the FCS in the frame. If it is correct, the bits are sent to the Network Layer for processing. If the FCS is incorrect, the frame is discarded.
- **Network Layer**—The IP addressing and other Network Layer information is verified and stripped away.
- **Transport Layer**—The segments are reassembled in the correct order; the TCP header and port identification are reviewed and stripped away leaving only upper-layer data. An acknowledgment is then transmitted to the sending station.
- **Session Layer**—Communication with upper layers is established.
- **Presentation Layer**—The data is decrypted and decompressed if necessary.
- **Application Layer**—The data can be viewed and responded to using an e-mail application.

The IP Protocol Suite Versus the OSI Reference Model

The initial research and creation of the IP suite of protocols was performed by the Defense Advanced Research Projects Agency (DARPA) under the U.S. Department of Defense (DoD). The IP suite was created to provide a secure and reliable transfer mechanism between different systems. The University of California-Berkeley added its own version of the IP protocol suite to its deployment of UNIX and the rest, as they say, is history.

IP is the protocol of the Internet and multiple platform environments. Today, just about any electronic device has an IP address, or will soon, to allow communication and networking.

The IP stack has four layers that map closely to the seven layers of the OSI model. The IP Protocol Suite vs. OSI Model Diagram shows the comparable layers and how they map to one another.

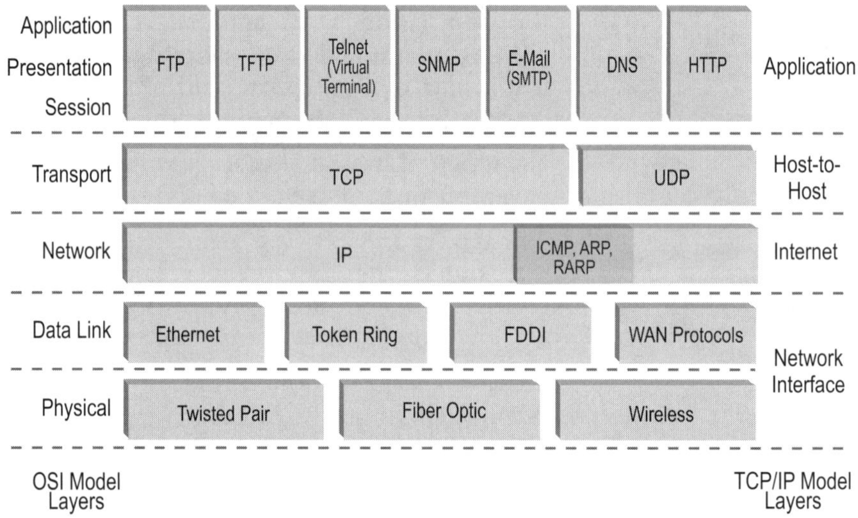

IP Protocol Suite vs. OSI Model

Application Layer

The Application Layer of the TCP/IP stack incorporates the top three layers of the OSI model: Application, Presentation, and Session. It is designed to provide user interface capabilities, node-to-node communication, and application support. Several types of services available at this layer are as follows:

File Transfer Services

- **FTP (File Transfer Protocol)**—Authenticated access for complete file services
- **TFTP (Trivial File Transfer Protocol)**—File transmission that requires no user intervention; used for backups, restores, and firmware upgrades

Network Management Services

- **Telnet**—Provides remote console/terminal capabilities using a dial-up, direct (console) access or network connection
- **SNMP (Simple Network Management Protocol)**—Monitors the network environment for critical events
- **DNS (Domain Name System)**—Provides Universal Resource Locator (URL) to IP address translation
- **DHCP (Dynamic Host Configuration Protocol)**—Assigns IP address information to host devices
- **BOOTP**—Allows diskless workstations to locate and download operating system and configuration files

Electronic Mail Services

- **SMTP (Simple Mail Transfer Protocol)**—Provides a generic e-mail gateway that translates between various e-mail formats
- **POP3 (Post Office Protocol version 3)**—The ability to send and receive mail and provide other e-mail handling services for a client
- **IMAP4 (Internet Message Access Protocol version 4)**—Client access to an e-mail server; more sophisticated format than POP3
- **MIME (Multipurpose Internet Mail Extensions) and S/MIME (secured)**—Allows e-mail attachments, various formatting, and embedded information

Web Services

- **HTTP (Hypertext Transfer Protocol)**—Fills client requests by sending Web pages
- **HTML (Hypertext Markup Language)**—The language used to create Web pages
- **JAVA**—A robust programming language used to provide Web-based input and applications

Host-to-Host Layer

The IP protocol suite Host-to-Host Layer falls directly in line with the Transport Layer of the OSI model. Remember that the Transport Layer is responsible for end-to-end transport services. This can be done with a reliable, connection-oriented method using TCP, or the unreliable, connectionless protocol UDP. The Comparison of TCP and UDP Table shows the differences between these two protocols.

Comparison of TCP and UDP

TCP	UDP
Connection-oriented	Connectionless
Virtual circuit made with three-way handshake	No initial setup communication provided
Provides flow control	No flow control
Uses acknowledgments	No acknowledgments
High overhead associated with extra services	Low overhead associated with reduced services
Segments large data streams, provides sequencing	Sequence numbers not provided
Provides complete reliability of service	Requires upper- and lower-layer protocols to provide reliability

TCP and UDP port numbers are assigned to each IP application so that they can be easily identified. The appropriate port number is included in the TCP or UDP header so that the receiving device knows how to handle the upper-layer information or request.

Internet Layer

The IP Internet Layer maps directly to the Network Layer of the OSI model. This layer has three main functions:

- **Routable protocols**—IP is a routable protocol because it has a hierarchical address. The address identifies both a network and a specific host. This address type is logical because it is assigned for a particular network but can easily be changed.
- **Routing protocols**—These protocols provide a means of routing and delivering messages using the best possible method. They make routing decisions based on the appropriate metric, and some can provide Quality of Service (QoS) route selection based on specific criteria.

- **Helper protocols**—These protocols provide helpful network assistance functions. They include ICMP, ARP, and RARP. The features and functions of each of these protocols are discussed in Module 5.

Data Link and Physical Layers

The IP model does not specify layer 2 or layer 1 protocols; thus, it maps exactly to the OSI model at the Data Link and Physical Layers. As with the OSI model, the Data Link Layer provides media access and a physical address for each node.

IP is independent of the Data Link Layer encapsulation type. This allows IP packets to be transferred via Ethernet, Token Ring, FDDI, ATM, frame relay, PPP, HDLC, and others. The appropriate physical address is included in the Data Link Layer header of the frame or cell before transmission. This address is associated with the source and destination IP address from the Network Layer so that the packet can be properly transmitted.

IP does not define any protocols at the Physical Layer. It is independent of this layer and can be transmitted over coax, UTP, fiber optic, wireless radio frequency, microwave, satellite, and a variety of public wide area network media.

Review Questions

1. Which layer of the OSI model includes routing devices and uses logical addresses to identify the sender and receiver?

 ____

2. Which layer of the OSI model provides end-to-end connectivity to send data across a network?

 ____

3. Which layer of the OSI model defines the signaling, connector types, and network topology, and sends 0s and 1s?

 ____

4. Which layer of the OSI model provides a user interface and means of communication with an e-mail program?

 ____

5. Which layer of the OSI model is subdivided into the MAC and the LLC layers?

 ____

6. Which layer of the OSI model provides security, representation, and data compression services?

 ____

7. Which layer of the OSI model establishes, maintains, and tears down a session, while keeping multiple communications separate?

 ____

8. What are the devices and PDUs at the bottom three layers of the OSI model?

 a. Physical

 ____

 b. Data Link

 ____

c. Network

____

9. What OSI model layers are associated with the IP protocol suite Application Layer? (Choose three.)
   a. Physical
   b. Presentation
   c. Network
   d. Session
   e. Transport
   f. Application
   g. Data Link
10. Which layer of the OSI model includes the TCP and UDP protocols?
    a. Network
    b. Transport
    c. Presentation
    d. Application
11. Which of the following protocols are associated with e-mail services? (Choose two.)
    a. HTTP
    b. SNMP
    c. SMTP
    d. ICMP
    e. POP
12. For sending Web requests and receiving Web pages, which protocol is used?
    a. SMTP
    b. HTTP
    c. SNMP
    d. Telnet
    e. FTP
13. IP is independent of the Data Link and Physical Layers. True or False?

Extended Activities

1. Write the proper layer of the OSI model for each description.

   a. Layer 4 Transport

   b. Layer 3 Network

   c. Layer 2 Data link

   Frames packets by adding new header information

   ____

   Responsible for routing traffic through the network

   ____

   Uses a port number as an address

   ____

   Uses a MAC address for transmission

   ____

   Is responsible for end-to-end connectivity

   ____

   Provides only best-effort delivery of packets

   ____

   Can perform windowing and flow control

   ____

   Uses a logical address for decision making

   ____

2. Match the following definitions with the proper term from the list at the end of the question.

   A physical address in hexadecimal format

   ____

The memory area where incoming transmissions are held until they can be processed

____

The process of securing data before transmission

____

A communication method for a reliable transport protocol

____

The process of discovering and maintaining network information

____

The response that indicates successful receipt

____

The process used to break data into smaller blocks for transmission

____

The device which reads the MAC address before performing any operations

____

The device which uses a logical address before determining the best path

____

The connectionless Transport Layer protocol

____

The process that allows a number of segments to be transmitted before a response is expected

____

Protocols that have a hierarchical address

____

The process that helps prevent transmissions from being accidentally dropped

____

A transmission that is addressed to all devices

____

The sublayer that provides identification of the network-layer protocol

____

The process that adds header information before transmission

____

a. Buffer
b. Segmentation
c. Connection-oriented
d. Acknowledgment
e. Switch
f. Broadcast
g. IP and IPX
h. Encapsulation
i. Flow control
j. Windowing
k. MAC
l. Encryption
m. UDP
n. Router
o. Routing updates
p. LLC

3. Write in the correct OSI model layer, associating it with each protocol.

   HTTP

   ____

   ICMP

   ____

   ARP

   ____

   Ethernet

   ____

   Telnet

   ____

   TCP

   ____

   SNMP

   ____

   UDP

   ____

   IP

   ____

   SMTP

   ____

   a. Application or upper 3
   b. Network
   c. Data Link
   d. Transport

Lesson 3—Network Devices

This lesson provides greater detail on the function of hubs, switches, routers, and multilayer switches. The lesson starts with a definition of each and offers insight into how each device handles network traffic.

Two important concepts are discussed:

- **A collision domain** represents all the devices that contend for bandwidth when they attempt to access the network. In an Ethernet environment, a collision may occur if more than one device tries to access the network at the same time. Devices such as switches, bridges, and routers are designed to break up collision domains. This prevents contention issues and, therefore, prevents collisions.
- **A broadcast domain** represents all the devices that receive a broadcast message. It is a good idea to reduce the size of broadcast domains to reduce the amount of unnecessary traffic received by all devices. Routers and layer 3 switches are both capable of physically breaking up broadcast domains. Virtual Local Area Networks (VLANs) can be used to logically define broadcast domains.

Hubs were the original network devices used to connect PCs, servers, and printers. Hubs were connected with bridges that allowed for some traffic isolation and more scalable networks. More sophisticated switching hubs and layer 2 switches have replaced hubs, although many hubs still operate in existing infrastructures.

Switches eliminate the need for bridges and offer complete collision management, as well as higher transmission speeds. Routers are used to segment a large network into smaller networks called "subnets." This isolates traffic, provides security, allows for growth, and offers access to the Internet or other WAN connections.

Objectives

At the end of this lesson you will be able to:

- Identify and describe layer 1 devices
- Identify and describe layer 2 devices
- Identify and describe layer 3 devices
- Describe other network devices
- Describe network security components

Key Point

Hubs, switches, and routers are the devices that transmit information through a network, and each has a specific purpose.

Layer 1 Devices

Layer 1 devices, or Physical Layer devices, are simple network components. They are designed to pass a signal without reading any addressing or performing any decision making processes. The most these devices can do is convert a signal from one form to another. Layer 1 devices commonly found in local area network (LAN) environments include repeaters, transceivers, and hubs.

Connecting to wide area networks (WANs) offers more options, including modems, codecs, CSU/DSUs, and multiplexers (MUX). These components are discussed in greater detail in Module 2. The function of repeaters and hubs is presented here.

Repeaters

A repeater is a component that fits inline on a cable or is embedded in another device. A repeater can perform the following tasks:

- Repeat a digital signal
- Extend the physical cable segment
- Change cable types

A repeater is used to repeat a digital signal exactly as it was originally generated. Signals degrade due to external interference, crosstalk, and overall impedance factors. A repeater takes the degraded signal, digitally re-creates it, then transmits it out of the other side. A repeater is different from an amplifier, which also works at the Physical Layer.

An amplifier is used to re-create and retransmit an analog signal. The difference is in the signal itself. An analog signal has various states of transmission. If noise or interference is introduced into the signal, it is transmitted together. An amplifier cannot tell the difference between the original signal and the line noise. It regenerates all of it and sends it along. Therefore, an analog transmission has less quality over long runs due to noise. By contrast, even if noise and interference are introduced into the digital signal, the 0s and 1s are regenerated exactly as the repeater reads them. This makes the digital signal cleaner and prevents it from degrading over long distance. Thus, repeaters are necessary to extend the cable segment and exceed specified distance limitations.

Finally, a repeater can change cable types. In the past, this was commonly done to change from the coax cable used in a bus environment to unshielded twisted pair (UTP) cable. When functioning in this manner, a repeater is sometimes called a transceiver.

Hub Technology

Hubs, similar to repeaters, work at the Physical Layer of the OSI model. As shown on the Hub Diagram, hubs allow devices to share the same bandwidth and provide two main services:

- Hubs allow more end stations to communicate with one another by extending the physical wire. They do this by changing the physical topology from a bus to a star, which provides easier installation and troubleshooting.
- Hubs repeat the electronic signal to all connected ports, except to the one that originally transmitted the data. A hub does not read or manipulate the traffic that crosses it but repeats the electronic information to enable the signal to be sent farther.

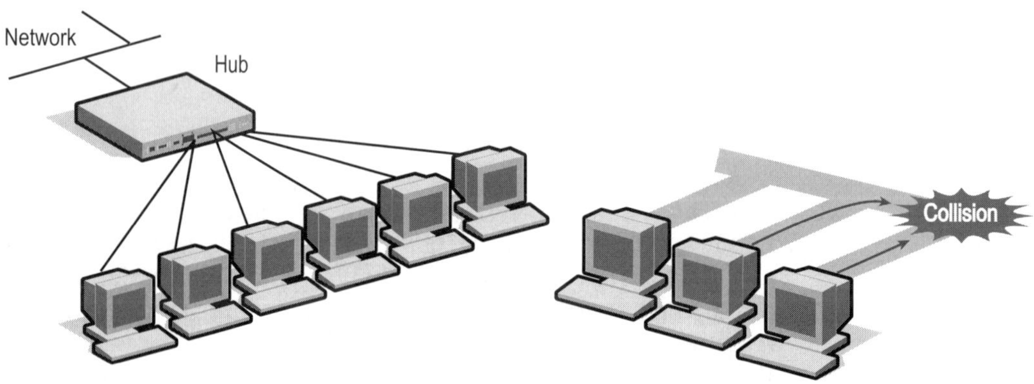

Hub

All the devices connected to a hub hear every signal that is generated; therefore, they are in the same broadcast domain. In addition, access to the media and collisions affect all devices because they are in the same collision domain. As discussed earlier in this lesson, collisions occur when more than one station listens to the wire, finds it available, and sends its data.

Because only one device can transmit at a time using a hub, the greater the number of devices on a network segment, the higher the chance for collisions. To help reduce traffic on an overpopulated network, hubs should be replaced by switches.

Hubs are often used in smaller networks where PCs, servers, and other network devices such as printers are all connected. Hubs can also be used as a central cable connecting point between the end station and a switching device. Considerations when you purchase a hub include:

- **Port density**—The number of ports needed is an important consideration. Allow for future growth. Multiple hubs can be stacked, enabling you to easily expand the number of available ports. Keep in mind, however, that connecting hubs together increases the size of the collision domain. More end devices means more traffic and more collisions, which reduces overall network performance.
- **Speed**—Speeds can range from 10 Mbps only to 100 Mbps only, or can include autosensing to allow for a mixed environment. This speed indicates the shared bandwidth.
- **Manageability**—Most hubs are simple plug-ins; however, management capabilities are available on the high-end models.

If a network requires many ports, variable speeds, and management capabilities, a switch is probably a better investment.

Layer 2 Devices

Layer 2 devices or Data Link Layer devices are more sophisticated than layer 1 devices. They are capable of reading address information and making decisions about how to handle the transmission. Network components found at layer 2 include NICs, bridges, and switches.

NIC

As discussed earlier in this lesson, NICs provide access to the network for the end device. They are installed in an expansion slot, as part of the motherboard, on the backplane of a laptop; or they are inserted in a PCMCIA slot. The system includes the physical or MAC address of the sending and receiving NIC in the frame header. The NIC has the following responsibilities:

- **Recognize** its own MAC address to retrieve frames from the network

- **Access** the network using the appropriate media access method such as Ethernet or Token Ring
- **Generate** the proper series and type of bits, based on media type; different standards apply for coax, UTP, STP, fiber optic, or wireless transmission

Bridges

Bridges are layer 2 devices that learn and store MAC addresses in a table. The bridge refers to this table to forward frames to the correct port and filter the traffic from all non-addressed ports. In the past, bridges were implemented in LAN environments where hub-to-hub communications were no longer efficient.

When traffic on a LAN started to cause performance problems, bridges reduced the load by dividing the network into separate segments. This worked because the filtering action of a layer 2 device created separate collision domains within the same network.

The nodes within each collision domain share the full bandwidth of the network only among themselves and not the entire network. This approach works best when most LAN traffic is local—in other words, when nodes within a department tend to communicate with one another much more than they do with nodes in other departments.

Bridge placement and network design was based on the 80/20 rule, meaning 80 percent of the traffic stayed local and 20 percent crossed the bridge. For example, if a server provides file storage for a department, much of the traffic in that department tends to be between that department's end devices and the server.

If a bridge is used to divide a LAN into two segments, the traffic on each segment will be approximately one-half what it was before. A relatively small proportion of network traffic will need to flow across the bridge, as illustrated on the Bridge Connectivity Diagram.

The technique called "traffic isolation" is an important tool for controlling network use. It can also be used to control traffic between segments and the network backbone.

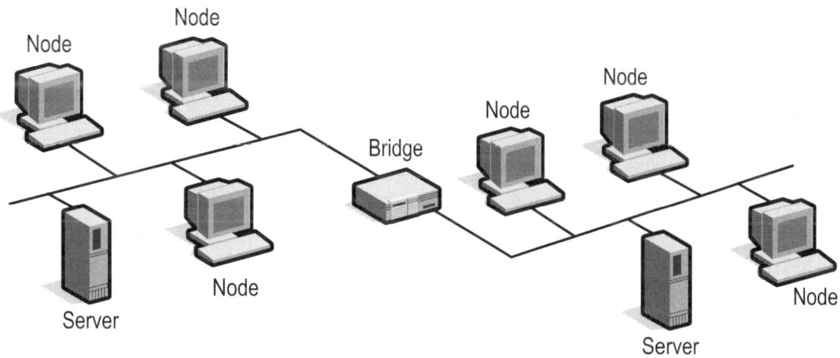

Bridge Connectivity

Note: This diagram shows only the bridge device. Typically, end devices connect to hubs, and hubs connect to bridges. The diagram has been simplified to show only the bridge in the network and the rest as Ethernet segments.

Bridges may sometimes be found in legacy networks, but are rarely installed anymore. After Internet usage became commonplace in organizations of all sizes, the 80/20 rule effectively "went out the window". Now, much of the network traffic travels between routed networks, and many organizations use tunnels on the Internet as their private WAN links, requiring the use of Layer 3 devices in the place of bridges.

Bridges were at a disadvantage, too, because they communicated at only 10 Mb, and were often designed for coax and AUI (attachment unit interface) cable connections.

For networks that still have hubs, and there are many, a small switch is used in place of the bridge. This is a cost-effective way of handling higher speeds, while not incurring the cost of a switch with a large number of ports.

Switch Technology

Layer 2 switches process frames using MAC address information from the Data Link Layer. A switch provides similar functionality as a software-based bridge. However, switching technology has exceeded bridge capabilities by using specialized hardware, called application-specific integrated circuits (ASICs). Switches offer scalability, low latency, and faster throughput (up to gigabit speed).

As you learned earlier in this lesson, switches help reduce traffic on a network because the switch makes each interface its own collision domain. This allows multiple devices to transmit data simultaneously without causing a collision.

As an analogy, a hub is like a single-lane road where all traffic has to share the same path. A switch is more like a freeway with multiple lanes and many overpasses, allowing vehicles to share the primary route without getting in one another's way.

To understand how this works, you need to review the operation of a switch. The Switch Diagram shows how contention is eliminated when each port gets its own virtual lane.

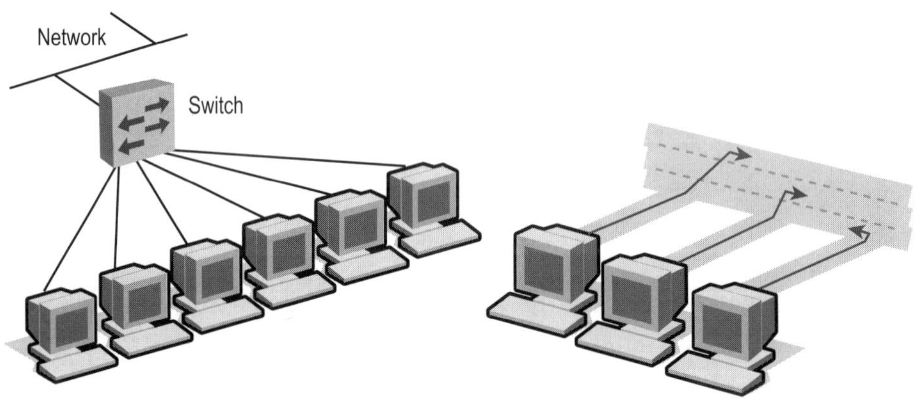

Switch

Remember from the Data Link Layer discussion in Lesson 2 that an Ethernet packet contains both source and destination MAC addresses. A switch reads every frame that is transmitted and creates a table with the source MAC address and interface where the frame was received.

This table is often called the MAC table, or filter table. The switch checks the MAC table for the destination address to determine whether its location is known. The switch handles transmission of the frame as follows:

- **Forwarding**—If the address is found in the MAC address table, the switch forwards the frame directly to the correct interface.
- **Filtering**—If the MAC address is found, no other interfaces receive the transmission. In this way, the switch filters unnecessary traffic by preventing it from being sent to other interfaces.
- **Flooding**—If the switch does not find the destination MAC address, it copies the frame out to all ports; this is called "flooding." Eventually, the receiving station replies and the switch updates its table with the new information.

A broadcast message is automatically sent to all ports and devices on every segment. Therefore, all devices and segments attached to a switch are said to be in the same broadcast domain.

To eliminate broadcast storms or a high volume of broadcasts propagating through the network, routers are implemented. In addition, routers are also necessary when dissimilar network topologies, such as Ethernet and Token Ring, are connected.

As with hubs, when you purchase switching devices, port density, speed, and manageability are all key considerations. Cisco provides an array of switch products, from the desktop environment to the high-end backbone solution. The number of ports can range from 12 to more than 100. Speeds vary from 10 Mbps, 100 Mbps, and 1,000 Mbps, and also provide autosensing capabilities on higher-end models.

Finally, manageability allows a network administrator to configure, monitor, and easily troubleshoot network configurations. In addition, many switches today allow logical segmentation with VLANs and the ability to prioritize traffic at the Data Link Layer.

Router Technology

Routers are layer 3 or Network Layer devices that perform a number of functions within a network. One of the most important is separating the physical network into segments. Each network segment becomes its own collision and broadcast domain. This reduces the volume of traffic that would lead to collisions and it prevents broadcast messages from propagating to all devices on the network. These are two important considerations in a large network environment.

Each network segment and every device is assigned a logical address. Depending on the protocols used, this could be an IP or an IPX address. The address itself is hierarchical, meaning that one portion of the address denotes the network and the other portion uniquely identifies a node. Note that routers use this information to locate a network and determine the best path to transmit data to that network. This process, however, makes routers slower than switches because a switch reads Data Link Layer headers, and a router has to read into the Network Layer header for its information.

When a router first starts up, it usually has no information about the network environment. Network routing table information can be manually entered as static routes or it can be dynamically learned using routing protocols.

Protocols such as RIP, IGRP, and OSPF supply route update packets that provide this information. Each device then builds and maintains a routing table used to transmit data. A routing table holds at a minimum the following three main components:

- **Network address**—Identifies the logical address of network segments known to the router. An entry must be kept for each protocol used on the network because the different addresses cannot be used interchangeably.
- **Egress interface (INT)**—Identifies the exit interface that is used when sending packets destined for another network.
- **Metric**—Identifies the value used to measure the distance to another network. This helps the router select the best path to send traffic through, based on the lowest metric. Each protocol has its own metric—for example, hops (the number of routers to pass through), bandwidth (the size or speed of the channel), or tick (the time in one-eighteenths of a second).

The Routing Table Diagram shows two routers, three network segments, and two end devices. The routing tables have been completed and show the network numbers, interface, and simple metric. The following steps are an overview of the routing process:

1. If a packet from Station 2.23 were destined for Station 6.15, the receiving router would strip off the Data Link Layer header, note the remote network address of 6.0, look it up in its table, and determine that it should be sent out of Interface Serial1 (S1).

2. The packet would be reframed with the router's MAC address as the source in the Data Link Layer header and sent from S1, traveling across the 4.0 network to the second router.
3. The second router would strip the Data Link Layer information and review the address. On finding it is destined for a local device, the router would reframe the packet and send it out of the Ethernet interface of the 6.0 network and on to the appropriate end device.
4. If an entry does not exist for a destination network, the packet is sent to the default gateway; or, if the default gateway does not exist, the packet is dropped.

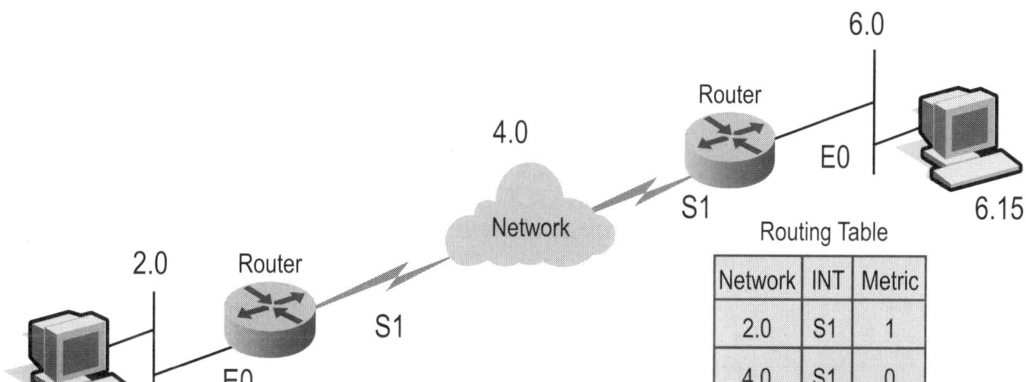

Routing Table

Network	INT	Metric
2.0	S1	1
4.0	S1	0
6.0	E0	0

Routing Table

Network	INT	Metric
2.0	E0	0
4.0	S1	0
6.0	S1	1

Routing Table

Note that routers read only the Network Layer address. In addition, when selecting the best path, routers look at the network and, if necessary, the subnet portion of the address. They do not bother with the host portion of the address when making routing decisions. The router leaves delivery to a host for a Data Link Layer device such as a switch.

Remember as well that the router must remove the Data Link Layer header information to read the network header. When reframing, the router replaces the original source address with its own MAC address. It may also change the destination MAC address as necessary, based on the next hop or device in the network path.

In addition to route selection and network segmentation, routers can also provide security. Network traffic can be blocked based on header information such as specific protocol, port number, or local address. An administrator can create an access list that filters specific traffic and then associates it with a router interface.

Inbound and outbound traffic is then controlled through that router interface. Along these lines, routers use the same information to provide quality of service (QoS) features such as bandwidth availability and high-priority routing.

Finally, routers provide interconnectivity. They allow communication between LAN and WAN environments, remote access to mobile users and telecommuters, and connectivity to the Internet. If VLANs are implemented in the network, routers can provide the link between them.

Routers can also be used to handle disparate network topologies such as Ethernet and Token Ring or FDDI. The router translates between the different media types and allows communication between different devices. When a router is translating between different protocols or providing connections to another network, it is acting as a gateway.

For example, when you configure IP address information on a desktop PC, you include a default gateway so that the PC knows which router is acting as the gateway and providing access to the Internet.

Not all routers function as gateways: only when they are doing protocol conversion or access to another network would they be considered a gateway. Otherwise, when making path selection and segmenting broadcast domains, the device is just a router.

A router may also have to "bridge" protocols that are considered non-routable. A non-routable protocol is one that does not have a hierarchical address or Network Layer implementation. Examples of non-routable protocols include Digital Equipment Corporation's Local Area Transport (DEC-LAT), IBM's Systems Network Architecture (SNA), Netbios, and Netbeui.

The router has to bridge these protocols to transmit them through the network. A router with this capability is sometimes called a "brouter" or bridging/router. Today, IP is the primary protocol used in both LANs and the Internet. However, legacy systems may still require the router to handle and, if necessary, translate multiple protocols.

When purchasing a router, you must first determine the function the router will be providing. Routers used for internal network segmentation have different requirements from routers that will be used for Internet or WAN connectivity. The following are a number of items to consider when making a router purchase:

- What protocols are used in the network (routable and non-routable)?
- What size network is the router connecting to (large, small)?
- How many and what type of LAN ports are needed?
- What routing protocols need to be supported?
- Will the router provide gateway/protocol translation services?
- How many LAN segments will the router support?
- What LAN speeds are needed now and in the future?
- Should the router have fixed or modular interfaces?
- Will the router provide Internet connectivity?
- Will the router provide WAN connectivity to branch offices?
- How many and what type of WAN ports are needed?
- Will the router provide firewall/security functions?
- Will the router need to perform address translation services?
- What WAN encapsulation types are needed?

These are only a few of the questions you must answer before selecting the correct router device. Cisco is known most for its router technology; it offers a wide selection of options and cutting-edge features in this area.

Layer 3 Switches

Layer 3 switches are packet switching devices that use the IP address in the network header to make filter and forwarding decisions. These devices use traditional and proprietary routing protocols to exchange routing information. They segment the network into physical broadcast domains and require different IP addresses on each interface, just as a router would.

Layer 3 switches are often faster than routers because they use ASICs instead of software decision making processes used on a router. This improves performance but is sometimes limited in upgrades if the hardware is manufactured to perform specific functions. In addition, switch backplanes are often more efficient because they process less information and perform fewer tasks than routers. These switches cannot translate protocols or connect different network topologies, but instead can focus on fast transmissions.

Layer 3 switches can perform the same packet-by-packet best-path determination as a router. However, many layer 3 switches have a more sophisticated learning and forwarding method than a router. A router looks up the destination IP network address in the packet and reviews its routing table to determine the best path to get there. A single transmission may have hundreds to thousands of segments all going to the same destination. The router looks each route up over and over again, methodically guaranteeing that they are all using the best path.

A layer 3 switch determines the best path, just as the router does. However, once it has sent information to that destination, it predicts that all other segments going to the same destination for that transmission could also use the original best path. Therefore, instead of determining the route over and over as a router might, it switches the information over the best path from that point forward.

This process is called "route-once-switch-many" and is an exceedingly fast and efficient method for transmitting packets. Layer 3 switches can also be called routing switches or switching routers. Unlike a router, these devices do not usually have WAN or Internet connectivity; however, that is changing as many vendors expand their product lines.

Other Network Devices

The following sections describe network devices that expand LAN and WAN services beyond traditional data communications over twisted pair cabling. All are components often found in contemporary networks.

DSLAMs

Digital Service Line Access Multiplexers (DSLAMs) are not LAN components. Rather, they are the equipment that allows service providers to offer xDSL services to its subscribers. DSLAMs are designed to filter traffic based on specific frequencies. xDSL service is delivered over Plain Old Telephone Service (POTS) lines. It uses the frequency above 4 Hz, which is set aside for the talk path that is used when you make a telephone call.

The upper frequencies offer high bandwidth download and low bandwidth upload transmissions. A DLSAM is inserted between the subscriber's local loop and the phone switches, which are used to switch calls and make circuit-switched modem connections. The DSLAM is designed to recognize traffic in the upper frequencies. Instead of passing this traffic to the phone switch, it moves it off to an optical network with a direct connection to an Internet service provider (ISP). In turn, this provides direct access to the Internet.

The DSLAM can allow the end user device to perform a connection-oriented process and remain active for up to two hours. It is activated as needed and terminated at a defined point. The other option, which is now more common, is always on. The line is provisioned to be always active. Keepalive communications are sent across the line to the customer premise equipment (CPE), which is a xDSL modem or router to maintain the logical circuit.

Cisco offers a number of high-end service provider and subscriber xDSL devices.

Voice Servers

Voice over IP and IP telephony services have become a more commonplace type of network traffic than in years past. Voice, communications, media, or call servers are a number of different names to identify the functions of an "IP centric" or IP-enabled Private Branch Exchange (PBX) or Networked Branch Exchange (NBX). Notice that many terms attempt to relay the same functionality. In an ever-changing market, each vendor has some method of differentiating its networked voice components from the others.

Generically, a voice server is a box that runs an operating system and voice-related applications. Although in the past, operating systems were usually proprietary, vendors have recognized the benefits of relying on open standard platforms like Microsoft NT and 2000, Linux, and UNIX.

The voice applications can provide the basic services of digit identification, call processing, route selection, and basic features like call forward, call transfer, and others. More advanced voice servers can provide a range of features similar to those found in tradi tional PBX environments.

The major benefit of IP communications and networked access is the ability to integrate services between the voice server and other components like voice mail, e-mail, unified messaging, fax services, call accounting systems, call management systems, automatic call distribution, and many others. In addition, IP communications ease integration with database information, which can be accessed using Interactive Voice Response (IVR) as self-service or through an agent query.

Voice servers have come a long way and still have a long way to go. Their designers are working to overcome the limitations of networks that are not up to the demands of toll-quality voice communications. This is a growing market that offers many promising developments.

Cisco offers the Universal Access Server, which can handle voice, fax, data, security, routing, gateway, and wireless communications.

Optical Network Devices

Optical network access devices provide the ability to connect to fiber optic transmission media "in the glass." This means that fiber optic is used throughout and no conversion from copper to light is necessary. Service providers that have high-density fiber optic backbones use this equipment to drop and insert information into the optical path.

In addition, multiplexing techniques such as coarse wave division multiplexing (CWDM) and dense wave division multiplexing (DWDM) allow the fiber optic media to be shared. The wave lengths are refracted and multiplexed to allow multiple transmissions across a single connection. This greatly improves the available bandwidth without changing the cable. Cisco offers a number of optical devices for customer, service provider, and wave division multiplexing purposes.

Network Security Components

Network security is a top concern in network administration and design. Daily, hackers are finding new ways to compromise networks of sizes ranging from home offices to global organizations. The following sections discuss components commonly used to protect networks from unauthorized access.

Firewalls

According to the National Computer Security Association (NCSA), a firewall is "a system or combination of systems that enforces a boundary between two or more networks." It is a controlled access point between one network and another.

There are many types of firewalls and applications for firewall use. The primary application in most networks today is a firewall between a private network and an external network such as the Internet.

An Internet firewall is a controlled access point that protects a private network from the outside world. It cannot stop attacks from malicious insiders, nor can it take the place of user education, and security policies and procedures. An Internet firewall is only part of an overall security plan. A firewall performs two related functions:

- Blocks external traffic from entering a private network.
- Permits internal traffic to exit a private network.

Some firewalls place greater emphasis on blocking outside traffic, whereas others emphasize permitting internal traffic to pass. Some firewalls permit only electronic mail (e-mail) traffic through them, thereby protecting the network against attacks other than those against the e-mail service.

More elaborate firewalls block traffic from the outside to the inside but permit users on the inside to communicate freely with the outside. Other firewalls provide less strict protections and only block access to certain services known to be problems.

Generally, firewalls are configured to protect against unauthorized interactive logins from an external network. This, more than anything, helps prevent tampering with machines on a network. Internet firewalls are also important because they can provide a focal point for security and auditing.

Firewalls often provide summaries to the administrator about what kinds and amounts of traffic passed through the network, how many attempts there were to break into it, and so forth.

Many features exist in firewall products. Firewalls are normally composed of both software and hardware products. Firewalls can be grouped into three primary categories, including:

- **Network layer firewalls (also called a packet filter)**—This type of firewall can read the IP address in the packet header to filter traffic. It can filter entire networks, subnets, or individual host IP addresses. This may be difficult to control because it blocks all traffic from certain systems, regardless of what communications they are attempting.

- **Application or port firewalls**—This type of firewall uses the port address in the transport header to make filter, or permit decisions. This can be somewhat restrictive since it blocks all access for everyone, not just some. For instance, if port 23 for Telnet is closed, no one, not even the administrator, can get in through that port for Telnet communications.
- **Hybrid firewalls**—This type of firewall has mutlilayer capabilities with the potential to read IP addresses, port numbers, and often even message contents. This allows granular control using a combination of IP and port information to make specific filter and permit test conditions.

Other firewalls can provide various services like pinhole. This allows an authorized connection to leave the network, while poking a hole for that session, for whatever source and destination port numbers were assigned. The pinhole closes as soon as the session is terminated. This type of firewall is handy for voice and some multimedia applications that do not use specific ports for every communication.

Proxy Servers

An application-level gateway allows a network administrator to implement a much stricter security policy than for a packet-filtering router. Rather than relying on a generic packet-filtering tool to manage the flow of Internet services through a firewall, special-purpose code (a proxy service) is installed for access to Internet services.

A proxy service acts as a "middleman" between a source and destination system. Instead of communicating directly with each other, the two systems establish a connection with the proxy server, which then exchanges messages between them.

If the network administrator does not install the proxy code for a particular application, the service is not supported and cannot be forwarded across the firewall. Also, the proxy code can be configured to support only those specific features of a service that the network administrator considers acceptable, while denying all other features.

This enhanced security comes with an increased cost. The gateway hardware and proxy service applications are expensive, additional time and knowledge is required to configure the proxy, and increased security means a decrease in service and transparency to users. As always, the network administrator must balance the organization's need for security with the user community's demand for ease of use.

Users are permitted access using proxy services, but they are never permitted to log in to the application-level gateway itself. If users are permitted to log in to the firewall system, an intruder could potentially compromise the effectiveness of the firewall. For example, after gaining root access, an intruder could install Trojan horses to collect passwords or modify the security configuration files of the firewall or proxy to create additional access holes.

AAA Services

Authentication, Authorization, and Accounting (AAA) services are the basis for securing everything within a network environment. Each operating system handles this process slightly differently, while providing the same functionality. Some operating systems are more secure and have much stronger access methods; others are easy for hackers to gain access to, using known bugs and security holes.

Third-party software products can be added to existing systems to provide these services using something other than the traditional user name and password. These types of systems are often implemented for remote access and require additional components such as a digital signature, or a digital key, which is constantly changing, or the correct response to a challenge.

In addition to securing remote access, many AAA systems are focusing on new technologies that provide more security. Biometrics have become popular methods for login and authentication, using voice recognition, fingerprint, hand shape, face characteristics, and the stuff movies are made of, retinal scan. Regardless of the methods used, AAA servers provide the following functions:

- **Authentication**—This first step is a validation that users are who they say they are. At a minimum a user name and password are required. Although probably the most common method of login, user name and passwords are only as secure as the people who use them. It is not uncommon to find that people have shared their passwords with someone else, or worse yet, written them down somewhere around their work area.
- **Authorization**—After a user or device is authenticated in the system, authorization validates what rights that user or device has. This could take the form of changing configurations and performing administrative tasks. It could also be more user-oriented such as the ability to send, receive, or change files and directories; print; and access network resources.

- **Accounting**—The accounting step logs and monitors the traffic and access made for authorized connections. This helps administrators track what is going on and audit network transmissions. Activities that are easy to track include file changes that have a new date, time, and ownership information. Another example would be access to Internet resources through a proxy server.

  Not all communications can be easily tracked or accounted for. Administrators may not turn on some of these features since they can affect network performance.

Review Questions

1. Hubs have one collision domain and one broadcast domain. True or False?
2. A router can switch frames by reading the MAC address. True or False?
3. A multilayer switch can transmit information based on MAC address, IP address, and/or port number. True or False?
4. A router decapsulates a frame to retrieve IP information. It then reframes the transmission with new MAC addresses before sending it to the next network. True or False?
5. A router and layer 3 switch both use routing protocols to dynamically learn about other networks and the best path(s) to reach them. True or False?
6. In addition to routing, which two functions can a traditional router also perform? (Choose two.)
   a. Fast switching
   b. Bridging non-routable protocols
   c. Creating a single collision and broadcast domain
   d. Providing a gateway to another network
7. A router reads what address in a packet?
   a. MAC address
   b. IP address
   c. Physical address
   d. Port address
8. What switch mode is used when the switch transmits information directly to its destination, based on a single MAC address?
   a. Flooding
   b. Filtering
   c. Forwarding
   d. Broadcasting

9. Which device type supports end-device connectivity and can define VLANs?
   a. Layer 2 switches
   b. Layer 3 switches
   c. Layer 4 switches
   d. Routers
10. Which of the following devices can read a MAC address? (Choose two.)
    a. Router
    b. Switch
    c. Bridge
    d. Hub
11. What network components could be used to provide security for traffic coming from the Internet? (Choose two.)
    a. Switch
    b. Firewall
    c. Hub
    d. Proxy server
12. What is the component used by a service provider to offer xDSL services to subscribers?
    a. DSLAM
    b. DSL router
    c. DSL modem
    d. DSL broadband server

Extended Activities

1. For what purpose is a hub most often used?

2. Why would an administrator implement a switch instead of a hub?

3. When would a router need to be included in designing a network?

Lesson 4—Network Topologies

The physical structure of a network, or its "topology," describes the physical arrangement of wires, connectors, and other devices that connect a group of communicating nodes. A network's topology has a powerful effect on its operation and efficiency.

A network topology is like a system of roads and highways. Over time, different types of road systems have been developed to meet various types of transportation needs. For example, the winding, interconnected streets of a suburban neighborhood are designed for low-speed travel between individual homes. In contrast, straight, wide superhighways provide high-speed travel between entire cities.

In a similar way, different network topologies have been developed to meet various communication needs. This lesson introduces the main topologies used in data networks. A single network may be based on only one of these topologies or combine several of them. The basic LAN topologies include: bus, star, extended star, ring, and star ring. The basic WAN topologies include: full and partial mesh, and service provider cloud.

Objectives

At the end of this lesson you will be able to:

- Compare physical and logical topologies
- Define the characteristics of a bus topology
- Define the characteristics of a star and extended star topology
- Define the characteristics of a ring and star ring topology
- Define the characteristics of a mesh and partial mesh topology
- Define the characteristics of a service provider cloud

Key Point

LANs and WANs can be built in a number of different topologies, each of which influences the network's physical and logical configurations, its size, and how devices connect and communicate.

Logical and Physical Topologies

There are two ways in which data networking professionals refer to topologies:

- Logical topologies show where signals go. They eliminate some details to make the important relationships easier to see.
- Physical topologies show more details about a network's connectors, cabling, and wide area links.

Physical Star, Logical Bus

To understand this difference, think of bus and star topologies. As we learned earlier in this module, signals travel exactly the same way in both bus and star topologies. However, for reasons described in this lesson, hardly anyone is wiring new bus networks. Ethernet LANs now use the more flexible star topology. Despite this fact, a broadcast network is usually diagrammed as a bus topology.

Therefore, the physical topology shown in the Physical Star Topology Diagram is equivalent to the Logical Bus Topology Diagram.

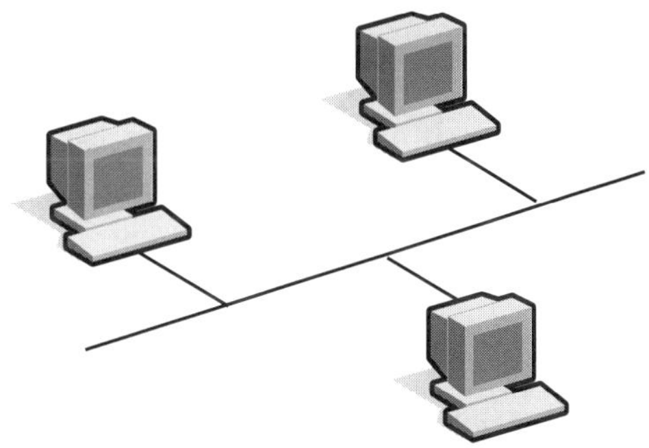

Logical Bus Topology

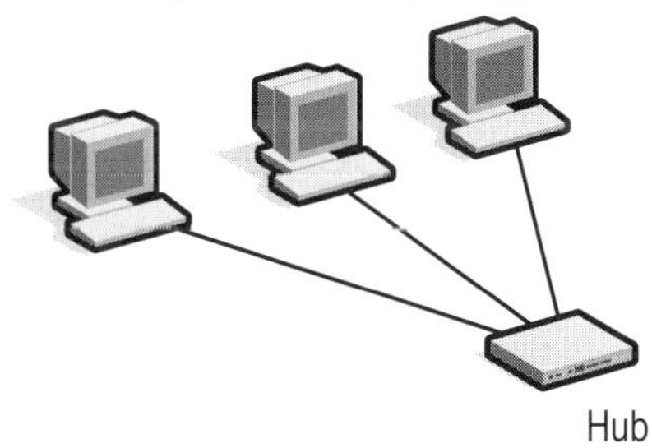

Physical Star Topology

As you can see, the logical diagram does not show the hub that connects the group of computers. However, the diagram of the bus makes it easy to see that all the devices directly share signals among themselves. Thus, when you see a bus diagram in this book or any other network text, remember that you are probably looking at a hub-centered star network.

Physical Star, Logical Ring

Ring topologies provide another good example of the difference between physical and logical diagrams. As we just learned, stations on a local area ring network are usually not connected directly to each other. Instead, they are all plugged in to a central multistation access unit (MAU). Thus, the physical diagram of a ring network looks almost identical to that of a broadcast network as seen on the Star vs. Ring Physical Topology Diagram.

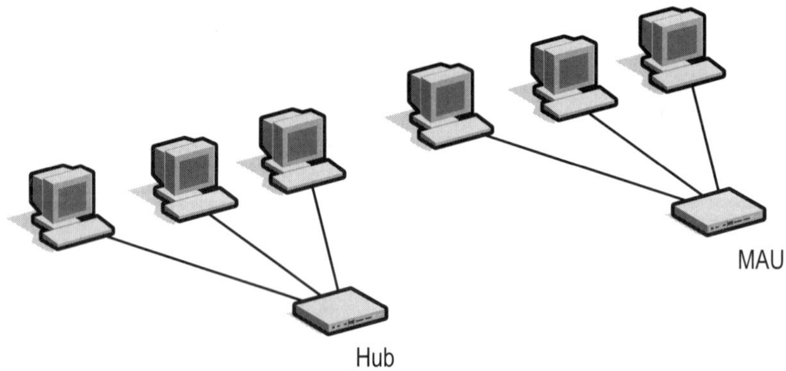

Star vs. Ring Physical Topology

It is easy to confuse these two networks. However, if we use logical diagrams, the difference between them is clear as seen on the Star vs. Ring Logical Topology Diagram.

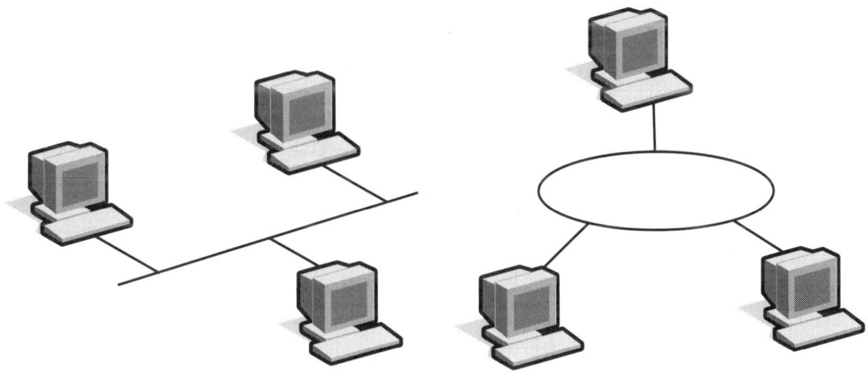

Star vs. Ring Logical Topology

Thus, when you see a LAN represented as a ring, remember that the devices are probably all connected to a central MAU.

Bus Topology

A bus topology is one of the simplest network designs and was the first topology used in LANs. A bus is a single electrical cable to which all devices in the network are connected (although the bus might be made up of many individual pieces of wire). This type of network structure is illustrated on the Bus Topology Diagram.

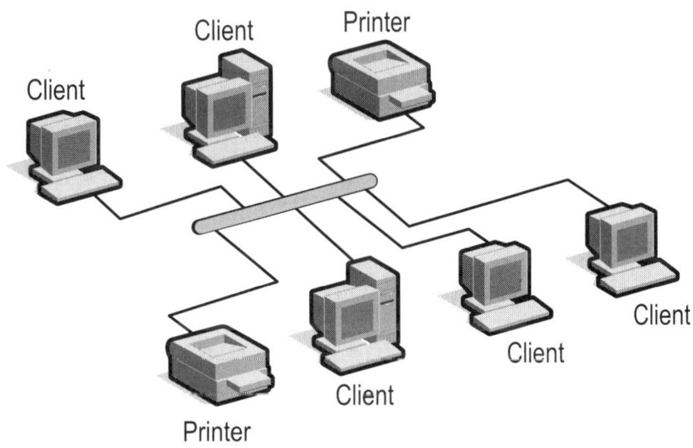

Bus Topology

The point where a device connects to the bus is called a "tap." Taps are made using different connection components, depending on the type of cable used for the bus.

When a node transmits data, the signal travels down the bus in both directions. Each node connected to the bus receives the signal as it passes that connection point. However, a node ignores any signal not specifically addressed to it. Because every node on the bus "hears" every message transmitted by any other node, all devices on a bus network are in the same broadcast domain.

When the signal reaches the end of the bus cable, a device called a "terminator" prevents the signal from reflecting back from the end of the wire. A terminator is an electrical resistor that essentially absorbs the signal energy.

If a bus network is not terminated, or the terminator has the wrong level of resistance, each signal may travel across the bus several times instead of just once. This problem reduces network performance because other nodes cannot transmit until the first signal dies down.

A bus topology is simple and easy to understand. However, if the bus cable breaks, the entire network may be disabled and is difficult to troubleshoot. In addition, moving, changing, or adding nodes on a bus means that the network is temporarily unavailable.

Star Topology

A star topology network is the most common type of LAN topology today. A star topology consists of multiple computers attached to a central signal-distributing device. Originally, the central device was a hub. This created a physical star but a logical bus. Similar to a bus, this configuration associates all end-devices in the same broadcast domain.

Networks designed today would have a switch as the central device. A switch acts as both a physical and logical star. Switches make filtering and forwarding decisions based on the MAC address in the frame.

Regardless of whether a hub or switch is used, each computer or end device is attached using a straight-through cable, as illustrated on the Star Topology Diagram.

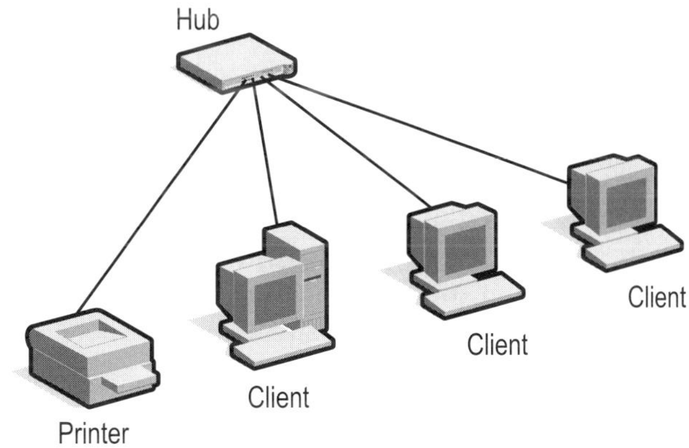

Star Topology

Star topologies provide the following advantages over bus topologies:

- Some hubs and switches have features that can detect defective cables and devices.
- End devices can be easily added and removed from a network.
- Network problems are easier to troubleshoot because suspect nodes can easily be disconnected.

In a star topology a single cable break only means that an end-device can no longer communicate with others. In a worst case scenario, the cable connecting the switch to the rest of the network breaks. In this case, the devices connected to the switch can communicate with each other; they just cannot connect to resources outside the switch.

However, in a star topology a new issue emerges: the hub or switch device becomes a single point of failure. If the device fails, many PCs, servers, printers, phones, and other end devices cannot communicate. Redundant hardware and software processes are built into higher-end switch devices to help prevent this problem.

Ring and Star-Ring

A "pure" ring topology consists of nodes connected in a series of point-to-point links, just as people join hands in a circle. Each node attached to the ring has one input and one output connection so that each node is connected to two links. When a node receives a signal on its input connection, it immediately passes it to the output connection. Thus, data flows only in one direction.

Like nodes on a star or bus network, a ring node only copies signals addressed to it. Each node can send messages by putting new bits onto the ring. A ring is susceptible to the same issues as a bus. Some technologies, therefore, use more than one ring, which can flow in opposite directions to prevent network outages.

A star-ring topology is built by combining ring and star concepts to obtain a reliable and serviceable configuration. A wire runs from each node to a central ring wiring hub, also called a multistation access unit (MAU). A star-ring is a physical star configuration; however, transmissions travel from node to node in a logical ring as the MAU copies each signal to each of its nodes in turn.

A star-ring topology requires more wire than a pure ring or bus. However, the MAU can eliminate problems caused by faulty hardware and connect multiple rings together. The MAU Connection Diagram shows how end devices connect to the logical ring and how a faulty device is bypassed in transmission.

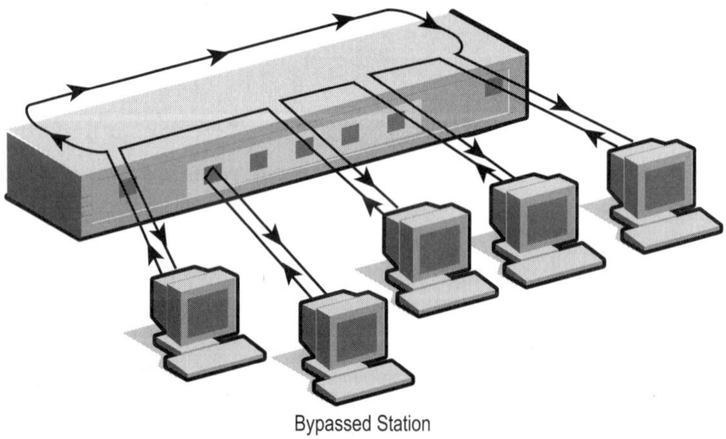

MAU Connection

Wide Area Topologies

As you learned at the beginning of this lesson, a WAN or a MAN is formed when two or more LANs are connected by point-to-point communication links. As the number of interconnected LANs increases, some networks develop a wide area star topology in which all branch offices connect to one central headquarters location. However, some organizations need each of their locations to be able to communicate directly with any other location, without routing through a central point.

Mesh

In a mesh topology, point-to-point links directly connect every site to every other site. Mesh networks are usually built over time as new sites are added to the overall network. The Mesh Network Topology Diagram provides an example of a mesh configuration.

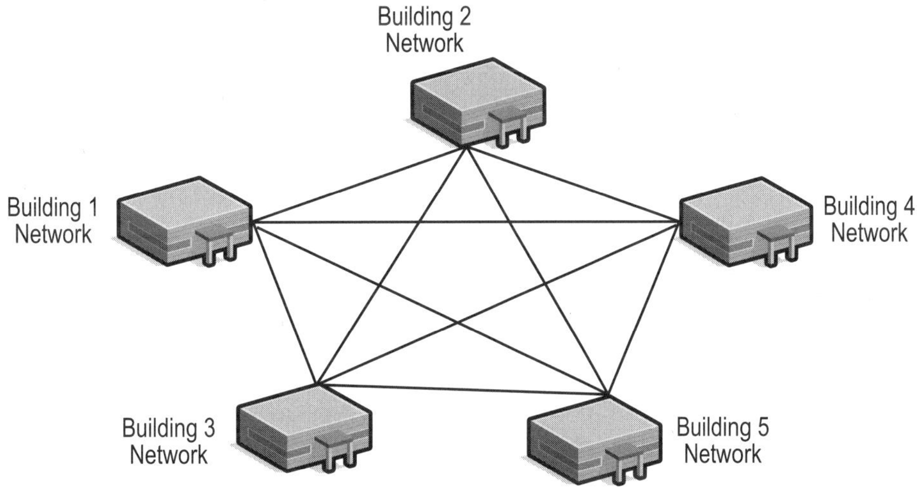

Mesh Network Topology

Mesh networks are fairly simple to understand. However, the number of point-to-point links increases sharply with the number of locations. For example, a three-site mesh network needs three links; however, four locations require six links, and five locations require ten links.

At that rate, it does not take long before the cost of a mesh network becomes very high. The benefit is that a mesh network provides extensive redundancy, which reduces the potential for transmission failure due to an outage.

Network Cloud

A network cloud, shown on the Network Cloud Diagram, is not really a topology. It is a representation of an unknown network structure, typically a transmission service offered by a networking service provider, such as a telephone company.

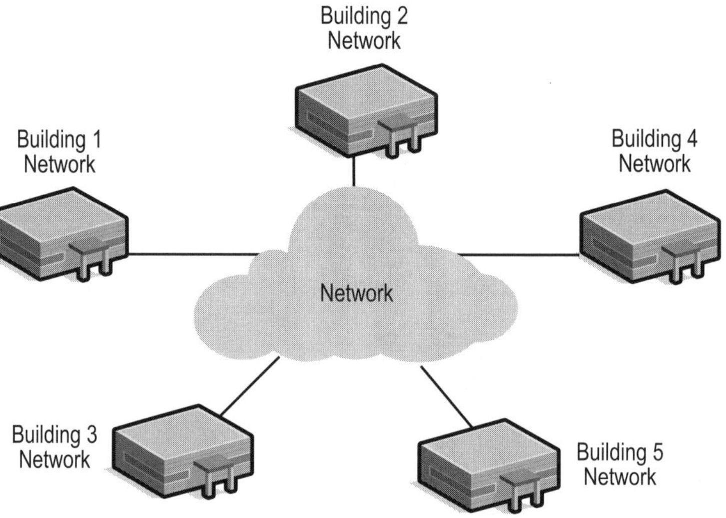

Network Cloud

The cloud symbol represents a private network of switching devices that may span a city, region, or nation. The network is drawn as a cloud because users of the service do not have any knowledge about the internal workings of that network. Only the service provider understands the topologies and connections that make up the paths between the switching sites within the cloud. The public telephone system and the Internet are two well-known examples of cloud networks.

To use the services of a cloud network, a company subscribes to the service, connects its locations to the edge of the cloud, and trusts the network provider to handle the details of moving traffic to its destination. Using a service provider's network usually means lower cost, less administration, and more flexibility over a mesh network. However, the possible drawbacks can be performance issues, security, and lack of network control.

Review Questions

1. Which of the following WAN topologies is managed and controlled by the network provider?
    a. A MAN
    b. A Mesh
    c. A Cloud
    d. A CN
2. An organization has decided that its point-to-point links are too costly to maintain. They have a reliable connection to the Internet with substantial bandwidth, as do all the branch offices. What network technology would allow them to securely transmit information between locations while reducing costs?
    a. Mesh
    b. Cloud
    c. VPN
    d. WAN
3. Which network topology uses coax cable with terminators?
    a. Bus
    b. Star
    c. Ring
    d. Star-ring
4. Which LAN topologies fail to function if a single wire is broken? (Choose two.)
    a. Mesh
    b. Star
    c. Ring
    d. Bus
5. Which components characterize a star topology? (Choose two.)
    a. UTP cable
    b. Coax cable
    c. Switch
    d. Terminators

6. What is the original network device used in a star configuration?
    a. Repeater
    b. Hub
    c. MAU
    d. Router
7. What defines the physical component in a star topology?
    a. The way the signal is transmitted
    b. The way the network components are cabled
    c. The way the network is addressed
    d. The protocol the NICs use
8. A hub is a physical star but a logical ___________?
    a. Ring
    b. Star
    c. Bus
    d. Mesh
9. What is the most common network LAN topology used in Ethernet networks?
    a. Star
    b. Bus
    c. Ring
    d. Mesh
10. What type of topology connects network devices through a MAU?
    a. Ring
    b. Star-ring
    c. Bus
    d. Mesh

Extended Activities

1. Match the following descriptions with the proper terms by choosing from the list at the end of the questions.

   The network topology that uses coaxial cable ______________

   The network topology that has a cable from a central network device running to each end device ______________

   The expensive, fully redundant WAN topology ____________

   The LAN topology that is often used in Token Ring networks and has a central access point ______________

   The network topology that connects the cable segment end-to-end, and for which a single cable break affects the entire network ______________

   The WAN network topology that uses a service provider instead of point-to-point leased lines ______________

   a. Ring
   b. Star
   c. Bus
   d. Cloud
   e. Mesh
   f. Star-ring

Summary

This module touched on many important concepts that will be expanded upon in later modules. Lesson 1 discussed PC and laptop components, including the all-important NIC. The lesson reviewed transmission and storage measurement terms. The three different numbering conventions were identified: binary, decimal, and hexadecimal. A conversion process was covered for each of these numbering schemes.

Lesson 2 provided an overview of networking and the OSI model, its seven layers and the types of devices found at the lower layers. If you are a network administrator, engineer, or designer, it is essential to understand the OSI model because it is used as a reference for all network devices, protocols, and hardware/software standards.

In this course, we review the OSI model when making comparisons. As fast as technology changes, you can rely on the fact that the OSI model will change very little, because it is the framework that all networking is based upon.

In addition to the OSI model, Lesson 2 diagramed how a transmission is framed to be sent across the network. It displayed how each of the bottom four layers encapsulate the information to be sent. It also compared the IP suite with the OSI model.

Lesson 3 discussed layer 1, 2, and 3 devices. Layer 1 devices are repeaters and hubs. These devices are unsophisticated and basically repeat a signal to extend the cable segment. Layer 2 devices have more capabilities to read and recognize the MAC or physical address.

NICs assign the source and destination MAC address into a frame, then access the media to send the transmission. Bridges and switches can read MAC addresses to make filtering and forwarding decisions.

Layer 3 devices include routers and layer 3 switches. Although these two devices can both read IP addresses and make best-path decisions, they are different in the way they go about their jobs.

This lesson ended by discussing some other network devices like DSLAMs, voice services, optical network devices, firewalls, proxy, and AAA servers.

Finally, Lesson 4 contrasted physical and logical network topologies. With that information, the lesson reviewed the characteristics of a bus, star, ring, star-ring, mesh, and cloud network topologies.

Module 1 Quiz

1. Which layer of the OSI model provides end-to-end delivery of segments?
   a. Network
   b. Session
   c. Transport
   d. Data Link
2. In which layer of the OSI model are repeaters found?
   a. Physical
   b. Data Link
   c. Network
   d. Transport
3. Which of the following is not a reason to use a reference model?
   a. Breaks a complex structure into smaller, easier-to-comprehend pieces
   b. Allows multiple vendors to develop products that can interact
   c. Requires everyone to use only a few select vendors when making network purchases
   d. Allows programmers to use a modular approach when developing software
4. When building a small network for 100 users, which components would be necessary for Internet access with security (Choose two.)
   a. Router
   b. Hub
   c. Firewall
   d. DSLAM
5. Which OSI model layer includes routers?
   a. Physical
   b. Network
   c. Transport
   d. Data Link

6. A large database file is moved from a user's hard drive into a centralized system where everyone can access it. The file is backed up regularly and secured. What type of network method is described here?
   a. Peer-to-peer
   b. Mesh
   c. Client/server
   d. Central access
7. What is the protocol that guarantees delivery and resides at the Transport Layer?
   a. UDP
   b. TCP
   c. IP
   d. IPX
8. You are troubleshooting an issue where a PC is not connecting to the network. What *physical* things should you check? (Choose two.)
   a. Is the cable properly plugged into the NIC and the wall jack?
   b. Are the correct protocols configured?
   c. Is the NIC's link light on?
   d. Is the correct software running on the PC?
   e. Can the PC share files?
9. Select a valid MAC address.
   a. 07:DH:C9:46
   b. 123.154.98.225
   c. 74:C0:91:66:34:B2
   d. 01:86:35:56:33
10. Other names for the address assigned to a NIC are: (Choose two.)
    a. Logical address
    b. Physical address
    c. MAC address
    d. Network address

11. Which layer of the OSI model adds both header and trailer information?
    a. Physical
    b. Network
    c. Transport
    d. Data Link
12. A NIC is installed in a PC. The NIC transmits bits as different voltages of electrical current. What type of media is this NIC using?
    a. Fiber optic
    b. Wireless
    c. Radio frequency
    d. Copper
13. Which service is not provided by routers?
    a. Best-path selection
    b. Translating between different topologies
    c. WAN connectivity
    d. Repeating a signal out of every port, except for the receiving port
14. Which of the following does a switch provide?
    a. All interfaces have the same collision and broadcast domains.
    b. All interfaces have the same collision domain but different broadcast domains.
    c. All interfaces have different collision domains but the same broadcast domain.
    d. All interfaces have different collision and different broadcast domains.
15. A hub creates which of the following physical network topologies?
    a. Bus
    b. Star
    c. Ring
    d. Mesh

16. Which of the following describe the address assigned to a NIC? (Choose three.)
    a. The address is 48 bits long.
    b. The address can easily be changed.
    c. The address is burned in at the factory.
    d. The address is in hexadecimal form.
    e. The address is in dotted-decimal notation.
    f. The address is 32 bits long.
17. Which of the following protocols are associated with e-mail services? (Choose two.)
    a. HTTP
    b. SNMP
    c. SMTP
    d. ICMP
    e. POP
18. A layer 2 switch is designed to read what address?
    a. MAC address
    b. IP address
    c. Logical address
    d. Port address
19. When purchasing a switch, which of these would not be considered when determining the requirements?
    a. Speed
    b. Port density
    c. WAN connections
    d. Manageability
20. Which layer of the OSI model has the PDU of a frame?
    a. Data Link
    b. Network
    c. Transport
    d. Physical

21. Which layer of the OSI model uses logical addresses?
    a. Network
    b. Data Link
    c. Physical
    d. Transport
22. At what layer of the OSI model does segmentation of large data streams happen?
    a. Transport
    b. Network
    c. Data Link
    d. Session
23. What happens when a router receives a packet with an unknown destination address?
    a. The packet is copied to all ports, except to the receiving port.
    b. The packet is broadcast across the network.
    c. The packet is forwarded to the default gateway.
    d. The packet is returned to the sender.
24. What happens when a switch receives a frame with an unknown destination address?
    a. The frame is copied to all ports, except to the receiving port.
    b. The frame is broadcast across the network.
    c. The frame is dropped.
    d. The frame is returned to the sender.
25. Which of the following items composes a router table?
    a. Router name, network name, network number
    b. Network address, interface, metric
    c. Network address, node address, interface
    d. Hop count, tick count, delay metric

26. What function is a router providing when it performs protocol conversion?
    a. Brouter
    b. Gateway
    c. Switch
    d. Forwarding
27. IP is independent of the data link and physical layers. True or False?
28. What does an IP address represent?
    a. The network and port
    b. The network and node
    c. The router and switch
    d. The sender and receiver
29. When Web requests are sent and Web pages are received, which protocol is used?
    a. SMTP
    b. HTTP
    c. SNMP
    d. Telnet
    e. FTP
30. When you create a small peer-to-peer network between two PCs to share files and printing, which components are necessary? (Choose three.)
    a. A router
    b. A cross-over cable
    c. A common protocol
    d. NICs
    e. A server

Module 2
Network Types

Networks are categorized based on their physical size, location, and method of connection. They are also categorized based on the services they perform. This module opens with a discussion of local area networks (LANs). LANs are made up of all the network resources, media connections, protocols, and applications that are used within a single building. LANs run network technologies such as Ethernet, Token Ring, Fiber Data Distributed Interface (FDDI), and Asynchronous Transfer Mode (ATM).

Ethernet is the most prevalent of these and, therefore, the majority of Lesson 1 is dedicated to a discussion of Ethernet components. Information included in Lesson 1 addresses IEEE specifications, carrier sense, multiple access with collision detection CSMA/CD, Ethernet frame headers, and the various speeds from 10-Mb to 10-Gb communications.

Lesson 2 provides a discussion of wide area networks (WANs). WANs are connections between LANs that provide interconnectivity for large, geographically dispersed businesses, remote communications, and Internet access. WAN facilities are provided by telecommunications companies and include everything from low-speed, dial-up analog connections to very high-speed optical carrier transmissions.

The WAN facility selected depends on the bandwidth needed, as well as on the associated costs. WANs function primarily at the Physical and Data Link Layers, although there are a few Network Layer protocols as well. WANs at the Physical Layer provide physical media, connectivity devices, signaling, and synchronization capabilities. WAN technologies at the Data Link Layer are used to encapsulate information, switch transmissions, and define the link access procedures.

Lesson 3 looks at a number of other network topologies. Campus area networks (CANs) are used to connect buildings that are close together. CAN connections are usually private wired and wireless media. For larger facilities, metro area networks (MANs) connect LANs that are distributed around a city. This is a common method for branch offices. Storage area networks (SANs) are increasing in popularity since they provide high-speed data access from a centralized location.

Content networks offer constantly developing technologies to improve delivery for the different types of traffic found on networks today. Virtual private networks (VPNs) provide access for mobile employees, allow lower-cost connections for branch offices, and allow businesses to connect to business partners, vendors, or major customers. VPN is a method that allows transmissions to tunnel through an existing network, in this case, the Internet.

Finally, Lesson 3 ends by comparing and contrasting Internet, intranet, and extranet terminology.

Lessons

1. Local Area Networks
2. WAN Fundamentals
3. Other Network Types

Lesson 1—Local Area Networks

Although Cisco supports other LAN topologies such as Token Ring and FDDI, this book and the exam focus mainly on Ethernet networking. Ethernet is a popular network platform because of its high speeds, ease of implementation and troubleshooting, and its expansion into Fast-Ethernet, Gigabit-Ethernet, and 10-Gigabit Ethernet technologies. This lesson explains some important Ethernet components that lay the foundation for future discussions.

To begin with, Ethernet traditionally used a contention-based method of media access. The Ethernet standard is defined as CSMA/CD. This means that end stations listen to the wire and transmit data when the wire is clear. If the line stays clear while sending, the transmission is delivered successfully. If another device transmits simultaneously, a collision occurs. Now that switches have replaced hubs in many network environments, contention is less of a problem.

Other topics discussed in this lesson include the different header types associated with Ethernet at the Data Link Layer. Header information is added to a packet to make an Ethernet frame. The process of adding header information is called "encapsulation."

This lesson ends with an overview of Ethernet transmission speeds of 10 Mb, 100 Mb, 1 Gb, and 10 Gb.

Objectives

At the end of this lesson you will be able to:

- Define International Electrical and Electronic Engineers (IEEE) LAN specifications
- Describe Carrier Sense Multiple Access with Collision Detection (CSMA/CD)
- Identify the components of an Ethernet frame header
- Describe 10-Mb Ethernet transmissions
- Describe 100-Mb Fast Ethernet transmissions
- Describe 1000-Mb Ethernet transmissions
- Describe 10-Gb Ethernet transmissions

Key Point

Ethernet is the predominate LAN protocol and has gained this status by providing fast and reliable network services.

LAN Standards

Local Area Networks (LANs) are the network components that are usually confined within a single building. This includes, but is not limited to, wire and wireless communication media, repeaters, hubs, bridges, switches, routers, gateways, servers, workstations, printers, network peripheral devices, operating systems, software applications, and protocols. Typically, the corporate entity that owns the network is also in charge of managing the network components. This includes cable and device installation, address assignment, maintenance, user access, troubleshooting, and a many other important tasks.

Several technologies are used in the LAN environment. Each one has its own characteristics of signaling, addressing, physical network topology, cable configuration, network interface card (NIC), and so on. LAN and WAN technologies used to encapsulate the data and access the media are found at the Data Link Layer of the Open Systems Interconnect (OSI) model.

Remember that the Data Link Layer is divided into two sublayers: Logical Link Control (LLC) and Media Access Control (MAC). This is the place in the OSI model where the logical connection from software and operating systems from the upper layers make a connection with the NIC and the physical media below. The details of these two sublayers are as follows:

- **Logical Link Control (LLC)**—The LLC sublayer is defined by the IEEE to be independent of the MAC sublayer below and of the Network Layer above. It was designed in this manner to reduce the requirements of the MAC sublayer and provide a common connection for all network types.

  LLC is a hand-off that helps the receiving device understand what to do with the packet at the Network Layer. For instance, a transmission is sent using IP and this information is included in the header of the LLC portion of the Ethernet frame. When the receiving device gets the frame and begins decapsulation, it sees that IP was used to package the information and hands the transmission to the internal IP stack for processing.

The same process would have worked at the LLC layer regardless if the LAN type were Ethernet, Token Ring, FDDI, or others. That is the benefit of a separate LLC layer: to have independence above and below.

- **Media Access Control (MAC)**—The MAC sublayer has the job of knowing how to access the network media. For instance, with Ethernet, the process is CSMA/CD; with Token Ring and FDDI, the process is wait until the token is available.

  The MAC sublayer also defines a connection to the Physical Layer. Here the NIC is responsible for putting the physical address of the sender and destination in the frame, as well as putting the transmission, in the correct format to send on the media. IEEE has also defined the specifications for the MAC sublayer, which are shown here in the LAN Specifications Table.

LAN Specifications

Data Link	LLC	Original Ethernet	IEEE 802.2					
	MAC		IEEE 802.3	IEEE 802.3u	IEEE 802.3z	IEEE 802.3ab	IEEE 802.5 Token Ring	FDDI
Physical								

Notice from the LAN Specifications Table that the original version of Ethernet was not associated with 802.2. It used a type field in place of the LLC in the frame header. Once the IEEE Ethernet specification was ratified, it built on the LLC component and changed the header accordingly. Some protocol analyzers, however, still show this field as the type field.

The IEEE standard is based on the original Ethernet specification created by DEC, Intel, and Xerox. The first specification was defined in the mid-1980s by the IEEE 802.3 committee and is not called Ethernet but Carrier Sense Multiple Access with Collision Detection (CSMA/CD).

Ethernet is a made-up name, whereas CSMA/CD is a working definition of how data is encapsulated and transmitted. Ethernet has evolved dramatically over the years and new specifications were developed and ratified by IEEE as follows:

- **802.3u**—Fast Ethernet specifies 100-Mb transmission over UTP CAT 5 or fiber optic cable
- **802.3z**—Gigabit Ethernet specifies 1000-Mb (1-Gb) transmissions over fiber optic cable
- **802.3ab**—Gigabit Ethernet specifies 1000-Mb transmissions over UTP CAT 5e cable

Other LAN standards include:

- **802.5**—Token Ring uses a ring topology and transmission speeds of 4 Mbps or 16 Mbps
- **FDDI**—An American National Standards Institute (ANSI) definition included under 802.5 because it uses a ring topology and token passing method similar to Token Ring

Ethernet CSMA/CD

Ethernet is a contention-based media access method that is defined at the Physical and Data Link Layers of the OSI model. Originally, it was a bus topology over coax cable. This means that only one frame can be sent along the network at a time and all stations review the frame to determine whether it is for them. Thus, all stations on a segment are in the same broadcast domain.

They are also in the same collision domain, which creates problems when more than one station sends a frame at the same time. Ethernet may use a hub configured as a physical star; however, it is still a logical bus. Today, switches have replaced many hubs to provide more efficient network transmissions.

To allow systems to share the network media and help reduce the number of problems with network access, Ethernet is based on CSMA/CD. To break this concept down into simpler terms, look at each piece of the name:

- **Carrier Sense**—A network node listens to the media for a digital signal to determine whether the line is available to transmit.
- **Multiple Access**—The bandwidth is shared, but two devices cannot transmit at the same time. The network node that sent data continues to monitor the media to make sure no other device tries to send simultaneously.

- **Collision Detection**—A collision happens when two devices send at the same time and their transmissions overlap. This is detected by a voltage spike on the wire. The devices involved in the collision issue a jamming signal to let others know they need to wait while the collision is cleared.

Sending a Frame

The Ethernet Send Algorithm Diagram illustrates the logic used to transmit a frame.

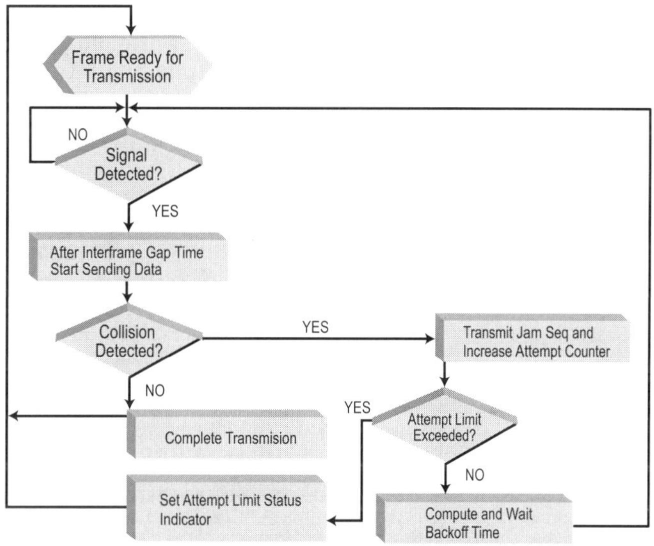

Ethernet Send Algorithm

Each node follows these steps to transmit a message:

1. Listen to the bus (the shared medium) to see whether any other node is transmitting (sensing the carrier signal does this). If a transmission is detected, continue listening until the channel is idle.
2. When no signal is detected, start transmitting the message.
3. While transmitting, listen to the bus. Compare the received message to what was transmitted. As long as they are the same, continue transmitting.
4. If the message received is not what was transmitted, assume a collision. Stop transmitting.

Note: The transceiver watches for a voltage threshold violation. Consequently, signal reflections and noise often appear as collisions.

5. Transmit a jam sequence to warn all other stations that a collision has been detected and to ensure that all network devices stop transmitting. The jamming sequence takes the form of 96 bits of alternating 1s and 0s.
6. Wait a random time and then start over with Step 1.

An important aspect of the CSMA/CD algorithm is the random-length interval (a few milliseconds [ms]) that a node waits before trying to retransmit when a collision occurs. Because the probability of two nodes waiting the same length of time is very small, a second collision is unlikely to occur. This ensures that nodes do not just keep "butting heads," with none able to access the bus.

On a heavily used network, collisions will occur, and time is wasted whenever this happens. Collisions are a major reason why performance of an Ethernet network decreases as the load increases.

Note that the node stops transmitting as soon as a collision is detected—that is the significance of the "CD" in CSMA/CD. Other similar protocols do not require a node to stop transmitting until the end of its message; thus, a significant amount of time is lost when any of the colliding nodes is transmitting a long message.

A potential problem with CSMA/CD is the time it takes for an electrical signal to travel from one point on the bus to another. This is called "propagation delay." In a large network, if two nodes, A and B, are at opposite ends of the bus and both start transmitting at the same moment, Node A might transmit the last bit of its message before the first bit has had time to reach Node B, and vice versa.

Neither node would detect a collision, yet the signal would be garbled. One way of solving this problem is to require that frames be at least long enough to prevent this situation, which is how Ethernet works.

Receiving a Frame

The Ethernet Receive Algorithm Diagram shows the sequence for receiving a frame.

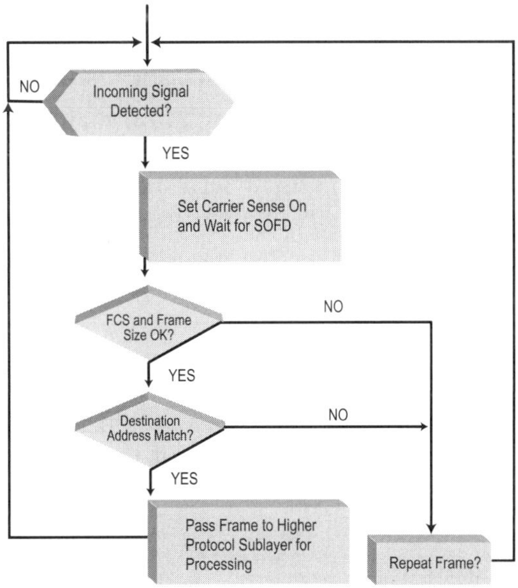

Ethernet Receive Algorithm

Ethernet is similar to an intersection with high bushes on all sides. Drivers approaching the intersection attempt to see whether any other traffic is coming and, if they do not see any, they speed into the intersection. If another driver also decides to speed into the intersection at the same time, there is a collision.

Other cars have to wait until the collision is cleaned up before they can proceed. The more cars approaching the intersection, the more likely problems will occur.

In the same way, more computers on a network result in a greater number of collisions. Therefore, switches or bridges isolate traffic and reduce the number of nodes on a given segment that is called a "collision domain."

Referring back to the original analogy, to reduce traffic and accidents, cars are directed to go through a rotary where all cars keep moving but do not get in one another's way. Reduce the number of nodes on a segment, and you reduce the traffic and the number of collisions.

Half-Duplex vs. Full-Duplex

Ethernet runs in either half-duplex or full-duplex mode. The original 802.3 Ethernet standard used half-duplex, meaning only one wire pair was used for sending and receiving digital signals in both directions. The other wire pair is used to perform the carrier sense, detect collisions, and transmit a jamming signal when necessary.

This, however, is only approximately 30 to 40 percent efficient, meaning 10-Mpbs Ethernet is transmitting approximately 3 to 4 Mbps in a large-network environment. Hubs transmit in half-duplex mode since they are a contention-based logical bus.

Full-duplex mode uses two wire pairs and creates a point-to-point connection between sending and receiving devices. This eliminates collisions and offers 100 percent efficiency. Full-duplex is determined and negotiated by the Ethernet port when it is powered on and initially communicates with a switch. The autosense feature allows a switch to determine the network speed (10, 100, or 1,000 Mbps) of the NIC and whether it can communicate in full-duplex mode.

Ethernet Frames

Remember from the review of the OSI model in Module 1 that the Data Link Layer is responsible for creating the Ethernet frame. It does this by adding its own information in the header and trailer, and encapsulating the packet passed from the Network Layer.

The header provides the information that computers need to successfully transmit data from the source computer to the destination computer. The Ethernet 802.3 MAC Layer Frame Diagram shows the specific fields found within the MAC header and trailer.

Note: The source and destination addresses referred to here are the physical or MAC addresses assigned to the computer's network interface card (NIC).

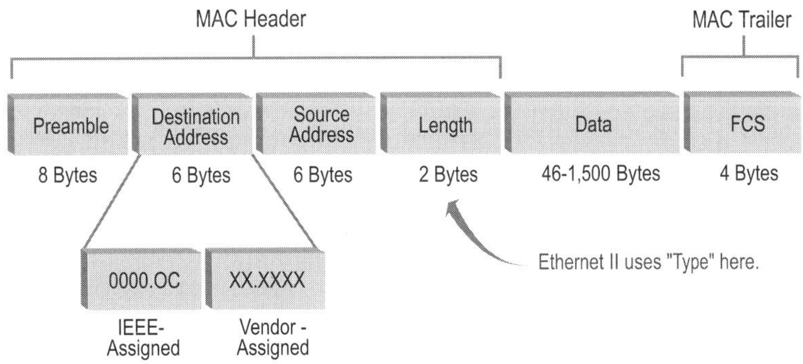

Ethernet 802.3 MAC Layer Frame

The fields of the Ethernet 802.3 MAC layer frame are explained below:

- **Preamble (8 bytes)**—Alternating 0s and 1s that let the receiver know a frame is being transmitted. The last byte is defined as the Start of Frame Delimiter.
- **Destination Address (6 bytes)**—The 48-bit hardware (MAC) address of the computer that is to receive the frame.
- **Source Address (6 bytes)**—The 48-bit hardware (MAC) address of the computer that is sending the frame.
- **Length (2 bytes)**—The length of the frame in bytes; Ethernet II uses Type instead of Length for this field.
- **Data (variable size from 46 to 1,500 bytes)**—LLC and upper-layer control information, in addition to a user's data. If the encapsulated data is less than 46 bytes "padding" bits (all 0s) are added to bring the data portion up to 46 bytes.
- **Frame Check Sequence (4 bytes)**—An error-detection feature. The sending computer determines the Frame Check Sequence (FCS) by applying an algorithm to all bits in the frame except to the preamble.

  The receiving computer does the same and, if the results match, the frame is accepted. If the results do not match, the receiver discards the frame. Depending on the transport protocol being used, a new frame may be retransmitted.

Minimum and Maximum Frame Sizes

The minimum size of an entire Ethernet frame is 64 bytes. In some instances, the data portion of the transmission does not have enough bits to reach the minimum size. Some legacy text editing programs, for instance, sent each keystroke as an individual transmission. Therefore, the data portion would be 8 bits of information and the rest would all be padding.

Another good example of frames that may not reach the minimum on their own is real-time transmissions. To prevent "packetization delay" (the time it takes to fill an entire packet to the minimum size), a real-time environment builds the frame with whatever information is currently available, then pads the remaining space to the correct size. Padding the frame ensures that the frame is long enough that the Destination Address (DA) field gets to the farthest node before the end of the frame is transmitted.

Frames that are smaller than 64 bytes are considered "Runts" and may be discarded as an error condition. The assumption is that frames smaller than 64 bytes may have been involved in a collision, since they would not normally be transmitted without proper padding. A number of network transmissions are smaller than the 64-byte minimum and are allowed to pass through because they have a special designation.

The maximum frame size for an Ethernet frame may vary depending upon which book you read. The two most common numbers that are traditionally given as the maximum size are 1,514 bytes and 1,518 bytes. When the Ethernet frame size is given as 1,518 bytes, it includes the FCS in the calculation. Since the FCS is 4 bytes long and some don't consider it to be part of the frame itself, 1,514 is also a viable number.

The IEEE has made some modifications to the Ethernet frame format to allow for the insertion of prioritization (802.1p) and VLAN (802.1Q) tag information. The addition of these fields requires the new maximum size to be changed to 1,522 bytes. Frames over the maximum size are considered "Giants," are counted as an error condition, and are usually discarded by the switch.

Destination Addresses (Unicast, Multicast, and Broadcast)

An Ethernet frame must include a MAC address that is used to identify where the frame should be delivered. If the MAC address is for a single device, and the switch knows the interface where the address is located, the frame is sent as a unicast.

Unicast means that the frame goes directly from the sender to the recipient, and no other devices see it. An Ethernet frame can be addressed to a group of nodes by setting one of the control fields in the DA. This allows multicasting of frames to several devices in the network simultaneously. When a frame is destined for all devices in a network segment, it is called a "broadcast." The MAC address of a broadcast is FF:FF:FF:FF:FF:FF.

Ethernet Transmission Speeds

In addition to the IEEE 802.3 number specification for Ethernet, there is also another identification method commonly used to indicate the speed of transmission, signal type, and media. This naming convention is descriptive and looks like the Ethernet Identification Method Diagram.

Ethernet Identification Method

The naming convention is broken down into the following pieces:

- **10, 100, 1000, or 10 G**—The first number in the name indicates the maximum transmission speed or bandwidth. The numbers represent 10 Mbps, 100 Mbps, 1000 Mbps (1 Gbps), and 10 Gbps, respectively.
- **Base**—The next word in the naming convention is used to identify the signal that Ethernet uses as a baseband signal. Baseband means that the signal is bounded and addressed to a designated destination. The destination may be a single device or a great number of devices in a broadcast situation.

  With baseband, the signal is targeted at a specific end point. Compare this with broadband, in which the signal is not addressed to any specific end point. Thus, if you have a receiving component tuned to the right frequency, you would be able to receive the transmission, just as anybody else would be able to. Examples of broadband signals are cable TV and radio.
- **2, 5, T, F, or some other letter** The last portion of the naming convention was originally used to specify the distance of the physical cable segment. 10Base2 allowed up to 185 meters (close to 200) and 10Base5 represented 500 meters for coax cable. UTP cable changed this standard to a T, Tx, T2, or T4. All of these indicate that twisted pair cable is used. The variations indicate that different pairs are used or is otherwise outside the normal specification.

UTP cable segments are a maximum of 100 meters. Another copper connection type is Cx, which is used over shielded twisted pair (STP) cable at 25 meters or less. If the name ends in F or Fx, fiber optic cable is used. The distance depends on the type of fiber. Other fiber optic specifications include Sx—short wavelength, Lx—long wavelength, LH—long haul, and several more.

Traditional Ethernet

Ethernet was originally specified at 10 Mb over coax cable in a bus topology (10Base2 and 10Base5). This was the first network infrastructure that provided new opportunities for communication. The bus topology was changed in most instances to a star configuration with a hub as the central connectivity device, and the cable was changed from coax to CAT 3 or CAT5 UTP. Ethernet was able to keep up for a period of time but eventually, as many corporate networks grew, collisions became a problem, which significantly reduced network performance.

Hubs were replaced with switches to improve overall network transmissions. In the new configuration 10 Mb was no longer shared between all connected devices as it was with a hub but dedicated to each end device connected to a switch port. Although this was a major improvement, 10 Mb couldn't keep up with growing network requirements.

Today, many users need access to high-end graphics and massive image files for scientific, medical, or engineering purposes. Database files have increased exponentially and timely retrieval is critical. Robust Web pages display animations, video, audio, and other multimedia components. Voice, video, and other real-time transmissions require speed for quality and performance. Network backups demand high bandwidth for transmission. Overall, we expect to get more in less time. For all these reasons, 10 Mb Ethernet has a tough time keeping up.

Fast Ethernet

Fast Ethernet, once reserved for backbone connections, server access, and only the most demanding computer users, has become the mainstay of most desktops today. Fast Ethernet meets the bandwidth requirements for the majority of desktop computers, printers, servers, new IP-based phones, and other network resources.

The Fast Ethernet standard (IEEE 802.3u) can send Ethernet frames at 100 Mbps over Category 5 UTP (100BaseTx) or fiber optic cabling (100BaseF). The frame format of Fast Ethernet is identical to that of 10-Mbps Ethernet; thus, a network can move up to the higher data rate if it can meet the following requirements:

- If UTP cabling is used, it must be Category 5 or higher.
- All NICs, hubs, and switches must support the 100-Mbps data rate.

In addition, a network may need to adjust its UTP wiring layout to meet the maximum distances allowed in the 100BaseTx standard. To provide such a high data rate, the longest UTP cable can be only 100 meters (m).

Smart network administrators plan for future upgrades to Fast Ethernet by using Category 5 cabling in all new installations, and by equipping all computers with NICs that support both 10- and 100-Mbps data rates. The slight extra cost of these components is more than offset by a simpler network conversion.

Gigabit Ethernet

Gigabit Ethernet has found its place in the LAN environment for backbone connectivity between network devices, server access, backup links, and storage area networks. Today, even desktops are demanding Gigabit throughput, and many computer vendors are offering 1-Gb NICs.

Gigabit Ethernet (IEEE 802.3z) provides throughput of 1,000 Mbps (1 Gbps). Like earlier versions, Gigabit Ethernet uses the frame format specified in the IEEE 802.3 standard.

The Gigabit Ethernet standard includes three specifications for optical fiber cabling and two specifications for copper:

- **1000BaseSX** ("S" for short wavelength) defines optical transceivers or Physical Layer devices for multimode fiber cabling using laser light at a wavelength of 770 to 860 nanometers (nm). This wavelength range is commonly referred to as 850 nm. 1000BaseSX transceivers are less costly than those found in products implementing the long wavelength specification described next.
- **1000BaseLX** ("L" for long wavelength) defines optical transceivers or Physical Layer devices for either multimode or single-mode fiber, using laser wavelengths of 1,270 to 1,355 nm (commonly called 1,350 nm).
- **1000BaseLH** ("LH" for long haul) is a multivendor specification that defines optical transceivers for Physical Layer devices that support distances greater than the 1000BaseLX specification. Each vendor has a set of transceivers designed to cover different distances. Although it is not an IEEE standard, many vendors are working to interoperate with IEEE 1000BaseLX equipment.

- **1000BaseCX** ("C" for copper) defines transceivers or Physical Layer devices for shielded copper cabling. A 1000BaseCX is intended for short-haul copper connections (25 m or less) within wiring closets.
- **1000BaseT** ("T" for twisted pair) specifies Gigabit Ethernet over four-pair Category 5 UTP copper cabling for distances up to 100 m. A 1000BaseT reaches gigabit speeds by supporting 250-Mbps full-duplex communications across each of the four wire pairs.

GBICs

Cisco offers a Gigabit Interface Converter (GBIC) for 1-Gb connections. This component allows for easy installation and easy reconfiguration as technology or media types change. The GBIC fits into a slot on a switch or router that is designed for this connection. The GBIC is then responsible for providing the correct signal, media access, and physical wired connectivity. Not only does this provide flexibility, it also allows for extra capabilities for network communications.

As an example, the 1000BaseLX/LH GBIC complies with all 802.3z specifications, but allows cable distances of up to 10 kilometers (6.2 miles). This extends the cable segment 5 km (3.1 miles) beyond the cable limit specified in the standard. Interchangeable GBICs are available for the both the fiber optic connections and the UTP and STP media types. Each one offers the appropriate connector.

As technology changes, GBICs can easily be pulled and replaced without replacing equipment. This offers a huge cost savings while still keeping up with the latest technologies.

10 Gigabit Ethernet

Formally ratified in June 2002, the IEEE 802.3ae standard for 10-Gigabit Ethernet outlines the cable types and technologies used to achieve this great bandwidth. A major benefit of using 10-Gb technologies is that it is built on the same principles of frame format, frame size, and switched full-duplex transmissions over single-mode and multimode fiber, making it easy to integrate into existing networks.

More important, this makes it possible to use Ethernet at the LAN at speeds of 10 Mbps, 100 Mbps, and 1000 Mbps while aggregating connections into a 10-Gbps backbone. Most network environments today are demanding greater backbone capabilities, as 1 Gbps connections are introduced into the desktop arena.

10-Gbps connections are useful for switch trunk links, server farms, disaster recovery, storage area networks, and any real-time or bandwidth intensive applications. Design and implementation is simplified, since 10 Gbps requires essentially the same knowledge and can use the same management and troubleshooting tools.

10 Gbps Ethernet has opened up an incredible new opportunity in the MAN and WAN environments as well. Service providers are deploying 10-Gbps Ethernet for both customer access and network backbone connections, with speeds matching Optical Carrier OC-192.

In this arena, the need for more speed is rarely ever met. Previously, the only viable options for high-bandwidth transmissions were Asynchronous Transfer Mode ([ATM] at 155 Mbps over OC-3) or Synchronous Optical Network ([SONET] at 622 Mbps over OC-12). These technologies require gateways to covert the transmissions, change the format, and add new addressing/header information. 10-Gb Ethernet is substantially faster, and can pass information end-to-end without gateway handling, layer 2 header conversion, or reformatting of any kind.

The 10-Gb standard includes two multimode and three single-mode cabling specifications, as follows:

- **10GBASE-S**—50.0 multimode fiber with an 850-nm laser light source. The S at the end of the standard is for serial transmission over a minimum of 65 meters.
- **10GBASE-LX4**—62.5 multimode fiber with a 1310-nm laser light source using Coarse Wave Division Multiplexing (CWDM) technology for a minimum distance of 300 meters.
- **10GBASE-LX4**—9.0 single-mode fiber with a 1310-nm laser light source using CWDM for a minimum distance of 10,000 meters.
- **10GBASE-L**—9.0 single-mode fiber with a 1310-nm laser light source and serial transmissions for a minimum distance of 10,000 meters.
- **10GBASE-E**—9.0 single-mode fiber with a 1550-nm laser light source and serial transmission for a minimum distance of 40,000 meters.

Review Questions

1. What is the basis for Ethernet technology?
   a. CMSD/CA
   b. CSMA/CD
   c. OSI model
   d. 16-Mbps transfer rates
2. What is the IEEE Ethernet specification for the MAC sublayer?
   a. 802.2
   b. 802.5
   c. 802.1
   d. 802.3
3. What is the IEEE Ethernet specification for the LLC sublayer?
   a. 802.2
   b. 802.5
   c. 802.1
   d. 802.3
4. What is the destination address in an Ethernet frame?
   a. The MAC address of the receiving device
   b. The MAC address of the sending device
   c. The IP address of the receiving device
   d. The IP address of the sending device
5. What is the transmission rate associated with 802.3z?
   a. 10 Mb
   b. 100 Mb
   c. 1000 Mb
   d. 10 Gb
6. What is the use of carrier sense in Ethernet technology?
   a. Sending data whenever ready
   b. Sending data when the token is passed to the device
   c. Asking the switch for permission to send
   d. Listening to the wire until no signal is heard

7. Why is the FCS at the end of an Ethernet frame?
   a. Determining the number of bits in the frame
   b. Telling the destination device that the frame has ended
   c. Providing error-checking capabilities
   d. Controlling the frame's transmission from source to destination
8. In the original Ethernet network environment, when more computers were added, what was likely to happen?
   a. The network would become more efficient at processing.
   b. The network would become more congested with more collisions.
   c. The network would become more congested with no additional collisions occurring.
   d. The network would get so busy it would eventually shut down.
9. What is the network configuration that allows signals to be sent and received simultaneously?
   a. Full-duplex
   b. Half-duplex
   c. CSMA/CD
   d. 10Base2

Extended Activities

1. How is a collision detected in an Ethernet network that uses UTP cable?

   ____

   ____

2. What is the MAC address of a broadcast frame?

   ____

   ____

3. What are the four standard specifications for Gigabit transmissions?

____

____

4. Where can 10-Gb Ethernet be used?

____

____

5. What is the connector in Cisco equipment that allows for 1-Gb transmissions?

____

____

Fill in the correct numbers for each description:

1. Length of the frame check sequence (FCS) trailer _________ bytes
2. Ethernet IEEE specification 802. _________
3. Minimum copper cable type for 100-Mb Ethernet CAT _________
4. Length of the destination MAC address _________ bytes
5. Minimum size of an Ethernet frame _________bytes
6. Minimum size for the data portion of the frame _________ bytes
7. Transmission capability of Fast Ethernet _________ Mbps
8. Length of a 100BaseT cable _________ meters
9. Maximum size of an Ethernet frame without a VLAN tag or FCS _________ bytes
10. Maximum size of an Ethernet frame with the VLAN tag and FCS _________ bytes

Lesson 2—WAN Fundamentals

Wide Area Networks (WANs) create connections between two or more LANs or campus area networks (CANs). You already know that all the network devices, media, and protocols that allow communication and shared network resources within a particular building or area compose a LAN. LANs use wired (mostly unshielded twisted pair [UTP] or fiber optic cable) and wireless connections to the desktop.

On a slightly larger scale, a CAN is best suited for large companies or educational facilities that require network connections between buildings located relatively close together. These connections may be hundreds of yards to a few square miles, depending on the size of the campus environment. Fiber connections are often used, as well as wireless bridges using antennas and line-of-sight connections.

A WAN and a metro area network (MAN) are similar in concept. A MAN connects a number of branch offices within a city, such as grocery chains or bank branches. MANs can use private media, meaning a business lays its own fiber connections or has their own microwave wireless connections.

However, most companies are not in the business of building, implementing, and maintaining these types of connections, and do not even try. Instead, they lease these services from local service providers to make connections to their branch locations. In most cases, MANs use local services, rather than long-distance services, which helps keep costs down.

The difference between a MAN and a WAN is mainly the distance between the connections. WANs typically run between geographic locations, including counties, states, and continents. They require both local and long-distance services, and their costs are significantly higher. This is directly related to the bandwidth requirements and the type of service used. The higher the requirements, the higher the cost for a WAN connection.

Businesses base their WAN connection decisions on speed, usage, cost, security, connection setups, availability, and other factors. Existing technologies can meet the current needs, and new WAN technologies are being created to improve performance and take networking into the future.

Objectives

At the end of this lesson you will be able to:

- Describe the global Internet
- Discuss WAN communications
- Identify WAN connectivity devices
- Define WAN and service provider terminology
- Compare the DCE and DTE functions
- Identify WAN bandwidth
- Discuss Physical Layer WAN components
- Discuss Data Link Layer WAN components

Key Point

WANs provide network connectivity across large geographical areas around the globe.

The Global Internet

As long as most of you can remember, there has been telephone service. When you want to make a call, you pick up the telephone, get dial tone, place your call, and possibly someone answers on the other end. Each subscriber connects to a local central office (CO), which provides their phone service: the access into the telephone network.

The public switched telephone network (PSTN) is composed of millions of miles of cable, wireless transmissions, telephones, codecs, fax machines, Private Branch Exchanges (PBX), service provider switches, and signaling systems. You may take for granted the intricacies of the PSTN because it is so common and easy to use. All of this has been evolving over the last 100 years or so, and provides a reliable and relatively inexpensive means of communication.

As the Internet Connections Diagram shows, the Internet is made up of the connections between all private networks. Internet connectivity is commonly used to access the World Wide Web (Web), but it goes beyond that. It is composed of millions of miles of cable and wireless transmissions, sometimes the same media that is used for voice communications. It is made up of networking devices like routers, gateways, firewalls, switches, channel service units/data service units (CSU/DSU), modems, multiplexers, xDSL routers, Digital Subscriber Line Access Multiplexers (DSLAMs), cable modems, and the list goes on and on.

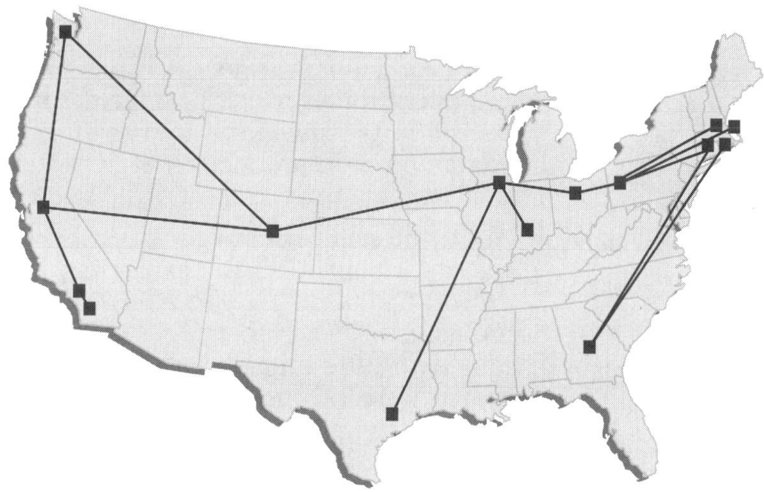

Internet Connections

To put the Internet in perspective, data connections have been evolving over the past 30 years or so, and technology has changed at a phenomenal rate. Even more astonishing, the Web as we know it today has only been available for around 10 years. Most consumers would not even recognize its original format of bulletin boards and newsgroups, compared to the media-rich Web that we know now.

The global Internet is a hierarchy of Internet service providers (ISPs) with routing capabilities, just as the PSTN has a hierarchy of telephone switching offices. However, in contrast, the Internet didn't really grow as gracefully. During the early history of the Internet, routers that connected the various networks composing the Internet were divided into two groups:

- The first group consisted of a small set of powerful core routers operated and maintained by the Internet Network Operations Center (INOC). These routers made up the core gateway system, maintained reachability information for all networks that made up the Internet, and exchanged routing information using the Gateway-to-Gateway Protocol (GGP). This was the original Internet backbone.

- The second group of routers consisted of a much larger set of less powerful, non-core routers controlled by individual organizations. These routers provided the link between the core system and individual local networks. This was before ISPs made these connections.

The core gateway system was designed to provide reliable and consistent routes for all possible destinations. It operated as the backbone that held the Internet together and made universal communication possible. Local networks attached to the Internet used the core as a transport or "long-haul" system.

As the Internet began to grow, many new routers had to be added to help interconnect the expanding network. In the past, such growth had taken place in a relatively unstructured and haphazard manner. New routers were added to the existing Internet system, with little concern for topological or other issues. The new routers were incorporated using GGP.

However, as the Internet continued to grow, this simple method of expansion did not scale well. As a result, the Internet began to evolve into a collection of separate sections called autonomous systems (ASs). ASs represent the large corporate and educational institution networks, which are controlled and maintained privately by the organization. These aren't really equivalent to LANs because they could span great distances over point-to-point, circuit-switched, or packet-switched WAN links to other networked locations.

Although the Internet is still expanding, there are more controls, monitoring, and standards, which help reduce some of the growing pains of the past. Access to the Internet is hierarchical, meaning there are levels that help organize and separate areas to reduce traffic. Exterior Gateway Protocols (EGPs) are used to communicate between ASs and ISPs.

ISPs provide connectivity into the network for businesses as well as home users. The major difference between subscribers is the amount of available bandwidth and how much reachability information is exchanged. All of this information right at your fingertips from halfway around the world in a matter of seconds is really an amazing accomplishment. It will be interesting, to see what the next 10 years bring.

WAN Communications

WANs are the connections between LANs or ASs. Unlike LANs, they are usually not completely controlled and maintained privately. WAN connections are made using a service provider. The business or home user who needs connectivity to a business, branch office, customer, vendor site, or the Internet must first subscribe to a WAN service.

This could be as simple as a dial-up modem connection over an analog telephone line, or it could be a multi-megabit SONET transmission. WAN services come in all shapes and sizes.

WANs have evolved from the days of sending data over the voice network using a dial-up or X.25 connection. Today WAN communications have many of their own protocols and transmission facilities. Traffic is a lot more demanding than just data. Today, all multimedia communications are transmitted over these connections, including, real-time, slow-motion, and streaming video; audio, music, instant text messages, animations, graphics, and voice; and plain old data, too.

Before this lesson goes into greater detail, it returns to the OSI model to help you determine where a device, connection, or encapsulation method is functioning. For WAN components, this is easy, since most of them are at the Physical and Data Link Layers. The WAN Components and the OSI Model Table shows how these stack up. The top layers of this model are shown with the IP suite since it is commonly used over WAN connections for e-mail, Web, file transfer, telnet, and other application services. The IP suite is not part of the WAN protocols; IP is independent of the WAN Data Link and Physical Layers, just as it is in the LAN environment.

WAN Components and the OSI Model

	Protocols	Devices and Connections
Application	HTTP, SMTP, FTP, Telnet, DNS	Web server, E-mail server, FTP server, DNS server, etc.
Presentation		
Session		
Transport	TCP and UDP	Firewall
Network	IP, BGP, X.25	Router, FRAD, Gateway, Firewall

WAN Components and the OSI Model (Continued)

	Protocols	Devices and Connections
Data Link	HDLC, PPP, Frame relay, ATM	Frame relay switch, ATM switch
Physical	EIA/TIA-232, EIA/TIA-449, V.35, X.21, EIA-530, RJ-48, RJ-11, F-Connector	Modems, Codecs, CSU/DSU, MUX, Asynchronous Dial-up, 56k leased lines, T1/DS1, DSL, Cable modem, SONET Optical Carrier

To better understand how the Internet works in terms of the OSI model, imagine a process familiar to everyone: accessing a Web page from home. The following is the process as it represents each layer of the OSI model:

1. First, you would use your Web browser, which requires Hyper Text Transfer Protocol (HTTP). DNS is also used at the upper three layers to resolve a domain name to an IP address used in Step 3.
2. HTTP uses TCP at the Transport Layer, adding the correct information such as port numbers, window size, acknowledgments, segment sequence numbers, and so forth.
3. IP is used at the Network Layer for logically addressing the packet. The IP address was determined from the DNS resolution in Step 1.
4. The Web request is encapsulated at the Data Link Layer by point-to-point protocol (PPP).
5. Finally, the bits are sent to the ISP over a dial-up connection, DSL, cable modem, or wireless media from your home.

When your request gets to the service provider (the cloud in most WAN diagrams), your request is added to many other Web requests that must be processed. Looking at this from the ground up, you have the following:

1. The service provider receives the bits sent from the appropriate connection media at the Physical Layer.

2. The service provider uses a special multiplexer at the Physical Layer to add your request to the millions of other requests going to the Internet backbone. Because there is a lot of other traffic, this pipe requires much more bandwidth than the connection from your business or home. Using fiber optic cable and built for speed, many service providers use Synchronous Optical Network (SONET) technology as a physical connection.
3. The service provider network may use ATM at the Data Link Layer to transport the information as cells that can be rapidly switched to their destination.
4. At the Network Layer, Border Gateway Protocol (BGP) uses the IP address of the packet to make routing decisions to determine the best path to deliver the request.

This is only one example of the process; however, it easily shows that each layer is dependant on the other for proper communication. Service providers can use any number and type of connections, media, and Data Link Layer protocols for transmission.

Service providers have no problem changing from one network to another by using gateway services to translate different protocols. They can easily change between copper, wireless, and fiber optic media as well using add/drop multiplexers to pick up and drop off traffic, based the appropriate media type.

It is also worth noting that X.25 is a Network Layer WAN protocol that does not require IP, but instead has its own hierarchical address that is almost identical to a telephone number. X.25 was a very reliable data transmission method. It is being replaced in many areas by frame relay.

WAN Connectivity Devices

The following subsections discuss WAN connectivity devices and their function.

Router (Default Gateway)

The first purpose of a router is to make best-path selection for all transmissions. But a router does not stop there. A router has full functionality: it can provide multiprotocol support and translation, security services, network and port address translation, WAN encapsulation services, LAN connectivity, remote access for branch offices, Internet access through an ISP, network segmentation, broadcast control, and a host of other services.

The router used to connect to the WAN or ISP is often called the "default gateway" because it is the only path to exit the LAN environment. Workstations and other routers in the network have the address of the default gateway. If LAN routers cannot determine the best path, or the destination is not within their tables, the LAN routers forward the transmission to the default gateway for handling.

This router is also often called a "border router," since it defines the border between internal and external communications. Many routers are built as modular units, which allows the network engineer to design the appropriate combination of connectivity. Encapsulation and interface options include, Ethernet, Token Ring, FDDI, ATM, frame relay, HDLC, PPP, and others.

WAN Switches

A frame relay or ATM switch is useful for service provider backbone connectivity. Switching at the Data Link Layer is much faster and more efficient than the process performed for path selection at the Network Layer. WAN switches are used in the service provider cloud to connect corporate networks together.

An example is a business connection using frame relay. The business has a router or frame relay access device (FRAD) as the customer premises equipment (CPE). This is necessary to act as a gateway between the LAN and WAN connections. The service provider makes the connection to a frame relay switch.

Inside the cloud, switches are used with virtual circuit connections, which reduce the amount of decision making and allow faster, more efficient transmissions. ATM switches are even more powerful because they have high bandwidth capabilities, run over fiber optic connections, and are designed for quality delivery of voice, video, and data.

Modems

A modem provides up to 56 Kbps dial-up capabilities for remote access or Internet connectivity. It converts digital information into an analog signal from the sender (modulation). At the receiving side it converts the analog signal back into a digital format (demodulation). Modems can be either synchronous or asynchronous. Asynchronous communications means the modem transmits a start and stop bit for every byte of information transmitted.

The speed of throughput depends on the quality of the connection, noise on the line, and compression ratio of the data. Synchronous modems establish a clock before transmission takes place and maintain the synchronization throughout. Modems are connected to analog local loops, which are also called plain old telephone service (POTS), tip and ring circuits, or loop-start lines.

Codecs

Codecs perform the exact opposite function of modems. Codecs take analog information and turn it into digital format. Analog information is received in the form of pitch and volume. The analog wave form is anything that creates noise or displays pictures; voice and video are two examples.

The information provided by voice and video is in various states. A codec uses a process called Pulse Code Modulation (PCM) to take the analog wave and convert it into a digital signal. A codec samples the original analog signal (4 kHz) at twice its original size (8000 times per second). It then converts the information into 8 bits (1 byte). Multiplying 8,000 X 8 = 64,000 or 64 K. This is the size of a DS0 in a T1, the exact amount of bandwidth necessary to place one phone call over a digital facility.

CSU/DSU

The CSU is the device that generates transmission signals on the digital local loop. It is used when making a connection to a 56-K leased line, Fractional T1, T1/E1, and so forth. The CSU provides access for voice communications over the same physical media. Voice is carried in 56-K or 64-K channels, allowing multiple phone calls to share the same physical wire. A CSU/DSU allows both data and voice to be transmitted together without getting mixed up.

Since data is better suited to a large pipe for transmission, the DSU bonds designated channels into one allocation of bandwidth. This allows data transmissions to be sent in digital form from sender to receiver. In many cases, the DSU functionality is provided by a router and not by a separate piece of equipment. A CSU is sometimes provided as a stand-alone component from the service provider.

WAN and Service Provider Terminology

To better understand WANs from the perspective of service providers, it is helpful to review a few telecommunications terms. WAN connections are made through the telecommunications network and are often provided by the same carriers that offer telephone service. The type of WAN service defines the standards for configuration, operation, and connection cost. The WAN Service Provider Diagram illustrates a few key telecommunications terms.

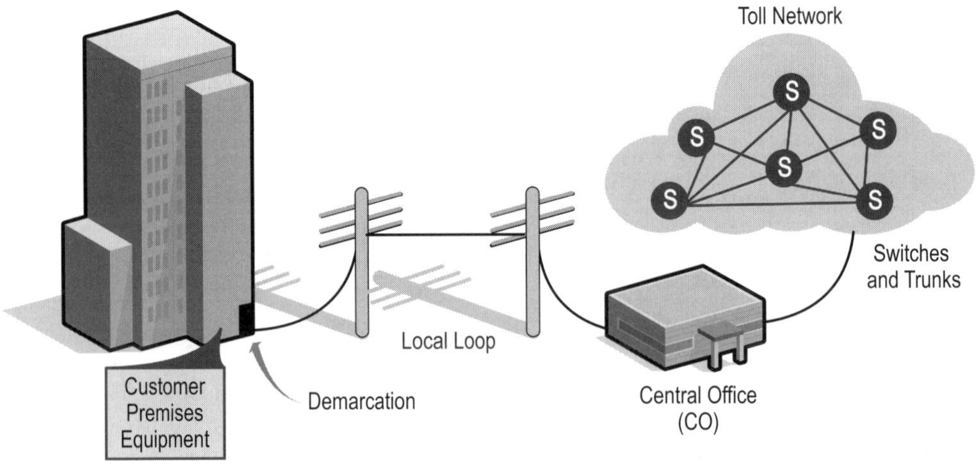

WAN Service Provider

- **Toll network**—In most WAN diagrams, the cloud represents the toll network. The toll network or public switched telephone network (PSTN) is a series of toll offices that house high-end switches tied together with trunk lines. The toll network provides an end-to-end connection from source to destination.

  The toll network is similar in concept to a LAN, only on a very large scale. They both have switches that connect customers, and trunk links that connect provider facilities. They make path selection decisions, establish connections, transmit information, and terminate connections.

- **Central office (CO)**—A CO is also called a "local exchange," "wiring center," "public exchange," or "point of presence (POP)." It is the location where a customer is connected to the WAN. The CO connects all telephone and transmission lines from a business or home. It has the responsibility of providing a physical connection, and switching calls and information transmissions to the correct location.

- **Point of presence (POP)**—The POP is a location where a service provider makes a connection to the PSTN or an ISP makes a connection to the Internet backbone. It may be collocated, meaning that it is a shared connection of equipment at the subscribers location.

It may also be a rental agreement for space at the telephone company location or telecommunication carrier. The equipment usually includes routers, frame relay and/or ATM switches, access services, and telephone switches.

- **Local loop**—A local loop, also called "the last mile," refers to the cable that connects the CO and the customer premises. This is usually copper wire; however, newer construction now offers fiber installations from the CO to the customer.
- **Demarcation point (demarc)**—The demarc is the location where a local loop is terminated into the physical jack located on the customer premises. All points after the demarc are the responsibility of the customer, not the service provider. The demarc is usually located in the telecommunications closet or basement.
- **Customer premises equipment (CPE)**—CPE is equipment connected to the demarc, either owned or leased by a customer. An example of CPE is a CSU/DSU, which is used for both telephone and data communications over a T1 line. A CPE can also be built into a router, similar to an ISDN port. In this case, a connection could be made directly from the demarc to the router.

Other terms that are also helpful when discussing WAN connections are:

- **Synchronous**—A communication process is considered synchronous if it maintains synchronization by sending a clocking signal. When connecting to a WAN service provider, the provider creates the synchronization clock. The CPE takes the clock and maintain the proper timing throughout transmission.

  When two pieces of equipment are connected back-to-back, for instance, two routers—the DCE sends the clock signal and the DTE takes the clock signal.
- **Asynchronous**—An asynchronous communication process does not use a clocking mechanism to maintain synchronization. Instead, it uses start and stop bits around each character. This slows transmission speeds and eats up valuable bandwidth. However, asynchronous communications are simpler and less costly than synchronous.

- **Analog**—This is a signal that transmits information using variable states in a wave pattern. Analog communications have frequency (the number of times the wave pattern changes) and amplitude (the height of the wave form). Analog signals can be used to transmit voice, video, and data.

  Analog is a natural state for voice and video since they have many values of information in the form of pitch (frequency) and volume (amplitude). Data is sent from a computer system in digital bits.

  When transmitted over an analog local loop, the digital bits must be converted into analog waves. This conversion process is performed by a modem, which MODulates and DEModulates the data stream from sender to receiver.

- **Digital**—Digital signals have only two possible states, 0 and 1, or on and off. This can be represented as electrical pulses (like Morse code) or light pulses (like turning a light switch on and off). Having only two discrete states means that the transmission can be reproduced exactly as it was originally transmitted.

DCE and DTE Functions

In addition to selecting the correct serial cable, you must determine which side is the DCE and which side is the DTE. Serial connections require the DCE device to establish synchronization by maintaining a clocking signal.

In most cases, the synchronization clock signal is issued by the service provider. The DCE would be the communication device such as a modem or CSU/DSU. The router would act as the DTE side of the serial connection, even though it is not the end device.

- **Data terminal equipment (DTE)**—This is a generic term for CPE that typically represents the end device that is used to input on the sending device and receive on the destination device. Examples of DTE could be terminals, PCs, printers, fax machines, telephones, and routers.
- **Data communication equipment (DCE)**—Also called data circuit-terminating equipment, this device provides connection for serial transmissions. In many cases, this device allows many DTE devices to communicate through a central WAN connection.

The DCE connects to a WAN or telecommunication service provider and can offer either synchronous or asynchronous transmission. Examples of DCE would be modems, routers, CSU/DSUs, and PBX/telephone switches.

It is also possible to connect two routers back-to-back over a serial connection without going over a WAN link. This is useful when the network needs to be extended but a WAN connection is not used. When a back-to-back link is made, one serial interface must be configured as the DCE, with clock rate set to a specific number. The other router is configured as the DTE. In this manner, the DCE provides the clock synchronization signal and, as usual, the DTE takes the clock signal. The service provider is not involved in this example.

The DCE/DTE Connections Diagram shows these two different scenarios. The first one is a connection through the service provider. Notice that in this example the DCE is the service provider and the DTE is the customer premises router. In the bottom diagram, a back-to-back router connection is shown with one as the DCE and the other as the DTE.

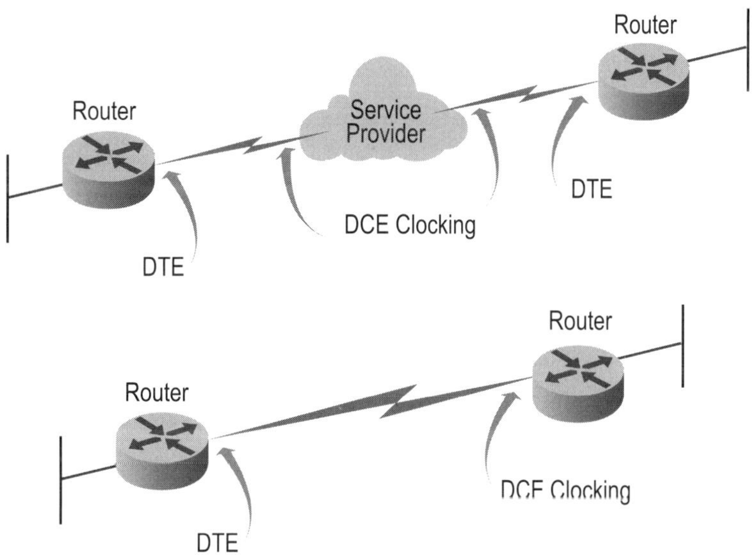

DCE/DTE Connections

WAN Data Transmission Rates

Local exchange carriers (LECs) offer traditional telecommunications services that use existing telephone company voice network facilities, and the copper local loop between a customer and central office (CO). The bottom rung of the point-to-point ladder is the analog connection, using modems to carry data over circuit-switched lines. At the top of the ladder are the higher-speed digital services, including Fractional T1 (FT1), T1, T3, and Synchronous Optical Network (SONET) Optical Carriers (OC1 to OC768).

The Physical Layer Technologies Table shows key Physical Layer technologies most often used for connection to a WAN. Associated data rates, physical media, and applications are also listed. Technology choices are based on need and economics.

Physical Layer Technologies

Technology	Data Rate	Physical Media	Application
Dial-up Modem	2400 Baud to 56 Kbps	Copper Twisted Pair	Internet and remote access for home office
Digital Data Service 56K Leased Line	56 Kbps	Copper Twisted Pair	Point-to-point connection for low bandwidth business applications
ISDN Basic Rate Interface (BRI)	128 Kbps Data, 144 Kbps Total	Copper Twisted Pair	Phone and data over 2 separate channels, or 128 Kbps (with out-of-band signal) for home office
Fractional T1	64 Kbps to 768 Kbps Cost makes it unlikely to subscribe to anything over this.	Copper Twisted Pair	Shared voice and data supplying remote connectivity and Internet for small to medium businesses.
T1/DS1	1.544 Mbps or 24 Channels (1.536 Mbps with 8 K of overhead.)	Copper Twisted Pair Optical Fiber Microwave	Shared voice and data on a point-to-point leased line, along with providing access to a frame relay service provider and Internet access for medium to large businesses

Physical Layer Technologies (Continued)

Technology	Data Rate	Physical Media	Application
E1	2.048 Mbps or 32 Channels	Copper Twisted Pair Optical Fiber Microwave	European equivalent of T1
xDSL	128 Kbps to 8 Mbps	Copper Twisted Pair	Internet connection for home office or small to medium business
Cable Modem	512 Kbps to 52 Mbps	Coaxial Cable	Internet connection for home office or small to medium business
T3/DS3	approximately 45 Mbps or 672 Channels	Copper Twisted Pair Optical Fiber Microwave	Large network connections providing voice and data, and Internet access for large businesses and call centers
E3	approximately 34.368 Mbps or 512 Channels	Copper Twisted Pair Optical Fiber Microwave	European equivalent of T3
OC1	51.48 Mbps	Optical Fiber	Backbone connections, Internet connectivity
OC3	155.52 Mbps	Optical Fiber	Large network backbone, Internet connectivity
OC12	622.08 Mbps	Optical Fiber	Service provider, large network, Internet backbone
OC24	1.244 Gbps	Optical Fiber	Service provider, large network, Internet backbone
OC48	2.488 Gbps	Optical Fiber	Service provider, large network, Internet backbone

Physical Layer Technologies (Continued)

Technology	Data Rate	Physical Media	Application
OC192	10 Gbps	Optical Fiber	Service provider and large networks backbone, used for 10Gbps Ethernet MAN and WAN services
OC768	40 Gbps	Optical Fiber	Largest optical carrier currently available

The basis for copper wire transmissions is a Digital Service 0 (DSO), which is a 64-Kbps channel. Transmissions that are lower than 64 K are considered subrate facilities. A T1 is built with 24 64 K DSOs for a total of 1.544 Mbps. A T1 can also be defined as a DS1 and a T3 can also be called a DS3. The European standards of E1 and E3 do not use the DS1 and DS3 terminology, although they, too, are based on multiples of the DSO.

Physical Layer WAN Components

In addition to the facilities that are provided by telecommunications companies, there are also the physical wired connections between the DCE and DTE components that reside at the Physical Layer. Cisco offers a proprietary 60-pin connector or a smaller "smart" serial WAN connector. The other cable end falls within the many different serial connector types listed below.

In addition to serial connectors, it is also common to see an RJ-48 connector, which looks similar to a LAN RJ-45 jack but uses a heavy-gauge, 4-wire cable.

- **EIA/TIA-232 (formerly RS-232)**—A DB-25 pin or DB-9 connection standard established by EIA/TIA. It is a common connector from a DCE to a DTE, or a serial port to a modem and supports 64-K transmissions over fairly short runs.
- **EIA/TIA-449**—DB-37 pin serial connection used for both DCE and DTE connections. It can support up to 2 Mb transmission with longer distance runs than the EIA/TIA 232.

- **EIA/TIA-612/613 High-Speed Serial Interface (HSSI)**—a 50-pin SCSI-II-type connector that provides DTE connection to T3 (45 Mbps), E3 (34 Mbps), and SONET STS-1 (51.82Mbps). The bandwidth depends on the service and connection equipment.
- **G.703**—BNC-style connector for Hybrid Fiber Coaxial (HFC) Cable, for CPE connections to the CO, with bandwidth capabilities up to E1 (2.048Mbps) rate.
- **V.35**—34 pin serial connection created by the International Telecommunication Union (ITU) and often used with T1 lines.
- **V.24**—ITU standard for DTE to DCE cable connections.
- **X.21**—37 pin serial connection used for both DCE and DTE connections. This connector is mainly found in Europe and Japan.
- **EIA-530**—DB-25 pin connection that can only be used for DTE connections (it is not DCE compatible).

Other WAN connectors include:

- **RJ-48**—Uses the same clear plastic clip as an RJ-45. However, the cable is shielded twisted pair, heavier gauge wire, and uses pins 1, 2, 7, and 8 for transmission. It is used with T1, Fractional T1, BRI, and subrate facilities.
- **RJ-11**—Also called "silver strand," this is the typical cable used for connecting a telephone to a wall jack. It has a smaller clip than an RJ-45 and uses pins 3 and 4. This cable and connector type is typically used for voice communications and xDSL connections.
- **F-Connector**—Used to connect a router to a cable TV service for Internet access.

Data Link Layer WAN Components

The Data Link Layer specifies the technologies that define methods for encapsulation, physical identification, and link access procedures (similar to the media access control in the LAN). At the Data Link Layer, encapsulation methods are as follows:

- **Cisco's High-Level Data Link Control (HDLC)**—The proprietary protocol that is the default encapsulation method for serial router connections. The Cisco version includes a field that allows it to differentiate between Network Layer protocols. It cannot be used between different vendors' equipment.

- **Synchronous Data Link Control (SDLC)**—The protocol developed by IBM to allow synchronous communications between mainframes and dumb terminals. It was the main communication method for long-distance communications in a Systems Network Architecture (SNA). The standard HDLC format uses the same header fields as SDLC since it was built on this technology.
- **Serial Line Internet Protocol (SLIP)**—An early protocol to allow dialup connection to the Internet. It was lacking in authentication and the ability to transmit multiple Network Layer protocols.
- **Point-to-Point Protocol (PPP)**—This protocol has effectively replaced SLIP and may do the same for HDLC. It provides two authentication methods, multiple Network Layer protocol support, error detection, compression, load balancing, and it is vendor-neutral. PPP is specified in RFC 1661.

Also at the Data Link Layer are methods that define how a connection will be established, how signals will be transmitted and how the overall communications will be controlled. These components are called Link Access Procedures (LAPs). The following is a short list of commonly used LAPs:

- **Link Access Procedure Balanced (LAPB)**—Balanced communications happen in-band, where signal information is sent along with the data transmissions. It is commonly used in X.25 networks and provides a high level of error detection.
- **Link Access Procedure, D Channel (LAPD)**—D channel communications happen out-of-band or clear channel. The signal information is sent over a separate channel (D channel) than the data transmissions (B channel). This is commonly used with ISDN PRI and BRI services.
- **Link Access Procedure, Frame mode bearer (LAPF)**—This link access procedure has similar characteristics to LAPD but it is designed for frame relay services. Frame relay is a service that uses a T1, as does ISDN PRI; therefore, the D channel can still provide out-of-band signaling. In addition, LAPF provides frame field information, structure, content, and addressing methods.

Review Questions

1. What is the device that is used to convert a digital signal to an analog signal for the sender?
   a. Codec
   b. CSU/DSU
   c. Modem
   d. DTE
2. What is the bandwidth of a digital signal created by a codec?
   a. 24 K
   b. 4 kHz
   c. 56 K
   d. 64 K
3. What is the transmission speed of a full T1/DS1?
   a. 128 K
   b. 1.544 Mb
   c. 1 Mb
   d. 144 K
4. Which of the following are at the Data Link Layer? (Choose two.)
   a. Modem
   b. ATM
   c. Frame relay switch
   d. Router
5. Which WAN protocol works at the Network Layer?
   a. X.25
   b. Frame relay
   c. PPP
   d. ATM

6. How is a WAN connection usually made?
   a. A business runs its own lines from point-to-point
   b. A business subscribers to WAN connections from a service provider
   c. A business makes a connection directly to the Internet backbone
   d. A business makes a logical connection to the cloud
7. Which WAN protocol is vendor-neutral and is used for dial-up and ISDN encapsulation?
   a. SLIP
   b. HDLC
   c. Frame relay
   d. PPP
8. What terms refer to the wired connection from the subscriber to the central office? (Choose two.)
   a. Local loop
   b. Last mile
   c. Wire line
   d. Bundled pairs
9. What is the location called where the telecommunications wiring is terminated on the customers premises?
   a. The POP
   b. Demarc
   c. End-point
   d. Local loop
10. What type of device is used to make a connection to a digital facility?
    a. Modem
    b. Codec
    c. CSU/DSU
    d. Repeater

Extended Activities

1. Match the following definitions with the proper terms by choosing from the list at the end of this question.
   a. A device that converts analog sounds into digital signals
   b. The process that is used to sample analog information and convert it to 64-K digital transmission
   c. A device that converts digital bits into an analog signal for the local loop
   d. A Network Layer device that is used as the default gateway to the Internet
   e. The slow, reliable transmission method being replaced by frame relay
   f. The point where the local loop terminates at the customer's location
   g. The dial-up method that offers authentication and multiple protocols
   h. A higher bandwidth protocol that uses virtual circuits to share a T1 line
   i. A very high bandwidth protocol designed to send voice, video, and data
   j. The piece of equipment that is required to send a clocking signal
   k. The network encapsulation protocol built for SNA by IBM
   l. The copper wire connection from the CO to the customer
   m. A serial connection that uses start and stop bits to maintain synchronization
   n. A network controlled by a signal entity that connects to the Internet
   o. The telecommunications network that includes switches and trunks
   p. The protocol that works with X.25 for signaling and transmission
   q. Equipment owned or leased by the customer—for example, a CSU/DSU
   r. WAN connections on a router that transmit 1 bit at a time
   s. A digital facility that has 24 DS0 channels of 64 K each

t. The company that provides Internet connections for businesses

u. A serial connection that uses a clocking signal to maintain synchronization

v. The location of the telecommunications service provider

w. The default proprietary serial encapsulation method for a Cisco router

x. The piece of equipment that takes a clocking signal from the DCE

y. The equipment that allows a connection to a T1 or E1

z. The link access procedure that is used with ISDN service

_______ Serial

_______ Synchronous connection

_______ Asynchronous connection

_______ Customer Premises Equipment (CPE)

_______ Data Communication Equipment (DCE)

_______ Data Terminating Equipment (DTE)

_______ Link Access Procedure Balanced (LAPB)

_______ Asynchronous Transfer Mode (ATM)

_______ Frame Relay

_______ Pulse Code Modulation (PCM)

_______ Toll network

_______ Internet Service Provider (ISP)

_______ Demarc

_______ Cisco HDLC

_______ Local loop

_______ T1

_______ Central Office

_______ PPP

_______ Autonomous System

_______ X.25

_______ Codec

_______ Link Access Procedure, D Channel (LAPD)

_______ SDLC

_______ Modem

_______ Channel Service Unit/Data Service Unit (CSU/DSU)

_______ Router

Lesson 3—Other Network Types

In addition to LANs and WANs, there are a number of other network types based on size, connection methods, and types of devices. The size of a network is measured by the number of devices or nodes that need to communicate, and where these nodes are in relation to each other.

This lesson discusses many of these network types, including campus area networks (CANs), metro area networks (MANs), storage area networks (SANs), content networks (CNs), and virtual private networks (VPNs). It also compares and contrasts intranet and extranet environments with the Internet.

Objectives

At the end of this lesson you will be able to:

- Review local area networks (LANs) and wide area networks (WANs)
- Identify the components of a CAN
- Identify the components of a MAN
- Identify the components of a SAN
- Identify the components of a CN
- Describe VPNs
- Compare and contrast intranets and extranets

Key Point

Other network types are defined by their size, connection methods, and types of devices.

LAN and WAN Review

LANs can range from a few nodes in a home office to several hundred nodes in a corporation. A LAN is made up of the wiring, network components, protocols, servers, PCs, and other peripheral devices typically confined to a single building.

WANs connect LANs together as shown in the LAN and WAN Connections Diagram. They are similar to MANs, but span longer distances. A WAN may include sites in the same country or multiple countries. WAN connections include leased line, circuit-switched, or packet-switched facilities by telecommunications or data transmission service providers.

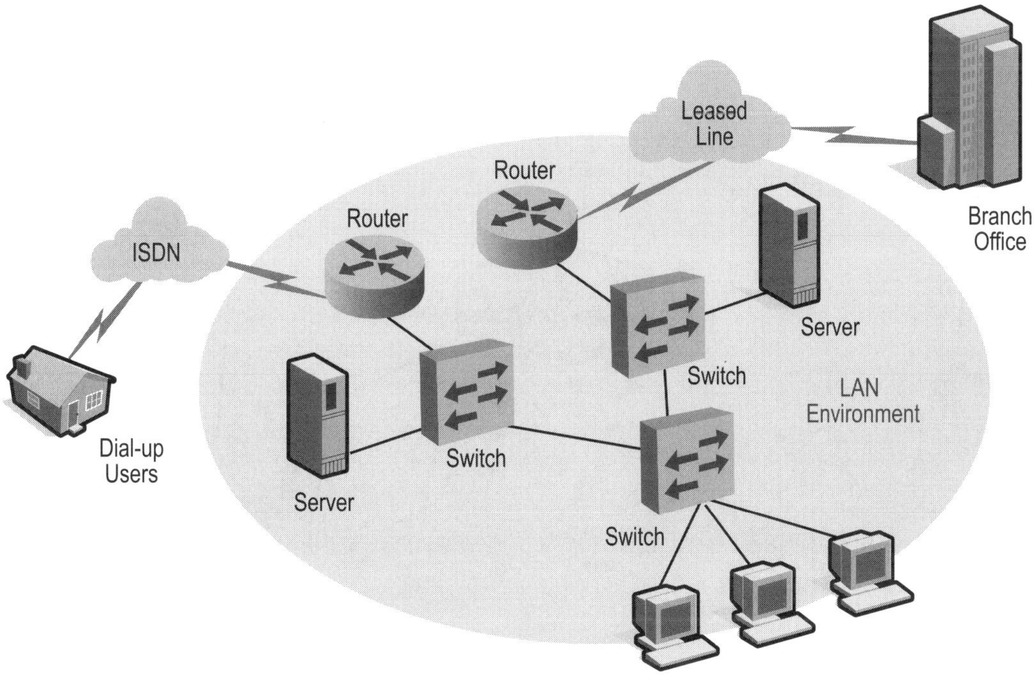

LAN and WAN Connections

CANs

Campus area networks consist of LANs connected across multiple buildings within a short distance of each other, usually on the same property or possibly across the street. CANs are often formed by very large organizations that have many buildings in close proximity to each other. Educational institutions are also good candidates, since a campus is the term used to discuss the property and buildings associated with a university or school.

Campus networks are built by connecting LANs to other LANs within an organization's networking infrastructure. In other words, the networking equipment used to connect LANs to form a campus network is owned and operated by the people in the organization.

When all the networking equipment and transmission systems belong to the organization that uses them, the infrastructure is called private facilities. The transmission links are usually fiber optic, copper, wireless radio frequency, or microwave, or a combination of several options. The Campus Area Network Diagram illustrates a typical campus and network connections between buildings.

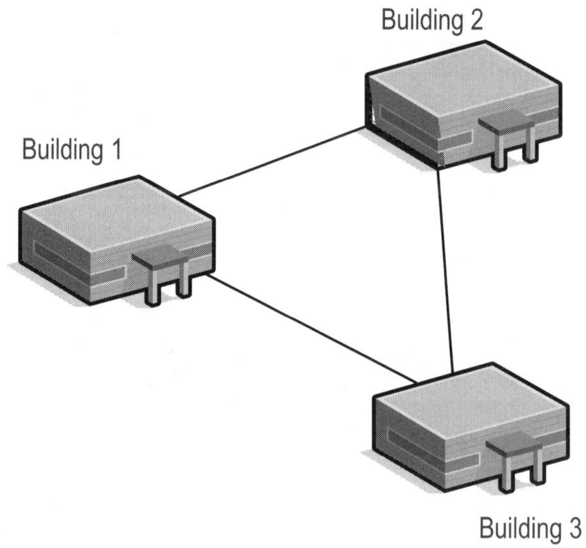

Campus Area Network

MANs

Metropolitan area networks are formed by connecting LANs in several locations across a city or small region. The links between LANs are typically leased from companies that provide telephone and data services. Depending upon distance, an organization may also be able to use private microwave transmission if they have line-of-sight capabilities.

Some companies even choose to run their own physically wired connections using fiber optic cable if they have right-of-way from point-to-point. For example, a business might interconnect several branch offices, as shown on the Metro Area Network Diagram. Banks, grocery, and other retail chains, or businesses with several locations in a city are all good candidates for MAN facilities.

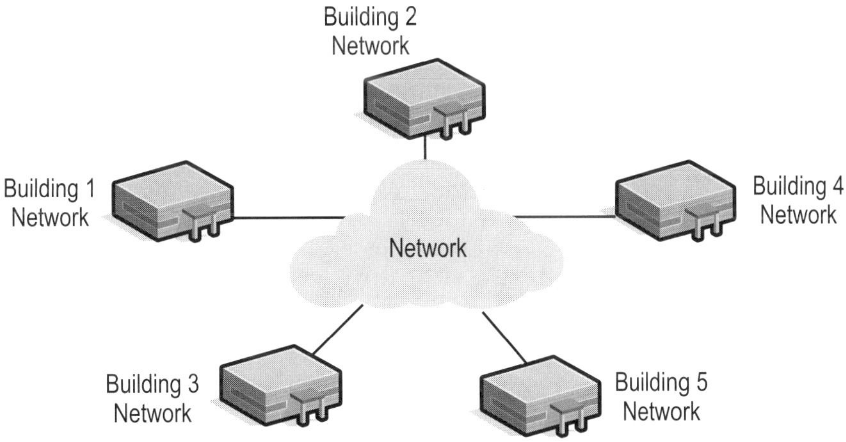

Metro Area Network

One of the primary differences between a MAN and campus network is that a campus network uses private facilities for interconnecting individual LANs, and a MAN uses public or shared facilities leased from a local telephone company. The difference between a MAN and a WAN is the general distance between systems.

WANs usually cover great distances and are more expensive for the long distance or long haul of transmissions. Typically, MANs are considered local since they are all within the same metropolitan area.

The connections between sites can include dial-up or circuit-switched connections for low bandwidth use. For higher-bandwidth digital facilities, the organization may select leased services like point-to-point lines, such as 56 K leased lines or T-carriers (fractional T1, T1, or T3).

Other options include switched services such as Integrated Services Digital Network (ISDN), frame relay, Asynchronous Transfer Mode (ATM), or Switched Multimegabit Data Service (SMDS), depending upon bandwidth requirements and type of transmissions.

Inside the service provider cloud at the metro area level there is usually a Synchronous Optical Network (SONET) ring. SONET allows very fast communications for all subscribers. Each business makes its connection using the appropriate facility, and the information is added to the bigger transmission media in optical format. When the transmission gets to its destination, it is converted back to an electrical signal that can be sent on a copper facility like a T1 for the receiving network.

SANs

Storage area networks are becoming increasingly popular as a means to share data in a completely distributed architecture. SANs connect storage devices (machines that contain large disk media) to all servers and clients that need access to files and applications. The storage devices can be accessed from a LAN, CAN, MAN, WAN, or VPN.

Servers can retrieve data from the storage devices regardless of their location. End users rarely realize a difference between local access and request for files on networked storage media. The following are benefits of SANs:

- **Scalability**—Network storage capacity can grow exponentially because it is not dependant on the limited resources in a single server. In addition, the nature of SANs allows data to reside in any location, but still be easily accessed and managed.
- **Ease of administration**—SANs can help reduce administration because of flexibility in data storage locations, server access, and the fact that they were designed with a single purpose: data storage. This streamlines administration for those systems, offloading tasks such as user administration, and e-mail services.
- **Return on investment**—The cost to design and implement SANs is initially high. However, the infrastructure can provide a fairly rapid return on investment in reduced administration, reduced network traffic, and soft costs such as more productive end users.
- **Reliability and availability**—Data can be stored concurrently (mirrored) in multiple locations. This provides redundancy for rapid data recovery.
- **Performance**—SANs increase server performance by reducing internal processing. By contrast, server-based storage requires processing to access the disk drives and retrieve files. With SANs, the server can be processing other requests and hand off the storage reads and writes to the appropriate storage device.

  In addition, multiple servers can access the storage media simultaneously, providing fast access to all requests.

Two options exist for the connection between server and storage media: FiberChannel and Internet Small Computer Systems Interface over IP (iSCSI). These connections offer high-speed communications with transmissions up to 1 Gb. Having the storage media separate from the servers allows for high performance because any server can access the data.

It also means that bottlenecks associated with servers that have high use or heavily congested network segments can be circumvented. Connections can be made using the FiberChannel or iSCSI, and switches for connections directly between servers, directly between storage devices, or from storage device to storage device.

This allows for many different communications methods using a high-speed link that is not susceptible to other network traffic. Thus, the SAN's only function is retrieving and sending data. It does not have to hear all the other miscellaneous broadcasts, packet transmissions to the Web, e-mail, printing, login authentication, routing updates, and so forth found on a typical network.

Another major benefit of this technology is that storage devices can be distributed at greater distances than the typical network components. SANs connections currently allow transmissions starting at 500 meters (approximately 1640 feet) and greater. It is projected that SANs will be able to connect devices up to 10 km (6.2 miles) in the near future.

Cisco offers the SN5420 Storage Router, which is built on IP and SAN technology. It can automatically identify and access storage devices on either FiberChannel or iSCSI connections. The management interface is easy to operate and provides simple connections between servers and storage devices.

CNs

Content networks are not so much a "type" of network as they are a "way" to network. Traffic transmitted across networks today have changed dramatically from the simple data files and e-mail that used to be sent. In addition to these traffic types, there are also various real-time voice, video, audio, multimedia, graphic formats, and sophisticated Web applications.

Content networking is a group of integrated services used to get a request filled and a response returned as quickly as possible, providing the highest level of service to each user's request. CNs are composed of new switching, routing, distribution, management, and network technologies that identify and transport information based on various criteria. This is a rapidly growing and changing environment.

The five components defined in Content Network technology include:

- **Content distribution and management**—A content distribution method that gets the information out to the network edge, from the servers where the content originated, to the content servers closer to the users' requests. This offers two management components that allow for content delivery and management, called business support system (BSS) and operations support system (OSS).

  Management features here enable an administrator to define content-delivery policies, access tracking for security monitoring, and refresh rates for information updates. Service providers can use this feature to track usage statistics for billing purposes.

- **Content edge delivery**—A component that provides access and content delivery to the end users or as close to them as possible. This component caches information for faster retrieval, while ensuring that content is also up-to-date. This reduces WAN bandwidth use and offers a level of security.
- **Content routing**—This component selects the best path within the network based on latency, protocols, congestion, reliability, policies, and so forth, to transmit content requests. This helps ensure the highest level of service for each type of traffic.
- **Content switching**—This component chooses the best server or content engine to fulfill a request based on load, availability, and use. It can also validate content location based on specific user request. This helps end users get exactly what they want, as quickly as possible.
- **Intelligent network services**—This component integrates a number of key network services to provide the best and most robust network throughput capabilities. This component identifies and handles traffic based on IP protocol, Quality of Service (QoS) routing capabilities, firewalls and security components, congestion control, prioritization, traffic shaping, bandwidth management, and VPN access.

Businesses have been driven over the last several years toward e-commerce from every direction. Not all business infrastructures were ready for the demands that many new applications and access requirements placed on their networks. Development in Web technologies, multimedia applications, voice over IP and IP telephony services, streaming audio and video, Webcams, Web radio and TV, Internet whiteboard, instant text messaging, network meeting, live chats, and so forth, have all pushed the envelope of network traffic.

These different traffic types also come with two new characteristics that have to be dealt with: demand for quality of service and high bandwidth requirements. Many organizations found that as they deployed e-commerce applications and users began taking advantage of many Internet features, their network performance degraded to unacceptable levels.

Content Networking is the organized group of network components and management functions that can bring order to the chaos. It allows network administrators to redefine where content is delivered and how it will be accessed. It brings distribution methods more in line with the existing network infrastructures, while still providing the quality that users demand.

Content Networking can provide increased productivity for employees, business partners, customers, and vendors by providing current information as quickly as possible.

VPNs

Virtual private networks provide a connection over a shared network that behaves like a dedicated link. VPNs are created using a technique called "tunneling," which transmits data packets across a public network, such as the Internet or other commercially available network, in a private "tunnel" that simulates a point-to-point connection. The tunnels of a VPN can be encrypted for additional security.

Many companies are using VPNs to provide connectivity to branch offices to reduce the cost of dedicated MAN or WAN links. An example VPN is illustrated on the Virtual Private Network Diagram.

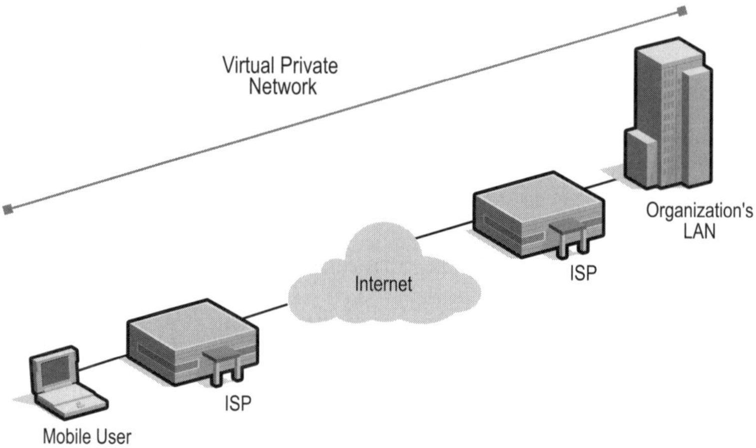

Virtual Private Network

This approach enables network traffic from many sources to travel through separate tunnels across the same infrastructure. It allows network protocols to traverse incompatible infrastructures. It also enables traffic from many sources to be differentiated, so that it can be directed to specific destinations and receive different levels of quality of service (QoS) handling. The main types of VPNs IT departments must support are:

- **Access VPNs**—Industry analysts predict that nearly 75 percent of corporate "knowledge workers" have at least one mobile computing device. IT organizations everywhere are struggling to meet this increasing demand for remote connectivity and deal with the resulting increases in network complexity and end-user support costs.
- **Internal VPNs**—IT must also support growing branch office connectivity. Particularly in organizations growing through acquisition or merger, the ability to rapidly integrate separate and frequently incompatible infrastructures can be critical to the success of business relationships.
- **External VPNs**—In addition, there is the emerging requirement to deploy extranets that support unpredictable relationships with customers and business partners. These connections create many management and security issues for the IT staff to cope with.

VPNs provide enterprises with a number of ways to immediately and substantially reduce the cost of remote access and branch connectivity. VPNs do this by taking advantage of the networking infrastructures and services of ISPs and other network service providers (NSPs). VPNs offer a cost-effective, scalable, flexible, manageable, and secure means of handling network growth; linking newly acquired business units; and supporting ad hoc business relationships.

Companies can get all these benefits while retaining central control over security and management of adds, moves, and changes. Enterprises deploying VPNs will have an increasing range of VPN-based services to choose from.

Tunneling is a method of transferring data packets over the Internet or other public network, while providing the security and features formerly available only on private networks. A tunneling protocol encapsulates the data packet in a header that provides routing information to enable the encapsulated payload to securely traverse the network.

Tunneling protocols in use for VPN communications today include point-to-point tunneling protocol (PPTP), layer 2 tunneling protocol (L2TP), and IP security (IPSEC).

Internet, Intranets, and Extranets

As a result of the dynamic growth of the Internet, new terminology is emerging almost daily. One source of confusion is the use of the terms Internet (capitalized), internet (not capitalized), intranet, and extranet.

Internet

When capitalized, Internet is generally considered the global TCP/IP network. In other words, the Internet that connects the world, which many people call the World Wide Web.

internet

When not capitalized, internet really refers to the internetworking or interconnection of two or more networks that use TCP/IP technology and protocols. This "internet" does not mean that a network is connected to the global Internet.

Intranet

Intranet refers to a "private Internet." It is a private, internal network that uses IP-based applications, tools, and routing; it is designed for private use by company personnel. An intranet is made up of all the network components within an AS. This could include LAN, CAN, SAN, MAN, WAN, and VPN connections for employees. Web content is created for access by internal users regardless of their method of connection.

For example, many companies store commonly used information as Web pages, and their employees use Web browsers to retrieve and view the documents. Intranet Web servers are hosted within the corporate network since they may provide access to confidential information and security is a concern.

The Web servers that provide intranet access use the same hardware, operating systems, and software as those that are used as Internet Web servers. The only difference is who accesses and how they access the intranet Web servers.

Extranet

An extranet includes both Internet and intranet capabilities. An extranet is a private intranet shared between closely aligned organizations. While it is external to each organization, it is not available to the general public. For example, a manufacturing company might work closely with a parts supplier for a specific product. Information about parts inventories could be stored in an extranet accessible to both companies.

An extranet provides somewhat secure connections and limited access to select external users. An extranet (external intranet) is a network segment, similar to a screened subnet, that offers controlled access to select Internet users. External users can view and sometimes update data stored on an internal network without traversing the internal network. This environment is typically set up to exchange information among a closely aligned group of organizations.

Memorable acronyms have been given to these type of services, such as:

- a business partners (business to business or B2B),
- a business and its chief suppliers (business to vendor or B2V), or
- clients (Business to customer or B2C).

A company can create an extranet to provide its business partners or customers direct access to product order information and account status housed in the organization's internal data warehouse systems. A dual-homed system acts as a proxy server for an application that runs on a server located on the extranet. The application acts as the proxy agent that retrieves the data from the internal systems and displays it for the user.

The Extranet Diagram illustrates an example of an extranet. The Internet client accesses the extranet Web system and is challenged by the system for a user name and password. Once logged in, the user requests information about a product.

The Web server, not the client, queries the internal database for the requested information, inserts it into a Web page template, and transmits it back to the browser. Customers get the information they need, without performing any operations that could interfere with the database.

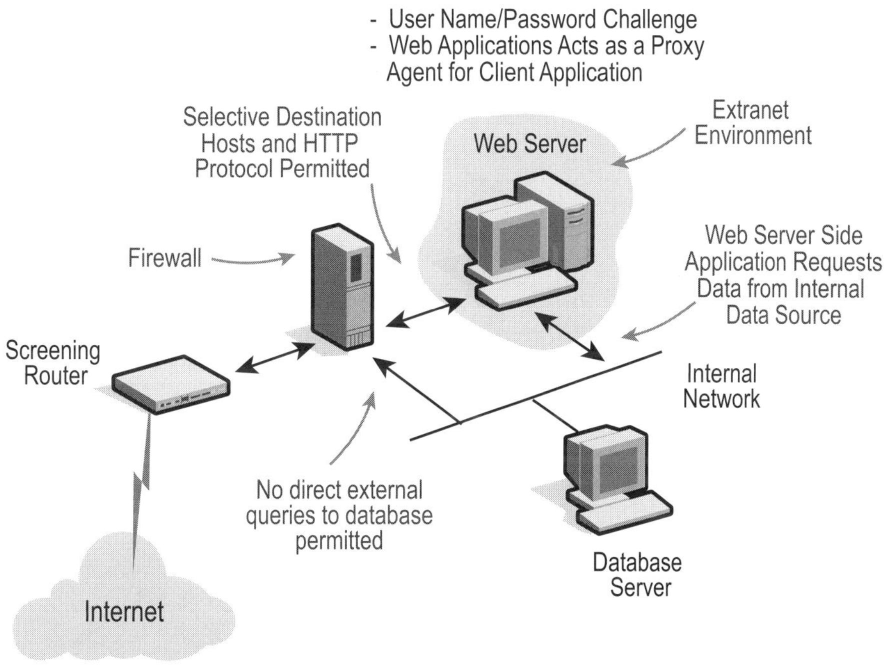

Extranet

Review Questions

1. A corporation has 15 branch offices dispersed throughout a big city. Until now, they have used modems to dial up and transmit files between the locations. What network type could they use to make the connections on a more permanent basis?

   a. CAN

   b. MAN

   c. WAN

   d. SAN

2. A company has locations throughout the United States and in three other countries. Information exchange is critical. What network type is used to make these connections?

   a. CAN

   b. MAN

   c. WAN

   d. SAN

3. An organization allows mobile users and people working from home to connect to the corporate network. The access is provided by the user's connection through the Internet. What network type is used?

   a. WAN

   b. MAN

   c. Access VPN

   d. Extranet VPN

4. Which type of network traffic is content networking not designed for?

   a. IP telephony

   b. Multimedia

   c. Streaming media

   d. Modem connections

5. What is the term given to Web content that is shared on a secure basis between two business partners?
   a. Internet
   b. Web
   c. Intranet
   d. Extranet
6. Which of the following is not a component in a CAN?
   a. IP communications
   b. SONET ring
   c. Routers
   d. Cable
7. What is the network type that is used to provide centralized access and alternate networking for storage devices?
   a. CAN
   b. WAN
   c. SAN
   d. CN
8. What access method allows VPNs to securely transmit information through the Internet?
   a. Hidden Transport
   b. Cloaking
   c. Tunneling
   d. Routing

Extended Activities

1. Match the following definitions with the correct terms from the list at the end of the question.

    a. Provides all the network connections owned and managed within a single building

    b. Connects LANs together that are all on one property with private wired or wireless media

    c. Manages and stores data for faster retrieval using Fiber-Channel or iSCSI connections

    d. Connects LANs together that are located in different parts of a city

    e. Connects LANs together using telecommunications lines for businesses that are distributed throughout the country or across the globe

    f. Allows connections into the network by tunneling through the Internet

    g. Individually handles different multimedia traffic with the highest levels of quality

    h. Internal Web site, used by employees only, that provides confidential information

    i. The connection of all autonomous systems into the Web

    j. A Web site set up for business-to-business communications of private information, not accessible by the general public

    ______ CN

    ______ CAN

    ______ Intranet

    ______ WAN

    ______ LAN

    ______ VPN

    ______ SAN

    ______ Internet

    ______ MAN

    ______ Extranet

Summary

This module defined all the different network types based on size, connections, facilities used, and purpose. Lesson 1 discussed LANs, with a primary focus on Ethernet. The lesson reviewed IEEE specifications, Ethernet frame headers, full-duplex and half-duplex communications, and the various transmission speeds associated with Ethernet.

Lesson 2 was an overview of WAN technologies. It discussed the global Internet and how businesses are connected together; it defined a number of service provider terms and also covered many WAN components. To connect to a WAN facility, the right equipment is important. Some options include modems, routers, CSU/DSUs, WAN switches, MUXes, and codecs. These devices all connect to telecommunications WAN facilities.

Lesson 2 provided a table that reviewed a number of different data transmission rates. The lesson also discussed serial and WAN connector types, and Data Link Layer protocols.

Lesson 3 was a description of several other network types. It discussed CANs and MANs, which extend the communication capabilities between branch offices and other locations. It discussed SANs as a means to store large repositories of data in various locations in the network and provide more efficient network access. Also covered was Content Networking, a method used to improve the quality and distribution of the various multimedia communications found in networks today.

Lesson 3 reviewed VPNs, which are network connections that allow transmissions to be tunneled through the Internet. This reduces costs normally incurred by long-distance WANs. The lesson ended with a discussion of intranets and extranets.

Module 2 Quiz

1. The part of the telephone network that includes all the switches and trunks used for transmission is called:
   a. The CO
   b. The toll network
   c. The local loop
   d. The demarc
2. The Cisco router side of a serial connection is what:
   a. A DB-25 connector
   b. A 60-pin proprietary connector
   c. An EIA/TIA-232 connector
   d. A DB-37 connector
3. An asynchronous connection uses what to transmit data while maintaining the connection:
   a. A clocking signal sent from the DCE
   b. A clocking signal sent from the DTE
   c. Start and stop bits around each character
   d. A digital pulse for synchronization
4. The wire connection made from the Central Office to your business is called the:
   a. Toll network
   b. Local loop
   c. Private line
   d. Leased line
5. Which serial encapsulation method allows for authentication and multiple protocol support for a dial-up connection?
   a. PPP
   b. SLIP
   c. ISDN
   d. CHAP

6. The WAN encapsulation type that has been almost completely replaced by Frame Relay for WAN connections is?
   a. ISDN
   b. X.25
   c. HDLC
   d. PPP
7. All of the following are valid serial connectors except:
   a. EIA/TIA-210
   b. V.35
   c. EIA/TIA-232
   d. EIA/TIA-449
8. What distinguishes a LAN from a WAN or MAN?
   a. Distance
   b. Use of public or private systems
   c. Use of routers, modems, and wireless bridges
   d. All of the above
9. Which of the following is not a WAN encapsulation type?
   a. ATM
   b. Frame Relay
   c. PPP
   d. Token Ring
10. Which of the following WAN services usually provides the highest bandwidth?
    a. T1
    b. T3
    c. DDS
    d. SONET
11. Ethernet operates at all speeds except which of the following?
    a. 16 Kbps
    b. 10 Mbps
    c. 1 Gbps
    d. 100 Mbps

12. Which of the following is the most popular LAN Data Link Layer technology?
    a. Token Ring
    b. FDDI
    c. SNA
    d. Ethernet
13. The CD in CSMA/CD refers to the ability of an Ethernet node to do which of the following?
    a. Access the physical medium
    b. Detect frame collisions
    c. Detect node failures
    d. Sense an electrical signal
14. The CS in CSMA/CD refers to the ability of an Ethernet node to do which of the following?
    a. Access the physical medium
    b. Detect frame collisions
    c. Detect node failures
    d. Sense an electrical signal
15. Collisions are normal on CSMA/CD LANs using switch devices for connectivity. True or False?
16. The majority of 10-Mbps Ethernet LANs use fiber optic technology. True or False?
17. CANs are used for identifying and prioritizing multimedia network traffic for the best service available. True or False?
18. Although they provide flexibility, VPNs are more costly than other WAN connections. True or False?
19. A T1 is the highest bandwidth copper wire facility. True or False?
20. SANs provide access to many multimedia application services like streaming audio and video feeds. True or False?

Module 3
Network Media

Network media is the foundation of communication capabilities. Without wired and wireless connections, transmission would be impossible. Before getting into more technical things such as switches and routers, here is an overview of how networks are connected together.

Lesson 1 starts out with a look at all the media types and their associated characteristics. The bounded media types that are included in Lesson 1 are unshielded twisted pair, shielded twisted pair, coaxial, and fiber optic cable.

Wireless connections also make up a substantial portion of many network environments today. Wireless communications include all transmissions that use the electromagnetic spectrum. This includes infrared, radio frequency (RF), microwave, and satellite. Lesson 1 ends with a comparison of all the media types.

Lesson 2 discusses the cable infrastructure commonly found in local area network (LAN) environments. It addresses cabling from an Ethernet perspective and starts the lesson with an overview of all the Ethernet specifications. Lesson 2 goes on to define straight-through and crossover cable pin configurations and when each type is used. It also discusses the components that are necessary to make a console connection using a rollover cable, serial converter, and Telnet application.

Lesson 3 is useful when making WAN connections. Most companies today have some sort of WAN connection, at the very least to the Internet. Other WAN connection types might include connections to branch offices, large customers, vendors, and mobile employees. WAN connections use serial transmissions that allow bits to be transmitted farther than typical LAN cabling.

WAN connections require synchronization, which is established by the service provider or by the DCE device in a back-to-back connection. Lesson 3 ends with a rundown of several different WAN connections. In addition to serial interfaces, there are ISDN BRI and PRI connections, ADSL, and cable modem.

Lessons

1. Network Media Types
2. Cabling the LAN
3. Cabling the WAN

Lesson 1—Network Media Types

A number of different media types are used in connecting networks. Copper cable is the most cost-effective and comes in three types: unshielded twisted pair (UTP), shielded twisted pair (STP), and coaxial. UTP cable is categorized by the number of twists per inch. CAT5 and CAT5e are the most common installation today.

CAT5e allows existing 100-Mb Ethernet communications, while providing for 1Gb future bandwidth as the network devices are upgraded or replaced. STP provides shielding to eliminate the possibility of external interference factors. It is not used as much today as it was when mainframes were the network servers.

Fiber optic cable is commonly used because of its high transmission capabilities, resistance to external interference, and high security. The two types of fiber optic cable are single-mode and multimode.

Wireless communications allow everything from very long distance via satellite to very short distance such as a wireless keyboard. They all use the electromagnetic spectrum to transmit information, just as radio waves give you music in your car. Under IEEE guidelines, wireless LANs are developing to provide complete flexibility in network access. Lesson 3 ends with a comparison of network media types.

Objectives

At the end of this lesson you will be able to:

- Identify the characteristics of unshielded and shielded twisted pair cable
- Identify the characteristics of coaxial cable
- Identify the characteristics of fiber optic cable
- Identify the characteristics of wireless communications
- Compare and contrast the media types

Key Point

Network technologies demand different physical media types. Unshielded twisted pair (UTP) and fiber optic cable are the most commonly wired media choices for network cabling. Wireless LAN communications are becoming more popular because they offer mobility.

UTP and STP Cable

Twisted pair cable consists of two or more pairs of thin, stranded, insulated copper wires twisted around each other to cancel Electromagnetic Interference/Radio Frequency Interference (EMI/RFI). Twisted pair cable is available in two standard varieties: unshielded twisted pair (UTP) and shielded twisted pair (STP). Recently, some manufacturers have offered a new type of twisted pair cable: screened twisted pair (ScTP).

UTP Cable

UTP is the most popular LAN cabling because it is inexpensive, light, flexible, and easy to install. It relies on precisely twisted pairs of wire to minimize EMI/RFI and is not shielded by an external conductor. The number of twists ranges from 2 to 12 per inch, depending on the type of cable. The UTP Cable Diagram illustrates this type of cable.

UTP Cable

Although UTP is similar in appearance to standard telephone cable, it must meet higher criteria to perform as data-grade cable. In particular, it is important to avoid using untwisted lengths of telephone-type cable to carry LAN traffic.

In recent years, two compatible, seven-level standards have been established for rating UTP cable by Electronic Industry Association/Telecommunications Industry Association (EIA/TIA) and the Underwriters' Laboratories (UL). The UL system uses the term "levels," and EIA/TIA uses the term "categories." Another slight difference is that the UL standard includes fire safety performance criteria similar to that specified by the NEC. Other than that, the EIA/TIA categories and UL levels are used interchangeably:

- **Category 1**—Analog and digital telephone communications, not suitable for data transmissions
- **Category 2**—Voice, ISDN, and data transmissions up to 4 Mb, used for Token Ring networks
- **Category 3**—Voice and data transmissions up to 10 Mb, Ethernet 10BaseT standard
- **Category 4**—Data transmissions up to 16 Mb, used for Token Ring networks
- **Category 5**—Data transmissions up to 100 Mb, Ethernet 100BaseT standard
- **Category 5e**—Data transmissions up to 1000 Mb (1 Gb), Ethernet 1000BaseT standard
- **Category 6**—Data transmissions up to 1000 Mb (1 Gb), higher-gauge wire than CAT5e

Higher-category UTP cables are made from higher-quality materials. Each higher category is also made with tighter cable twists and variable twist patterns for increased resistance to interference; in Category 5, those twists continue right up to the connector. A minimum of Category 5 is recommended for today's data network installations.

It is possible to combine network sections that use different cable categories. However, it is better to use the same category throughout a network. Many analysts recommend installing only Category 5e cable to provide sufficient bandwidth capacity for future needs.

Special care must be taken when installing Category 5 cabling systems. Not only must the cable meet specifications; in addition, only the highest quality connectors must be used. When Category 5 cable is connected, no more than 0.5 inch (1.3 centimeters [cm]) of the twist must be unraveled, a sometimes-difficult task that requires skilled installers.

Care must also be taken not to exceed the bend radius of the cable or otherwise crimp it. This can cause a misalignment of the twisted pair and lead to transmission errors.

In addition, twisted pair cables must be terminated on connectors of the same category of cable or higher. For example, if Category 5 cable is terminated on Category 3 connectors, that part of the installation usually performs at Category 3 data rates.

The "T" in 10BaseT stands for twisted pair. Thus, this term represents a network running 10 Mbps, using baseband signaling, over twisted pair cable. 10BaseT adapters typically include the transceiver circuitry, and like 10Base2 adapters, do not require an external transceiver. 100BaseT offers 100 Mbps transmissions.

Both 10BaseT and 100BaseT use a star topology. Each station is individually connected to a port on a multiport hub, which provides a central wiring point for each station connection or segment. The hub functions as a repeater and transceiver, receiving incoming signals from all stations, then broadcasting them to every station attached to the hub.

In other words, if one computer transmits a signal, all stations attached to the same hub receive that signal. (However, only the intended recipient processes the message.)

The 10BaseT Ethernet Configuration Diagram illustrates end devices connected to a hub in a star topology. This configuration consists of an Ethernet hub using UTP cable to connect eight workstations. In today's networks the hub would be replaced with a switch.

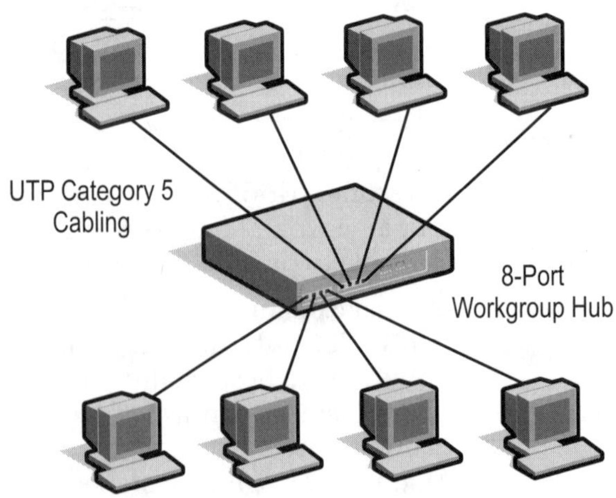

10BaseT Ethernet Configuration

Each end of the twisted pair cable is equipped with an RJ-45 connector, which is similar to a standard snap-in telephone connector, as illustrated on the RJ-45 Plug and Receptacle for UTP Diagram. All 10BaseT components, such as NICs and hub ports, use the same connectors, making installation fast and easy. A new device is connected by snapping a cable directly into the device NIC on one end and a hub or switch port on the other end.

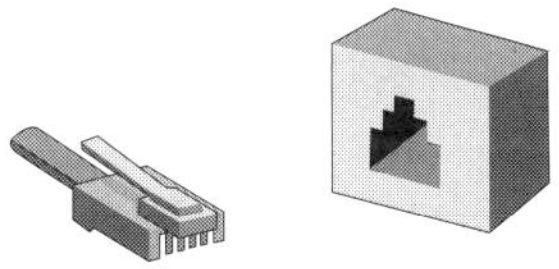

RJ-45 Plug and Receptacle for UTP

UTP is one of the most popular wiring standards due to its lower cost and relative ease of installation. In addition, its star topology allows for efficient management, maintenance, fault isolation, and reconfiguration of a LAN.

A hub or switch can be located in a central location, such as a wiring closet. In many offices, network cables run from the wiring closet, through the walls or ceiling, to each work area. Each cable is terminated at a wallplate near each workstation; thus, attaching a new computer to the network is as simple as plugging in a telephone.

A computer is connected to the wallplate, then the other end of the cable is connected to the hub or switch in the wiring closet, as illustrated on the UTP Connections at Wallplate Diagram. Hubs and switches can also be interconnected to enlarge a LAN.

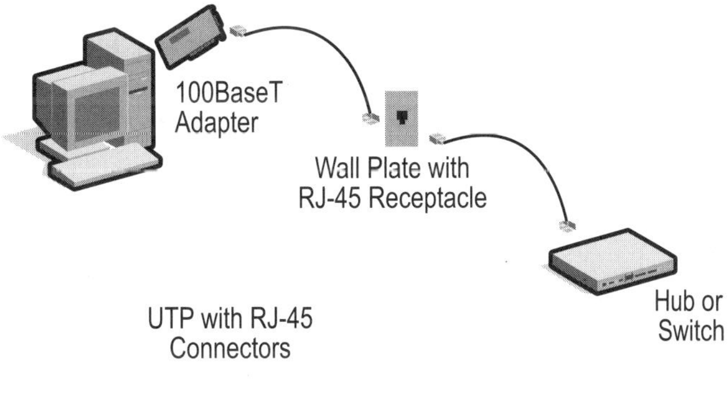

UTP Connections at Wallplate

Category 5 UTP cable is commonly used to wire 100BaseT networks. Category 3 cable is adequate for a 10-Mbps data rate, but network designers typically install Category 5 or 5e to ensure that the network wiring can support future upgrades to faster data rates. This approach is wise because the labor needed to install new cable is much more expensive than the slight increase in cable cost from Category 3 to Category 5.

The maximum distance for UTP cable is 100 meters. This is the specified distance from end device to repeater, hub or switch and applies to 10BaseT, 100BaseT and 1000BaseTx.

STP Cable

STP cable consists of two or more twisted pairs of copper wire surrounded by flexible insulation, a foil shield, and an outer plastic sheath. In some types of multiwire STP cable, individual twisted pairs may be surrounded by their own foil shield. The foil shield helps dissipate EMI, particularly at data rates of 16 Mbps or higher. The STP Cable Diagram illustrates this type of cable.

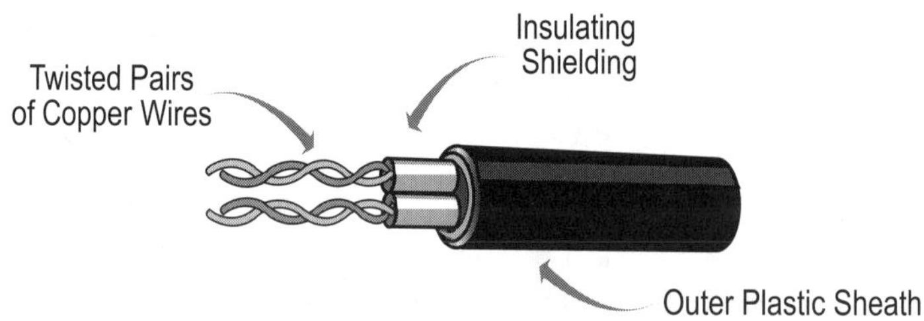

STP Cable

STP wiring was the original cable specified for ring topology networks, such as Token Ring and Fiber Distributed Data Interface (FDDI). STP provides considerably more resistance to EMI/RFI than UTP; however, it is also more bulky, less flexible, and more expensive to install.

Coaxial Cable

Coaxial cable was one of the first types of cable used in LANs. It typically consists of a central copper or copper-coated conductor surrounded by flexible insulation, a shield of copper wire mesh, and an outer plastic jacket. The Coaxial Cable Diagram illustrates the construction of this type of transmission medium.

Coaxial Cable

The shield serves as the second conductor (to complete the electrical circuit), and acts to prevent EMI/RFI. This physical design makes coaxial cable fairly expensive and generally harder to install than other types of cables.

Coaxial cable was designed to support Ethernet networks using bus topologies. Each type of coaxial cable is identified by a number called the radio government (RG) standard. But when the first Ethernet networks were developed, each type of LAN specified a particular type of cable.

Thus, coaxial cable is commonly identified by the name of the type of Ethernet LAN it implements, rather than its RG standard number. For example, it is more common to hear someone ask for "10Base2 coax" than "RG-58." The Coaxial Cable Types Table lists the two most common types of coaxial cable, their RG standard, and the maximum Ethernet bus length each can support.

Coaxial Cable Types

LAN Type	Cable Type	Maximum Distance (meters)
10Base2 (Thin Ethernet)	RG-58 A/U, RG-58 C/U	185
10Base5 (Thick Ethernet)	RG-8, RG-11	500

10Base5

10Base5 is the standard for using thick, RG-8-type coaxial cable to implement 10-Mbps baseband Ethernet networks using a bus topology. The "5" in the name represents 500 meters (m), which is the maximum length of a network bus using this cable. Thus, the term "10Base5" means "**10** Mbps, using **base**band signaling, and no longer than 500 m."

10Base5 cable is also called "Thicknet" or "Yellow Wire." This cable includes two layers of foil shielding and an additional copper mesh shield. In a 10Base5 network, a separate transceiver device connects a computer to the main bus cable to transmit outgoing signals and receive incoming signals. The transceiver connects to the computer's NIC by means of a separate transceiver cable called an "attachment unit interface (AUI)."

10Base2

10Base2 is the standard for using thin, RG-58-type coaxial cable to implement 10-Mbps baseband Ethernet using a bus topology. The number "2" in 10Base2 stands for approximately 200 m (to be precise, 185 m), which is the maximum length of this type of network bus.

10Base2 is also called "Thinnet," "ThinLAN," and "Cheapernet." 10Base2 uses twist-on T-connectors, called "BNC connectors," to attach to NICs (adapters) and other devices. In most 10Base2 implementations, the network adapter performs the transceiver functions.

The first and final T-connectors in the series include a 50-ohm terminating resistor to eliminate reflected signals on the unterminated cable. The 10Base2 Adapter and Cable Diagram illustrates these two components.

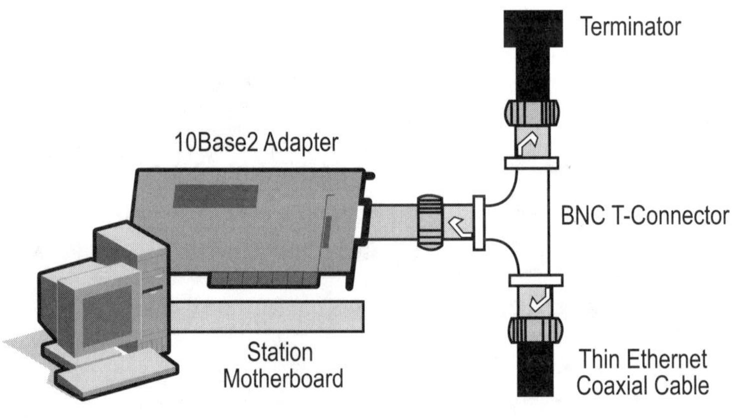

10Base2 Adapter and Cable

The 10Base2 Wiring Rules Table lists various parameters to consider when using this cable to wire an Ethernet system. The reason for some of these minimum and maximum values will become clear when you learn about the Ethernet protocol.

10Base2 Wiring Rules

10Base2 Parameter	Value
Maximum data rate	10 Mbps
Maximum repeaters between transceivers	4
Maximum stations per segment	30
Maximum coaxial segment without a repeater	185 m
Maximum coaxial length with repeaters	925 m

Coaxial cable, including 10Base2 and 10Base5, has good EMI/RFI resistance provided by its shielding. However, coaxial cable is bulky and relatively difficult to install through wire ducts and other spaces in a building. In addition, a cable break anywhere along a bus can disable the entire network segment.

Most important, Ethernet networks over coaxial cable are limited to 10 Mbps. As network users and applications require more bandwidth, coaxial cable has been overtaken by twisted pair and fiber optic cable. Coaxial cable can still be found in older networks; however, it is not typically used in new installations.

Fiber Optic Cable

A fiber optic cable is a thin strand of glass or plastic, coated with a protective plastic jacket. It is so thin that the glass fibers bend easily. A beam of light can be trapped within a fiber so that the optical cable essentially becomes a pipe that carries light around corners.

Fiber optic networks can support high data rates, theoretically as high as 50 Gbps. An optical fiber can carry a light signal for a long distance (typically up to 2 kilometers [km]) before the signal must be strengthened. Because light is not appreciably affected by electromagnetic fields, optical signals are immune to EMI/RFI. This makes fiber a good choice for "noisy" environments with many electrical motors, such as elevator shafts and factories.

In addition, fiber does not corrode, making it well suited for high-humidity and underwater environments. Optical fiber is also a highly secure medium because it is difficult to splice into a fiber optic cable without detection.

The primary disadvantage of fiber optic cable is its cost. Fiber optic cable and equipment are relatively expensive in terms of both materials cost and installation. However, industries that need the high capacity and secure features of fiber find it well worth the investment. For example, nearly all long-distance telecommunication lines are fiber optic.

Fiber Communication Systems

The basic model for a communication system includes a transmitter and receiver, connected by optical fiber cabling. In typical fiber optic systems, each device contains both a transmitter and receiver, combined in a single transceiver unit. Because fiber optic cable must be cut to present the light beam to a receiver, only point-to-point connections can be made; a bus cannot be constructed.

Transmitter

A transmitter includes the following components:

- **An encoder**—Converts the input data signal into digital electrical pulses
- **A light source**—Converts the digital electrical signal to light pulses
- **A connector**—Couples the light source to the fiber through which the light rays travel

The transmitter accepts digital electrical signals from a computer. A diode converts the digital code into a pattern of light pulses (on and off) that are sent out to the receiver through the optical fiber.

There are two basic types of light sources for fiber optic systems:

- **Light emitting diodes (LEDs)**—Use less power and are considerably less expensive than lasers. LEDs can be used with multimode cable and are the most common light source. LEDs provide a bandwidth of approximately 250 megahertz (MHz).
- **Laser diodes**—Are used for long-distance transmission over single-mode cable. Laser light is more powerful because laser light waves are radiated in phase, which means the crests and troughs of all light waves are perfectly aligned with one another. This alignment or coherence creates a signal with much less attenuation and dispersion than noncoherent light. Laser diodes can provide much higher bandwidth (up to a theoretical maximum of 10 gigahertz [GHz]).

Note: Never look into a fiber optic cable to see whether light is present. The infrared laser light used in fiber optic LANs is invisible but can permanently damage your sight in an instant.

Receiver

A receiver converts the modulated light pulses back to electrical signals and decodes them. It includes:

- A photodetector that converts the light pulses into electric signals
- An amplifier, if needed
- A message decoder

Fiber Optic Cable Construction

Optical fiber cable consists of three parts, as shown on the Fiber Optic Cable Diagram:

- **Core**—A solid fiber of highly refractive clear glass or plastic that serves as the central conduit for light. The diameter and consistency of the core varies, depending upon the specification of the fiber.
- **Cladding**—A layer of clear glass or plastic with a lower index of refraction. When light traveling down the core reaches the boundary between the core and cladding, the change in refractive index causes the light to completely refract or bend back into the core. The cladding of each fiber completely contains light signals within each core. This effect is called "total internal reflection."
- **Coating**—A reinforced plastic outer jacket that protects the cable from damage.

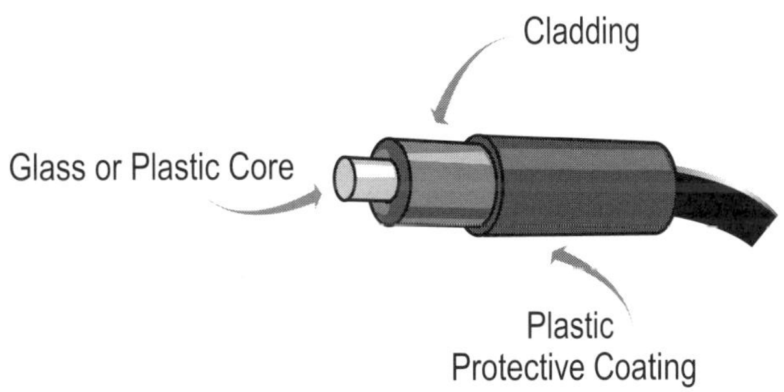

Fiber Optic Cable

Fiber Optic Dimensions

Fiber optic cable is very thin. The diameters of fiber optic cores and cladding are specified in micrometers (µm). The thinnest fiber optic cable (single-mode) typically has a core diameter of 5 to 10 µm (0.005 to 0.010 millimeter [mm]). Thicker fiber optic cable (multimode) ranges from 50 to 100 µm in core diameter. In comparison, human hair is approximately 100 µm thick.

Fiber optic cable is specified in terms of its core and cladding diameter. For example, the most common type of fiber optic cable for LAN installations is 62.5/125-µm cable, where 62.5 refers to the core diameter and 125 refers to the cladding diameter.

The core diameter is called the "aperture" because it determines the maximum angle from which the cable can accept light. Total internal reflection only occurs when light strikes the cladding at a shallow angle. If the angle is too steep, some or all of the light penetrates the cladding itself, causing signal loss.

Each fiber optic core conducts light in one direction only. Therefore, to send and receive, devices are usually connected by two fiber optic strands. These may be single-strand (simplex) cables, or duplex cables containing two fiber optic strands. Duplex cables are more commonly used than simplex cables.

Fiber cables can also consist of several bundles, as illustrated on the Multiple Bundle Fiber Optic Cable Diagram. These are used for high-capacity backbones for outdoor connections between campus buildings. Because light signals are completely contained within each fiber, no coating or shielding is necessary between fibers. However, reinforcing strands are usually added to increase the pulling strength of the cable.

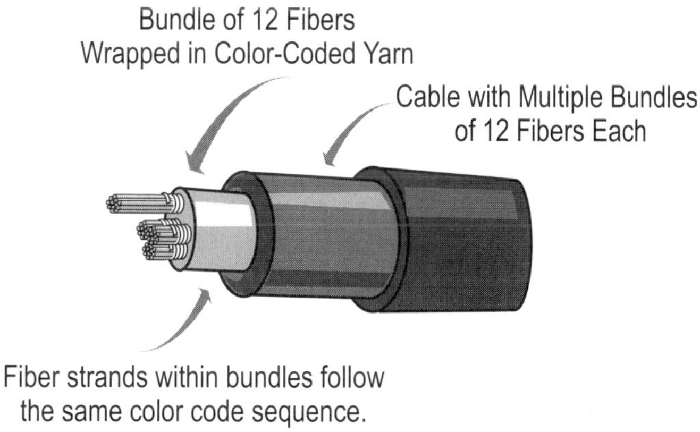

Multiple Bundle Fiber Optic Cable

Types of Fiber Optic Cable

Fiber optic cable is available in two general types:

- Multimode fiber which is wide enough to carry more than one light signal. (Each signal is called a "mode.")
- Single-mode fiber which is thin and can carry only one light signal.

Multimode Fiber

Each light signal or light ray that passes through a cable is called a "mode." Multimode fiber optic cable is wider than single-mode cable; thus, it has enough room for more than one light ray. These light signals are separated by different angles of reflection as they travel down the core.

Because multimode signaling separates light signals by angle, not all light rays travel the same distance. Some light rays travel nearly straight through the core, while others bounce off the cladding many times before reaching the far end of the fiber, as illustrated on the Multimode Fiber Diagram.

With modes traveling different distances but at the same speed, the spread of the signal increases over time and can cause data errors due to the overlapping of light pulses. This problem is called "modal dispersion."

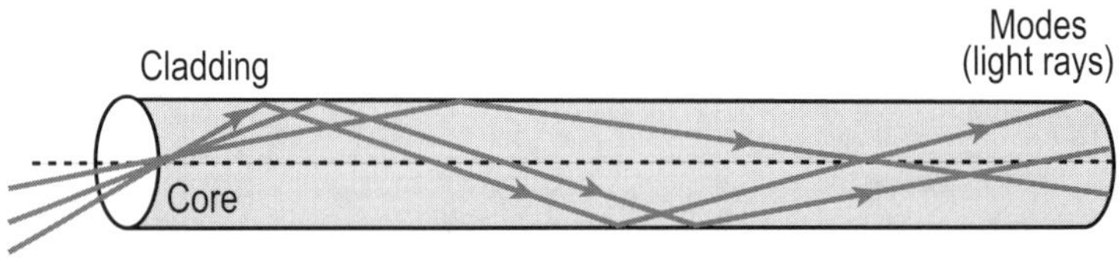

Multimode Fiber

The construction of a multimode fiber can either cause or fix this problem. There are two types of multimode fiber: step-index and graded-index fiber.

Step-Index Fiber

The standard type of optical fiber, called "step-index fiber," consists of only two transparent layers (core and cladding) and cannot compensate for the multimode signal dispersion effect.

Graded-Index Fiber

The core of a graded-index fiber cable has several transparent layers, each with a different refractive index. This planned inconsistency allows light modes to travel at different speeds through the core. Thus, all modes reach the far end of the fiber more uniformly. The most commonly specified fiber optic cable is 62.5/125-µm multimode graded-index.

Single-Mode Fiber

Single-mode fibers have diameters sized to the wavelength they are designed to carry. A typical single-mode fiber core diameter is 8 µm. Only one mode will propagate through fiber with this core diameter. Single-mode fibers are generally step-index fibers. Because only one mode travels along the fiber, the problem of diffusion does not occur in single-mode fibers.

Single-mode fibers require laser diode transmitters. By using this coherent light source, single-mode fiber optic cable can support longer transmission distances than multimode fiber. Distances range from a few miles to as many as 20 miles.

New technologies called Dense Wavelength Division Multiplexing (DWDM) allow single-mode fiber to carry multiple transmissions by refracting the light into separate color spectrums. However, the transmission is multiplexed into "white" light then demultiplexed back into separate transmission on the receiving end.

Installing Fiber Optic Cable

Fiber optic cable is difficult to install correctly; therefore, it requires well-trained, careful, installation technicians. This, combined with the time-consuming nature of each connection, makes fiber optic cable the most expensive cable to install. Because of this need for training and experience, many organizations hire specialists to install fiber optic networks.

Connections and splices of fiber optic cable are particularly difficult to make. Each end of the cable must be cut off at perfect right angles, the ends polished by hand or machine, and the cable precisely aligned to the connector.

Like copper wire connectors, the snap-in connectors that terminate optical fibers provide a simple way to link one fiber to another, or to a device. However, the nature of optical transmission means that fiber connectors must do their job at a higher level of precision. While it is fairly simple for copper connectors to make a secure electrical connection with copper connectors, fiber connectors must precisely align the ends of two very thin fibers.

There are many different types of fiber connectors and many of them are proprietary. The EIA/TIA-568 standard specifies two connector types, illustrated on the Fiber Optic Connectors Diagram:

- SC connectors, which are preferred. These snap-in connectors include both one-fiber and two-fiber plugs.
- ST ("straight tip") connectors, which are allowed in legacy installations. These bayonet-style connectors use a push-and-twist motion to attach one multimode or single-mode fiber.

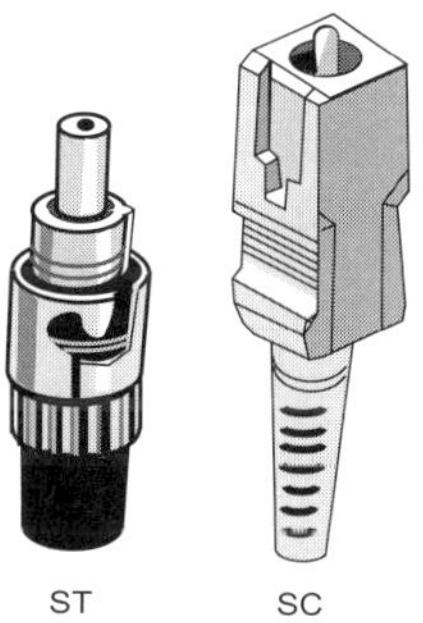

Fiber Optic Connectors

Wireless Communications

Radio waves are increasingly used to carry voice and data signals through open space. Wireless transmission has traditionally been used where it is impossible or too costly to install fixed cable, such as in historic buildings or rough terrain. However, radio-based mobile communication, both voice and data, is growing exponentially as consumers demand the flexibility and convenience of cell phones and wireless data networks.

The term "wireless" usually does not mean that a signal is carried using radio technology all the way. Most wireless transmission uses the cable-based telephone system as much as possible, shifting to radio transmission only when necessary.

Wireless Protocols

Wireless LANs interface with the rest of a LAN system in one of two ways:

- At the Physical Layer using existing Data Link Layer protocols
- At the Data Link Layer using proprietary protocols

Wireless technologies that provide a new Physical Layer channel can be implemented in relatively simple devices that use standard Data Link Layer protocols such as Ethernet. This approach has the benefits of high interoperability with existing LAN equipment because all devices use the same MAC sublayer protocol, higher speed, lower cost, lower power requirements, and smaller device size.

The Data Link Layer wireless technique requires proprietary protocols and hardware for both the Data Link and Physical Layers. This technique produces more sophisticated (and costly) devices than implementing wireless technology as a purely Physical Layer technique.

The Electromagnetic Spectrum

Radio waves are one part of the electromagnetic spectrum, which includes all types of radiated energy, such as radio waves, infrared waves (heat), visible light, and x-rays. This spectrum is illustrated on the Electromagnetic Spectrum Diagram.

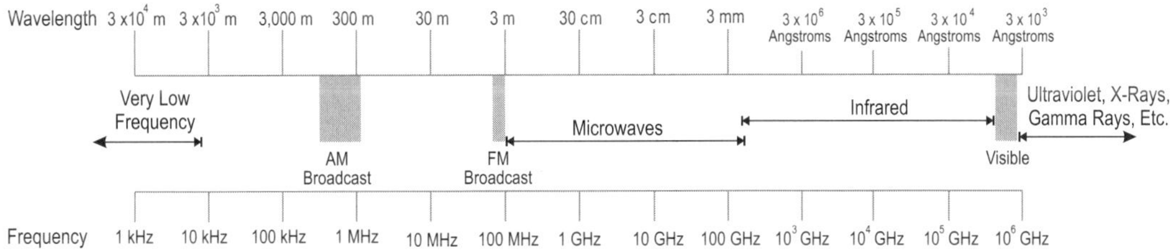

Electromagnetic Spectrum

At first glance, the electromagnetic spectrum seems very wide; however, not all of it is useful for sending signals through open air. The sun interferes with any messages sent in the visible light spectrum, and the atmosphere absorbs ultraviolet light. X-rays and gamma rays (and beyond) are so short that they pass through most receivers without being detected.

Thus, to transmit signals, we must use wavelengths that are longer than visible light: infrared, microwaves, and radio. In general, we call these wavelengths the "RF spectrum."

We identify parts of the RF spectrum by either of the following measurements:

- **Wavelength** is the physical distance between the crests of a wave, as illustrated on the Wavelength Diagram. As you can see on the Electromagnetic Spectrum Diagram, these phenomena are arranged in order of their wavelengths. Some radio waves are as long as 30,000 m, while the wavelength of infrared energy ranges from 3 mm to 0.003 mm. Shorter wavelengths are measured in angstroms: 1 angstrom is one ten-millionth of a millimeter (10^{-9} m).
- **Frequency** measures the number of times per second that a wave moves from the highest point, through the lowest point, then back to the highest point again. Frequency is measured in cycles per second or Hertz (Hz). One Hz equals 1 cycle per second, 1 kilohertz (kHz) equals 1,000 Hz, 1 MHz equals 1 million Hz, and 1 GHz equals 1 billion Hz.

Either of these measurements is equally good for identifying parts of the RF spectrum because they are directly related to each other. As the wavelength of energy becomes shorter, so does its frequency. Thus, if one person says "the 100-GHz band," and another says "the 3-mm range," they are both talking about the same part of the spectrum.

Wireless Networking Applications

There is a staggering number of uses for radio transmission. However, wireless transmission in data networks tends to fall into the following categories:

- **Point-to-point microwave systems**—Used for making connections between buildings or external wireless bridged communications
- **Satellites**—Used for moderate to long-distance communications
- **Cellular systems and Personal Communications Services (PCS)**—Used for cell phone and now text and Web-based information delivery to cell phones and related devices
- **Wireless LANs**—Used for end-user connectivity of laptops, PCs, and network peripherals
- **Short-range infrared transmission**—Used for wireless keyboard, mouse, and other input/output devices; can also be used for data transmissions

Remember that each of these wireless applications is based on the same principles. In each case, a transmitter modulates a carrier wave, and a receiver detects and demodulates that wave.

IEEE 802.11 Wireless LAN Standards

The IEEE Project 802.11 committee drafted a standard for LAN interoperability based on a minimum bandwidth of 1 Mbps. This consists of a wireless MAC sublayer protocol that can interface with a variety of Physical Layer protocols corresponding to vendor approaches to the technology.

In Europe, the European Telecommunications Standards Institute (ETSI) and the Conference European des Postes et des Telecommunications/European Conference of Postal and Telecommunications Administrations (CEPT) are responsible for broad-scale standardization. The European version of the IEEE 802.11 standard is ETSI Res 9.

Spread-spectrum systems that comply with 802.11 can operate in three nonlicensed frequency bands, commonly called the Industrial, Scientific, and Medical (ISM) bands:

- 902 to 928 MHz
- 2.4 to 2.483 GHz
- 5.725 to 5.875 GHz

High-frequency carrier signals can carry data faster than low-frequency signals, because each cycle of a radio wave can be modulated in various ways to represent one or more digital bits. In other words, the more cycles per second a signal provides, the more data it can carry. Therefore, of the three ISM bands, most new wireless LAN development is occurring in the 2.4- and 5-GHz ranges.

The IEEE 802.11 standard defines the basic technology of wireless networking. However, that approach can only deliver 1- to 2-Mbps throughput at a maximum distance of 300 feet. Thus, the IEEE 802.11 committee and other working groups have continued working to develop better standards and protocols that will enhance the growth and development of this new technology. These new 802 wireless standards include:

- **802.11b**—This direct-sequence, spread-spectrum communication method can deliver a maximum raw throughput of 11 Mbps. The technology, currently used in most wireless office LANs, operates within the 2.4-GHz range.
- **802.11a**—This approach uses orthogonal frequency-division multiplexing, over multiple parallel channels, to deliver a raw data rate of up to 54 Mbps. In the United States, this technology operates in several portions of the 5-GHz range. (Channel hopping occurs within the assigned band of frequencies.) However, there is more competition for this part of the spectrum in Europe and Asia; thus, fewer channels will be available for 802.11a there.
- **802.11g**—After much debate and anticipation, IEEE ratified 802.11g in June 2003. 802.11g delivers up to 54 Mbps using orthogonal frequency-division multiplexing in the 2.4-Ghz band. Basically, it uses the same encoding method as 802.11a in the same frequency as 802.11b. This allows for backward compatibility with 802.11b components by allowing the 802.11g devices to "step down" to the lower bandwidth (11 Mb) as needed.

  However, for devices needing the higher bandwidth capabilities, the wireless Access Points and NICs in use will have to be physically replaced. This is because, although the frequency is the same, the coding method is different. Access point locations may also have to be moved closer together to achieve data rates anywhere close to 54 Mb.

  As stated earlier in this lesson, a major drawback to the 2.4-Ghz frequency is the number of other devices that contend for the same range. This can also diminish the practical bandwidth of the new 802.11g components. Many vendors have developed and manufactured products during the ratification process. This means that the standard in many cases is catching up to the market. However, some vendors missed the boat by implementing proprietary solutions in their equipment to achieve higher bandwidth or alleviate issues with distance.

Therefore, it is important, when considering wireless equipment, to verify that it meets the specifications of the ratified 802.11g standard. For more information, review the IEEE Web site at **www.standards.ieee.org**.

Because these wireless standards all operate at the Physical Layer, they can support existing Data Link Layer protocols such as Ethernet. At the same time, 802.11a and 802.11b each use a different part of the spectrum and a different method of spread-spectrum transmission. For these reasons, they are incompatible with each other.

Comparison of Media Types

The Media Characteristics Table compares the most common transmission media.

Media Characteristics

	Media Type					
Characteristic	**Twisted Pair**	**Coaxial Cable**	**Fiber Optic**	**Microwave**	**Satellite**	**Wireless LANs**
Capable of digital transmission	Good – distance-sensitive	Better–less distance-sensitive	Best – much less distance-sensitive	Yes	Yes	Yes
Prone to attenuation	Most	Less	Least	Yes	Much less than ground-based microwave	Yes
Prone to electrical interference	Yes	Somewhat	No	Yes	Less than ground-based microwave	Yes

Media Characteristics (Continued)

	Media Type					
Character-istic	**Twisted Pair**	**Coaxial Cable**	**Fiber Optic**	**Micro-wave**	**Satellite**	**Wireless LANs**
Cost of installation	Moderate	Moderate	Moderately high	High	Very high	Moderately high
Cost of associated equipment	Low	Moderately high	High	High	High	Moderately high
Bandwidth	Medium to high	Medium	High	High	High	Varies
International transmission	No	Yes	Yes	Yes	Yes	No
Appropriate for broadcast video	No	Yes	Yes	Yes	Yes	No
Strengths	Inexpen-sive, easy to install	High bandwidth	Long-distance transmis-sion, high security	Rugged terrain and mobile tele-phones	Very long-distance transmission	Mobile transmission without delay
Drawbacks	Susceptible to interference	Limited to 45 Mbps, hard to install	Expensive and hard to install	Vulnerable to eaves-dropping, may be distorted by poor weather	Noticeable propaga-tion delay	Susceptible to interference

Review Questions

1. When is UTP cable preferred over fiber optic?
   a. When there is little electrical interference
   b. When cost is no object
   c. When going long distances
   d. When security is very important
2. Which connector type is used with Thinnet coaxial cable?
   a. RJ-45
   b. RG-58
   c. BNC
   d. RJ-11
3. Which of the following cable types can transmit data the longest distance?
   a. Thinnet
   b. UTP
   c. STP
   d. Fiber optic
4. What is the maximum number of repeaters that can be used to extend the cable distance with coaxial cable?
   a. 2
   b. 3
   c. 4
   d. 5
5. How are bits represented on fiber optic cable?
   a. Electrical signals
   b. Pulses (on/off) of light
   c. Changing wavelength
   d. None of the above

6. Which of the following are the two primary types of light sources in fiber optic cables?
    a. UTP and STP
    b. Laser diode and LED
    c. Multimode and single-mode
    d. EMI and RFI
7. Which of the following are the two types of fiber optic cables?
    a. UTP and STP
    b. Laser diode and Light Emitting Diode
    c. Multimode and single mode
    d. EMI and RFI
8. Which of the following describes the purpose of cladding in a fiber optic cable?
    a. To reflect light as it passes through a cable
    b. To amplify the light signal
    c. To increase the propagation of light
    d. To decrease the angle of reflection
9. Which of the following is a 802.11 wireless technology most often used for?
    a. Replace cabled LANs
    b. Point-to-point transmission
    c. Low data rate applications
    d. Replacement of Ethernet in LANs
10. In a typical 10BaseT network, which of the following is the maximum distance a signal can be sent over twisted pair?
    a. 100 m
    b. 1,000 m
    c. 10 km
    d. 200 m

Extended Activities

1. Fiber optic cable is not sensitive to electrical noise. True or False?
2. Single-mode fiber uses laser diodes to generate a light signal. True or False?
3. If light strikes the cladding at too steep an angle, the light will bounce too many times, causing the signal to travel too slowly. True or False?
4. Twisted pair cable is used mostly for high bit rates over long distances. True or False?
5. Twisted pair wires are twisted to make the cable stronger for ease of installation. True or False?
6. 10Base2 uses a terminating plug at the ends of the bus. True or False?
7. UTP cable is used extensively in data networks. True or False?
8. Which wireless transmission method uses direct sequence spread spectrum?
   a. 802.11
   b. 802.11b
   c. 802.11a
   d. 802.11g
9. Which connector types are standard with fiber optic cable? (Choose two.)
   a. ST
   b. RJ-45
   c. SC
   d. LM
10. What radio frequency is used for 802.11b and 802.11g wireless?
    a. 915 Mhz
    b. 5.4 Ghz
    c. 2.4 Ghz
    d. 2.9 Ghz

Lesson 2—Cabling the LAN

This lesson discusses the physical media types used to connect network and end devices together. It begins with an identification chart that outlines the different cable and connector types used in various Ethernet environments. Category 5 or higher UTP cable with an RJ-45 connector is the most common and cost-effective desktop configuration.

You will learn about the pin requirements for straight-through and crossover cables. A straight-through cable is used to connect different network device types. A crossover cable changes the pins from 1 to 3 and 2 to 6, "crossing over" the transmit to receive. It is used to directly connect two like network devices. A review of LAN connectors, RJ-45, AUI, and fiber optics follows. A LAN diagram displays how the infrastructure is cabled internally.

This lesson also discusses the configuration and use of a rollover cable. This cable type allows a PC to connect to a router or switch for configuration and monitoring. This special cable plugs into a serial interface on the PC and the console port of the network device. The pin configuration of the rollover cable, and the steps used to make a console connection conclude the lesson.

Objectives

At the end of this lesson you will be able to:

- Identify Ethernet cabling standards
- Define UTP straight-through and crossover cable configurations
- Recognize LAN connectors and cable configurations
- Define rollover cable configuration
- Set up a console connect to a switch or router

Key Point

Ethernet has a broad range of specifications for different cable types and bandwidth options.

Ethernet Cable Specifications

As shown in the Ethernet Cable and Connector Types Table, a number of Ethernet cable specifications are defined at the Physical Layer. These are IEEE 802.3 industry standards that determine how a network is physically laid out. They are labeled using the speed, baseband signal, and a cabling specification as shown in the table.

Ethernet Cable and Connector Types

IEEE	Specification	Cable Type	Maximum Cable Length	Connector Type	Speed (Mbps)
802.3 Ethernet	10Base2 Thinnet	Coaxial cable	185 meters	AUI and/or BNC	10
	10Base5 Thicknet	50-ohm coaxial cable	500 meters	AUI and/or BNC	10
	10BaseT	Category 3, 4, 5, or 5e UTP	100 meters	RJ-45	10
802.3u Fast Ethernet	100BaseTX	Category 5 or 5e UTP (two pairs)	100 meters	RJ-45 and MII	100
	100BaseT4	Category 3, 4, 5, or 5e UTP (four pairs)	100 meters	RJ-45 and MII 40-pin connector	100
	100BaseFX	Multimode fiber	400 meters	Duplex Media-Interface Connector ST	100
802.3ab	1000BaseT	Category 5 or 5e UTP (four pairs)	100 meters	RJ-45	1,000
802.3z Gigabit Ethernet	1000BaseCX	Copper STP	25 meters	Special DB-9, HSSDC	1,000
	1000BaseSX	62.5- and 50-micron core multimode fiber	500 meters	780-nm laser, SC Connector	1,000
	1000BaseLX	9-micron single-mode fiber	3 to 10 km	1,300-nm laser, SC connector	1,000

UTP Cable Configurations

This course, and any career in networking, requires some knowledge of cabling configurations. Standard cabling used for WAN or fiber connections is difficult to make and is usually purchased or installed professionally. However, UTP cable is easy to configure and terminate. This section provides a basic pinout for both straight-through and crossover cables. Keep in mind that a number of standards are available and different pinouts can be used to match jack configurations.

UTP cable is composed of eight copper wires, each wrapped in a very thin, color-coded plastic sheathing. The wires are then twisted into four pairs, which are held in an outer plastic casing.

The pairs are divided between Transmit and Receive, or Tip and Ring (terms originating with telephone connections). Either way, they refer to the direction of flow, and the positive or negative charge given to a pair. To simplify identification, the wires are color coded and can be easily seen when they are in a clear RJ-45 connector or when a cable is spliced.

The cabling is unshielded (it has no heavy outer cladding) because the twisted wires protect each other and help reduce outside electrical interference and cross talk. Cables are categorized by the number of twists per inch; the higher the number, the more twists and the better the cable's performance on a network.

Cabling specifications are defined by EIA/TIA and AT&T. Two standards are provided by EIA/TIA: 568A and 568B; AT&T's standard is 258A. The RJ-45 Pinout Configurations Table represents two common cable color and number associations, which are important when making data cables.

RJ-45 Pinout Configurations

Pin Number	Signal	EIA/TIA-568A	AT&T 258A or EIA/TIA-568B
1	Transmit +	White/Green	White/Orange
2	Transmit -	Green/White	Orange/White
3	Receive +	White/Orange	White/Green
4	Not used	Blue/White	Blue/White
5	Not used	White/Blue	White/Blue

RJ-45 Pinout Configurations (Continued)

Pin Number	Signal	EIA/TIA-568A	AT&T 258A or EIA/TIA-568B
6	Receive -	Orange/White	Green/White
7	Not used	White/Brown	White/Brown
8	Not used	Brown/White	Brown/White

The standard Ethernet connector is an RJ-45, similar but larger than the one used for a telephone. The name stands for "Registered Jack," with 45 referring to a specific wiring configuration. When facing an RJ-45 connector with the clip down, pin 1 is on the left and pin 8 is on the right.

To make a cable, cut the plastic outer cladding, separate the pairs, and trim as necessary, align them using the specifications for either a straight-through, crossover, or rollover cable, and then crimp the RJ-45 connector on the end using a special crimping tool.

Straight-Through Cable

A straight-through cable has the same wiring configuration on both ends. To see this, hold up both connectors in the same orientation. The Straight-Through Cable Pinout Configuration Diagram shows the EIA/TIA-568B specification.

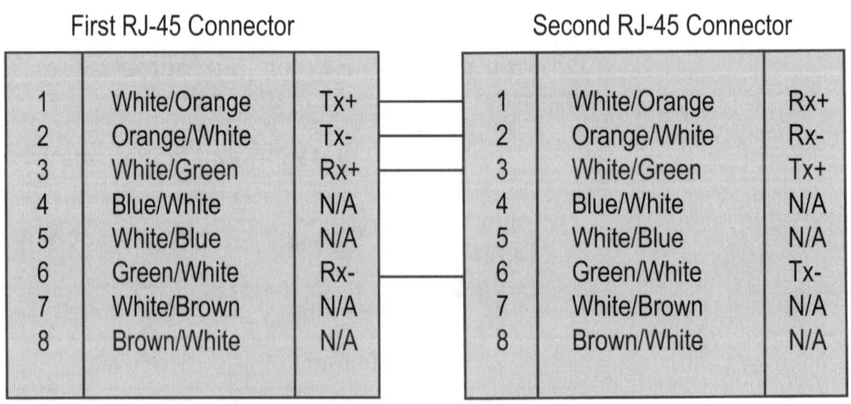

Straight-Through Cable Pinout Configuration

Straight-through cables are used for:

- Patch cables from a personal computer (PC) or server to a hub
- Patch cables from a PC or server to a switch
- Cables between a router and a switch

Crossover Cable

A crossover cable changes the pin configuration, where pin 1 crosses to pin 3 and pin 2 crosses to pin 6, as illustrated on the Crossover Cable Pinout Configuration Diagram.

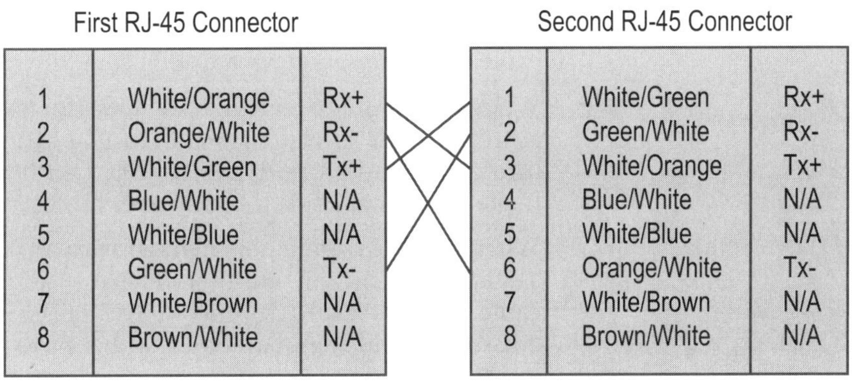

Crossover Cable Pinout Configuration

Crossover cables are used for:

- Connecting a switch to a switch
- Connecting a switch to a hub
- Connecting a PC or server to another PC or server
- Connecting a hub to a hub
- Connecting a router to a router

Straight-Through vs. Crossover Cable

A quick rundown of when to use straight-through versus crossover cables was just discussed. But sometimes it is difficult to decide. When trying to determine which type of cable to use, remember the odd X theory or remember that "two wrongs don't make a right." There should always be an odd number of Xs when you are cabling devices.

Remember, too, that unless it is an uplink port, a switch or hub port counts as an X port. In addition, the following guidelines should help you decide which type of cable to use when connecting devices:

- When cabling between different devices (for example, switch to router, switch to PC, or PC to hub), use a straight-through cable. The network device in this case provides the X.
- When cabling between like devices (for example, switch to switch, router to router, or PC to PC), use a crossover cable into any standard port NOT marked with an X. This would make one X, which is the crossover cable.
- When cabling from a port marked with an X on one device to a standard port on another device, use a straight-through cable. In this example one of the ports is performing the crossover, resulting in an odd number of Xs.
- When using the X port on both devices, use a crossover cable because both ports and the cable together make three crosses, again an odd number of Xs.

The Straight-Through vs. Crossover Cable Diagram shows examples of cabling between two switches. The first image shows a cable going into an unmarked port on one device and an X port on the other device; therefore, a straight-through cable is used. The second image shows a crossover cable going between two devices, using the X ports on each.

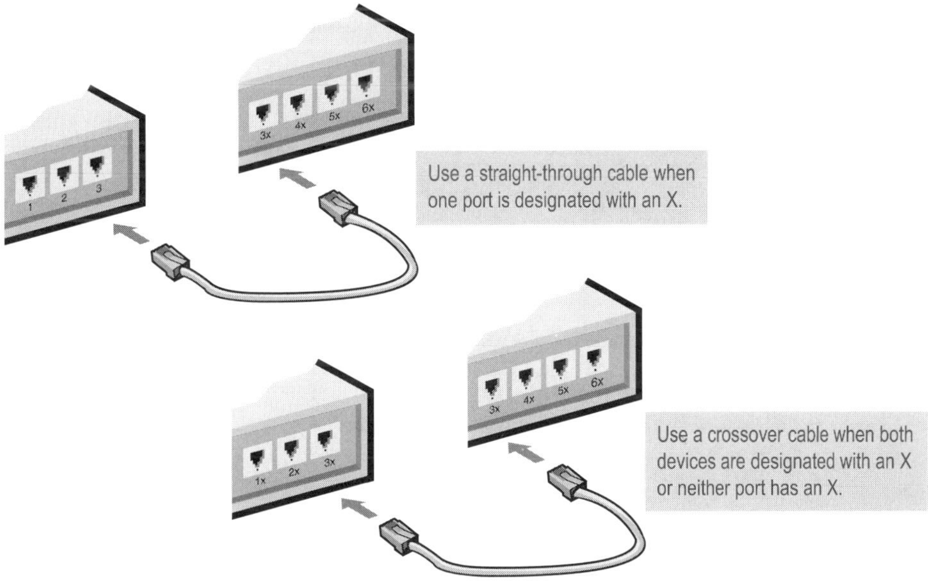

Straight-Through vs. Crossover Cable

Some network devices have autosensing capabilities. Regardless of whether you use a straight-through cable or a crossover cable, the port senses it and adapts accordingly.

LAN Connectors and Cable Configurations

The types of connectors found on LAN devices are usually RJ-45, fiber, BNC, or AUI DB-15. Although older equipment AUI and BNC ports may still be in use, they have a 10-Mbps limitation and are often replaced with newer hardware. The RJ-45 connector ports are labeled numerically and usually have a link, error, and possibly speed LED indicator.

A link LED indicates that a physical connection has been made and is usually green. An error condition may be shown by the same LED and is usually orange. The speed indicator may show an autosynchronization of 10 or 100 Mbps. When a light is off, a physical connection is not possible.

Fiber optic ports are also available on many devices and have two connections, generally labeled "Tx" and "Rx" for transmitting and receiving connections, respectively. The LAN Connectors Diagram illustrates the different connector ports on a LAN switch device.

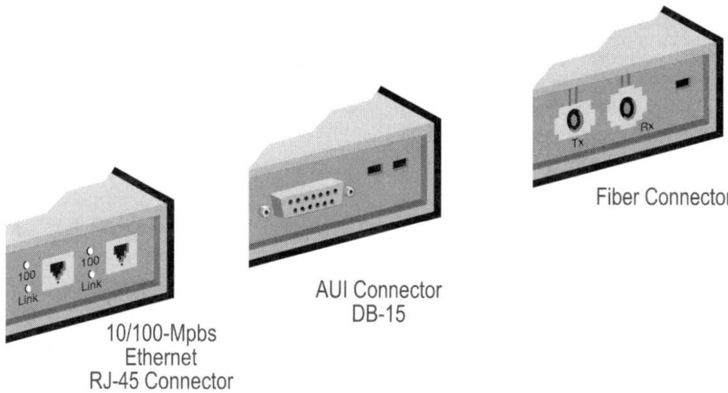

LAN Connectors

Gigabit Interface Converter

Cisco offers a special connection for gigabit communications, called a Gigabit Interface Converter (GBIC). This is a hot-swappable interface that allows connectivity over CAT5/5e twisted pair, single-mode fiber, or multimode fiber. Hot-swappable means that the interface can be removed and replaced without turning the equipment off.

A switch or router has a slot that the GBIC fits into. The GBIC component itself is about half the size of a deck of cards. The input/output plug interface is specific to the technology, as follows:

- 1000BaseT (UTP Cat 5/5e)
- 1000BaseSX (multimode)
- 1000BaseLX/LH (single-mode 3 to 6 miles)
- 1000BaseZX (single-mode 40 to 62 miles)

This modular approach allows network designers a lot of flexibility when building equipment. It also allows connections to be easily changed between devices or exchanged when a different cable connection is required. For more information about the different types and a look at the GBIC, access the Cisco Web site at **www.cisco.com** and search for GBIC.

Cabling the LAN

A LAN configuration usually remains inside a single building and connects PCs, servers, and peripheral devices to a network using hubs and switches. (Although bridges can be used as well, their popularity has waned substantially.)

A typical Ethernet LAN cable scheme is explained as follows:

- PCs are connected to workgroup hubs or switches using a straight-through cable running 10 or 100 Mbps, depending on the system requirements. Systems requiring faster throughput are generally put on a faster connection.
- The workgroup hubs or switches usually connect to a high-speed switch at 100 Mbps, using a crossover UTP cable, or at 1 Gbps using fiber optic cable.
- Servers can be attached directly to this switch as well, or to a multilayer switch at 100 Mbps using a straight-through UTP cable, or again at 1 Gbps using either a copper or fiber optic connection.
- If two switches are used, they should be connected with a crossover cable at 100 Mbps. Fiber optic uplinks are more commonly used between switches. This allows speeds of up to 1 Gbps. New methods and cable configurations now provide 10-Gb connectivity.
- Finally, the multilayer switch is connected to a router using a straight-through cable, at 100 Mbps, 1 Gbps, or 10 Gbps.

The LAN Cabling Diagram shows a typical LAN cable scheme.

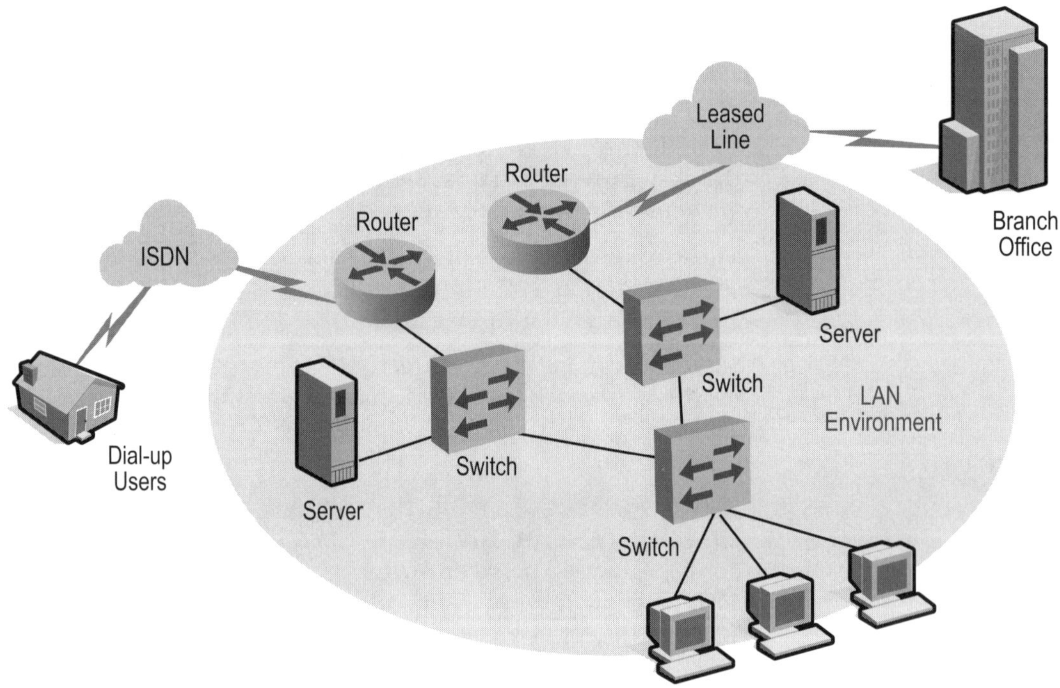

LAN Cabling

Rollover Cable

A rollover cable is shipped with Cisco devices and is used to connect a terminal or PC with a switch, or router for configuration. This is a special cable with RJ-45 connectors on both ends. A DB-9 or DB-25 serial adapter is then made or purchased that plugs the cable into the PC.

The pinout is the complete reverse on each side using the following pins: 1-8, 2-7, 3-6, 4-5, 5-4, 6-3, 7-2, 8-1. When looking at a rollover cable in the same orientation, the colors on each side are exactly the opposite. Notice from the Rollover Cable Diagram that each side is the opposite of the other; however, only pins 1, 3, 6, and 8 are used for communication.

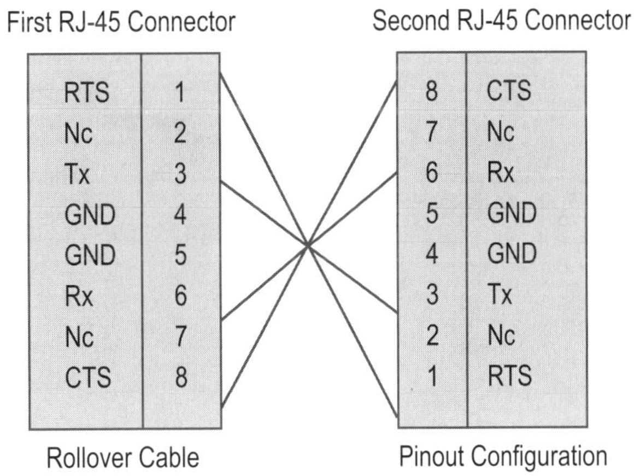

Rollover Cable

Setting Up a Console Connection

To first configure and monitor any Cisco device, you need to make a console connection. The process for establishing out-of-band console access is as follows:

1. Connect to the device by buying or making a rollover cable. (Use the pin configuration just discussed.) Connect the cable to the console port on the device and the serial port of a PC using the appropriate adapter: DB-9 or DB-25.
2. Access a terminal emulation software package. If running Microsoft Windows 95, 98, 2000, or NT, from Start, select Programs, select Accessories, select Communications, and then select HyperTerminal. Terminal software can also be purchased or downloaded from the Internet.
3. Configure the terminal software for the correct COM port number, 9600 bps, 8 data bits, no parity, 1 stop bit, and no flow control. The Console Connection Screen Capture shows the proper configuration.

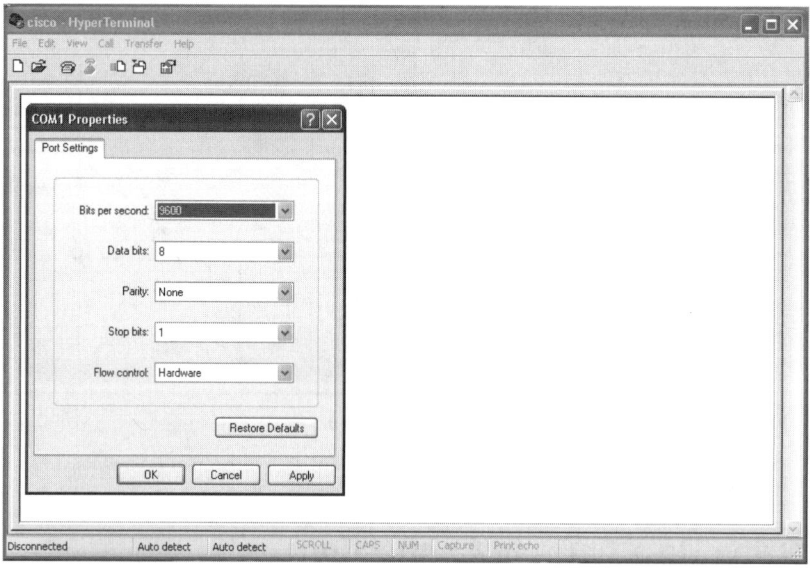

Console Connection

4. Press **ENTER** several times until a login prompt is displayed. Log in and access the device. The login process will be discussed in detail later.

Note: The auxiliary (AUX) port can be also used to make an out-of-band modem connection to any device. However, the AUX port and passwords must be configured using the console port. The settings for the AUX port are 9600 bps, 8 data bits, no parity, and 1 stop bit.

Review Questions

1. What is the name of the Gigabit connector found in Cisco equipment?
   a. Giga-connect
   b. GBIC
   c. Gigabit Fiber
   d. Giga-speed link
2. What is the proper pin configuration used for a rollover cable?
   a. 12345678 to 87654321 using 1, 3, 6, and 8
   b. 12345678 to 12345678 using 1 to 3, and 2 to 6
   c. 12345678 to 12345678 using 1, 2, 3, and 6
   d. 12345678 to 87654321 using 4, 5, 7, and 8
3. Which of the following media types can support 1-Gb transmissions? (Choose three.)
   a. CAT 3
   b. CAT 5e
   c. Multimode fiber
   d. Single-mode fiber
   e. 802.11g wireless
4. Which layer of the OSI model specifies LAN media, cables, wireless, and connectors?
   a. Data Link
   b. Physical
   c. Network
   d. Transport
5. Which standards organization defined the 568A/B specifications?
   a. ANSI
   b. IEEE
   c. EIA/TIA
   d. IETF

6. Which of the following is supported by a GBICs interface? (Choose two.)
   a. 10BaseT
   b. 100BaseT
   c. 1000BaseT
   d. 1000BaseFx
7. What items are necessary to set-up a console connection? (Choose two.)
   a. straight-through cable
   b. rollover cable
   c. Telnet software
   d. IP address
   e. NIC
8. Where is 1-Gb transmission most often found in a medium-sized LAN infrastructure? (Choose two.)
   a. desktop
   b. backbone
   c. trunk links
   d. WAN links
9. What is the first color wire in the 568B standard?
   a. Orange
   b. White/Orange
   c. Green
   d. White/Blue
10. Which of the following support Fast Ethernet standard 802.3u? (Choose two.)
    a. 100BaseCx
    b. 100BaseTx
    c. 100BaseFx
    d. 100Basex

Extended Activities

1. What are the correct cable types in the following situations (straight-through cable, crossover cable, or rollover cable)?

   a. Straight-through cable

   b. Crossover cable

   c. Rollover cable

   Connecting two hubs together ______________________

   Connecting a PC to a hub ______________________

   Connecting a hub to a switch ______________________

   Connecting a switch with an X port to a switch with a regular port ______________________

   Connecting a router to a router ______________________

   Connecting a router to a switch ______________________

   Connecting a hub to a router ______________________

   Connecting two PCs ______________________

   Connecting a switch X port to a switch X port

   ____

   Connecting a PC to the console port of a router

   ____

2. What is a console connection used for?

   ____

   ____

   ____

   ____

   ____

   ____

3. Which pins are different in a crossover cable from one end to the other?

   ____

4. Identify each cable type, based on the Pin Configuration Diagram.

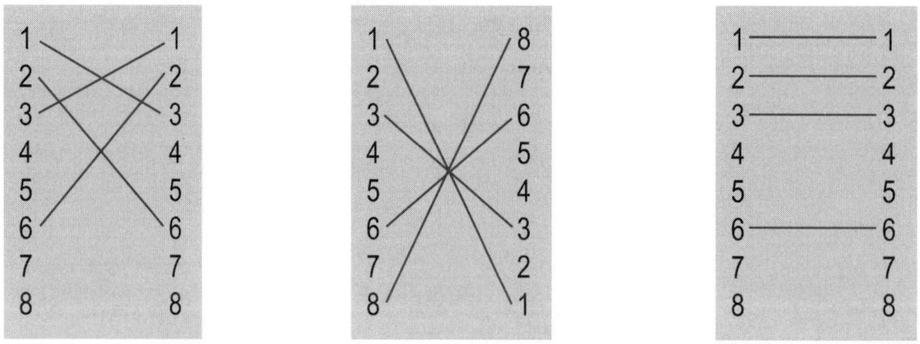

______________________ ______________________ ______________________

Pin Configuration

Lesson 3—Cabling the WAN

Up to this point, you have learned about LAN concepts and configurations. LAN administration can take up the majority of any network engineer's time. However, WAN connections are also important in network administration. These connections provide communication between branch offices, customers, vendor sites, and the Internet. Regardless of size, most organizations use some type of WAN connection. This lesson covers cabling WAN connections.

Objectives

At the end of this lesson you will be able to:

- Define WAN services and their associated connections
- Identify WAN serial connector types
- Describe router connectivity
- Identify connections on a router backplane
- Make an ISDN BRI connection to a router
- Make an ADSL connection to a router
- Make a cable modem connection to a router

Key Point

WAN connections are varied, depending upon the service provider, type of connection, and distance factors. Serial connections are used in the WAN environment because bits sent one at a time are able to travel farther.

WAN Services and Connections

There is a direct correlation between the physical media that is used for WAN connections and the WAN service method used to transmit information. You can best understand this by looking at the WAN Services and Connections Table. The remainder of this lesson discusses the physical connections.

WAN Services and Connections

WAN Service	Cisco HDLC	PPP	Frame Relay	ISDN BRI ISDN PRI	xDSL	Cable Modem
Facility	DS0 through DS3			BRI or T1	POTS line	Coax Cable
Connector	EIA/TIA 232, 449 X.21, V.24, V.35 EIA/TIA 612/613 HSSI			RJ-48 Different wire and pinout than an RJ-45	RJ-11 Same as phone wire and jack	G.703 BNC connector

The objective of WAN connectivity is to expand the internetwork by providing external access. This may include, but is not limited to:

- Dial-in or dial-out capabilities using a traditional modem and analog phone line
- Dial-on-demand routing or point-point capabilities using an ISDN BRI (144 Kbps) circuit
- 56 Kpbs leased-line connection for point-to-point low-bandwidth requirements
- 64 Kpbs to full T1 (1.54 Mbps) and ISDN PRI services for point-to-point branch office or Internet connectivity
- Frame relay services over a T1 for branch office connectivity
- xDSL service or cable modem for Internet connectivity
- T3/DS3 (45 Mbps) communications for high-speed branch office and Internet connections
- Fiber optic connections for ATM and SONET communications

As the WAN Cabling Diagram shows, WAN connections are created through routers and can be either dedicated lines used continuously, or dial-on-demand type connections for home users or equipment servicing.

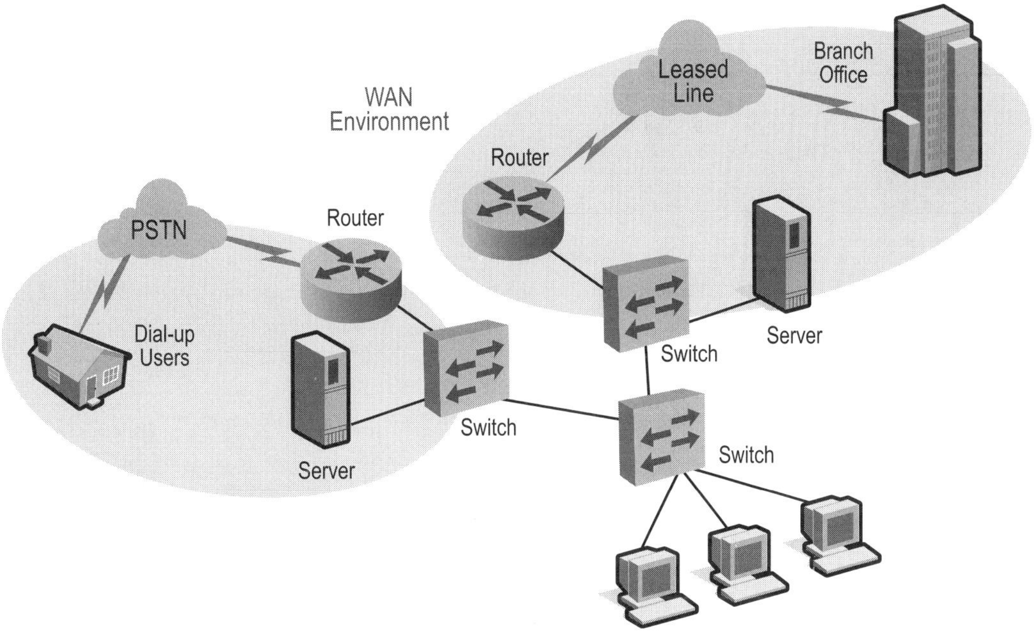

WAN Cabling

Physical Serial and WAN Connectors

Cabling standards and transmission media are at the Physical Layer in WAN connections. When purchasing a serial cable, it is important to know both the router connection and the interface connector type on the other end. Cisco offers a standard proprietary 60-pin connector or a smaller "smart-serial" connector for many WAN connections. This makes Cisco routers compatible with the many different provider requirements, while maintaining a vendor standard.

It is common to see a V.35 for synchronous communications like a T1. It is also common to see an RJ-48 connector that looks similar to a LAN RJ-45 jack but uses a heavier-gauge 4-wire cable. EIA/TIA-232, also called RS-232, is used for asynchronous communications like dial-up modems. The Serial Connectors Diagram shows some of the options available for WAN connections.

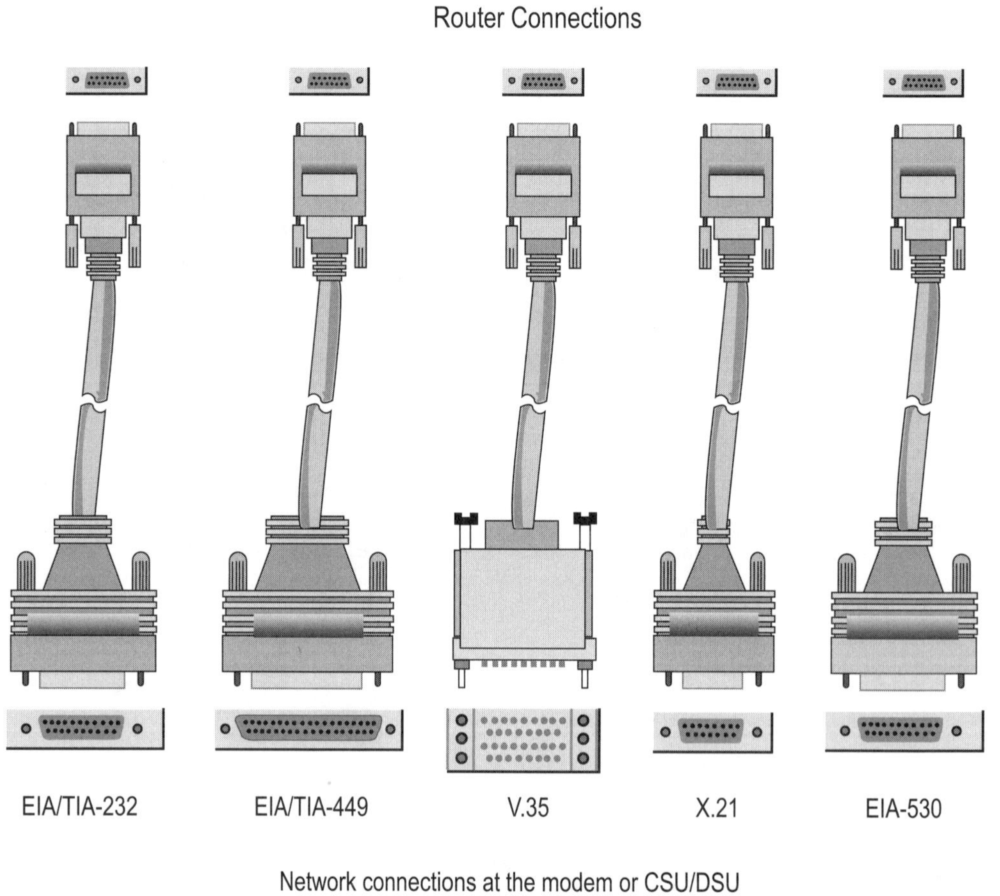

Serial Connectors

Although not all cables are shown on the diagram, Cisco serial cables support the following WAN connection standards:

- **EIA/TIA-232 (formerly RS-232)**—A DB-25 pin connection standard established by EIA/TIA. It is a common connector from a DCE to a DTE, or a serial port to a modem. This type of connection is also offered as a 9-pin connector.
- **EIA/TIA-449**—DB-37 pin serial connection that can be used for both DCE and DTE connections.
- **EIA/TIA-612/613 High Speed Serial Interface (HSSI)**—A 50-pin SCSI-II-type connector that provides DTE connection to T3 (45 Mbps), E3 (34 Mbps) and SONET STS-1 (51.82 Mbps).

- **G.703**—BNC-style connector for Hybrid Fiber Coaxial (HFC) cable with bandwidth capabilities of up to the E1 (2.048 Mbps) rate.
- **V.35**—34 pin serial connection created by the International Telecommunication Union (ITU) and often used with T1 lines.
- **X.21**—DB-37 pin serial connection used for both DCE and DTE connections. Mainly found in Europe and Japan.
- **EIA-530**—DB-25 pin connection that can only be used for DTE connections (it is not DCE-compatible).
- **RJ-48**—Uses the same clear plastic clip as an RJ-45; however, the cable is shielded twisted pair, heavier-gauge, four-wire cable and uses pins 1, 2, 7, and 8 for transmission. Used with T1, Fractional T1, BRI, and subrate facilities.
- **RJ-11**—Also called "silver strand," this 6-wire cable is typically used for connecting a telephone to a wall jack. It has a smaller jack than an RJ-45 and uses pins 3 and 4. This cable and connector type is used for voice communications and xDSL connections.

Serial data transmission is used for WAN connections because it allows a signal to travel farther. A serial connection sends bits of data one at a time through a single channel. In contrast, a parallel connection sends a number of bits simultaneously. Serial channels use an electromagnetic or optical frequency range to carry the bits of data. This frequency is measured in cycles per second, called "Hertz (Hz)," and creates the bandwidth used to transmit data. Bandwidth can also be expressed in bps.

Standard serial channels currently available carry from 2,400 bps to 45 Mbps, which is a T3/DS3 line. Data throughput greater than this is possible, but it is outside the scope of this book.

Comparing Serial Connections

In WAN communications, a number of different terms are used for the ability to transmit information, some of which include:

- **Frequency**—Represents the spectrum or band of communication that carries a signal. Specified in cycles per second (Hz), or how often the signal changes state. Voice communications use approximately 3 kHz (3000 Hz) for analog communications.
- **Bandwidth**—Represents the total capacity of data transmissions available on the line.

- **Speed**—A generic term that is a cross between bandwidth and bits per second. Basically, how much information can be transferred over a specific amount of time.
- **Bits per second (bps) or kilobits per second (Kbps)**—A count of each 0 and 1 that is transmitted across a particular connection in 1 second. Can be used to calculate how much information is transferred in a specific period of time; similar to speed.
- **Baud**—A term which does not refer to the cable transmission, but instead to the ability for a modem to send information over an analog line. Baud and bps are not equivalent.

Distance and bandwidth capabilities are two important factors to consider when selecting serial cable types. Based on the cable quality, shielding, connector types, and external interference factors, there are distance limitations for serial cables. Standards have been established as guidelines to help network designers limit cable to the appropriate length for optimal performance. Standards for bits per second and the lengths they support for the EIA/TIA-232 and EIA/TIA-449 are shown in the EIA/TIA-282 and -449 Standards Table.

EIA/TIA-232 and -449 Standards

Bits per Second (bps)	Distance in Meters	
	EIA/TIA-232	EIA/TIA-449
2,400	60	1250
4,800	30	625
9,600	15	312
19,200	15	156
38,400	15	78
115,200	3.7	—
1.54 Mbps (T1)	—	15

Notice that with serial cables, as the speed increases, the cable distance must decrease. This is to account for signal attenuation. It is possible to run a serial cable longer than the specified distance, but it means a reduction the in overall throughput.

This table also shows that for longer-distance serial connections, the EIA/TIA-449 is clearly the better choice. For short-run connections, EIA/TIA-232 (RS-232) is the typical cable connection.

Router Connectivity

In addition to selecting the correct serial cable, you must determine what will be considered the Data Communications Equipment (DCE) and what will act as the Data Termination Equipment (DTE). Serial connections require the DCE device to maintain synchronization by sending a clocking signal.

The receiving side is the DTE, which takes the clock signal and establishes communication. In most cases, the DCE synchronization clock signal is issued by the service provider. Therefore, the customer premise equipment (CPE) would be considered the DTE side of the serial connection.

It is also possible to connect two routers back-to-back over a serial connection without going over a WAN link. This is useful when the network needs to be extended but a WAN connection is not used. When a back-to-back link is made, one serial interface must be configured as the DCE, with the clock rate set to a specific number. The other router will be configured as the DTE.

In this manner, the DCE provides the clock synchronization signal and, as usual, the DTE takes the clock signal. The service provider is not involved in this example.

The DCE/DTE Connections Diagram shows these two different scenarios. The first one is a connection through the service provider. Notice that in this example, the DCE is the service provider and the DTE is the customer premises. In the second image, a back-to-back router connection is shown, with one router as the DCE and the other as the DTE.

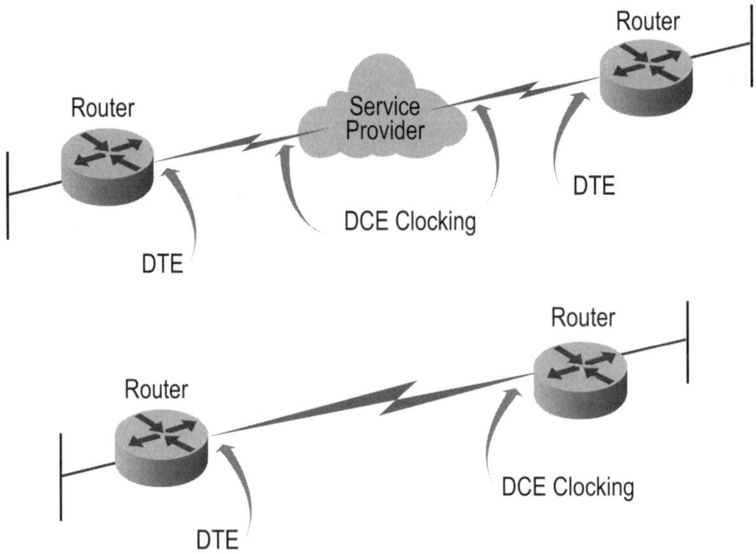

DCE/DTE Connections

Connections on a Router Backplane

To make a WAN connection, routers can have either a fixed backplane or modular backplane. A fixed configuration means you get what you ordered: the available ports are the only options. A modular backplane allows different components to be added, changed, swapped out, or upgraded as necessary. Most routers have a number of ports that are fixed, with the option of adding a WAN Interface Card (WIC).

To access these ports when configuring the router, you have to provide the port type and port number, that is, "Serial0." When configuring a modular interface, you have to provide port type, slot number, and port number, that is, "Serial 1/0." The Router Backplane Diagram shows some of the ports available for WAN connections.

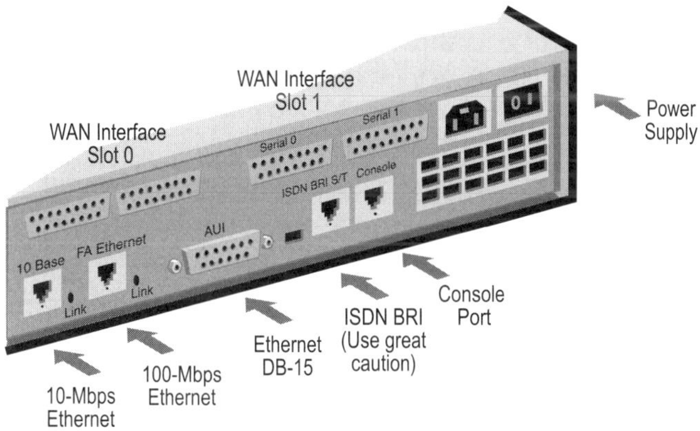

Router Backplane

In addition to the Ethernet and console port available on this router, there are also several WAN options. This router has an ISDN BRI S/T interface, which means that before this device can connect to the service provider, it must be connected to a Network Termination 1 (NT1) device. Another option would be an ISDN U interface, which is considered the NT1 device.

Across the top of the router, there are four Cisco proprietary serial connections. These could be used to support different WAN connections, such as dedicated leased lines using frame relay, HDLC, or Point-to-Point Protocol (PPP).

On the router side, the 60-pin serial connector is used. The type of connection on the other side depends on your service provider or on other end device requirements. Examples of different serial connectors discussed earlier in this lesson include EIA/TIA-232, EIA/TIA-449, V.35, X.21, and EIA-530.

ISDN BRI Connection to a Router

Integrated Services Digital Network-Basic Rate Interface (ISDN BRI) allows dial-on-demand or dial-back connectivity through two 64-Kbps B channels and one 16-Kbps D channel. The B or bearer channel is used for circuit switched data transmission. The D channel is used for out-of-band signaling, like connection establishment, flow control, acknowledgments, and connection teardown.

The type of ISDN BRI port is determined by the equipment purchased and who is providing the NT1 device. The NT1 is an ISDN component that provides the connection between the ISDN service provider and the customer. In North America, the customer usually owns the NT1 component. This could be a device called an NT1 but, for this class, the NT1 would be integrated into the router.

An NT1 can be easily identified because the ISDN BRI port is labeled with the letter U. The U reference point is the connection between service provider and NT1.

Outside North America, it is common for the service provider to manage the NT1 device. In this case, the ISDN BRI interface is labeled as an ISDN BRI S/T. This indicates that the NT1 is provided by some other device.

The connection is made with a specially configured twisted pair cable with an RJ-48 connector. Although the plug and jack look the same as an RJ-45, they are different. An ISDN BRI cable with an RJ-48 plug is four-wire, heavier-gauge cable, with a different pin configuration and higher signal strength.

A word of caution here: non-ISDN devices should never be connected using these ports. ISDN BRI ports create voltages that could damage or ruin any other device.

ADSL Connection to a Router

Asymmetric Digital Subscriber Line (ADSL) is a service that offers high-speed Internet access over existing analog telephone lines, also called Plain Old Telephone Service (POTS) lines. ADSL is a popular option for virtual office/home office users and companies. The service is inexpensive and does not usually require new cabling.

Cisco offers the 827 ADSL Router, which has one ADSL port.

The ADSL connection port is a standard RJ-11 jack. This uses a typical telephone cable, which is sometimes called silver-strand or ribbon cable. The RJ-11 has the same shape as an RJ-45 connector, but it is smaller because it is only a 6-wire cable instead of 8-wire like UTP. The RJ-11 uses only pins 3 and 4 for transmission.

Pin 3 is considered the ring (receive) side and pin 4 is considered the tip (transmit) side. One end plugs into the router and the other end plugs into any wall jack. ADSL service must be activated on the telephone line to provide connectivity. Filters are often provided for wall jack replacement and inline to the phone to help reduce interference for older telephones.

Cable Modem Connection to a Router

Another option for high-speed Internet access that rivals ADSL service is cable modems. This service is delivered through the wire that provides cable television. Frequencies are split off to provide separate bandwidth for data transmissions.

In addition, many cable service providers now offer telephone service over the same cable. Small companies and home office users find cable modem bandwidth and price very attractive.

Cisco offers the uBR905 Router to provide cable connectivity.

This router has an F-connector that looks like the connection on the back of a cable-ready TV or cable set-top box. The connector twists into place and connects to the cable wall jack. To reduce cable TV and data transmission interference, a high-pass filter is usually installed.

Review Questions

1. Which part of a serial connection is responsible for the clock signal and synchronization?
   a. DTE
   b. DCE
   c. Router
   d. Cable
2. Which serial cable type has a typical DB-9 or DB-25 connector and is the same standard identified under two different committees? (Choose two.)
   a. RS-232
   b. EIA/TIA-449
   c. EIA/TIA-232
   d. RJ-232
3. What is the connector on a Cisco uBR905 that is used to connect to the cable TV network?
   a. RS-232 connector
   b. RJ-48 connector
   c. F-connector
   d. AUI connector
4. What is the ISDN BRI interface labeled if the router has an integrated NT1?
   a. S/T
   b. BRI
   c. U
   d. R
5. What is the distance limitation for an RS-232 cable at 9600 bps?
   a. 10 meters
   b. 15 meters
   c. 20 meters
   d. 30 meters

6. What is the connector that is used in the router for an ADSL connection?
    a. RJ-11
    b. RJ-45
    c. RJ-48
    d. RJ-232
7. What connector type is typically associated with BRI connectivity?
    a. RJ-11
    b. RJ-45
    c. RJ-48
    d. RJ-232
8. When making a back-to-back serial connection, one router is configured as the DCE. What must the other device be configured as?
    a. DCE
    b. BRI
    c. DTE
    d. Serial
9. Which of the following would be considered WAN connections? (Choose two.)
    a. RJ-45
    b. RJ-48
    c. RJ-11
    d. AUI

Extended Activities

1. Match the following terms to the correct descriptions for serial cables and connectors.

   a. EIA/TIA-232 (formerly RS-232)

   b. EIA/TIA-449

   c. EIA/TIA-612/613 (High Speed Serial Interface HSSI)

   d. G.703

   e. V.35

   f. X.21

   g. EIA-530

   h. RJ-48

   i. RJ-11

   DB-25 pin connection that can only be used for DTE connections, not the DCE side ____________

   BNC style connector for Hybrid Fiber Coaxial (HFC) Cable ____________

   The same plug as RJ-45, but different heavy-gauge, four-wire cable and different pins ____________

   A 50-pin SCSI-II-type connector used for T3, E3, and SONET ____________

   Used to connect telephones and ADSL service, also called silver strand ____________

   DB-37 pin DCE and DTE connections, mainly found in Europe and Japan ____________

   Very common DB-25 or DB-9 pin connection standard established by EIA/TIA ____________

   DB-34 pin connection created by the ITU and often used with T1 lines ____________

   DB-37 pin connection used for both DCE and DTE connections ____________

Summary

Media and connectors are an important part of LAN and WAN connectivity. Without them, nothing would be able to communicate. This module began by discussing the characteristics associated with different media types. Lesson 1 reviewed twisted pair, coaxial, and fiber optic cable. It also discussed wireless communication methods that can be used for both long- and short-distance communications. Lesson 1 finished by comparing the different media types.

Lesson 2 discussed cabling in the LAN environment. Ethernet is the major focus for this book, since it is the most widely used network topology. Ethernet standards were discussed, as well as bandwidth possibilities and distance limitations.

Depending upon the cable type, Ethernet has a number of different connector options, which include: BNC, AUI, RJ-45, SC, and ST. Cisco offers a special interface called a Gigabit Interface Converter for 1 Gb transmissions. Different GBICs are available to plug into switches or routers that represent the correct cable type. This allows complete flexibility for changing media types without the need to replace the device.

Lesson 2 ended with a discussion of making a console connection. The console port on a switch or router allows an administrator to make an out-of-band connection for configuration purposes. It requires a special type of cable called a rollover cable, a serial interface adapter, and a Telnet application.

Lesson 3 discussed cabling in a WAN environment. Serial cables and connectors are used to make a WAN connection. Serial transmission means that 1 bit is sent at a time, which allows transmissions over greater distances than typical LAN media.

Different WAN services use different WAN media, but Cisco has standardized its serial interface to two types. This way Cisco does not have to change the router backplane. Instead, customers just buy the correct cable based on their needs. A number of other connections are also available on routers, which include ISDN BRI S/T or U interface, RJ-11 ADSL connection, and an F-connector for cable Internet access.

Module 3 Quiz

1. The type of cable used in a 10BaseT network is:
   a. STP
   b. UTP
   c. Coaxial
   d. Fiber
2. The type of connector used in a 10BaseT or 100BaseTX cabling scheme is:
   a. AUI
   b. DB-9
   c. RJ-11
   d. RJ-45
3. What UTP category cable can only be used for voice communications?
   a. 3
   b. 4
   c. 5
   d. 1
4. A rollover cable is used to:
   a. Connect a switch to a hub
   b. Connect a switch to a router
   c. Connect a terminal to a router for configuration
   d. Connect two like devices together
5. The maximum cable length in a 10baseT network, also called a "home run," is:
   a. 200 meters
   b. 100 meters
   c. 500 meters
   d. 25 feet

6. In a DTE/DCE serial connection, which of the devices provides the clocking signal?
   a. DTE
   b. DCE
   c. Modem
   d. Physical Layer topology
7. Cisco provides a proprietary serial connection on routers that has how many pins?
   a. 9
   b. 15
   c. 25
   d. 60
8. The Base in 10Base2, 10Base5, and 10BaseT stands for:
   a. Broadband
   b. Broadbase
   c. Baseband
   d. Backbone
9. If cabling from a switch to a switch and one port is marked with an X, the cable type should be:
   a. Crossover
   b. Straight-through
   c. Rollover
   d. Serial
10. What is the connector type that is used for 1000BaseT or 1000BaseSX communications?
    a. GBIC
    b. RJ-45
    c. Gigastack
    d. Gigachannel

11. What is the IEEE standard that covers 11-Mb wireless communications?
    a. 802.11
    b. 802.11a
    c. 802.11b
    d. 802.11g
12. When making a console connection to a device, which of the following components would not be necessary?
    a. An IP address
    b. A rollover cable
    c. A serial converter
    d. A Telnet application
13. When cabling a WAN, what connector is used for ADSL connectivity?
    a. RJ-45
    b. RJ-11
    c. RS-232
    d. GBIC
14. Which of the following terms would be used to measure transmissions on a serial WAN cable connection?
    a. baud
    b. Kbps
    c. kHz
    d. 10BaseT
15. What is considered a common maximum distance an 802.11 signal can travel between endpoints while still delivering up to 2 Mbps throughput?
    a. 100 feet
    b. 300 feet
    c. 500 feet
    d. 1000 feet

16. What best describes UTP cable? (Choose two.)
    a. UTP cable standards are built on categories
    b. UTP cable standards are built on types
    c. UTP cable is twisted to reduce external interference
    d. UTP cable is shielded to eliminate external interference
17. Which fiber optic cable standard would be best suited for long-distance runs?
    a. Multimode
    b. Single-mode
    c. Laser mode
    d. Stepgrade index
18. What source is used to send bits over a multimode fiber optic connection?
    a. Electrical pulses
    b. LED
    c. RF
    d. Laser
19. When a router has an ISDN BRI "U" connection, what is the function of that device?
    a. It is acting as a frame relay access device
    b. It is acting as a DTE
    c. It is acting as an NT1
    d. It is acting as a DCE
20. What is the minimum cable requirement for 100BaseT?
    a. CAT1
    b. CAT3
    c. CAT5
    d. CAT5e

Module 4
Switching Fundamentals

Anyone studying network communications needs a fundamental understanding of switching concepts. Before switches, all network nodes shared the LAN architecture. Though this arrangement was functional, it often resulted in problems.

Lesson 1 explains the problems administrators experienced when working with a shared LAN architecture. For example, physical distance limitations were set on cable used in Ethernet environments to maintain reasonable signal quality and to prevent collisions caused by transmissions coming from both ends of the network at the same time. Additionally, all nodes in a shared LAN architecture were part of the same collision and broadcast domains, meaning that all devices had to both share the bandwidth on a network segment and wait until the network was clear before transmitting. An increase in the number of end devices connected to the shared media resulted in an increase in network traffic, unnecessary broadcasts, and more collisions. This combination seriously impacted network performance.

Lesson 2 introduces LAN (layer 2) switches that can help reduce many shared architecture problems. Switches isolate collisions by learning MAC addresses and recording them in a MAC address table. Using a frame's destination MAC address to transmit the frame directly to the end device, switches filter each transmission from all other ports. Hence, a switch creates a single collision domain on each port. Since end devices no longer have to contend with other nodes for network resources, they work much more efficiently and the network performance improves dramatically.

Lesson 3 discusses VLANs, which take this performance enhancement one step further. VLANs are logical broadcast domains defined on a layer 2 switch device. A switch with VLAN capabilities can not only control collisions, but broadcast traffic as well. VLANs allow administrative definition of workgroups, project teams or whatever is necessary for traffic isolation, broadcast control and security. Although VLANs take a little time to properly design, they can greatly reduce the amount of physical recabling and moving equipment. Administrators can make VLAN membership changes and associate devices throughout the building even if they are on different floors or different switches. Routers or layer 3 devices are used to allow communication between VLANs.

Lessons

1. Shared LAN Architectures
2. LAN Switching
3. Virtual LANs

Lesson 1—Shared LAN Architectures

Networks are inherently limited by a number of factors. To begin with, cables are physically limited in the distance that a signal can travel. This is caused by the overall strength of the signal, external interference factors, cable quality and connectors. Another physical distance limitation has to do with the way Ethernet is designed to carrier sense before transmission. With long cable segments, two devices might hear that the line is clear, only to have a collision.

All devices that share network bandwidth are considered to be in the same collision domain. All devices that hear a broadcast message are considered to be in the same broadcast domain. Large collision or broadcast domains mean poor network performance. Therefore, a proper network design is intended to reduce collision and broadcast domains using layer 2 and layer 3 devices.

Objectives

At the end of this lesson you will be able to:

- Identify the segment distance limitations for different cable types
- Explain how to extend the cable segment
- Describe broadcast, multicast, and unicast transmissions
- Define a collision domain
- Define a broadcast domain
- Describe the major bandwidth consumers in a network
- Explain how to create multiple collision domains

Key Point

A collision domain is the area where all devices contend for access and share network bandwidth. A broadcast domain is the area where all devices receive a broadcast frame.

Segment Distance Limitations

Signals that are transmitted across cable segments can travel only a certain distance before the signal strength is degraded. The reduction in signal quality is called "attenuation" and it happens because of external interference factors such as electromagnetic interference (EMI) and radio frequency interference (RFI). It can also be caused by crosstalk (bleed-over between signals on other wire pairs), improperly terminated wall jacks or cable plugs, and damaged wire.

Logistically, a signal can only be transmitted so far before signal strength is reduced to an unacceptable level. Fiber optic cable is not prone to interference factors such as EMI and RFI. Multimode fiber is also vulnerable to certain transmission problems. Certain types of fiber can have issues with refracted signals overlapping or transmissions arriving at different rates resulting in errors.

Beyond the physical media limitations, Ethernet standards had to define distance limitations for cable segments because of carrier sense multiple access with collision detection (CSMA/CD). Remember that Ethernet network interface cards (NICs) must first "listen" to the wire to see if another device is using it before they attempt transmission.

If the cable segment is overly long, devices on opposite ends may not detect a transmission and think the line is clear to send. This will result in collisions and reduce overall network performance. For this reason, Ethernet standards define maximum cable lengths for coax, UTP, and fiber optic cable.

Once a switch is introduced, the possibility of a collision is reduced; however, the physical issues of signal attenuation still exist. In addition, as bandwidth increases, the cable segment length typically decreases. Given all factors, signal quality cannot be maintained over long distances at high speeds.

Think about this from a different perspective—that of driving your car. If you drive your car at only 10 miles per hour down a street, you are less affected by potholes, narrow lanes, side traffic, oncoming cars, poor lighting, the condition of your vehicle, your tires, driving capabilities, and so forth. If you drive your car at 100 miles per hour, these factors play a significant part in your ability to maintain that speed.

The Ethernet specification and associated cable length are shown in the Ethernet Cable Segment Limitations Table:

Ethernet Cable Segment Limitations

Ethernet Specification	Segment Length
10Base2	185 meters
10Base5	500 meters
10BaseT, 100BaseT, TX, T2, T4	100 meters
10BaseFL	2000 meters
100BaseFX	400 meters
1000BaseCX	25 meters
1000BaseLX	550 meters if 62.5 μ or 50 μ multimode fiber 10 km if 10 μ single-mode fiber
1000BaseSX	250 meters if 62.5 μ multimode fiber; 550 meters if 50 μ multi-mode fiber

Extending the LAN Segments

Although these segment lengths are important guidelines, they do not match up with the needs of business. Office and device locations cannot all be within, say, 100 meters of each other if you are using UTP cable. Some may fall easily into the range, whereas others are too far and cannot be moved. To extend the physical cable segment, you must extend the signal strength.

Devices that can perform this function include hubs and repeaters found at the Physical Layer of the OSI model. Hubs and repeaters take an electric signal and regenerate it as it was originally created. Thus, if noise or interference are introduced, the signal is reproduced and transmitted as it was in its original state.

Layer 1 devices do a good job of improving signal quality, which allows transmissions over greater distances. However, hubs and repeaters cannot address the second reason for specific cable lengths, which is related to collisions. All devices connected to a hub contend for or share network bandwidth. This is called a "collision domain," which is discussed later in this lesson.

Other network devices can also repeat the signal to extend the cable segment. Bridges, switches, and routers perform this function, in addition to providing a range of other more important services. The major difference is that these devices are used to improve performance in an Ethernet network by reducing or preventing collisions.

Unicast, Multicast, and Broadcast Transmissions

Three different addressing methods can be used at both the Data Link Layer and the Network Layer to identify and communicate with end devices. The three types are as follows:

- **Unicast**—A transmission sent as a unicast is addressed to one specific end point. The transmission goes from a single sender to a single destination. The frame contains a specific MAC and a specific IP address for only the destination host device. A switch reads the MAC address and does its best to send it directly to the proper port, based on information in the MAC address table.
- **Multicast**—Multicast transmissions are intended for a number of devices. The transmission goes from a single sender to a specified group of devices at the same time. For a multicast to work, the devices have to join a group or otherwise identify themselves. For instance, at the Data Link Layer, this could be used to communicate with all NICs manufactured by a specific vendor, based on the first 3 bytes of the MAC address. Multicast is also used at the Network Layer and is identified with a Class D address.
- **Broadcast**—Transmissions sent as a broadcast are intended for every device within the broadcast domain. It is a "calling all devices" sort of transmission from a single sender to all end points. End nodes that do not need to hear the transmission discard it. A broadcast is sent at the Data Link Layer using the MAC address of FF:FF:FF:FF:FF:FF. At the Network Layer, the IP address for a broadcast has all 1s in the host position, for instance 172.16.40.255.

As you will see in Lesson 2, bridges and switches are designed to learn the MAC address of the source (sending) device. Multicast and broadcast addresses are the destination address; they can never be a source address. Therefore, bridges and switches do not attempt to learn multicast and broadcast addresses. Instead, a multicast or broadcast is handled like a flooded frame and sent out all ports except the one where it was initially received.

Collision Domains

A collision domain represents all the devices that contend for bandwidth when attempting to access the network. In an Ethernet environment, a collision can occur if more than one device tries to send a transmission at the same time. This is possible in a bus topology where every device shares the same cable segment.

It is also possible on networks where end devices are connected using hubs. All hosts connected to a hub are in the same collision domain. With a bus or hub configuration, the more nodes on the network, the more traffic. As traffic increases, collisions do as well. This is just like traffic on a road. The more cars you get driving on the same road, the more likely they are to get in an accident. When accidents occur, other traffic is stopped until the accident is cleared. The same scenario happens in a collision domain. As more hubs are connected together, the collision domain gets larger. That means as more devices need to share the bandwidth, there will be more collisions, and more system impact because of those collisions.

Devices such as switches, bridges, and routers are designed to break up collision domains. By learning addresses and filtering traffic, these devices eliminate the possibility of a collision. A switch port is an individual collision domain. This means the end device does not have to share bandwidth or consider collisions when transmitting. It even saves the time it takes to perform carrier sense to verify that no other device is sending.

In the end, it means better network performance and fewer transmission delays. Returning to the driving analogy, if you were the only driver on a deserted road, you would not have to worry about other cars and you would be able to travel at the full speed of the road.

Broadcast Domains

A broadcast domain represents all the devices that receive a broadcast message. One example of a broadcast that is very common is an address resolution protocol (ARP) request. Before a PC can transmit a frame, it must have the MAC address of the end device. An ARP request is sent as a broadcast to contact the end device and retrieve the MAC address. In a busy network, PCs may send hundreds of these a day.

Since ARPs are sent as a broadcast, every device receives it, even if they have nothing to do with the request. It is a good idea to reduce the size of broadcast domains to reduce the amount of unnecessary traffic received by all devices. This broadcast traffic not only affects the network; it also affects the devices on the network.

To use an analogy, think of a small company that has an attendant who answers the phone and announces all calls over the paging system. If there are only a few employees, this may be distracting but you could still get work done.

In a very large corporation, hearing the announcements for hundreds of calls a day may get so distracting that no one could do any work. All employees would have to hear the page, decide if it is for them, and either take the call or go back to work.

Routers and layer 3 switches are both capable of physically breaking up broadcast domains. VLANs on layer 2 switches can also be used to logically define broadcast domains. Layer 3 devices and VLANs break up broadcast domains by using Network Layer address information. This allows them to differentiate between network segments and filter traffic. Small, well-designed broadcast domains reduce broadcast traffic only to the devices that should receive them.

In the end, this reduces the unnecessary broadcast traffic for everyone else on the network. To finish the analogy with the paging system, the large company may decide that paging all calls is not working. Instead, they may have an attendant answer the calls for a particular department, then make the announcement for a much smaller group.

Bandwidth Consumption

In addition to physical segment limitations, collision concerns, and broadcast traffic, another problem plagues bus- and hub-based architectures. The problem is bandwidth consumption. When networks were first built, people were used to "sneaker-net." This network topology required the user to put the file for transmission on a diskette and walk it to its destination.

Needless to say, this topology was short-lived and was quickly replaced with cables and network devices.

The point is that files were relatively small—at first, small enough to be carried on a disk or transmitted across a slow dial-up modem connection.

Times have changed and, as PCs and servers have increased in capabilities, so have the demands on the network. It used to be that only text characters in word-processed documents and numbers in spreadsheets were being sent. Nowadays, anything goes.

Multimedia capabilities allow PC and servers to do many extraordinary things with the right software applications and peripheral devices. The following is a list of some of the more bandwidth intensive applications:

- **Medical and scientific imaging**—Huge, graphically intensive photographs and drawings
- **Data warehouse and databases**—Large repositories of data
- **Computer aided drafting, design, manufacturing, or engineering**—Large image files for blueprints, technical specification drawings, and manufacturing instruction sets
- **Video**—Real-time, slow-motion, or streaming video feeds
- **Audio and music**—Accompanying video, prerecorded, or real-time streaming audio
- **Voice**—Only a small amount of bandwidth is needed, (around 64k), although voice depends on guaranteed bandwidth for quality
- **Desktop publishing**—Large files that include graphics, text, and special formatting
- **Wed applications**—Combining many multimedia components

Review Questions

1. Which of the following addresses is a broadcast?
   a. AB:CD:10:93:BD:87
   b. F0:93:24:51:BA:C6
   c. FF:FF:FF:FF:FF:FF
   d. EE:EE:EE:EE:EE:EE
2. Which of the following are definitions of a collision domain? (Choose two.)
   a. All devices that hear a broadcast message
   b. All devices that repeat a transmission
   c. All devices that share network bandwidth
   d. All devices that contend for network access
3. Which devices could be used to break up collision domains? (Choose two.)
   a. Bridge
   b. NIC
   c. Switch
   d. Hub
4. Which of the following are reasons for physical segment limitations?
   a. The signal degrades over distance
   b. The possibility for collisions in a bus or hub architecture
   c. External interference factors
   d. all of the above
   e. Both a and c
5. What definitions can be associated with a unicast? (Choose two.)
   a. A one-to-one transmission
   b. A one-to-many transmission
   c. The destination address of AB:96:35:92:15:64
   d. The destination address of FF:FF:FF:FF:FF:FF

6. Which components can be used to segment broadcast domains? (Choose three.)
   a. Layer 2 switches
   b. Bridges
   c. VLANs
   d. Layer 3 switches
   e. Routers
7. What statements best describe traffic in a collision domain? (Choose two.)
   a. As traffic increases, available bandwidth increases.
   b. As traffic increases, available bandwidth decreases.
   c. As traffic increases, collisions increase.
   d. As traffic increases, collision subside.
8. What is the distance limitation for Ethernet using 10BaseT or 100BaseT?
   a. 185 meters
   b. 500 meters
   c. 100 meters
   d. 1000 meters
9. Which Ethernet specification does not transmit at 10Mb?
   a. 10BaseT
   b. 100BaseT
   c. 10Base2
   d. 10Base5
10. What is an example of a common network broadcast?
    a. An ARP request
    b. A frame transmission
    c. Streaming video
    d. Database access

Extended Activities

1. Referring to the Network Device Diagram, how many collision domains and broadcast domains are associated with each device?

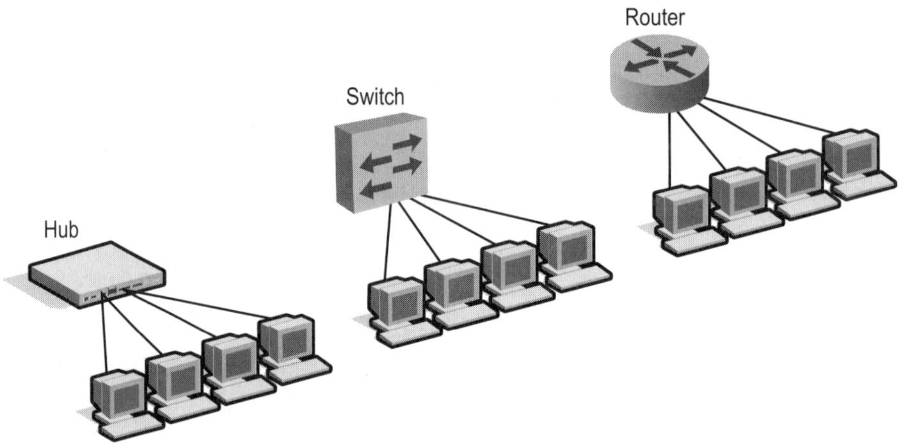

Network Device

a.	Hub	Collision Domains ____________ Broadcast Domains ____________
b.	Switch	Collision Domains ____________ Broadcast Domains ____________
c.	Router	Collision Domains ____________ Broadcast Domains ____________

Lesson 2—LAN Switching

Before beginning this module on switching you will review the switch's predecessor, the bridge. This lesson begins with a quick comparison of bridging and switching technology. Then it discusses the main functions of a switch: to learn and maintain a list of addresses on the network, and to filter or forward data across the network.

This lesson describes how frames are transmitted through a switch and the different switch types available. It also defines different switching methods, redundant network topologies, the potential for active loops and how to prevent them with spanning tree algorithms.

Objectives

At the end of this lesson you will be able to:

- Explain how LAN switching is performed
- Identify the features of LAN switches
- Compare the different switching techniques
- Describe various bandwidth options for Ethernet switches
- Describe switching at other layers
- Describe how frames are processed
- Describe redundancy and active loops in a bridged or switched network
- Explain how Spanning Tree Algorithm controls active loops in a switched network architecture

Key Point

Switches have the ability to isolate traffic, break up collision domains, and forward frames quickly from node to node. Today's switches are based on ASICs, which provide very fast decision-making and processing capabilities.

LAN Switching

Not too long ago, bridging technology was prevalent. Bridges were popular because they broke a large network into smaller segments or separate collision domains. Isolating traffic eases media contention issues and allows the network to expand while increasing overall performance.

A bridge is a Data Link Layer device that connects two or more LAN segments together. It learns and stores the MAC addresses of network nodes. Then it makes decisions about when to transmit data to another segment (forwarding) or when a transmission should be blocked since the nodes reside on the same segment (filtering). Finally, a bridge uses Spanning Tree Algorithm-based protocol [Spanning Tree Protocol (STP)], to prevent active loop problems with redundant network links.

Switches provide newer technology and, although more advanced, they still provide the same basic functions as a bridge. Like bridges, switches can connect multiple network segments, isolate traffic, ease media contention, and increase overall network performance.

Switches can also learn addresses, filter or forward frames, and prevent loops from creating network problems. Whereas bridges have a few ports used to connect multiple hubs, switches directly connect network devices to allow the highest throughput and performance. There are other differences as well, as listed in the Comparison of Bridges and Switches Table.

Comparison of Bridges and Switches

Bridge	Switch
Software-based technology	Hardware-based ASICs
Limited port availability (usually fewer than 16 ports)	Very high port density (100+ on some switches)
One spanning tree instance per bridge	Many spanning tree instances per switch
Slower processing capability (10 to 30 percent throughput lost due to bridging protocol requirements)	Faster overall processing capability (little or no throughput lost due to reduced overhead compared to bridges)

Regardless of the device, careful consideration should go into planning network segments, and bridge or switch placement. Because bridges have a very limited number of ports, hubs are required to connect a large number of devices.

When you use a bridge, 80 percent of the traffic should remain within the same segment because it would be very ineffective to constantly forward traffic between segments.

In a switched environment, however, adequate ports are usually available. Thus, all end nodes should be directly attached to a switch port instead of through a hub. Using a hub with a switch automatically changes full-duplex capability to half-duplex mode. Full-duplex transmission is achieved by using two separate circuits of the media, therefore eliminating Ethernet collisions.

A switch is designed to provide direct point-to-point connection and take advantage of full-duplex transmission capabilities. If a number of end nodes are connected first to a hub, and then share a switch port, the devices can only transmit in half-duplex mode because they are sharing the same media and must be able to detect collisions.

Thus, when you are upgrading a legacy network from bridges to switches, you should remove the hubs and connect all end nodes directly to switch ports to increase network performance.

LAN Switch Features

Having advanced beyond bridges, Data Link Layer switch devices now incorporate many features that provide enhanced performance and network efficiency. The following are a few of the most common features and the services they provide:

- **Individual collision domains**—LAN switches break up collision domains by learning MAC addresses and making filter/forwarding decisions. Every interface on the switch represents its own collision domain, which means that the potential for collisions is almost nonexistent.

  Individual collisions domains are sometimes called "micro segmentation." The only time that a collision would be possible is if two or more devices shared the switch port using a hub for connectivity.

- **Full-duplex capability**—As stated earlier, once the possibility of collisions is removed, the devices no longer have to perform carrier sense to share the wire, nor do they have to listen to make sure a collision did not disrupt their transmission. This allows the end device to use both transmit and receive capabilities at the same time, which is called "full-duplex." This greatly increases the end device's communication capabilities.
- **Wire-speed transmissions**—Since there are no collisions, the end device can consume all the bandwidth without concern about contention. It does not have to share the line and therefore can take advantage of the full bandwidth capacity. This is called "wire speed" (or sometimes "media rate") because it is based on the capacity of the wiring itself. As discussed in Module 3, unshielded twisted pair (UTP) category 3 (CAT3) cable can support 10 Mbps, and CAT5 can support 100 Mbps. Therefore, the installed network cabling determines the wire-speed at which the switch operates.
- **Simultaneous communications**—The switch is designed to handle many simultaneous transmissions for all ports. When one device sends to another, the switch keeps that transmission separate from all others and delivers it directly to the addressed end device.

  The switch's ability to handle multiple transmissions is exponentially larger than the sum of all the ports' capacity. What this means, is that the switch's backplane has greater capacity than the bandwidth of all the ports added together.

Switching Techniques

A switch can use two different methods to read and transport frames through a network. As the Switch Types Diagram shows, each switch type reads and handles a frame differently.

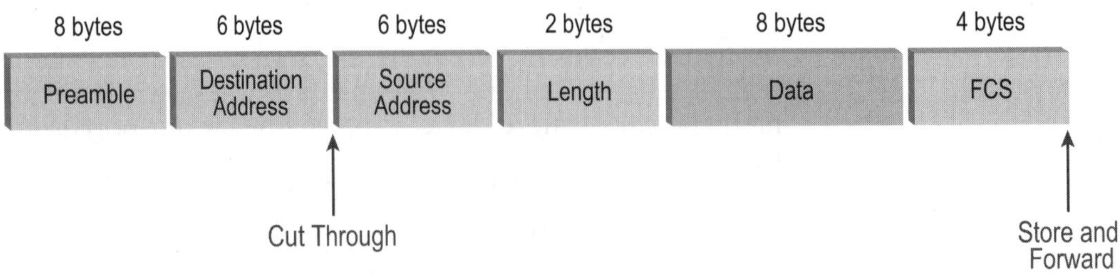

Switch Types

Cut-Through

Using the cut-through method, a switch identifies the destination address from the frame header and immediately forwards it to the appropriate port designated in the MAC address table. The processing time is constant, regardless of the frame size, because only the destination address is read in each instance.

Some switches read and maintain an error count for the cyclical redundancy check (CRC) in the trailer of the frame. If too many errors are detected, the switch can be programmed to change to the store-and-forward mode.

Along with cut-through, some switches offer an additional feature called fragment-free, runt-free, or modified cut-through. This means the switch will validate that an Ethernet frame is at least 64 bytes in length before transmitting it. This helps the switch reduce errors and retransmissions by dropping problematic frames before they get to their destination.

Store-and-Forward

Using the store-and-forward method, the switch reads an entire frame into the buffer, and both the source and destination addresses are identified. The switch performs a cyclical redundancy check (CRC) to validate the Frame Check Sequence (FCS). Store-and-forward provides error free delivery by checking each frame for the following:

- **Giant frames**—Frames larger than the maximum transmission unit for Ethernet of 1518 or 1522 bytes (if IEEE 802.1p/Q header is included)
- **Runt frames**—Frames smaller than the minimum size of 64 bytes
- **Invalid frames**—Frames in which the computation of the CRC and the FCS do not match

In each case, the switch discards the frame. All frames that have valid FCS and are within the appropriate size parameters are rapidly switched to their destination.

Store-and-forward has the highest processing time (processing latency) through the switch. On the positive side, it also has the highest degree of assurance that each frame is good. Unlike cut-through, which has a constant rate of transmission, store-and-forward latency varies, based on the size of the frame. Remember that an Ethernet frame can range in size from 64 to 1,518 bytes.

Although cut-through switching provides a fast means of frame transmission, it is limited in its processing ability. Many switch devices today have advanced features like frame queuing/prioritization (802.1p), VLANs (InterSwitch Link - ISL or 802.1Q), and multilayer switching and filtering.

The cut-through method of switching only allows the destination address to be read, thus preventing better processing and decision making. When better processing and decision making are required, the store-and-forward mode is used to take advantage of the information provided by reading the entire frame.

Ethernet Switch Bandwidth

Ethernet switches were first developed for 10-Mb communications. All ports offered 10-Mbps transmissions over UTP CAT3 or CAT5 wire. Using a star topology allowed for easier cable management and troubleshooting than the bus environment did previously. Or, if coming from a hub environment, the switch offered individual collision domains, which greatly improved network performance.

Though the physical network still only provided 10Mbps bandwidth, the switch guarantees this bandwidth to each and every port, rather than requiring that all nodes share it as they did when configured on a bus or hub. Switch devices that run at 10 Mb are covered under the Ethernet standard 10BaseT (10 Mb, baseband signal, twisted pair wire, 100 meters).

Fast Ethernet offered port speeds of 100 Mbps. At first, these were only used for uplink or trunk links between switch devices. Using the principle that the network backbone should be the fastest connection, this makes sense. However, the demand for bandwidth to the desktop meant that 100-Mb ports could no longer be reserved for just the backbone.

As more and more manufacturers produced high speed NICs, the switch manufacturers had to respond. At the same time, they had to be conscious of the network devices that required backward compatibility.

Some network peripherals only support 10-Mb communications. These devices need to be supported going forward. The answer was NICs and switches that could support both speeds. So manufacturers developed 10/100-Mb devices. These could be either 10 Mb or 100 Mb, depending upon the end device's capability. In the early releases, the bandwidth had to be manually configured for one or the other.

Later, 10/100 Mb autosensing switches made their name by detecting the speed of the NIC and automatically connecting at that speed. This reduced network administration. But some NICs that do not support the autosense feature can create transmission errors on the network. For this reason, be sure to check the NIC documentation to determine the best way to configure the device. Switch devices that provide 100-Mb communications fall under the Fast Ethernet standard 100BaseT.

Switches that support 10 Mb and 100 Mb allow both speeds within the same switch. This just means that some end devices send faster than others, depending upon their equipment.

This capability is not available in Token Ring, where there are also two speeds: 4 Mbps and 16 Mbps. However, based on the method of communication, these two speeds cannot run on the same ring. So the fact that Ethernet allows both speeds is a great benefit. It allows networks to be upgraded, one card at a time and provides backward compatibility.

With 100-Mb switched connection to the desktop, it is only proper to have a faster backbone. Therefore, 1-Gb ports are used for trunk links between switches, and connections to routers or other network equipment. In some switches, these ports can be combined to achieve even greater transmission capabilities.

This concept is called Link Aggregation Groups (LAGs) and can provide a substantial amount of bandwidth. This is important because as times change, 1-Gb bandwidth requirements to the desktop are now becoming more and more common. NIC manufacturers are creating 100/1000-Mb cards. Some manufacturers are even building these cards onto the motherboard to improve overall performance.

As this becomes more common, the demand for closet Gigabit switches increases. UTP CAT5e wire is a minimum, using all four wire pairs to achieve this communication capability.

In addition, these switches are built with a Gigabit Interface Converter (GBIC) instead of traditional ports. The GBICs allow for easy exchange, upgrade, and replacement as the technology or wiring changes. Switches that provide 1-Gbps transmissions over twisted pair cable fall under the Gigabit Ethernet standard 1000BaseTx.

Very high end and expensive switch devices support 10-Gbps communications. These are used for backbone connectivity in large corporate networks, as well as metro area networks (MANs), and soon in wide area networks (WANs). Considering the trend, it is interesting to speculate how long it will be before there is a demand for 10-Gb communications at the desktop.

Multilayer Switch Technology

Switching technology has expanded beyond frame switching at the Data Link Layer. ASICs and software allow switch manufacturers to build devices that can read multiple layer header information, and perform filtering and forwarding decisions.

The function of a switch is to read the appropriate header information and get the transmission to its destination as quickly as possible. Switching technology is used as follows:

- **Layer 2 switches**—These are the traditional frame switching devices discussed earlier in this lesson. They read MAC addresses in the data link portion of the frame to make filter and forward decisions. These devices define each interface as its own collision domain, with all interfaces belonging to the same broadcast domain.

  VLANs can be used on layer 2 switches to logically define broadcast domains/network segments. Many layer 2 switches can also prioritize transmissions, based on predefined priority values. This helps real-time information get to its destination more quickly.

- **Layer 3 switches**—These are packet-switching devices that use the IP address in the network header to make filter and forwarding decisions. These devices use traditional and proprietary routing protocols to exchange routing information. They segment the network into physical broadcast domains and require different IP addresses on each interface, just as a router would.

  Layer 3 switches are often faster than routers because they use ASICs instead of the software decision-making processes used on a router. This improves performance, but is sometimes limited in upgrades, because the hardware is manufactured to perform specific functions.

  In addition, switch backplanes are often more efficient than routers, because they have less processing or fewer tasks to perform. These switch devices cannot translate protocols or connect different network topologies, but instead can focus on fast transmissions. Layer 3 switches can perform the same packet-by-packet best-path determination as a router. However, many layer 3 switches have a more sophisticated learning and forwarding method than a router.

A router looks up the destination IP network address in the packet and reviews its routing table to determine the best path to get there. A single transmission may have hundreds to thousands of segments, all going to the same destination. The router would look each one up over and over again, methodically guaranteeing that they were all using the best path.

A layer 3 switch determines the best path just as the router does. However, once it has sent information to that destination, it predicts that all other segments going to the same destination for that transmission can also use the original best path. Therefore, instead of determining the route over and over as a router might, it switches the information over the best path from that point forward.

This process is called "route-once-switch-many" and is a very fast and efficient method for transmitting packets. Layer 3 switches can also be called routing switches or switching routers. Unlike a router, these devices do not usually have WAN or Internet connectivity, however that is changing as many vendors expand their product lines.

- **Layer 4-7 switches**—These switches are most often software-programmed into a switch device to look at the transport header and into the upper-layer message information. These switches can use TCP and UDP port numbers to switch transmissions to the proper service as quickly as possible. They can also be used to filter or handle unwanted traffic on the network using the port number in the same way as a layer 4 firewall.

  Switches may also be able to look into the content for upper-layer information and filter/forward specific transmissions. In this way, special handling could be provided for real-time multimedia, text messaging, real-time stock quotes, weather or news feeds, and many other kinds of information.

  Educational institutions have found these switches help to block music-sharing services and messaging services that do not have specific port numbers to catch with a firewall.

  Layer 4-7 switching is much slower than the first two because the switch has to read deeper into the headers and content to determine how the transmission should be handled. It is also slower because the variability of decision making makes it difficult to switch using ASICs and much of it must be done with software for flexibility.

- **Multilayer switches**—These devices combine more than one layer into a single device. For instance, a multilayer switch may have layer 2 connectivity with layer 3 processing capabilities to route between VLANs and access other parts of the network. Devices with multilayer capabilities create efficiencies because they can switch frames, packets, or messages, depending on the destination.

Regardless of the layer(s) they function at, switches provide a robust and powerful network solution, which is an integral part of many network designs now and in the future. When network routers can no longer keep up with demand, many will be replaced with layer 3 or multilayer switch devices to improve performance.

Process of Switching Frames

A switch uses a MAC address table or filter table to associate network nodes and their port numbers. This table allows a bridge or switch to make decisions about how to handle network traffic. The table is stored in the content-addressable memory (CAM) and is empty when a device is initially started. Switches perform the following high-level functions:

- Learn MAC addresses and store them in a MAC address table
- Read the frame header to make the appropriate transmission decisions, based on the MAC address, and possibly priority and VLAN number
- Filter the frame from all ports not specifically addressed in the destination address field
- Forward the frame directly to the port specified in the address field
- Flood a frame that has a MAC address not in the MAC address table
- Broadcast a frame that includes a broadcast address of FF:FF:FF:FF:FF:FF

The following sections provide more details on how this works.

Learning Network Addresses

Because a switch is a Data Link Layer device, it learns and stores only the physical or MAC address of the network interface card (NIC) burned in by the manufacturer. The process of learning all the network node addresses is best described using an example of what happens as data is transmitted. The Learning MAC Addresses Diagram shows how a switch learns addresses.

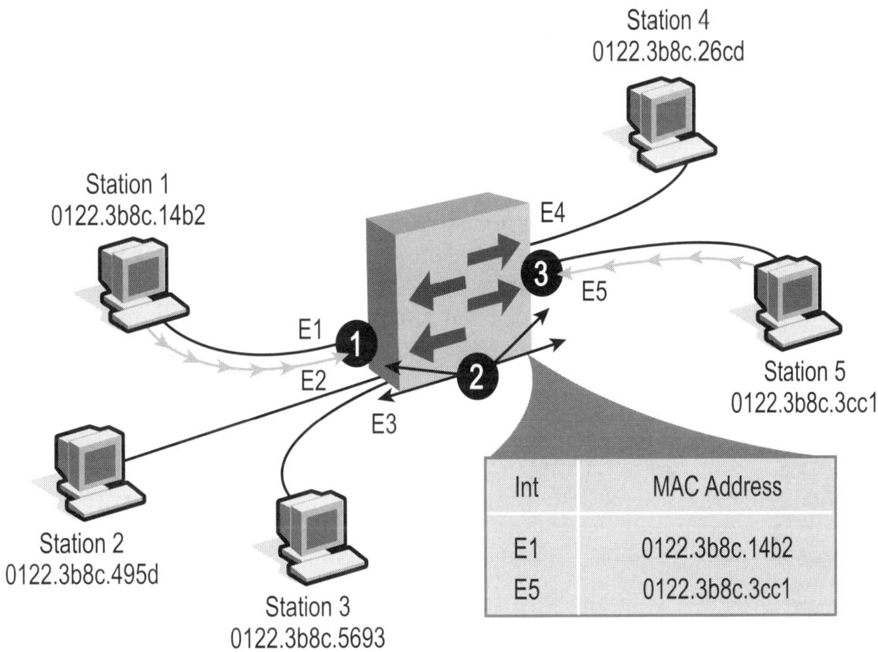

Learning MAC Addresses

The process of a switch learning addresses is as follows:

1. Station 1 sends a frame destined for Station 5. The frame is temporarily stored in the switch's buffer because no MAC address entries are available to designate which port to send the frame to. It makes note of Station 1's MAC address and the port where the frame was received.
2. Having no other MAC address entries, the switch sends the frame out of all network ports, except the one at which it was received. This process, called "flooding," is a very inefficient use of the network bandwidth; however, it is necessary to establish the MAC address table.

3. After Station 5 receives the frame, it sends back an acknowledgment. Station 5's address and associated port are added to the MAC address table. A point-to-point connection has been established because the switch has learned the addresses of the two devices. All future frames can go directly from Station 1 to Station 5 without flooding the network.

When another end node sends a frame, the switch references its MAC table, looking for an associated entry, and goes through the entire process again. In this way, the switch eventually learns the MAC addresses of all network nodes and caches them in memory. To maintain this table of information, an aging process is used. Aging requires entries to be removed if devices have not communicated with the switch over a specified period of time.

Frame Forwarding/ Filtering

The efficiency of a switched network is based on the point-to-point connections it makes. After the MAC address table is established, the switch no longer has to flood the network when a new frame is received. Instead, it identifies the destination address and checks its table to locate the appropriate port.

Then the switch forwards the frame directly to the destination device and blocks or filters it from all other ports. Using the earlier example, the Filtering/Forwarding Diagram illustrates the process when Station 1 again sends data destined for Station 5.

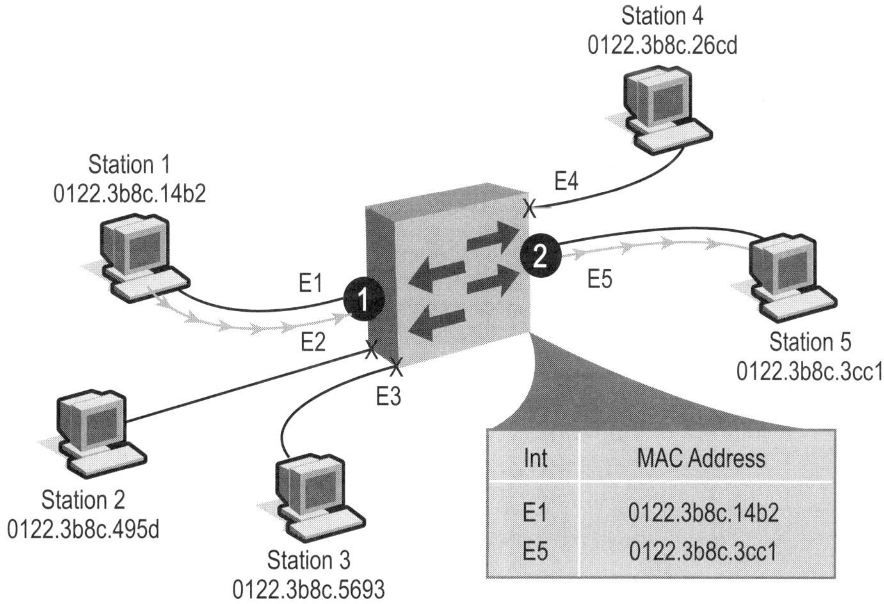

Filtering/Forwarding

The filtering/forwarding process is as follows:

1. The switch receives the frame, identifies the destination address, looks it up in the MAC address table, and finds the correct port.
2. The switch then sends the frame to only the specified port associated with the destination device.
3. The switch filters the frame from being sent out of any other ports, saving bandwidth on the associated links.

Redundancy and Active Loops

When networks were designed many years ago and bridges were in place, the architect who designed them would build them without any looped connections. This meant that the bridge had only one way in or out. As networks grew, a new objective became important, and that was for a stable and reliable network. To help achieve this goal, designers would include more than one cable, and sometimes more than one way to get from one network to another.

While redundancy of devices and cabling helped reduce network outages, it created an entirely new problem: active loops. An active loop is created when there is more than one connection to a network from two bridges or switches. Whereas a designer might create redundant links on purpose, sometimes this can happen accidentally as the network expands without reviewing all connections.

The Active Loops Diagram illustrates a topology containing an active loop. Active loops can be a severe problem for bridge- and switch-based networks.

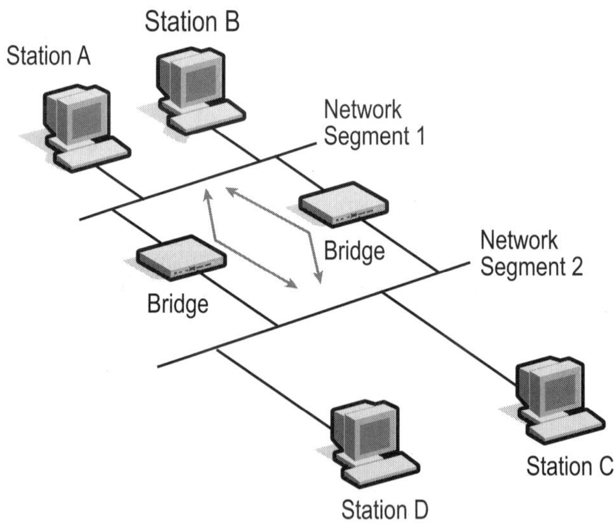

Active Loops

The three biggest problems with active loops are as follows:

- **Duplicate frames**—Every time Station A sends a frame to Station C, a separate instance of the frame is forwarded by each bridge. This results in two identical frames traversing the internetwork to the destination host. This redundant traffic can quickly degrade overall network performance. The bigger problem, however, is that the receiving system views the duplicate frames as an error and discards them both. Not getting a proper acknowledgment, Station A transmits them again, and the problem repeats itself.
- **MAC address table thrashing**—A bridge or switch learns and records the MAC address of the sending device in its MAC address table. If a loop exists, a frame may traverse one link at one time and go over a different link the next time. This can create a situation in which the switch updates its table over and over again with new port information. It's called thrashing because the addresses never remain valid and the processing capability of the switch is consumed with the updates. The switch can no longer forward frames.
- **Broadcast storm**—Remember that a broadcast message is sent out of all ports, except the one that it was received on. If there is a loop, a single broadcast could be transmitted through the network indefinitely, going in one side then out the other. A broadcast storm would consume all the available bandwidth, degrading network performance and preventing other transmissions.

The problem of active loops in a bridged network has been recognized and addressed by a networking standards committee of the Institute of Electrical and Electronic Engineers (IEEE). The IEEE standard for preventing active loops in bridged and switched networks is 802.1D. The solution is more commonly called the Spanning Tree Algorithm (STA) or the Spanning Tree Protocol, and has become a basic part of bridge and switch functionality.

Spanning Tree Algorithm

A spanning tree is a set of device-to-device paths through the network such that there is one, and only one, path between any two devices. STA constructs a spanning tree through a series of bridge-to-bridge negotiations. These negotiations determine which paths remain enabled for transmissions and which path(s) remain at least temporarily disabled.

As a result of these negotiations, one port on each bridge in the tree is placed in a forwarding state. All others are placed in a blocked state. This process ensures a single path between any two devices on the network and prevents the formation of active loops.

In other words, STA creates a logically loop-free network topology by not using certain paths; that is, by putting the redundant paths in a blocked mode. In the Sample Spanning Tree Diagram, the left part of the diagram shows a meshed topology containing loops, in which each dot represents a switch.

The image on the right shows how spanning tree is included in the meshed topology to eliminate loops. One bridge is chosen as the root bridge and begins negotiations to eliminate redundant paths.

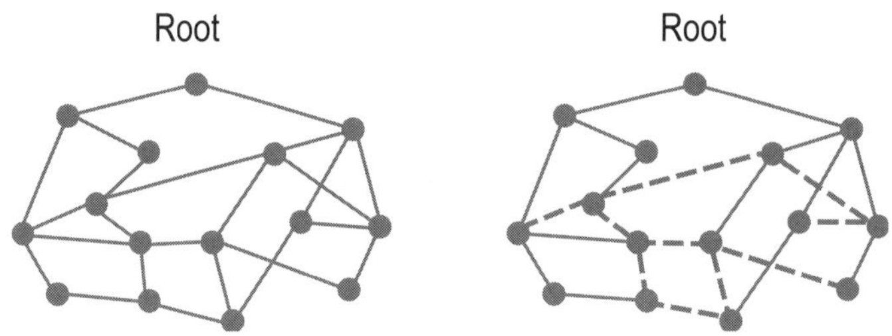

Sample Spanning Tree

STA further provides that if, for any reason, the unique path fails, the participating bridges can reactivate blocked ports to create a new spanning tree. Thus, STA allows internetworks implemented by bridges to have some path redundancy without the problems associated with active loops. With this feature, STA allows networks to recover quickly and automatically if a bridge/switch or section of network cabling fails.

Review Questions

1. List the similarities between a bridge and a switch.

2. List the differences between a bridge and a switch.

3. What percentage of traffic should remain on the same network segment when using a bridge?

4. When an end node is connected directly to a switch port, will it be able to transmit in full-duplex or half-duplex mode? Explain.

5. When is a frame flooded?

6. When is a frame forwarded?

7. When is a frame filtered?

8. How much of the frame is read before it is forwarded with cut-through?

9. How much of the frame is read before it is forwarded with store and forward?

10. Which switch method has the longest latency (delay) and why?

Extended Activity

Using the Switched Network Diagram and the information following this question, create the MAC address table for this switch in the order that frames are sent and received. Remember that entries are only made for the source address and associated port. Also keep in mind that frames are acknowledged by the receiving device.

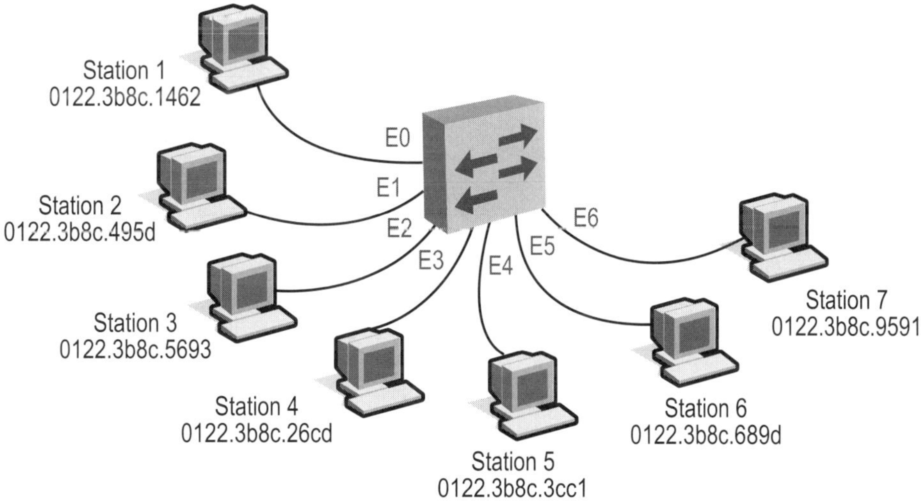

Switched Network

Port	MAC Address

Station 1 sends data destined for Station 7.

Station 4 sends a frame to be received by Station 3.

Station 2 sends data with a destination address of Station 4.

Station 5 sends a frame to Station 6.

Lesson 3—Virtual LANs

A VLAN is a switching technology that allows a network administrator to define security boundaries, create more bandwidth by segmenting broadcast domains, and provide a flexible and scalable network environment. VLANs also allow administrators to accommodate user and business needs without unnecessary physical reconfiguration.

VLAN membership can be defined based on port or MAC address. This lesson discusses many of the key terms and concepts associated with VLANs. It describes the need for VLANs, as well as the characteristics and benefits of using VLANs. It also discusses the types of VLAN membership and how transmission is handled when communicating between VLANs.

Objectives

At the end of this lesson you will be able to:

- Identify the need for VLANs
- Describe the characteristics and benefits of a VLAN
- Identify the VLAN components
- Describe the options for VLAN membership
- Explain how communication between VLANs is performed

Key Point

VLANs are created on switches and provide the administrator an amazing amount of flexibility when configuring a network. VLAN membership can be defined based on similar application, location, workgroup requirements, security, traffic flow, broadcasts, and many other considerations.

The Need for VLANs

You learned in Lesson 1 that a layer 2 switch device breaks up collision domains but maintains one broadcast domain for all connected end nodes. This could become a problem if hundreds of nodes are connected and some of them create a great deal of broadcast traffic. For example, many of the new multimedia applications are incredibly bandwidth- and broadcast-intensive. Add to that the possibility of faulty hardware or old network designs that cannot keep up with current requirements, and you have a networking nightmare. Day-to-day work cannot be done because network performance is slow and unreliable.

Administrative staff and sometimes entire departments are often scattered throughout a building. Company standards often require groups to work together that may be physically separated in the building. Without a lot of time and physical reconfiguration, it is difficult to stay on top of the changing business environment.

Physically locating PCs and network devices according to work patterns, traffic isolation, and security can become challenging. Traffic isolation becomes important, especially for real-time traffic versus data transmission. Physical network infrastructures may not accommodate new and different traffic types, or be able to separate them properly.

Characteristics and Benefits of VLANs

Fortunately, VLANs can fix many of these problems without replacing existing switches or physically reconfiguring a network infrastructure. A VLAN allows different users to work together and communicate within the same broadcast domain, regardless of their physical location.

A VLAN logically segments a big broadcast domain (the entire switch or several switches connected together) into smaller broadcast domains (workgroups or departments). This greatly reduces network traffic and therefore improves network performance. VLANs also allow an administrator to create a more secure network environment because the administrator has complete control over network access.

The VLAN Diagram shows how physical network requirements, such as traffic control, flexibility, and security, can be handled using a VLAN.

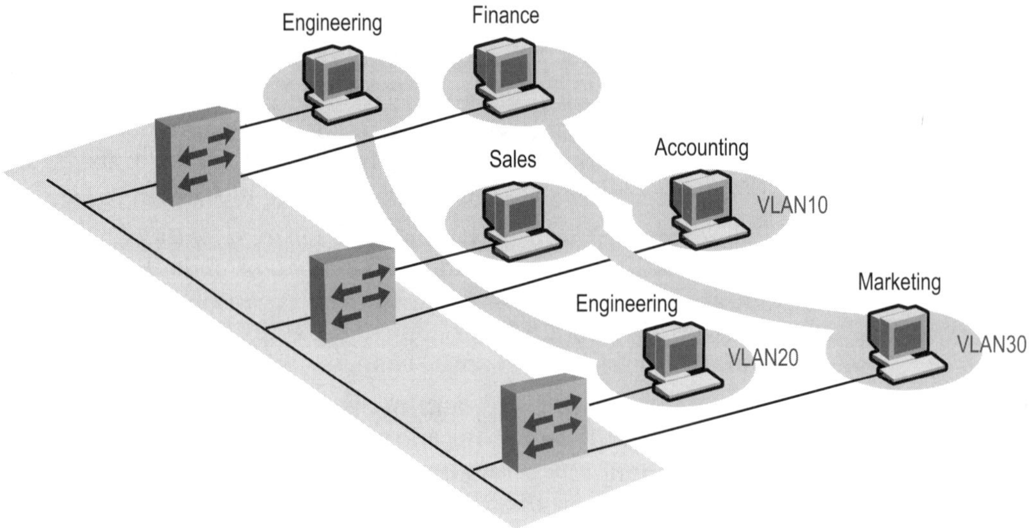

VLAN

VLAN handles these physical network requirements:

- **Traffic control (broadcast segmentation)**—When a VLAN is created, the administrator determines which devices should be able to communicate with each other. All members of a VLAN are in the same broadcast domain. They receive broadcasts from devices in the same VLAN, but not from devices in different VLANs. Therefore, VLANs provide a logical segmentation of a network. This not only keeps traffic for key groups together; it also reduces network traffic to all other devices outside the VLAN.
- **Flexibility/scalability**—An administrator's job is tough enough without having to keep up with the company's adds, moves, and changes. New resource demands placed on a network can make it difficult to maintain network performance. VLANs reduce administrative time and costs by providing more flexible and efficient network configuration.

An administrator can make assignments based on workgroup needs, project teams, or type of application, instead of physi cal location. Equipment does not have to be relocated and cabling does not have to change. The administrator can modify the VLAN settings from any Telnet connection to the switch. As a network grows or new application requirements put a higher demand on network services, an administrator can manage it by adding more VLANs.

- **Security**—In a traditional network, routers are used to create security because they segment a network and allow an administrator to determine who can communicate with whom. Layer 2 switch devices can also provide security using VLANs. Because frames are only received by devices in the same VLAN and are otherwise filtered to all other VLANs, a more secure environment is created.

  A router or layer 3 switch must be added to the infrastructure to allow devices from one VLAN to talk with devices of a different VLAN. This provides a secure environment while still allowing flexibility in configuration.

  Another common security problem in some organizations is network intrusion. An unauthorized user could access a network and monitor or intercept traffic by plugging into an open network port. Because VLAN membership is highly administered, only very specific access is available, greatly reducing the potential for a security breach.

VLANs Components

- **Layer 2 switches**—A simple VLAN configuration could reside on a single switch or, in more complex environments, a VLAN can span multiple switches. Each configured VLAN acts as its own complete switch environment. Each VLAN learns addresses, makes filtering/forwarding decisions, and prevents loops as if it were its own separate switch device. When a frame is received from a port, it is only forwarded to other ports in the same VLAN.
- **Routers or layer 3 switches**—To communicate between VLANs, a router, layer 3 switch, or router switch module (RSM) must be implemented to provide internetworking capabilities. This allows packets to be moved between the different logical network segments, just as they would if configured as physical segments.

- **Trunk links**—A trunk allows a VLAN to span across multiple devices, such as switches, routers, and servers. Trunk links can carry traffic for multiple VLANs. A trunk port is most often configured on Fast Ethernet (100 Mbps) or Gigabit Ethernet (1000 Mbps) ports used for backbone connection.

  After a trunk link is established, all VLANs communicating between the two devices automatically use that link. If the administrator does not want a particular VLAN to use the trunk, he or she must manually remove the VLAN from the trunk.

- **Encapsulation or frame tagging options**—The two encapsulation or frame tagging options that are used to identify and maintain separation between VLANs are Cisco's Inter-Switch Link (ISL) and IEEE 802.1Q:
  - **ISL**—This frame tag method is a Cisco proprietary protocol that encapsulates the original frame with VLAN-specific identification fields. It functions only when connecting all Cisco network devices. ISL came before IEEE 802.1Q was specified.
  - **IEEE 802.1Q**—This is the industry standard for VLAN tags that allows communications between different vendors' equipment. 802.1Q adds a shim (a small piece of header information) that includes both a prioritization and VLAN.

VLAN Membership

After an administrator has determined the needs of an organization based on common requirements, security, and traffic control, the administrator can create VLANs. The administrator must perform some up-front design and configuration work to set up VLANs and assign memberships. However, after they are configured, processes like add, moves, and changes are easily performed using the CLI, without physically recabling or changing network infrastructure.

VLAN membership can be assigned statically or dynamically. Regardless of how it is assigned, a station can only belong to one VLAN at a time, unless it has more than one network interface card (NIC). There are a few exceptions to this scenario, but they are outside the scope of this discussion:

- **Static membership (port-based)**—An administrator specifically assigns a port to a particular VLAN. Initially, this process can be time consuming. Static assignments work well in a network where the user environment is relatively stable and does not change constantly. All ports are static-members of VLAN1 by default.
- **Dynamic membership (MAC-based)**—An administrator can dynamically configure port assignments by using a VLAN Membership Policy Server (VMPS). This is available on higher-end switch devices, such as the Catalyst 6000, or on an external server. Other Catalyst switch devices support dynamic membership by retrieving information from a VMPS.

  A database of MAC addresses provides dynamic membership with an associated VLAN assignment. When an end node attaches to a network, the MAC address is read by the switch and located in the VMPS database. The connection is then assigned to the correct VLAN for the period of time it is active. This works well in an environment where mobility is important. For example, salespeople or field technicians can plug a laptop into the network and access the network resources they need from any location.

Communicating Between VLANs

VLANs are logical segments instead of the traditional physical segments. Even though they are logical, they still have the same characteristics as a physical segment. For example, they are used for broadcast control, they isolate traffic, and they have a different network address for each segment. What this means is that a VLAN, like a router interface, represents a subnetwork. Therefore, the VLAN is assigned an appropriate IP address and subnet mask.

Since each VLAN represents its own subnet, traffic moving from one VLAN to another must be transmitted at the Network Layer. This means it must be handled by a router or layer 3 switch. Multilayer switches can perform both the end-device VLAN connectivity and connect the VLAN segments, all in the same device. In a more traditional scenario, a router is used to connect the VLAN segments together.

Either way, this connection is performed using a trunk link. The trunk link is a high-speed (100-Mbps or 1-Gbps) connection that transmits all VLAN and other switch traffic. A router that performs the function of routing between VLANs is often called a "router-on-a-stick" or a "one-armed-router." This is because traffic enters and leaves the device over the same physical trunk link.

The Connecting VLANs with a Router Diagram shows the physical configuration required for this to take place.

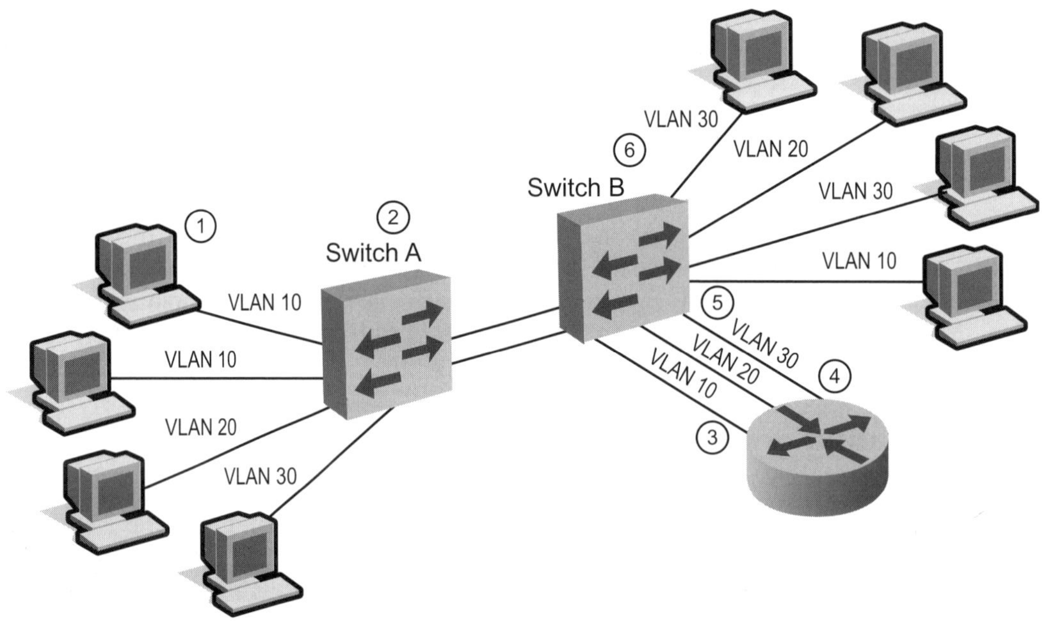

Connecting VLANs with a Router

The end device is not aware of its VLAN membership or how its traffic is being handled. When transmitting to systems in a different VLAN, the process is the same if they were being transmitted to another physical segment. The steps from end to end are as follows:

1. The PC sends a transmission destined for a system that is in another VLAN.
2. The switch receives the frame and recognizes that it is not in the same VLAN or logical network segment.
3. The switch hands the frame to a Layer 3 device (Layer 3 switch or router)
4. The Layer 3 device reads the IP address of the destination and identifies where to send it, based on routing table entries. The device forwards it to the correct egress interface.
5. The transmission is received into the VLAN of the recipient.
6. The switch reads the MAC address of the destination device, looks it up in the MAC address table, and forwards it to the proper destination port.

Review Questions

1. What are the VLAN frame tagging methods available on Cisco switches? (Choose two.)
   a. ISL
   b. 802.1D
   c. 802.1Q
   d. VLAN-ID
2. A VLAN has which of the following characteristics? (Choose two.)
   a. A VLAN creates logical broadcast domains.
   b. A VLAN creates physical broadcast domains.
   c. A VLAN provides administrative flexibility.
   d. A VLAN requires more day-to-day administration than traditional networks.
3. In a network created with VLANs, what has to be performed when a person takes on a new project and needs to be part of a different LAN segment?
   a. The administrator must recable the users connection.
   b. The administrator must reterminate user's connection.
   c. The administrator must change the switch port.
   d. The administrator must Telnet into the switch to change VLAN membership.
4. What method is used to dynamically assign VLAN membership?
   a. Port-based
   b. DHCP assignment
   c. MAC-address-based
   d. IP-address-based
5. VLANs can be created on which device?
   a. Hub
   b. Layer 2 switch
   c. Bridge
   d. Layer 3 switch

6. What devices could be used to communicate between VLANs? (Choose two).
    a. Layer 2 switch
    b. Repeater
    c. Layer 3 switch
    d. Router
7. In VLANs, what is the connection between two switches called?
    a. Uplink
    b. Trunk link
    c. Connection link
    d. LAN link
8. What VLAN membership assignment method is best suited for networks that are static and in which equipment does not move often?
    a. MAC-based
    b. Port-based
    c. IP-address-based
    d. VLAN-tag-based
9. What are reasons to design and configure VLANs? (Choose two.)
    a. They are easy to initially set up.
    b. They require very little hardware.
    c. They create small, logically defined broadcast domains.
    d. They allow complete and flexible administrative control.
10. What are names for the router that can be used for connectivity between VLANs? (Choose two.)
    a. One-armed router
    b. Router-on-a-stick
    c. Fast-forward router
    d. Trunk router

Extended Activities

1. Match the following components with their associated description.

   a. 802.1Q

   b. MAC address

   c. Traffic isolation

   d. ISL

   e. Security

   f. Layer 2 switch

   g. Router

   h. Trunk

   i. Broadcast

   j. Port-based

   The proprietary method Cisco uses to identify VLAN information in a frame is a _________

   The cable connection between two switches that share VLAN information is a _________

   The device that is necessary to communicate between VLANs is a _________

   The IEEE standard for VLAN tag headers is _________

   The type of traffic that VLANs logically control is _________

   The device where end nodes are connected for VLAN membership is a _________

   The VLAN membership assignment that is based on the cable connection is _________

   The node information used for assigning dynamic VLAN membership is a _________

   The VLAN feature that allows the administrator to control who is talking to whom is _________

   The VLAN feature that separates transmissions based on type of information is _________

Summary

This module addressed a number of key features associated with switching technologies. It started with problems that are often encountered in old network topologies. These problems include transmitting over long physical cable segments, collision domains, broadcast domains, and high bandwidth use. Layer 2 and multilayer switching is the answer to all these problems.

A layer 2 switch repeats a signal to extend transmission distances. It also breaks up collision domains, eliminating network contention issues. Using VLANs, a layer 2 switch can also logically break up broadcast domains. Controlling and isolating traffic to that extent creates more available bandwidth for the resource-intensive applications used in most networks today.

Module 4 Quiz

1. Why should hubs and repeaters not be used to interconnect entire LANs?
   a. They are too expensive.
   b. They are too powerful.
   c. They do not manage traffic efficiently enough.
   d. They cannot connect different physical media.
2. At which OSI layers do switches reside? (Choose three.)
   a. Data Link Layer
   b. Physical Layer
   c. Transport Layer
   d. Network Layer
3. Can switches switch two frames simultaneously?
   a. Yes
   b. No
4. Which of the following devices isolate traffic in an Ethernet network?
   a. Bridge
   b. Switch
   c. Router
   d. All of the above
5. Performance will likely increase in an Ethernet network when which of the following occurs?
   a. Switches are replaced by hubs.
   b. Routers are replaced by hubs.
   c. Switches are replaced by bridges.
   d. Hubs are replaced by switches.
6. What is a broadcast frame?
   a. A frame addressed to "all nodes"
   b. A frame addressed to one node but received by all nodes on the same hub
   c. A frame transmitted over a wireless LAN
   d. A frame sent to a specific destination address

7. Switches are needed in which of the following situations?
   a. Too many collisions on the LAN
   b. Remote connection of two LANs over a WAN link
   c. Broadcast storms
   d. All of the above
8. Consider a 10BaseT network that has four workgroup hubs. Each hub connects eight nodes. Each of the workgroup hubs is connected to one another. The network administrator decides to connect each of the four hubs to a central switch instead of to one another. What is the effect of this change?
   a. Each of the hubs has 10-Mbps bandwidth to share among its end devices.
   b. Each of the hubs has 2.5-Mbps bandwidth.
   c. Each of the nodes has 10-Mbps bandwidth.
   d. Each of the nodes has 1/32 of the 10-Mbps bandwidth.
9. Consider a network that has three workgroup hubs, with each hub connected to six nodes. Each of the three hubs is connected to an individual port on a switch. How many collision domains and broadcast domains are in this network?
   a. One collision domain, one broadcast domain
   b. Three collision domains, one broadcast domain
   c. Three broadcast domains, one collision domain
   d. Three collision domains, three broadcast domains
10. Consider a network that has three workgroup hubs, with each hub connected to six nodes. Each of the three hubs is connected to an individual port on a router. How many collision domains and broadcast domains are in this network?
    a. One collision domain, one broadcast domain
    b. Three collision domains, one broadcast domain
    c. Three broadcast domains, one collision domain
    d. Three collision domains, three broadcast domains

11. VLANs are implemented using which type of device?
    a. Bridge
    b. Gateway
    c. Repeater
    d. Switch
12. Which of the following best describes the functionality of a VLAN?
    a. Grouping of nodes logically that are physically separated
    b. Grouping of nodes physically in one single routing domain
    c. Replace passive hubs for performance purposes
    d. Provide for performance improvements over traditional routed networks
13. The primary reason to build a VLAN is to:
    a. Separate servers from workstations
    b. Group segments together to form logical traffic patterns
    c. Increase reachability of broadcast traffic
    d. Provide for increased segment-switching capabilities
14. Which of the following is not a way to define VLAN membership?
    a. By Layer 1 protocol
    b. By MAC address
    c. Dynamically
    d. By Port
15. A method of automatically joining a VLAN group might be based on:
    a. MAC address
    b. Vendor equipment type
    c. Application type
    d. Physical Layer characteristics

16. When a switch adds information inside the MAC layer header to communicate VLAN information, it is using:
    a. Frame tagging
    b. Table maintenance
    c. TDM
    d. Packet tagging
17. A broadcast domain is the area of a network where:
    a. All packets are sent to all routers.
    b. All frames with an all Fs MAC destination address are sent to all devices.
    c. All messages are sent to all applications.
    d. Frames are isolated to switch ports.
18. Decreasing a broadcast domain effectively: (Choose two.)
    a. Increases reachability
    b. Decreases performance
    c. Increases available bandwidth
    d. Increases security
19. Use of equipment from multiple switch vendors when implementing a VLAN relies on:
    a. Use of IP-only networks
    b. Use of IEEE Ethernet
    c. Use of standards such as 802.1Q
    d. Use of standards such as 802.2
20. Routers are used with switched VLANs for which of the following purposes?
    a. Route information between VLANs
    b. To provide security
    c. To provide access to WANs
    d. All of the above

Module 5
IP Protocol Suite

Today, the Internet Protocol (IP) suite, or Transmission Control Protocol TCP/IP, as it is often called, has a presence in almost every aspect of networking and computer systems. In addition, its scope has broadened to include many devices that need information access and connectivity to the Internet, such as wireless phones, WebTV systems, cars, and other components.

However, IP is much more than just the 32-bit address used for identification. It is a complete suite of applications and protocols that provide user interaction, data retrieval, electronic mail (e-mail), data transmission, routing protocols, streaming, real-time media, and much more.

The "IP Protocol suite" is therefore a more accurate name than the commonly used term "TCP/IP." As this module will help clarify, many applications and services do not use TCP at all; instead they use User Datagram Protocol (UDP).

The three lessons in this module give you an overview of the entire IP suite. The first lesson is about protocols at the Network or Internet Layer. These include the routable protocol IP that is used for hierarchical addressing, fragmentation, and best-effort delivery. Also included are some helper protocols used with IP, such as Internetwork Control Message Protocol (ICMP), Address Resolution Protocol (ARP), and Reverse Address Resolution Protocol (RARP). The lesson ends with an overview of Dynamic Host Control/Configuration Protocol (DHCP) and how it is used to allocate IP addresses and other important configuration settings to network devices.

Lesson 2 reviews the components at the Transport or Host-to-Host Layer: TCP and UDP. TCP provides a reliable, connection-oriented means of transport for IP. It is commonly used for all data transmissions that rely on dependable transmission. Yet, with dependability comes overhead, and TCP can be bulky and slower than its counterpart UDP. By contrast, UDP is a connectionless, unreliable transport protocol. It is commonly used for real-time transmissions like voice, video, and streaming media. UDP has very low overhead, which makes it fast. It depends on upper- and lower-layer protocols for reliability and therefore streamlines transmissions at the Transport Layer.

Lesson 3 lists and describes a select group of IP applications. These applications are grouped into file transfer, network management, e-mail, and Web services. The applications provide a user interface as well as specific program functionality.

For reference, the Request for Comment (RFC) document number is included for each application type. This section also tells you which Transport Layer protocol is used by each application and the application's assigned Transport Layer port address.

Lessons

1. Network Layer Protocols
2. Transport Layer Overview
3. Upper-Layer IP Applications

Lesson 1—Network Layer Protocols

This lesson reviews the most important part of the protocol suite, IP. IP is used to provide a hierarchical addressing structure, a best-effort delivery method, and, if necessary, to fragment packets to accommodate different network Maximum Transmission Units (MTUs). IP has its own header at the Network Layer, which includes the IP addresses of the source and destination.

Part of this header, called the ToS or Type of Services field, has gained a lot of press lately. The ToS, which went unused for many years, is now being used to help in Quality of Service (QoS) route decision making. An application or device can use this field to define how the transmission should be handled, based on precedence, delay, throughput, and reliability.

At the Network Layer, IP depends on several protocols to provide network services and logical-to-physical address translations. ICMP is the protocol that provides network messages so that devices know the status of a transmission, can detect connectivity, provide flow control, get addressing information, and learn that a route is unreachable. `Ping` is an example of a command that is provided by ICMP echo requests/echo reply messages to test host-to-host connectivity.

ARP and RARP are two other helper protocols at the Network Layer. ARP is used to determine the Media Access Control (MAC) address when an IP address is known, and to complete the MAC header of a frame. RARP gets an IP address when the MAC is known, which helps a workstation to acquire an IP address from a DHCP server.

Objectives

At the end of this lesson you will be able to:

- Review the IP protocol suite
- Define the function of IP
- Identify the components of an IP header
- Discuss the ToS field
- Identify the protocol field
- Describe the purpose of ICMP
- Describe the purpose of ARP and RARP
- Describe the function of DHCP

Key Point

The IP protocol suite is made up of numerous protocols at the upper layers of the OSI model. IP is only one small portion of the suite, and it depends on many other protocols to provide user applications, end-to-end transmission capabilities, address assistance, control messages, and routing in the network.

IP Suite Review

At the start of a module on the IP protocol suite, it makes sense to review how IP compares with the OSI model. Although most books and network people use the term TCP/IP in reference to the OSI model, TCP/IP is only a segment of the total group of protocols that work together. This lesson focuses on the Network Layer, which includes IP, ICMP, ARP, and RARP. Although not displayed on the diagram, the process of using DHCP completes this lesson.

Lesson 2 discusses the Transport Layer protocols TCP and UDP in greater detail. Lesson 3 gives you a brief overview of several commonly used IP applications. The IP Suite vs. the OSI Model diagram shows where each protocol is located.

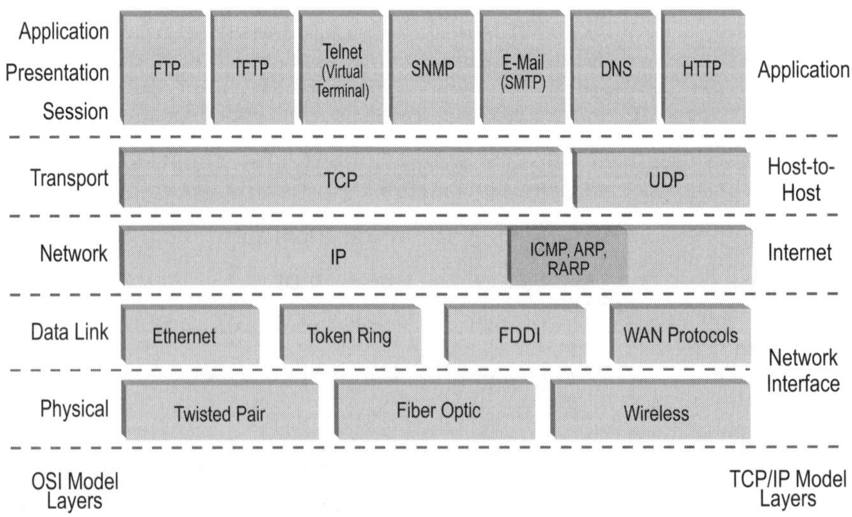

IP Suite vs. OSI Model

Internet Protocol

IP is the quintessential element of the Internet or Network Layer. The IP protocol provides the following services:

- **Hierarchical addressing**—The Network Layer is responsible for adding a header that includes the IP address information of the source and destination devices. An IP address is hierarchical, meaning that it represents different levels: an entire network, possibly a subnetwork segment, and a single host device. Routers and other Layer 3 devices use this hierarchical address to make decisions about how to handle the packet and the best path to get to the destination. This is called "routing," and IP uses a number of routing protocols to perform this function.
- **Connectionless, best-effort delivery**—Each packet is routed through the system independently of all other packets. No connections or logical circuits are established at the Network Layer. By itself, IP has little data error control. IP provides a 16-bit header checksum, calculated from the header's length, that receiving stations use to validate a packet. The receiving station discards packets with invalid checksums. There are no end-to-end or hop-by-hop receipt acknowledgments. There are no provisions for the retransmission of lost or corrupted data. And there are no packet-sequencing or flow-control mechanisms. IP depends on TCP at the Transport Layer for reliable transmission services. If UDP is used, IP is only a best-effort delivery method.
- **Fragmentation**—Individual network segments can set varying maximum packet sizes, called the Maximum Transmission Unit (MTU). In most cases, segmenting is a job handled at the Transport Layer by TCP. However, in a routed network, packets may traverse different network topologies that may have different MTUs. The sending and receiving hosts have no knowledge of these MTU variances. Therefore, although the source station's Transport Layer protocols have efficiently divided the data stream into segments, and the IP module has built packets for efficient delivery across its directly connected network, the resulting packets may eventually be fragmented to match another network segment's MTU and then reassembled at the destination.

An IP software module resides in all hosts and network devices running the IP protocol stack. These modules share common rules for logical address, header interpretation, fragmentation, and reassembling. Additionally, the IP protocol suite includes procedures for route decision making and other helpful functions, such as Address Resolution Protocol (ARP), Reserve Address Resolution Protocol (RARP), and Internet Control Message Protocol (ICMP). These protocols are discussed later in this lesson.

IP Header

To better understand IP, take a look at the header information that is added to the data passed from the upper layers, as shown on the IP Header Diagram.

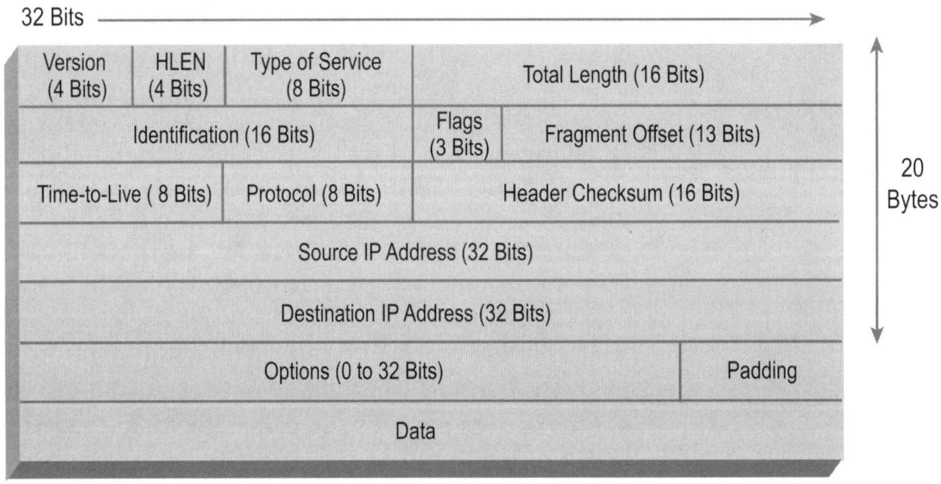

IP Header

The IP header is 20 bytes long in addition to the upper-layer data, which varies. The IP header consists of the following fields:

- **Version (4 bits)**—Defines the use of IP version 4 (IPv4) (current version) or IP version 6 (IPv6) (future 128-bit addressing scheme). This field ensures that the sender, receiver, and intervening gateways agree on the correct packet format. The most widely used IP version is version 4; IPv6 is now in testing and limited deployment. These bits read 0100 for IPv4.

- **Header Length (HLEN) (4 bits)**—Identifies the length of the IP header in 32-bit words. IP headers must be a minimum of 20 bytes long. IP options can extend the field by 4 bytes (32 bits) at a time. The most common header, which contains no padding or IP options, measures 20 bytes long and has an HLEN field of 5 (0101).
- **Type of Service (ToS) (8 bits)**—Because IP is a best-effort protocol, few implementations use the ToS fields as RFC791 defines them. Instead, Quality of Service (QoS) applications used for such delay-sensitive, bandwidth-intensive services as video and Voice over IP (VoIP) modify these bits to suit their needs. Network devices all along the packet's route must recognize these bit settings and provide the appropriate network services for QoS to be provided. Not all routing devices or routing protocols have the capability to decipher ToS/QoS bits, which means the transmission will default to IP's best-effort delivery methods. This field is discussed in greater detail later in this lesson.
- **Total Length (16 bits)**—Identifies the length of the packet with both header and upper-layer data. The maximum size is 65,535 bytes, and all hosts must be able to handle a packet of at least 576 bytes.
- **Identification (16 bits)**—Each packet must have a unique identification number so that receiving hosts can reassemble the fragmented packet.
- **Flags (3 bits)**—Determine whether fragmentation is necessary and, if so, control fragmentation counts. If a network device is preparing to send a packet longer than the network MTU and sees the `Don't Fragment Bit` set, it returns an ICMP error message to the sender and discards the packet. All fragments but the last have the `More Fragments Bit` set to 1.
- **Fragment Offset (13 bits)**—Specifies the fragment's location in the original packet. The first fragment has offset 0, and the remaining fragments are measured as 8-byte units, representing the fragment's beginning in relation to the start of the original payload.
- **Time-to-Live (TTL) (8 bits)**—Identifies the amount of time a packet should be allowed to traverse a network without being delivered. Each gateway (router or Layer 3 device) the packet traverses decrements this field by one. After the packet's TTL expires, the next network device removes it from the network. Because network devices almost always forward

a packet in less than 1 second, the TTL is used as the packet's hop count. After this time expires, the packet is dropped by the next device and an ICMP time exceeded message is returned. Setting a TTL prevents undeliverable packets from endlessly circulating through a network.

- **Protocol (8 bits)**—Specifies which Transport Layer protocol was used to create the message carried in the Data area of a packet. Similar to a how port numbers are used to identify upper-layer applications for the Transport Layer, a protocol number identifies the Transport Layer protocol for the Network Layer. This allows communication between Layers 3 and 4 by identifying and passing data to the appropriate protocol. The two most common protocols used at this handoff point are TCP and UDP, as shown on the Protocol Numbers Diagram.

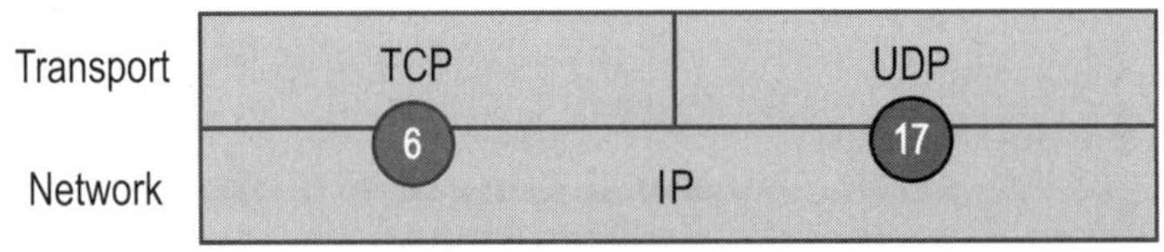

Protocol Numbers

TCP uses protocol number 6, whereas UDP uses protocol number 17. Other upper-layer protocol possibilities include:

- **ICMP**—protocol number 1
- **Interior Gateway Routing Protocol (IGRP)**—protocol number 9
- **IPv6**—protocol number 41
- **ICMP for IPv6**—protocol number 58
- **EIGRP**—protocol number 88

These protocol numbers, along with many others, are controlled by the Internet Assigned Numbers Authority (IANA). To get a complete listing of all available protocol numbers refer to RFC 1700.

- **Header Checksum (16 bits)**—Provides the results of a cyclical redundancy check (CRC) performed on the IP header only. Because some Header fields change as the packet traverses the network (for example, the TTL or the ToS bits), each hop where the header is processed recomputes the checksum.

- **Source IP Address (32 bits)**—Identifies the IP address of the sending host. The source IP address does not change as the packets traverse the network.
- **Destination IP Address (32 bits)**—Identifies the IP address of the receiving host. The destination IP address does not change as the packets traverse the network.
- **Options (0 to 32 bits)**—This variable-length field is used for options such as recording the route taken, specifying the route to be taken, and timestamping. The option field can be zero or more bits long.
- **Padding**—If necessary, padding means that binary 0s are added to guarantee that the IP header ends at a 32-bit boundary.
- **Data (variable)**—Consists of upper-layer protocol data.

A Closer Look at the ToS Field

The first 3 bits in this field are the priority or precedence bits, and indicate how the packet should be handled. The next four bits in the ToS field are labeled D-T-R-C and indicate Delay, Throughput, Reliability, and Cost as values. At this point, however, the cost bit and the last bit are not in use, but available for future use. This combination of bits in the Network Layer header helps identify and prioritize traffic when you are using a routing protocol that provides Quality of Service (QoS) like Open Shortest Path First (OSPF).

Many protocol analyzers and network documentation calls this area the diffserv code point (DSCP). (Differentiation Services are described in RFCs 2474 and 2475.) As stated earlier in this lesson, not all routing protocols support this priority information; therefore, QoS cannot be guaranteed even if a value has been set. The ToS Field Diagram shows how this part of the header is divided at the bit level.

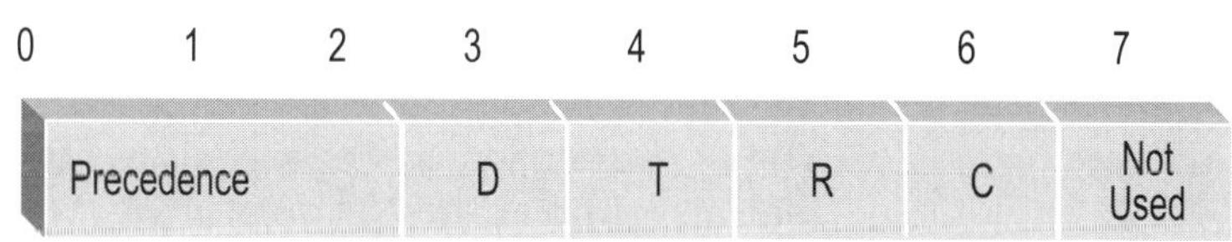

ToS Field

Precedence Bits

The ToS field Precedence bits (bits 0-2) are used by a source host to convey to other devices on the internetwork a packet's relative importance (precedence). These bits were designed to provide a mechanism that would allow a router to treat certain packets as more important than other types of traffic. For example, a network can only accept packets above a certain precedence at times of high network load. This field's values range from 0 (low) to 7 (high). The bits can be set as follows, from highest to lowest:

111—Network Control

110—Internetwork Control

101—Critical

100—Flash override

011—Flash

010—Immediate

001—Priority

000—Routine

D-T-R-C Bits

Until recently, most network devices ignored the ToS field D-T-R-C bits (bits 3 through 7). With the introduction of the Open Shortest Path First (OSPF) routing protocol, IP routers began to support ToS routing. RIP does not use this field when making the best path selection. The D-T-R-C bits are described as follows:

- **Bit 3: D-(Delay) bit**—Used by a source host to request either low delay or normal delay. The defined bit states are: 0–Normal delay, 1–Low delay.
- **Bit 4: T-(Throughput) bit**—Used by a source host to request either high or normal throughput. The defined bit states are: 0–Normal throughput, 1–High throughput.
- **Bit 5: R-(Reliability) bit**—Used by a source host to request either high reliability or normal reliability. The defined bit states are: 0–Normal reliability, 1–High reliability.
- **Bits 6-7**—Reserved for future use. The defined bit states are: 00–Reserved.

The IP Header Screen Capture shows the contents of header information found at the Network Layer. You can compare the descriptions given here of each field with a real transmission in a production environment. Notice that, as stated, the length of the IP header is 20 bytes.

This protocol analyzer uses the name Differentiated Services Field in the place of the ToS field discussed earlier in this lesson. This terminology is more common today, although in this example, no values are set in this field to provide QoS.

Also notice the Fragment fields, Time to live value, and Protocol pointing to TCP at the Transport Layer. The last piece of valuable information in the IP header is the Source and Destination IP addresses.

```
⊞ Frame 392 (60 on wire, 60 captured)
⊞ Ethernet II
⊟ Internet Protocol, Src Addr: 198.152.12.67(198.152.12.67), Dst Addr: 135.35.88.52 (135.35.88.52)
    Version: 4
    Header length: 20 bytes
  ⊟ Differentiated Services Field: 0x00 (DSCP 0x00: Default; ECN: 0x00)
      0000 00.. = Differentiated Services Codepoint: Default (0x00)
      .... ..0. = ECN-Capable Transport (ECT): 0
      .... ...0 = ECN-CE: 0
    Total Length: 40
    Identification: 0xc89b
  ⊟ Flags: 0x00
      .0.. = Don't fragment: Not set
      ..0. = More fragments: Not set
    Fragment offset: 0
    Time to live: 59
    Protocol: TCP (0x06)
    Header checksum: 0x0502 (correct)
    Source: 198.152.12.67(198.152.12.67)
    Destination: 135.35.88.52 (135.35.88.52)
⊞ Transmission Control Protocol, Src Port: 8000 (8000), Dst Port: 1573 (1573), Seq: 355811802, Ack: 615302370,
```

IP Header

Helper Protocols

At the Internet or Network Layer, three main helper protocols are used with IP to provide a complete networking environment. These three protocols are ICMP, ARP, and RARP.

ICMP

As its name implies, Internet Control Message Protocol (ICMP) is a management and messaging protocol. Unlike e-mail messaging, ICMP is for important communications between routers in a network, as well as for communication to end-devices. A few of the main functions performed by ICMP are as follows:

- **Echo Request/Echo Reply**—Most people working with or learning about computers and network technology are familiar with the PING command. This helpful ICMP feature is really an echo request and echo reply. Using `PING` allows you to determine communication and connectivity up to the Network Layer from the sender to the receiver. If an echo reply is successful, communication can be established. If an echo reply fails, this could indicate problems at the lower layers in the connection between the two devices. It is also possible that echo request/echo reply services have been blocked by a firewall or access list to prevent `ping`'s use in a malicious attack, sometimes referred to as the "ping of death."

- **Address Request/Address Reply**—Although network broadcasts are continuously sent out by means of routing protocols, in some instances, a router needs more immediate information. In that case, the router sends out an address request to retrieve IP address information about another device.
- **Subnet Mask Request**—ICMP issues a subnet mask request to learn about the internetwork environment and addressing structure.
- **Destination Unreachable**—Routers exchange and maintain routing tables that provide the best path through a network. If a packet is received that is addressed to a network not in the table, the router attempts to send it to the default gateway. If a default gateway is not set, the router drops the packet and returns an ICMP destination unreachable message to the source.
- **Source Quench**—An ICMP source quench message informs the sender that the receiving host's buffer is full. The sending device waits for additional information before continuing transmission. This data flow method prevents packets from being dropped due to heavy traffic and inability to process more data once the buffer is full. In data networking, the source quench is often called a "choke" packet because it tells the sender to suspend transmitting until the source has had time to process the original transmissions.
- **Timestamp/Timestamp Reply**—This combination of ICMP services checks the time it takes to traverse a particular network segment.
- **Time Exceeded**—Each packet includes a time-to-live (TTL) number that prevents it from circling a network indefinitely if it cannot be delivered. When a router receives a packet and the TTL has expired, the router returns a time exceeded message to the sender and drops the packet. The process of performing a traceroute to detect the path used to communicate with another device uses an ICMP time exceeded message. When a traceroute is performed, the TTL is set to one. Each receiving device issues a time exceeded error message. The hops reported to the screen are each of the ICMP messages being returned.
- **Parameter Problem**—A router reads the header of every packet. If it detects a faulty packet structure, it notifies the sender with a parameter problem ICMP message.

- **Redirect**—A router knows it should never have to send a packet out of the same interface through which it was originally received. If it does, there is an error in a routing table, which provided incorrect routing information. An ICMP redirect message indicates that this has taken place and attempts to prevent it in the future.

From this list, it is evident that ICMP provides an invaluable function in the network environment. Without it, many networking features would not be available or network functionality would be drastically limited.

ARP

An IP hierarchical address is helpful for locating a single network and, more specifically, for locating a single device in a very large internetwork. However, only a Layer 3 device can understand this address format. Other Layer 2 devices use a physical or MAC address to locate a particular device in a local area network (LAN) segment. To complete all the delivery requirements, the upper-layer data must include an IP or logical address, as well as the physical or MAC address for the receiving host.

Remember that encapsulation adds header information to the upper-layer data and decapsulation removes it. If both addresses are not included, the upper-layer data may have a difficult time traversing the many different devices that make up the internetwork.

This is where Address Resolution Protocol (ARP) comes into play. ARP is another component of the IP suite that is used to identify MAC addresses when the IP address is known. It stores the IP-to-MAC-address information in the ARP cache in memory. This table is frequently updated with new entries, and old devices are eliminated. The following steps outline how ARP is used to update the ARP cache and add MAC address information:

1. If a host wants to send data to another system on the same subnet that is not in its ARP cache, it sends an ARP request to find the MAC address for the receiving host. This ARP request is broadcast with the destination IP address provided by the upper-layer protocol.
2. The receiving system hears the broadcast and replies with its MAC address.

3. If the destination IP address is not in the same subnetwork, a router or other layer 3 device is queried. This function is called proxy arp and must be enabled for the router or other layer 3 device to respond with its own MAC address. The router would then be responsible for sending an ARP to the next hop to determine the next MAC address.

The ARP Diagram shows a sending host making an ARP broadcast request for the MAC address of the destination device.

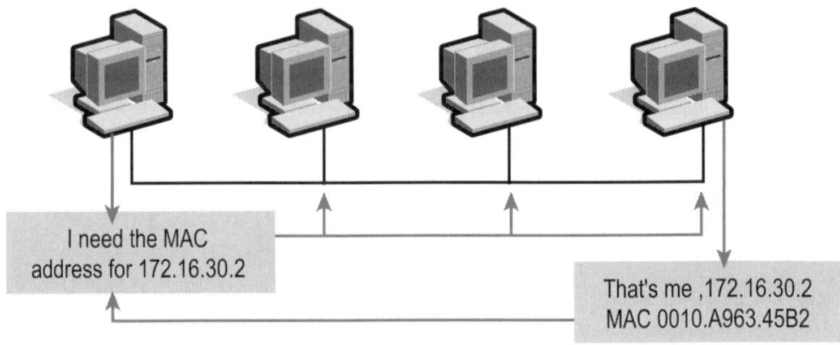

ARP

The ARP Request Screen Capture shows how the ARP request would be displayed in a protocol analyzer. Notice how the Destination address is set to ff:ff:ff:ff:ff:ff and, lower on the screen, the Target MAC address is 00:00:00:00:00:00. This indicates that the ARP is being sent as a broadcast to all devices within the same segment. Also notice, under Info, that the request is written as Who has IP address, Tell the requesting IP address.

```
Source             Destination        Protocol  Info
00:50:da:68:ea:1a  ff:ff:ff:ff:ff:ff  ARP       Who has 192.168.30.2? Tell 192.168.30.4
⊞ Ethernet II
⊟ Address Resolution Protocol (request)
    Hardware type: Ethernet (0x0001)
    Protocol type: IP (0x0800)
    Hardware size: 6
    Protocol size: 4
    Opcode: request (0x0001)
    Sender MAC address: 00:50:da:68:ea:1a (3COM_68:ea:1a)
    Sender IP address: 172.16.30.4  (172.16.30.4)
    Target MAC address: 00:00:00:00:00:00 (XEROX_00:00:00)
    Target IP address: 172.16.30.2 (172.16.30.2)
```

ARP Request

The ARP Reply Screen Capture shows the information that is returned for the original request. This transmission is sent directly back to the requestor, as a unicast. In addition, the transmission now has the essential information of a MAC address for the requesting device.

```
Source              Destination         Protocol  Info
00:50:da:68:d2:91   00:50:da:68:ea:1a   ARP       192.168.30.2 is at 00:50:da:68:d2:91
⊞ Ethernet II
⊟ Address Resolution Protocol (request)
    Hardware type: Ethernet (0x0001)
    Protocol type: IP (0x0800)
    Hardware size: 6
    Protocol size: 4
    Opcode: request (0x0001)
    Sender MAC address: 00:50:da:68:d2:91 (3COM_68:d2:91)
    Sender IP address: 172.16.30.2 (172.16.30.2)
    Target MAC address: 00:50:da:68:ea:1a (3COM_68:ea:1a)
    Target IP address: 172.16.30.4  (172.16.30.4)
```

ARP Reply

RARP

As the protocol name implies, Reverse Address Resolution Protocol (RARP) does exactly the opposite (the reverse) of ARP. As stated earlier in this lesson, ARP determines a MAC address when the IP address is known. RARP, on the other hand, finds an IP address when the MAC address is known.

RARP is not generally used for delivering network data. Workstations or devices that receive their network configuration from a Dynamic Host Configuration Protocol (DHCP) server usually use RARP. With RARP, the sending device knows its own MAC address. To get IP address information, the device sends a DHCP request as a RARP, with the MAC address included, to a server for its IP address assignment.

DHCP Overview

MAC addresses are Layer 2 addresses that are burned into the network interface card (NIC) by the manufacturer. IP addresses, on the other hand, are logical, meaning that they need to be assigned and configured on a device or host. This configuration can be performed manually with physical access to the host. When you configure an address in this manner, it stays the same until someone changes it. The IP address becomes part of the configuration for the device and is loaded and used while the system is active.

The benefit to this type of assignment is that there is a specific number that remains the same and identifies a specific device. Usually such an assignment is made when it is necessary for the address to stay the same. Examples of when addresses are directly assigned to a device might be printers, servers, switches, and router interfaces.

In these examples, the IP address must stay the same for clients to locate them. As for the network equipment, the IP address must stay the same so that routing protocols can build their tables and the devices can be accessed using Telnet for configuration purposes.

As these examples show, it makes sense to have a specific assignment manually configured. For many years, this was the only way to assign IP addresses. But with the number of hosts that are in many corporate networks today, manually assigning and changing IP addresses would be a full-time job. In addition, it is critical that each device have a unique IP address. When you are making hundreds of assignments, however, it is difficult to keep track of where they were assigned and eventually human error will create a duplicate entry. It can be fixed easily enough, but overall this process is just too time consuming and not accurate enough.

Dynamic Host Configuration Protocol (DHCP) is a service that clients use to request and download IP addressing and configuration information. DHCP can be used to dynamically or statically assign IP addresses to host devices. When assigning a dynamic address, the DHCP server first reviews which network segment the request came from. It then assigns the host an available address from a pool of addresses for that segment.

In dynamic assignment, the IP address is leased to the requestor for a specific period of time—three days by default. Lease times can be shortened to allow more devices to use the available IP address pool.

With dynamic assignment, the IP address for a given host can change frequently. Therefore, it doesn't work well for devices that require a specific address assignment at all times. Dynamic assignment may also make it difficult to track Internet access and raise other security issues because a host address could change before being identified.

Static assignment works much as the manual configuration discussed earlier in this lesson. It allows a specific address to be assigned to a specific host. The difference is that instead of an administrator physically assigning the address on the device itself, DHCP distributes a specific address to the device every time an address is requested. A static DHCP assignment means that when a request is heard from a certain MAC address, the DHCP server looks for the specific IP address to assign.

Therefore, a host given a static assignment gets the same IP address every time it makes a request. Going one step further, static addresses do not have to fall under the same lease process as dynamic addresses because they are always associated with a single host.

Regardless of the method used, DHCP servers can provide IP address, subnet mask, default gateway, DNS, TFTP, and WINs server addresses, as well as many additional components. DHCP servers can also pass vendor-specific device configuration information using option codes, and provide a mechanism for automatic address renewal.

Many Internet service providers (ISPs) and LAN administrators use the leasing mechanism to oversubscribe their address ranges, signing more clients than they have addresses to support. Further, DHCP reduces network administration workload because clients need not be configured manually. Microsoft clients, such as Windows 98 and Windows 2000, configure themselves "out of the box" to use DHCP when the IP protocol stack is installed. Other OSs that run IP, such as Linux and Mac OS, support DHCP as well. RFC 2131 specifies DHCP.

DHCP Operation

Whereas BOOTP defines only two steps (client BOOTREQUEST and server BOOTREPLY), DHCP RFC 2131 defines eight. Four of these steps enable the client to successfully acquire a lease from a server: DHCPDISCOVER, DHCPOFFER, DHCPREQUEST, and DHCPACK. You will learn about these steps in the following sections.

As in BOOTP, a DHCP client requests an address and a server responds. The DHCP Client Initialization Diagram illustrates the DHCP client/server interaction when a client initializes.

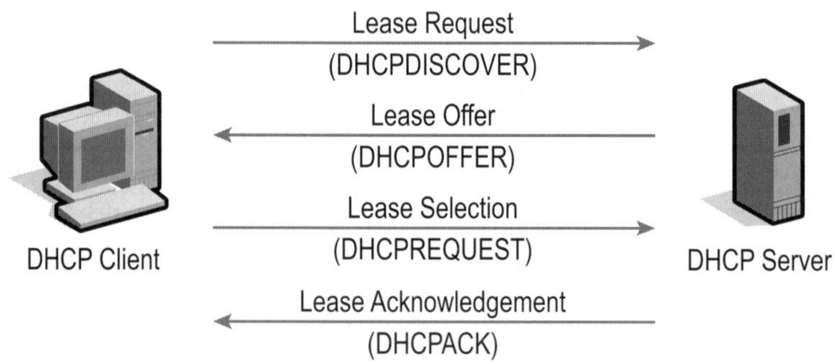

DHCP Client Initialization

When a DHCP client first initializes, it loads a limited version of TCP/IP and takes the following lease acquisition steps to obtain an IP address lease from a DHCP server:

1. The client broadcasts a DHCPDISCOVER message to its local subnet. At this point, the client is in the initialization state.
2. A DHCP server (or servers) responds to the DHCPDISCOVER message with a DHCP offer (DHCPOFFER) message.
3. If no server responds, the client does not initialize TCP/IP. Instead, it continues to resend DHCPDISCOVER messages until it receives a response.

   Note that a feature built into Windows 2000 and later, called "IP autoconfiguration," allows these DHCP clients to alternately select an address from the Microsoft-reserved 169.254.0.0/16 network. Thus, if a client cannot locate a DHCP server, it can still enable TCP/IP by choosing one of these addresses. Clients can communicate on the local network until a DHCP server becomes available. The clients continue to transmit DHCPDISCOVER packets every five minutes until a server answers.
4. When the client receives an offer (or offers), it enters the SELECTING state. It then selects from the received offers a preferred offer, and builds a reply. If more than one server responds to the DHCPREQUEST, the client normally chooses the first offer it receives.
5. The client enters the REQUESTING state by replying to the selected server with a DHCP request (DHCPREQUEST) message.

6. The offering server replies to the DHCPREQUEST with a DHCP acknowledgment (DHCPACK) message.
7. When the client receives the DHCPACK, it configures its TCP/IP properties and joins the network, entering the BOUND state.

In some cases, a DHCP server can return a DHCP negative acknowledgment (DHCPNAK) message in response to the client's DHCPREQUEST message. This occurs if a client requests a duplicate or invalid address. The client initialization process fails in this case, and the client must restart from Step 1.

Review Questions

1. Which protocol would be used when the IP address is known, but MAC address information needs to be determined?
   a. ARP
   b. RARP
   c. ICMP
   d. PING
2. What is the protocol number associated with TCP?
   a. 17
   b. 6
   c. 9
   d. 12
3. Which ICMP message represents a response to a ping command?
   a. echo request
   b. echo response
   c. echo reply
   d. ping reply
4. Which IP header is used by the ICMP protocol to indicate that the transmission should be dropped because it exceeded its life?
   a. TTL
   b. Destination unreachable
   c. echo reply
   d. ARP
5. What IP service distributes an IP address to a device based on its location in the network or its MAC address?
   a. RARP
   b. DHCP
   c. IP
   d. Router

6. Which protocols are found at the Network Layer? (Choose all that apply.)
   a. TCP
   b. IP
   c. UDP
   d. ICMP
   e. RARP
   f. HTTP
   g. ARP
7. Which values represent a current IP address? (Choose two.)
   a. 48 bits
   b. 32 bits
   c. 4 octets
   d. 6 bytes
8. Which terms best describe IP transmissions? (Choose two.)
   a. Best-effort delivery
   b. Guaranteed delivery
   c. Connection-oriented delivery
   d. Connectionless delivery
9. What is the ToS byte in an IP header used for?
   a. Identifying the segment number of the packet
   b. Defining the IP route
   c. Identifying the correct exit interface
   d. Providing precedence and QoS information useful in route selection
10. RARP is best described as which of the following?
    a. Determining the IP address when the MAC address is known
    b. Changing the MAC address from one destination to another
    c. Getting the MAC address when the IP address is known
    d. Dynamically learning network routes

Extended Activities

1. Match the following definitions with the correct ICMP process

   When transmitting to an unknown address, the packet is dropped and this ICMP message is sent back to a host ____________________

   The response provided when a ping command is successful ____________________

   Message transmitted when the TTL field in a packet has expired ____________________

   Used by the ping command to indicate communication ability ____________________

   Used for flow control to let the sending device know the destination buffer is full ____________________

   Checks the time is takes to traverse a segment of network ____________________

   Used when a packet has the wrong path and must be rerouted over the same interface through which it was received ____________________

   Request by a router to get addressing information about a network ____________________

   Used when a bad packet structure is identified ____________________

   Routers use this ICMP to learn about the network mask of an address ____________________

   a. Echo Request

   b. Echo Reply

   c. Address Request/Address Reply

   d. Subnet Mask Request

   e. Destination Unreachable

   f. Source Quench

   g. Timestamp/Timestamp Reply

   h. Time Exceeded

   i. Parameter Problem

   j. Redirect

Lesson 2—Transport Layer Overview

This lesson takes a detailed look at how the Transport Layer Internet Protocols work. When data must be sent between two applications on an IP network, the applications use the services of TCP and IP, plus local area network (LAN) and wide area network (WAN) protocols for the particular network.

TCP is the connection-oriented, reliable protocol most often used when transmitting data. TCP requires a lot of overhead for the connection process, flow control, acknowledgments, segmenting, and sequencing. Data is not delay-sensitive; therefore, being slowed by overhead is not a problem. However, for real-time transmissions or for transmissions that happen frequently, TCP services are overkill.

Although many people in the data networking world are inclined to call everything TCP/IP, it is only half the equation. User Datagram Protocol (UDP) is also a Transport Layer protocol, used for connectionless transmissions. It is normally coupled with applications such as Simple Network Management Protocol (SNMP), Domain Name System (DNS), routing protocols, and real-time transmissions such as voice and video. UDP cuts out all the overhead by relying upon upper or lower layer protocols for assistance in circuit establishment and flow control.

This lesson ends with a discussion of the logical, Transport Layer port numbers used to identify the upper-layer information to the receiving system. The port number is inserted by the sending device to indicate the Application Layer information. The destination device "listens" for requests on these logical ports to provide specific services. In addition, the ports can be used to filter traffic through a firewall or speed it through the network using layer 4 switching capabilities.

Objectives

At the end of this lesson you will be able to:

- Discuss TCP functionality
- Identify the components of a TCP header
- Discuss UDP functionality
- Identify the components of a UDP header
- Identify source and destination port numbers

Key Point

TCP and UDP ports are logically assigned numbers that represent a particular application. They do not reference a physical port on a network device.

TCP Components

Remember from the Host-to-Host Layer discussion at the beginning of Lesson 1 that TCP is connection-oriented and reliable. What does this really mean in networking terms? TCP manages data transfers between different systems. It does this with a number of very important functions, including connection establishment, segmentation, sequencing, and acknowledgments, as well as flow control and windowing. You can see some of these functions in the TCP segment header shown later in this section.

Connection Establishment

When data is being sent from one computer to another using TCP, a connection must first be established. Because TCP is a connection-oriented protocol, the two communicating computers must first create a virtual connection before any data is transmitted. This process is called a "three-way handshake" and is shown on the Three-Way Handshake Diagram.

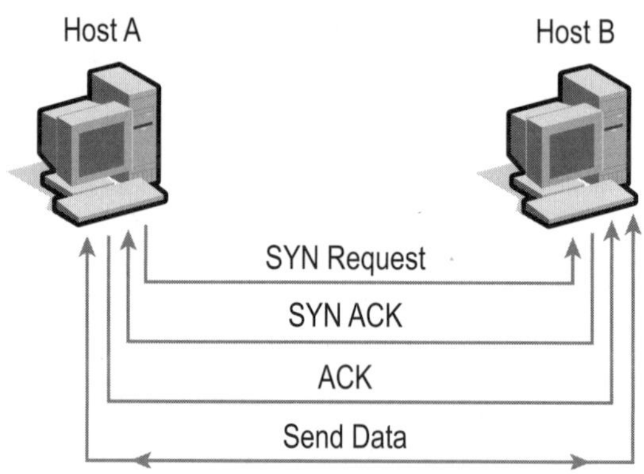

Three-Way Handshake

The process is as follows:

1. The sending host, Host A, sends a synchronization request that includes a sequence number, for instance 250. The first transmission establishes the initial sequence number (ISN). This number is used to track the connection and maintain orderly transmissions.

   As the Three-Way Handshake Diagram shows, the sending host transmits a sequence number and synchronization request, for example (seq 250, SYN). To keep the diagram simple, it shows the steps but not the numbers.

2. The receiving system host, Host B, responds with its own sequence number (500) and an acknowledgment of Host A's sequence number, incremented by one (251). This tells Host A that the request was successful and communication can be established. In response, the receiving host transmits (seq 500, ack 251, SYN, ACK) back to the original sender.

   Notice that the sequence number is made up by the receiving device, and the acknowledgment number is the sender's sequence number, incremented by one. This tells the sender what the receiving host expects as the next segment. This second step is considered a synchronization acknowledgment.

3. Upon receipt of the acknowledgment, Host A sends an acknowledgment of Host B's sequence number (501), which is also incremented by one. At this point, the virtual circuit is created and data transmission can take place. To finish the example, the transmission is from the sender to receiver, as follows: (seq 251, ack 501, ACK).

   Notice that the segment number is the same as the one provided in the acknowledgment during the last step. Also note that the acknowledgment number is incremented by one to indicate that the synchronization is complete.

Now that you have read all the steps, here is a more succinct view of this process, using the same example.

Step 1 HOST A → seg 250, SYN → HOST B

Step 2 HOST A ← seq 500, ack 251, SYN, ACK ← HOST B

Step 3 HOST A → seg 251, ack 501, ACK → HOST B

TCP uses individual sequence numbers instead of relying on some type of synchronization signal from a network. To verify that a particular virtual circuit is valid, it continues to use the sequence numbers created in the original connection establishment throughout the transmission. If a significant delay in transmission ensues, one or both hosts may request to verify the connection with another synchronization process.

Segmentation, Sequencing, and Acknowledgments

TCP is responsible for breaking upper-layer data into manageable segments. When data is segmented by TCP, a sequence number and forward reference acknowledgment are added. At the destination end, the host resequences the message as the segments are received.

The receiving host uses the forward reference acknowledgment to indicate that it received the last segment and asks the sending host to send the next one. Any unacknowledged segments are automatically retransmitted by the sender.

In addition, if an acknowledgment is not received within a specific period of time, the sending host retransmits. The Acknowledgment and Windowing Diagram illustrates how these two components work together to provide a more efficient use of the network bandwidth.

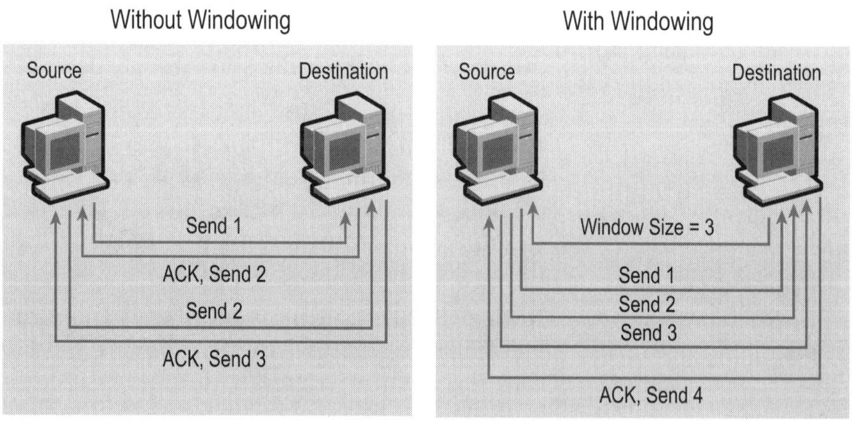

Acknowledgment and Windowing

Flow Control and Windowing

The process of acknowledgment can be bandwidth-intensive, as shown on the first part of the Acknowledgment and Windowing Diagram. Without a window set, one segment is sent and one acknowledgment is the reply. This would take place for the entire transmission and be a waste of network bandwidth. With the high-capacity devices on networks today, it makes sense to provide a more efficient means of data flow control.

When a session is first established, the receiving host reports a "window" size. The window size represents the number of bytes that can be buffered on the receiving system's NIC before an acknowledgment is sent. This can dramatically reduce the amount of network traffic and still provides an extremely reliable transport mechanism.

Window sizes can vary throughout the connection. Each acknowledgment may provide the same or different window size, called a "sliding window," based on buffering capabilities or network congestion. This allows the best balance of network throughput.

Notice on the "without windowing" side, from the Acknowledgment and Windowing Diagram, that the sender would send one transmission and wait for the acknowledgment. Then it would send the next transmission and wait for the next acknowledgment. Think of this as eating in a strange restaurant, where the waiter brings you each bite of food, lets you sample it, and then allows you to order another bite. It would take a long time to eat a meal this way, as it would take a long time to complete a transmission this way.

On the side "with windowing," the systems can communicate how many segments can be sent before the acknowledgment is transmitted. As you can see in the diagram, the systems agreed on three segments: the sender will send three transmissions before expecting an acknowledgment.

This would be like ordering an appetizer, getting your salad, then getting the main course, and finally dessert. Although three segments are shown here for simplicity, in reality the window size is indicated in octets.

With this window technique the waiter would bring out whole plates of food, one at a time, and ask if you wanted anything else. This is a much more efficient use of the waiter's time and yours, not too mention how much traffic is cut out going back and forth.

Terminating a Connection

When transmission is complete, the sending device performs an orderly shutdown of the connection. This lets the receiving system know that no more information will be received. The steps are somewhat similar to those performed during the three-way handshake. The termination steps are as follows:

Step 1 HOST A → seq 300, FIN = 1 → HOST B

Step 2 HOST A ← seq 550, ack 301, FIN = 1 ← HOST B

Step 3 HOST A → seq 301, ack 551, FIN = 0 → HOST B

Step 4 Connection terminated

Notice that the sequence and acknowledgment works just as it did during the three-way handshake. When termination is requested, the control field changes from SYN, ACK, or both to FIN, indicating that the transmission is finished. If the hosts want to transmit information again, they must establish a new connection with another three-way handshake. Look for the control fields in the TCP header to see where the hosts set this information.

TCP Header

As you saw earlier in this lesson, upper-layer data is broken into smaller segments at the Host-to-Host or Transport Layer. If TCP is the protocol used for connection-oriented services and reliability, a TCP header is added to the segment. The TCP header is 20 bytes long, and provides important information such as sequence and acknowledgment numbers, source and destination ports (for upper-layer applications), window size, error control, and other possible options.

The TCP Header Diagram shows the fields included in this type of header.

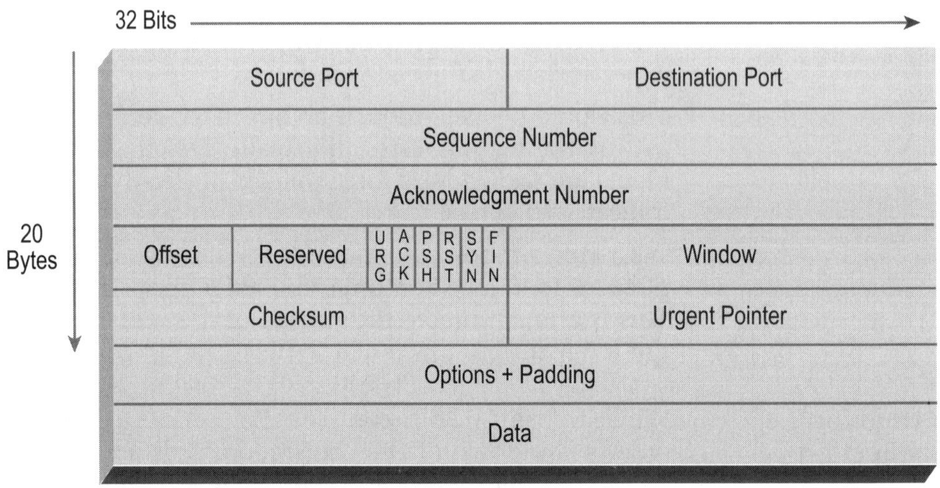

TCP Header

The TCP header fields are as follows:

- **Source Port (16 bits)**—Used as a reference to identify the sending process; a randomly generated number.
- **Destination Port (16 bits)**—Identifies the receiving application; selected from the well-known or vendor-specific application port numbers.
- **Sequence Number (32 bits)**—Assigned to the segment to ensure proper resequencing and acknowledgement of the segment to which it is assigned.
- **Acknowledgment Number (32 bits)**—Identifies the segment expected next. It is a forward reference number.
- **Header Length (Offset)**—Represents the number of 32-bit words in the header.
- **Reserved (6 bits)**—Are always set to zero.
- **Code Bits (6 bits)**—Establishes and controls setup and termination of the session; from left to right, the code bits are:
  - URG—Indicates Urgent Pointer field is significant
  - ACK—Indicates Acknowledgment field is activated
  - PSH—Used for data transmissions
  - RST—Used to resequence the connection
  - SYN—Used to sequence numbers or for three-way handshake
  - FIN—Indicates no more data from sender; terminates connection
- **Window (16 bits)**—Identifies the sliding window buffer of the receiving device.
- **Checksum (16 bits)**—Provides the calculated error check of the header and data fields.
- **Urgent Pointer (16 bits)**—Identifies the end of data marked "urgent."
- **Options + Padding (0 to 32 bits)**—Can include information about the maximum TCP segment size.
- **Data (varies)**—Consists of upper-layer protocol data—that is, the information being sent.

It is helpful to see the contents of a TCP header for a transmission that was sent across a production network. The TCP Header Screen Capture was taken from a protocol analyzer. It shows how each TCP field is displayed and the values that are typical to each section.

```
⊞ Frame 390 (54 on wire, 54 captured)
⊞ Ethernet II
⊞ Internet Protocol, Src Addr: 135.35.88.52 (135.35.88.52), Dst Addr: 198.152.12.67 (198.152.12.67)
⊟ Transmission Control Protocol, Src Port: 1573 (1573), Dst Port: 8000 (8000), Seq: 615302369, Ack: 355811802, Len: 0
    Source port: 1573 (1573)
    Destination port: 8000 (8000)
    Sequence number: 615302369
    Acknowledgement number: 355811802
    Header length: 20 bytes
  ⊟ Flags: 0x0011 (FIN, ACK)
      0... .... = Congestion Window Reduced (CWR): Not set
      .0.. .... = ECN-Echo: Not set
      ..0. .... = Urgent: Not set
      ...1 .... = Acknowledgment: Set
      .... 0... = Push: Not set
      .... .0.. = Reset: Not set
      .... ..0. = Syn: Not set
      .... ...1 = Fin: Set
    Window size: 64211
    Checksum: 0x9cca (correct)
```

TCP Header

UDP Components

Although TCP provides for complete reliability when data is transmitted through a network, it also requires a lot of overhead, not just in the header size, but in the requirements for session establishment, creation of a virtual circuit, sequencing, and acknowledgments. For data, this process is necessary to ensure successful transfer. However, for some network functions, that kind of overhead is just too expensive (in terms of header size or delay).

Thus, many upper-layer protocols provide their own reliability and error-checking mechanisms. If they were to use TCP, the redundancy would be a waste. Instead, UDP provides an excellent alternative, replacing reliability with lower overhead and greater speed.

Keep in mind that UDP provides no flow control, acknowledgments, segmenting, sequencing, or connection establishment. That is what makes it unreliable and connectionless. When data is sent from the upper layers to be transmitted by UDP, a small header is added and it is sent.

Real-time transmissions like voice and video commonly use UDP for transmission. This may be confusing since UDP is unreliable; however, in reality, UDP is the best method for this type of traffic. Voice and video transmission rely on other protocols to provide circuit establishment and flow control. In most cases, TCP is involved in establishing the end-to-end connection that the devices use to communicate.

Once connected, the transmission headers can be streamlined for faster delivery. In addition, real-time transmissions should not be retransmitted, if dropped or incomplete. Instead, it is better for the viewer or listener to predict what the information was. Continually sending acknowledgments would slow down real-time traffic and, furthermore, acknowledgments are unnecessary because the sender does not retransmit in this environment. Thus, UDP provides a low-overhead, efficient means of getting real-time and other constant traffic through the network.

UDP is also often used with: routing protocols, SNMP traffic that sends constant network notifications or updates, and the DNS name resolution process. In the first two examples, if a transmission gets dropped or the content is corrupt, another update is sent on a predefined time interval. Therefore, it is not necessary to be reliable by providing all the TCP services. As for DNS, if a name resolution process fails, the client would be informed and would probably make a new name resolution request.

UDP Header

A UDP header is always the same size: 8 bytes. This includes four UDP components and the data. The UDP Header Diagram shows these fields.

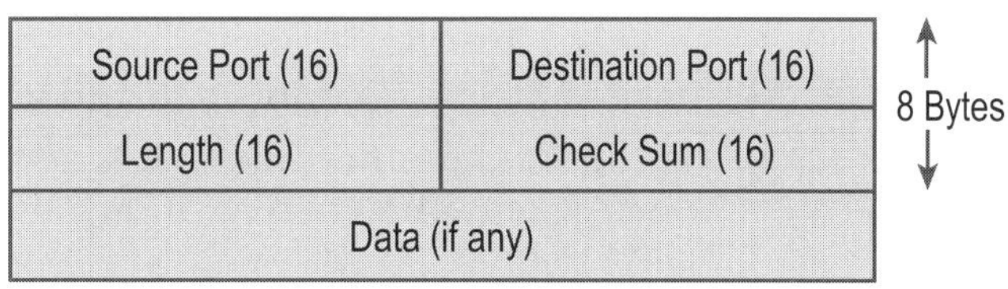

UDP Header

The UDP header fields are as follows:

- **Source Port (16 bits)**—Used as a reference to identify the sending process; a randomly generated number
- **Destination Port (16 bits)**—Identifies the receiving application; selected from the well-known or vendor-specific application port numbers
- **Length (16 bits)**—Provides the total length of the UDP header and data

- **Checksum (16 bits)**—Provides the calculated error check of the header and data fields
- **Data (varies)**—Consists of upper-layer protocol data

Notice that only the most important fields are used from the TCP header. Everything else is stripped off to provide a small, clean UDP header. Fewer fields mean less overhead and less bandwidth use.

The UDP Header Screen Capture shows the simple contents found in the header fields when UDP is the transport protocol. Notice that there are substantially fewer lines and values associated with the UDP header, when compared to the TCP Header Screen Capture shown earlier.

```
⊞ Frame 17 (214 on wire, 68 captured)
⊞ Ethernet II
⊞ Internet Protocol, Src Addr: 192.168.10.19 (192.168.10.19), Dst Addr: 192.168.10.100 (192.168.10.100)
⊟ User Datagram Protocol, Src Port: 2120 (2120), Dst Port: 3010 (3010)
    Source port: 2120 (2120)
    Destination port: 3010 (3010)
    Length: 180
    Checksum: 0x6c8b
  Data (26 bytes)
```

UDP Header

Source and Destination Port Numbers

Notice that the first two fields of both the TCP and UDP headers are the source and destination port numbers. They are important. The source port is a number higher than 1023 that is dynamically assigned by the sending host. This helps the communication devices maintain connection and identify the proper session.

The destination port number is assigned based on the IP application requested. This port number tells the receiving Transport Layer what to do with the data upon arrival.

As a standard, software developers created and organized a list of port numbers controlled by the Internet Assigned Numbers Authority (IANA). Port numbers are assigned in ranges, which have been given the following specifications:

- Numbers 0 through 1023—Well-known ports
- Numbers 1024 through 49151—Registered ports used for vendor-specific applications
- Numbers 49152 through 65535—Dynamically assigned ports

Although only a small list of all possible assignments, the Port Numbers Diagram shows several TCP and UDP ports. Notice that the port number assigned to DNS straddles both TCP and UDP. This is because DNS uses TCP for server zone transfers (database updates between DNS servers). It then uses UDP for name resolution. (For a complete listing of well-known port numbers, refer to **http://www.iana.org/assignments/port-numbers**.)

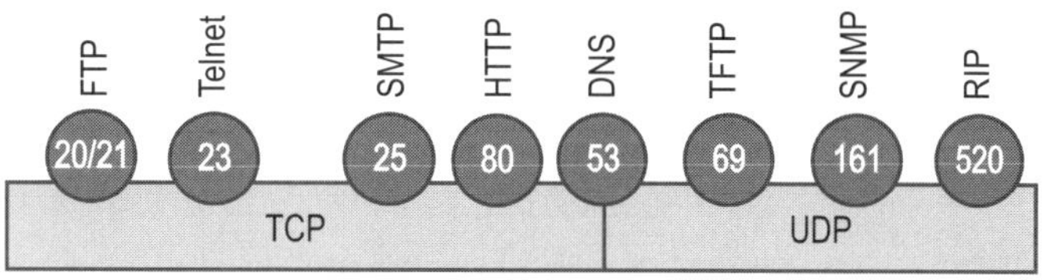

Port Numbers

Port numbers can be helpful for filtering traffic through a firewall or access list. A firewall can be a service that runs on a router, server, or network appliance that filters traffic moving between networks. In most cases, the traffic moves between a corporate network and the Internet. Access lists are test statements that match traffic to determine if it should be permitted or denied transport. Access lists are more commonly used within the LAN.

In either case, port numbers logically identify traffic that can then be used for filtering. For instance, the TCP port number 25 (SMTP) is often opened in the firewall to allow e-mail to be sent and received. On the other hand, an administrator may want to block Telnet traffic from entering the network from the Internet, and therefore denies TCP port number 23 (Telnet).

Having 65,535 possible port numbers would require a lot of administration to determine which ones to use. In most cases, they are all denied, and only certain ones are activated or allowed on an as-needed basis.

Port numbers can also be useful to multilayer switching devices that can read the port number and determine the best path to get to that destination. This goes beyond the IP address and provides a connection to the upper-layer information for faster transport of certain applications.

Review Questions

1. What port number is used for telnet services?
   a. 23
   b. 26
   c. 80
   d. 21
2. If an administrator wanted to prevent FTP traffic from entering the network from the Internet, what port number should be blocked in the firewall?
   a. 21
   b. 23
   c. 25
   d. 28
3. Which of the following are characteristics of TCP? (Choose two.)
   a. Unreliable
   b. Uses acknowledgments
   c. Provides no flow control
   d. Connection-oriented
4. Which transport protocol works best for real-time transmissions?
   a. TCP
   b. UDP
   c. IP
   d. HTTP
5. What is the IP port range called for numbers from 0 – 1023?
   a. Registered ports
   b. Well-known ports
   c. Designated ports
   d. Dynamic ports

6. Which fields are in a UDP header? (Choose two.)
   a. Source port
   b. Acknowledgment
   c. Sequence number
   d. Destination port
7. Which value tells TCP how to arrange the segments back into the original transmission?
   a. Segment number
   b. Source port number
   c. Sequence number
   d. Acknowledgment number
8. What is the length of a source or destination port?
   a. 8 bits
   b. 4 bytes
   c. 16 bits
   d. 32 bits
9. What does a system do before transmitting using TCP?
   a. Performs a three-way handshake
   b. Sends a ping packet
   c. Sends a hello packet
   d. Listens on the proper port
10. What is the description of a window when using TCP?
    a. A window is the connection process between two devices.
    b. A window is the opportunity to send before the connection is lost.
    c. A window is the number of segments that can be received before the destination device sends an acknowledgment.
    d. A window is the interface through which the user accesses the application connected to TCP.

11. What is the first step to make a connection to another device using TCP?
    a. Sending host transmits a SYN
    b. Sending host transmits an ACK
    c. Sending host transmits a SYN, ACK
    d. Sending host transmits a FIN
    e. None of the above
12. What is the first step to make a connection to another device using UDP?
    a. Sending host transmits a SYN
    b. Sending host transmits an ACK
    c. Sending host transmits a SYN, ACK
    d. Sending host transmits a FIN
    e. None of the above
13. If the connection was established with an initial sequence number of 200 and the receiving host set its sequence number to 950, which connection establishment process is correct for the second step?
    a. seq 950, ack 201, SYN, ACK
    b. seq 200, ack 950, SYN, ACK
    c. seq 201, ack 951, SYN, ACK
    d. seq 200, ack 951, ACK
14. When TCP is ready to close a connection, what happens first?
    a. The sending host transmits a FIN, ACK.
    b. The receiving host transmits a FIN.
    c. The sending host transmits a FIN.
    d. The receiving host transmits a FIN, ACK.

15. What happens if a transmission sent using TCP does not reach its destination?
    a. The sending system does not get an acknowledgment and retransmits.
    b. The receiving system recognizes that it is missing a segment and requests a retransmission.
    c. IP running on a router recognizes the dropped packet and recovers it from memory.
    d. The segment is lost because IP cannot recover it.

Extended Activities

1. Match the following applications with the correct transport protocol by writing them in the correct side of the table.

   HTTP, DNS name resolution, SNMP, SMTP, FTP, TFTP

TCP	UDP

2. Write the port number for each protocol next to the application in the table in Extended Activity 1.
3. Copy the six flag code bits used in a TCP header and write a brief explanation of each in the space provided.

____

____

____

____

____

____

4. Match the following by writing either TCP or UDP after each description.

   Connection-oriented ___________

   Built-in flow control ___________

   Low overhead, efficient ___________

   Reliable ___________

   Unreliable ___________

   No acknowledgments ___________

   Segments and sequences ___________

   Connectionless ___________

   Sends acknowledgments ___________

   Large header, many fields ___________

   Used for real-time transmissions ___________

5. Using the TCP Screen Capture, answer the following questions.

```
⊞ Frame 390 (54 on wire, 54 captured)
⊞ Ethernet II
⊞ Internet Protocol, Src Addr: 135.35.88.52 (135.35.88.52), Dst Addr: 198.152.12.67 (198.152.12.67)
⊟ Transmission Control Protocol, Src Port: 1573 (1573), Dst Port: 8000 (8000), Seq: 615302369, Ack: 355811802, Len: 0
    Source port: 1573 (1573)
    Destination port: 8000 (8000)
    Sequence number: 615302369
    Acknowledgement number: 355811802
    Header length: 20 bytes
  ⊟ Flags: 0x0011 (FIN, ACK)
      0... .... = Congestion Window Reduced (CWR): Not set
      .0.. .... = ECN-Echo: Not set
      ..0. .... = Urgent: Not set
      ...1 .... = Acknowledgment: Set
      .... 0... = Push: Not set
      .... .0.. = Reset: Not set
      .... ..0. = Syn: Not set
      .... ...1 = Fin: Set
    Window size: 64211
    Checksum: 0x9cca (correct)
```

a. What is the destination port number?

   ____

b. What is the source port number?

   ____

c. What is the destination IP address?

   ____

d. What is the source IP address?

____

e. Which transport protocol is used?

____

f. What is the flag fields set to?

____

g. Is the content of the header validated as correct or incorrect?

____

Lesson 3—Upper-Layer IP Applications

As you learned earlier in this module, the upper three layers of the OSI model are grouped together. The services of the Application, Presentation, and Session layers are all required when protocol applications are defined. This lesson looks at the IP suite protocols that provide file transfer, network management, e-mail and Web services.

Objectives

At the end of this lesson, you will be able to:

- Define the IP application protocols used for file transfer
- Define the IP application protocols used for network management
- Define the IP application protocols used for e-mail services
- Define the IP application protocols used for Web services

Key Point

IP applications provide a user interface and program functionality. In addition to those mentioned here, there are many other standard and vendor-specific IP applications.

File Transfer Applications

The two protocols used for file transfer are File Transfer Protocol (FTP) and Trivial File Transfer Protocol (TFTP). They are necessary for sending or receiving files between different system types. Both protocols provide a user interface that allows the person transmitting files an option for when to use one application over the other. Each protocol has its own characteristics and specific functions, as discussed next.

FTP

FTP was originally defined by Request for Comment (RFC) 959. It uses the TCP transport protocol to provide connection services and reliable transmission on ports 20 and 21. FTP allows administrative control of file systems by requiring a login authentication using a specific user ID (or anonymous for general access).

The administrator can then define what file/directory levels can be accessed and what FTP services can be used. This protocol provides a complete set of file transfer services, including displaying a list of directories, files, and file sizes. It allows for copying, moving, creating, and deleting directories and files.

You can use FTP at a command line in many operating systems. To do so, you must have knowledge of the commands necessary to retrieve (get) and send (put) files from another system. You can also do this using a graphical user interface (GUI) that allows you to drag and drop files and folders from the local system to the remote location and visa versa.

Many Web servers also use FTP for file downloads. When the new process is initiated, the browser window changes from HTTP to FTP with the appropriate address location. Using FTP through a Web browser may eliminate the need to log in, but it provides only limited access to download specific files without the host of other FTP functions.

TFTP

The word trivial in the name indicates that this protocol is simple, requires no authentication, and is transported using UDP. TFTP does not require a login, thus security is minimal, and TFTP needs no user intervention. Unlike FTP, it does not provide any browsing or directory access features, only send and receive.

Diskless workstations use TFTP along with the Bootstrap Protocol (BOOTP), discussed later in this lesson, to initialize. Because TFTP is simple and small, it can be embedded in a device's read-only memory (ROM). Network devices, such as routers and switches, use TFTP for software and firmware upgrades and can download configuration information from a central TFTP server. RFC 1350 defines TFTP, which uses port 69.

Network Management Applications

A number of protocols are used to aid in network administration by allowing configuration access, network monitoring, name resolution, and address assignment.

Telnet

Telnet is a terminal emulation program that allows a Telnet client to access another device as if the client were directly connected terminal console. A Telnet session can be established with a direct cable connection, by means of a modem connection or through the network or the Internet using TCP/IP. Telnet provides a command line or menu-driven terminal screen as the user interface.

Telnet configures and manages switches, routers, and many other network devices. Microsoft Windows Operating Systems offer Telnet capabilities in the **Communications | Accessories** section. This is the Microsoft's license of Hilgraeve Inc.'s HyperTerminal program. Numerous other Telnet applications come with an operating system and can be purchased as a separate application or are sharewhare, freely available for download from the Internet. RFC 854 defines Telnet.

SNMP

Simple Network Management Protocol (SNMP) is a standardized network management scheme. A central network management station (NMS) uses SNMP to collect data from other network computers or software processes called "agents." SNMP defines the collected data's format; it is up to the central station or network manager to interpret it.

SNMP features low network resource requirements, portability, and widespread acceptance. SNMP includes an agent and administrative component. The agent is configured to detect (trap) critical network issues, such as high bandwidth use, downed links or servers, loss of communication, or high error counts.

The agent then sends a message to the administrative component indicating the problem. This can be logged for informational purposes, or specific actions can be programmed to respond and attempt to solve the issue. SNMP uses UDP for transport because response information is frequent and the connection-oriented nature of TCP would require too much time and overhead. RFC 1157 defines SNMP.

RMON

Remote Monitoring (RMON) supplements SNMP. Whereas SNMP gathers network information from a single Management Information Base (MIB) and presents to the monitoring station a view of a collection of separate entities, RMON defines additional MIBs that allow monitoring stations to view the network as a whole. RMON uses RMON probes, sometimes called RMON agents, which are either firmware built into a network device or a special hardware device designed to monitor a network segment and its devices.

An RMON probe tracks and analyzes network traffic, and gathers statistics, reporting this information to the monitoring station. RFC 1757 defines RMON and RFC 2021 defines the more advanced, Layer 3 RMON2.

DNS

Domain Name System (DNS) is virtually a necessity for Internet access because it translates the easily remembered domain and hostnames into IP addresses used to locate a network device. Before DNS services were available, systems relied on host files to associate names to IP addresses. This became difficult to administer for a large number of devices or if there was an address change on the network. Every host file on every workstation in the network would have to be updated with new addresses or changes.

DNS provides a centralized name resolution database running on a DNS server. Client applications, such as Telnet or browsers, contact DNS servers when using fully qualified domain names (FQDNs), also called Universal Resource Locators (URLs), to resolve these names to IP addresses.

IP uses numerical logical addresses to find hosts across a routed network. Thus, to find a server on the Internet, the application needs to know the server's IP address. DNS looks up the URL, for example **http://www.cisco.com**, in its database and returns to the client the corresponding IP address (198.133.219.25).

A DNS server can be located inside a corporate network to resolve both internal and external addresses. Public DNS servers offer address resolution services on the Internet by providing pointers to high-level domains such as .com, .net, .biz, .org, and others.

DNS uses both TCP and UDP at the Transport Layer. A DNS server uses TCP when performing a zone transfer. This is the process that copies a DNS database in whole or parts to another DNS server. Because it can be a large amount of data, TCP is necessary to ensure reliable transport from one system to the other.

DNS uses UDP when providing name resolution services. UDP is unreliable, but name resolution is not a mission-critical transmission. If you type in a Web address and it does not resolve to an IP address because the request is lost, you would press the **Enter** key again, and the resolution process would be retried.

With the millions of resolution requests a busy public DNS server receives each day, it would slow the process substantially if TCP were used for resolution. In any case, for both zone transfers with TCP and name resolution services with UDP, DNS uses port number 53. For more information, RFCs 1034 and 1035 define DNS.

BOOTP

Bootstrap Protocol (BOOTP) is a method by which diskless TCP/IP hosts can automatically find their IP address, find a BOOTP server's address, and download a file from which they can boot. A single BOOTP message specifies many items a workstation might need at startup, including its gateway to the Internet (a router port address) and a DNS server's address.

BOOTP is more than just IP addressing information. It can download entire operating systems and configuration files to an end-device that does not store this information locally. RFC 951 describes BOOTP.

DHCP

Dynamic Host Configuration Protocol (DHCP) is a protocol TCP/IP clients use to locate and download IP addressing and configuration information. It is similar to BOOTP in that it allows a client to download information.

However, BOOTP was designed for downloading the operating functions of a device. DHCP expects that the client requestor has an operating system and therefore transmits only configuration information such as IP address, subnet mask, default gateway, DNS, TFTP, and WINs server addresses, as well as other components. Whereas a BOOTP administrator must manually identify requesting hosts and their corresponding information, DHCP blindly passes information to any host that requests it. DHCP servers can pass vendor-specific device configuration information using option codes and provide a mechanism for automatic address renewal, based on a lease period.

Mail Services

The protocols in mail services allow electronic mail messages to be sent, received, opened in different e-mail viewing tools, embed graphics or additional formatting, attach files, provide e-mail security, and convert between different e-mail formats. Most systems send e-mail to a server first. If they send messages directly to a client and the client is unavailable, the message may be lost or transmissions may fail.

Sending messages to a central location like an e-mail server, allows the message to wait until the client needs to view the information. The messages are stored on the server until the client requests them. Then the server is responsible for allowing the client to view the messages or download them directly to the local machine for storage.

To use a postal system analogy, SMTP is like a mail carrier, responsible for transporting mail between e-mail systems. Post Office Protocol (POP) and Internet Message Access Protocol 4 (IMAP4) are like the post office, responsible for receiving, storing, and forwarding mail. Multipurpose Internet Mail Extension (MIME) has the ability to send packages, in addition to letters, through the post office.

SMTP

Simple Mail Transfer Protocol (SMTP) is the Internet standard protocol for transferring e-mail messages from source to destination. SMTP relies on TCP for reliable transport. Unlike other communication protocols that use binary codes in structured fields, SMTP uses plain English headers.

SMTP defines a set of processes to transfer e-mail messages between mail systems; it does not define the programs used to store messages on a server. Many different messaging platforms exist today that can send and receive e-mail and other associated information like attachments, calendar items, task lists, voice mail, and so forth. SMTP is only used for transmission; it is not used for storage or client retrieval.

SMTP is generic enough to be used by the majority of IP-based e-mail systems. However, there are proprietary mail systems that use their own protocols for transport. Mail gateway software is necessary to convert between non-SMTP and SMTP-based systems. RFC 821 defines SMTP.

MIME

MIME is used with SMTP for supporting more than just standard ASCII text files. Using MIME, many different types of data can be sent through e-mail. Examples of MIME-supported data types are:

- **Binary information**—Word-processed documents or spreadsheets
- **Graphic images**—Graphic Interchange Format (GIF) or Joint Photographic Experts Group (JPEG) files
- **Video**—Moving Pictures Expert Group (MPEG) files
- **Audio**—Waveform Audio (WAV) files

MIME is an SMTP extension. It enables multiple objects that represent body text, character sets, and attachment information to be encoded and transported within a single message. Exceptions include ASCII, images, and audio fragments. RFC 1341 initially described MIME; this has been superseded by RFCs 1521 and 2045.

MIME creates an "envelope" around the attachment consisting of several header fields that indicate the MIME version, the message's content, the type of encoding used, and other extended fields. Although MIME does use an encoding technique before transmission, it is widely available and not very secure.

S/MIME

Secure/MIME (S/MIME) is a specification for secure electronic messaging. In 1995, software vendors created S/MIME to solve a real problem: interception and forgery of e-mail. Protecting sensitive data is a concern, especially in a world where e-mail has become a common communication method.

The S/MIME specification was designed to be easily integrated into e-mail and messaging products. S/MIME uses digital signatures and public-key encryption to ensure that hackers do not tamper with messages in transit.

S/MIME encrypts the message and encloses it in a digital envelope that can only be opened by someone holding the sender's public key. S/MIME has replaced MIME functionality while providing security in the majority of e-mail applications today.

POP

POP is used to transfer information from a mail server to a user's computer so users can read, delete, or otherwise manage their e-mail; POP3 is the latest version. A POP mail server stores e-mail until the client requests it. The user accesses the mail server by means of a desktop e-mail program, such as Lotus Notes, Eudora, or Outlook, and downloads messages. The POP3 server is responsible for authorizing access in the form of a user name and password.

IMAP4

IMAP is another protocol for e-mail message retrieval. The latest version, IMAP4, is similar to POP, but it supports some additional features. POP requires you to first download messages before you can work with them.

With IMAP4, you can search for keywords in your e-mail messages while the messages remain on the mail server. As a result, you can download only those messages you choose. Like POP, IMAP uses SMTP for communication between the e-mail client and the server. RFC 1730 defines IMAP4.

Web Services

Web service protocols support browser-based communications over the Internet and private internetworks (intranets). Web services operate based on the client/server model, in which a user uses a Web client (browser) to request information in the form of Web pages from a Web server. The Web server answers the client by returning to the browser the requested information in the form of text, images, multimedia content, and executable applications and scripts.

Browsers (HTTP)

A Web browser is a TCP/IP client application that allows a user to retrieve hypertext documents from an intranet or Internet server. An intranet server is a Web server that resides within an organization's network and provides private information to internal users. An Internet Web server has public access through the World Wide Web.

Regardless of where it is located, a Web server can use the same operating system, Web server application, and protocol for transmission. A client makes a request using a Web browser and the domain name, URL, or IP address of the destination server. The Web request is sent using HTTP to the associated Web server.

The Web server is listening for HTTP and fills the Web requests by providing the home page or index of files available at that server location.

RFCs 1945 and 2616 define HTTP as the Application Layer protocol browsers use to request and transmit documents between a client and an HTTP server.

One reason Web servers can handle thousands and perhaps millions of requests per hour is that Web connections are stateless. That is, after the browser downloads the requested document, picture, or media file, the server disconnects that session.

A browser opens multiple simultaneous sessions, one for every file (link) it accesses. Every time a client browser wants to retrieve a document, by clicking on a link, a separate request is sent to the server. Because the browser/server connection drops after the browser retrieves the file, if a user spends several hours reading a particular Web page, the server has no knowledge of it.

The client browser maintains the file(s) open in local memory until the user moves on to another page or closes the browser. The most common tools used to create and program Web pages are HTML and, for Web applications and scripts, Java, and JavaScript.

HTML

The Web browser's job is to display documents retrieved from Web servers. These documents are HyperText Markup Language (HTML) documents. HTML is text-based formatting language used to generically format text using a variety of tags and attributes. The Web browser reads the HTML document and displays it as indicated by the HTML formatting language. Because the browser provides the intelligence to format and display HTML documents, these documents are generally small.

Java

Java is an advanced object-oriented programming language used to build dynamic Web sites that interact with the user based on the user's choices and decisions. Java applications can be run on virtually any type of computer and operating system with a Java compiler installed. Java code is meant to be portable from computer platform to computer platform with few to no changes. For this reason, Java is said to be "platform-independent."

JavaScript

JavaScript is a scripting language that can be added to an HTML page to increase the page's capabilities. Like other scripting languages, JavaScript is interpreted. In other words, the browser reads the script one line at a time, then performs the instructions as indicated by the script.

JavaScript, like HTML, is written in plain text format. This makes it easy to insert JavaScript into a Web page, using a text editor or HTML authoring tool. Because it is written in text format, JavaScript can be easily delivered (embedded in an HTML page) over the Internet to be run on a client computer.

Review Questions

1. Which application is used to send messages between different e-mail systems?
   a. SNMP
   b. Telnet
   c. SMTP
   d. HTTP
2. What is the protocol used for transmitting Web information between client and server?
   a. HTML
   b. SMTP
   c. FTP
   d. HTTP
3. Which application can download an entire operating system and configuration?
   a. DNS
   b. DHCP
   c. BOOTP
   d. FTP
4. DNS can resolve information between which components? (Choose two.)
   a. URL
   b. FTP
   c. Port number
   d. MAC address
   e. IP address
5. Which of the following can be delivered using a DHCP server? (Choose three.)
   a. IP address
   b. MAC address
   c. Default gateway
   d. DNS server address
   e. Operating system
   f. Configuration file

Extended Activities

1. Compare and contrast FTP and TFTP by filling in the following table:

	FTP	TFTP
Transport protocol		
Port number		
Login requirements		
Type of file access		
Human intervention required?		
Commonly used for		

2. Perform a Web search to find sites that provide information on the following protocols. After researching, list the RFC that defined each protocol and the date the RFC was established.

   a. FTP ______________
   b. TFTP ______________
   c. Telnet ______________
   d. SNMP ______________
   e. RMON ______________
   f. DNS ______________
   g. BOOTP ______________
   h. DHCP ______________
   i. SMTP ______________
   j. MIME ______________
   k. IMAP4 ______________
   l. HTTP ______________

Summary

This module provided a foundation of knowledge about the IP protocol suite. This important network protocol is more than just IP. It is a complete group of protocols, all dependent upon one another for services and functionality. Although the IP protocol suite was developed many years ago, new protocols are constantly being added and old protocols updated to provide improvements in functionality as well as new services.

Lesson 1 discussed the IP protocol, including the Network Layer header information. The lesson also reviewed the helper protocols ICMP, ARP and RARP. Lesson 1 ended with a discussion of DHCP used for distributing IP and network configurations to end devices.

Lesson 2 provided more insight into the Transport Layer protocols of TCP and UDP. TCP is a reliable, connection-oriented protocol that offers many services to IP, such as reliable, end-to-end transport. UDP, on the other hand, is a connectionless protocol that is not reliable.

When UDP is used, IP is only a best-effort transport that relies on upper- or lower-layer protocols for circuit connections, flow control, and other services. This lesson also discussed the well known port numbers that identify upper-layer applications at the Transport Layer.

Lesson 3 discussed the applications commonly associated with IP. These include HTTP for the Web, SMTP for e-mail, FTP and TFTP for file transmission, SNMP for network management, and Telnet for remote console capabilities. Other protocols were also discussed in this lesson.

Module 5 Quiz

1. Which IP component communicates messages about unreachable networks, dropped or faulty packets, and devices on which the buffer limit has been exceeded?
   a. ARP
   b. TCP
   c. ICMP
   d. RARP
2. In which OSI model layer are TCP and UDP found?
   a. Network Layer
   b. Transport Layer
   c. Data Link Layer
   d. Application Layer
3. Which of the following is the connection-oriented, reliable delivery protocol?
   a. IP
   b. UDP
   c. TCP
   d. ICMP
4. Which port number is assigned to the Telnet application?
   a. 23
   b. 21
   c. 53
   d. 69
5. Which of the following definitions correctly describes ARP?
   a. A protocol that identifies the sending station's IP address
   b. A protocol that identifies the receiving station's IP address
   c. A protocol that identifies the IP address when the MAC address is known
   d. A protocol that identifies the MAC address when the IP address is known

6. Which of the following definitions correctly describes RARP?
   a. A protocol that identifies the sending station's IP address
   b. A protocol that identifies the receiving station's IP address
   c. A protocol that identifies the IP address when the MAC address is known
   d. A protocol that identifies the MAC address when the IP address is known
7. A ping is really which of the following?
   a. An expired TTL message
   b. An echo reply to an echo request
   c. A reply to an information request
   d. A reply to a redirect request
8. Fragmenting at the Network Layer allows for what?
   a. Different MTUs on a network
   b. Smaller overall packet sizes
   c. Larger overall packet sizes
   d. Different protocol requirements on a network
9. What is the protocol number for TCP?
   a. 17
   b. 6
   c. 9
   d. 11
10. The length of a UDP header is always what?
    a. 10 bytes
    b. 8 bytes
    c. 20 bytes
    d. 18 bytes
11. TFTP uses which protocol for transmission?
    a. UDP
    b. TCP
    c. ICMP
    d. ARP

12. Which of the following is not true regarding DNS in the IP protocol suite?
    a. Port number 53 identifies it.
    b. It uses TCP for zone transfers between DNS servers.
    c. It uses ARP to deliver the proper IP address to a diskless workstation.
    d. It uses UDP for name resolution.
13. RARP is often used for which task?
    a. Defining the best path through an internetwork
    b. Providing an IP address, given its MAC address
    c. Proving a MAC address, to the sending host when the IP address is known
    d. Proving upper-layer protocol information for the IP header
14. Which of the following is the connection-oriented process of establishing communication between two devices using TCP/IP?
    a. Synchronization
    b. Three-way handshake
    c. Acknowledgment
    d. Agreement
15. Which of the following is not an IP application?
    a. HTTP
    b. Telnet
    c. TCP
    d. SMTP
16. Which IP applications are associated with e-mail services? (Choose two.)
    a. SNMP
    b. EMP
    c. SMTP
    d. POP

17. Which of the following applications use TCP for transport? (Choose four.)
    a. SNMP
    b. SMTP
    c. HTTP
    d. FTP
    e. TFTP
    f. Telnet
18. Which of the following are found in a UDP header? (Choose two.)
    a. Source port
    b. acknowledgment
    c. Destination port
    d. IP address
19. What is the first step in a three-way handshake?
    a. The sender transmits a SYN to the receiver
    b. The receiver sends a SYN to the sender
    c. The receiver sends an ACK to the sender
    d. The sender transmits a PSH to the receiver
20. Which network service is used to dynamically deliver IP address, subnet mask, default gateway, and other IP and vendor-specific information to a host device?
    a. DNS server
    b. BOOTP server
    c. TFTP server
    d. DHCP server

Module 6
IP Addressing, Subnetting, and Routing

IP version 4 (IPv4) was built on an addressing scheme designed during the mid-1970s. For the most part, it has proven to be an effective identification plan based on a 32-bit number displayed in dotted decimal format. Decimal numbers are those numbers that we read and write every day. An IP address can include decimal numbers from 0 through 255, which is the largest number that can be represented in a single byte or octet. The addresses are considered dotted decimal because periods are used between the decimal numbers to delineate each octet (8 bits or 1 byte).

Keep in mind the decimal and binary number conversion process discussed previously as a foundation for this module. This is important because routers and other network devices read IP addresses at the bit level, as either a 0 or 1. Being able to make the conversion not only provides perspective on what the computer reads, it also is necessary to better understand what is happening at the bit level during the subnetting process.

An IP address is really two pieces of information: a network portion and a unique host portion. IP addresses have been grouped together into classes of addresses. Lesson 1 provides the characteristics and the number of networks and hosts available for assignment in each address class. It also presents a discussion of the default subnet masks used for each class of address, a description of broadcast addresses, and a list of the private addresses excluded from each address range. The lesson ends with a brief discussion of IP version 6 (IPv6), a new addressing scheme, and Classless Interdomain Routing (CIDR) or supernetting.

Lesson 2 focuses on subnetting, beginning with the subnetting process and ending with a number of examples. Many different methods for subnetting exist, and each one has its own benefits and drawbacks. The method used in this book focuses on a handy subnetting table. This table helps with the decimal-to-binary conversion process and vice versa, identifies the bits used for network numbers and hosts, locates the correct subnet mask, and pinpoints the first network number. This subnetting table, along with a few simple math equations, provides everything necessary to make subnetting computations.

Subnetting is a skill that should not be taken lightly. It includes a must-know skill-set that is required on almost all computer or network-related tests. You may even be required to calculate subnet information on the job in design process, implementation, or troubleshooting connectivity. Work through all the problems, and spend the time necessary to learn subnetting. Although challenging, it will be much easier to answer the questions after you have struggled through it a few times.

Lessons 3 and 4 deal with the IP routing process and protocols, respectively. Routing is necessary to select the best path through a network. Routers and layer 3 switch devices make path decisions based on a metric. Routing protocols are grouped by their location as either Interior Gateway Protocols (IGPs) (found inside an autonomous system [AS]) or Exterior Gateway Protocols (EGPs) (between ASs). Dynamic routing protocols are then further defined as to how they make path decisions and exchange routing information. Three types of routing protocols exist: distance vector, link state, and hybrid. Lesson 4 provides an overview of Routing Information Protocol versions 1 and 2 (RIPv1 and RIPv2), Interior Gateway Routing Protocol (IGRP), Enhanced IGRP (EIGRP), and Open Shortest Path First (OSPF). It finishes with a description of Border Gateway Protocol version 4 (BGPv4), which is considered an EGP.

Lessons

1. IP Addressing Basics
2. IP Subnetting
3. Routing Basics
4. Routing Protocols

Lesson 1—IP Addressing Basics

Working in the computer industry requires an understanding of IP addressing and routing, and possibly even subnetting. Most of us understand what an IP address is or, more specifically, what it looks like; however, we may not completely understand what is going on behind the scenes. This lesson begins by defining the dotted decimal notation that makes up an IP address. It then goes into detail about the division of IP address numbers and hierarchy for each class of address.

In addition to an IP address, a subnet mask is also necessary to define how the address will be viewed. Each class of address has a specific default subnet mask that must be applied. Due to the limited number of unique IP addresses, private addresses have been excluded from the assignable address ranges. These addresses are not registered and can be used by any organization within their corporate network. This lesson discusses the private address numbers.

The lesson also discusses the different broadcast and multicast methods used to communicate with all devices or groups of devices on a network segment. It ends with an overview of IPv6 addressing and characteristics, as well as information about CIDR.

Objectives

At the end of this lesson you will be able to:

- Describe the IP address structure
- Identify reserved IP addresses
- List the IP address classes and their numerical ranges
- Identify the default subnet mask for each address class
- Identify the private addresses
- Describe the uses for broadcast and multicast addresses
- Describe IPv4 address allocation
- Compare and contrast IPv4 and IPv6
- Discuss the characteristics of CIDR

Key Point

Current IP addresses are 32 bits or 4 octets. These addresses are broken into different classes: Classes A, B, C, D, and E. Each one defines a specific number range and default subnet mask. Each class of address also has a specific number of unique networks and unique hosts per network.

IP Address Overview

An IP address is a number assigned to any device that needs to communicate using the IP protocol suite. It is a logical Network Layer address that is administratively assigned and can be changed as needed. This allows hosts with different operating systems (OSs) to interoperate, in addition to providing Internet connection. Packets sent across a network include a source IP address and destination IP address. This is required to locate the network and specific host to which the packet is being delivered.

One of the most important things about an IP address is that it is hierarchical, meaning it represents two components. One is the network and the other is a specific host. Without a hierarchical address structure, routing tables could contain over 4 billion entries, requiring significantly more memory and processing power. The majority of routers do not have the capacity to even get close to this number. In fact, even the largest Internet routers cannot generally hold more than approximately 60,000 routing entries. Even if they could, the routing processes under this burden would be slow and inefficient. Instead, routers use the network portion of the address to determine the best path to get to another network. The host portion of the address is used for unique identification of a single device.

To obtain the network portion of an IP address, you need to register with an Internet service provider (ISP) that will assign one or more IP addresses in a range. These addresses represent an organization, unique from all other companies. Because only a limited number of assignable unique IP addresses are available, ISPs must be conservative in address distribution. Therefore, many organizations use private IP addresses for their internal use; these addresses have been excluded from the assignable address ranges.

Note: To actually connect to the Internet using a private address, you use the Network Address Translation (NAT), which is outside the scope of this book.

Regardless of where an IP address comes from, a default subnet mask is applied to the address to identify the host and network portions. The network portion of the address does not usually change from one host to another on a network. A network administrator can further subnet the addresses to define segments within a network environment.

The following list presents characteristics of an IPv4 address:

- The entire address is 32 bits in length.
- The address may be represented in decimal notation (for example, 192.168.15.12), hexadecimal notation (for example, C0.A8.0F.0C), or binary notation (for example, 11000000.10101000.00001111.00001100).
- The address is equally divided into four 8-bit octets, separated by periods.
- The lowest possible decimal number in any given octet is 0.
- The highest possible decimal number in any given octet is 255.
- An IP address with a host portion of all 0s is considered the address of the network itself, or the address of the wire. This is not a valid assignable host address.
- An IP address with a host portion of all binary 1s, or decimal 255, is considered the broadcast address of the network and communicates with all nodes within the particular network segment. This is also not a valid assignable host address.
- The first leftmost portion (most significant) of the IP address represents the network.
- The last rightmost portion (least significant) of the IP address represents the host.
- The number of bits used to represent either the network or host depends on the class of address and subnet mask.

The IP Address Diagram presents a typical 32-bit IP address.

192.168.15.12

IP Address

Reserved IP Addresses

Before actually identifying the classes of address, it is important to identify those address types that are excluded from assignment. The first one is excluded as a network address. Before classful addressing was designed and IP addresses widely used, a special type of address was defined. This address is called a "local loop-back" and is used to test network communication capabilities locally for a device. The IP address assigned for local loopback purposes is 127.0.0.1. As a result, this Class A address block is unassignable for networks or hosts.

The address of the network or wire itself also cannot be assigned as a host address. The definition of a network address is all 0s in the host portion of the address. This is not a valid host address because it is the address of the wire. If a host was accidentally assigned this address, it would cause unexpected network problems. A router uses the network address to make routing decisions. Examples of network addresses for an entire enterprise may look like 12.0.0.0, 172.16.0.0, or 201.45.65.0. In these examples, the zero in the host portion of each address indicates the network. However, after subnetting has been performed, especially with a Class C address, the network number may no longer be so obvious. For example, the addresses 201.45.65.16, 201.45.65.32, 201.45.65.48, and 201.45.65.64 are all examples of subnet addresses using the subnet mask 255.255.255.240. They have all zeros in the host portion of the address, although this is not apparent from looking at the decimal value. We will discuss how this works in the lesson entitled "IP Subnetting." For now, just note that you cannot have all 0s in the host position because that represents the network/subnet.

Another excluded address type is broadcast address. A broadcast address is designed to communicate with a large number of hosts simultaneously. To accomplish this, a broadcast uses all 1s in the portion of the address that represents the hosts. For example, to communicate with all hosts on a particular segment, the host portion of the address is set to all 1s. Using the examples from above,

12.255.255.255, 172.16.255.255, and 201.45.65.255 are all considered broadcasts. However, for the remaining subnet addresses discussed earlier, 201.45.65.31, 201.45.65.47, 201.45.65.63, and 201.45.65.79 are the respective broadcast addresses. These numbers have all 1s in the host position and are therefore considered invalid as a host assignment. If assigned, the system will not respond with an error message; however, the network segment could encounter problems.

Note: To exclude all 0s and 1s from the assignable host address range, subtract 2 for all host calculations.

IP Address Classes

Initially, IP classes were not used when assigning addresses. This changed for ease of administration and assignment purposes. It also changed because hierarchy is important for a router to make path selections. Without a hierarchical structure to the IP address scheme, a router would be burdened with a huge number of addresses to store and sort through when making routing decisions. As an example of something you are more familiar with, think about trying to call someone using the person's Social Security number. The telephone network equipment would have to record every person's Social Security number and then identify where they lived and how to connect to their telephone. Not only would it be very difficult to store this information, but it would be virtually impossible for the telephone switch to place your call and get it to the proper telephone in a timely manner. The switch would have to sort through millions of numbers to find the right one and then determine where to send the call. Instead, the telephone network uses a hierarchical number plan.

Without getting too technical, in North America, the first three digits generally represent the geographic area, large portion of a state, or metropolitan area. The next three digits represent the local exchange, a smaller area of the network within the geographic location. This narrows the search to anywhere from 2 to 25 square miles. Finally, the last four digits represent a single subscriber's telephone number. Notice that in using the hierarchy, the telephone switch goes from a large area to a smaller area and then to one specific location, all in a matter of seconds.

Although IP addresses are also hierarchical, they were not defined in the same manner as a telephone numbers. As the example indicated, a telephone number in North America has a fixed hierarchy: (area code) local exchange-subscriber. With IP addressing, the hierarchy has been divided between classes of addresses. This was necessary based on how the addresses were originally assigned, and in order to best utilize the available address space.

The five defined classes of IP addresses and their characteristics are discussed in the following five sections. The first characteristic is the binary rule and the associated decimal number range that represents each class. IP address classes and their numerical values are defined in Request for Comment (RFC) 796. The next characteristic is the default subnet masks associated with Class A, B, and C addresses, defined in RFC 917. A subnet mask is used to defined the hierarchy, similar to the telephone number example above. The final characteristic is the private IP address ranges, which are defined in RFC 1918 for Classes A, B, and C. Private addresses can be used inside a corporate network, but are not allowed in the public Internet space. To change a private address into a public address for accessing the Internet, use NAT.

Class A

Class A address characteristics are as follows:

- The first bit of a Class A address must be a binary 0.
- The Class A address range is from 1.0.0.0 through 126.255.255.255.
- Exclusion: Although part of the Class A allocation of address numbers, the address 127.0.0.1 and the entire range cannot be used, because it is reserved as a local loopback address.
- The default subnet mask for a Class A address is 255.0.0.0. The first octet defines the network and the remaining three octets identify available host bits

  (NNNNNNNN.HHHHHHHH. HHHHHHHH.HHHHHHHH).
- The Class A address range has 126 possible networks (2^7 -2).
- The Class A address range has 16,777,214 assignable hosts per network (2^{24} – 2).
- The Class A private network address range that cannot be used for Internet connectivity is 10.0.0.0 to 10.255.255.255. These addresses can be assigned for internal corporate use, but will not provide Internet access.

Class B

Class B address characteristics are as follows:

- The first 2 bits of a Class B address must be binary 10.
- The Class B address range is from 128.0.0.0 through 191.255.255.255.

- The default subnet mask for a Class B address is 255.255.0.0. The first two octets define the network portion and the remaining two octets identify available host bits

  (NNNNNNNN. NNNNNNNN.HHHHHHHH.HHHHHHHH).
- The Class B address range has 16,384 possible networks ($2^{14} - 2$).
- The Class B address range has 65,534 assignable hosts per network ($2^{16} - 2$).
- The Class B private network address range that cannot be used for Internet connectivity is 172.16.0.0 to 172.31.255.255.

Class C

Class C address characteristics are as follows:

- The first 3 bits of a Class C address must be binary 110.
- The Class C address range is from 192.0.0.0 through 223.255.255.255.
- The default subnet mask for a Class C address is 255.255.255.0. The first three octets define a network and the remaining octet identifies available host bits

  (NNNNNNNN.NNNNNNNN. NNNNNNNN.HHHHHHHH).
- The Class C address range has 2,097,152 possible networks ($2^{21} - 2$).
- The Class C address range has 254 assignable hosts per network ($2^{8} - 2$).
- The Class C private network address range that cannot be used for Internet connectivity is 192.168.0.0 to 192.168. 255.255.

Class D

Class D address characteristics are as follows:

- Class D addresses are reserved for multicast groups.
- They are not used for network/host address assignment.
- The first 4 bits of a Class D address must be binary 1110.
- The Class D address range is from 224.0.0.0 through 239.255.255.255.

Class E

Class E address characteristics are as follows:

- Class E addresses are used for experimental and research purposes.
- They are not assigned to any production network environments.

- The first 5 bits of a Class E address must be binary 11110.
- The Class E address range begins at 240.0.0.0.

To get a better understanding of what this really means, the IP Address Classes Diagram shows each class of address along with the associated bit positions. Keep in mind that with a subnet mask, you can always use more bits for networking, leaving fewer bits for a host. When subnetting, you must use at least the default number of assigned network bits (8 bits for Class A, 16 bits for Class B, and 24 bits for Class C). This concept is further discussed in the lesson entitled "IP Subnetting."

Class A	0	Network	.	Host	.	Host	.	Host
Class B	10	Network	.	Network	.	Host	.	Host
Class C	110	Network	.	Network	.	Network	.	Host

IP Address Classes

Calculating IP Address Classes

Refer to the Converting Binary to Decimal Table (from Module 1, Lesson 1), which can be used as an easy reference for identifying the range for each class of address. The IP Address Class Calculation Table shows how this works with some new information. When calculating address classes, remember the following rules:

- Class A's first bit (0) indicates the address range is from 1 through 127. (Note that 127 cannot be used as a network address, because it is assigned as the local loopback address; thus the range is really 1 to 126.)
- Class B's first 2 bits (10) indicate the address range is from 128 to 191.
- Class C's first 3 bits (110) indicate the address range is from 192 to 223.
- Class D's first 4 bits (1110) indicate the address range is from 224 to 239. Remember, however, that Class D addresses are not used for network/host address assignment.
- Class E's first 5 bits (11110) indicate the address range is from 240 to 247. Class E addresses are reserved for experimental use.

IP Address Class Calculation

	Class A	Class B	Class C	Class D	Class E			
Subnet Bit	128	192	224	240	248	252	254	255
Base 2	2^7	2^6	2^5	2^4	2^3	2^2	2^1	2^0
Bit Value	128	64	32	16	8	4	2	1
Class A first	**0**	0	0	0	0	0	0	1 = 1
Class A last	**0**	1	1	1	1	1	1	1 = 127
Class B first	**1**	**0**	0	0	0	0	0	0 = 128
Class B last	**1**	**0**	1	1	1	1	1	1 = 191
Class C first	**1**	**1**	**0**	0	0	0	0	0 = 192
Class C last	**1**	**1**	**0**	1	1	1	1	1 = 223
Class D first	**1**	**1**	**1**	**0**	0	0	0	0 = 224
Class D last	**1**	**1**	**1**	**0**	1	1	1	1 = 239

Notice the row at the top of the table. This row of numbers was created by adding each value in each bit position, from left to right. A brief rundown of how the top row is calculated is presented below. If you put a 1 in each bit position from left to right, then determine the decimal value, the end results are as follows:

10000000	128 = 128
11000000	128 + 64 = 192
11100000	128 + 64 + 32 = 224
11110000	128 + 64 + 32 + 16 = 240

11111000	128 + 64 + 32 + 16 + 8 = 248
11111100	128 + 64 + 32+ 16 + 8 + 4 = 252
11111110	128 + 64 + 32 + 16 + 8 + 4 + 2 = 254
11111111	128 + 64 + 32 + 16 + 8 + 4 + 2 + 1 = 255

Also, notice that each class of address fits neatly between the numbers in the top row, as follows:

Class A	00000001 – 01111111 = 1 to 126 (127 is the local loopback address and cannot be used.)
Class B	10000000 – 10111111 = 128 to 191
Class C	11000000 – 11011111 = 192 to 223
Class D	11100000 – 11101111 = 224 to 239
Class E	11110000 – 11111111 = 240 to 255

Default Subnet Masks

Just as there are different classes of IP addresses, there are also different default subnet masks. A subnet mask is used to mask off a portion of an address that represents a network. The longer the subnet mask, the more bits used for networks, and the smaller the subnet mask, the fewer bits used for networks. The network portion of the address is always at the beginning because it represents the largest portion in the address hierarchy. Routers use the network portion of the address to make the best path selections. When looking at a subnet mask, the network portion is represented or masked with binary 1s starting from the left, as shown below. (Class D and E addresses are not discussed here because they cannot be used for network or host IP address assignment.)

Class A	255.0.0.0 in binary: 11111111.00000000.00000000.00000000
Class B	255.255.0.0 in binary: 11111111.11111111.00000000.00000000
Class C	255.255.255.0 in binary: 11111111.11111111.11111111.00000000

It is important to note that any number in the same position as the default subnet mask value of 255 will always stay the same. This is why it is called a "mask." The following three sections provide examples that represent Class A, B, and C network environments using the appropriate default subnet masks.

Class A

- Given an IP address of 12.191.65.200, the default subnet mask is 255.0.0.0.
- All 8 bits of the first octet are used for the network.
- The number 12 in the first position will never change throughout the entire organization's network.
- The last three octets are available for subnetworks and host assignment. In this example, .191.65.200 represents a unique host assignment.

Class B

- Given an IP address of 179.22.63.111, the default subnet mask is 255.255.0.0.
- All 16 bits of the first two octets are used for the network.
- The numbers 179.22 in the first two positions are the same for all hosts throughout the company, because they represent the assigned corporate network.
- The last two octets with the numbers .63.111 represent the host assignment.

Class C

- Given the IP address of 201.35.160.14, the default subnet mask is 255.255.255.0.
- All 24 bits of the first three octets are used for the network.
- The numbers in the first three octets of 201.35.160 will never change.
- The last octet is available for subnetworks and host assignment (in this case, .14).

Keep in mind that these are the defaults. Given this, do you think it is possible to have a Class A address with a subnet mask of 255.255.255.0? Most people assume this is a Class C subnet mask and could not be used for a Class A address. Remember that a subnet mask does not define the class of address. Rather the first number in the IP address defines the class. Once the class is determined, the proper default subnet mask can be applied. For the example of using a Class A address with 255.255.255.0, it simply means that more bits are being used for the network portion; thus, fewer bits are available for the host. Creating subnets is the topic of the lesson entitled "IP Subnetting."

Private IP Addresses

Before Internet access became common in the mid-1990s, many organizations assigned their own IP addresses for internal system communications. However, as more and more organizations got access to the Internet, this was no longer acceptable. Specific addresses were acquired by organizations from a Domain Name System (DNS) registrar or ISP. Using another organization's address is a violation of the IP address numbering plan and could result in a fine. To prevent this, RFC 1918 defines specific addresses that are excluded from the public IP address numbers and are considered private. These addresses can be used by any organization, regardless of the IP address(es) or class of address they were assigned by their service provider. The three private IP addresses are shown in the Private Address Ranges Table.

Private Address Ranges

Range	Description
10.X.X.X	16,777,214 possible host addresses
172.16.X.X – 172.31.X.X	16 networks with 65,534 hosts per network
192.168.X.X	254 networks with 254 hosts per network

The X in various positions in each address indicates this number can be changed by an administrator. These private addresses have been excluded from each address class and are not assigned to any organization for public use. In addition, 172.16.X.X through 172.31.X.X is a range of addresses that allows a network administrator to define different network segments. Also notice that the Class C address of 192.168.X.X only has the first two octets assigned, instead of all three. This allows some creative numbering, in which an administrator can configure network numbers such as 192.168.1.0, 192.168.2.0, 192.168.3.0, 192.168.4.0, and so forth.

Private addressing works on the premise that there are many host devices that do not need to access or be accessed through the Internet. Connecting to the Internet is the only time a device needs a public address. To be located inside an organization's network, a device simply needs a unique IP address. Private addressing helps conserve the limited number of assigned IP addresses. NAT can be used to convert a private IP address used internally into a public IP address that can access the Internet. NAT is covered in Interconnecting Cisco Network Devices, the second course in this certification.

Broadcast Addresses

A broadcast is a message addressed with the destination of all devices on a particular network. It works by placing all binary 1s in the proper location of the IP address. You should be familiar with the following three types of broadcasts:

- **Flooding broadcast**—A flooding broadcast is also considered a local network broadcast. The number is all binary 1s or 255.255.255.255, regardless of the network IP address. Routers do not propagate these types of broadcasts, so the traffic stays local to a particular network. All hosts in the same network receive the broadcast.
- **All subnets broadcast**—Note from earlier discussions that an organization is provided an IP address and, depending on the address class, a certain portion of that address never changes. The remaining octets or bits can be used for subnets and unique host IDs. With an "all subnets broadcast," the organization-assigned number stays the same and all remaining bits are changed to binary 1s. This means that the broadcast will reach all hosts on all subnetworks. For example, if an organization is assigned the Class B IP address of 185.72.0.0, the all subnets broadcast would be 185.72.255.255. Some portion of the third octet would more than likely identify subnetworks, while the last octet would probably identify the hosts. Routers read and forward all subnet broadcasts. This is similar to the concept of having a public address system in an elementary school and broadcasting to all classrooms that everyone must attend an assembly.
- **Directed broadcast**—A directed broadcast is more specific because it only goes to the hosts within a single subnetwork. A directed broadcast has binary 1s in only the host portion. Using the example from above, if a subnet is 185.72.16.0, then the directed broadcast is 182.72.16.255. This broadcast would be sent to all hosts within the 16.0 network. Referring to our example of the public address system throughout an entire elementary school, a directed broadcast would only address students in the fifth grade. All other speakers would be silent except those in the fifth grade classrooms.

Broadcasts are reserved addresses that cannot be assigned to any host. They are set aside to contact all hosts within a particular network environment. Keep this in mind during the subnetting process described in the lesson entitled "IP Subnetting." Determining the broadcast address is an important step in the calculation process.

Multicast Addresses

As just stated, broadcasts are designed to communicate with all devices in a subnet or network. This can get noisy if only a few devices need to hear a message. With a broadcast, a message is indiscriminately sent to all devices within a specific area. Devices that do not need the message, review its contents and discard it. The problem lies in the fact that the end device still has to hear the message and use its own processor to review it. This can become a big problem in networks with large broadcast domains, where many devices are hearing messages that do not concern them.

Routers, layer 3 switches, and virtual local area networks (VLANs) are designed to break up broadcast domains into smaller segments. This helps reduce the amount of unnecessary broadcast traffic from being propagated to other subnets. However, because broadcasts are verbose, they need to be limited. In certain situations, we can accomplish this by using the concept of multicast.

Class D IP addresses provide a way to identify a group of devices that have similar communication needs. For example, routers using a specific routing protocol such as OSPF are all grouped to communicate together. Other routing protocols send routing updates as broadcast messages to all devices. This creates a lot of unnecessary traffic for hosts to read if they are not routers. When using a protocol such as OSPF, the routers use specific Class D addresses to communicate using a multicast within the group. This eliminates the unnecessary broadcast traffic that is sent to all devices. Only those devices that have the correct Class D address are members of the multicast group and will receive the message. Keep in mind that a device would have its normal Class A, B, or C address for unique identification purposes. It would also have a Class D address to be included as part of the multicast group.

Multicast can also cut down on traffic in another way. Typically speaking, when a transmission is sent, it is addressed to a single end device as a unicast (one-to-one). If the transmission needed to be sent to 15 devices simultaneously, the information would still be sent as a unicast. It would travel from the sender to the 15 individual devices as 15 separate transmissions through the network. By using a multicast method, however, this same transmission could be sent as one single message, but addressed to all devices in the specific multicast group.

As an example, consider a classroom lab with 15 personal computers (PCs) that need to be reimaged after every class is over. Imaging is a process that allows an OS and configuration to be sent to a PC without going through extensive manual installation. Traditionally, this reimaging process means that the server would send out 15 huge image files to the 15 individual PCs. This would significantly slow both the network and imaging process. Instead, using a multicast group with a Class D address, the server could send out one image and all devices would receive it at exactly the same time. This reduces the traffic from 15 separate images with exactly the same content, to a single image sent to all 15 PCs. The transmission time is decreased significantly.

IP Address Allocation

During the 1980s when the government was first privatizing the Internet, IPv4 was more than sufficient to handle the total of 213 Internet hosts. By the late 1980s, the host count had increased to over 2,000 and was growing rapidly. By 1996, the number of hosts had risen to over 500,000, and by 1999, the count was over 50,000,000. This rapid growth gave rise to a number of IPv4 problems, the most prevalent being the limited number of IP addresses available.

From January 2000 to January 2002, the number of Internet World Wide Web (Web) sites grew by 383 percent. The Internet Growth in Millions of Hosts Diagram illustrates the growth in the number of Internet hosts between January 1997 and January 2002.

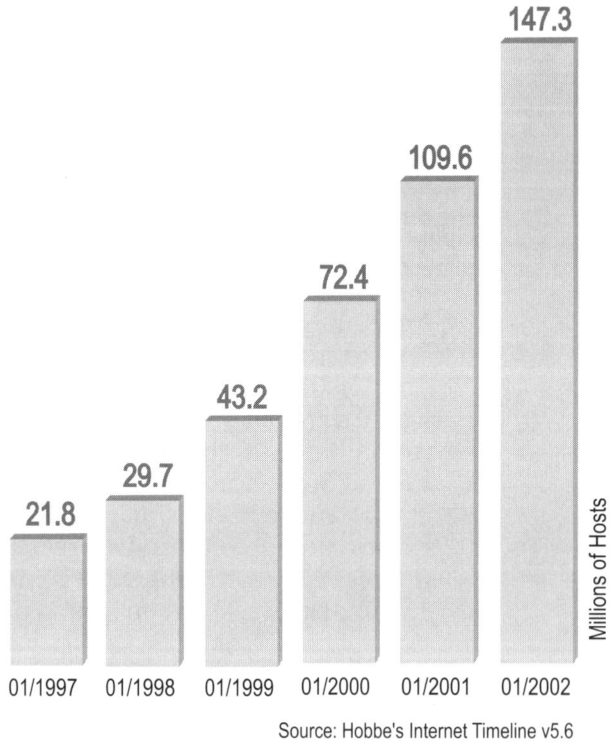

Internet Growth in Millions of Hosts

The Internet is a network of networks, composed of many individual carriers and ISPs. Each of these individual networks needs globally unique IP address ranges for their routers, subnetworks, and customers. Before those addresses can be assigned to hosts, an organization must be assigned a network address that represents the AS to the Internet. Based on the knowledge you now have about classful addressing, you can see that there are just over 16,500 Class A and B network addresses that can be assigned. These addresses were given out to government entities, educational facilities that helped develop the Internet, and large organizations. The remainder were made available to ISPs for distribution.

Obviously, the limited number of available Class A and B addresses cannot meet world-wide addressing needs. Far more Class C addresses are available (2,097,150) for assignment, but even these are now in limited supply. Additional, most organizations would need several Class C addresses to support all their hosts.

All in all, the current version of IP address allocation numbering has worked up to this point. It will not be able to sustain the growth of the future. For now, steps such as private addressing with NAT allow businesses to communicate internally and access the Internet while still conserving address usage. CIDR (discussed shortly) is a method that helps service providers manage their address allocations, as well as reduce routing tables. IPv6 is planning to help revolutionize the number structure and address allocation to support future communications.

IPv4 vs. IPv6

RFCs to modernize and improve IP were submitted to the Internet Society (ISOC) and Internet Engineering Task Force (IETF) as early as 1995. IETF appointed a formal group to study the next IP generation, already called IPv6. RFC 2460, which replaces the original RFC 1883, specifies IPv6 as the IPv4 replacement and handles many different protocol issues at once.

IPv6 expands IP addresses from the current 32 bits to 128 bits. The benefits of these larger addresses include:

- **Allows continued Internet expansion**—Expanding the addresses to 128 bits ensures that the Internet will not exhaust its address supply in the near future. Addresses that are 128 bits allow for 2,128 personal addresses. This greatly expanded address range ensures that we can assign everything from cellular phones to personal digital assistants (PDAs) to wrist-worn communicators their own IP address. This address space can keep pace with the ever-expanding array of PCs, printers, IP telephones, and other IP address network peripheral devices.
- **Improves routing efficiency**—Longer IP addresses allow for aggregating addresses by hierarchies of network, access provider, geography, corporation, and other groupings. Such aggregation should increase router lookup speed and reduce router memory requirements, making routing more efficient.
- **Accommodates non-IP addressing formats**—The long address space provides adequate room for translations of Internetwork Packet Exchange (IPX), network service access point (NSAP), Ethernet Media Access Control (MAC) addresses, and other non-IP addresses into IPv6 addresses. This allows existing networks to connect to the Internet with a minimum of address reconfiguration, and reduces setup, debugging, and maintenance loads on network managers.

These next two subsections compare the IPv4 and IPv6 addressing formats.

For IPv4:

- 4 octets or 32 bits
- 4,294,467,295 total IP addresses
- Example address: 172.16.30.5
- 10101100.00010000.00011110.00000101

For IPv6:

- 16 octets or 128 bits
- 3.4 x 10^{38}
- Example address: 9072:AB71:9AD4:84BD:FE22:CD01:674F:43BE
- 1001000001110010:1010101101110001:1001101011010100:1000010010111101:1111111000100010:0110110100000001:0110011101001111:0100001110111110

In addition to the change in address size, RFC 2460 also identifies and fulfills a number of other key components. IPv6 offers security and encryption, quality of service (QoS) features, network recognition and automatic addressing, mobility, and the list goes on and on.

CIDR

Several studies performed in the early 1990s determined that Internet backbone router routing tables would exceed 60,000 entries by mid-1994. This led the studies' authors to declare that when the tables reach this number of entries, the routers would not be able to handle any more. Unless a solution was found soon, this meant the end of the Internet's growth. RFC 1338, written in 1992, proposed a method to control Internet routing table sizes and IP address use, called "supernetting" or "address aggregation." The authors' motives for this proposal, according to the RFC, were as follows:

- The Class B address space was nearing exhaustion. Although they did not need all the host addresses a Class B network supplied, most medium-sized networks needed more host addresses than a Class C network could provide. Thus, many Class B addresses went unused.

- The Internet router tables were growing beyond the capacity of software and network administration capabilities at the time.
- The 32-bit IP address space was also approaching exhaustion.

To address the first two concerns, the authors proposed to distribute aggregated blocks of Class C IP addresses to network service providers. The service providers, having exclusive possession of these address blocks, could then suballocate these addresses to their customers. Customers, as well, could suballocate addresses further. This address allocation technique required little in the way of host configuration changes, instead requiring that network routers support this mechanism.

Routers that support address allocation are called "classless routers." Classless routers pass, as part of their routing table updates, both the network number and prefix. The term CIDR describes the requirement that routers performing address allocation support classless routing, and that they aggregate routing table entries obtained from routers within their routing domains.

RFC 1519 renders RFC 1338 obsolete, and introduces CIDR as the strategy for replacing the classful routing processes of assigning Class A and B network addresses to large networks. Instead, ISPs and carriers are assigned an aggregate block of Class C addresses. CIDR uses address prefixes to represent the aggregated Class C address spaces.

An aggregated address is represented by a 32-bit-long, dotted decimal network address, and includes a prefix to represent the block of Class C addresses composing the aggregate. For example, the address 198.64.0.0/16 represents a block aggregate of 256 Class C networks, ranging from the first network address (198.64.0.0) to the last (198.64.255.0). In classful addressing, this range of addresses would have to be advertised and maintained in the routing tables as 256 separate entries (198.64.0.0, 198.64.1.0, 198.64.2.0, 198.64.3.0, ... 192.64.255.0). With CIDR, all those entries can be combined into a single classless entry of 198.64.0.0/16. It will then be up to the service provider to manage and assign the address allocations. And, it will be the work of the routers to find the appropriate route given the information provided.

The CIDR Sample Prefixes Table lists the numbers of aggregate Class C networks and host addresses available for some common CIDR block prefixes. Note that the smaller the prefix, the more Class C networks and host addresses available. Large organizations are assigned an address with a smaller prefix, and then suballocate their address blocks across their subnetworks. RFC 1466 states that, in most cases, no organization will be assigned a prefix smaller than 18 bits (/18 prefix). If an organization needs more than 64 networks or 16,384 hosts, it should consider applying for a Class B address.

CIDR Sample Prefixes

CIDR Prefix	Equivalent Subnet Mask	Number of Aggregate Class C Networks	Number of Host Addresses Available*
/24	255.255.255.0	1	256
/23	255.255.254.0	2	512
/22	255.255.252.0	4	1024
/21	255.255.248.0	8	2048
/20	255.255.240.0	16	4096
/19	255.255.224.0	32	8192
/18	255.255.192.0	64	16,384
/17	255.255.128.0	128	32,768

* This number includes the address of the wire and broadcast. Subtract 2 from each value for the actual number of assignable hosts.

To provide a simplistic overview of how a prefix equals a subnet mask, all you have to understand is that the prefix is defined by all the 1 bits turned on to mask the network address. For instance, converting 255.255.255.0 from our earlier example to binary gives you 11111111.11111111.11111111.00000000. Counting all the 1s should equal 24 (8 + 8 + 8); this is displayed as the prefix /24.

Review Questions

1. What is the total length of the current IP address?

2. An octet is made up of how many bits?

3. What is the Class B address range?

4. What is the private Class B address range?

5. What address is reserved for local loopback and cannot be assigned as a network?

6. If all the host bits are set to 0s, what does the IP address represent?

7. If all the host bits are set to 1s, what does the IP address represent?

8. The default subnet mask of 255.255.255.0 is used for which address class?

9. Given a subnet mask of 255.0.0.0, for which address class(es) could this be used?

10. The decimal number 255 indicates how many 1s are being used?

11. Who receives a broadcast message?

12. What address class is used by multicast groups?

____

13. How many possible networks are available in the Class A address?

____

14. Which address class has the most available hosts?

____

15. Which address class has the least number of available hosts?

____

16. What is the private Class C address?

____

17. What is the Class C address range?

____

Extended Activity

Provide the correct class and subnet mask for each IP address below. Then, using the default subnet mask, identify the numbers of the network portion and host portion of each IP address.

IP Address	Address Class	Default Subnet Mask	Network Portion	Host Portion
192.168.10.3				
14.18.254.201				
145.192.10.1				
127.0.0.1				
182.168.3.10				
213.245.10.5				
91.16.20.7				

Lesson 2—IP Subnetting

Companies use either public or private IP address ranges. Using a default subnet mask allows them a specific number of hosts based on the class of address used. The default subnet mask defines only a network portion and host portion of the IP address. However, most companies have a more complex network environment that uses routers, layer 3 switches, or VLANs. Remember that these components are used to provide security, break down broadcast and collision domains, and segment network traffic. Routers can also provide wide area network (WAN), Internet, and remote access connectivity. When layer 3 devices or VLANs are present in a network, subnetting is required. This creates additional hierarchy in the address by defining network, subnet, and host portions.

We need to learn a few calculations to determine the correct subnet mask. This lesson provides an understanding of the calculation process, including determining the resulting number of subnetworks and hosts, identifying the correct subnet mask, and identifying the IP address range available for assignment, as well as the network and broadcast addresses.

Keep in mind that there are many different ways to do these calculations. You may have already seen or learned how to calculate this information differently. You can use whatever method you feel most comfortable with or adopt this method. What matters is that you are able to do the calculations and obtain the correct answer. It is definitely worth spending the time it takes to learn this material by practicing. You may not need to do a lot of subnetting on the job, but at least you will understand an IP address and subnet mask when you see one. In addition, if you take networking or TCP/IP certification exams, you will repeatedly perform subnet calculations.

One last note: although it is possible, using special commands, to use high and low subnets, this lesson does not teach that. The majority of subnetting materials do not allow a 0 network, and that standard will be maintained here for consistency. (Cisco equipment does provide the ability to use the 0 network using the global configuration command **`ip subnet-zero`**.) Remember, too, that the host portion of an address cannot be all 0s (addresses the network itself) or all 1s (used for broadcasts). Keeping these points in mind, let us learn how to subnet.

Objectives

At the end of this lesson you will be able to:

- Explain why subnetting is used
- Describe the process used in subnetting
- Identify the number of networks and hosts available using a particular subnet mask
- Define subnet, network number, address range, and broadcast
- Complete Class A, B, and C subnetting examples
- Calculate subnetting problems given different information
- Describe the process of using logical AND to determine the subnetwork address

Key Point

Subnetting is the process of taking bits from the host portion of an IP address and giving them to the network portion. A subnet mask is used to define which portion of the IP address is network, which portion is subnetwork, and which portion remains available for host assignment.

Why Subnet?

The lesson entitled "IP Addressing Basics" discussed having one large network and using the default subnet mask associated with the address class assigned to a company. This works well in a small organization with a very limited network infrastructure that is free of routers. However, this network environment is not typical in a larger organization. Subnetting is the process of segmenting one large network into smaller pieces. This process is beneficial for a number of reasons:

- **Traffic reduction**—When a large network is broken into smaller networks (subnetworks) using a router or layer 3 switch, the result is less overall network traffic. This is because broadcast traffic that would normally circulate through the entire network is not forwarded by routers.

- **Traffic isolation**—It is often desirable to isolate traffic based on application type, protocol, or resource requirements. A perfect example might be the separation of data and real-time multimedia applications. Data needs guaranteed transport, but is less concerned about delay. Real-time applications, on the other hand, are delay-sensitive but are often less concerned about reliability.
- **Security**—One large network broken into subnets also provides the benefit of added security. Using routing protocols and access lists, an administrator can determine which networks and subnetworks are allowed to communicate.
- **Network performance**—Less traffic means better network performance. When local traffic in a subnetwork stays local, it has less impact on the network infrastructure as a whole.
- **Expansion capabilities**—Many small subnetworks allow for growth. Scalability is part of every corporate environment, and a network is no different. Using subnets allows for future growth, meaning that more subnetworks can be added without having a major impact on overall network performance. Without subnets, adding more devices and traffic would have significant impact on a network.
- **Troubleshooting**—Smaller networks are easier to troubleshoot than one large network. With subnetting, it is easier to target and troubleshoot a particular network than to try and find a problem in the entire infrastructure. It also helps reduce the number of devices that may be impacted by an outage in another part of the network.
- **WAN connections**—Connections made to branch offices and other geographic locations are possible because of routers. The idea of breaking up one large network and distributing it across the nation, or the world, would not be a reality without routers and subnets.
- **Logical segmentation**—Many networks are now logically segmented using VLANs on layer 2 switches. This allows an administrator to define a group of devices that should be in the same logical broadcast domain because they share similar traffic or have similar security needs.

As discussed earlier, IP addresses have a hierarchy based on their address class. Using the default subnet mask, the hierarchy only includes a network portion and a host portion. For some small networks, this level of hierarchy is sufficient. However, for the reasons just discussed, subnets are used to add another level of hierarchy between network and host. This level of hierarchy is similar to the local exchange of a telephone number. The network portion of the assigned IP address will not change based on the address class. The Internet Assigned Numbers Authority (IANA) is responsible for overseeing IP address distribution, domain name services, and other protocol numbering associated with the Internet. Individual groups under IANA represent geographic areas for number assignment. In North America, the group is American Registry for Internet Numbers (ARIN), who has a repository of addresses that are assigned to an ISP for distribution. ARIN is responsible for, among other things, maintaining an accurate database of address usage.

Companies and educational organizations get their IP address(es) from an ISP. For address conservation, many organizations use private addresses internally and one or two public addresses to access the Internet. After the network portion is assigned or a private address is used, the network administrator can determine the number of subnetworks and hosts that the current and future network environment requires. Then, using the subnet calculation process discussed next, the appropriate subnet mask can be determined and applied.

So far, the discussion has been about the logical aspects of IP addressing. Physically, a subnet is a smaller portion of a larger network. Subnets are often called "segments" and represent physical or logical broadcast domains. Routers and layer 3 switches break up broadcast domains; therefore, each connection to a router, or a layer 3 device, is considered a subnet. A VLAN is considered a logical broadcast domain and although it functions on a layer 2 switch, it is also considered a subnet. In each case, the segment is assigned a different subnetwork IP address. Each subnetwork has its own range of unique host addresses, as well as a broadcast address used to communicate with all hosts on the subnet.

The Process of Subnetting

To subnet an assigned IP address, you must first start with the default subnet mask. The default subnet mask is based on the class of address assigned and cannot change in a classful environment. From there, you can identify the number of bits available to use between network numbers and host addresses. It is important to remember that subnetting takes host bits and turns them into subnetwork bits. The more subnetworks you assign, the fewer the number of hosts that will be available on each subnetwork. The reverse is also true: the fewer the number of subnetworks assigned, the more bits that are available to assign as unique hosts.

Although it takes a little practice, the process of subnetting is very systematic and applicable, regardless of the address class. It may look slightly different from Class A to Class C, but the process remains the same. As noted earlier, you can perform this process many ways. Use any method you have learned or find comfortable. If you like the method described below, use it. It is a very big-picture overview. The rest of this lesson breaks the steps down into more specific details. We end with a summarized version of how to actually perform the calculations. Do not get caught up in the details of each step, but try to see the big picture. It is like riding a bike: if you had to attempt this task only as individual steps, you would never get moving. Instead, by thinking about the process as a whole, you are able to ride that bike. Although it is not easy the first time, it gets better with practice. An overview of the subnetting process is as follows:

1. Determine the number of (sub)networks currently required and allow for future growth. This includes each router interface and wide area connection, Layer 3 switch, or VLAN. Note that the connection between two routers shares the same subnetwork address.
2. Determine the number of hosts on the existing network and allow for future growth. A host is any computer, server, printer, switch, IP telephone, PDA, or other network device that resides on a particular network. Each node that requires an IP address is considered a host. Each router interface is also assigned an IP address.
3. From these two calculations, determine which subnet mask to use. Start with the default subnet mask for the address class you are assigned, and add bits (taken from the host) to the network portion to create the new subnet mask.
4. Determine the network address for each subnetwork. This is the first address and it represents the network itself. It is also referred to as the address of the wire. The host portion of this address will end in binary 0s.

5. Determine the broadcast address for each subnetwork. The broadcast is used to communicate with all hosts on the subnetwork simultaneously. The broadcast is the last number before the next network address. The host portion of this address will be all binary 1s.

6. Determine the range of addresses available for host assignment. All the remaining addresses between the network number and the broadcast address are available for assignment to hosts. Each host must have a unique IP address to function properly on the network.

The next few sections provide a more detailed explanation of how each component is calculated. The Subnetting Table provides valuable information used in subnetting.

Subnetting

Subnet Bit	128	192	224	240	248	252	254	255
Base 2	2^7	2^6	2^5	2^4	2^3	2^2	2^1	2^0
Bit Value	128	64	32	16	8	4	2	1

The first two steps in the subnetting process include determining the number of networks and hosts per network. In most cases, unless you work for a company that is just starting up, this has already been done. It is very probable, however, that growth was not accounted for, or the company has an address change and you may be asked to perform this process again. At the very least, you will be asked to calculate the number of networks and hosts on an exam.

Step 1—Determine the Number of Networks

To determine the number of networks, you must identify the number of different network connections made using router and layer 3 switch interfaces, including both local area network (LAN) and WAN connections. Do not forget to account for all VLANs as well. On the Example Network Diagram, notice that each connection between routers is considered its own network. Each network must be assigned a network address to allow communication.

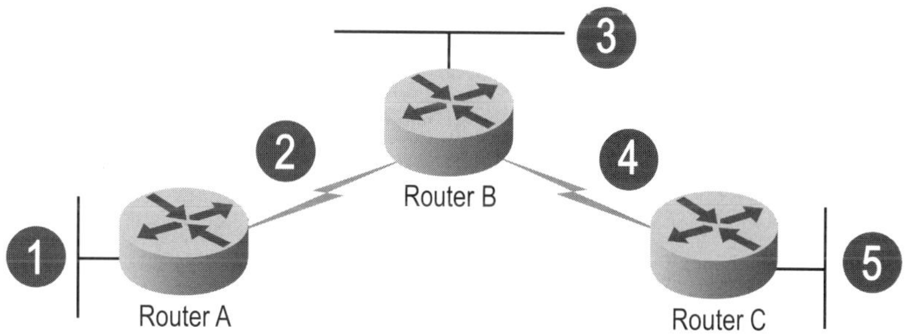

Example Network

In this example, five subnetworks must be defined:

1. Ethernet segment off Router A
2. Serial connection between Router A and Router B
3. Ethernet segment off Router B
4. Serial connection between Router B and Router C
5. Ethernet segment off Router C

The formula for calculating the number of bits required to provide five networks is as follows:

$2^n - 2$ = at least 5

The first number in this equation is 2, because we are working with binary numbers (0 and 1). The 2 to the nth power provides the total number of possible networks using every possible combination of bits. The number 2 is subtracted from the result, because networks with all 0s and all 1s are considered invalid. (Note: Many vendors now allow the zero-based subnet address to be used. However, for test purposes, traditional calculations are required, which do not include this address range.)

From this formula, we need to calculate what "n" must be to get at least 5. Let us calculate a few examples as follows:

$2^2 - 2 = 2$

$2^3 - 2 = 6$

This last equation worked, indicating that 3 bits would provide six different combinations. That exceeds the requirement of five subnetworks.

A simpler way to tackle this without performing a specific calculation is to refer to the Subnetting Table presented earlier. Look on the bottom row of the table for a number that is greater than the requirement by at least two. After you have a number on the bottom row that works, look up to the middle row in the table. As discussed, 2^3 provides enough networks to fulfill the above requirement. The exponent also provides the number of bits that will be taken from the host portion and used for networks. (Do not worry about the location of this number in the table; it is just a reference to help with the calculation). In this case, 3 bits are necessary, as determined by looking at the exponent.

To complete the network calculation, assign the first 3 bits of this octet as the network, by placing Ns in the first three positions under the table starting from the left. These 3 bits represent the bits taken from the host and given to the network. They are in the first position because the network always comes first in an IP address. This process is shown on the Determining the Network Bits Diagram. For simplicity, note that the diagram shows only a single octet, not an entire IP address. At this point, the address class does not matter.

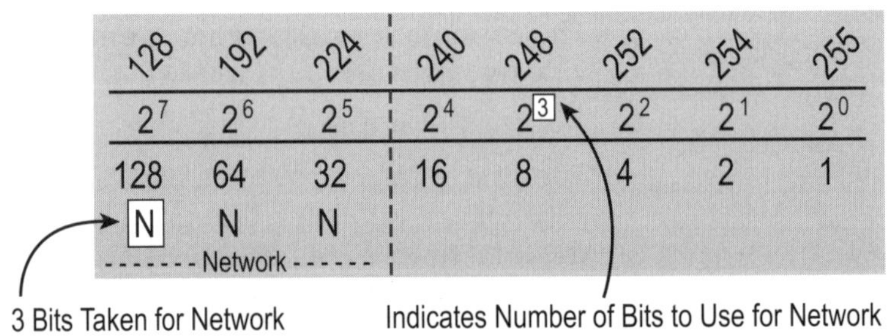

Determining the Network Bits

Step 2—Determine the Number of Hosts

After you have calculated the number of bits used for the different network addresses, the remaining bits are available for the host. In the example, 3 bits were determined to be necessary to fulfill the network requirements and were indicated on the diagram using the letter N. Using a single octet (Class C address in this case), we can now determine the number of bits still available to assign to hosts. Refer to the Determining the Network Bits Diagram. How many bits are still available? It looks like 5 bits are still available. You can also determine this by using simple math. If an octet contains 8 bits, and 3 bits are used for networks, that leaves 5 bits that can be used for hosts (that is, 8 - 3 = 5). The host bits can be easily identified by writing Hs in all the remaining positions.

Next, to determine how many unique hosts 5 bits will accommodate, use the following equation:

$2^h - 2$ = number of unique hosts

This is the same formula originally used to calculate the number of networks, with the exponent changed to "h" to identify it is being used on hosts. Knowing that 5 bits are left, the equation becomes $2^5 - 2 = 30$. Or, for an easy reference, use the Subnetting Table. Look for 2^5 in the middle row of the table, then look directly below for the number 32. Subtract 2 for invalid hosts, and the remaining number is 30 possible hosts per network. The Determining the Host Bits Diagram shows the bits used for both networks and hosts.

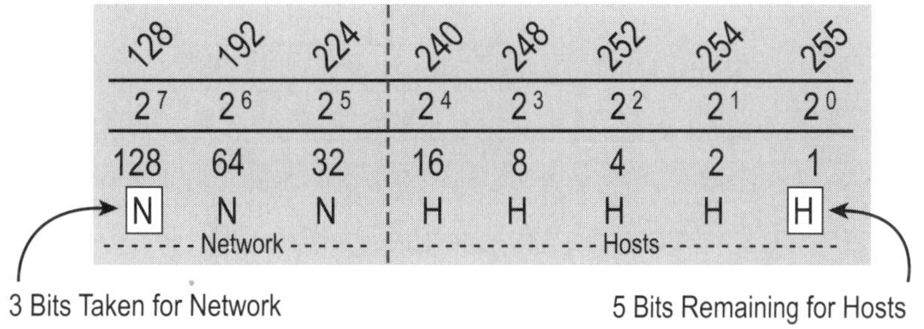

Determining the Host Bits

When using the equation $2^n - 2$, count the bits that have been defined as Ns during the first step. In this case, 3 bits were defined as Ns. For the equation $2^h - 2$ to determine hosts, replace "h" with the number of H bits that remain for host assignment. Only use the table as a reference for determining the value of the equation.

A summary of the steps detailed in this section follows:

- **Step 1**—Determine the number of current and future networks required. Use the formula $2^n - 2$, or look on the bottom row and directly up to the exponent on the Subnetting Table, to determine the number of bits to take from the host portion and assign to the network.
- **Step 2**—Determine the number of hosts required per network segment. Use the formula $2^h - 2$, or the table, to determine the remaining bits available after the networks have been determined.

This process will be reviewed for each address class later in this lesson.

The last four steps of this process go together. After you have one part, the rest just fall into place. The following four steps are shown on the Subnetting Diagram:

- **Step 3**—Define the subnet mask being used
- **Step 4**—Define all possible network numbers
- **Step 5**—Define the broadcast address for each network
- **Step 6**—Define the address range available to assign hosts

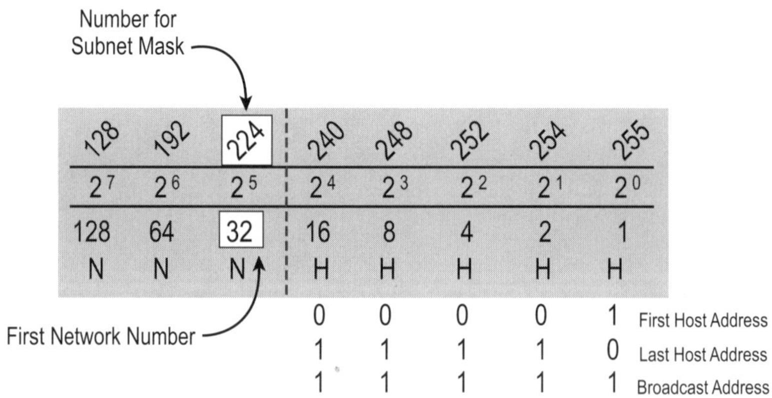

Subnetting

Step 3—Define the Subnet Mask

This step is easy using the table from the previous example. Refer to the Subnetting Diagram, which includes all the information you need to calculate the subnet mask. Notice a line is drawn between the bits assigned to the network (the Ns) and those available for hosts (the Hs). If you look to the left of this line at the top row, you see the number 224. This is the number used in the subnet mask if 3 bits are taken for subnetworks.

Now the diagram only shows one octet; however, it does not really matter which address class is used. Use the information shown in the Address Class Using 224 in the Subnet Mask Table.

Address Class Using 224 in the Subnet Mask

Address Class	Default Subnet Mask	New Subnet Mask
Class A	255.0.0.0	255.224.0.0
Class B	255.255.0.0	255.255.224.0
Class C	255.255.255.0	255.255.255.224

Notice that the default portion of the subnet mask never changes. It cannot, because it is a defined part of the address class. The remaining octets can be used for subnetwork assignment – this is what subnetting is all about.

Step 4—Define the Network Numbers

Looking at the bottom row of the table on the Subnetting Diagram, to the left of the line is the first network number of 32. Notice that it is in the same position directly below the subnet mask, which makes it a "dead giveaway." A little more math and we can calculate all the possible network numbers for this example. Remember that six networks are possible using 3 bits ($2^3 - 2 = 6$). Start with the first network number of 32, and add 32 over and over six times to get the remaining network numbers. The network numbers are calculated as follows: 32 + 32 = 64, 64 + 32 = 96, 96 +32 = 128, 128 + 32 = 160, and 160 + 32 = 192. This works regardless of the address class, as the Calculating the Network Numbers Table indicates.

Calculating the Network Numbers

Network	Class A Example	Class B Example	Class C Example
1st network	10.32.0.0	172.16.32.0	192.168.10.32
2nd network	10.64.0.0	172.16.64.0	192.168.10.64
3rd network	10.96.0.0	172.16.96.0	192.168.10.96
4th network	10.128.0.0	172.16.128.0	192.168.10.128
5th network	10.160.0.0	172.16.160.0	192.168.10.160
6th network	10.192.0.0	172.16.192.0	192.168.10.192

Notice from the table that only the subnetted portion of the address changes for each example. The first portion of the address does not change because of the default subnet mask.

Another way to determine the network numbers is to use a binary method. The process is simple with a few networks, but becomes very time-consuming if too many network numbers are necessary. In that case, the previous method of just adding the first network number to itself is the most efficient. It is good to use this method just to double-check your addition. It also allows you to see the bits in action. Keep in mind that only one of these two methods is necessary to use. They both return the same results, and the second method is only shown in the Binary Network Numbers Table to prove where the network numbers came from. It will not be reviewed in the other examples.

Binary Network Numbers

Subnet Bit	128	192	224	240	248	252	254	255	Network Number
Base 2	2^7	2^6	2^5	2^4	2^3	2^2	2^1	2^0	
Bit Value	128	64	32	16	8	4	2	1	
32 =	0	0	1						172.16.32.0
64 =	0	1	0						172.16.64.0
96 =	0	1	1						172.16.96.0
128 =	1	0	0						172.16.128.0
160 =	1	0	1						172.16.160.0
192 =	1	1	0						172.16.192.0

Remember from the current problem that 3 bits are being used, which provides six networks. The network numbers of all binary 0s and 1s are invalid and cannot be used. To see how the appropriate network numbers are created with the Class B subnet mask of 255.255.224.0, use the Binary Network Numbers Table. Notice that the numbers defined with the bit combinations are exactly those that were defined using the addition method above; therein lies the proof.

Only the first 3 bits were used in this example, because those are the network bits. Notice how each possible binary combination is used, excluding all 0s and all 1s.

Step 5—Define the Broadcast Address for Each Network

Now that all the possible networks have been determined, defining the broadcast address is very simple. The broadcast address is one less than the next network number. For Class A and Class B addresses, this includes some octets with all binary 1s or 255. Using the Calculating the Network Numbers Table and inserting columns for the broadcast addresses results in the Defining the Broadcast Addresses Table.

Defining the Broadcast Addresses

Network	Class A Network Address	Class A Broadcast	Class B Network Address	Class B Broadcast	Class C Network Address	Class C Broadcast
1st network	10.32.0.0	10.63.255.255	172.16.32.0	172.16.63.255	192.168.10.32	192.168.10.63
2nd network	10.64.0.0	10.95.255.255	172.16.64.0	172.16.95.255	192.168.10.64	192.168.10.95
3rd network	10.96.0.0	10.127.255.255	172.16.96.0	172.16.127.255	192.168.10.96	192.168.10.127
4th network	10.128.0.0	10.159.255.255	172.16.128.0	172.16.159.255	192.168.10.128	192.168.10.159
5th network	10.160.0.0	10.191.255.255	172.16.160.0	172.16.191.255	192.168.10.160	192.168.10.191
6th network	10.192.0.0	10.223.255.255	172.16.192.0	172.16.223.255	192.168.10.192	192.168.10.223

Step 6—Define the Address Range Available for Host Assignment

Although we have run out of room in the table above, just like the other five steps, this step is also easy. After you know the network number and broadcast address, all the numbers in between are available for host assignment. The host address range is one more than the network number and one less than the broadcast. The Class A Complete Subnet Example Table, Class B Complete Subnet Example Table, and Class C Complete Subnet Example Table provide the starting and ending host addresses for these address classes.

Class A Complete Subnet Example

Network	Class A Network Address	Starting Host Address	Ending Host Address	Class A Network Broadcast
1st network	10.32.0.0	10.32.0.1	10.63.255.254	10.63.255.255
2nd network	10.64.0.0	10.64.0.1	10.95.255.254	10.95.255.255
3rd network	10.96.0.0	10.96.0.1	10.127.255.254	10.127.255.255
4th network	10.128.0.0	10.128.0.1	10.159.255.254	10.159.255.255

Class A Complete Subnet Example (Continued)

Network	Class A Network Address	Starting Host Address	Ending Host Address	Class A Network Broadcast
5th network	10.160.0.0	10.160.0.1	10.191.255.254	10.191.255.255
6th network	10.192.0.0	10.192.0.1	10.223.255.254	10.223.255.255

Class B Complete Subnet Example

Network	Class B Network Address	Starting Host Address	Ending Host Address	Class B Network Broadcast
1st network	172.16.32.0	172.16.32.1	172.16.63.254	172.16.63.255
2nd network	172.16.64.0	172.16.64.1	172.16.95.254	172.16.95.255
3rd network	172.16.96.0	172.16.96.1	172.16.127.254	172.16.127.255
4th network	172.16.128.0	172.16.128.1	172.16.159.254	172.16.159.255
5th network	172.16.160.0	172.16.160.1	172.16.191.254	172.16.191.255
6th network	172.16.192.0	172.16.192.1	172.16.223.254	172.16.223.255

Class C Complete Subnet Example

Network	Class C Network Address	Starting Host Address	Ending Host Address	Class C Network Broadcast
1st network	192.168.10.32	192.168.10.33	192.168.10.62	192.168.10.63
2nd network	192.168.10.64	192.168.10.65	192.168.10.94	192.168.10.95
3rd network	192.168.10.96	192.168.10.97	192.168.10.126	192.168.10.127
4th network	192.168.10.128	192.168.10.129	192.168.10.158	192.168.10.159
5th network	192.168.10.160	192.168.10.161	192.168.10.190	192.168.10.191
6th network	192.168.10.192	192.168.10.193	192.168.10.222	192.168.10.223

Notice from each of the example tables the following characteristics:

- The broadcast address is one less than the next network number.
- The starting host address is one more than the network address.
- The ending host address is one less than the broadcast address.
- The network addresses are always even numbers.
- The broadcast addresses are always odd numbers.
- The numbers on the top row of the subnetting table are the only options for subnet mask assignment.
- The numbers on the bottom row of the subnetting table are the only options for network address numbers.

Class A Subnetting Example

Because Class A is first, let us start with this class for a complete subnetting example.

The company is assigned a Class A IP address of 14.0.0.0. The default Class A subnet mask is 255.0.0.0.

At least 58 networks must be created, with a few extra networks for future growth. At least 20,000 addresses must be available to assign to hosts on each network. (This example does not really represent a production environment, because a network designer would never assign so many hosts to each subnet; it is really more for applying the method of subnetting.)

1. **Determine the number of networks using the formula $2^n - 2$ = at least 58 or look on the bottom row of the Subnetting Table for a number that is greater than 58 by at least 2.**

   Referring to the Class A Subnetting Diagram, you can see that $2^6 = 64 - 2 = 62$ networks. This meets the requirement of at least 58 networks, with a few available for growth. The exponent number indicates that 6 bits will be used to create 62 networks. As depicted on the diagram by Ns in the bottom row starting from the left, the network reserves the first 6 bits of the octet.

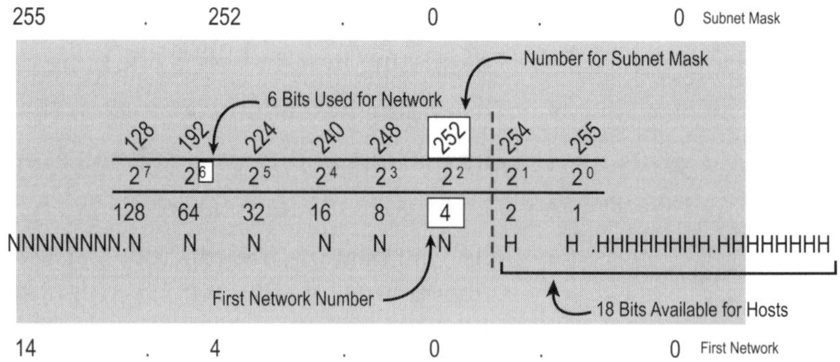

Class A Subnetting

2. **Determine the number of hosts using the formula $2^h - 2$ = at least 20,000.**

   After 6 network bits are put in place on the Class A Subnetting Diagram, how many bits are available for hosts? Notice from the diagram that 2 bits are in the second octet, plus both of the last two octets are still available, for a total of 18 bits. Using the equation $2^h - 2$, this provides $2^{18} - 2 = 262{,}142$ hosts. The remaining bits provide more than the required number of hosts per subnet.

3. **Determine the subnet mask.**

   With the 6 network bits in place, a line is drawn after the last bit. The number in the top row to the left of the line is the new subnet mask number. Notice from the Class A Subnetting Diagram that this corresponds to 252. Adding to the default Class A network mask, the new subnet mask is 255.252.0.0.

4. **Determine the network numbers.**

   At least 62 networks are possible, thus we will not cover all of them here, but we will at least get started. The first network is the number on the bottom row, directly under the subnet mask, 14.4.0.0. The next network is 4 added to itself to get 14.8.0.0, and again to get 14.12.0.0, and again to get 14.16.0.0.

The Class A Subnetting Example Table presents these network addresses in the second column.

Class A Subnetting Example

Network	Network Address	Starting Host Address	Ending Host Address	Broadcast Address
1st network	14.4.0.0	14.4.0.1	14.7.255.254	14.7.255.255
2nd network	14.8.0.0	14.8.0.1	14.11.255.254	14.11.255.255
3rd network	14.12.0.0	14.12.0.1	14.15.255.254	14.15.255.255
4th network	14.16.0.0	14.16.0.1	14.19.255.254	14.19.255.255
5th network	14.20.0.0	14.20.0.1	14.23.255.254	14.23.255.255

5. **Determine the broadcast address.**

   Remember that the broadcast address is one less than the next network number. For the first network of 14.4.0.0, the last number before the next network is 14.7.255.255, which is the broadcast address. For the second network of 14.8.0.0, the last number before the next network is 14.11.255.255. Notice that the number that is one less than the next network is in the second octet. The last two octets are all binary 1s or 255. Refer to the last column in the Class A Subnetting Example Table to see the associated broadcast addresses.

6. **Determine the assignable host address range.**

   All the numbers between the network address and broadcast address are available to assign to hosts. Remember that a host cannot be all 0s (network) or all 1s (broadcast); this was accounted for in the last two steps. For the first network, the host address range is 14.4.0.1 through 14.7.255.254. For the second network, the host address range is 14.8.0.1 through 14.11.255.254.

Now let us pull it all together so that it is easier to understand. The Class A Subnetting Example Table includes calculations for the first five networks. The Class A network specifications are as follows:

- Assigned IP address: 14.0.0.0
- Networks = $2^6 - 2 = 62$
- Hosts per subnet = $2^{18} - 2 = 262{,}142$
- Subnet mask: 255.252.0.0

Class B Subnetting Example

Now for a Class B example using the same basic process, only this time the numbers have moved over an octet. Changes will be made to the third octet instead of the second octet as in Class A.

The company is assigned a Class B IP address of 181.55.0.0. The default Class B subnet mask is 255.255.0.0.

At least 30 networks must be created, which accounts for future growth. At least 2,000 addresses must be available to assign to hosts.

1. **Determine the number of networks using the formula $2^n - 2$ = at least 30 or the Subnetting Table.**

   Referring to the Class B Subnetting Diagram, you can see that $2^5 = 32 - 2 = 30$ networks. This is exactly the number of networks the company requires, including networks for future growth. The exponent indicates 5 bits will be used for subnetting. Reserve the 5 bits by placing an N in the correct position on the diagram, and this step is complete.

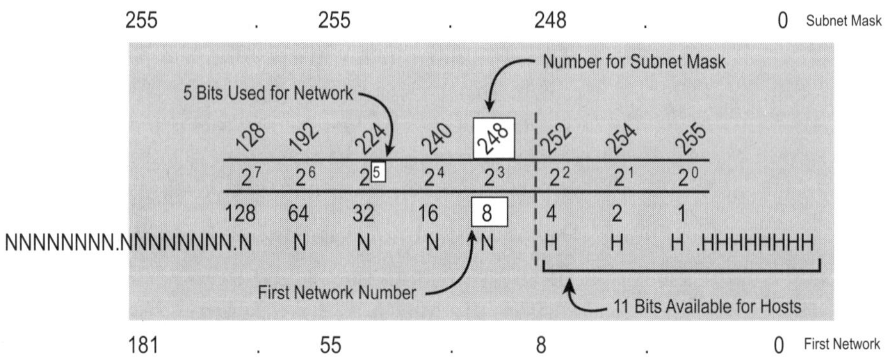

Class B Subnetting

2. **Determine the number of hosts using the formula $2^h - 2$ = at least 2,000.**

   After the 5 network bits are put in place, how many bits are available for hosts? There are 3 bits in the third octet, plus the 8 bits in the remaining octet in a Class B address, for a total of 11 bits. Using the equation $2^h - 2$, this information provides $2^{11} - 2 = 2,046$ hosts. This meets the requirement of 2,000 hosts, with 46 hosts available in each subnetwork for future growth.

3. **Determine the subnet mask.**

   With the 5 network bits in place, draw a line after the last bit (between the Ns and Hs). The number in the top row to the left of the line is the subnet mask number. In this case, the subnet mask is 255.255.248.0.

4. **Determine the network numbers.**

   There are at least 30 possible networks, thus we will not cover all of them here, but we will determine a few for starters. The first network is the number on the bottom row, directly under the subnet mask, 181.55.8.0. The next network is this number (8) added to itself to get 181.55.16.0, and again to get 181.55.24.0, and again to get 181.55.32.0.

5. **Determine the broadcast address.**

   Remember that the broadcast address is one less than the next network number. For the first network, the broadcast address is 181.55.15.255. For the second network, the broadcast address is 181.55.23.255.

6. **Determine the host address range.**

   All the numbers between the network address and the broadcast address are available to assign to hosts. Remember that a host cannot be all 0s (network) or all 1s (broadcast); this was accounted for in the last two steps. For the first network, the address range is 181.55.8.1 through 181.55.15.254. For the second network, the address range is 181.55.16.1 through 181.55.23.254.

Now let us pull it all together so that it is easier to understand. The Class B Subnetting Example Table includes the first five networks. The Class B network specifications are as follows:

- Assigned IP address: 181.55.0.0
- Networks = $2^5 - 2 = 30$
- Hosts per subnet = $2^{11} - 2 = 2,046$
- Subnet mask: 255.255.248.0

Class B Subnetting Example

Network	Network Address	Starting Host Address	Ending Host Address	Broadcast Address
1st network	181.55.8.0	181.55.8.1	181.55.15.254	181.55.15.255
2nd network	181.55.16.0	181.55.16.1	181.55.23.254	181.55.23.255
3rd network	181.55.24.0	181.55.24.1	181.55.31.254	181.55.31.255
4th network	181.55.32.0	181.55.32.1	181.55.39.254	181.55.39.255
5th network	181.55.40.0	181.55.40.1	181.55.47.254	181.55.47.255

Class C Subnetting Example

Class C addresses can be a little trickier because the only bits available for subnetting are in the last octet. This means that the numbers for network, host address ranges, and broadcast all reside within the last 8 bits, but the process is exactly the same. This is where it is really important to understand what is going on at the bit level, which a lot of textbooks do not include. Now, let us go through the process as we have done for Classes A and B.

The company is assigned a Class C IP address of 222.101.85.0. The default Class C subnet mask is 255.255.255.0.

At least six networks must be created, which accounts for future growth. At least 30 addresses must be available to assign to hosts, which also allows for future growth.

1. **Determine the number of networks using the formula $2^n - 2$ = at least 6.**

   Referring to the Class C Subnetting Diagram, you can see that $2^3 = 8 - 2 = 6$ networks. This meets the company's requirement, which accounts for future growth. The exponent indicates that 3 bits will be used for subnetting. Place Ns in the first three positions of the octet on the diagram.

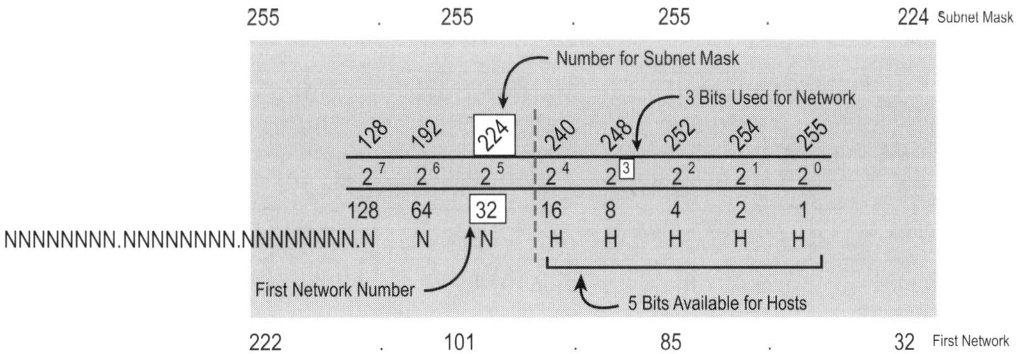

Class C Subnetting

2. **Determine the number of hosts using the formula $2^h - 2$ = at least 30.**

   After 3 network bits are put in place, how many bits are available for hosts? There are only 5 bits left in this last octet to use for host assignments. Using the equation $2^h - 2$, this information provides $2^5 - 2 = 30$ hosts. Again, this is perfect; exactly 30 unique hosts fulfill the requirement.

3. **Determine the subnet mask.**

   With the 3 network bits in place, draw a line after the last bit. The number in the top row to the left of the line is the subnet mask number. In this case, the subnet mask is 255.255.255.224.

4. **Determine the network numbers.**

   There are at least six possible networks, included in the Class C Subnetting Example Table. The first network is the number on the bottom row of the Class C Subnetting Diagram, directly under the subnet mask, 222.101.85.32. The next network is this number (32) added to itself to get 222.101.85.64, and again to get 222.101.85.96, and so on.

Class C Subnetting Example

Network	Network Address	Starting Host Address	Ending Host Address	Broadcast Address
1st network	222.101.85.32	222.101.85.33	222.101.85.62	222.101.85.63
2nd network	222.101.85.64	222.101.85.65	222.101.85.94	222.101.85.95
3rd network	222.101.85.96	222.101.85.97	222.101.85.126	222.101.85.127
4th network	222.101.85.128	222.101.85.129	222.101.85.158	222.101.85.159
5th network	222.101.85.160	222.101.85.161	222.101.85.190	222.101.85.191
6th network	222.101.85.192	222.101.85.193	222.101.85.223	222.101.85.224

5. **Determine the broadcast address.**

   Remember that the broadcast address is one less than the next network number. For the first network, the broadcast address is 222.101.85.63. For the second network, the broadcast address is 222.101.85.95.

6. **Determine the assignable host address range.**

   All the numbers between the network address and the broadcast address are available to assign to hosts. Remember that a host cannot be all 0s (network) or all 1s (broadcast); this was accounted for in the last two steps. For the first network, the address range is 222.101.85.33 through 222.101.85.62. For the second network, the address range is 222.101.85.65 through 222.101.85.94.

Let us summarize what we just calculated. The Class C Subnetting Example Table includes all six possible networks. The Class C network specifications are as follows:

- Assigned IP address: 222.101.85.0
- Networks = $2^3 - 2 = 6$
- Hosts per subnet = $2^5 - 2 = 30$
- Subnet mask: 255.255.255.224

Class C subnetting may almost be easier than the other classes if you look at the bits. Everything is right there in one octet. Remember that the starting host address is one more than the network. The ending host address is one less than the broadcast. And, the broadcast address is one less than the next network number. It is really pretty simple to figure out with a little practice.

Subnetting From Another Perspective

At times you will be asked to answer different types of subnetting questions. The purpose of testing is to make sure you know the material inside and out. Before you go to take an exam, we will look at subnetting from a few different angles, just to make sure it is understood. We will review the type of questions you might encounter, and go through the process to find the correct answers. Below are three examples of typical IP subnetting questions that differ from the preceding examples.

Given an IP address of 170.45.0.0 and a subnet mask of 255.255.240.0, determine the number of networks and hosts.

Using the Subnetting Table introduced earlier, you can draw a line to the right of the subnet mask as shown below. Then write in Ns to the left of the line and Hs to the right of the line.

Subnetting

Subnet Bit	128	192	224	240	248	252	254	255	
Base 2	2^7	2^6	2^5	2^4	2^3	2^2	2^1	2^0	
Bit Value	128	64	32	16	8	4	2	1	
	N	N	N	N	H	H	H	H	. HHHHHHHH

It is easy to see that 4 bits are before the line and 4 bits are after the line. Keep in mind that a Class B address means that another octet and its 8 bits are available for the host's assignment, for a total of 12 bits. To answer the question, calculate the following equations by counting the N and H bits:

Networks	$2^n - 2 = ?$	$2^4 - 2 = 14$
Hosts	$2^h - 2 = ?$	$2^{12} - 2 = 4{,}094$

Thus, the answer to the question, given a Class B address and a subnet mask of 255.255.240.0, is 14 networks and 4,094 hosts per network.

Given an IP address of 199.30.82.0 and a subnet mask of 255.255.255.192, what are the first two networks, their address ranges, and broadcast addresses?

Refer to the Subnetting Table and place a line to the right of the subnet number. This points us right to the network information used to answer this question. The number in the bottom row directly under the subnet is the first network.

Subnetting

Subnet Bit	128	192	224	240	248	252	254	255
Base 2	2^7	2^6	2^5	2^4	2^3	2^2	2^1	2^0
Bit Value	128	64	32	16	8	4	2	1

Add that number to itself (64 + 64 = 128) to determine the next possible network address. The Two-Network Example Table shows the details.

Two-Network Example

Network	Network Address	Starting Address	Ending Address	Broadcast Address
1st network	199.30.82.64	199.30.82.65	199.30.82.126	199.30.82.127
2nd network	199.30.82.128	199.30.82.129	199.30.82.190	199.30.82.191

Using the address and subnet mask of 170.45.0.0 and 255.255.240.0, respectively, which two of the following are on the same subnetwork?

a. 170.45.33.23

b. 170.45.49.114

c. 170.45.47.67

d. 170.45.30.241

To figure this out, you need to fill in the Address Table as follows.

Address Table

Subnet Bit	128	192	224	240	248	252	254	255
Base 2	2^7	2^6	2^5	2^4	2^3	2^2	2^1	2^0
Bit Value	128	64	32	16	8	4	2	1

Save Subnet Example

Subnet Address	Starting Host Address	Ending Host Address	Broadcast Address
170.45.16.0	170.45.16.1 **d**	170.45.31.254	170.45.31.255
170.45.32.0	170.45.32.1 **a c**	170.45.47.254	170.45.47.255
170.45.48.0	170.45.48.1 **b**	170.45.63.254	170.45.63.255
170.45.64.0	170.45.64.1	170.45.79.254	170.45.79.255

There are more numbers that can be assigned, but this is enough to answer the question. With the Save Subnet Example Table filled out, associate each letter of the answer options with one of the subnets. Answer a is a host address in subnet 170.45.32.0 (the second one down), so write an "a" in that row. Answer b is a host address in the third subnet, so "b" is written on the third line. Answer c is a host address in the second subnet; write in "c" on line two. Answer d is a host address in the first subnet, so "d" is written on the first row. Looking at the table, it is easy to see after working the problem that the correct answer is that a and c are in the same subnet. Without actually doing the calculation this would be difficult to determine. We are often likely to simply pick the numbers that are closest together; however, as this example proves, that method does not work for this type of problem.

Working the problems when you already have the subnet mask is no more difficult than the previous examples using the Subnetting Table. The Subnetting Table is easy to create and works for the majority of subnetting questions. If used properly, it can be an invaluable tool in the subnetting process. Once you get good at subnetting, or if you do it a lot, you will probably use a subnet calculator for this work. However, do not cheat yourself now. It is better to struggle through and learn it than fumbling through this topic and becoming dependent on a calculator. Calculators cannot be used in the exam; thus you are going to have to do it by hand anyway.

Now that you have seen the process and reviewed a number of problems, the following is a quick recap of the subnetting process. This is a good page to bookmark as a reference to the steps discussed in detail in this lesson. There will be times when you need all of the steps together, and other times when you only need one or two. If you forget the process, just go back to the steps and try it again. Do not be afraid to put pencil to paper and practice subnetting a lot. You can read this section over and over; however, until you try some problems, it will never sink in.

The method explained in this book is dependent on the Subnetting Table.

Subnetting

Subnet Bit	128	192	224	240	248	252	254	255
Base 2	2^7	2^6	2^5	2^4	2^3	2^2	2^1	2^0
Bit Value	128	64	32	16	8	4	2	1

As a summary of the subnetting process, the following list presents the basic steps:

- Determine the requirements for the problem. If it is number of subnetworks, count all router, layer 3 switch interfaces, and VLANs. The number of hosts is often just provided as part of the problem. **Look at the bottom row of the Subnetting Table for a value that is greater than the requirement by at least two.**
- **Look directly up to the exponent value, which defines the number of bits.** If the requirement is for subnetworks, write Ns under each position in the table starting from the left. If the requirement is for hosts, write Hs under each position in the table starting from the right. Fill the other side in with either Ns or Hs to complete the table.
- **Draw a line between the Ns and Hs. Look to the top row of the table to determine the new subnet mask.** The value to the left of the line on the top row is appended to the default subnet mask.
- **Check your work to make sure that enough bits have been made available for both subnets and hosts. Use the formula $2^n - 2$ = subnetworks and $2^h - 2$ = hosts per network.** Fill in the formulas by counting the number of Ns and Hs put in place during the last step. Remember that only one octet is addressed with the Subnetting Table. Make sure to include any remaining octets when using a Class A or Class B address.

- **Determine the network addresses to fill in the first column of the table.** This can be done using the binary method, making all the possible combinations of 0s and 1s to the left of the line. Another way to determine the network addresses is to look at the decimal number on the bottom row of the table to the left of the line. Then add that number to itself for as many times as there are subnetworks calculated in the last step.
- **Determine the broadcast addresses to fill in the last column of the table. The broadcast address is one less than the next network number.** Thus, if the entire first column is filled in, simply use it to calculate the broadcast addresses and fill in the last column.
- **Determine the assignable host address range.** The host address range is all the values between the network and the broadcast. To fill in the remainder of the table, the first possible host value is one more than the network. The last possible host value is one less than the broadcast.

Using Logical AND to Determine the Subnetwork Address

Now that you have a fairly complete picture of the entire process, there is one more calculation that may come in handy. It is a process called "logical ANDing." It is useful to determine a subnetwork address from a complete IP host address. Logical ANDing can help you see why a subnet mask is considered a mask in the first place. It shows that where there are 1 bits in the subnet mask, the associated address value will remain the same.

To get a better understanding of this process let us review it with an actual address and subnet mask. The address for this example is 192.168.45.171 and the subnet mask is 255.255.255.224. First, perform this process as follows:

1. Write the IP address as binary. The table used for the subnetting process can be helpful to make this conversion.
2. Write the subnet mask in binary directly under the IP address.
3. "AND" the two numbers together using the following principles:

   Any positions with 1 AND 1 = 1

   Any combination of 0 AND 1 = 0 (that is 0 AND 1 = 0, 1 AND 0 = 0, 0 AND 0 = 0)

4. Convert the binary number back to decimal to see the subnetwork address.

Following these steps, let us work the problem with 192.168.45.171 and 255.255.255.224:

1. Following Steps 1 and 2 of the previous process, write the IP address and subnet mask directly over one another in binary:

   192.168.45.171 11000000.10101000.00101101.101 | 01011

   255.255.255.224 11111111.11111111.11111111.111 | 00000

2. AND these two numbers together:

   11000000.10101000.00101101.101 00000

3. Convert the binary name back to decimal to reveal the subnetwork number:

   11000000.10101000.00101101.10100000 = 192.168.45.160

This tells us that the host address 192.168.45.171 belongs on subnetwork 192.168.45.160 given the subnet mask of 255.255.255.224. Notice that this is easy to see if you draw a line after the last bit of the subnet mask. The value that is returned as all 0s in the host position is the address of the subnetwork or, as it is sometimes referred to, the address of the wire.

Just to make sure you understand, let us try one more example, this time with a Class B address. The given address is 172.16.98.221 and the subnet mask is 255.255.252.0. Use the steps to determine the subnetwork address for this host.

172.16.98.221	10101100.00010000.011000 | 10.11011101
255.255.252.0	11111111.11111111.111111 | 00.00000000
AND	10101100.00010000.011000 | 00.00000000

10101100.00010000.01100000.00000000 = 172.16.96.0

Given the information, the host address 172.16.98.221 is on subnetwork 172.16.96.0.

Review Questions

Refer to the Subnetting Table as necessary for the following questions.

Subnetting

Subnet Bit	128	192	224	240	248	252	254	255
Base 2	2^7	2^6	2^5	2^4	2^3	2^2	2^1	2^0
Bit Value	128	64	32	16	8	4	2	1

1. What class(es) of address can use the subnet mask of 255.255.240.0?

   ____

2. With a Class C address and subnet mask of 255.255.255.192, how many networks can be assigned?

   ____

3. Using the same information from Question 2, how many hosts can be assigned?

   ____

4. When subnetting, bits are taken from the host portion and given to the network. True or False?
5. When subnetting, the default subnet mask must always be used, then subnet bits are added as necessary. True or False?
6. The subnet mask 255.255.255.0 can be used with a Class A address. True or False?
7. Using a Class B address and 6 bits for networks, what is the subnet mask?

   ____

8. Using a Class A address and 10 bits for networks, what is the subnet mask?

   ____

9. Using a Class C address and 3 bits for networks, what is the subnet mask?

____

10. Which two binary number combinations cannot be used for host assignments, and why are these two combinations reserved?

____

11. Given the subnet mask 255.255.248.0, used with a Class B address, how many bits are used for subnetworks?

____

12. Given the subnet mask 255.255.255.224, used with a Class C address, how many bits are used for subnetworks?

____

13. Given the subnet mask 255.255.248.0, used with a Class A address, how many bits are available for hosts?

____

14. Given the subnet mask 255.255.254.0, used with a Class B address, how many bits are available for hosts?

____

Extended Activities

Complete each of the following problems using the necessary information from this lesson and the Subnetting Table.

Subnetting

Subnet Bit	128	192	224	240	248	252	254	255
Base 2	2^7	2^6	2^5	2^4	2^3	2^2	2^1	2^0
Bit Value	128	64	32	16	8	4	2	1

1. Given a Class B address of 129.120.0.0 and the requirement for at least 60 networks, provide the following:
   a. Subnet mask

   ____

   b. Actual number of networks

   ____

   c. Number of possible hosts

   ____

   d. First network address

   ____

2. Given a Class C address of 198.100.45.0 and the requirement for at least 30 hosts per network (no requirements for the number of networks have been given), provide the following:
   a. Subnet mask that allows 30 hosts

   ____

   b. Number of networks

   ____

   c. Missing information for all the networks

Network	Network Number	Starting Host Address	Ending Host Address	Broadcast Address
1st network				
2nd network				
3rd network				
4th network				
5th network				
6th network				

3. Given a Class B address of 171.92.0.0 and a subnet mask of 255.255.240.0, provide the following:
   a. Number of networks

   ____

   b. Number of hosts

   ____

   c. Missing information for the first three networks

Network	Network Number	Starting Host Address	Ending Host Address	Broadcast Address
1st network				
2nd network				
3rd network				

4. Given a Class C address of 200.4.82.0 and the requirement for at least 14 networks, provide the following:
   a. Number of available hosts

   ____

   b. Subnet mask

   ____

   c. Missing information for the first five networks

Network	Network Number	Starting Host Address	Ending Host Address	Broadcast Address
1st network				
2nd network				
3rd network				
4th network				
5th network				

5. Which of the following addresses are in the same network as 172.16.54.14 with a subnet mask of 255.255.240.0? (Choose two.)
   a. 172.16.49.230
   b. 172.16.64.14
   c. 172.16.46.255
   d. 172.16.62.255
6. What is the broadcast address for the second network using an address of 197.36.91.0 and subnet mask of 255.255.255.192?
   a. 197.36.91.64
   b. 197.36.91.128
   c. 197.36.91.127
   d. 197.36.91.191
7. Given the address 200.47.30.0 and the subnet mask of 255.255.255.248, with the requirement of 10 networks and 8 hosts, which of the following statements is correct?
   a. There are enough bits for both networks and hosts.
   b. There are enough bits for networks, but not for hosts.
   c. There are not enough bits for networks, but there are enough for hosts.
   d. There are not enough bits for networks or hosts.
8. On what network number does the host address 10.14.54.23 with a subnet mask of 255.252.0.0 reside?
   a. 10.4.0.0
   b. 10.10.0.0
   c. 10.12.0.0
   d. 10.14.0.0
9. What is the second network address given the number 192.168.40.0 and the subnet mask of 255.255.255.248?
   a. 192.168.40.1
   b. 192.168.40.8
   c. 192.168.40.12
   d. 192.168.40.16

10. A company is currently using the subnet mask of 255.255.255.192 with a Class C address. The company has grown in size and the network engineer is changing the network infrastructure. The new requirement is for at least seven subnets, with growth potential for at least four additional subnets in the near future. What should the subnet mask be changed to in order to accommodate the new requirements?

    a. 255.255.255.224

    b. 255.255.255.240

    c. 255.255.255.252

    d. 255.255.224.0

11. A client is having problems communicating with another network device. The IP address of Host A is 192.168.111.62 with a subnet mask of 255.255.255.224. Host B has an IP address of 192.168.111.65 with the same subnet mask. Both devices physically reside on the same network segment. Why can't they communicate?

    a. The subnet mask is wrong for Host B.

    b. The IP address for Host B is misconfigured; it does not have the correct address for the subnet where it is located.

    c. The two devices do not have the proper communication software installed.

    d. The router is not forwarding packets between the two subnets.

12. A network administrator wants to assign addresses to router interfaces that are connected back-to-back. Only two host addresses are required on each subnet. A lot of subnets need to be assigned. Which subnet mask can be used to create the most number of subnets with only two hosts per subnet?

    a. 255.255.255.240

    b. 255.255.255.248

    c. 255.255.255.252

    d. 255.255.255.254

13. Which address is not on the same subnetwork as all the other addresses given the Class B IP address 172.16.X.X and the subnet mask 255.255.248.0?

    a. 172.16.16.24

    b. 172.16.23.95

    c. 172.16.24.200

    d. 172.16.18.111

14. A network administrator has just been hired and is reviewing the existing network infrastructure. The corporate network is assigned a Class A address. There are currently 85 subnets in use. The company is projecting growth of approximately 15 new subnets per year. The network administrator needs to determine the correct subnet mask that will support current needs and future network growth over the next five years. What subnet mask should be used?

    a. 255.240.0.0

    b. 255.255.0.0

    c. 255.255.192.0

    d. 255.254.0.0

15. A person is installing some new equipment on a network. All devices are physically located and must have addresses in the same subnet to communicate properly. The person is given the following addresses to assign the equipment: 192.168.10.20, 192.168.10.22, 192.168.10.24, and 192.168.10.26. The subnet mask in use is 255.255.255.248. Which addresses are incorrectly assigned? (Choose two.)

    a. 192.168.10.20

    b. 192.168.10.22

    c. 192.168.10.24

    d. 192.168.10.26

Lesson 3—Routing Basics

Routing is the process of moving information from one place to another based on a hierarchal address. Routing is performed at the Network Layer of the Open Systems Interconnection (OSI) model by routers and layer 3 switch devices. This lesson provides a foundation for understanding how the routing process works. It discusses IP routing using static routes, default routes, and dynamic routing protocols. To get a better understanding of how this works, we look at the difference between routed and routing. The lesson goes on to discuss the components of a routing table, and then walks step-by-step through the transmission process. The lesson ends with an overview of the key features of routing protocols, as well as the values associated with routing metrics.

Objectives

At the end of this lesson you will be able to:

- Describe the IP routing process
- Describe the method routers use to make path selection
- Distinguish between routed and routing protocols
- Identify the components of a routing table
- Explain a simple routing process from sender to receiver
- Identify the characteristics of routing protocols
- Identify the values associated with routing metrics

Key Point

Routing is an essential part of getting information from one host to another in a network. Hierarchical Network Layer addresses and routing protocols make route selection possible.

IP Routing

The Internet is a large collection of networks and hosts interconnected by routers. Routers are specialized devices that connect two or more packet-switching networks. Routers function as intermediate packet switches that forward traffic from one network to another. Routers are also called "gateways" in Internet literature. The IP protocol suite was designed to provide communication services that allow an individual host to communicate with any other host on any of the networks that make up the Internet or an enterprise network.

If a host on one network wishes to communicate with a host on another network, the source host must transmit the packet to a router directly connected to its local network. There are many ways a host can learn the identity of the appropriate router: through static routes, default routes, and dynamic routing protocols. After receiving a transmission, the router forwards the packet through the interconnected system of networks and routers until it eventually reaches a router attached to the same network as the destination host. This final router delivers the packet to the switch or hub, and then on to a specified host on its local network.

Path Selection

A router makes its forwarding decisions based on the information contained in a routing table. This information includes the destination network number, rather than the actual physical address of each destination host. Because the routing table is based on network numbers rather than host addresses, the amount of information a router needs to maintain in its routing table is directly proportionate to the number of networks that make up the internetwork. This reduces the routing table's size, because a router does not have to maintain information about every single host connected to the internetwork.

Three types of IP routing methods exist:

- **Static routing**—These routes are configured by a network administrator. They reduce router overhead, require no bandwidth to pass updates, and are often used for troubleshooting, network changes, or across slow WAN links. Disadvantages include high administration to configure, update, and maintain the routing entries and poor scalability on large networks.
- **Default routing**—These manually configured routes are designed to send any packets without an assigned route to the next hop router by means of a default router port. These can only be used on routers with a single outside interface. Default routers, also called "default gateways," are the only path for leaving a network.
- **Dynamic routing**—These routes are learned by routers sharing routing information. Dynamic routing protocols pass routing updates between each other to learn different path options and create routing tables. Dynamic routing protocols include RIP, IGRP, EIGRP, and OSPF.

Routed and Routing Protocols

IP is considered a routed or routable protocol because it has a hierarchical Network Layer address. This address uniquely identifies every host within a network environment. The router cannot use a MAC address to locate a device because a MAC address does not have the proper type of hierarchy. For a router to pass traffic, it must have a routed protocol. Besides IP, other routable protocols include IPX used in Novell NetWare environments, and X.25 used for packet-switched WAN environments.

Other protocols found in LAN environments today are not routed protocols because they do not have the proper addressing format for a router to use and make the best path selection. Instead, the router must act like a bridge to connect these protocols together for transmission at the Data Link Layer. When a router is working in this manner, it is sometimes referred to as a "brouter." This means that it bridges the nonroutable protocols, while routing the rest. Nonroutable protocols include Network Basic Input/Output System (NetBIOS), Systems Network Architecture (SNA), Banyan VINES, and AppleTalk.

Routing protocols are used to exchange information between routing devices. Routing protocols have very specific features that allow them to build routing tables, share the information with neighboring devices, calculate a metric value for each path, and determine the best path based on the metric value. Routing protocols are considered dynamic because they update routing table information as a network changes. Without a routing protocol, an administrator would be required to configure static routes to perform path selection. The routing protocols that will be discussed in further detail include RIP, IGRP, EIGRP, OSPF, and BGP.

Routing Tables

A router examines its routing table to determine how to forward a packet. If the destination is on a directly attached network, the router delivers the packet without using the services of another router. If the destination is on a remote network, the router must send the packet to another router closer to the final destination. The route to a remote network can be statically configured or dynamically learned through a routing protocol such as RIP, IGRP, or OSPF.

Routers can use a combination of static and dynamic techniques to obtain information needed for their routing tables. Each router first establishes an initial set of routes that are directly connected through egress (exit) interfaces on a device. A router will then exchange routing table information with other devices based on the method appropriate to the routing protocol being used. After the initial routing table has become memory-resident, the router must have the ability to respond to new routes or changes in the network topology. Updates can be made to static routes by an administrator. More commonly, a router learns about path changes from other routers using the same dynamic routing protocols.

A routing table holds the following information at a minimum:

- **Network address**—This is the network and subnetwork portion of an IP address. This concept is discussed in the lesson entitled "IP Addressing and Subnetting."
- **Egress interface**—This is the interface that transmissions exit to get to another network.
- **Metric**—A metric is a value used by a router to determine the best path to another network.

Other values such as time, next hop address, owner, and administrative distance value can also be included in a routing table.

Simple Routing Process

The method for transmitting a packet from one host to another over an internetwork is shown on the Simple Routing Process Diagram. This example involves a source host (Host A), destination host (Host B), two intermediate routers, and three distinct networks segments. The IP and Ethernet addresses for each host and router port are also presented.

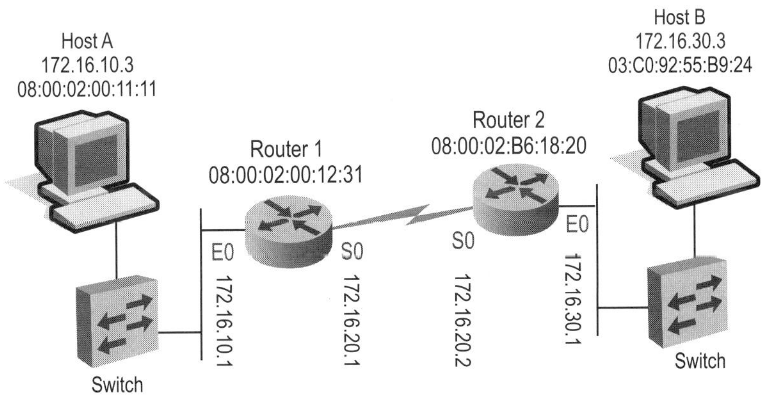

Simple Routing Process

The path a packet takes is not determined by a single central source, but is the result of examining each routing table used in the journey through a network. Each router defines only the next hop in the path and relies on the next-hop router to send an IP packet on its way. In very broad terms, routing involves taking bits off the wire, removing the frame header, and reading the IP packet address. The router reviews its routing table to determine the best path. The packet is then reframed and transmitted to the egress interface to continue on its way. The following sections provide a more detailed explanation of the process.

Host A on Network 172.16.10.0 wishes to make a connection to Host B on Network 172.16.30.0 using the Telnet protocol. As the packet moves from router to router, the IP header defined by Host A remains constant and does not change. The only addresses that change as the packet moves toward its final destination are the source and destination MAC addresses in the Ethernet header.

Because Host A and Host B are on different networks, Host A must use the services of an IP router. The switch that Host A is connected to can only transmit to other devices within the same network segment. Upon initialization, Host A learned that the IP address of its default gateway is 172.16.10.1. As a result, Host A knows it must use Router 1 to transmit a packet to any host residing on a different network. Before Host A can send the first frame, it must have the MAC address of Host B. Because it has the IP address but not the MAC address, Host A will broadcast an Address Resolution Protocol (ARP). Router 1 will see the broadcast and instead of forwarding it, the router will reply to Host A with its own MAC address. In this way, the router is a proxy ARP, because it is only an intermediate device and not the final destination. Host A will put the router's MAC address into the Ethernet header and transmit the frame.

The Sample Ethernet Frame Diagram shows the MAC address of the router, Host A's MAC address, the Type field indicating an IP transmission, and the source and destination IP addresses.

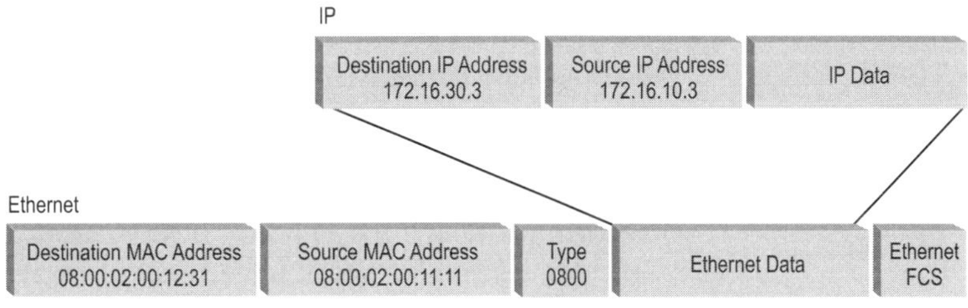

Sample Ethernet Frame

Upon receipt of the bits, Router 1 removes the Ethernet header and reviews the destination IP address in the Network Layer header. It then locates the route to Network 172.16.30.0 in its routing table out Serial interface 0. Router 1 knows that the destination network is one hop away, and that it must forward the packet to Router 2 at IP address 172.16.20.2. If Router 1 does not have the appropriate MAC address in its ARP cache, it will send an ARP broadcast and wait for Router 2 to respond.

Router 1 reframes the packet with a new Ethernet header and the MAC address of Router 2. Notice that the destination and source MAC addresses have changed from the Sample Ethernet Frame Diagram, to the content of the Sample Ethernet Frame First Hop Diagram. The destination MAC address (Router 1) from the first diagram, has now become the source MAC address. The new destination MAC address is for Router 2, the next hop in the network path. Also note that the destination and source IP addresses have not changed. They must remain intact for the final destination device to be located and acknowledgments sent back to the original sender.

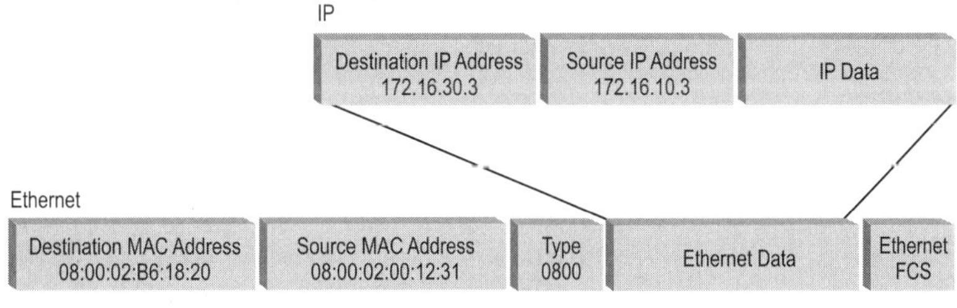

Sample Ethernet Frame First Hop

Upon receiving the bits, Router 2 removes the Ethernet header, and reviews the packet for the destination network IP address. Router 2 locates the route on interface Ethernet 0 that is directly connected. If the MAC address of Host B is not found in its ARP cache, Router 2 broadcasts an ARP request to determine the MAC address of the destination device. Host B responds with its MAC address and Router 2 reframes the transmission with the new information. It moves its own MAC address and the new source, and leaves the Network Layer header contents intact. This change can be seen on the Sample Ethernet Frame Transmission to Host B Diagram. After the frame is rebuilt, it is sent out the Ethernet 0 egress interface of Router 2.

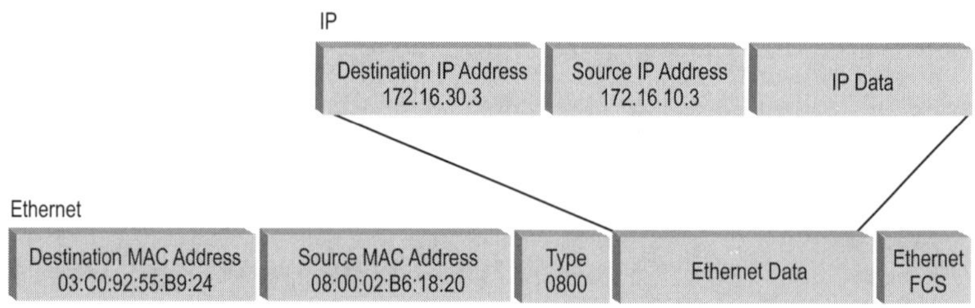

Sample Ethernet Frame Transmission to Host B

Router 2 transmits the frame to the local switch. The switch reads the MAC address and locates the proper interface in the MAC address table for Host B. When the transmission is received by the network interface card (NIC), Host B recognizes its MAC address, performs a calculation on the Frame Check Sequence (FCS), then decapsulates the rest of the frame. Recognizing that it was sent as IP, Host B sends the contents to the IP protocol stack for processing. IP passes the segment to TCP, which examines the port number and passes the message to the input queue for the Telnet process. Host B responds to the request and the entire process is repeated in the opposite direction.

Routing Protocols

Routing algorithms were designed at a time when systems were beginning to communicate over something other than a modem and telephone line connection. They developed along with hierarchical addresses that could provide a means of differentiating between the network and host in one single address. Early attempts could pass traffic but not very gracefully. Some of the earliest inventors set out objectives that all routing protocols should be able to perform. To be successful, these standards have been maintained.

Over the years, routing protocols have evolved and improved to include many new QoS mechanisms for very specific path selection. Not all routing protocols have kept up, but some such as RIP still maintain a position because they are easy to administer and continue to work. The following list briefly describes the requirements of all routing protocols:

- **Best path selection (optimization)**—Routing protocols are designed to locate the best path for each and every packet transmitted. A router uses a metric that it calculates based on the values or criteria it deems important. Each routing protocol uses a different metric to make its decisions. Thus, a route one router would select may be different based on a different routing protocol. In addition, with routing protocols that support QoS capabilities, a router may make different path selections based on the traffic type.
- **Low resource requirements (simplicity and low overhead)**—Maintaining routing protocol communications should be only one small portion of a router's resources. Process and memory can better serve transmission purposes, if not constantly performing administrative tasks such as updating routing tables. It is important for routing protocols to consume as few device resources as possible. This is also true for a network. Although information exchange is important, it must be weighted with network bandwidth utilization for exchanging and maintaining routing information.
- **Dynamic routing (robustness and stability)**—Routing protocols are designed to update information on a constant basis. This allows routers to always be aware of a network status and when changes affect certain connections. The routing protocol must be designed not only to allow updates as needed, but also handle network outages without significant impact. If a link fails, the router needs to respond to the incident while maintaining as much traffic transmission as possible.

- **Rapid convergence**—When a network outage is experienced, a router must quickly determine how to deal with the problem. To communicate properly, all routers must possess a knowledge of the connected networks. Convergence is the process in which all routers are in a state of "agreement" on the network topology. This means that each routing table has a complete list of the network addresses and methods to access them. Rapid convergence is important to get information transmitting again. The router cannot begin processing until convergence is complete. This can severely impact a network that has a routing loop, or physical link problem that fluctuates up and down.

Routing Metrics

A routing metric is what a routing protocol uses to make its path selection. This information is calculated by the routing protocol and stored in a routing table. When a packet is received, the router reads the Network Layer address, and then references the routing table. Based on the metric, the router decides which path to choose and sends the packet to the appropriate egress interface.

Some simple routing metrics may only base decisions on a single factor. For example, IP RIP uses a handoff point (hop) count when deciding the best path. More sophisticated routing protocols can use a combination of these values to select the best path. As stated earlier, some even make packet-by-packet path selection based on the type of traffic and its needs for transmission.

Possible values found in routing metrics can include:

- **Hop count**—A value that represents the number of routers/layer 3 devices from sending router to destination network. It is a simple metric to calculate: just add one for each router. However, it does not take into account the bandwidth of the links between the routers. For example, assume two routers are connected with redundant links, one at 10 megabits per second (Mbps) and the other at 100 Mbps. The router calculates the two routes and finds both of them are one hop regardless of the connection used. With hop count alone, the router is not aware of the difference between the bandwidth to select the 100-Mbps link. It simply sees both links as equal, and may select either path.
- **Ticks**—Transmission time calculated to 1/18th of a second. It is combined with hop count for IPX RIP.

- **Bandwidth**—The actual capability of the media. It represents the total bandwidth of the line, not what is available for transmission. The range is 1,200 bits per second (bps) to 10 gigabits per second (Gbps). With a default configuration over serial connections, bandwidth is often miscalculated. All serial links default to the bandwidth of a T1, which is 1.54 Mbps. If any other connection is used (for example, 64, 128, or 512 kilobits per second [Kbps]), the serial interface should be changed to the appropriate setting. Otherwise, the router will use the wrong information when making path selection based on default information.
- **Delay (throughput)**—The amount of time it takes to transmit packets through a network in tenths of milliseconds. This value has a number of contributing factors, such as bandwidth, network congestion, latency in processing, distance, queuing, and number of intermediate hops.
- **Reliability**—A value that quantifies the error rate based on keepalive packets across a link.
- **Load**—The amount of traffic found on a particular link or using a router resource. This helps indicate connections that are heavily used and often congested, versus a road less traveled.
- **Cost**—A value assigned by a network administrator. This value can be based on one or more of the previous metric values or designated by an administrator. In most cases, cost does not refer to the financial cost of a link, but rather an arbitrary number chosen to meet specific criteria.

Routing to the Internet

The majority of network environments today connect to the Internet. Generally, a border router is designated to provide the Internet connection, make route decisions, and often act as a firewall. To network devices and hosts, the border router is considered the default gateway. Remember that a gateway provides protocol conversion and connection to another network. When a router cannot find a network IP address in its own routing table, it sends the packet to its defined default gateway. If a default gateway is not set, the packet will be dropped. Transmissions destined for the Internet must use a default gateway/border router, as shown on the Border Router Internet Connection Diagram.

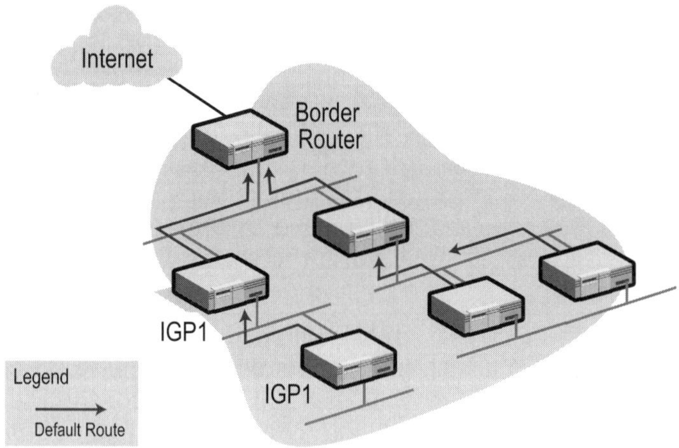

Border Router Internet Connection

A border router connects the internal subnetworks to the Internet. The internal routers run an IGP, which is a routing protocol used to share routing information within an AS. IGP is an umbrella term that represents routing protocols used inside a LAN/WAN environment controlled by one organization. IGPs include RIP, IGRP, EIGRP, and OSPF. The border router runs an EGP to share routing information with exterior routers. EGP is an umbrella term used to define routing protocols that connect ASs. The only EGP currently in use is BGPv4.

The interior nodes pass routing information between each other and the border router, but are not aware of routes to networks outside their AS. Instead, when the interior routers need to access a host on an exterior network, they send the packets to the port specified in their default route entries. As a result, routing is simplified, because only internal routes must be included in routing tables within the AS. A single default route is used for all routes that are otherwise not recognized. Once in the Internet, transmissions are switched and routed with precision using IP address information. The only difference is that MAC addresses are not used in the Data Link Layer header as they were in the LAN.

Review Questions

1. Which of the following could be used to create a routing metric? (Choose two.)
    a. Hop count
    b. MAC address
    c. Encapsulation type
    d. Bandwidth
2. What things are included in all routing tables at a minimum? (Choose three.)
    a. Network address
    b. MAC address
    c. Egress interface
    d. Ingress interface
    e. Metric
3. Which of the following are considered routing protocols? (Choose two.)
    a. IPX
    b. RIP
    c. OSPF
    d. IP
    e. SNA
4. Which of the following are considered routed protocols? (Choose two.)
    a. IPX
    b. RIP
    c. OSPF
    d. IP
    c. SNA

5. Which metric value takes into consideration the maximum transmission capacity of a connection?
   a. Bandwidth
   b. Hop count
   c. Delay
   d. Throughput
6. When a router transmits information, what does it do with the MAC portion of the header?
   a. Leaves the MAC header intact
   b. Reframes the packet with a new MAC header using its address as the destination and using a new source
   c. Reframes the packet with a new MAC header using its address as the source MAC, and performs an ARP to determine the new destination MAC address
   d. Puts IP address information in place of the MAC address
7. What happens to the destination IP address when a packet is sent through a router?
   a. It is changed to a new IP address.
   b. An ARP is performed to determine whether a different address is necessary.
   c. Nothing changes with the destination IP address when sent through a router.
   d. The router changes only the source IP address, not the destination IP address.
8. Which of the following is not a form of IP routing?
   a. Default
   b. Static
   c. Dynamic
   d. Automatic

9. Which characteristics describe the goals of a routing protocol? (Choose two.)
   a. Reliability
   b. Continuous broadcasting
   c. Rapid convergence
   d. Address resolution
10. Which routing metric is generally administratively defined?
   a. Hop count
   b. Bandwidth
   c. Delay
   d. Cost

Extended Activities

1. Label each of the following terms as either routed, routing, or nonroutable:

   IP __________

   RIP __________

   OSPF __________

   NetBIOS __________

   IGRP __________

   IPX __________

   SNA __________

   a. Routed
   b. Routing
   c. Nonroutable

2. Match the following terms with the appropriate description:

   A route path that is administratively defined ______________

   A routing metric that defines the amount of time to transmit end-to-end, also called "throughput" ______________

   When all routers agree and have the same routing information in their routing tables ______________

   The exit interface a router sends information to for transmission ______________

   The value that represents a count of each router from one network to another ______________

   A protocol that has a hierarchical Network Layer address ______________

   The routing process that uses routing protocols ______________

   a. Egress interface
   b. Routed protocol
   c. Static route
   d. Convergence
   e. Dynamic routing
   f. Delay
   g. Hop count

Lesson 4—Routing Protocols

This lesson discusses routing protocol categories according to where they are used: whether internal or external to an AS. The protocols used internally are called IGPs; those that are used between ASs are called "inter-autonomous system routing protocols" or EGPs. IGPs are categorized based on how they perform routing functions and exchange routing information. The three main routing categories are distance vector, link state, and hybrid. RIPv1, RIPv2, and IGRP all have characteristics of distance vector routing. OSPF is considered a link state routing protocol and EIGRP is a hybrid protocol. The majority of the lesson provides details on each of these protocols.

In addition, it discusses the administrative distance number, which is used to identify the most believable protocol if more than one is configured. The lesson ends with information about BGPv4, the EGP used to exchange reachability information with other ASs on the Internet.

Objectives

At the end of this lesson you will be able to:

- Identify the gateway protocols (IGPs and EGPs)
- Compare and contrast distance vector and link state routing protocols
- Describe RIPv1 and RIPv2
- Describe IGRP, EIGRP, and OSPF
- Discuss the use of administrative distance numbers
- Describe BGP

Key Point

Routing protocols are categorized based on whether they operate internally (IGPs) or externally (EGPs). IGP dynamic routing protocols are also categorized as distance vector, link state, or hybrid.

Gateway Protocols

As you may know, routers connect networks. They allow information to pass from one host, through a network, to a host in another network. This transmission could happen from your PC to someone in a different department within your organization. Or, it could be carried through the Internet to someone in a different country. Groups of routers and network boundaries are defined around corporate entities and education institutions. These areas or domains have their own management, administrative control, and address assignments, as well as network and routing protocols.

Each independently controlled network environment is referred to as an AS. IANA, the same organization that oversees all IP address distribution, also defines AS numbers. IANA distributes these 16-bit numbers to the Internet registrars: ARIN (The Americas, Caribbean, and Africa), RICE-NCC (Europe), and APNIC (Asia-Pacific region). Routers within an AS use these assigned numbers to identify and distinguish themselves from other ASs connected to the Internet.

Routers that exchange routing information with another device are referred to as neighbors or peers. Routers that belong to the same AS are called "interior neighbors," and routers that belong to different ASs are called "exterior neighbors."

IGPs

Routers within a single AS communicate using one of several dynamic routing protocols, known generically as IGPs. Continuous communication is necessary to dynamically update routing and reachability information within each router so it accurately reflects the current state of the network topology. Performance is the key requirement of an IGP. The routing algorithm should respond immediately to failures and find the lowest-cost path to a destination network. IGP examples include RIP, OSPF, IGRP, and EIGRP.

EGPs

Communications between routers that belong to different ASs require an additional protocol. This type of protocol is referred to as an EGP. Routers that run an EGP to advertise reachability also need to run an IGP to obtain information from within their own AS. Each AS administrator is free to select an IGP that best fits their needs; however, all ASs must use the same EGP. The only EGP currently in use is BGPv4.

At least one router in an AS is designated as the border router. This router provides the Internet connection, makes route decisions, and often acts as a firewall. To network devices and hosts, this device is considered the default gateway. Remember that a gateway provides protocol conversion and connection to another network. When a router cannot find the network IP address in its own routing table, it sends the packet to its defined default gateway. If a default gateway is not set, the packet will be dropped. Transmissions destined for the Internet must use the default gateway/border router.

The Autonomous Systems Diagram shows the relationships between IGPs, the EGP, and border routers when connecting through the Internet. A border router connects the internal subnetworks to the Internet. The internal routers and the AS ingress interface on the border router all run an IGP. The IGP selected depends upon the network requirements. The border router runs an EGP on its egress interface to the Internet. This allows it to share routing information with exterior routers.

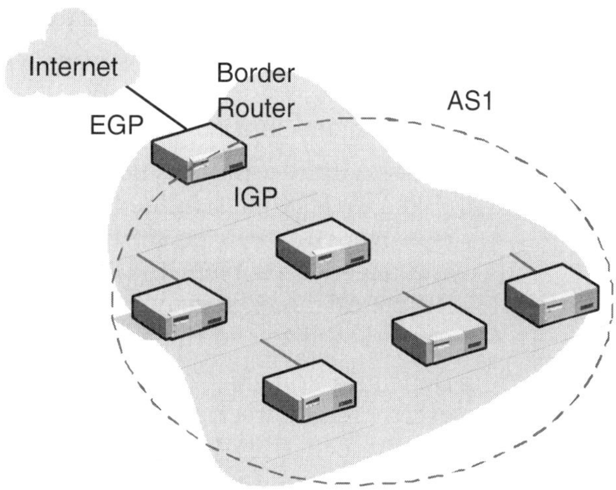

Autonomous Systems

Types of Dynamic Routing Protocols

Computer networks use two types of dynamic routing protocols to maintain their routing tables and calculate the shortest path to a destination. They are Distance-Vector Algorithms (DVAs), also known as Bellman-Ford Algorithms, and Link-State Algorithms (LSAs), also known as Shortest Path First (SPF) or Dijkstra Algorithms. All routing algorithms must use routing metrics stored in routing tables to select the best path to a destination. The shortest path between networks is determined by examining all routes to the destination and selecting the route having the smallest metric or cost. The metric value can be hop count, bandwidth, transmission delay, an administratively defined cost, or a composite metric created from two or more individual metrics.

Distance Vector Algorithms

In DVAs, a router sends its neighbors a vector of distances or metrics for all possible network destinations (its routing table). The router is not aware of what the actual path is, only the direction it should go. DVA routers create tables by exchanging routing information. They update the tables by incrementing their own information with that of a neighbor router. This secondhand information is not always the most accurate; thus, in this way, DVAs are often called "routing by rumor." DVAs send complete routing tables as broadcasts on a predefined basis. Each router then has to evaluate the received table with its own table to determine whether any differences exist.

DVAs have been in use for many years. As a result, many sample implementations are available, and they are well understood by software developers.

DVAs require only a small number of central processing unit (CPU) cycles to determine the shortest route to a distant network. However, this can be misleading because of the potential slow convergence problem that may require multiple updates. These simple calculations may have to be performed many times before routes stabilize and the network enters a state of convergence.

Depending on the size of a network, the amount of information exchanged between neighbors can be quite large. This is especially true in a routing domain containing many networks and a complex topology. In DVAs, each router transmits information to its neighbors about its routes to every other destination network. It is impossible for other routers to check this information for accuracy and, as a result, it is difficult for a router to automatically ignore information provided by misbehaving routers. In addition, because the information transmitted by each router is a function of the information it receives from its immediate neighbors, identifying a misbehaving router supplying inaccurate data is quite difficult.

A change in the routing table of a single router can result in a chain of updates. It can take a considerable amount of time for this information to reach all other routers in the routing domain. As a result of the slow propagation of routing information, DVAs can form routing loops, and be slow to converge. This slow convergence can lead to route instability and increased overhead. Finally, DVAs do not scale well and experience problems in very large networks because of the potential for slow convergence.

Routing protocols that fall into this category are RIPv1, RIPv2, and IGRP. Each has distance vector characteristics and shortfalls. IGRP is the most sophisticated of the options, providing a higher hop count, manageability for more sophisticated networks, and an enhanced routing metric. An easy, nontechnical way to remember that these protocols are associated with distance vector is that they all have an "R" in their names and the word vector ends in "r."

Link State Algorithms

In LSAs, each router must know the entire network topology before computing the shortest path to each destination network. Initially, routers using an LSA send Hello packets to neighbor devices to establish an adjacency. Each router exchanges this information so it can build a complete database and topology map of the entire network infrastructure. The routers do not exchange information if nothing changes on the network. This makes LSA-based networks quieter than DVA networks.

When a change happens, the router that detected it sends a link state advertisement to its neighbors. Each router floods the update messages to every other router in the routing domain as a multicast. These messages contain the metric and state of each of the router's attached links. Routes are consistent because every router is using the identical routing algorithm on an identical database. Each node has all the information required to calculate the minimum-cost route from itself to any other network in the routing domain. This allows for more sophisticated route decision making and knowledge about the status of a network link.

Each router maintains a consistent view of the network, thus eliminating problems of looping and slow adjustment to changes in network conditions. Misbehaving routers are easier to detect when using an LSA, because each router maintains an identical link-state database. Because each router reports on the state of its own links to its neighbors, information from a suspect router can be compared to what a neighbor router is reporting. The link may be considered operational only if each end of the link agrees on the link's state.

LSAs can eliminate problems that occur in very large networks because of their ability to partition an AS into areas. The LSA is calculated on a per-area basis. Interarea destinations are learned from routers connected to more than one area.

An excessive amount of memory and communication overhead may be required in large networks, because each router must maintain an up-to-date database containing the entire network topology. LSAs require a larger amount of CPU time per calculation compared to DVAs. However, because new routes are calculated directly, rather than converging toward the solution, the additional CPU requirements are offset by the need to only perform the calculation once.

The routing protocols associated with LSA work on the shortest path first principles. The most common one in use today is OSPF, because it is vendor-neutral and offers very granular administrative control. Two others include the Intermediate System to Intermediate System (IS-IS) and the Novell Link Services Protocol (NLSP). An easy, nontechnical way to remember that these routing protocols are associated with LSA is that they all have an "s" in their names, just like link state.

To get a better understanding of how these routing algorithms work, let us consider a real-life scenario of getting directions to a particular destination. Driving in your car, you are like a packet being transmitted through a network.

Let us first look at how distance vector would handle our scenario. Assume you ask someone for directions to your destination. Just as a router looks up the address of the destination, the person tells you, "Take a left here and go to the first stop sign, then ask the next person you see how to get there." You follow the directions, drive to the stop sign and ask the next person. They tell you, "Take a right and drive until you get to the traffic light, then ask the next person you see." You drive to the traffic light and ask the next person, and they give you one more direction. This process happens over and over as you find your way, never really knowing where the next step will lead, but trusting you will eventually get to your destination.

Notice that the process is time-consuming and not very well thought out. In addition, if someone gives you bad information, you could be going in circles. Finally, no one has provided any information about the best way to get to the destination, or alternate routes in case of a traffic accident or construction. In all cases, they are expecting the next person to give you correct information. Although it does not take much to make this process work, it is not a very sophisticated way of getting to your destination.

Now let us look at the scenario from the LSA perspective. You are getting ready to go somewhere, and you have decided to plan ahead a bit. You ask your neighbors that have been to the destination how to get there. One of them gives you very detailed directions over the telephone. So detailed, in fact, that you are not only able to write them down step by step, but you can also draw a map of where to go. You call another neighbor and ask them to confirm, and they tell you a different way they found to be faster. You look on a map of the area and find out that some of your route includes a four-lane highway, some of it two-lane roads, and the final route is residential. To help in decision making, you listen to the news to verify the traffic situation. Finally, you take the map and directions, make your decision on which route to take, and you are off.

While driving, your friend calls and tells you they just drove the same direction you are heading and construction has caused a traffic jam. They recommend you try another route. Without hesitation, you review the map and go a different direction. Notice from this analogy that it took more time initially to prepare for the trip. However, in the end, it offered you a knowledgeable route selection process, and the flexibility of handling a traffic problem by knowing alternate routes.

This analogy offers two ways of going about the same process. This is basically how the two different routing protocols of DSA and LSA handle the process of exchanging routing information and making best path selections.

Hybrid Protocols

Hybrid routing protocols combine features and functions of both DVA and LSA. For example, it is beneficial to have the low administration and setup requirements that DVA provides. To gain the benefits of LSAs, it is helpful to reduce network traffic, provide a sophisticated metric, allow larger networks, and provide rapid convergence. A hybrid routing protocol aims to provide the best of both worlds.

EIGRP is just that. It is a Cisco proprietary method for improving the network performance of IGRP. It maintains the composite metric values, as well as ease of configuration and support for larger networks that IGRP had already incorporated. It enhances

IGRP in the form of providing rapid convergence in the event of an outage. It provides a more sophisticated calculation process for updating routing table information. It also supports using different subnet masks in a single network, called "variable length subnet masking (VLSM)." VLSM is discussed in the Interconnecting Cisco Network Devices course.

RIP

RIP, a distance vector protocol, was designed for relatively small networks. To prevent problems associated with routing loops, RIP routes can have a maximum hop count of 15. RIP considers a network 16 hops away unreachable. This limits the size to a diameter of 15 routing devices. This limitation is necessary because every RIP router exchanges entire routing tables as a broadcast every 30 seconds. As the number of routers increases, there is an even sharper increase in the number of RIP broadcasts on the network. RIP sends these broadcasts using User Datagram Protocol (UDP) on Port 520. RIP is not concerned that UDP is connectionless and unreliable. If a routing table packet gets dropped, the router knows that another will be sent in 30 seconds.

A RIP router cannot see a network beyond its adjacent routers, and must depend on its neighbors for correct routing information. RIP uses hop count as its metric. This means that when a routing table is received from a neighbor, the new entry is incremented by one and updated in the table. The router always assumes that if the router was two hops for the neighbor, it will be three hops for them. If it is four hops for the neighbor, it will be five hops for them, as so on. This is why it is sometimes called "routing by rumor," in that a router only knows what other routers tell it.

As discussed earlier, having a hop count as a metric is not very sophisticated. The router would not be able to determine the bandwidth of the link or base its path selection decisions on anything other than the number of hops.

RIPv1 was created before the development of subnet masks for IP addresses. Therefore, it does not transmit subnet information with network addresses, and is considered classful only. When subnetting became common, RIPv2 was created to handle this additional routing information. Among other things, RIPv2 added a subnet mask or prefix field to the update information. Supporting this field allows for classless routing. This means that networks can use different network numbers and subnet masks in different areas of the network and still be properly accessed. RIPv2, therefore, offers support for VLSM.

IGRP

Because IGRP is a Cisco proprietary routing protocol, using it on a network requires that all internetwork routers are Cisco routers. IGRP improves upon IP RIP in a number of ways:

- IGRP increases the maximum hop count to 255, with a default of 100. This makes IGRP suitable for even the largest networks.
- IGRP's default metrics are the link's bandwidth and delay; however, it can also build a composite metric using the link's reliability, load, and maximum transmission unit (MTU). An administrator can define the values and weight of importance in the routing decision. Without administrative configuration, IGRP will automatically provide a more sophisticated view of the network than RIP.
- The IGRP default update period is three times that of RIP. IGRP sends updates every 90 seconds. This means less traffic on the network.
- Like RIPv1, IGRP is a classful routing protocol. IGRP does not pass subnet information within the route update packets.

  IGRP broadcasts its entire routing table to adjacent neighbor routers. IGRP differs from RIP in that it uses AS numbers to designate a routing domain. Route updates are limited to the routers within a specific AS. This allows administrative control over the routing table exchange.

As mentioned earlier, IGRP can create a composite metric of several individual metric variables. For each path within an AS, IGRP records the bandwidth, accumulated delay, MTU, hop count, reliability, and load. Although the protocol records the MTU and hop count variables, they are not used to calculate the composite metric. Instead, these variables are passed with route update messages to help other routers characterize the path. The router weighs each metric variable, assigning bandwidth the most importance. When a network consists of one topology, such as an all Token Ring or 100-Mbps Ethernet network, the routers determine the best path based only on the hop count. On a mixed-media network, such as a combined 10- and 100-Mbps Ethernet network, the routers choose the path with the lowest composite metric.

EIGRP

EIGRP is a Cisco proprietary routing protocol that enhances IGRP's capabilities. Both protocols use the same routing composite metric of bandwidth and delay as defaults. The path selection process is identical regardless of the protocol. However, this is where the similarities end.

EIGRP has the following characteristics:

- **Faster convergence**—EIGRP use the Diffusing Update Algorithm (DUAL) to provide rapid convergence when a link fails or network topology changes. This process is fast because only the devices affected by the change are involved in the computation. In addition, the loop-free environment is calculated and all devices synchronize simultaneously. Rapid convergence is very important to keep traffic moving through the network, and provides a level of resilience in case an outage does occur.
- **Larger network environment**—EIGRP has a maximum hop count of 224 devices. However, it does not add to the hop count until 15 routers have been traversed. This greatly extends the physical limitations of the network, and allows EIGRP to be a very scalable routing protocol solution.
- **Partial updates**—When a change takes place, EIGRP sends only update information. This drastically reduces the bandwidth used during transmission. It also reduces the processing overhead of reviewing entire routing tables and speeds the convergence process. EIGRP uses multicast and unicast whenever possible. This reduces the unnecessary traffic that is often generated by other dynamic routing protocols which broadcast updates.
- **Neighbor identification**—Routers using EIGRP identify themselves to their neighbors using Hello packets when they first start up on a network. In addition, they stay in communication with each other using these small Hello packets to maintain their knowledge of each other. If a Hello packet is not received in a specified period of time, the router realizes it has lost communication with a neighboring device, and begins the recovery/update process. This is called "neighbor discovery" and "neighbor recovery."

- **Redundancy**—DUAL is also used to identify a feasible successor. This means that when routing information is exchanged, the router will look for the least-cost route to a particular network. It will also look for other routes that are advertised to the same segment through a different loop-free connection. It adds this information to its table as a feasible successor. If one connection fails, the successor can automatically be used. This is yet another reason why EIGRP is fast to converge.
- **VLSM support**—EIGRP includes the subnet mask when exchanging route information. This allows different subnet masks to be used in various parts of the networks, and packets to get to the proper destination.
- **Reliable transport**—EIGRP uses reliable transport methods when necessary to ensure the proper routing information is received. This reduces the need for constant updates or retransmissions. If reliable transport is not necessary, the overhead is reduced by using a best-effort delivery.
- **Protocol-independent**—EIGRP can be used with IP, IPX, and AppleTalk protocols.
- **Route summarization**—An administrator can control how routing information is sent. EIGRP allows routes to be summarized during the exchange process. This keeps routing table size manageable and reduces bandwidth for updates. Special handling is also offered for stub networks, which defines what information should be exchanged in and out of the stub area.
- **Authentication**—EIGRP allows a simple password or more sophisticated Message Digest 5 (MD5) hash to be used for authentication between neighbor devices. This prevents malicious and inaccurate route updates from being added to the network.

OSPF

OSPF was developed by the IETF in 1988. It solves RIP's main problems, while providing many new features in a vendor-neutral environment. Two of the main things IETF wanted to address were network size and routing metrics. OSPF was designed without boundaries, meaning that regardless of the size, OSPF can grow with any network. OSPF supports configurable metrics, allowing an administrator to assign each path a cost value based on a combination of factors, such as bandwidth, reliability, delay, and hop count. For example, a fast T1 line could be assigned a cost metric of 10, while a slower 56-Kbps line would get a cost metric of 100. OSPF always selects the path with the lowest-cost metric, regardless of hop count. Of course, an administrator can include hop count with other factors when determining the cost of a route.

OSPF communicates with neighbor devices using Hello packets. They build neighbor adjacencies, a relationship that helps them better understand the network connections around them. They build their own routing tables with firsthand information from neighbor devices. After that, orderly update procedures help reduce network traffic, exchanging only update information as link-state advertisements.

OSPF exchanges entire routing tables every 30 minutes just to validate all entries and stay current. OSPF packets are sent as multicasts to other OSPF routers, and acknowledged to ensure reliability. This greatly reduces the network traffic found with RIP's constant broadcasts of unchanged information. All routing exchanges are authenticated. This allows only "trusted" routers to participate in routing within an AS, and prevents both accidental and malicious routing table corruption inside an OSPF-based system. OSPF uses either TCP or UDP at the Transport Layer over Port 89. It has its own built-in Network Layer protocol. Other features of OSPF include:

- **Equal-cost multipath routing**—This allows a router to perform load balancing over multiple routes with equal costs. Recognizing the entire network topology means that OSPF is also resistant to routing loops.
- **Subnet mask exchange**—This allows the use of variable-length subnet masks. This feature extends the IP subnet addressing model and allows network managers to make efficient use of the IP address space.
- **Faster convergence**—OSPF sends link-state advertisements when updates are encountered. This allows routers to quickly recognize the change, update tables, and recompute their network topology map.
- **Support for area routing**—This allows a network manager to limit network-wide traffic by partitioning the AS into subdomains. Area routing provides another level of information hiding, reduces network traffic, and protects routing within an area from outside interference.

- **Support for type-of-service (ToS) routing**—OSPF allows a sending host to use the IP packet header ToS field to request one of several classes of service (CoSs) from an OSPF router. This gives the option of providing QoS routing based on the special needs of different traffic types.

The Dynamic Routing Protocols Table compares these IGPs based on a number of key characteristics. No one routing protocol is better suited than another for any or all networks. That is precisely why options exist. It is then up to the administrator to decide what is most appropriate. For a vendor-neutral solution, RIP or OSPF are used depending on the size and complexity of the network. In a Cisco environment, IGRP or EIGRP are often selected because they can optimize network performance on Cisco routers.

Dynamic Routing Protocols

Characteristics	RIPv1	RIPv2	IGRP	EIGRP	OSPF
Vendor-neutral	X	X			X
Convergence time	Slow	Slow	Slow	Very rapid	Fast
Support for VLSM		X		X	X
Metric	Hop count	Hop count	Bandwidth and delay	Bandwidth and delay	Cost factor Bandwidth by default
Type of routing protocol	DVA	DVA	DVA	Hybrid	LSA
Size of network supported	Maximum 15 hop radius	Maximum 15 hop radius	Up to 255 hops (100 by default)	224 hops*	Very large networks

* EIGRP does not actually count a hop until 15 routers have been traversed; therefore, the limitation of 224 hops actually allows thousands of routing devices.

Administrative Distance Numbers

Before moving on to BGP, it is important to discuss one last concept: administrative distance numbers. A router uses these numbers to determine the most "believable" path that should be selected to route packets across a network. This is important, because some routers may have more than one routing protocol, as well as static routes configured. The router could get confused with so many options to choose from. However, its decisions are greatly simplified using administrative distance numbers.

These numbers, determined by a standards board, are assigned to each routing process and protocol. When a static or dynamic routing protocol is configured on a router, it automatically associates the default administrative distance with that route. When reviewing its routing tables, the entry with the lowest administrative distance number will be used to route the packet through the network. This means that even though there may be a route with a better metric path, the entry will be ignored if the route does not have the most believable administrative distance number.

The Administrative Distance Numbers Table presents the routing protocols just discussed with their associated administrative distance numbers. The lower the number, the more believable the route; the higher the number, the less believable the route.

Administrative Distance Numbers

Type of Route	Administrative Distance Number
Static	1
EIGRP	90
IGRP	100
OSPF	110
RIP	120
Unreliable route	255

Notice how the Cisco protocols EIGRP and IGRP are given priority over the vendor-neutral options. Only the routing protocol with the lowest administrative distance number will be used to route packets through a network. If more than one routing protocol is configured, the other protocols will continue to broadcast their routing information in hopes of someday being selected for packet routing. This means a lot of unnecessary traffic is on a network that could be eliminated by removing extraneous routing protocols that are not actually being used for routing.

For example, if both IGRP and RIP are configured on a router, only IGRP will be used for route selection. RIP will continue to broadcast its routing tables every 30 seconds even though they will never actually be used. To eliminate unnecessary network traffic, turn off all redundant routing protocols. By the way, no routing protocols are configured by default. It is up to an administrator to configure routing protocols on each device.

BGP

Border Gateway Protocol (BGP) is an inter-autonomous system routing protocol, meaning that it communicates between ASs. This is the routing protocol of the Internet, used for AS connectivity as well as communications between ISPs. The primary function of a BGP-speaking system is to exchange network reachability information with other BGP systems. Using this information, routers can construct a map of connected ASs using the AS number for identification of the path. BGP uses the map to prune routing loops and enforce some policy decisions at the AS level.

BGP runs over TCP, a reliable transport protocol present in virtually all commercial routers and hosts. This means TCP handles update message segmentation, acknowledgment, retransmission, and sequencing. Any TCP authentication scheme can be used with BGP's own authentication mechanisms. The BGP error notification mechanism assumes TCP supports a "graceful" connection closure, delivering all outstanding data before closing a connection. BGP establishes its connections over TCP well-known Port 179.

When two BGP-speaking routers establish a TCP connection, they exchange messages to open and confirm the connection parameters, and then they exchange their entire BGP routing tables. Each router sends updates as its routing table changes. BGP does not require periodic refreshes of the entire BGP routing table. Therefore, a BGP speaker must retain the current version of the entire BGP routing table of all its peers for the duration of the connection.

BGP sends keepalive messages periodically to test the connection. Notification messages are sent in response to errors or special conditions. If a connection encounters an error condition, a notification message is sent and the connection is closed.

Hosts executing BGP need not be routers. A nonrouting host, such as a gateway (protocol converter), could exchange routing information with routers by means of an EGP or IGP. The non-routing host could then use BGP to exchange routing information with a border router in another AS. When BGP routers exchange routing information between ASs, they are using Exterior BGP (EBGP), also known as External BGP. A BGP router can also exchange route information with BGP routers within the same AS; in this case, it is running Interior BGP (IBGP) or Internal BGP.

Review Questions

1. What routing protocol is used for small network environments that want little administration and have different vendor's equipment?
   a. OSPF
   b. IGRP
   c. EIGRP
   d. RIP
2. Which of the following are considered distance vector routing protocols? (Choose two.)
   a. OSPF
   b. IGRP
   c. EIGRP
   d. RIP
3. Which routing protocol is considered a hybrid?
   a. OSPF
   b. IGRP
   c. EIGRP
   d. RIP
4. Which routing protocol is considered an LSA?
   a. OSPF
   b. IGRP
   c. EIGRP
   d. RIP
5. Which routing method has the lowest administrative distance?
   a. Static routes
   b. IGRP
   c. EIGRP
   d. RIP

6. Which components do IGRP and EIGRP use as defaults in their composite metric? (Choose two.)
   a. Cost
   b. Hop count
   c. Bandwidth
   d. Delay
   e. Load
7. What is used to identify neighbors and establish adjacencies when using OSPF?
   a. Hello packets
   b. Broadcasts
   c. MAC addresses
   d. Routing tables
8. Which protocol is considered an EGP?
   a. RIP
   b. IGRP
   c. OSPF
   d. BGPv4
9. What is the maximum reachable hop count with RIPv2?
   a. 15 hops
   b. 30 hops
   c. 16 hops
   d. 90 hops
10. Which routing protocols are vendor-neutral? (Choose two.)
    a. RIP
    b. IGRP
    c. OSPF
    d. EIGRP

Extended Activities

1. Match the following descriptions with the correct component:

   Cisco's proprietary routing protocol that has a composite metric ______________

   An inter-AS routing protocol that exchanges reachability information on the Internet ______________

   A routing protocol type that is sometimes called "routing by rumor" ______________

   An administratively defined routing metric value used with OSPF ______________

   The metric value used by RIP ______________

   The general category that groups routing protocols internal to an AS ______________

   The routing protocol that calculates a network topology map and communicates using multicasts ______________

   The category of routing protocol that combines the best of DVA and LSA ______________

   The routing protocol that sends broadcasts of an entire routing table every 30 seconds ______________

   The term used to describe routing protocols external to an AS ______________

   The enhanced version of Cisco's routing protocol that is considered a hybrid ______________

   The category of routing protocol that has a more sophisticated knowledge of the network topology ______________

   a. IGP
   b. EGP
   c. DVA
   d. LSA
   e. RIP
   f. OSPF
   g. IGRP
   h. EIGRP
   i. Cost
   j. Hop
   k. BGP
   l. Hybrid

Summary

This module started out with laying the foundation on the hierarchy of an IP address, the different classes of address and their associated subnet masks. The current IP addressing structure is 32 bits or 4 octets in length. The hierarchy of the address is divided between a network portion and subnet portion as defined by the subnet mask. Each address class has a specific number range and default subnet mask assignment. Lesson 1 discussed the allocation of IP addresses, and the special use of broadcast and multicast addresses. It ended with a discussion of the growing demand and dwindling supply of addresses. IPv6 and CIDR are two methods that will provide a long-term solution. IPv6 offers 128-bit or 16-octet IP addresses expressed in hexadecimal format. CIDR offers routing table management by aggregating addresses together. It also helps conserve addresses by combining contiguous Class C addresses together.

Lesson 2 provided an explanation of the subnetting process. It went through the subnet calculations with a handy subnetting table as a reference, then added a few simple equations to finish it off. Three different examples were provided for Class A, B, and C addresses. Subnetting questions can be worded in many different ways. Sometimes it is necessary to perform a complete calculation to get the information to provide an answer. Other times, only one or two steps in the whole process will be used. A list of the steps is included at the end of the lesson as a handy reference and guide when going through the subnetting process. Subnetting is one of those things that takes a while to understand. It is also something that if you do not use it, you will lose it. Therefore, spend enough time in this area to be very proficient in answering all the different types of questions at the end of Lesson 2, as preparation for the real exam.

Lesson 3 provided a high-level overview of general routing principles, including how routing is performed. It discussed such things as routed versus routing protocols, the contents of routing tables, and how routers exchange information. It also discussed the path determination process and the metric values routers use to select the best path for transmission.

Lesson 4 provided more details on the categories of routing protocols. First, routing protocols are grouped together based on where they route. Routing protocols found inside an AS are considered IGPs, while those outside or between ASs are considered EGPs. Next, the lesson reviewed the categories of routing protocols based on how they route. This category includes distance vector, link-state, and hybrid. The lesson then provided an overview of RIP, IGRP, EIGRP, OSPF, and BGP.

Module 6 Quiz

1. When subnetting, where do the extra bits come from?
   a. From the existing subnet mask
   b. From the host portion and given to the network
   c. From the network portion and given to the host
   d. From the IP address assignment
2. How many network bits are used with a Class C address and subnet mask of 255.255.255.248?
   a. 6
   b. 5
   c. 4
   d. 3
3. Given the IP address 22.0.0.0 and subnet mask 255.224.0.0, what is the network number of the first subnet created?
   a. 22.32.0.0
   b. 22.64.0.0
   c. 22.128.0.0
   d. 22.16.0.0
4. If 3 bits are used for subnetting with a Class C address, how many bits are available to use for hosts?
   a. 4
   b. 6
   c. 5
   d. 3
5. What is the default subnet mask for a Class B address?
   a. 255.0.0.0
   b. 255.255.0.0
   c. 255.255.255.0
   d. 255.255.255.255

6. All of the following are true regarding a broadcast address except which?
   a. The host portion is made up of all 1s.
   b. This address can also be used as a host assignment.
   c. This address is used to communicate with all hosts on a network segment.
   d. A Class A or B broadcast will include the number 255.
7. What is the first octet of a Class A address range?
   a. From 0 – 127
   b. From 1 – 126
   c. From 127 – 192
   d. From 1 – 127
8. If using a Class C address and 14 networks are required, what is the appropriate subnet mask?
   a. 255.255.255.248
   b. 255.255.255.240
   c. 255.255.255.224
   d. 255.255.255.252
9. What is the IP address class that is used for multicast groups?
   a. Class B
   b. Class C
   c. Class D
   d. Class E
10. What is the IP address that is used for local loopback and is therefore invalid as a network number?
    a. 128.0.0.1
    b. 126.0.0.1
    c. 127.0.0.1
    d. 125.0.0.1

11. How many bits is a current IP address?

    a. 32

    b. 8

    c. 16

    d. 4

12. What is the equation to determine the possible number of hosts or networks?

    a. $2^n - 2 =$

    b. $2^n =$

    c. $2^n / 2 =$

    d. $2^n * 2 =$

13. What is the correct broadcast address for the first network given an IP address of 197.68.144.0 and subnet mask of 255.255.255.248?

    a. 197.68.144.15

    b. 197.68.144.24

    c. 197.68.144.31

    d. 197.168.144.48

14. Which of the following is not a possible host address given an IP address of 200.1.60.0 and subnet mask of 255.255.255.224?

    a. 200.1.60.32

    b. 200.1.60.45

    c. 200.1.60.66

    d. 200.1.60.93

15. Which IP address class can have a maximum of 254 unique hosts?

    a. Class A

    b. Class B

    c. Class C

    d. Class D

16. What is the binary number for the decimal number of 164?
    a. 10100100
    b. 11000000
    c. 10100011
    d. 10001111
17. What must the first binary digits of a Class C address always be?
    a. 01
    b. 10
    c. 110
    d. 1110
18. All of the following are reasons to subnet except which?
    a. To break a big network into smaller pieces
    b. To reduce network traffic
    c. To allow substantially more hosts
    d. To allow for easier administration and troubleshooting
19. Given a network address of 175.144.16.0 and subnet mask of 255.255.248.0, what is the correct IP address range for this network?
    a. 175.144.16.1 – 175.144.31.254
    b. 175.144.16.1 – 175.144.23.254
    c. 175.144.16.0 – 175.144.23.255
    d. 175.144.16.1 – 175.144.31.255
20. Which characteristics correctly represent an IPv6 address? (Choose two.)
    a. 64 bytes
    b. 128 bits
    c. 32 bits
    d. 16 octets

21. Which of the following are benefits of CIDR? (Choose two.)
    a. Route aggregation and smaller routing tables for ISPs
    b. Multicasting all routing updates
    c. Better use of Class C address allocation
    d. Sophisticated hop count routing metric
22. Which address could be used for multicast transmission?
    a. 186.190.200.200
    b. 222.10.185.111
    c. 224.0.15.1
    d. 245.65.0.10
23. A DHCP server is used to dynamically distribute IP addresses. Host A receives address 185.63.14.37 with a subnet mask of 255.255.255.224. Host B receives address 182.63.14.52 with the same subnet mask. Which description best describes how these devices are connected to the network?
    a. The two hosts are on the same subnetwork.
    b. The two hosts are in different VLANs.
    c. The two hosts are in different physical segments.
    d. A router separates the two hosts.
24. A network administrator is given the following addresses for static assignment: 199.200.52.8, 199.200.52.9, 199.200.52.10, and 199.200.52.11. The subnet mask is 255.255.255.248. Which address will not work given the information provided?
    a. 199.200.52.8
    b. 199.200.52.9
    c. 199.200.52.10
    d. 199.200.52.11
25. What is the network address for the host 45.23.191.52 with a subnet mask of 255.252.0.0?
    a. 45.12.0.0
    b. 45.16.0.0
    c. 45.20.0.0
    d. 45.22.0.0

26. What is the subnet mask given the prefix /22?
    a. 255.255.255.0
    b. 255.255.252.0
    c. 255.255.240.0
    d. 255.255.248.0
27. Which IGP is typically used in very large, sophisticated networks with many different vendors' equipment?
    a. RIP
    b. BGP
    c. OSPF
    d. EIGRP
28. What is the most current EGP available?
    a. BGPv4
    b. RIPv1
    c. OSPFv2
    d. IPv6
29. What is the network address of the host 185.63.175.88 with the subnet mask of 255.255.240.0?
    a. 185.63.162.0
    b. 185.62.175.0
    c. 185.63.160.0
    d. 185.63.170.0
30. What are characteristics of IGPs? (Choose two.)
    a. They are used within an AS.
    b. They are used between ASs.
    c. It is an umbrella term that covers routing protocols such as RIP and OSPF.
    d. It is an umbrella term that covers the routing protocols of the Internet.

Module 7
WAN Technologies

Up to this point, we have been discussing local area network (LAN) concepts and configurations. LAN administration can take up the majority of any network engineer's time. However, wide area network (WAN) connections are also important in network administration. These connections provide communication between branch offices, customers, vendor sights, and the Internet. Regardless of size, most organizations currently use some type of WAN connection. This module is dedicated to describing WAN concepts and configurations.

The module begins with a discussion of WAN connectivity to the public switched telephone and data network. It then defines the different connection types, including point-to-point leased lines, and packet- and circuit-switched networks. The measurements of WAN bandwidth are discussed. In addition, techniques for multiplexing traffic across a single physical wire are also reviewed.

Lesson 2 defines a number of Data Link Layer encapsulation methods, including High-Level Data Link Control (HDLC), Point-to-Point Protocol (PPP), Integrated Services Digital Network (ISDN), Digital Subscriber Line (DSL), frame relay, and Asynchronous Transfer Mode (ATM). This lesson also discusses Synchronous Optical Network (SONET), a Physical Layer protocol for transmitting information over a fiber optic cable.

Although this module touches on a number of key WAN technologies, it only scratches the surface of what is available in the WAN arena. For now, the information presented will better inform you about WAN encapsulation types, basic telecommunications principles, and common Internet and remote access communication methods.

Lessons

1. WAN Overview
2. WAN Access Technologies
3. Modems

Lesson 1—WAN Overview

A LAN consists of all the components that internally make up a corporate network environment. However, more and more, companies must have connections to other businesses, branch offices, customer and vendor locations, and the Internet. Sometimes a single WAN connection is necessary, while other times several WAN connections are required. A WAN is a communications channel that spans a geographic area. In today's technology environment, WAN connections do more than simply transmit data. They are required to transmit video, voice, and data, and are also subject to other multimedia requirements.

The concept of a WAN can be difficult to comprehend, because WANs incorporate services provided by someone else outside an organization. Most companies do not have the money, time, or resources to create their own WAN connections. Therefore, they lease them from a service provider. Diagrams in most documentation show WAN connections as a cloud between two businesses. While this does not help explain the components inside the cloud and how they work together, the cloud represents the many different technology options available.

No one defined technology is used for WAN connections. This lesson sheds some light on the cloud. (All the possible WAN technologies are outside the scope of this book.) We begin by discussing the three basic categories of WAN links: circuit-switched connections, packet-switched connections, and dedicated leased lines.

Objectives

At the end of this lesson you will be able to:

- Describe a WAN
- Define circuit switching and packet switching
- Describe point-to-point leased lines
- Define WAN bandwidth
- Describe various multiplexing techniques
- Define physical, logical, and virtual circuits

Key Point

WAN connections do more than simply transmit data. They must now also transmit video and voice communications and are subject to meeting many other multimedia requirements.

WAN Connections

WAN connections are necessary for almost any business. They are used to connect to branch offices, the Internet, customers, vendors, and telecommuters. WAN connections are often overlooked and misunderstood because they are part of the telecommunications network and cover a large range of technologies.

A few terms are important to understand before proceeding. Three WAN connection types are available based on customer requirements: circuit-switched connections, packet-switched connections, and dedicated leased lines. Each type has its advantages and disadvantages, and all three can meet the needs of an organization. Some technologies only allow a single connection type. Others have the ability to provide different connection types to fulfill any specification. The Types of WAN Connections Diagram shows how the different connections are made physically.

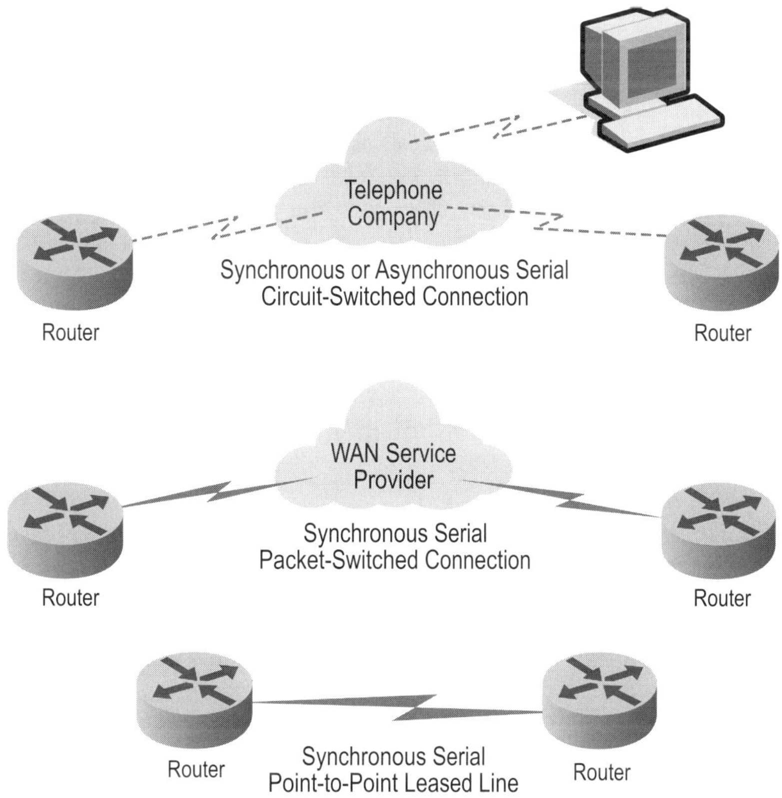

Types of WAN Connections

Circuit-Switched Connections

Circuit switching is the method used when making a telephone call. A dedicated path is created from the sender to the receiver for the duration of the transmission. The connection must be established before sending, and terminated when finished. This dedicated connection provides security and guarantees bandwidth in advance. This can also be a drawback if only a small portion of the bandwidth assigned is needed during transmission. The remaining bandwidth is wasted because it cannot be used by any other transmissions. Another drawback is if some portion of the link fails, the circuit is disconnected and must be reestablished.

Addressing information is only necessary when establishing a circuit. This reduces the amount of necessary header information. Because the circuit path is determined during call setup, no decision making takes place during the transmission.

To use an analogy, think of a circuit-switched network as a train on a track. After the connection is made, it can only follow the predefined path for the duration of transmission. Luckily, the train does not have to worry about congestion on the track because it is a dedicated line. The conductor does not have to think about which way to go, because the track offers only one way while the train is running. Modems, telephones, and ISDN are all examples of circuit-switched connections because they "dial up" before transmission and terminate when complete. These technologies use the public switched telephone network (PSTN) for their services. Circuit-switched networks can work in either a mesh or cloud topology.

Packet-Switched Connections

A packet-switched connection provides point-to-point or multipoint connections using virtual circuits. Virtual circuits are logical connections within a physical link. Unlike a dedicated leased-line connection, a packet-switched network allows the physical media to be shared. This greatly reduces the cost of service over a dedicated leased line if the traffic is more bursty in nature. Data traffic is often bursty because it requires a lot of bandwidth for specific amounts of time, and then may not use it again for a while. Packet-switched networks are not dedicated to any one transmission. Instead, they provide shared, on-demand access to a network.

To get information to the right place, special headers with addressing information are added to identify the source and destination. Routing and switching decisions are made throughout the transmission. This means that the best route is selected each time; however, it also slows things down when determining which path to choose. Dynamic route selection means that if a link fails or is highly congested, another route can easily be chosen and the transmission sent a different way. Speeds for packet-switched synchronous transmissions are similar to leased lines, from 56 kilobits per second (Kbps) to 45 megabits per second (Mbps) and up.

To use another transportation analogy, think of packet-switched networks as similar to a car on a road. There are many roads that allow you to get from one place to another. They are shared by other drivers, and provide additional routes in case a problem is encountered. However, because the cars all have to share the same roadway, traffic congestion could cause transmission to slow down. And, because there are so many different roads to choose from, drivers must make many decisions on what the best route is to get to their destination.

Packet-switched connections in a WAN are used in a cloud topology and require Network Layer hierarchical addresses for transmission. X.25 is a true packet-switching technology. Internet Protocol (IP) with PPP, HDLC, frame relay, and ATM all have characteristics of packet/frame/cell switching capabilities.

Point-to-Point Leased Lines

A leased line is a point-to-point connection from one location to another. It is dedicated to a customer, and is not shared with other companies. This provides a high level of security and guaranteed bandwidth. A leased line is also relatively fast because no setup process is required to create the connection. It is on all the time, regardless of whether it is being used. Dedicated lines are often used for connections between branch offices or to the Internet. However, they can be costly, especially when they are not used to their full capacity. Leased lines are synchronous serial lines that can run from 56 Kbps to speeds of a Digital Signal level 3 (DS3) facility at 45 Mbps and up.

Dedicated lines can be public or private. A private line is one in which a business pays for the cable or wireless media to be run from one location to another. This can be very expensive over long distances, and requires a level of knowledge that most companies do not have. A public dedicated line is leased from a provider that creates and maintains the physical and logical connection. You can think of dedicated lines as a private road connecting two locations. Although there is only one way in and out, the road is yours alone.

Leased lines are connected to a channel service unit/data service unit (CSU/DSU), which brings a digital signal from the subscriber, provides synchronization, offers loopback testing, and allows connection to the WAN circuit. The CSU/DSU is the digital device that replaces the functions of a modem in an analog dial-up scenario. Dedicated lines are used in mesh network topologies.

WAN Data Transmission Rates

Local exchange carriers (LECs) offer traditional telecommunications services that use existing telephone company voice network facilities and the copper local loop between a customer and central office (CO). The bottom rung of the point-to-point digital facilities is the Dataphone Digital Service (DDS), also called "Digital Data Service." DDS is considered a subrate facility because it provides connection bandwidth in increments from 2,400- to 56-

Kbps leased lines. A subrate facility is any transmission path that operates at less than a Digital Signal level 0 (DS0) or 64 Kbps. A CSU/DSU is used to make the connection to this facility.

At 64 Kbps, a DS0 is one channel of a T1 or E1 line. One DS0 provides the necessary bandwidth to make a digital telephone call. A T1/DS1 used in North America is made up of 24 DS0s, which provides a total bandwidth of 1.544 Mbps. The value of 1.544 Mb commonly referenced as the bandwidth of a T1 includes 8 Kb of overhead. The usable bandwidth of a T1 is therefore actually 1.536 Mbps. Fractional T1 (FT1) services are offered in many areas and allow subscribers to determine the appropriate number of channels (DS0s) they need to fulfill their bandwidth requirements, while reducing costs over a full T1. Although it is possible to assign any number of channels to a fractional T1, the service is impractical after about 11 to 12 channels. At that point a full T1 is most cost effective. E1 is the European equivalent (also used in Latin and Central America) of the T1 and has 32 DS0s for a total of 2.048 Mbps. For higher bandwidth transmissions, in North America the next terrestrial facility is a T3, also called a "DS3." This is made up of 672 DS0s, for a total bandwidth of 43.008 Mbps or 45.736 Mbps. The European technology closest to this is an E3, which has a bandwidth of 34.368 Mbps. A CSU/DSU is used to connect to a T1 or E1.

The WAN Bandwidth Table provides a review of these technologies in addition to others, such as a dial-up modem, ISDN, DSL, and cable modem, discussed later in this module. The table includes transmission rates, media, and applications.

WAN Bandwidth

Technology	Data Rate	Physical Media	Application
Dial-up modem	2400 baud to 56 Kbps	Copper twisted pair	Home office, Internet, low-bandwidth remote access
DDS 56-Kbps leased line	56 Kbps	Copper twisted pair	Low-bandwidth digital facility, point-to-point
ISDN-Basic Rate Interface (BRI)	128 Kbps data, 144 Kbps total	Copper twisted pair	Home or small office phone and data over two separate channels, or 128 Kbps together, out-of-band signal D channel

WAN Bandwidth (Continued)

Technology	Data Rate	Physical Media	Application
Fractional T1 (FT1)	64 Kbps to 768 Kbps	Copper twisted pair	Small- to medium-business line, shared between voice and data, remote connectivity, internet
T1/DS1	1.544 Mbps* or 24 channels 1.536 usable	Copper twisted pair Optical fiber Microwave	Medium to large business, can be shared with voice and data, point-to-point leased line, access to frame relay service provider, internet access
E1	2.048 Mbps or 32 channels	Copper twisted pair Optical fiber Microwave	European standard similar to T1, but with higher bandwidth; otherwise, same application
xDSL	128 Kbps to 8 Mbps	Copper twisted pair	Many varieties of DSL service; bandwidth determined by distance from CO, quality of line
Cable modem	512 Kbps to 40 Mbps	Coaxial cable	Shared media; can provide high bandwidth; contention based media
E3	34.368 Mbps or 512 channels	Copper twisted pair Optical fiber Microwave	European standard similar to T3; large network connections, shared between voice and data
T3/DS3	45 Mbps or 672 channels 43.008 Mbps usable	Copper twisted pair Optical fiber Microwave	Large network connections, shared between voice and data, Internet access, call centers

Multiplexing Methods

Mutliplexing is a technique that allows different information streams to be transmitted over the same physical media. Mutliplexing defines the method for adding information to a line and removing (demultiplexing) it from the line while maintaining its separation and integrity from other concurrent transmissions.

TDM

Time division multiplexing (TDM) combines many digital bit streams with relatively low bit rates into a single bit stream with a relatively high bit rate. It is, in essence, a way for many slow communications channels to "time share" a very fast channel. The advantage is that the cost per bit transmitted on a single fast channel is lower than on multiple slower channels.

TDM is accomplished by interleaving data from several bit streams. This can be done on a bit basis or byte basis, called "bit interleaving" or "byte interleaving," respectively. The TDM Diagram illustrates this concept. During time interval 1, 8 bits from source channel 1 are transmitted. During successive intervals, bytes from successive source channels are transmitted on the output channel. A complete set of values from each input channel is called a "frame."

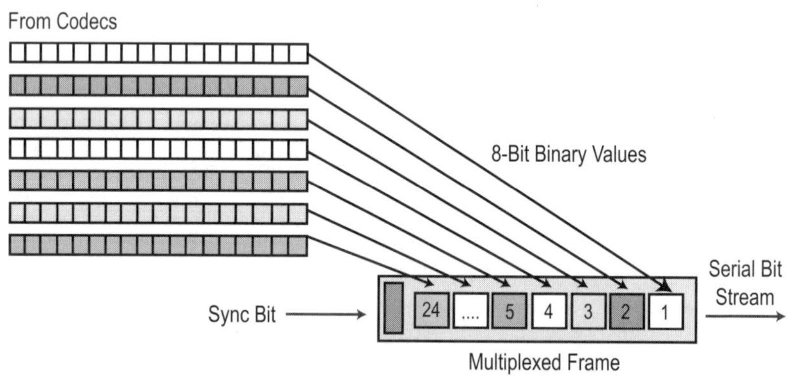

TDM

Two types of TDM exist: synchronous TDM (STDM) and asynchronous TDM (ATDM). In STDM, the multiplexing device assigns time slots. If a time slot is not filled with data, it is wasted. This is inefficient, because devices do not transmit consistently, wasting a lot of bandwidth. ATDM allows time slots to be allocated on demand with all time slots being filled during transmission.

FDM

Frequency division multiplexing (FDM) was developed to allow a trunk line with only two pairs of wires to carry multiple transmissions simultaneously. Because of limitations in the technology first developed for FDM, a voice channel was standardized at 4 kilohertz (kHz) of bandwidth. An additional 600 hertz (Hz), between 3.4 and 4 kHz, was necessary to separate the channels on a multiplexed line, so one channel would not interfere with the next. This vacant frequency band is known as a "guardband."

A device such as a channel bank, CSU/DSU, or multiplexer (MUX) is used to separate the different transmissions into various frequencies called "channels" or "carriers." Each carrier is a steady signal of a certain frequency. By convention, channel 1 is assigned the highest frequency band, channel 2 the next highest frequency, and so forth. Using this method, each frequency can be used for a different telephone conversation or data communication, thus allowing much greater use of the physical media.

WDM

Wavelength division multiplexing (WDM) is a multiplexing technique used for optical fiber. WDM has two different formats: coarse WDM (CWDM) is generally used over short-haul connections such as in LAN and metropolitan area network (MAN) environments, and dense WDM (DWDM) is used in long-haul WAN connections. WDM uses multiple light wavelengths to transmit signals over a single optical fiber. WDM is like a prism that takes a beam of light and refracts it into several wavelengths of separate colors. Each wavelength carries information at rates as high as 2.5 gigabits per second (Gbps).

With optical technology advances, WDM has seen more and more wavelengths, or channels, squeezed into an optical fiber. Aggregate rates as high as 1 terabit, or 1 trillion bits per second (bps), are possible with this technology. Thus, WDM is actually more like FDM in that separate channels within a transmission pipe are each carrying a stream of data. This technology is being used to move IP, SONET, and ATM traffic simultaneously through the same fiber media.

SM

Statistical multiplexing (SM) is a method that best utilizes the available bandwidth by dynamically allocating it on an as-needed basis. It is useful when transporting variable bit rate (VBR) streams of information, such as video, voice, audio, and data, over the same bandwidth. SM multiplexes all the different streams into a single constant bit rate (CBR) transmission path. This means far more efficient use of the overall available bandwidth and improved quality of service (QoS). Unlike the other multiplexing technologies, SM can reallocate and adjust the bandwidth over time, providing optimal use of a channel for each transmission.

Physical, Logical, and Virtual Circuits

When making a WAN connection, it is important to understand the difference between physical and logical circuits. What is seen as a wired connection may have little to do with the type of information and number of communications that can be transmitted across the connection.

A physical circuit is the actual wired or wireless media used for transmissions. The physical circuit can carry information in the form of analog or digital signals, and is the "pipe" that communications are sent through. An example of a physical circuit is a two- or four-wire T1 used for digital transmissions. Another example is an analog local loop, also called a "plain old telephone service (POTS) line," which is the primary connection for residential customers.

A logical circuit defines the use of the physical media. Using special encoding, signaling, and multiplexing techniques allows the physical circuit to be used for a number of different communication channels. For example, the T1 uses a DS1 that allows a total bandwidth of 1.54 Mbps for communication. However, with the right equipment, encoding, and signaling a T1 can also transmit 24 DS0s. This means that over a two- or four-wire physical circuit, 24 separate communication channels are available. That equals 24 telephone calls that can be placed simultaneously over one physical circuit.

Another example uses the analog POTS line. With DSL service and the right equipment, the logical circuits could be the voice path used for talking on the telephone, an alternate voice path for call waiting, a low-bandwidth DSL upload channel, and a high-bandwidth DSL download channel. Only one local loop is required; however, it can be used to make calls and cruise the Internet at the same time.

A virtual circuit is also logical in the method it uses for transmission. A virtual circuit defines whether the transmission path is always available or is dynamically established when information needs to be sent. Two types of virtual circuits exist: permanent virtual circuits (PVCs) and switched virtual circuits (SVCs).

PVC—A PVC behaves like a dedicated connection between source and destination endpoints. A PVC always establishes a predefined path between these two endpoints. The circuit is always on, meaning it is always available for transmission. Although this reduces the time it takes performing initial setup processes, it means that the connection is fixed between the two communication points. Frame relay and ATM are examples of technologies that use PVCs. Similarly, DSL and cable modem services offer always-on access to the Internet.

SVC—An SVC is analogous to a public-switched telephone service, in that calls can be made dynamically between a source endpoint and any destination endpoint in a network. The end devices establish a connection on demand and disconnect when communications cease. This provides a bit of flexibility for endpoint connections, but requires time to establish the circuit before transmission can take place. A dial-up modem connection is a very basic SVC process of call setup, transmission, and call termination. X.25 is an older technology that used this same process to send data. Today, ATMs often uses SVCs for more flexible connectivity options.

Review Questions

1. Which multiplexing technique combines different communication signals by assigning each a time slice?
   a. FDM
   b. TDM
   c. SM
   d. DWDM
2. What is the transmission bandwidth of ISDN-Basic Rate Interface (BRI) service?
   a. 1.54 Mbps
   b. 64 Kbps
   c. 2.048 Mbps
   d. 128 Kbps
3. The increment of measure for a single channel is a DS0. What is the bandwidth of a single DS0?
   a. 64 Kbps
   b. 56 Kbps
   c. 128 Kbps
   d. 1.54 Mbps
4. A company has implemented a full mesh WAN topology connecting three remote offices with dedicated connections that are always on. What type of WAN circuits are being used?
   a. Circuit-switched connections
   b. Point-to-point leased lines
   c. Packet-switched connections
   d. Virtual circuits
5. How many DS0s are grouped together to make a T1/DS1?
   a. 10
   b. 15
   c. 20
   d. 24

6. Which of the following best describes a circuit-switched connection?
   a. A dedicated line between two endpoints that is always active
   b. A logical link that provides a virtual connection to an endpoint
   c. A connection that is established on demand and terminated upon completion
   d. A connection that switches transmissions on a packet-by-packet basis
7. Which component is required to connect to a digital facility? (This component may be an external device that plugs into a T1 or an integrated component.)
   a. Router
   b. Repeater
   c. CSU/DSU
   d. Modem
8. What is the bandwidth associated with a DS3?
   a. 64 Kbps
   b. 10 Mbps
   c. 128 Kbps
   d. 45 Mbps
9. Which circuit connection type uses bandwidth by efficiently switching information using addresses included in a header?
   a. Circuit-switched connection
   b. Point-to-point leased line
   c. Packet-switched connection
   d. Virtual circuit
10. Which communication methods use circuit-switched transmissions? (Choose two.)
    a. Modem
    b. ISDN
    c. X.25
    d. IP

Extended Activities

1. Match the following components with the appropriate description:

   DS1 ______

   Circuit-switched ______

   Packet-switched ______

   Point-to-point leased line ______

   DS0 ______

   PVC ______

   SVC ______

   TDM ______

   FDM ______

   a. A dedicated physical wired circuit that connects two endpoints
   b. A logical circuit that is always on, acting like a physical circuit
   c. A multiplexing technique that uses different frequencies for transmissions
   d. Transmission bandwidth of 24 DS0s
   e. A physical connection that is established as information needs to be sent
   f. A logical circuit that is activated on demand to switch information
   g. A multiplexing technique that uses different time slots
   h. A 64-Kbps circuit used for a single telephone conversation
   i. A transmission method that uses addressing to make routing decisions

Lesson 2—WAN Access Technologies

This lesson discusses many of the technologies at the Data Link and Physical Layers of the Open Systems Interconnection (OSI) model. The protocols PPP and HDLC often rival each other when transmitting over serial and ISDN lines. PPP is vendor-neutral and offers a few more advanced features than HDLC. ISDN provides two options: Basic Rate Interface (BRI) (144 Kbps) and Primary Rate Interface (PRI) (1.54 Mbps).

DSL services are becoming very popular because they provide a low-cost alternative for Internet access over existing telephone lines. Frame relay is a Data Link Layer encapsulation method that sends information into a frame relay service provider network. Frame relay can greatly reduce the cost of long-distance leased lines, because connections are made locally.

ATM is a fast transmission method that was designed for voice, video, and data. It typically transmits 53-byte cells over an Optical Carrier level 3 (OC3) at 155 Mbps. SONET is the Physical Layer implementation that provides the optical carrier for ATM. It is built on the OC1 and incremented to provide very high bandwidth capabilities.

Objectives

At the end of this lesson you will be able to:

- Define the characteristics of PPP and HDLC
- Define different ISDN services
- Describe xDSL types and implementation
- Define the characteristics of frame relay, ATM and SONET

Key Point

WAN access technologies are found at the Data Link and Physical Layers of the OSI model; knowledge of these technologies will help enable the creation of efficient and stable wide area networks.

PPP

PPP has several features that include an encapsulation method and data link functions, and provides transmission for dynamic IP address allocation. PPP has benefits over Serial Line Internet Protocol (SLIP) and HDLC because it is not proprietary in nature and allows multiple Network Layer protocol transmissions. It can be used over synchronous or asynchronous lines, and provides connectivity between different vendors' products.

PPP has become the encapsulation method of choice for IP communications. PPP uses the same encapsulation framing format as HDLC, replacing the proprietary field with a protocol. When transmitting across a serial link with PPP as the encapsulation type, the appropriate Data Link Layer header is added, as shown on the PPP Header Diagram.

PPP Header

Next PPP uses its Data Link Layer component, Link Control Protocol (LCP), to provide important services. LCP is the workhorse behind PPP. It is responsible for negotiating, testing, and establishing the connection between sender and receiver. Then it maintains the connection, detects errors, and provides security, compression, and load balancing.

LCP also provides authentication to validate the connecting devices. PPP has two authentication methods: Password Authentication Protocol (PAP) and Challenge Handshake Authentication Protocol (CHAP). If authentication is accepted, LCP hands off to the Network Layer. After the transmission is complete, LCP tears down the connection.

The PPP Network Layer component is Network Control Protocol (NCP). NCP is responsible for identifying, selecting, and configuring the protocol(s) to be transmitted between sender and receiver. The various protocols that can be identified and sent by means of PPP include IP, Internetwork Packet Exchange (IPX), and Cisco Discovery Protocol (CDP), as well as others.

HDLC

HDLC, a connection-oriented Data Link Layer protocol, is based on IBM's Synchronous Data Link Control (SDLC) protocol. It has relatively little overhead, which improves performance. HDLC is a bit-oriented protocol that frames characters and provides a checksum. On the downside, standard HDLC is only designed to run a single Network Layer protocol, such as IP, IPX, or Systems Network Architecture (SNA), over a connection. Because HDLC does not have any header fields that include protocol-specific information, it cannot keep multiple protocols separate. In addition, it does not offer an authentication method for securing connections.

Although HDLC is an industry standard for serial connections, each vendor that offers HDLC encapsulation has a slightly different header format. Cisco Systems has added a proprietary field that allows Cisco HDLC to identify and differentiate multiple Network Layer protocols over the same physical connection. However, the difference in header formats means that HDLC, in most cases, only works when communicating between devices from the same vendor. HDLC is the default encapsulation type for serial interfaces on Cisco routers. It can be used with dedicated point-to-point or multipoint connections. Cisco's implementation can also provide authenticated access.

Because HDLC is the default method for Cisco serial links, it is not necessary to configure HDLC encapsulation. The serial interface automatically adds a Cisco proprietary HDLC header to data as it is sent across a connection. As stated, Cisco's HDLC header is proprietary because it includes a protocol type field that allows different upper-layer protocols to be sent and differentiated over a serial link. This is not the standard HDLC format, however. The HDLC Header Comparison Diagram presents the differences in the fields.

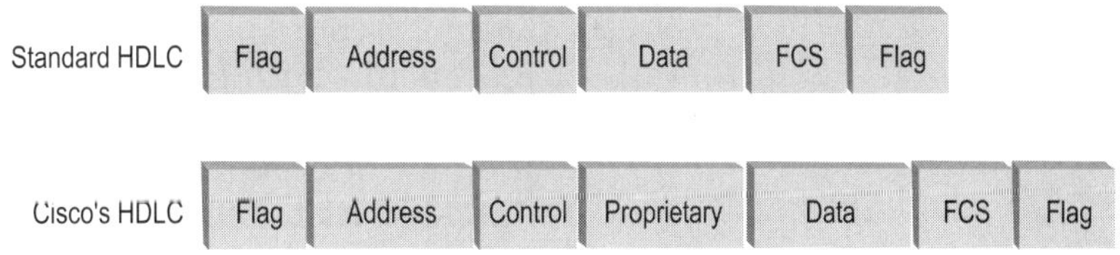

HDLC Header Comparison

ISDN

We subscribe to ISDN in the same way we subscribe to voice services. (Of course, the end office must offer ISDN.) ISDN is a combination of encapsulation and signaling methods. It was designed to transmit voice, video, data, and other multimedia communications over the same physical link.

ISDN provides access to digital channels. Two types of channels are available for subscriber use:

- **D channel**—This channel is used to transmit signal information (such as digits), perform call setup, maintain the circuit, and tear down the call path. A separate channel for signaling is called "clear channel signaling (CCS)" or "out-of-band," because it is separated from the information being sent. CCS eliminates the problem of distinguishing control signals from data. Two or more bearer (B) channels share the D channel which saves bandwidth. D channels are either 16 or 64 Kbps depending upon the service.
- **B channels**—These channels operate at 64 Kbps and are used to carry circuit-switched data, voice, fax, slow-scan video, and so forth. They are called "bearer" channels because they bear the load of whatever they are transmitting. The signal is kept separate in the D channel.

ISDN offers two types of services, chosen depending on bandwidth and access needs. A business might require more than one kind of service, just as they might require more than one telephone line. The services types include:

- **Basic rate interface**—Also known as BRI, this service provides one 16-Kbps D channel and two 64-Kbps B channels, and is sometimes referred to as "two B plus D" or "2B+D." Although this service can provide 144 Kbps of usable capacity, the D channel is normally reserved for signaling; therefore, only 128 Kbps of bandwidth are available for transmission. BRI service can be used as two telephone lines, or one telephone line and one 64-Kbps data channel, or combined to provide 128 Kbps of data bandwidth.

- **Primary rate interface**—Also know as PRI, this service is structured around the bandwidths of T1 (1.544 Mbps) for North America and Japan. It includes a 64-Kbps D channel and 23 – 64-Kbps B channels. Primary rate service is also known as "23B+1D." When using an E1 facility in Europe, Australia, or Central and Latin America, PRI is 30 B channels, 1 primary D channel, and a backup D channel, which is often described as 30B+2D. E1 provides up to 2.048 Mbps of bandwidth.

DSL

DSL was developed as a way to offload much of the modem traffic that was tying up central office (CO) telephone switches as more subscribers gained access to the Internet. DSL uses the existing twisted pair telephone wires connecting homes and businesses to the local exchange carrier (LEC) or CO. The talking path (POTS) used for voice conversations and additional features such as three-way calling or call waiting only takes up a very small portion of the bandwidth available on the copper wire (local loop). xDSL can use this extra higher-frequency bandwidth by distributing it for upstream and downstream traffic.

The "x" often shown in the name of xDSL indicates a variable that is used to represent the various types of DSL service. When a specific type is provided, the x is replaced with the letter that describes the exact technology. xDSL is offered as Asymmetric DSL (ADSL) and ADSL Lite, Symmetric DSL (SDSL), Rate Adaptive DSL (RADSL), DSL over ISDN line (IDSL), High-data-rate DSL (HDSL), and Very high-data-rate DSL (VDSL). This lesson discusses the characteristics of ADSL and SDSL, as well as the defined standards, speeds, modulation techniques, and distance limitations of each.

Asymmetric DSL (ADSL) distributes the bandwidth asymmetrically. In other words, ADSL provides more downstream (to the user) bandwidth than upstream (from the user) bandwidth. The majority of target applications for digital subscriber services are asymmetric. Internet access, remote LAN access, multimedia access, and specialized personal computer (PC) services all feature high-data-rate demands downstream to a subscriber, but relatively low-data-rate demands upstream. Regardless of the bandwidth allotment, all of these arrangements operate in a frequency band above POTS, leaving POTS independent and undisturbed, even if a premise's ADSL modem fails.

Full-rate ADSL, also called "G.DMT" has been standardized under the American National Standards Institute (ANSI) specification T1.413 Issue 2. It has downstream transmission capability from 128 Kbps up to 8 Mbps. Upstream transmissions are possible between 64 Kbps and 1.024 Mbps. Distance and line quality are major factors in the transmission rates. The maximum distance for ADSL service from subscriber to CO is 18,000 feet.

ADSL uses one of two multiplexing techniques to achieve the high bandwidth and allow simultaneous upstream and downstream transmission. ADSL originally used Carrier-less Amplitude/Phase modulation (CAP), achieving speeds from 256 to 7,168 Kbps downstream and 91 to 1,088 Kbps upstream. Discrete Multi-Tone (DMT) is part of the ANSI T1.413 standard that allows for faster transmission speeds up to 8,064 Kbps downstream and 1,024 Kbps upstream.

Typically speaking, ADSL service is considered circuit-switched because it uses a connection through the CO. The service provider may offer ADSL as either access-on-demand connection or always on. Access-on-demand is usually less expensive and allows subscribers Internet access when they want it through a process similar to a dial-up connection. An always-on connection is there as soon as a PC is booted up and Internet service is requested.

SDSL uses the available bandwidth to offer equal bandwidth on upstream and downstream channels. SDSL is more useful in environments where there is an equal amount of transmissions and requests to and from the Internet. Companies or home office users that have established virtual private network (VPN) connections find SDSL beneficial. SDSL is helpful in this type of environment because there is usually no typical pattern of transmission, but rather a need for bandwidth in both directions.

SDSL does not have a specific standard as yet defined. It commonly uses the digital encoding and multiplexing technique called "2B1Q" (2 binary 1 quaternary). For practical purposes, SDSL offers 768 Kbps in both directions. It has a general distance limitation of 22,000 feet from the CO.

xDSL Implementation

There are numerous other xDSL standards, encoding/multiplexing methods, and usage. Additional varieties will be developed and available as demand increases and technology improves. Vendors that build DSL equipment must comply with the international standards for compatibility.

To get DSL service, the subscriber's line is tested for quality and upper-frequency bandwidth. A technician at the CO can usually indicate whether the service is available based on the results of the test. If the line passes, the person or business subscribes to DSL service just as they would get a telephone line. In most cases, no new wire is installed, and the service is delivered over the existing telephone line(s).

Residential subscribers receive a DSL communication device that they plug into the Ethernet port of their PC. They plug the other port into a standard wall jack for a telephone. It is often necessary to put filters on the other wall jacks/telephones in the house to prevent interference. In a business environment, DSL service is provided using a specialized DSL router or interface in an existing data router.

On the provider side, the CO or competitive service provider must install specialized equipment to provide access. The CO must have a Digital Subscriber Line Access Multiplexer (DSLAM) that picks up the higher-frequency DSL traffic from the standard POTS traffic for each subscriber. The DSLAM then multiplexes each traffic stream with many other subscribers and transmits it onto its own network, typically ATM over SONET or 10-Gigabit Ethernet, which is becoming a popular option. The traditional POTS voice conversations are switched as they are normally through the PSTN.

Some service providers are extending service availability by installing DSLAMs into new housing developments and business complexes that would otherwise be too far from their local CO to receive service. The xDSL Implementation Diagram shows a subscriber's access to the CO and onto the Internet.

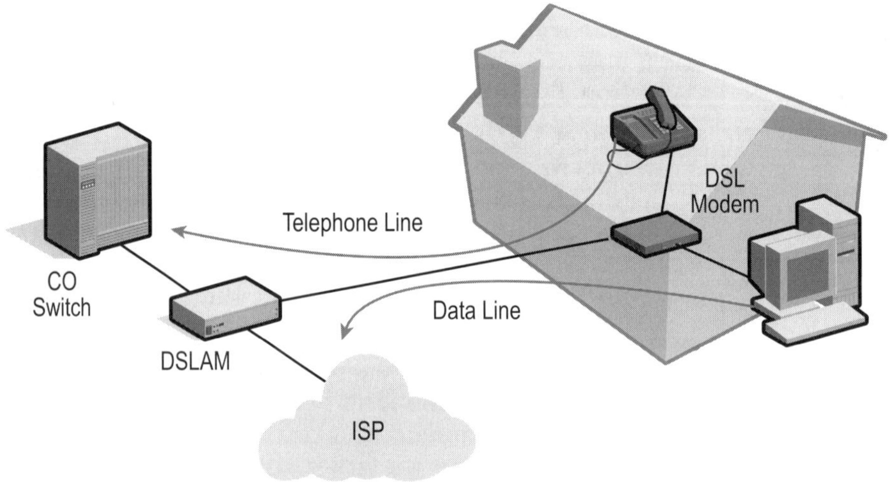

xDSL Implementation

xDSL Pros and Cons

The various DSL options give business and residential subscribers more options for services. Because xDSL service is provided over existing telephone lines, it is a very cost effective method for high-speed Internet access. Subscribers can add additional lines for higher bandwidth, again at a much lower cost than similar bandwidth options. DSL service does not affect the telephone line (POTS); therefore, a person can talk on the telephone and use the Internet at the same time. If, for some reason, the DSL service is down or the DSL modem fails, the POTS line will not be impacted. The service is always on, preventing the time it takes to make a dial-up connection.

Service providers are having a difficult time managing requests for service in many areas where subscribers are farther from the CO than the specified distance. Availability is one of the major obstacles yet to be overcome. Although DSL services are available in a majority of metropolitan areas, overly long loops, multiple wire splices, and poor quality lines prevent reasonable bandwidth, if there is any service at all. In addition, many residential lines were installed with load coil or filter devices to segment and compress the voice frequencies. This helps reduce interference from upper and lower frequencies, improves voice quality, and allows the signal to travel farther. However, these components block out the upper frequencies, preventing DSL access unless they are removed or a new line is run.

Frame Relay

Frame relay has replaced many X.25 connections because of its higher performance. Frame relay removes the majority of overhead used by X.25. Instead, frame relay relies on upper-layer protocols for error detection and some flow control. In addition, communication lines have become more stable since X.25 was the best choice for a WAN protocol.

Frame relay uses PVCs to establish a communication channel from the customer premises equipment (CPE) to the frame relay service provider. This is more cost-effective than a dedicated long-distance point-to-point link, because the connection is local. Frame relay is a well-suited protocol for higher-bandwidth, bursty data transmission requirements than its predecessors of X.25 and standard dial-up connections.

When customers are interested in frame relay services, they must first get a fractional or full T1 connection from the frame relay service provider to their premises. This line may or may not be provided by the same company as the frame relay services. Next, it is necessary to sign a contract that defines the committed information rate (CIR). This is the average throughput that the service provider will guarantee for a specified period of time. The CIR could be up to 1.544 Mbps, which is the maximum bandwidth of the T1.

The customer must also have the CPE to support the frame relay connection. This can be a router or frame relay access device (FRAD). The router or FRAD is considered a data terminal equipment (DTE) device because it is on the subscriber side. It synchronizes with the provider's frame relay switch, which acts as the data communication equipment (DCE) that provides the clock signal for synchronization.

Frame relay is a connection-oriented, Data Link Layer protocol. It provides a data encapsulation method as well as establishes a virtual circuit. To create a PVC between the CPE and the frame relay switch at the service provider, a signal called a "Local Management Interface" (LMI) is used. There are three different LMI formats: Cisco, ASNI, and Q.933a. The service provider will indicate which LMI standard should be configured to achieve an active connection. Once established, LMI is also responsible for sending "keepalives," which are a network heartbeat to maintain the PVC in an active status.

As a Data Link Layer protocol, frame relay must have an appropriate address to add to the frame header. Frame relay adds a data link connection identifier (DLCI), which is a 10-bit address that identifies the virtual circuit. This address is locally significant. Within the service provider cloud, the information is switched and routed accordingly using DLCI and IP address information.

Frame relay offers point-to-point and multipoint connection options. Each endpoint must be a frame relay subscriber with a local connection. The Frame Relay Header Diagram shows the contents after the packet is encapsulated with frame relay information.

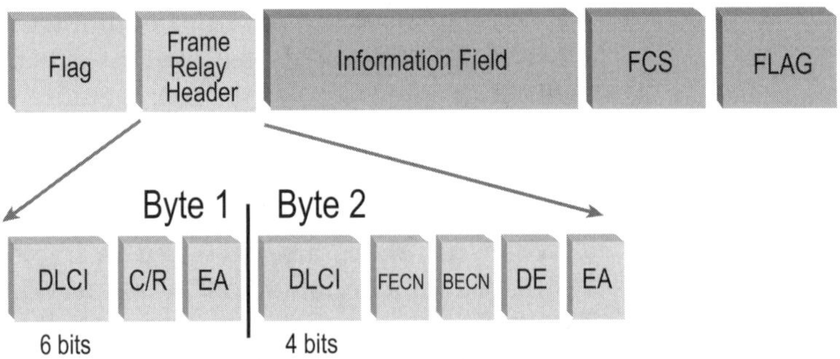

DLCI: Data Link Connection Identifier
C/R: Command/Response Field Bit
EA: Address Extension Bit (allows 3- or 4-byte header)
FECN: Forward Explicit Congestion Notification
BECN: Backward Explicit Congestion Notification
DE: Discard Eligibility Indicator

Frame Relay Header

Frame relay is a connection-oriented but unreliable protocol. Typically, these two characteristics would not be found together, but it all goes back to the CIR. When the CIR is negotiated, customers determine how much bandwidth they need and how much they are willing to pay for. The idea is that the network will not be constantly busy and therefore more data will be transmitted than paid for. However, if the customer sends data over the CIR, the frame relay switch will tag any frames that exceed the amount as "discard eligible" (DE). If frame relay switches in the cloud are experiencing congestion, they can drop any frames flagged with DE to help reduce traffic. This is what makes frame relay unreliable. However, when using Transmission Control Protocol (TCP)/ IP, if an acknowledgment is not received within a specified period of time, the source will assume something happened and retransmit. Therefore, frame relay is dependent on upper-layer protocols for flow control and recovery.

ATM

ATM was designed to transmit voice, video, and data simultaneously at very high speeds. ATM breaks all information down into 53-byte cells, which allows it to switch the cells very quickly through a network. ATM was designed with speed in mind, and therefore runs over very fast transmission media, often a copper DS3 at 45 Mbps or more commonly an OC3 at 155 Mbps. Because of its capabilities, ATM is most often found inside provider networks. Large corporate networks also use ATM connections as their backbones, as well as for access to the Internet to meet the increasing need for bandwidth.

ATM is a Data Link Layer protocol that is both connection-oriented and reliable. It provides inherent QoS features because of the way it handles different information. ATM initially breaks all transmissions into 53-byte cells. The payload of voice, video, audio, or data is 48 bytes in length. The ATM header is 5 bytes. This means that large data transmissions do not get any more space than small voice or video transmissions. This prevents delay-sensitive real-time information from getting held back by lengthy data packets. Because all cells are equal size, they get equal network access. The ATM Cell Header Diagram shows the contents of the cell.

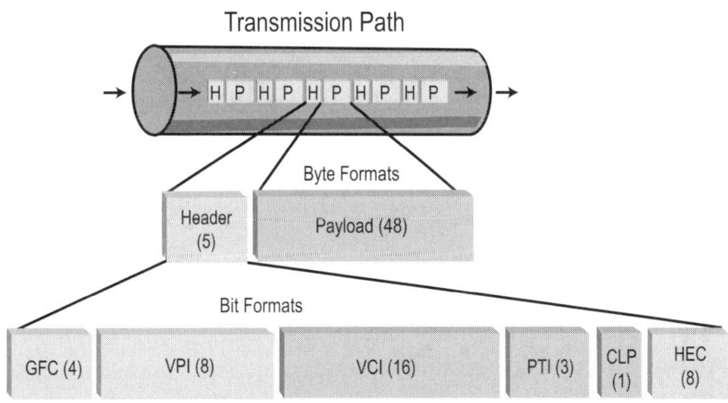

ATM Cell Header

The fact that ATM is connection-oriented at the Data Link Layer also cuts down on overhead. By establishing a PVC or SVC end-to-end, ATM can reduce the amount of addressing that is necessary during the transmission process. For example, when ATM defines its virtual circuit, it then establishes virtual paths that contain virtual channels (VCs). To stretch this concept a bit, think of a virtual circuit as a highway, with the virtual path being one direct lane (for instance, eastbound), and the VCs as being three lanes of the highway. To keep traffic separate, the cell header includes a virtual path identifier (VPI) as well as a virtual channel identifier (VCI). It is like saying that you drove to work today on I-70 eastbound in lane 2. Each VC is allocated to voice, video, or data, which means that this traffic is kept separate while getting equal and adequate throughput. The ATM Virtual Circuit Diagram shows how the VC is divided.

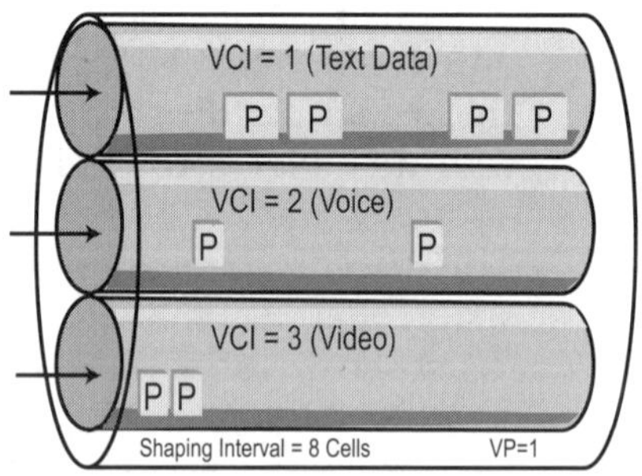

ATM Virtual Circuit

SONET

SONET is a technology at the Physical Layer of the OSI model. The SONET standard defines a signal hierarchy similar to T-carriers, but extending to much higher bandwidths, as presented in the SONET Data Rates Table.

SONET Data Rates

Facility	Bandwidth	Application
OC1	51.48 Mbps	Backbone connections, Internet connectivity
OC3	155.52 Mbps	Large network backbone, Internet connectivity
OC12	622.08 Mbps	Service provider, large network, Internet backbone
OC24	1.244 Gbps	Service provider, large network, Internet backbone
OC48	2.488 Gbps	Service provider, large network, Internet backbone
OC192	10 Gbps	Service provider and large networks backbone, used for 10-Gbps Ethernet MAN and WAN services
OC768	40 Gbps	Largest optical carrier currently available

The basic building block is the Synchronous Transport Signal level 1 (STS-1) 51.84-Mbps signal, chosen to accommodate a DS3 signal. The hierarchy is defined past STS-48, that is, 48 STS-1 channels for a total of 2,488.32 Mbps, capable of carrying 32,256 voice circuits. The STS designation refers to the interface for electrical signals. The optical signal standards are correspondingly designated OC1, OC3, and so forth. Current OC rates are as high as OC768 (40 Gbps).

SONET began as a U.S. standard, and was later incorporated into the international standard Synchronous Digital Hierarchy (SDH). SDH has been standardized by the International Telecommunication Union-Telecommunications Standardization Sector (ITU-T). SONET/SDH meets the worldwide need for standardization. SONET uses the term OC or STS as the data rate descriptor. SDH uses Synchronous Transport Mode (STM).

SONET offers important advantages for those who use switched networks for communications:

- The SONET standards provide a low-level platform upon which other protocols, such as the WAN encapsulation types described in this section, can be based.
- SONET makes it possible for subscribers to purchase equipment that interfaces "in the glass" with switched public networks. For example, SONET interfaces are available for ATM and ISDN.
- Optical carriers make multimedia application requirements combining data, voice, and video images both technically and economically feasible.
- SONET provides direct, transparent interfaces to Layer 2 WAN protocols, such as ISDN and ATM. For example, SONET appears to ISDN interfaces as a continuation of the ISDN network, which is based on copper cable.

The SONET standard includes extensive network operation and management facilities. A significant portion of the SONET bandwidth is allocated for out-of-band control signaling for this purpose. This management system has its own OSI-compliant communications architecture. SONET is the building block for ATM transmission in the service provider network. As more and more corporate and education organizations need increased bandwidth, many are building their own ATM/SONET rings with fiber optic cable. In addition, they can also make very high-speed Internet connections directly to a service provider using this technology.

A technology made possible using OC192 capabilities is 10 Gbps Ethernet. It is being leveraged first as a service provider network backbone. MAN and WAN connectivity is then offered to corporate customers. Eventually large corporate networks will find themselves making similar advancements to achieve high-bandwidth connections as well.

Review Questions

1. Which technology transmits information in a cell format?
    a. Frame relay
    b. ISDN
    c. ATM
    d. PPP
2. What are characteristics of PPP that differentiate it from HDLC? (Choose two.)
    a. PPP is vendor-neutral.
    b. PPP is a Physical Layer protocol
    c. PPP inherently supports multiple Network Layer protocols.
    d. PPP was built on SDLC technology.
3. In which layer of the OSI model is SONET found?
    a. Network
    b. Transport
    c. Data link
    d. Physical
4. What logical circuit makes frame relay connection-oriented?
    a. Dial-up connection
    b. PVC
    c. SVC
    d. Dedicated point-to-point leased line
5. Which encapsulation type is considered the default for a serial interface on a Cisco router?
    a. PPP
    b. ISDN
    c. HDLC
    d. Frame relay

6. Which DSL service type provides high bandwidth upstream and low bandwidth downstream?
   a. RADSL
   b. ADSL
   c. SHDSL
   d. xDSL
7. Which channel in ISDN service is used to transmit circuit-switched data or voice?
   a. B channel
   b. D channel
   c. I channel
   d. Q channel
8. What is the Physical Layer implementation for ADSL service?
   a. Coaxial cable
   b. 10BaseT cable
   c. POTS line
   d. Fiber optic
9. What will happen to information that exceeds the CIR in frame relay?
   a. It will not be transmitted.
   b. It will be returned to the sender.
   c. It will be flagged as DE and sent.
   d. It will be transmitted to its destination without any changes.
10. Which disadvantages limit DSL implementation? (Choose two.)
   a. Distance
   b. Telephone line
   c. Quality of wire
   d. Bandwidth

Extended Activities

1. Match the following technologies with their associated components. Each technology has two correct answers.

   PPP _____ _____

   HDLC _____ _____

   ISDN _____ _____

   ADSL _____ _____

   Frame relay _____ _____

   ATM _____ _____

   SONET _____ _____

   a. Uses LMI
   b. Provides OC
   c. 2B+1D
   d. POTS line
   e. Cells
   f. LCP
   g. Default serial encapsulation
   h. Physical Layer fiber
   i. VPI/VCI
   j. Built on SDLC
   k. PRI and BRI
   l. CIR
   m. PAP and CHAP
   n. High downstream, low upstream

Lesson 3—Modems

Modems are Physical Layer devices that have been around for many years. They are designed to take a digital signal and convert it to an analog wave that can be transmitted over an analog facility such as a standard telephone line. Modem technology has changed a lot over the past years, due to standards that have helped achieve faster transfer rates and higher bandwidth. The highest modem standard is now V.92, which provides features that allow for faster communications.

Another line that is readily available and is now being used for Internet access is the cable used for transmission of cable television. Cable providers have improved the quality of the lines, incorporating Hybrid Fiber and Coaxial (HFC) cable into sophisticated transmission media. This allows for very high-bandwidth potentials at a greatly reduced cost over other traditional high-speed transmissions. The only limitation is that cable modems share bandwidth in a specific cable area. That is, the more subscribers that use the line, the less bandwidth that is available to others. This lesson introduces both traditional dial-up modems and the newer cable modem technology.

Objectives

At the end of this lesson you will be able to:

- Identify the characteristics of analog modems
- Define analog modem standards
- Discuss the characteristics of cable modems
- Define how cable modems work
- Identify the pros and cons of cable modem technology

Key Point

Advances in both modem technologies and modem standards make possible the transmission of a wide variety of data, including audio, voice, and video.

Modem Concepts

Modems are Physical Layer devices. Portions of the public telephone network can carry only analog signals. Therefore, digital signals must be converted to analog form by a process called "modulation." Digital computer signals (baseband) are converted to analog signals for transmission over analog facilities, such as the local loop. Modulation modifies the form of a carrier wave (electrical signal) so it can carry intelligent information on some sort of communications medium. The opposite process, converting analog signals back into the original digital state, is referred to as "demodulation." A modem is responsible for performing this conversion. The Modem Connection Diagram presents a very simplified view of this process.

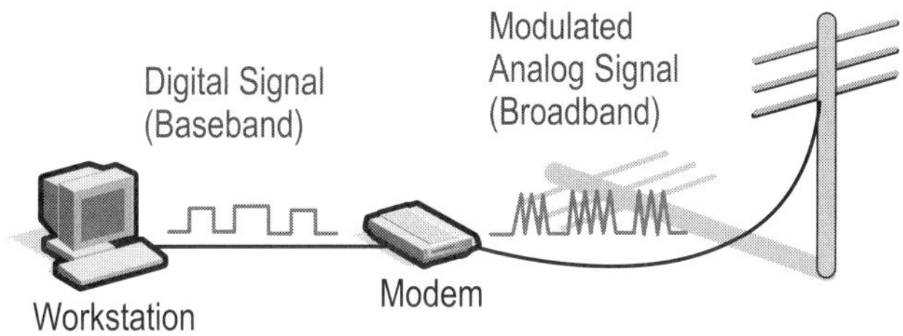

Modem Connection

An internal modem is a card that plugs into a PC or server motherboard bus. An internal modem can also be a card that plugs directly into a router chassis. These cards contain their own serial port on board, and use the computer or router's power supply. External modems are normally self-contained in their own case (or rack-mounted in commercial versions), have a separate power supply, and connect to a computer by means of an RS-232 serial cable to one of the serial ports on the back of a PC. Many PC modems also have a Universal Serial Bus (USB) cable connection as an alternate option. An external modem may also attach to the serial port of a router for WAN connectivity, or the auxiliary port for administration console connection.

Generally, modems are classified as either synchronous or asynchronous. A synchronous modem contains a clock source and phasing circuits, while an asynchronous modem does not. In synchronous transmission, data is sent continuously in regular, clocked intervals. Asynchronous modems do not need clocking sources because each data character is framed by start and stop bits. These modems synchronize on every character; a PC modem is considered an asynchronous modem.

Analog Modem Standards

Standards govern the signals required to set up, transmit, and terminate calls. For a "handshake" to occur, modems must be compatible. "Handshaking" refers to the initialization process that two or more computers go through before they are able to communicate. Control signals are exchanged between the modems to establish the connection. Modems are often capable of operating at several different speeds. Users can adjust operation speeds by means of software commands or changes in components, wires, or switch settings. A modem's fallback rate refers to its ability to detect poor line conditions and lower transmission speeds to prevent errors. For example, a modem operating at 28.8 Kbps may fall back to 19.2 or 9.6 Kbps when line conditions deteriorate.

When discussing modems, the terms baud, bps, bytes, and characters per second (cps) are used. Baud, named after the 19th century French inventor Baudot, originally referred to the speed a telegrapher could send Morse code. It later came to mean the number of times per second a signal changes state. A bit is a single binary piece of data that can be represented by a 0 or 1; thus, it may appear that bps and baud are the same. However, phase shifting and other modulation and data-handling techniques allow more than 1 bit to be transmitted with each baud in high-speed modems. That is, 28,800 bps can be transmitted with a substantially lower baud rate of 3,600 8-bit cps. Therefore, the proper term to use when talking about high-speed modems is bps.

The following standards have been created by the International Telecommunications Union (ITU) to address various modem communication capabilities and include newer technologies as they became available:

- **V.22bis**—This is the original international standard that provided simultaneous transmit and receive capabilities (full-duplex). This standard provides 2,400 bps at 600 baud.
- **V.32/V.32bis**—This standard offers full-duplex data communications over telephone lines at 4,800 or 9,600 bps at 2400 baud. V.32 modems automatically adjust their transmission speed based on the quality of the lines. This standard also includes a provision for an optional fall-forward feature. This allows a modem to actively poll a line, determine when con-

ditions improve, and then reset itself to the highest rate conditions warrant. This can be a very valuable feature, because a small line impairment at the beginning of a lengthy file transfer could turn a 30-minute telephone call into an expensive 3-hour data transfer. With fall forward, a modem might only be at the lower speed for a few minutes.

- **V.34**—V.34 is the standard for full-duplex modems for data communications across telephone lines at up to 28.8 Kbps. Like V.32, V.34 modems can adjust their transmission speed based on line quality. This standard was originally V.FC (developed by Rockwell International). Modems were then developed with an extension of the 1994 V.34 standard that supported speeds up to 33.6 Kbps (AT&T and USR Courier). It is sometimes difficult to achieve the higher connection rates, due to poor line conditions.
- **V.42**—This standard offers the same transfer rate as V.32. It improved performance over poor quality telephone lines by including better error correction methods, thus making it more reliable. V.42 can be used with digital telephone networks.
- **V.90**—V.90 is the standard for full-duplex modems for data communication across telephone lines at up to 56 Kbps downstream. The V.90 standard specifies that there may only be one analog-to-digital conversion in the path between a carrier and modem. The upstream data transmission is limited to approximately 35 Kbps.
- **V.92 with V.44**—ITU has introduced a new modem standard that offers 56 Kbps downstream and 48 Kbps upstream. It allows for both asynchronous and synchronous communications. It includes three new features that help provide this performance: quick connection, Modem on Hold (MOH), and Pulse Code Modulation (PCM) upstream. Quick connect means that the modem "trains" itself to the service provider connection for faster dial-up access. It uses MOH to allow a user to decide how to handle an incoming call without complete service disruption. It uses PCM upstream to boost the upload transmission rate to 48 Kbps. Finally, many V.92 modems utilize the V.44 compression algorithm, which can provide high compression ratios (up to 50 percent) before transmission.

Cable Modem Technology

Cable technology has been deployed to homes and business throughout North America and other countries as a means to deliver an extensive number of channels to subscribers. The network is composed of coaxial cable to the home or office building. Fiber optic cable is used for higher bandwidth in the cable provider's network. This combination of media is referred to as an HFC network. The entire bandwidth of the media is not consumed by the television and music communications that are being transmitted. Using specialized equipment, the cable service provider can allow high-bandwidth upstream and downstream data transmission. In addition, many providers are also incorporating telephone service onto the cable facility.

Cable modem technology provides for very high bandwidth capabilities. It is possible, considering the frequencies and utilization, to achieve transmission rates up to 40 Mbps. However, a more conservative estimate puts bandwidth at around 8 Mbps for the average subscriber. Unlike other technologies, cable modems cannot make any bandwidth promises. Cable access occurs over shared media. All subscribers that are connected to the same cable segment from the headend share the allotted bandwidth for that segment. Thus, as the number of requests increases, the available bandwidth for other users sharing that physical media decreases. Cable providers try to prevent this by not oversubscribing areas and adding bandwidth as demand increases.

How Cable Modems Work

The Internet by Means of a Cable Modem Diagram provides an overview of cable modem access over an HFC network. HFC networks are composed of a fiber feeder from a cable head end to a neighborhood optical node serving several hundred homes. A signal travels from the node to each home over coaxial cable. A network interface unit (NIU) inside a home includes a cable modem and other electronics.

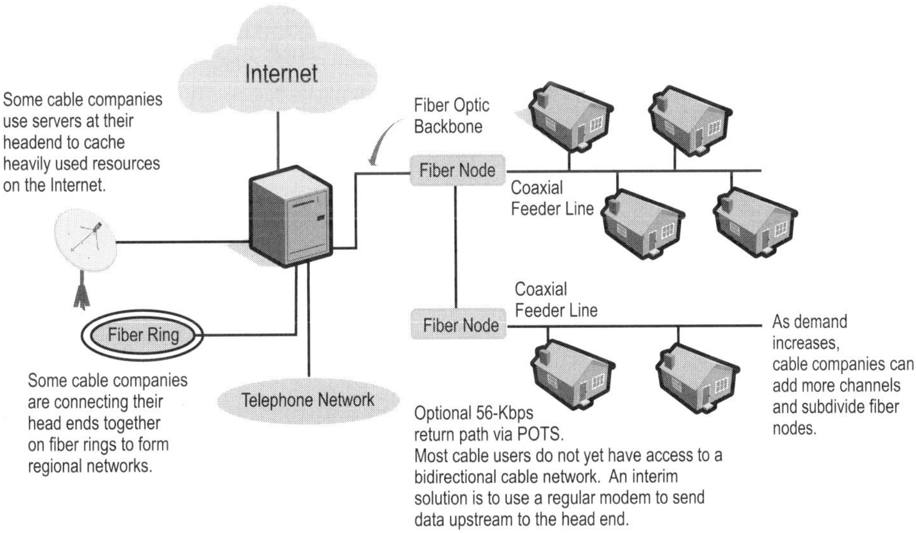

Internet by Means of a Cable Modem

A cable modem is a complex device incorporating a tuner, which separates data signals from broadcast streams (video) from telephony; parts from network adapters, bridges, and routers; network management software agents, which enable a cable company to monitor operations; and encryption devices. Each cable modem has an Ethernet port. As a result of this configuration, up to three cable wires can be provided from the NIU: a coaxial wire delivering broadcast video to a television, an Ethernet wire connecting to a PC, and a twisted pair of wires connecting to a telephone.

The most common cable modems create a downstream data stream out of one of the 6-MHz television channels that occupy the spectrum between 50 and 750 MHz. Common cable modems create an upstream channel carved out of the currently unused band between 5 and 42 MHz. The current HFC cable network uses a 750-MHz spectrum, equivalent to 110 downstream channels of 6-MHz bandwidth (a Federal Communications Commission [FCC] limit) each. Spectrum bandwidth from 5 to 42 MHz is reserved for upstream signaling and telephony. Using 64-quadrature amplitude modulation (QAM), downstream transmission can occur at rates as high as 30 Mbps.

The downstream channel is continuous; however, it is divided into cells or packets, with each packet addressed to a particular subscriber. The downstream portion of the spectrum supports a mix of analog video, digital broadcast, interactive video, telephone, and data services. Downstream transmission does not disturb transmission of television signals to the television set. Upstream transmission rates vary by modem vendor. To avoid collisions, systems are being designed to place each upstream packet onto the network with control signals embedded in the downstream information stream.

Two types of cable modems exist: two-way cable modems and telephone return cable modems. Telephone return cable modems allow subscribers of cable networks that have not been upgraded for two-way communication to obtain the benefits of high speed on the downstream link. The majority of cable modems in use today are telephone return modems.

Cable Modem Pros and Cons

In today's business environment, low-cost options and flexibility are important. Home users, corporate decision makers, and educational facilities are all looking at faster access through media technologies that are already in place. Cable technologies provide high-speed access at a very affordable price. Cable service providers have made significant improvements to the HFC cable plant in most metropolitan areas. This allows for a wide area of coverage. In addition, cable modems do not suffer the same distance limitations that impact xDSL services.

On the service provider side, an extensive amount of work, cable, and equipment goes into making Internet data transmissions and telephone service available. At the onset, many cable service providers oversubscribed their media. Remember that cable media are shared and, therefore, other users connecting to the same segment will impact transmission speeds and available bandwidth. Some cable companies gained a bad reputation in the beginning, before they were able to compensate for the high demand by adding the appropriate infrastructure to support it.

Review Questions

1. What was the first modem standard that was internationally recognized?
   a. 2400 baud
   b. V.22bis
   c. V.32bis
   d. V.92
2. Which feature is associated with the V.92 standard?
   a. Provides quick connect
   b. Supports V.44 compression
   c. Provides asynchronous and synchronous communications
   d. Provides all of the above capabilities
3. What type of cable is used to connect an external modem to a PC? (Choose two.)
   a. Phone cable
   b. Serial cable
   c. USB cable
   d. Ethernet cable
4. Which modem feature of the V.92 standard offers 48 Kbps upstream?
   a. Fast forward
   b. V.44 compression
   c. PCM upstream
   d. ADSL
5. What type of wiring is associated with the cable network?
   a. All coaxial
   b. Fiber optic
   c. Copper telephone lines
   d. HFC
   e. All of the above

6. Which modem standards can transmit 56 Kbps for downstream transmissions? (Choose two.)
   a. V.32
   b. V.44
   c. V.90
   d. V.92
7. What is the main location where all HFC or coaxial cables are connected and receive transmissions?
   a. Hub
   b. Switch
   c. Headend
   d. CO
8. Which of the following describe the benefits of using cable modem technology? (Choose two.)
   a. Very high potential bandwidth
   b. Lower cost than point-to-point leased lines
   c. Ability to connect to any branch office
   d. Access over existing copper telephone lines
9. Modems and cable modems operate at which layer of the OSI model?
   a. Physical
   b. Data Link
   c. Network
   d. Transport
10. Which technology is in the direct competition with cable modems?
    a. Dial-up modems
    b. T1 carrier
    c. xDSL
    d. ATM

Extended Activities

Answer true or false for each characteristic associated with modem and cable modem technology.

Dial-Up Modem Technology

1. Provides access to the Internet over existing telephone lines
2. Allows a user to talk on the telephone while using the modem
3. Has a maximum upstream limit of 56 Kbps
4. Offers a range of standards that define bandwidth and compression
5. Provides analog-to-digital conversion on the sending side
6. Can achieve downstream transmission rates of 56 Kbps
7. Provides synchronous or asynchronous communications

Cable Modem Technology

1. Can provide access to the Internet
2. Provides symmetric bidirectional communications
3. Uses the existing and updated coax cable network used for cable television
4. Some interference caused by channels for television signal and Internet access
5. Cable line shared by neighbors up to the headend
6. Allows transmission of video, voice, data, and music
7. Can provide high-bandwidth transmission rates
8. Offers a full-time connection

Summary

This module covered WAN technologies by starting with a description of connection types. There are three options for connections: circuit-switched, packet-switched, and point-to-point leased lines. Each one has specific characteristics and pros and cons. A business may select one or more options to fulfill their communication needs. Other terms introduced in Lesson 1 included bandwidth, data transmission rates, multiplexing techniques, and physical, logical, and virtual circuits (PVCs and SVCs).

Lesson 2 provided an overview of the many Data Link and Physical Layer WAN protocols. PPP, HDLC, frame relay, and ATM are all Data Link Layer encapsulation methods. HDLC was one of the earliest implementations and maintains its status as the default encapsulation method for serial links. However, PPP has a number of features that outweigh HDLC capabilities. PPP can provide multiple Network Layer support while still being vendor-neutral. It also offers two authentication methods, as well as compression and load balancing. ISDN can use either HDLC or PPP for encapsulation and transmission over its BRI or PRI service.

xDSL is a service that offers faster Internet access than a traditional modem over the existing telephone lines. xDSL uses the upper frequencies above the talking path for communication. This allows a user to talk on the telephone while using the computer for Internet access. xDSL has many different configurations and standards that are maintained by international organizations.

Frame relay uses up to T1 facilities to provide connection-oriented switched communications. It greatly reduces the costs that would normally be experienced using point-to-point leased lines. ATM and SONET work together to provide very high-bandwidth transmission. SONET is the Physical Layer fiber optic ring that offers OC standards. ATM uses an OC3 for 155 Mbps cell-switched transmissions. Both ISDN and ATM were designed for transmitting voice, video, and data.

Lesson 3 presented information about modem technologies, including traditional modems designed to use the PSTN, as well as cable modems that use the coax cable plant for cable television. Modems are used to modulate a digital signal into an analog format on the sending side. The modem on the receiving side demodulates the information, converting the transmission from analog back to digital format. Although slower than other communication methods, traditional dial-up modems offer low cost and readily available access to the Internet and other locations. Modem technology is still evolving to help provide new features and services. Cable technology provides an even faster alternative to dial-up modems. It has the potential for very high bandwidth while keeping costs low.

WAN technologies are an important part of any network administrator's knowledge base. They are necessary because business today is not self-contained. Companies, branch offices, vendors, customers, and virtual office employees all need the ability to communicate with one another. In addition, everyone wants access to the Internet. Whether for entertainment or productivity, it is a necessity in today's world.

Module 7 Quiz

1. Which of the following identifies a virtual circuit in a frame relay network?
   a. DLCI
   b. FECN
   c. BECN
   d. CBS
2. Which of the following best characterizes CIR, as referred to in frame relay networks?
   a. Guaranteed average data transmission rate
   b. Guaranteed maximum data transmission rate
   c. Number of bits that can be transmitted in a given time interval
   d. Number of bytes that can be transmitted in a given time interval
3. Which of the following technologies is considered the lowest in the protocol stack?
   a. Packet switching
   b. X.25 packet switching
   c. Frame relay
   d. SONET
4. Which functions does a modem perform? (Choose two.)
   a. Amplify analog signals
   b. Convert digital signals to analog signals for the sender
   c. Repeat digital signals
   d. Convert analog signals to digital signals for the receiver
5. Which of the following is an example of a modem specification?
   a. T1
   b. T3
   c. EIA-232-D
   d. V.90

6. Which of the following best describes a DTE?
   a. End device or node in a network
   b. Communicating device maintained by a telephone company
   c. High-speed switch
   d. CSU/DSU
7. A T1 line type is equivalent to the ____________ standard.
   a. DS0
   b. ISDN-BRI
   c. DS1
   d. E1
8. Which of the following is a fiber optic technology?
   a. T3
   b. T1
   c. SONET
   d. Ethernet
9. Which of the following are the building blocks for SONET?
   a. STS-1
   b. 51.84 Mbps
   c. 48 Kbps
   d. 64 Kbps
   e. Both a and b
10. What is the primary difference between a packet-switched network and circuit-switched network?
    a. A circuit-switched network is point-to-point.
    b. A packet-switched network deals with packets, and a circuit-switched network deals with circuits.
    c. The route a packet travels over a packet-switched network is always the same, whereas the route a packet travels in a circuit-switched network is never the same.
    d. The route a packet travels over a packet-switched network can be different, whereas the route a packet travels over a circuit-switched network is always the same for the length of the session.

11. Which of the following is true of both ATM and frame relay?
    a. They are both connection-oriented.
    b. They were both developed for voice and data.
    c. They are both Data Link Layer protocols
    d. They both use cells to transmit information.
12. What does VPI/VCI in the ATM header identify?
    a. Virtual path, virtual channel
    b. Virtual point, virtual circuit
    c. Virtual PVC, virtual communication
    d. Virtual path, valid channel
13. What is one disadvantage of cable modem communication?
    a. Very high bandwidth
    b. Low-cost alternative to other communication methods
    c. Available on the cable television wired network
    d. Shared media access to the head end
14. Which of the following protocols were initially designed for multimedia (voice, video, and data)? (Choose two.)
    a. Frame relay
    b. T1 and T3
    c. ATM
    d. ISDN
15. Which of the following describes FRAD?
    a. A device used to send voice technology over an IP network
    b. A router used to connect LANs using frame relay
    c. A switch that interfaces ATM to an Ethernet network
    d. A frame relay application
16. Which factors affect xDSL line performance? (Choose two.)
    a. The standards supported by the connecting modems
    b. The number of B channels provisioned on the xDSL link
    c. The number of splices and noise on the local loop
    d. The distance from the subscriber to the CO

17. What is the major difference between a LAN and a WAN?
    a. Type of cabling used to configure a network
    b. Distance between nodes in a network
    c. Type of devices used to connect workstations to a network
    d. Type of NIC used
18. Which of the following is the fastest line speed?
    a. T1
    b. SONET
    c. Frame relay
    d. BRI
19. Which of the following best describe PPP? (Choose two.)
    a. Authentication services
    b. Proprietary headers
    c. Multiple Network Layer protocol support
    d. Default encapsulation method for frame relay
20. Which of the following best describes ADSL?
    a. Analog-to-digital conversion at the local loop
    b. Digital-to-analog conversion at the local loop
    c. High speed to the subscriber, low speed from the subscriber
    d. High-speed data transfer from the subscriber, low-speed transfer to the subscriber
21. What is the payload portion of an ATM cell?
    a. 53 bytes
    b. 48 bytes
    c. 1.54 Mbps
    d. 128 Kbps
22. What is the ATM transmission rate over an OC3?
    a. 1.54 Mbps
    b. 45 Mbps
    c. 51.5 Mbps
    d. 155 Mbps

23. Which technology is made up of 23B+1D?
    a. Frame relay
    b. V.90 modem standard
    c. ISDN-BRI
    d. ISDN-PRI
24. What is the signal standard used by frame relay to establish and maintain a PVC?
    a. DLCI
    b. LMI
    c. CIR
    d. DE
25. Which authentication methods are associated with PPP? (Choose two.)
    a. PAP
    b. Secret password
    c. CHAP
    d. PVC

Module 8 Configuring and Operating Cisco IOS Devices

This module is the foundation necessary for understanding the Internetwork Operating System (IOS) found on the majority of Cisco Systems equipment. The IOS is a software image stored in the memory of the device. The IOS provides an administrative interface for configuration and management purposes, reliable network functionality, security, scalability, and, of course, connectivity. Although other interface options exist, Lesson 1 focuses on the command-line interface (CLI), which requires an administrator to provide the correct command syntax to initiate configuration changes and monitor network activity. The CLI provides a Help feature that includes a list of available commands at any given level. It also provides a number of error responses in the event a command is typed incorrectly. Lesson 1 finishes by introducing the two main levels of access into a router or switch: user EXEC mode and privileged EXEC mode, sometimes called "enable mode."

After reviewing the basics of the CLI, Lesson 2 provides specific information about Cisco's workgroup switches. It begins with the startup, power on self test (POST) process that uses the light-emitting diodes (LEDs) of a switch to indicate functionality or error conditions. It then proceeds through a few familiarizing steps in the CLI, such as the login process, using Help features, and showing configuration files.

Lesson 3 provides similar information to that in Lesson 2, but for a router. We first review the startup and initial setup routine of a router. Then we cover the process of logging in and using the help commands, as well as the edit keys and commands. The lesson also includes using the history buffer to recall commands and viewing the initial configuration.

Lesson 4 lists the different router configuration modes, including global configuration, interface, subinterface, line, and routing protocol configuration modes. Each mode has a different command prompt for easy identification. This lesson reviews configuration commands used to start or shut down an interface, configure Internet Protocol (IP) addresses, hostnames, and interface descriptions, as well as clock rate and bandwidth settings for a serial interface. The lesson ends with a few show commands that an administrator can use to verify these configuration settings and validate that an interface is functioning properly.

Lessons

1. Cisco IOS Software
2. Switch Startup
3. Router Startup
4. Router Configuration

Lesson 1—Cisco IOS Software

The IOS is the foundation for functionality in a Cisco router or switch. It is a necessary and vital component; a Cisco device cannot operate without the IOS. This lesson begins by identifying the features of the IOS. It then goes on to discuss how network devices are configured, as well as the methods used to connect to each device for configuration and monitoring purposes. It also reviews the startup process that happens for both a router and switch. This process includes checking the hardware in the POST, finding and loading an IOS, and then finding and loading a configuration file. The last portion of this lesson discusses the functions of the CLI and the different EXEC modes: user and privileged.

Objectives

At the end of this lesson you will be able to:

- Identify the features of the Cisco IOS
- Define how network devices are configured
- Discuss the basics steps in device startup
- Describe how to connect to a Cisco device
- Access and use the CLI
- Recognize the different EXEC modes

Key Point

The IOS provides an administrative interface for configuration and management purposes, reliable network functionality, security, scalability, and, of course, connectivity.

Cisco IOS Features

Like any network device, Cisco routers and Catalyst switches use underlying software code to provide their functionality. Numerous versions of the IOS are implemented on Cisco hardware; however, the commands are fairly similar across the board. In addition to providing a CLI and the ability to configure a device, the IOS also provides the following network services:

- **Connectivity**—Provides high-speed data transmission between devices
- **Scalability**—Increases network capacity by adding new devices or upgrading technology on an as-needed basis
- **Reliability**—Provides network redundancy and stability to offer reduced outages and dependable network access
- **Functionality**—Implements select protocols and device features to provide a complete network solution
- **Security**—Allows an administrator to manage network access and control unauthorized usage

Network Device Configuration

When you purchase a new router or switch, the manufacturer has already loaded it with the IOS. This means that, out of the box, it has the functionality that is characteristic of the Cisco IOS. As listed above, this includes connectivity, scalability, reliability, protocol and device features/functionality, and security.

Because all networks are different, it would not make any sense for a vendor to provide specific configurations for each and every individual client. Not only would this be incredibly time consuming, it would also reduce corporate security. The specific protocols, addresses, and security policy implementations are unique to each business, and should not be shared with anyone outside that organization. There are times when third-party implementation or network design specialists are involved in installing and configuring equipment. In that case, the concern over security changes, because they have a business relationship during the project.

In general, when setting up a Cisco router or switch, the following steps must be considered:

- **Configure the proper Network Layer addresses**—On a router, an IP address and subnet mask are assigned to each router interface because they represent subnet or network segments. In contrast, a switch is assigned one IP address for the entire device (excluding virtual local area networks [VLANs]), which is used for management purposes.
- **Configure network functionality**—The interfaces must be enabled for communication and configured with the appropriate settings. On a router, the static or dynamic routing protocol requires configuration. On a switch, it is important to review the Spanning Tree Protocol (STP) configuration or other methods to prevent active switching loops.

- **Configure administrative access**—The initial configuration is performed through the console port on either a switch or router. Future configuration and device management is usually performed from a remote Telnet session. It is therefore necessary to configure virtual terminal and possibly modem auxiliary (AUX) settings for access.
- **Configure security**—Initial security settings are passwords for console, AUX, and Telnet communications. An encrypted password is also configured for access to the administration command interface called "privileged EXEC mode." Eventually more sophisticated security measures can be taken on either a switch or router associated with connectivity and traffic flow.

When a Catalyst switch is purchased and installed, it arrives from the manufacturer with a number of key configurations already established. The settings specific to your network, such as IP address and password, need to be configured. However, out of the box, the switch is basically ready to "cable" and run without too much administration.

When a Cisco router is purchased and installed, it arrives from the manufacturer without any preset configurations. Unlike a switch, however, a router cannot perform many functions without a configuration. To simplify this process, the router includes initial autoinstallation code called "setup." Setup provides a number of basic configuration settings in a menu-driven format.

Device Startup Process

Regardless of whether it is a switch or router, three main functions take place when a device is first started. The startup process is called "bootup," and is initiated by code burned into the hardware of the device. This code is called the "bootstrap" or "bootloader," and is used to perform the following functions:

1. **Run the POST.** This is a diagnostic test of all internal components, such as the memory, central processing unit (CPU), and ports, to verify they are working properly. The microcode used during POST is stored in read-only memory (ROM), and activated every time a router or switch is powered up. POST tests verify the hardware functionality for device components. This helps ensure that problems will not be encountered later due to faulty hardware.

2. **Find and load the IOS.** Upon completion of the hardware tests, the bootstrap process is initiated. Like POST, the bootstrap is also a microcode stored in ROM. The bootstrap executes other programs, in this case, locating and loading the IOS. This provides all the device functionality and features discussed earlier.
3. **Find and load the configuration.** Administrative settings entered during setup or through device configuration are stored in a configuration file. These settings are loaded after the IOS to provide the communication capabilities specific to your network. Like the special settings on your computer, routers and switches also have a configuration that provides important settings, such as a hostname, IP addresses, routing protocol configurations, and much more.

Connecting to a Cisco Device

There are a number of ways to connect to a switch or router to monitor or configure its settings. Initially, the connection must be made through a console port, because the other possible connection options require configuration. A list of several different connection options and how each one is accomplished is as follows:

- **Console port**—The console port physically connects a terminal with a network device using a rollover cable. The device is configured using terminal emulation software (for example, HyperTerminal) on a workstation to access the CLI. The default settings for the terminal emulator are 9600 baud, 8 bits, no parity, and 1 stop bit (9600-8N1).
- **AUX port**—The AUX port is used when supporting a remote device by means of a modem. This method can only be used after the AUX port is configured using the console connection. The requirements for making an AUX connection are a straight-through serial cable, a 14.4 kilobits per second (Kbps) modem, and the proper personal computer (PC) software. Note that not all Cisco devices have an AUX interface.
- **Compact disc read-only memory (CD-ROM)**—Some switch devices can load software configuration utilities directly from CD-ROM (called "Cisco's Fast Step"), which provides a very simple configuration interface used from a Microsoft Windows workstation.

- **Telnet session**—A Telnet session can be used to access a device through a terminal emulation software product after IP is configured. Telnet can provide an interface from a PC or through another network device such as a router or switch.
- **Trivial File Transfer Protocol (TFTP)**—A configuration file can be saved to a network server using TFTP, and downloaded to the device at a later time. This can be used to back up the IOS or configuration settings, or quickly change a configuration.
- **Internet download**—Configuration files can also be downloaded using a World Wide Web (Web) browser. Examples of a browser-based configuration include Cisco's Virtual Switch Manager (VSM) and CiscoWorks2000. IP must be first configured on the device so that Netscape or Microsoft Internet Explorer can make a connection.

The first three methods are considered out-of-band management, because they provide a physical connection to the device and do not use the network for communication. The last three methods are considered in-band management because they each utilize network connectivity and an IP address must be configured on the device before communication can be achieved. This class focuses on configuring Cisco devices using the CLI with either a console connection or through a Telnet session.

The CLI

The IOS of Cisco routers and switches is frequently accessed using a CLI. An interface that uses a command line means that it has specific commands that are required to be entered to configure and monitor a device. These commands are typed in directly at a specific prompt to perform the desired function. In most cases the command does not execute on the device until **ENTER** is pressed. At that point, the typed command is parsed (read by the device) and executed (acted upon). If the command is typed correctly, the device will respond by performing the function requested. This may mean that it updates a configuration with new settings, displays statistics information for monitoring, estab lishes a new connection to another device, or any number of other possibilities. If, however, the command is typed incorrectly or not available at the current prompt, the device will return an error message or attempt to locate the error command as a host for Telnet purposes.

It is not uncommon these days for professionals entering the networking industry to be most comfortable with a graphic user interface (GUI). This is the interface that Windows, Apple/Macintosh and X Windows in UNIX are based on. It allows settings and access using a mouse and provide a user-friendly environment.

Coming from this scenario, the CLI may be a bit difficult to understand at first. The commands are very specific and require exact sequence and spelling. However, over time the commands will become natural and, with enough practice and hands-on work, you can often type them without thinking much about the actual syntax. After you get used to the commands, you may even find that CLI provides a faster and more efficient way to configure settings. Examples include applying the history buffer (a list of previously typed commands) to reenter commands that are often repeated. This allows an administrator to type the command once, and then use the UP ARROW key (similar to the DOS key or command line in UNIX) to retrieve a previously typed command.

Another way the CLI can provide efficiencies is by allowing commands to be copied and pasted at the command prompt. With a little knowledge, these can even be scripted to automate some settings or configurations. For those familiar with a CLI, Cisco's CLI will simply require you to remember new and specific commands. You will already feel a comfort level with the way commands are typed and executed, and find shortcuts and Help features easier to master.

Cisco's CLI has the following characteristics:

- Each command is typed using specific command syntax.
- The command is parsed and executed after ENTER is pressed.
- The CLI has a hierarchy with different levels of functionality, including two EXEC modes and numerous configuration modes.
- The prompt changes to indicate the current level or mode. This allows an administrator to recognize the proper command options for that level.
- Different commands are available depending upon the EXEC or configuration mode. The commands will only be recognized and executed when typed at the proper level.

The benefit of gaining a solid understanding of the CLI is that it is a primary configuration and management interface for Cisco routers and switches. Although the CLI differs by device and IOS version, once the basics are established, knowledge of the CLI allows you to move from one device to another without having to learn a completely new way of doing things., it is also nice not having to search for where a check box was put, or deal with drop-down options that do not include the one you want, which can happen when using a GUI.

EXEC Modes

Two EXEC modes are available in the CLI for routers and switches: user EXEC and privileged EXEC. EXEC is the portion of the CLI that allows commands to be executed, hence the name. Depending upon which EXEC mode you are currently in, the CLI prompt and available commands will be different.

User EXEC Mode

The user EXEC mode allows a very limited number of functions, mainly to monitor or review switch or router settings. It does not allow any configuration changes or the ability to reload the software settings. Initial access to a switch or router begins in user EXEC mode. This mode can be easily identified by the ">" (greater than) symbol.

A switch without a hostname assignment has the following prompt:

```
>
```

A switch with a hostname assignment has the following prompt:

```
sw2950>
```

Notice that for a switch, there is no hostname or device identification before the prompt upon initial startup.

A router without a hostname assignment has the following prompt:

```
router>
```

A router with a hostname assignment has the following prompt:

```
Router1>
```

All routers initially have the same prompt. This can get very confusing when moving between devices for configuration or monitoring. Therefore, it is advisable to assign each device a hostname that can be used to differentiate it from other routers or switches. The hostname can be anything an administrator decides is helpful in unique device identification. In the previous examples, sw2950 and Router1 are the hostnames for the switch and router, respectively. Notice how the prompt changes to indicate the hostname.

To leave user EXEC mode, the lowest level of access, and end the connected session, type **exit** or **logout** at the prompt. The device initial access screen will again be displayed.

To move to the next level, from user EXEC mode to privileged EXEC mode, use the command **enable** or **en** for short. For switches and routers, type the appropriate command type as follows:

>enable (on a switch)

router>**enable** (on a router)

Privileged EXEC Mode

The privileged EXEC mode allows all monitoring, configuration, and debugging commands to be entered. This is the mode required for administrative access to a device. Also called "enable mode," it provides an extensive set of commands that an administrator can use to verify configurations, view traffic statistics, and back up or restore the configuration and IOS. This mode allows the processing of the device to be interrupted or administratively changed. Privileged EXEC mode provides access to the next level of the hierarchical structure that allows global configuration, and other more specific configuration levels on the device.

This mode is generally password-protected for security purposes, although no password is initially set. As stated earlier, privileged EXEC mode is entered by typing **enable** at the user EXEC prompt, then supplying the appropriate password if requested. If the password is correct, the session will switch to privileged EXEC mode and the prompt will change to #. The # symbol indicates enable mode has been entered and administrative options are available. To return to user EXEC mode, simply type **disable** or **exit** at the # prompt. The switch and router prompts will initially look as follows in privileged EXEC mode:

(on a switch)

router# (on a router)

Review Questions

1. Which process is initiated when a device is started for the first time?
   a. POST
   b. Find and load an IOS
   c. Find and load the configuration file
   d. Check all ports
2. Where are configuration and show commands initiated on a router?
   a. GUI
   b. POST
   c. CLI
   d. MENU
3. Which mode allows you to view only a few statistics screens?
   a. Privileged EXEC mode
   b. User EXEC mode
   c. Setup mode
   d. Enable mode
4. Which modes have the same meaning? (Choose two.)
   a. Privileged EXEC mode
   b. User EXEC mode
   c. Enable mode
   d. Configuration mode
5. Which prompt correctly identifies user EXEC mode on a Catalyst 2950 series switch?
   a. `#`
   b. `switch#`
   c. `switch*`
   d. `>`

6. Which mode allows commands that can interrupt the device's processing capability?
   a. User EXEC mode
   b. Privileged EXEC mode
   c. Setup mode
   d. Access mode
7. Which command is used to go back one configuration level or leave privileged EXEC mode?
   a. **`end`**
   b. **`bye`**
   c. **`exit`**
   d. **`user`**
8. What are two methods of in-band management of a Cisco device?
   a. Console port
   b. Telnet
   c. TFTP server
   d. AUX port
9. Which of the following are considered features of the Cisco IOS? (Choose three.)
   a. Security
   b. Configuring IP address
   c. Functionality
   d. Reliability
   e. EXEC modes
10. What is the purpose of the POST process?
    a. Configure a device with initial settings
    b. Test functionality and verify hardware components
    c. Load the bootstrap process
    d. Load the IOS

Extended Activities

1. Name three out-of-band methods to communicate with a switch device, and describe how each one is connected.

 ____

 ____

 ____

2. Name three in-band methods to communicate with a switch device, and describe how each one is connected.

 ____

 ____

 ____

3. Describe the three major steps in the device startup process.

 ____

 ____

 ____

4. Name the two EXEC modes and describe how each one is used.

 ____

 ____

 ____

 ____

5. List and describe the five features provided by the Cisco IOS.

Lesson 2—Switch Startup

With a little background on STP, from the module entitled "Switching Fundamentals," it is time to begin getting our feet wet. A good place to start is an overview of the Cisco IOS. This lesson looks at the switch startup process, and how to make a console connection and configure a device for the first time. To wrap up the IOS basics, we will discuss the CLI, and the different modes of configuration and operation, as well as a number of basic help and show commands to become familiar with the switch environment. This lesson focuses on commands used with the 1900 and 2950 series Catalyst switch devices.

Objectives

At the end of this lesson you will be able to:

- Recognize the startup process on a Catalyst switch
- Verify the results of the LEDs during the switch POST
- Verify the switch bootup output display
- Review the factory default configuration for Catalyst 1900 switches
- Review the setup configuration process for Catalyst 2950 switches
- Log in to a switch and recognize the EXEC modes
- Use the Help features available in the switch CLI
- Use basic configuration commands on a switch
- Display the initial switch configuration

Key Point

When a switch starts up, a Telnet screen shows the messages generated by the OS as it is initialized. An administrator can view this information along with monitoring the LEDs to verify functionality.

Initial Switch Startup Process

When powering up a switch for the first time, a number of steps and procedures should be followed. Once powered up, the switch goes through a series of system checks and notifies the administrator of any error conditions. The process for starting a switch is as follows:

1. **Make all the appropriate cable connections**—This includes network connections to other devices as well as end nodes.
2. **Make a connection from a PC or laptop to the switch using the console port and a rollover cable**—This will be used to configure and monitor the switch in the future. (Other ways to make a terminal connection were reviewed in the lesson titled "Cisco IOS Software.") Open a Telnet session using HyperTerminal or other appropriate application using the correct connection parameters (usually COM1, 9600, 8, No, 1, Hardware).
3. **Plug a power cable into the power supply**—Many Catalyst switches do not have an on/off button, so when the power cable is plugged in, the device automatically starts up. At that point, the switch goes through the boot sequence.
4. **View the POST process as it is performed by watching the LEDs on the front of the switch**—Also, view the Telnet application screen to watch as the switch verifies hardware and loads the IOS.

Status of LEDs

Upon starting a switch, it begins the POST, which performs routines to check the hardware. The LEDs on the front panel of the switch are shown on the Switch Chassis LEDs Diagram, and are used to help an administrator determine the outcome of the POST process.

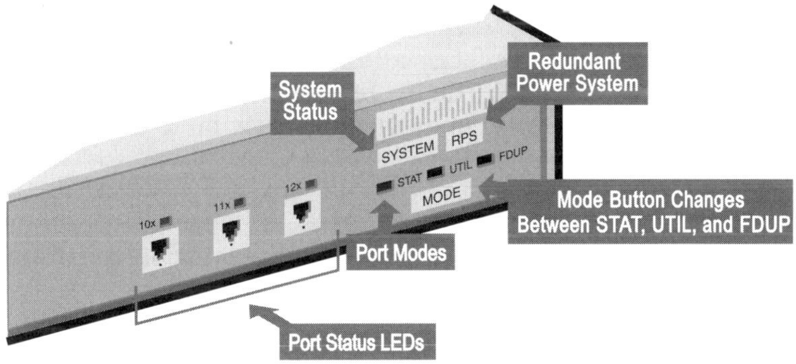

Switch Chassis LEDs

The following information is applicable to the Catalyst 1900 and 2950 series switches. Other switches may vary from this description based on the number of ports, port definitions, and sequence of events. Check your switch documentation to verify the POST and status of LEDs.

First, all port LEDs flash green to verify working order of the lights, and indicate the POST process has begun. On a 24-port switch, port LEDs 1 through 16 are each assigned to a specific test process and are all initially lit in solid green. The LEDs can respond to the POST as follows:

- The green LED goes out indicating the test has passed successfully.
- The LED changes from green to amber at the point of failure, and the system LED also changes to amber.

Remember that the POST is not checking the port itself but hardware components, such as the memory, console port, timers, and overall port functionality. Upon completion of the entire POST, the LEDs all blink again as they did in the beginning, then turn off. The list of all components represented by specific LEDs is presented in the Port LEDs Table.

Port LEDs

LED No.	Associated Component Being Tested
16x or AUX	FATAL—Embedded control unit (ECU) dynamic random-access memory (DRAM) The AUX port is used on a 12-port switch instead of Port 16x.
15x	Not used
14x	Not used
13x	Not used
12x	FATAL—Forwarding engine
11x	FATAL—Forwarding engine static random-access memory (SRAM)
10x	FATAL—Packet DRAM
9x	FATAL—InterSwitch Link Transmission (ISLT) Application Specific Integrated Circuit (ASIC)
8x	FATAL—Port control/status
7x	FATAL—System timer interrupt
6x	FATAL—Content Addressable Memory (CAM) SRAM
5x	NONFATAL—Real-time clock: The switch cannot restart itself automatically in the case of a power loss. The switch can forward packets and otherwise perform normally.
4x	NONFATAL—Console port: The device cannot be accessed using the console port. It can be accessed using a Telnet session in-band or through the AUX port.

Port LEDs (Continued)

LED No.	Associated Component Being Tested
3x	FATAL—CAM
2x	NONFATAL—Burned-in address (MAC address): The device uses the default Ethernet MAC address and will forward packets normally.
1x	NONFATAL—Port Loopback: This LED indicates the port failed the functionality test. Verify which ports failed using the console screen. Do not attempt to communicate using the ports that failed the port loopback test.

Note: Fatal errors indicated by LEDs 16x, 12x, 11x, 10x, 9x, 8x, 7x, 6x, and 3x will render the switch device useless. This will require technical support from Cisco and may require that the device be serviced or replaced. Nonfatal errors indicated by LEDs 5x, 4x, 2x, and 1x allow the device to continue processing, but may limit one or more functions of the device.

Upon completion, all LEDs flash momentarily then go out. In addition to the port LEDs that are checked during the POST process, the functions of a number of other LEDs on the switch should be understood. The Switch Chassis LEDs Diagram and the Switch LEDs Table explain what the additional LEDs are used for and how to detect an error condition. Green usually indicates proper functionality, whereas an amber light indicates an error condition. Pressing the mode button allows you to toggle through the port status, bandwidth utilization, and full-duplex operations of the switch. These will not only light the appropriate mode LED, but will also light necessary port LEDs. Finally, in addition to the LEDs on the device itself, any errors detected during the POST process will also be displayed on the console terminal screen.

Switch LEDs

LED Label	Function
System LED	Off—Indicates device does not have power Solid Amber—Indicates a system failure or error state; may be detected during the POST or operation Solid Green—Indicates the system is operational and functioning normally
Redundant Power Supply (RPS) LED	Off—Indicates redundant power supply is not installed or device does not have power Solid Amber—Indicates redundant power supply is installed, but not operational Flashing Amber—Indicates redundant power supply is powering the device because the internal power supply has failed Solid Green—Indicates redundant power supply is working properly Flashing Green (2950)—Indicates redundant power supply is connected and supplying power to another device, making it unavailable
UTIL LED (Bandwidth Utilization Mode)	Catalyst 1900 series switch: On a 12-port switch: LEDs 1-4 = 0.1 to < 1.5 Mbps LEDs 5-8 = 1.5 to < 20 Mbps LEDs 9-12 = 20 to 140 Mbps On a 24-port switch: LEDs 1-8 = 0.1 to < 6 Mbps LEDs 9-16 = 6 to < 120 Mbps LEDs 17-24 = 120 to 280 Mbps

Switch LEDs (Continued)

LED Label	Function
UTIL LED (Bandwidth Utilization Mode) (continued)	CCatalyst 2950-12, 2950-24, 2950C-24, and 2950T-24 series switches: Amber—Indicates the switch traffic has hit maximum bandwidth utilization of the switch backplane since powered on Green and Amber—Uses a weighted scale to define bandwidth utilization. Green LED has an amber background. All LEDs on—Indicates 50% or more of total bandwidth Far-right LED off—Indicates more than 25% but less than 50% of total bandwidth Only the first LED on—Indicates less than 0.0488% of total bandwidth used Other switch models vary. Check the Cisco Web site or documentation for specific LED status information.
STAT LED (Port Status Mode)	Off—Indicates no connection established Solid Amber—Indicates the specific port is not forwarding traffic. This could indicate it was disabled by the administrator, or disabled by a process such as STP or an unsecured MAC address trying to access a secured address port. Flashing Green and Amber—Indicates there is a link failure in the port. This could include collision frames, cyclic redundancy check (CRC) errors, a chattering network interface card (NIC), or transmission alignment problems. Solid Green—Indicates a link has been made Flashing Green–Indicates activity/traffic passing through the port
FDUP LED (Full-Duplex Mode)	Off—Indicates port is transmitting in half-duplex mode Solid Green—Indicates port is configured and transmitting in full-duplex mode

Switch Bootup Process

If no fatal errors are found when the hardware is checked and verified, the device begins the system startup routine, which loads the switch IOS image. After the IOS is loaded, the device searches for and applies the appropriate software configurations. These factory default settings are initially preconfigured in the Catalyst switch memory. The process of additional basic configuration will be addressed later in this lesson.

Upon bootup, the switch generates a message from the IOS as it initializes. The terminal displays the screen presented on the Menu Console Login Screen Capture.

```
Catalyst 2950 Management Console
Copyright (c) Cisco Systems, Inc. 1993-2001
All rights reserved.
Enterprise Edition Software
Ethernet Address: 00-50-BD-98-76-B2

PCA Number: 78-3251-97
PCA Serial Number: B7A0295X6Q3
Model Number: WS-C2950-24-EN
System Serial Number: B7A02A71M59
Power Supply S/N: PHI09314A74
-----------------------------------------------
1 user(s) now active on Management Console.

        User Interface Menu

                [M] Menus
                [K] Command Line
                [I] IP Configuration

Enter Selection:
```

Menu Console Login

This screen provides information about the switch's Ethernet address and various serial numbers. It also provides the User Interface menu, with the following selections:

- M—Menu interface (type the letter "M" to enter)
- K—Command Line interface (type the letter "K" to enter)
- I—IP Configuration options (type the letter "I" to enter)

This course uses the CLI for all configurations, so select the letter "K" during the labs.

From this point, an administrator is able to enter the CLI, review the existing settings, and make any necessary changes. The next few sections provide a quick overview of basic commands and helpful features to get started configuring a Catalyst switch. For class purposes, a Catalyst 1900 and/or 2950 switch will be referenced.

Factory Default Configurations for Catalyst 1900 Switches

Direct from the factory, the Catalyst 1900 switch comes configured with a number of default settings. The preconfigured settings allow for initial basic communication. Additional configuration is required to meet specific corporate network requirements. The list of default settings is as follows:

- IP address = 0.0.0.0
- Cisco Discovery Protocol (CDP) = Enabled
- Switching mode = Fragment-free
- 100BaseT port = Autonegotiate duplex mode
- 10BaseT port = Half-duplex
- Spanning Tree = Enabled
- Console password = None

Setup Configuration Process for Catalyst 2950 Switches

Unlike the Catalyst 1900, the 2950 does not come preconfigured with setup parameters. Instead, it provides a simple setup process that allows for rapid and simplified initial configuration to get the device online as quickly and easily as possible. This setup process is very similar to the one required for a router. The following prompts require input during the setup process:

```
--- System Configuration Dialog ---
At any point you may enter a question mark '?' for help.
Use ctrl-c to abort configuration dialog at any prompt.
Default settings are in square brackets '[ ]'.

Continue with configuration dialog? [yes/no]:
Enter IP address: ip_address
Enter IP netmask: ip_netmask
Would you like to enter a default gateway address?
[yes]:
IP address of the default gateway: ip_address
```

```
Enter a hostname: host_name
Enter enable secret: secret_password
Would you like to configure a Telnet password? [yes]:
Enter Telnet password: telnet_password
Would you like to enable as a cluster command switch?
Enter cluster name: cls_name
```

Fill in each prompt with the appropriate information. Upon completion, the switch displays all entries and asks for confirmation to save the configuration. To change a setting created during the setup process, or add new configuration settings, access the device using the CLI. To accept the configuration, use the **y** or type **yes** when the device prompts `Use this Configuration? [yes/no]:`

CLI and EXEC Modes

After a connection to the device has been made, you have access to the Menu Console Login screen presented earlier. Typing **K** at the menu screen provides access to the CLI, Cisco's traditional console environment. Every command entered is interpreted (parsed) by the IOS and then the corresponding operation is carried out. This is why it is considered the IOS software EXEC session, because it executes commands. Two access levels exist within the CLI: user EXEC mode and privileged EXEC mode.

User EXEC Mode

The user EXEC mode allows a very limited number of functions, mainly to monitor or review the switch settings. It does not allow any configuration changes or the ability to reload software settings, or disrupt switch processing. When initially accessing a switch device, it begins in user EXEC mode. User EXEC mode can be easily identified with the > symbol or right arrow at the end of the switch's hostname. To end the connected session, from user EXEC mode use the command **`logout`** or **`exit`**.

Privileged EXEC Mode

The privileged EXEC mode allows all monitoring, configuration, and debugging commands to be entered. This mode, also called "enable mode," has the ability to change device configuration as well as interrupt switch processing. Therefore, it is typically password-protected for security purposes, although no password is initially set. Privileged EXEC mode is entered by typing **`enable`** at the user EXEC > prompt, then supplying the appropriate password. If the password is correct, the session switches to privileged EXEC mode and the prompt changes to #. The # symbol indicates enable mode has been entered and administrative options are available.

Privileged EXEC mode provides access to configure terminal mode on the device. This is the next level of access that allows global configuration commands to be set. To return to user EXEC mode from privileged EXEC mode, simply type **`disable`** or **`exit`** at the # prompt.

Note: The bold font in the command syntax throughout this course indicates the exact text that should be typed.

The Switch CLI Screen Capture shows the Menu interface, and the user EXEC mode prompt that is displayed when accessing the switch's CLI. It also shows the process of accessing privileged EXEC mode by entering the **`enable`** command and the subsequent prompt change.

```
        User Interface Menu

                [M] Menus
                [K] Command Line
                [I] IP Configuration

Enter Selection:K

        CLI session with the switch is open.
        To end the CLI session, enter [Exit].

>enable
#
```

Switch CLI

In either mode, commands can be typed in manually or copied from a text editor. The **TAB** key provides autorecognition and can be used to complete a command. To use this feature, simply begin typing the command up to the first three letters, then press the **TAB** key. If the command is recognized, it will automatically be completed. If there are similar commands, or not enough letters have been supplied to identify it from other commands, you may have to provide more information before using the **TAB** key for completion.

In addition, many IOS commands will be recognized by the first few letters, making it unnecessary to type the entire command. For example, the command #**`show running-config`** could also be typed and recognized as #**`sh run`**. As with most systems, the **ENTER** key lets the system know the command is complete and begins execution. If the command is not recognized by the device, it will attempt to resolve the command to an IP address and Telnet to the unknown command as if it was a hostname.

Switch Help Features

Cisco's IOS software on the Catalyst 1900 and 2950 switches provide handy and easy-to-use features that greatly aid overall administration. First, it displays console error messages, that provide a pointer to a syntax error in a command. This makes it easier to identify and correct syntax problems. Next, it provides a command history buffer, which maintains a running accumulation of previous commands for quick review, reentry, or correction. The history buffer can be accessed using the **UP ARROW** or **DOWN ARROW** to locate the desired command. Finally, it provides context-sensitive help in the following two specific formats:

- **Command syntax help**—This format is used to identify available commands and their usage. To access command syntax help, type a **?** at the command prompt. A listing of all available command options at the current level is displayed. You can also use this command syntax help to get the sequence of commands that must be typed. In that case, begin the command, leave a space, and finish with a **?** where the remainder of the command is unknown. When the Help feature shows <cr>, the command is complete and the **ENTER** key (carriage return) should be used to parse and execute the command.
- **Word help**—This format allows an administrator to get more specific assistance on a specific command. To use this option, begin typing the letters of the command and use the **?** (without any spaces) at the location where the word is unclear. A complete list of commands available that begin with the characters typed is displayed.

Keep in mind that available commands and associated help screens will change based on the EXEC mode you are currently in. User EXEC mode has very limited command availability, whereas privileged EXEC mode has a more broad range of options.

Basic Configuration Commands on a Switch

After an administrator has entered privileged EXEC mode, the administrator has access to configure the device. A hierarchy of configuration modes are available, depending upon what settings are being implemented or changed. For basic configuration of the entire switch, use the global configuration mode. This mode is used to establish settings associated with the device itself, such as hostname, IP address, and default gateway. Remember that you must first be in privileged EXEC mode (identified by the #) before entering the configuration command. After you have entered global configuration mode, the prompt changes to `(config)#`. The following lines display the commands to move from user EXEC mode to global configuration mode:

```
>enable
#configure terminal
(config)#
```

The command **`configure terminal`** can be reduced to **`config t`** or **`config term`**. All commands typed in this mode will be executed as soon as the **ENTER** key is pressed. All commands take effect immediately, meaning the switch does not have to be restarted. The configuration is stored in the nonvolatile random access memory (NVRAM) of the switch, which is available even after the device is power cycled.

In global configuration mode, the hostname, IP address, subnet mask, default gateway, and many other parameters can be set. On a switch, the hostname and IP addressing information makes a remote console connection to the device for management purposes. The following sections provide the syntax for each item listed above. Remember that you can always use the context-sensitive help to determine a particular command. You can also use the **TAB** key to finish commands for which you have provided at least three characters.

Host Names

A hostname is the name given to the device by an administrator to uniquely identify it on the network. It changes the command prompt to provide easy, memorable identification of the device. Most organizations have specific naming conventions to define how the device should be identified. The name can be any combination of letters, numbers, and other characters such as dash or underscore. To set or change a hostname, use the following command after the global configuration prompt:

```
(config)#hostname hostname
```

An example of this command is:

```
(config)#hostname Switch_1900
Switch_1900(config)#
```

Notice that after the command is entered, the prompt changes to the hostname you set.

IP Addresses and Subnet Masks

The IP address and subnet mask are assigned together, because they are directly related. An IP address and subnet mask are necessary to manage the switch using a Telnet session, for Simple Network Management Protocol (SNMP) management, or to connect through the VSM by means of a Web browser. This section provides the syntax necessary to set an IP address. For classroom purposes, the instructor will provide the appropriate information to configure your device. In a production environment, the network design will provide the IP address, subnet mask, and default gateway.

When assigning an IP address to the 1900 switch, a single address is assigned to the actual device. However, when assigning an IP address to the Catalyst 2950 where VLANs have been configured, each VLAN is assigned an IP address and subnet mask. To set the IP address and subnet mask in global configuration mode, use the following command on a 1900 series switch:

```
Switch_1900(config)#ip address ip-address subnet-mask
```

An example of this command is:

```
Switch_1900(config)#ip address 172.16.10.3 255.255.255.0
```

On a 2950 switch, an IP address needs to be assigned to the management VLAN, called "VLAN 1." Any additional VLANs created must have their own IP address assignments. To configure VLAN1 and others, use the following commands:

```
Switch_2950(config)#interface vlan vlan_number
Switch_2950(config-if)#ip address ip-address subnet-mask
```

An example of this command is:

```
Switch_2950(config)#interface vlan 1
Switch_2950(config-if)#ip address 172.16.20.1 255.255.
255.0
```

Default Gateways

A default gateway is a pointer to the routing device that routes traffic between different networks. It is the device that is directly connected to the switch and carries packets not deliverable in the local segment. To communicate with this device and use it as a means to access another network, the switch must be aware of the router's IP address. The network design will dictate the default gateway IP address in a production environment.

To assign the default gateway, use the following command:

```
Switch(config)#ip default-gateway gateway-ip-address
```

An example of this command is:

```
Switch(config)#ip default-gateway 172.16.10.1
```

Note: For switches designated as multilayer or Layer 2-3 switches that have IP routing capabilities, it is not necessary to configure a default gateway.

To view these configuration changes, you must return to privileged EXEC mode, using either the **exit** command or **CTRL+Z**. Typing **exit** will take you back one level. Using **CTRL+Z** will take you directly to privileged EXEC mode. From global configuration mode, these two steps perform the same function.

Using the Show Commands

It is important to become familiar with the commands used to verify the configurations and review statistics information for the switch. The show commands provide this ability. These commands can be used in either user or privileged EXEC modes, although user mode has fewer capabilities. Four show commands are listed here, along with the information they provide. Each command description includes a screen capture, showing the type of information displayed after entering the command.

The command **show version** (or **show ver**) displays important information about the software version number, hardware configuration, device uptime, configurations, and boot files, as well as a base Ethernet address. This command can be used in either EXEC mode. The Show Version Command Screen Capture presents the information displayed using this command.

```
switch1>en
switch1#show version
1900A uptime is 0day(s) 06hour(s) 55minute(s) 41second(s)
cisco Catalyst 1900 (486sx1) processor with 2048K/1024K bytes of memory
Hardware board revision is 5
Upgrade Status: No upgrade currently in progress.
Config File Status: No configuration upload/download is in progress
15 Fixed Ethernet/IEEE 802.3 Interface(s)
Base Ethernet Address: 00-30-80-C7-01-80

switch1#
```

Show Version Command

The command **show running-config** (or **show run**) displays the configuration currently being run on the device. This includes the hostname, IP address(es), and interface configurations. Because the resulting display is more than one screen, press **ENTER** to review it line-by-line, or press the **SPACEBAR** to go page-by-page. Each section is separated for easy review with a ! symbol. This command can only be used in privileged EXEC mode. The results of this show command are illustrated on the Show Running-Config Command Screen Capture.

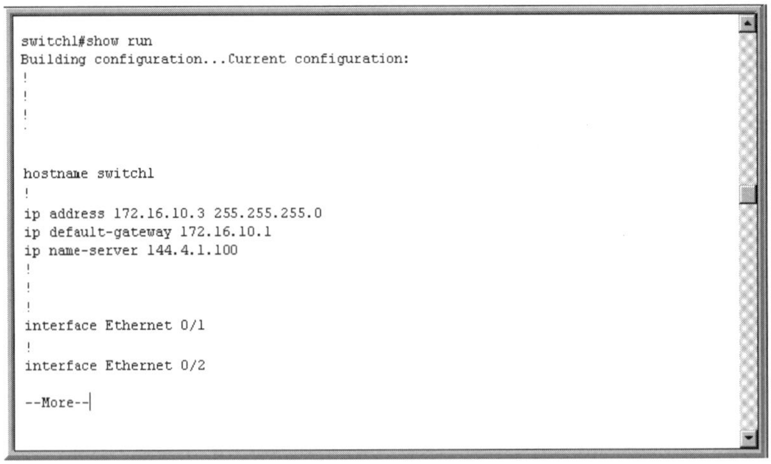

Show Running-Config Command

The command **show interface** (or **show int**) allows the review of each interface and its configuration. To access a specific interface, you must provide the interface identifier. This command, which can only be executed in privileged EXEC mode, also displays past one page, so press **ENTER** for single-line review or **SPACEBAR** for additional pages. The Show Interfaces Command Screen Capture presents the information displayed using this command.

```
switch1#show int
Ethernet 0/1 is Suspended-no-linkbeat
Hardware is Built-in 10Base-T
Address is 0030.80C7.0181
MTU 1500 bytes, BW 10000 Kbits
802.1d STP State:  Forwarding     Forward Transitions:  1
Port monitoring: Disabled
Unknown unicast flooding: Enabled
Unregistered multicast flooding: Enabled
Description:
Duplex setting: Half duplex
Back pressure: Disabled

    Receive Statistics                        Transmit Statistics
-------------------------------------  -------------------------------------
Total good frames                    0  Total frames                         0
Total octets                         0  Total octets                         0
Broadcast/multicast frames           0  Broadcast/multicast frames           0
Broadcast/multicast octets           0  Broadcast/multicast octets           0
Good frames forwarded                0  Deferrals                            0
Frames filtered                      0  Single collisions                    0
Runt frames                          0  Multiple collisions                  0
No buffer discards                   0  Excessive collisions                 0
                                        Queue full discards                  0
```

Show Interfaces Command

This specific screen capture includes various lines and associated information as follows:

- Line 1—Indicates whether a specific Ethernet port is currently enabled or disabled
- Line 2—Shows the type of built-in interface (in this example, 10Base-T)
- Line 3—Shows the Media Access Control (MAC) address for this port, which will be incremented an appropriate number from the base address
- Line 4—Indicates the maximum transmission unit (MTU) size and bandwidth (BW) speed
- Line 5—Indicates whether STP is being used, and the current port state
- Lines 6-11—Indicate the settings that have been configured for this interface, and what duplex mode is currently running

Additional lines show statistical information and error counts for the interface.

The command **`show ip`** is used to view the IP-related settings for the switch. The Show IP Command Screen Capture presents the information available using this command on a Catalyst 1900.

```
switch1#show ip
IP Address: 172.16.10.3
Subnet Mask: 255.255.255.0
Default Gateway: 172.16.10.1
Management VLAN:  1
Domain name:  routersim.com
Name server 1: 144.4.1.100
Name server 2: 0.0.0.0
HTTP server : Enabled
HTTP port :  80
RIP : Enabled

switch1#
```

Show IP Command

Notice that the **`show ip`** command provides the IP address and subnet mask assigned to the device. It also shows the default gateway, management VLAN number, name and Hypertext Transfer Protocol (HTTP) server address(es), and routing protocol.

Review Questions

1. Put the following switch startup processes in the correct order:

   _____ Hardware checks are performed during the POST.

   _____ All network cable connections are made, including to the console port.

   _____ Configuration files are located and their settings applied.

   _____ The operating system (OS) loads to perform system startup routines.

   _____ The power cable is plugged in, because there is no on/off switch on the device.

   _____ The User Interface menu options are displayed on the screen.

2. Put the following EXEC mode scenarios in the correct order, from where the CLI screen begins by default:

   _____ The administrator types **`enable`** at the appropriate prompt.

   _____ Login access takes you to the > prompt.

   _____ The prompt displays #.

   _____ The administrator is prompted for a password.

   _____ Configuration commands can be used on the system.

3. Explain what happens when the following commands or keystrokes are entered at the command prompt:

   a. **`?`**

   ____

   b. **`show ?`**

   ____

   c. **`show ver[TAB]`**

   ____

   d. **`UP ARROW`**

   ____

e. **`DOWN ARROW`**

____

f. **`enable`**

____

g. **`disable`**

____

4. What is the name given to the Help feature that allows an easy review of previously used commands?

____

5. Provide the syntax for the command that allows you to view the configuration currently running on the device.

____

____

6. Provide the syntax for the command that allows you to view how an interface is configured.

____

____

7. Provide the syntax for the command that displays information on the base address and hardware settings.

____

____

8. Provide the proper name for each of the following acronyms:

   a. POST

   ____

   b. CLI

   ____

   c. IOS

   ____

d. LED

____

e. TFTP

____

f. STP

____

Extended Activities

To obtain hands-on experience using the commands outlined in this lesson, visit the Student Resources section of WestNet Learning's Web site at **http://www.westnetlearning.com**.

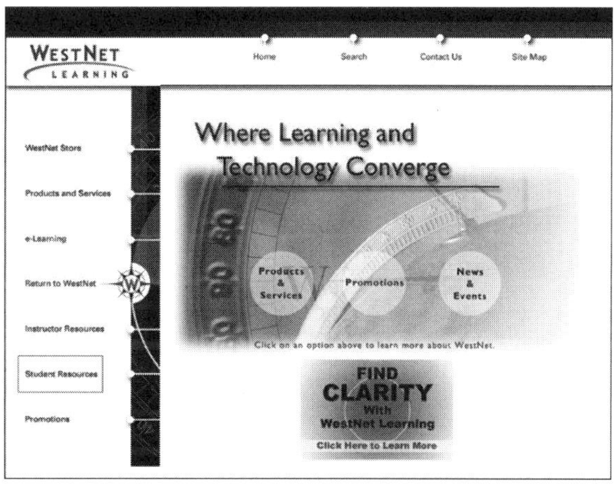

To enter the site, use your e-mail address to login and then type in this course's ISBN number. After you're in the Resources pages, look for the Suggested lab options associated with this module and lesson. Then answer the following questions.

1. What EXEC mode is initially active?

____

2. What commands are available at this level?

____

3. What command is used to access privileged EXEC mode?

   ____

4. How did the prompt change?

   ____

5. When using `?`, how many more commands are available at this level?

   ____

6. Type **`show version`**, and note the response.

   ____

7. What is the MAC address for this device?

   ____

8. Type **`show run`[TAB]**. After you have pressed the **TAB** key, how does the command change?

   ____

9. Press **ENTER**. What type of information is displayed from the running-config?

   ____

10. Is there a hostname and IP address on this device?

    ____

11. What keystroke allows you to see more information in the running-config file, line-by-line?

    ____

12. How about page-by-page?

    ____

13. When the running-config is finished, type **`show int`** to review the interfaces. What is the MTU, BW, and network topology of this port?

    ____

14. What is the MAC address for the first interface?

____

15. How is this different from the base device MAC address?

____

16. What is the STP port state for this interface?

____

17. At the prompt, type **`show ?`** (Make sure there is a space between the word and ?.) Note all the possible show command options.

____

18. Use one of the show commands discovered with the `?` feature, and describe the information provided.

____

19. Use the **UP ARROW** to review the commands you used during this exercise. What is this feature called?

____

Lesson 3—Router Startup

As stated earlier, the Cisco IOS is very similar between routing devices. This makes it easy to administer a large network, because you only have to remember a certain number of commands that can be used on many Cisco products. This lesson looks at the commands used to access and configure a Cisco router. It begins with the Help features, editing keys, and error messages. It then discusses configuration modes and the many different configuration options available on a router and each interface. The password section of this lesson shows how to set up passwords for the many entry points into a device. The lesson ends with some show commands that can verify the interface and configurations entered for a router.

Objectives

At the end of this lesson you will be able to:

- Recognize the startup process on a Cisco router
- Identify the steps involved in the setup process
- Log in to a router
- Access Help features in the CLI
- Identify the output of the command history
- Use editing keys and functions
- Recognize command error messages

Key Point

Many of the commands used with the Catalyst switch IOS are the same for Cisco's routers. They both have a similar CLI, which makes it easy to learn and remember commands. In addition, the Help feature is always available to provide the proper syntax.

Router Boot Sequence

Three main functions take place during the router boot process. The three steps are virtually the same for a router as for a switch. The first step is a hardware check or POST to verify the physical components of the device. The second step involves finding and loading the IOS. Finally, the device finds and loads a configuration file to provide its basic settings. The three steps are described here in further detail:

1. **Run POST**—This diagnostic process verifies that the internal components, such as the memory, CPU, and ports, are all working properly. The microcode used during POST is stored in ROM, and activated every time a router is turned on. The POST process ensures that problems will not be encountered later due to faulty hardware.
2. **Find and load the IOS**—A special code, the bootstrap code, is used to locate, load, and run the Cisco IOS software. After loading, the bootstrap is not used until the router is powered off/on or reloaded. The bootstrap code reads the configuration register to find and load the IOS. As stated earlier, the IOS is loaded from flash memory by default. It is stored in a compressed format, and must be uncompressed before being moved into random access memory (RAM) for faster access. Some router models, including the Cisco 2500 series used in the classroom, do not have enough RAM to store the entire IOS image. Those devices simply run the IOS directly from flash memory.
3. **Find and load the configuration**—Like the special settings on your computer, a router also has a configuration that provides important settings, such as a hostname, IP addresses, routing protocol configurations, and much more. Some of these settings can be created during the initial setup process discussed later in this section. Manual configuration commands must also be set in a router; many of these commands are presented in the next section. After the router is configured, the settings must be saved in the startup-config file and stored in NVRAM. Each time the device is restarted, it finds and executes the contents of the startup-config file to provide the router's functionality. If the startup-config file is not found in the designated location (NVRAM by default), the router begins an autoinstallation process to set up an initial configuration.

Initial Configuration With the Router Setup Program

The setup process is a simplified way to configure a router when a startup configuration is not located. The setup routine provides a step-by-step process, which prompts an administrator for input. The information entered is then added to the startup configuration for that device. It is also loaded into RAM and run on the router. This process is suitable for basic configuration only. Additional configuration can then be performed from global configuration mode (discussed later) for more advanced settings.

During the setup process, the default option associated with a particular question is shown in square brackets ([ ]). To activate that option, simply press **ENTER**. To break out of the setup routine, press the **CTRL+C** keys together. If necessary, an administrator can manually start the setup process from global configuration mode using the command:

```
Router(config)#setup
```

Two router setup modes exist, basic management and extended configuration, as described in the following sections.

Basic Management

Basic management mode quickly configures a router with the most minimal settings necessary for initial connectivity and administration. Because it is not the default setup routine, an administrator has to answer the question "`Would you like to enter basic management setup?`" with a "**`yes`**." Notice that on the System Configuration Dialog Screen Capture, the user does not enter basic management, but instead begins the extended configuration process.

```
          --- System Configuration Dialog ---

Continue with configuration dialog?  [yes/no]: y

At any point you may enter a question mark for help.
Use Ctrl + C to abort the configuration dialog at any prompt.
Default settings are in square brackets  [   ].

Basic management setup configures only enough connectivity for
management of the system, extended setup will ask you to
configure each interface on the system.

Would you like to enter basic management setup? [Yes/no]: n
```

System Configuration Dialog

Extended Configuration

To enter this setup mode, you must answer "**no**" when asked "`Would you like to enter basic management setup?`" The extended configuration mode presents more questions that allow an administrator to configure a hostname, passwords, networking protocols, IP addresses, and interface settings. Upon completion, this configuration displays all of the configured settings, and asks whether you want to save them, start over, or exit the setup process.

After you enter extended configuration mode, you are prompted to review the current interfaces on the router. This list varies greatly depending on the model of the device you are using. The Interface and Password Setup Screen Capture is applicable to a Cisco 2501 router, which has one attachment unit interface (AUI) Ethernet port and two serial interfaces, as well as the standard console and AUX ports (which are not shown). The administrator is prompted for a hostname to assign the device; the default hostname is Router. It is best to create a unique name that describes the device location or network function. The hostname assigned below only changes the prompt on the router. It is advisable to make the hostname the same as the assigned domain name; however, this is not required. Well-assigned hostnames make it easier for an administrator to identify devices, and can also be used for Telnet access to devices and name resolution (discussed later).

```
First, would you like to see the current interface summary? [Yes]: y
Interface    IP-Address  OK? Method  Status                 Protocol
Ethernet0    unassigned  YES unset   Administratively down  down
Serial0      unassigned  YES unset   Administratively down  down
Serial1      unassigned  YES unset   Administratively down  down

Configuring global parameters:
   Enter host name [Router]: Router1

The enable secret is a password used to protect access to
priviledged EXEC and configuration modes. This password, after
entered, becomes encrypted in the configuration.
   Enter enable secret: networking

The enable password is used when you do not specify an enable secret
password, with some older software versions, and some boot images.
   Enter enable password: Cisco

The virtual terminal password is used to protect access to the
router over a network interface.
   Enter virtual terminal password: telnet1
```

Interface and Password Setup

Setting passwords is another important step in the setup process. As the Interface and Password Setup Screen Capture shows, you are prompted to set three different passwords. The characteristics and properties of these passwords are as follows:

- **Enable secret**—The word "enable" means this password is used to move from user EXEC mode to privileged EXEC mode. To do this, type **`enable`** or **`en`** at the `Router>` prompt. If an enable password is set, you will be prompted to enter the password before proceeding into privileged EXEC mode. Enable secret means that the password will be encrypted with a Message Digest version 5 (MD5) (one-way) hash and, therefore, is more secure from intrusion.
- **Enable password**—This password is not encrypted in the configuration file by default; however, it can be encrypted with a weak algorithm when the **`service password-encryption`** command is given. The enable password is not normally used if an enable secret password exists. The enable password is a fall-back option for previous IOS versions, and can also be used for troubleshooting or accessing a boot image.
- **Virtual terminal password**—The virtual terminal password authenticates Telnet access into a router. It is set for all Telnet ports, and prevents Telnet access to the device unless the proper password is provided. Keep in mind that this is the first step to accessing a device across a network. Once in, a user telneting into a router has to provide the enable secret password to actually have privileged EXEC access to the device.

Note: The enable secret and enable passwords should not be the same. You will be warned once, however, if you set them to be the same a second time, you will not get another warning. In some documented instances, neither password will then work and access to the device will be denied. Also, because the enable password is either plaintext or easy to decrypt, setting the two passwords to be the same greatly weakens the security of the enable secret password.

After you have finished entering the appropriate passwords for a router, the setup process begins asking questions about the routing protocols that will be used on this device. Although this class focuses on configuring and networking with IP, many additional protocols are available for configuration, as the Networking Protocol Options Screen Capture shows.

```
Configure SNMP Network Management? [no]: enter
    Community string [public]: enter
Configure LAT? [no]: enter
Configure Appletalk? [no]: enter
Configure DECnet? [no]: enter
Configure IP? [yes]: enter
    Configure IGRP routing? [yes]: enter
    Configure RIP routing? [no]: enter
Configure CLNS? [no]: enter
Configure IPX? [no]: enter
Configure Vines? [no]: enter
Configure XNS? [no]: enter
Configure Apollo? [no]: enter
```

Networking Protocol Options

Although not being set up at this time, a brief description of each protocol option follows:

- **SNMP**—Monitors and manages network traffic statistics.
- **Digital Equipment Corporation's (DEC's) Local Area Transport (LAT) Protocol**—Used to connect terminals to DEC hosts.
- **AppleTalk**—Used primarily with Apple/Macintosh computers and printers.
- **DECnet**—Supports DEC's Digital Network Architecture (DNA).
- **IP**—Configured on a router, with two possible routing protocol options: Routing Information Protocol (RIP) and Interior Gateway Routing Protocol (IGRP) (default protocol). These two distance-vector protocols are used to exchange routing information.
- **Connectionless Network Service (CLNS)**—Is an International Standards Organization (ISO) standard for the Network Layer of the Open Systems Interconnection (OSI) model.
- **Novell's Internetwork Packet Exchange (IPX) Protocol**—A legacy Network Layer protocol used in Netware environments.
- **Banyan Virtual Integrated Network Services (VINES)**—Based on protocols derived from the Xerox Network System (XNS).
- **XNS**—Provides key elements of Banyan VINES and Novell's IPX protocols.

- **Apollo**—Used for routing within Apollo domains and communication between Apollo workstations.

As shown on the Networking Protocol Options Screen Capture, pressing **ENTER** in reply to each question indicates the default option was chosen. Notice that the only protocol configured for this device is IP, with IGRP used for routing.

The next setup requirement is configuring the router interfaces. You are prompted to configure each one individually, and are given different options based on the type of interface. As shown on the Interface Configuration Screen Capture, an IP address and subnet mask are assigned to the Ethernet 0 port on this device. In addition, the administrator declined configuration options for both of the serial interfaces.

```
Configuring Interface Parameters:

Do you want to configure Ethernet0 interface? [yes]: enter
  Configure IP on the interface? [no]: y
     IP address for this interface: 172.16.10.1
     Subnet mask for this interface [255.255.0.0]: 255.255.255.0
     Class B network is 172.16.0.0, 24 subnet bits; mask is /24

Do you want to configure Serial0 interface? [yes]: n
Do you want to configure Serial1 interface? [yes]: n
```

Interface Configuration

Upon completion of all options, the device will generate a configuration that includes all the settings created during the setup process. You should carefully review this configuration and make sure it is correct. After reviewing the contents, you are prompted to select from three different options:

- [0]—Go to IOS command prompt without saving this config.
- [1]—Return back to the setup without saving this config.
- [2]—Save this configuration to NVRAM and exit.

The first two options erase all values provided during the setup process. By selecting Option 0, the administrator now has access to the command prompt, as if the administrator had used the **CTRL+C** key combination to break out of the setup routine. By selecting Option 1, the entire setup process is started over. This is handy if something is not correct when the configuration is reviewed at the end. However, it can be too time consuming to reset all the values. It would be easier to save the configuration, and then edit the incorrect settings. The last option, Option 2, saves the configuration so that it will be available if the router is restarted at any time. It will then move you to the command prompt for further access or configuration.

The last diagram in this series, the Configuration and Save Options Screen Capture, shows an example of the options entered during the setup process. By pressing **ENTER**, the administrator saved the settings to NVRAM, and now has access to the command prompt.

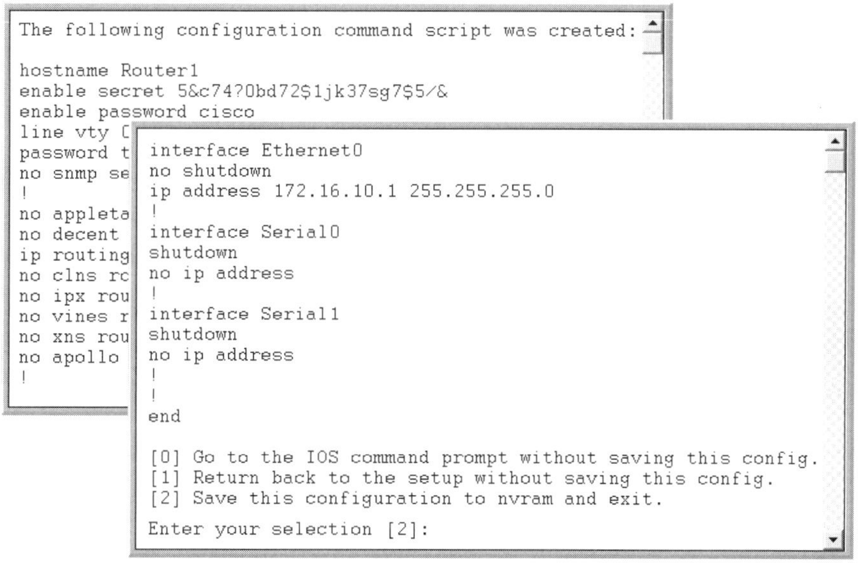

Configuration and Save Options

Basic Commands for Help, History Buffer, Editing, and Error Messages

This section covers the basic Help features provided as part of the Cisco CLI. Help can be used in user EXEC, privileged EXEC, or any configuration mode. It is a very useful tool, offering the next expected word or syntax component. Another useful feature included in the IOS is a history buffer that stores a set number of previously used commands. This can be helpful when reviewing past entries, or simply to prevent a lot of unnecessary typing. A full range of editing CTRL characters provides the ability to easily edit previously typed commands. This is useful when you have a very lengthy command with a simple error. Instead of retyping the entire command, you can use the Edit features to make the change. Finally, as with any system, error messages are provided when commands are entered incorrectly. Cisco's console error messages can help pinpoint a problem by identifying syntax issues, incomplete commands, or ambiguous entries.

Context-Sensitive Help

Any good system has a Help feature that acts as a guide to let you know how commands should be entered and, for that matter, what commands are available. The Cisco IOS provides context-sensitive help. Two Help features are available: one provides all possible commands, and the other provides syntax help.

To obtain general help about all available commands in a particular mode, press the **?** key after the router prompt. This works exactly the same way as it does with the Catalyst switch CLI. Fewer commands are available in user EXEC mode than in privileged EXEC mode.

To get help with a specific command, type the first few letters of the command, then press **?**. For example, if you want help on all possible commands that start with the letters CL, use the command `Router#`**`cl?`**. The router will respond with the two commands **`clear`** and **`clock`** as options. This is helpful if you have an idea of the command you are looking for, but not the proper wording.

To get help on the syntax of a particular command, type the portion of the command you know, and where you are unsure of the next option, use **?**. For example, if you are trying to set the clock on a device, you begin with the command **`clock ?`**. The Help feature would then return the next possible option or options. It also maintains the last command typed at the prompt, so you only need to add to it. This is particularly handy with long, complicated commands. The Help Feature Screen Capture shows the process of obtaining help at each step using the **`clock`** command as an example.

```
Router>en
Router#cl?
clear clock
Router#clock ?
      set  Set the time and date

Router#clock set ?
hh:mm:ss  Current Time

Router#clock set 12:31:00 ?
<1-31> Day of the month
MONTH  Month of the year

Router#clock set 12:31:00 8 may 2001
Router#
```

Help Feature

History Buffer

The history buffer is a set number of previously typed commands stored in memory. This may help an administrator easily recall a previously used command, or identify what commands have been entered on the device in the past. It can also be very useful in tracking changes, or simply preventing you from retyping commonly used commands. By default, the history buffer contains the last 10 commands entered. The following options allow you to access a command in the history buffer:

- **UP ARROW** or **CTRL+P**—Displays the current command, then moves upward through each previous command in the list.
- **DOWN ARROW** or **CTRL+N**—Displays the current command, then moves downward through each consecutive command in the list.
- **CTRL+R**—Displays the current command, then moves downward through each consecutive command in the list.
- `Router#`**`show history`**—Displays the entire contents of the history buffer.

To change the size of the history buffer and store more commands, use either of the following commands:

`Router#`**`terminal history size`** *`number`*

`Router#`**`history`** *`number`*

The first command changes the history buffer size only for the current session. The second command changes the history buffer for all sessions. The maximum size of the buffer is 256 entries. The History Buffer Screen Capture presents an example of previously typed commands in a history buffer. It also shows the history buffer size being changed to 25 entries.

```
Router1#show history
en
config t
hostname Router1
exit
show run
show history

Router1#terminal history size 25
Router1#
```

History Buffer

Edit Keys

The CLI includes a set of editing keys that allow you to easily make changes to commands. Assume you have entered a very long command string, only to find that you misspelled the first word. The edit keys help you move around the command and modify the string. The IOS feature that provides this capability is called "enhanced editing mode" and is enabled by default. Enhanced editing can be turned off if you have scripts that do not interact well, or you do not care for this feature. The following commands enable and disable, respectively, the extended editing capabilities:

```
Router#terminal editing
Router#terminal no editing
```

The Extended Editing feature offers a number of CTRL key combinations that provide horizontal movement on the command line. The following is a list of these editing key sequences and the functions they perform:

- **TAB**—Completes an entry if enough characters have been typed to distinguish a command
- **BACKSPACE**—Removes a character to the left of the cursor
- **CTRL+Z**—Moves from configuration mode back to privileged EXEC mode

- **CTRL+U**—Erases an entire line from the command prompt
- **CTRL+W**—Erases a word in the command string
- **CTRL+D**—Erases a single character to the right of the cursor
- **CTRL+A**—Moves the cursor to the very beginning of the command string
- **CTRL+E**—Moves the cursor to the very end of the command string
- **ESC+B**—Moves the cursor backward a single word
- **ESC+F**—Moves the cursor forward a single word
- **CTRL+B**—Moves the cursor backward a single character
- **CTRL+F**—Moves the cursor forward a single character

Keep in mind that when you use a command that causes information to scroll off the screen, the word `--MORE--` is displayed. Two options can be used to view more information:

- **SPACEBAR**—Pressing the **SPACEBAR** key displays the next entire page of available information.
- **ENTER**—Pressing **ENTER** only shows one additional line at a time, which may be helpful when looking for a specific line, but can be very time consuming for long files, such as the startup-config file.

Pressing the **ESC** key returns the cursor to the prompt.

Error Messages

Error messages are provided by the CLI to help identify a problem in a command. Four possible error conditions may be triggered in response to incorrect user input. The Error Messages Screen Capture shows all four error conditions and their text messages.

```
Press RETURN to get started.

Router>
Router>en

Router#display
Translating 'display' ...domain server (255.255.255.255)
% Unknown command or computer name, or unable to find computer address
________________________________________

Router#show con
%Ambiguous command: "show con"
________________________________________

Router#clock
% Incomplete command.
________________________________________

Router#terminal history seze
                           ^
% Invalid input detected at '^' marker.

Router#
```

Error Messages

The four possible error conditions are:

- **`% Unknown command or computer name, or unable to find computer address`**—If a command is entered that is completely unrecognized by a device as a valid command, it will attempt to resolve it as a hostname. The device tries to resolve the name to attempt a Telnet connection into a remote device. Notice in the screen capture that the word `display` was typed. Display is not a valid command, thus the router attempts to translate the word `display` using any form of name resolution, in this case a broadcast address. Because it is not resolved as the hostname of any device, Telnet is not possible and the error message is returned.

  When first working with a router and command line, you may type in unidentifiable commands fairly frequently. Having to wait for each mistake to attempt name resolution and contact, especially in a large network, can be time consuming. To disable the Name Resolution feature and prevent this error message from responding, use the following command from global configuration mode:

  `Router(config)#`**`no ip domain-lookup`**

- **`% Ambiguous command`**—This error condition indicates that not enough of the command was provided for the system to distinguish it from more than one possible command option. In the example presented on the Error Messages Screen Capture, the command fragment **`show con`** was entered. A router has two possible commands that begin with this syntax: **`show controllers`** and **`show configuration`**. To prevent this error message, at least one more letter must be typed to differentiate between the two possibilities. You can check that enough distinguishable characters have been typed and automatically complete the command by using the **TAB** key.
- **`% Incomplete command`**—An incomplete command means that additional syntax is required but has not been provided. All commands have specific keywords or values that must be typed in the correct order for the command to be complete. To determine the next required command component, use the **`?`** key to get help with the remaining options. Using **`?`**, the command is considered complete when help displays <cr>, which indicates carriage return (ENTER key) is all that remains.
- **`% Invalid input detected at '^' marker`**—This error message lets you know that a command is missing or, in many cases, is mistyped or misspelled. The "^" symbol is used to point out the location where the problem exists. The exact error location can still be difficult to determine when a word has been left out, or the command looks correct otherwise.

Review Questions

1. Which of the following are characteristics of the enable secret password? (Choose all that apply.)
   a. The password is encrypted.
   b. The password is used to gain access to a device by means of Telnet.
   c. The password takes you from user EXEC mode to privileged EXEC mode.
   d. The password is used for older versions of the IOS and for boot images.
2. Which of the following are the initial setup modes?
   a. Basic and extended
   b. Low-level and high-level
   c. User and privileged
   d. Automatic and manual
3. All of the following can be configured during the initial extended setup process except which?
   a. Router hostname
   b. IP addresses for the interfaces
   c. Passwords
   d. Name server IP address

Extended Activities

If a router is available in the classroom, work in teams to start it up and configure an initial setup. Make sure that the router used for this and future activities is not a production device and is used for lab purposes only.

1. Locate a rollover cable. They are generally flat with exactly the opposite pinouts in the RJ-45 connectors.
2. Plug the cable into the router's console port, and into the serial converter (RJ-45 to DB-9) that plugs into the computer's COM port.

3. Open a terminal emulation program. There are a few ways to do this, and you can use one of two methods. Start at a command prompt, type **TELNET** and press **ENTER**. Alternately, from a Microsoft Windows-based computer, go to Start | Programs | Accessories | Communications | HyperTerminal.
4. Set the terminal emulation program to communicate Direct to COM1 (or appropriate COM port).
5. Turn the router on, and watch as the POST process and IOS load is performed.
6. If no startup-config file is located, the router will then prompt you to begin the autoinstallation process using Setup. If setup does not start automatically, perform the following steps:

```
Router>enable
Router#config t
Router(config)#setup
```

7. Go through the setup configuration process, providing a hostname, passwords, and network protocol configuration (IP only), and setting an IP address and subnet on the interfaces.
8. Upon completion, review your configuration as shown on the screen.
9. When prompted, select Option 1 to restart the setup process without saving your configuration.
10. Disconnect the cables from the previous steps, and allow another team to work through the lab activity.

To obtain hands-on experience using the commands outlined in this lesson, visit the Student Resources section of WestNet Learning's Web site at **http://www.westnetlearning.com**.

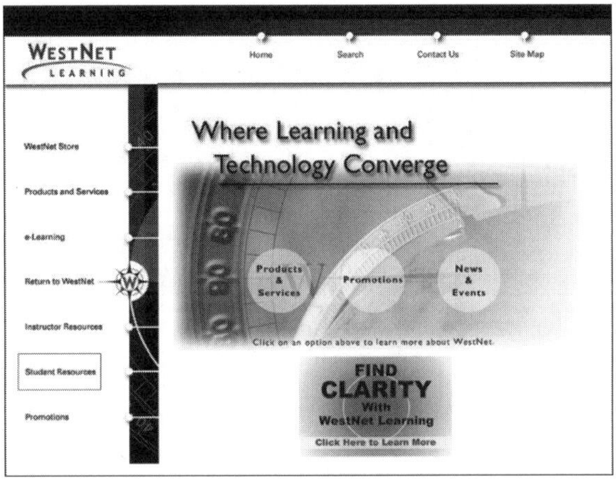

To enter the site, use your e-mail address to login and then type in this course's ISBN number. After you're in the Resources pages, look for the Suggested lab options associated with this module and lesson. Then answer the following questions.

1. Define the action taken when using the following keys or edit functions:

   a. ESC

   ____

   b. SPACE BAR when ---MORE--- is displayed

   ____

   c. ENTER when ---MORE--- is displayed

   ____

   d. CTRL+B

   ____

   e. CTRL+C in setup mode

   ____

2. How many commands are kept in the history buffer by default?

3. Write the command that can be used to change the history buffer size to 25 commands?

4. What command is used to display the contents of the history buffer?

5. What keystroke could be used to view the last command entered?

6. What error message would be displayed if a command is typed without all the required words?

7. What error message would be displayed if a command is misspelled?

8. What error message would be displayed if not enough distinguishing letters were provided for the device to recognize the syntax of the command?

Lesson 4—Router Configuration

Beyond the user EXEC and privileged EXEC modes are configuration modes. The first level up from privileged EXEC mode is called "global configuration mode" and is used to set parameters that are necessary for the entire device, such as a hostname and security features like username and password. From here, you can also access specific configuration modes for interfaces, subinterfaces, controllers, lines, and routing protocols. Each one has appropriate commands specific to that component. To leave a higher-level configuration mode and return to global configuration, use the **exit** command. In many instances, it may be necessary to return directly to privileged EXEC mode, to do this use the **CTRL+Z** keys together. From there, show commands can be used to display configuration and statistical information. Privileged EXEC mode can also be used to save the running configuration where all settings are initially entered into the startup configuration, which is saved permanently.

Objectives

At the end of this lesson you will be able to:

- Access various configuration modes
- Configure global settings
- Configure router interfaces
- Configure IP address settings
- Verify interface configuration using show commands
- Save the configurations into startup-config

Key Point

The IOS has a hierarchy of configuration levels. Global configuration mode is accessed from privileged EXEC mode. Major commands are used to access additional and more specific configuration modes, such as interface, subinterface, controller, line, and routing protocol. The prompt changes to indicate the current mode. The major command must be followed by one or more subcommands that provide the actual configuration.

Global Configuration Mode

Now for the real power: global configuration mode. As an administrator, sometimes you will need to configure and reconfigure router settings. Global configuration mode allows you to do just that. It also provides access to the many additional layers of configuration available after you have entered this level of management.

To begin, let us take a look at the three possible initial global configuration options. If you enter the command **config** at the privileged EXEC mode prompt, the system will ask whether you want the `terminal, memory, or network` option, as follows:

```
Router#config
Configuring from terminal, memory or network [terminal]?
ENTER
Router(config)#
```

- **Config terminal**—The **config terminal** command accesses global configuration mode and the configuration information currently held in RAM. Every command typed is automatically parsed and executed as soon as **ENTER** is pressed. These commands are entered directly into the running-config file stored in dynamic random access memory (DRAM). If, however, it is not manually saved to NVRAM, these changes will be lost when the router is restarted. Notice that the prompt changed from `Router#` to `Router(config)#` to help identify the level of access at the command line. Remember, to get word or context-sensitive help, use **?**. In addition, the **UP** and **DOWN ARROW** keys and edit commands can also be used. **Configure terminal** is the default mode, because it activates all commands immediately. It is up to the administrator to make sure those commands are permanently saved. After initial setup, use **config terminal** for any further configuration changes or additions.
- **Config mem** (memory)—This configuration option reads information from the startup-config file stored in NVRAM, which is not erased after a restart. Keep in mind that during the configuration process, the startup-config file will be placed into RAM and will overwrite the existing running-config file.

- **`Config net`** (network)—Using this option allows configuration of a file from a TFTP server. The configuration information is retrieved from the TFTP server and overlays the existing running-config file in RAM. Be careful with this method because settings are entered into the running-config file as they are read from the TFTP server. For example, a line in the configuration file stored on the TFTP server could change the IP address of the Ethernet interface. That line would be read and applied before the rest of the configuration file is downloaded. This would prevent the router from communicating with the TFTP server, and disrupt the rest of the download process.

To exit global configuration mode and return to privileged EXEC mode, you can use one of three options:

```
Router(config)#exit
Router(config)#end
Router(config)#CTRL+Z
```

You may recall that the setup process configures a router for the first time. This process provides a question-and-answer format for configuring the device. However, it is usually only performed once to get the basic configuration setup and connect to the device. From that point forward, an administrator uses the **`configure terminal`** mode to provide additional settings or change the existing configuration. The next two sections present commands used to set a hostname for the device and display banner messages. Later in this lesson, you will use global configuration to set up passwords for the device. For now, let us get started with the basics.

Configuring a Host Name

The first configuration that should take place is setting up or changing the hostname to identify a router. To set or change a hostname for a device, enter global configuration mode and use the following command:

```
Router(config)#hostname name
```

For example:

```
Router(config)#hostname RouterB
```

Once entered, the prompt immediately changes to reflect the new hostname: `RouterB(config)#`.

Configuring a Banner Message

The following list describes several different types of banner messages that can be configured and displayed on a router:

- **Incoming banner**—Displays when a connection is made to a device, but before the login process has taken place
- **Login banner**—Displays for console or virtual terminal connections
- **EXEC banner**—Displays after **`enable`** and the password to enter privileged EXEC mode are typed
- **Message of the day banner (motd)**—Displays information about device maintenance, network changes, or access restriction information

To provide a disclaimer to anyone accessing the device, companies most often use banner messages. At least one of them usually includes wording such as "`Only authorized users may access this device! If you are not authorized, please exit this device immediately.`" Banner messages are optional, and are simply used to display text information.

The Host Name and Banner Message Configuration Screen Capture shows the commands necessary to make these settings. Notice the Help feature was used to determine all banner options available. The `banner motd` was selected. When setting a message of the day banner, a delimiting character is used. The character in this example is a #, and is used to begin and end the message text. Between the delimiting characters, the text can be multiple lines as necessary.

```
RouterB>en
RouterB#config t
Enter configuration commands, one per line.  End with CNTL/Z.

RouterB(config)#hostname RouterB

RouterB(config)#Banner ?
  LINE      c banner-text c, where 'c' is a delimiting character
  exec      Set EXEC process creation banner
  incoming  Set incoming terminal line banner
  login     Set login banner
  motd      Set Message of the Day banner

RouterB(config)#banner motd #
Enter TEXT message.  End with the character '#'.
Only authorized users may access this device!
If you are not authorized, please exit the device immediately!
#
RouterB(config)#
```

Host Name and Banner Message Configuration

Other Configuration Modes

From global configuration mode, there is an additional hierarchy of more specific configuration levels. This includes access to configure interfaces, subinterfaces, lines, controllers, and routing protocols for both IP and IPX. Accessing a specific configuration level requires a major command. This means the prompt will change and access to a new level will be granted. Major commands are displayed in the Configuration Modes Screen Capture and listed in more detail below. These commands are only used to move from global configuration mode to a specific configuration mode. They do not provide any configuration in themselves.

```
RouterB#config t
Enter configuration commands, one per line.  End with CNTL/Z.
RouterB(config)#int e0
RouterB(config-if)#exit
RouterB(config)#int e0.1
RouterB(config-subif)#exit
Router(config)#controller T1 1
Router(config-controller)#
RouterB(config)#line vty 0 4
RouterB(config-line)#exit
RouterB(config)#router rip
RouterB(config-router)#exit
RouterB(config)#
```

Configuration Modes

For configuration purposes, a subcommand is required. A subcommand can be issued only after the major command has been used to change the prompt and configuration level. Subcommands can perform functions such as assign passwords, provide login access, define bandwidth and clock rate, enable or disable an interface, associate a network for routing, and much more. To keep this straight, just remember that a major command is used to move and provide access to specific levels in the command hierarchy. Subcommands are then used to define the configuration or display information. In any case, the **`exit`** command will move you out of the current level. Using **CTRL+Z** will return you to privileged EXEC mode from any configuration mode.

You should be familiar with a number of other configuration levels and associated prompts. The Configuration Modes Screen Capture presents several possibilities. Lines have been added to help distinguish between each command and prompt. Notice that the **`exit`** command is used to return to global configuration mode and move to a different configuration level. Accessing and configuring commands in these other levels will be discussed as appropriate throughout this class.

The major commands shown on the screen capture are:

- **`(config-if)#`**—The interface configuration mode displays the same prompt regardless of the interface being configured. This can be somewhat confusing when changing several interfaces at the same time. To access and configure a particular interface, use:

  `Router(config)#`**`int`** *`port-type number`*

  For example:

  `Router(config)#`**`int e0`** or `Router(config)#`**`int s0`**

  The resulting prompt is:

  `Router(config-if)#`

- **`(config-subif)#`**—The subinterface configuration mode sets up multiple logical interfaces on a single physical port. This is helpful when configuring certain wide area network (WAN) connections, or when configuring multiple protocols. Subinterfaces are not required to be assigned in consecutive order. A subinterface is configured and accessed with a physical interface number and subinterface number as the following example shows:

  `Router(config)#`**`int e0.1`** or

  `Router(config)#`**`int e0.2`**

  The resulting prompt is:

  `Router(config-subif)#`

- **(config-controller)#**—This configuration mode is used to access configuration parameters necessary for a WAN environment. Controllers are associated with ports that connect to a T1 (1.54 Mbps total bandwidth) used primarily in North America. A controller can also be used to access an E1 (2.038 Mbps total bandwidth) used primarily in Europe, and Central and Latin America. The controller configuration mode requires that T1 or E1 be specified, in addition to the number of the interface. The syntax for this command and prompt is as follows:

  Router(config)#**controller {T1 | E1}** *number*

- **(config-line)#**—This prompt is used by an administrator to configure settings for the console, auxiliary, and Telnet lines. Each line type requires different syntax to access it; however, the resulting prompt is always (config-line)#:

  Router(config)#**line console**—Sets direct connection access through the console port and a rollover cable

  Router(config)#**line auxiliary**—Sets AUX port configuration for remote administration by means of a modem

  Router(config)#**line vty 0 4**—Sets Telnet access for all five incoming connections

  The resulting prompt is:

  ```
  Router(config-line)#
  ```

  At the line configuration level, you can set passwords, login requirements, modem settings for the AUX port, banner messages, and access lists for security. The process of setting passwords for these lines is discussed later.

- **(config-router)#**—Router configuration is accessed when setting up IP routing protocols and their associated components. Routing protocols communicate network path selection information between routing devices. A number of router configuration options can be set up at this level. We will focus on RIP and IGRP. The following syntax sets up these two protocols:

  Router(config)#**router rip**

  Router(config)#**router igrp number**

  Both of these commands result in the following prompt:

  ```
  Router(config-router)#
  ```

Configuring Ethernet and Serial Interfaces

A router's interfaces provide network connectivity capabilities; thus, it is important for them to be configured properly. The correct way to identify and access a particular interface varies depending on the device. If a router has fixed interfaces, meaning it has a single backplane that cannot be changed, the interface is labeled with port type and number (for example, E0 [Ethernet 0]). If a device is modular (with the exception of the Cisco 4000 series router), meaning it has expansion slots where interface cards are plugged in, the interface is labeled with port type slot number and then port number (for example, Ethernet 0/0). Notice that routers identify the first interface with the number 0, and the second with the number 1. The following are a few examples. The first two will work using the Cisco 2501 router; the remaining examples may be included on other router devices.

To access the first fixed 10-Mbps Ethernet port, use:

```
Router(config)#interface ethernet 0 or
Router(config)#int e0
```

To accesses the first fixed serial interface, use:

```
Router(config)#interface serial 0 or
Router(config)#int ser0
```

To access the modular Ethernet interface in the first slot, first position, use:

```
Router(config)#interface ethernet 0/0 or
Router(config)#int e0/0
```

To access the second Fast Ethernet (100-Mbps) interface, use:

```
Router(config)#interface fastethernet 1 or
Router(config)#int fa1
```

To access the first ISDN-Basic Rate Interface (BRI) interface, use:

```
Router(config)#interface bri0 or
Router(config)#int bri0
```

Notice that like most commands in the Cisco CLI, these can be reduced to a few basic characters and still be understood. However, if you really like to type, you can finish out the command as well. Also remember that you can use the **TAB** key to finish a command.

In addition, when you have accessed an interface, the prompt will change as shown in the preceding section to `Router(config-if)#`. There is no need to exit the interface configuration mode to access another interface. Simply type in the next interface name and the device moves configuration access to the next port. This can be confusing, however, because the prompt `Router(config-if)#` never changes to indicate which interface is currently being worked on. To verify the last interface accessed, use the **UP ARROW** key. To exit the interface configuration level and return to global configuration mode, use the `exit` command. To completely exit global configuration mode, use **CTRL+Z**.

Setting an IP Address

Each interface on a router is its own subnetwork, and the router communicates between these different networks. To do that, each interface must have its own IP address.

Let us look at the basic syntax. To configure IP on an interface, access the appropriate interface using one of the appropriate commands just discussed, then execute the following commands:

```
Router(config)#int e0
Router(config-if)#ip address 192.168.10.1 255.255.255.0
```

Notice the syntax includes the command **ip address** (**ip addr**). The assigned IP address is then provided. This address varies based on your corporate requirements. Each port must be assigned a unique network number. The last part is the subnet mask, which is the default Class C subnet mask in this example.

It is worth noting that for more complex network environments, it may be necessary to assign more than one IP address to an interface. If you simply type the **ip address** command again, it will overwrite any previous IP address assignment. Instead, you must include the command **secondary** at the end of the standard IP address assignment syntax, as shown in the following example:

```
Router(config)#ip address 192.168.20.20 255.255.255.0
secondary
```

Another option is to configure different IP addresses using subinterfaces.

Using Descriptions

It is a very handy and good administrative practice to label your interfaces with descriptions. This helps anyone working with the device determine where an interface is connected, and what purpose it serves. The description can be viewed in running and startup configurations, as well as by using the **show interface** command. We discuss viewing this information in the next section. To set a description, access the interface and then use the following commands:

```
Router(config)#int e0
Router(config-if)#description Executive LAN 9th floor
Router(config-if)#int s0
Router(config-if)#desc WAN connection to Dallas
circuit:84d92adb1
```

The first command accesses the first Ethernet port. This command is not necessary if you are already in interface configuration mode after setting the IP address. The next line shows an example of text that might be used as a description. The command consists of the word **description** (**desc**) and up to 80 characters of text. Notice that instead of exiting interface configuration, we simply changed to the serial 0 interface, and the prompt stayed the same.

Configuring Serial Interfaces

A serial interface creates WAN connections, but it can also connect routers back-to-back in a network environment. When making a serial connection between two devices, one side must provide the clock signal used for synchronization. When making a WAN connection, the service provider will be configured as the data communications equipment (DCE) and provide synchronization. In that case, the connected router will always function as the data terminal equipment (DTE) and receive the clock signal.

In a back-to-back configuration, one router must act as the DTE and the other router acts as the DCE. The connecting cable identifies each device as either DCE or DTE. After this is determined, it is necessary to configure the clock signal on the router that will function as the DCE. You can easily remember that the DCE provides the clock signal, given that clock and DCE both include the letter "C."

When connecting routers back-to-back, to set the clock rate, access the serial interface on the router that serves as the DCE. Then type in the **clock rate** command and provide an appropriate speed in bits per second (bps). Your options are 300 to 4,000,000 bps. A typical clock rate is 56,000 bps (or 56 Kbps). Use the following commands to set the clock rate:

```
Router(config)#int s0
Router(config-if)#clock rate 56000
```

Another important serial interface setting is bandwidth. By default, all serial interfaces are configured at a T1 circuit or 1.544 Mbps. This does not represent all configurations and, in fact, is not even used by a device to understand the available bandwidth. Routing protocols such as IGRP and Open Shortest Path First (OSPF) use the bandwidth setting to determine the best route through a network. The higher the bandwidth for a route, the more likely the route will be used. Because all serial interfaces default to a T1 circuit, however, there is no distinction between the actual available bandwidth. This is not an issue with Ethernet interfaces that automatically recognize their bandwidth capabilities. Unlike clock rate, bandwidth is set in Kbps, from 1 Kbps to 10,000,000 Kbps (or 10 gigabits per second [Gbps]). The command used to set bandwidth for a 64-Kbps connection is shown in the following example:

```
Router(config-if)#bandwidth 64
```

Configuring Ethernet Media Types

Several of the router models have more than one Ethernet connector media type. The media type is used to identify which connector and cable type is being connected. AUI is the original Ethernet connectivity method for connecting to coaxial cable, and looks similar to a serial interface. Another option is standard unshielded twisted pair (UTP) cable with an RJ-45 connector. These are labeled 10BaseT and 100BaseT depending on whether the connection is 10-Mbps Ethernet or Fast Ethernet at 100 Mbps. The "T" at the end of the standard is used to indicate twisted pair. The 2500 series Ethernet routers use the AUI connector as the default connector type, while the multiple LAN port models, such as the 3600 series routers, may provide a combination of AUI and RJ-45 Ethernet connections.

A final option is using a media independent interface (MII) connector. This configuration supports 100BaseT4 Ethernet, which achieves 100 Mbps data rates over four pairs of Category 3, 4, or 5 UTP cabling. It requires a special transceiver and is only available on select models. To configure the Ethernet media type, use the following command in interface configuration mode for the correct Ethernet port:

```
Router(config-if)#media-type {aui | 10baset | 100baset |
mii}
```

For example, to configure Ethernet 0 as a 10BaseT standard UTP configuration, use the commands:

```
Router(config)#int e0
Router(config-if)#media-type 10baset
```

Starting or Shutting Down an Interface

One of the most important commands is starting an interface, or shutting it down. This is important when making physical connections and establishing communication. When an interface is shut down, no communications can pass between the directly connected devices. When an interface is started, a connection can be established and the devices can communicate.

After you have finished configuring an interface, make sure it is communicating by using the **no shutdown** command. If you want to stop an interface from communicating, use the **shutdown** command. Keep in mind that the **shutdown** and **no shutdown** commands only work in interface configuration mode.

To turn off an interface and prevent communication, use the following command:

```
Router(config-if)#shutdown or shut
```

To turn on an interface and allow communication, use the following command:

```
Router(config-if)#no shutdown or no shut
```

Notice that the **no shutdown** command was issued for the Ethernet 0 interface on the Interface No Shutdown Command Screen Capture. After this command is executed, the router returns the `%LINEPROTO-5-UPDOWN:` status message indicating the state was changed to "up." It also shows the `%LINK-3-UPDOWN:` status message indicating whether communication has been established. This is determined with the `changed state to up` message. If the attached device is shut down, another `%LINK-3-UPDOWN:` status message will be displayed indicating its state was changed to down. The **no shutdown** command must be issued on both devices to open the link and establish communication.

```
routera>en
routera#config t
Enter configuration commands, one per line.  End with CNTL/Z.
routera(config)#int e0
routera(config-if)#no shut
%LINEPROTO-5-UPDOWN: Line protocol on Interface Ethernet0, changed state to up
%LINK-3-UPDOWN: Interface Ethernet0, changed state to up
routera(config-if)#
```

Interface No Shutdown Command

Setting Passwords

Network routers should be secure, because they provide access to the network, as well as network functionality. If someone were to gain access to a device and change settings, the network could be severely impacted. Therefore, it is important to set passwords to protect routers from unauthorized access. To add an additional layer of security, it is also a good idea to encrypt the passwords. Without encryption, the passwords are displayed and can be easily read from both running-config and startup-config. Encryption makes a password unreadable by displaying a random mix of characters. It is important to note that the encryption algorithm Cisco uses for all passwords, except the enable secret password, is inherently weak.

While it is a good idea to encrypt all passwords to prevent casual observers from gaining access to routers, you should also physically guard access to configuration files. To manually encrypt all passwords, in addition to the secret password, use the following command before making any password settings:

```
Router(config)#service password-encryption
```

An encrypted password and regular enable password are presented on the Enable Passwords Screen Capture. The first password was entered as **`enable secret`**, meaning it was automatically encrypted. Notice in the configuration toward the bottom of the screen, the cryptic row of characters next to `enable secret`. The next command is **`enable password`**, which, by default, is not encrypted. This password is shown in clear text and can be easily read at the bottom part of the diagram.

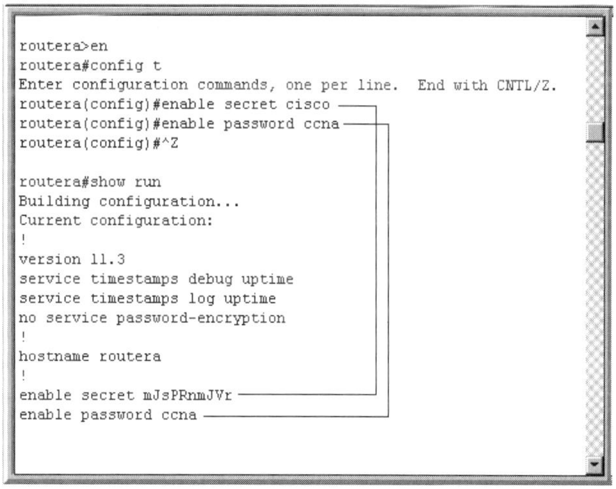

Enable Passwords

Enable Passwords

Enable passwords are used to gain entry to privileged EXEC mode from user EXEC mode. Remember that the command to make this transition is **`enable`**, which is where the enable password comes from. Enable passwords can be configured during the initial setup routine, discussed earlier in this lesson. However, you will most likely want to change these passwords on occasion. The enable secret password is encrypted using MD5 and cannot easily be read or deciphered. The enable password is not encrypted except as noted above, and is only used with older versions of the IOS or when using a boot image for troubleshooting or maintenance purposes. These passwords should be set to different words, preferably something difficult to guess.

To configure an encrypted password used when entering enable mode, use the following command in global configuration mode:

```
Router(config)#enable secret word
```

Replace "word" with your password. However, do not type "enable secret password," because this would set the password to "password."

To configure a nonencrypted password used with boot images and older versions of the IOS, use the command:

```
Router(config)#enable password word
```

Console Passwords

A console password gains access to a router through the console port on a device directly connected to a computer. Although this connection is usually more secure because routers are generally stored in a locked closet or are otherwise less accessible, it is still a good idea to set a console password. When a console password is set, you will be prompted to enter it before you are able to see the initial router prompt. If an enable password is set, you will also have to provide this second password to access privileged EXEC mode. To access the console port and set a console password, use the following commands:

```
Router(config)#line console 0
Router(config-line)#login
Router(config-line)#password word
```

The first line accesses the console port; notice that the prompt changes to `(config-line)#`. The second command **`login`** tells the system that login authentication is required. The third command line sets the password when you replace "word" with the appropriate password for this device.

There are two other console configuration settings that should be discussed before moving on. The first command is used to control the amount of time a connection will wait before timing out and returning to the initial prompt. By default the session will time out after 10 minutes. This provides an element of security, in case an administrator walks away from the device for a period of time without first exiting privileged EXEC mode. Anyone who found the device in this mode could possibly view configurations or make changes that could impact network communications. In a more controlled and secure environment, it may be necessary for an administrator to leave the device for a period of time to check connectivity elsewhere or make cable changes in another location. Upon return the administrator would have to go through the login process again if he or she had been away more than 10 minutes. To prevent the device from timing out and remain connected until the administrator logs out, use the following command in line console configuration mode:

```
Router(config)#line console 0
Router(config-line)#exec-timeout 0 0
```

The other command administrators find helpful is used to prevent the typing of console messages for disrupting commands. For instance, if an administrator accesses an interface and types the command **`no shut`**, the router will respond by bringing the interface up and displaying the status. This is one or more lines of message that would get garbled with the commands the administrator is typing at the time. To prevent this from happening, use the configuration command:

```
Router(config-line)#logging synchronous
```

When entered, the **logging synchronous** command allows messages and commands to be displayed on individual lines without getting mixed up. This makes it easier to read messages. It also helps prevent syntax errors with garbled or interrupted commands.

Telnet Passwords

After a Telnet password and IP address are assigned to a router, the device can be accessed using terminal emulation software from virtually anywhere in the network. This presents a much higher level of security concerns because it is more difficult to control. The number of available simultaneous Telnet sessions varies with the IOS version and router model. For example, the Cisco 2501 router used in class, with the standard version of the IOS, offers five possible simultaneous Telnet sessions. If the router is using an enterprise IOS version, this number may be significantly higher. You can determine the number of possible Telnet sessions by entering global configuration and using the following command:

```
Router(config)#line vty ?
  <0-4>   First line number
```

The second line shows the information returned by the router. In this example, five Telnet sessions, labeled 0 to 4 (first to last), are available. It is easiest to configure all five Telnet session passwords at the same time, and advisable to set them the same. Unless you are the only administrator in your organization, it is difficult to determine which Telnet session you will be granted. If the passwords were different for each Telnet line, you would have to guess your connection, and provide the correct password. To set all the Telnet passwords, use the following syntax:

```
Router(config)#line vty  0  4
Router(config-line)#login
Router(config-line)#password word
```

To access all five Telnet session lines, use the **line vty 0 4** command. Notice that after the VTY line is accessed, the remainder of the prompts and commands look identical to those used in the console password configuration. Also note that like the console password, you will be prompted for a password as soon as a connection is made to the device, but before you receive the router prompt. If an enable password is also set, you will have to provide that as well to enter privileged EXEC mode.

Auxiliary Passwords

The AUX port makes a remote connection to a router using a modem. This is fairly secure in itself because dial-up information must be known to make the connection. However, it can also be more of a problem to trace, because the person making the connection to the device might not even be on the network or in the same building. The auxiliary password works like the console or VTY (Telnet) passwords, prompting at the point a connection is made to the device, but before entry is granted. To configure an auxiliary password, use the following commands:

```
Router(config)#line aux 0
Router(config-line)#login
Router(config-line)#password word
```

Notice again that the syntax is the same as that used for both the console and VTY lines. Also keep in mind that the second command **`login`** is important because it tells the device that login authentication is required. Without providing that, the device will not prompt for a password.

To provide additional security and allow individualized access, an administrator can create usernames and passwords for login access to VTY, consoles, and AUX lines. This is a two-step process. First the administrator has to create a list of usernames and passwords on the device in global configuration mode. The command to do this is as follows:

```
Router(config)#username name password word
```

For example, when setting up John, Mary, and Jack with access, the following commands are necessary:

```
Router(config)#username john password donttell
Router(config)#username mary password verysecure
Router(config)#username jack password nooneknowns
```

To require a login username when accessing the console, Telnet, or AUX lines, replace the command **`login`** with **`login local`**. This tells the device to prompt for a username in addition to the password. Each password is encrypted and case sensitive. Type the second command as follows to configure all Telnet lines for user authentication:

```
Router(config)#line vty 0 4
Router(config-line)#login local
```

Note: Remember that passwords are case sensitive.

To prevent all login access to any of the line levels, use the command **`no login`**. By default, only the console line is activated. The VTY and AUX lines do not provide login until configured to do so.

Verifying the Configuration With Show Commands

To view all the configurations that have been made throughout this lesson, you can use the following **`show`** commands.

Show Interface Ethernet0

To view configuration settings that were made for all interfaces on the router, use the command `Router#`**`show interface`**. To display information for a particular Ethernet interface, use the command `Router#`**`show int e0`** to access the first Ethernet port. Each individual interface can be accessed one at a time using this syntax by changing the number. The Show Interface Ethernet0 Command Screen Capture displays the typical information seen when using this command.

```
router#show int e0
Ethernet0 is up, line protocol is up
  Hardware is Lance, address is 0000.0c8d.5c9d (bia 0000.0c8d.5c9d)
  Internet Address is 172.16.20.1 /24
  MTU 1500 bytes, BW 10000 Kbit, DLY 1000 usec, rely 255/255, load 1/255
  Encapsulation ARPA, loopback not set, keepalive set (10 sec)
  ARP type: ARPA, ARP Timeout 04:00:00
  Last input 00:00:04, output 00:00:07, output hang never
  Last clearing of "show interface" counters never
  Queueing strategy: fifo
  Output queue 0/40, 0 drops; input queue 0/75, 0 drops
  5 minute input rate 0 bits/sec, 0 packets/sec
  5 minute output rate 0 bits/sec, 0 packets/sec
     396 packets input, 41743 bytes, 0 no buffer
     Received 58 broadcasts, 0 runts, 0 giants, 0 throttles
     0 input errors, 0 CRC, 0 frame, 0 overrun, 0 ignored, 0 abort
     0 input packets with dribble condition detected
     472 packets output, 47379 bytes, 0 underruns
     0 output errors, 0 collisions, 2 interface resets
 Text Omitted
```

Show Interface Ethernet0 Command

The following bullets provide a brief description of each line or component displayed using the **show interface** command:

- **Ethernet0 is up, line protocol is up**—The first part indicates that the interface is physically configured and enabled. Other options include down (physical) and administratively down (disabled). The second half defines whether the Data-Link Layer protocol set is sending/receiving and can use the interface. Options include up or down. Different line states will be discussed in further detail later.
- **Hardware**—This line displays the hardware type and burned-in address (BIA), also called the MAC address of the device.
- **Internet address**—The configured IP address is shown with a prefix instead of subnet mask.
- **MTU, BW, DLY, rely, and load**—This line specifies the maximum transmission unit (MTU), which indicates the size of the frame. (Ethernet frames are typically 1,500 bytes.) `BW` stands for bandwidth; it represents the interface capabilities (10,000 kbps = 10 Mbps). The last three items are delay (`DLY`), reliability (`rely`), and `load` of the line. These values are calculated over a 5-minute period and used as appropriate to make path selection. When a protocol such as EIGRP or OSPF is used.
- **Encapsulation**—This line identifies the encapsulation type. **Loopback** and **keepalive** indicate whether these have been set.
- **Last input**—This is the time since the last packet was received. **Last output** is the time since the last packet was sent. **Output** `hang` indicates whether an interface had to be reset because of transmission timeout. The numbers are displayed in hours, minutes, and seconds. Over 24 hours shows days and hours.
- **Last clearing**—This line indicates the time since the counters displayed below were reset to zero. Routing statistics such as delay, reliability, and load that affect routing protocols are not reset.
- **Queuing strategy**—This indicates packets are sent first in, first out. Other priority options may also be displayed.

- `Output and input queue`—The first value represents the number of packets waiting to be processed in the output and input queues, respectively. The second number after the slash is the actual size of the queue. If the number of packets waiting exceeds the maximum queue size, they will be dropped, which is indicated by `drops`, the last statistic on that line.
- `5 minute input rate` and `5 minute output rate`—These lines indicate the average number of bps and packets per second that have been received or sent by the router over the last 5 minutes. These numbers are a weighted average over the time period and can only provide a general estimate of the statistics during the time period.

Several statistics are displayed together. The individual purpose of each is as follows:

- `Packets input`—Indicates the number of received packets that are error-free (not discarded).
- `Bytes`—Indicates the total number of bytes, including the frame header of all transmissions.
- `No buffer`—Indicates the transmission had to be dropped because the buffer was full. A high no buffer count may be an indication of an Ethernet broadcast storm.
- `Received broadcasts`—Indicates the number of multicast or broadcast packets received. If broadcast domains are designed properly, the broadcast statistic should be less than 20 percent of the number of input packets. Otherwise, review the broadcast traffic patterns to see how the segment could be improved.
- `Runts`—Indicates the number of Ethernet frames that are smaller than the required minimum of 64 bytes. Runts are discarded and are usually caused by collisions or external interference. Any number other than 0 is checked to determine the cause.
- `Giants`—Indicates the number of Ethernet frames that are larger than the MTU of 1,518 (now 1,522 bytes). Giants are discarded and are often caused by incompatible or proprietary header fields.
- `Throttles`—Used in low memory as a flow-control method to slow down transmissions and process each packet consecutively.

- **`Input errors`**—Counts the number of errors for incoming packets from the list of options above and below. Some packets may have more than one error, making this statistic hard to validate.
- **`CRC`**—Performed by the router to compute the cyclic redundancy check (CRC) value specified by the sender. If the two calculations do not match, the packet header is considered invalid. Check for bad network interface cards (NICs), collisions, or external interference factors.
- **`Frame`**—Indicates the frames received with CRC errors and an incorrect number of octets. Check for bad NICs, collisions, or external interference factors as you would when troubleshooting a CRC error.
- **`Overrun`**—Indicates the rate of incoming transmission that exceeded the hardware buffer on the receiving (next hop) device.
- **`Ignored`**—Indicates incoming packets that are ignored because there are no internal buffers for processing. This buffer is different from the no buffer statistics. This can be caused by broadcast storms and high bursts of traffic.
- **`Input packets with dribble condition detected`**—This informational statistic indicates frames that are slightly longer than the specified MTU but were processed by the router.
- **`Packets output`** and **`bytes`**—Indicate, respectively, the total number of packets and bytes (including frame header) transmitted by the router.
- **`Underruns`**—Indicates the number of times the router could not keep up with transmissions being received. This is not always reported.
- **`Output errors`**—Indicates the number of all errors transmitted from an interface. As with input errors, some packets may have more than one error, making this statistic hard to validate.
- **`Collisions`**—Indicates the number of retransmissions required due to Ethernet collisions. The cause of this error could be overlong cable segments or too many repeaters.
- **`Interface resets`**—Indicates the number of times an interface has been reset. This may be caused by transmission delays, slow or absent keepalives, clock signal problems, loopback problems, or interfaces that are shut down on one end, but are trying to communicate on the other.

Show Interface Serial0

A serial interface has a lot of the same statistics as an Ethernet interface. If using the command **show interface**, serial interfaces will be displayed directly after all Ethernet interfaces are displayed. To get statistics specific to the serial interface, use the command `Router#`**show interface s0**, replacing the number with the appropriate number for each serial interface as necessary. The Show Interface Serial0 Command Screen Capture displays the information typically found in this statistics screen. Refer to the previous bullets for details about certain statistics.

```
router#show int s0
Serial0 is up, line protocol is up
  Hardware is HD97530
  Internet Address is 172.16.30.1 /24
  MTU 1500 bytes, BW 64 Kbit, DLY 1000 usec, rely 255/255, load 1/255
  Encapsulation HDLC, loopback not set, keepalive set (10 sec)
  Last input 00:00:04, output 00:00:07, output hang never
  Last clearing of "show interface" counters never
  Input queue: 10/75/0 (size/max/drops); Total output drops: 0
  Queueing strategy: weighted fair
  Output queue: 3/1000/64/0 (size/max total/threshold/drops)
  Conversations 1/1/256 (active/max active/max total)
  Reserved Conversations 0/0 (allocated/max allocated)
  5 minute input rate 0 bits/sec, 0 packets/sec
  5 minute output rate 0 bits/sec, 0 packets/sec
Text Omitted
```

Show Interface Serial0 Command

When using **show interface** for both Ethernet and serial interfaces, the first line displays the physical connection status, then the Data Link Layer protocol status. The following bullets list possible conditions and describe what each one means:

- **Serial0 is up, line protocol is up**—The interface is communicating properly both physically and at the Data Link Layer encapsulation protocol.
- **Serial0 is up, line protocol is down**—The interface has physical connectivity, meaning the interface is enabled and passing traffic. However, the Data Link Layer protocol is not able to communicate. This could be due to an encapsulation problem, such as different encapsulation types configured on either side. It could also be caused by the wrong clock rate, no synchronization, or the interface not sending keepalives to maintain interface status.

- **Serial0 is down, line protocol is down**—This indicates that traffic is not being passed due to both a physical and logical problem. Usually this indicates a cable is disconnected or damaged and is not able to send traffic. It is also possible that the remote interface on the other side of the cable is shut down.
- **Serial0 is administratively down, line protocol is down**—This indicates that the interface is shut down and therefore is not sending traffic. To active it, go to the appropriate interface and use the command **no shut**. If the connection is otherwise good, the receiving interface is enabled, and the encapsulation is configured correctly, the status should change to `interface is up, line protocol is up`.

This information can help an administrator determine what action to take when trying to resolve a communication problem on an interface.

Show Controller Serial0

Another show command that is useful when working with serial interfaces is **show controller**. This is particularly helpful when trying to determine which serial interface should be configured as the DCE and which will be the DTE in a back-to-back router connection. Typically a clock signal is provided by the central office (CO) or service provider that the router connects to for WAN communications. In this case the router simply synchronizes with the provided clock signal. However, there are times when routers are connected through serial interfaces and cables that do not go through the CO. Therefore, the device that has the serial cable end labeled DCE will be responsible for providing the clock signal. The DTE-side device, based on the DTE side of the cable, will take the clock signal and synchronize to it. Using the command **show controller s0**, the administrator can easily determine which side to configure the clock rate, without having to see the physical cable. This command displays the information presented on the Show Controller Serial0 Command Screen Capture.

```
Router#show controller serial 0
HD unit 0, idb = 0x121C04, driver structure at 0x127078
buffer size 1524 HD unit 0, V.35 DCE cable
Text Omitted
```

Show Controller Serial0 Command

Show Running-Config

Another valuable show command, **`show running-config`**, displays the configuration currently active and running on a router. This configuration is composed of all the settings created in configuration mode, including the device hostname, passwords, and banner messages, as well as interface configurations, such as IP address, description, and shutdown status. To access this information and verify all the configuration settings made, use the command:

Router#**show run** or

Router#**show running-config**

The running-config file is stored in DRAM and provides the settings necessary for a router to function at any given time. All new configurations are automatically added to memory and activated immediately. However, they are not permanently saved. For now, let us take a look at the Show Run Command Screen Captures, which display the contents of DRAM and the current router configuration.

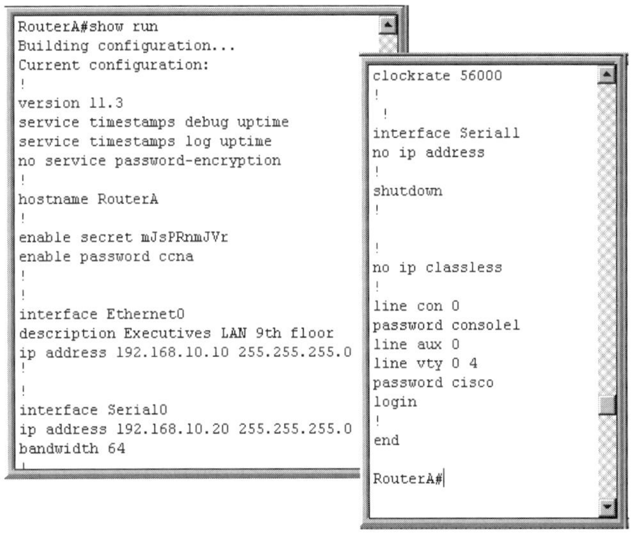

Show Run Command

Notice from the screen captures that the **`show run`** command was entered in privileged EXEC mode. It then queries DRAM and builds the current configuration, which takes a few seconds to generate. This command supplies the IOS version, timestamp, password encryption information, hostname, and enable passwords. The exclamation points provide separation between sections. The next portion of the config provides information for the

Ethernet 0 interface, which includes a description and IP address. Serial 0 is configured and displays an IP address, bandwidth, and clock rate. The running-config file also shows ports that are shut down. It is not specified whether the Ethernet 0 and Serial 0 ports are up and communicating. Notice in the next panel, however, that the Serial 1 interface is shut down. In addition, Serial 1 is not configured with any settings at this time. Finally, the console and VTY lines have passwords set that were not encrypted and can easily be read. To indicate the running-config is complete, the word **`end`** is displayed.

Using the show commands discussed above, you can easily verify a router configuration. **`Show running-config`** is a command used frequently to display current settings or verify any changes made to a router. This display gets longer and more detailed as new configurations are added. **`Show interface`** and **`show run`** are informational commands. Others will be used throughout this class and during administration to obtain more information about a device. A limited number of show commands are available in user EXEC mode. To get a list of the available show commands in either user or privileged EXEC mode, use the helpful feature **`show ?`**.

Verifying and Saving the Configuration

Just as they do on a switch, show commands issued on a router verify the router's configuration. Unlike a switch however, the current running-configuration is not automatically saved. Therefore, it is important for an administrator to save the configuration so that it is available even if the router is turned off. In addition, it is a good idea to back up the IOS and configuration files to another location for recovery purposes.

Remember that the **`show run`** command displays the contents of the configuration currently running on a router from DRAM. The running-config file is volatile, meaning that if a router is powered off, the settings in DRAM will be lost. Over time many settings may be configured on a router, and the router runs them as soon as they are entered. However, they must be saved manually into NVRAM to make sure they are not lost after a restart. Just think how difficult it would be if a production router was restarted and none of the settings were saved. Where would you begin? Hopefully you have a backup, a printout of the configuration, or a really good memory.

Fortunately, the process of saving a configuration is very simple. The running-config file is stored in DRAM and is volatile. The startup-config file is stored in NVRAM and is saved even after a restart. To view the contents and verify whether the two configurations are the same, use the following commands.

To access the configuration in DRAM (volatile), use:

`Router#`**`show run`** or

`Router#`**`show running-config`**

To access the configuration in NVRAM (permanent), use:

`Router#`**`show start`** or

`Router#`**`show startup-config`**

To access the startup configuration in NVRAM in IOS versions 10.3 and earlier, use:

`Router#`**`show config`**

To save a new configuration, or make sure an existing configuration is saved, use the **`copy`** command. Copy can be used for several functions, including copying the saved configuration to current, copying the current configuration to saved, and backing up or restoring the IOS and configuration files from a TFTP server.

The command **`copy run start`** saves the current configuration for future use. All settings currently running on the device will now be available upon future restarts. The **`copy run start`** command completely overwrites the contents of the NVRAM startup-config file. When this command is issued, a router will respond with `Building Configuration...... [OK]`. The proper syntax for the command is:

`Router#`**`copy run start`** or

`Router#`**`copy running-config startup-config`**

Another copy command, **`copy start run`**, reverts the current configuration back to the saved settings. This may roll back a change that has not yet been saved but is causing problems. This command basically overwrites or overlays DRAM, and therefore the router must activate any differences from the startup configuration to the current running-config file. When this command is executed, a router responds by changing the interface shutdown status as appropriate. It indicates the copy is complete with the message `%SYS-5-CONFIG_I: Configured from memory by console.` The syntax for the **`copy start run`** command is as follows:

Router#**copy start run** or

Router#**copy startup-config running-config**

The Copy Commands Screen Capture shows the **copy run start** and **copy start run** commands and the results of using each one.

```
RouterA#copy run start
Building configuration...

[OK]


RouterA#copy start run
%LINEPROTO-5-UPDOWN: Line protocol on Interface TokenRing0, changed state to down
%LINK-5-CHANGED: Interface TokenRing0, changed state to initializing
%LINEPROTO-5-UPDOWN: Line protocol on Interface TokenRing0, changed state to up
%LINK-3-UPDOWN: Interface TokenRing0, changed state to up
%SYS-5-CONFIG_I: Configured from memory by console
RouterA#
```

Copy Commands

Review Questions

1. When configuring the clock rate, what will the command prompt look like?

   a. `Router(config-if)#`

   b. `Router(config-line)#`

   c. `Router(config-controller)#`

   d. `Router(config-subif)#`

2. Assume the **`show interface`** command displays the following: `Ethernet 0 is administratively down, line protocol is down`. What is the status of the interface?

   a. The interface is functioning normally and sending traffic.

   b. The interface is not functioning normally, but is still passing traffic.

   c. The physical interface is functioning properly, but Ethernet is not configured correctly.

   d. The interface is shut down.

3. Which is considered a major command?

   a. **`clock rate 56000`**

   b. **`no shut`**

   c. **`int e0`**

   d. **`ip address 172.16.50.1 255.255.255.0`**

4. What configuration command could be used along with a username and password to authenticate each person's access individually?

   a. **`login`**

   b. **`authentication`**

   c. **`user login`**

   d. **`login local`**

5. From the prompt `Router(config)#`, which methods could be used to go back to privileged EXEC mode? (Choose two.)

   a. **`exit`**

   b. **`disable`**

   c. **CTRL+Z**

   d. **`enable`**

6. What would the prompt look line when configuring Telnet access?
   a. `Router(config)#`
   b. `Router(config-line)#`
   c. `Router(config-if)#`
   d. `Router(config-vty)#`
7. Which show command would be used to indicate which side is the serial DCE connection?
   a. **`show interface s0`**
   b. **`show running-config`**
   c. **`show dce`**
   d. **`show controller s0`**
8. Which of the following are true regarding the encrypted enable password? (Choose two.)
   a. They are entered using the command **`enable secret`** *`word`*.
   b. They are case sensitive.
   c. They are sent across the network as clear text.
   d. The are entered using the command **`enable encrypted`** *`password`*.
9. Which commands could be used to enter global configuration mode? (Choose two.)
   a. `Router#`**`configure terminal`**
   b. `Router>`**`global config`**
   c. `Router#`**`configure memory`**
   d. `Router#`**`config t`**
10. Match the following with the correct description:

    Serial0 is up, line protocol is up _______

    Serial0 is up, line protocol is down _______

    Serial0 is down, line protocol is down _______

    Serial0 is administratively down, line protocol is down _______

a. The device has been shut down.

b. The device is physically connected but not communicating.

c. The device is communicating at the Physical and Data Link Layers.

d. The device is configured but not communicating.

Extended Activities

To obtain hands-on experience using the commands outlined in this lesson, visit the Student Resources section of WestNet Learning's Web site at **http://www.westnetlearning.com**.

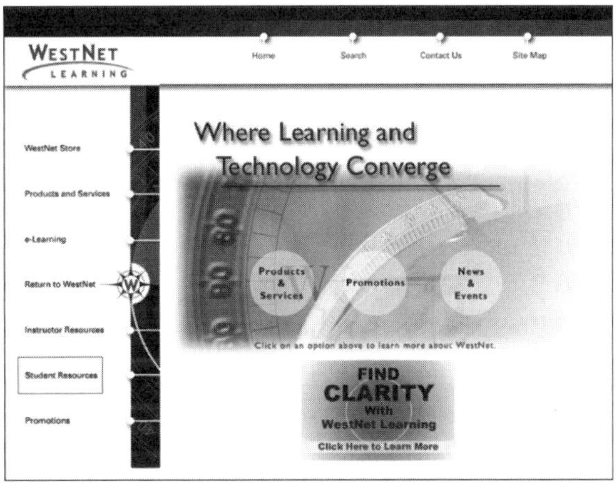

To enter the site, use your e-mail address to login and then type in this course's ISBN number. After you're in the Resources pages, look for the Suggested lab options associated with this module and lesson. Then answer the following questions.

1. After typing the command **`config t`**, what does the resulting prompt look like?

   ____

2. What command is used to assign a hostname?

   ____

3. What command is used to set a message of the day banner?

   ____

4. What command configures an encrypted enable password?

____

5. What command configures a nonencrypted password?

____

6. What command is used to access the first Ethernet interface?

____

7. How did the prompt change to indicate you are in interface configuration mode?

____

8. What are two possible ways to exit global configuration mode?

____

9. What command is used to display the current configuration?

____

10. What command is used to configure the clock rate on the serial interface?

____

11. On which side of the serial connection must the clock rate be set?

____

12. What is the default bandwidth across a serial interface?

____

13. What command is used to activate an interface?

____

14. What command is used to deactivate an interface?

____

15. What command is used to save a configuration?

____

Summary

Switches and routers play a very important role in a network environment. They provide security, scalability, connectivity, and network functionality. Lesson 1 presented an overview of the Cisco IOS found on many network devices. It also discussed the CLI, the administrative and monitoring interface. Lesson 2 discussed the physical startup process for a switch. It also discussed how to log in to the switch, and reviewed a number of Help features and show commands. Lesson 3 did the same for a router. The router startup is somewhat similar to a switch, however, if a router does not find a startup configuration file, it will perform a setup process that allows for simple configuration. The CLI functions are almost identical in the EXEC modes, Help feature, and many show commands. A router, however, has several different configuration modes, mainly to configure serial interfaces and router parameters.

Lesson 3 also reviewed the available configuration modes, and discussed how to view the configuration files. Lesson 4 ended this module with more configuration commands. The commands introduced in this lesson include those necessary to configure and start or shut down Ethernet and serial interfaces, set IP address(es), assign a router a hostname, and a number of other basic configuration options. This lesson ended with a few show commands that verify the configuration settings.

The Summary of Commands Table summarizes the syntax of the various commands introduced in this module.

Summary of Commands

Command Prompt, Syntax, and Options	Description
`Enter Selection: [M] Menu, [K] command line, [I] IP configuration`	Provides user interface options. K is selected to access the CLI, which is used to access user EXEC mode on the switch.
`Switch>`**`enable`** or **`en`**	Enters privileged EXEC mode, also called "enable mode."
`Switch>`**`exit`** or **`logout`**	Ends the current connected session.
`Switch#`**`disable`** or **`dis`**	Leaves enable mode and returns to user EXEC mode.
`?`	Provides context-sensitive help at any location.

Summary of Commands (Continued)

Command Prompt, Syntax, and Options	Description
`Switch#`**`show version`** or **`sh ver`**	Displays the IOS version, hostname, hardware, network interfaces, base Ethernet address, and so forth.
`Switch#`**`show runnning-config`** or **`sh run`**	Displays the current configuration of the switch, including the hostname, IP settings, and interface configurations.
`Switch#`**`show interface`** *`[port]`* or **`sh int`**	Shows all interfaces on the switch; a single port can also be displayed. Includes port state, interface type, MAC address, MTU size, STP configuration, and other settings.
`Switch#`**`show ip`**	Displays address, subnet, gateway, VLANs, domain name, name, and HTTP server IP addresses.
`Switch#`**`config t`**	Enters global terminal configuration mode, prompt changes to `Switch(config)#`, and allows configuration commands to be entered.
`Switch(config)#`**`exit`** or **`CTRL+Z`**	Exits global configuration mode.
`Switch(config)#`**`hostname`** *`host_name`*	Assigns a hostname to the switch; the prompt reflects the name.
`Switch(config)#`**`ip address`** *`ip-address subnet-mask`*	Sets an IP address and subnet mask on the switch, which is used to Telnet in to the switch from the network.
`Switch(config)#`**`ip default-gateway`** *`gateway-ip-address`*	Sets the IP address for the network's default gateway.
`Router>`**`en`** or **`enable`**	Moves from user EXEC mode to privileged EXEC mode. The prompt changes to `Router#`.
`Router#`**`dis`** or **`disable`**	Moves from privileged EXEC mode back to user EXEC mode.
`Router>`**`logout`** or **`exit`**	Logs out of user EXEC mode.
`Router#`**`show history`**	Displays the last 10 commands by default.
`Router#`**`terminal history size`** *`number`*	Changes the history buffer size from 10 up to 256 commands for the current session.
`Router#`**`history`** *`number`*	Changes the history buffer size from 10 up to 256 commands for all future sessions.

Summary of Commands (Continued)

Command Prompt, Syntax, and Options	Description
Router#**terminal editing**	Allows the TAB, CTRL, and ESC keys to be used for edits.
Router#**terminal no editing**	Prevents the special edit keys from being used.
Router#**config t**	Enters global terminal configuration mode.
Router(config)#**exit** or **Ctrl+Z**	Exits configuration mode and goes back to privileged mode.
Router(config)#**hostname** *hostname*	Sets the hostname for a router. The prompt changes.
Router(config)#**banner motd #** *message* **#**	Sets a message of the day banner. Others are available.
Router(config)#**int** *port-type number* Router(config)#**int** *e0*	Accesses interface configuration mode using the port type (for example, Ethernet or serial) and number. The prompt changes to Router(config-if)#.
Router(config)#**int** *port-type number.number*	Accesses subinterface configuration mode by specifying the port type, physical number, and then logical subinterface number. The prompt changes to Router(config-subif)#.
Router(config)#**line vty 0 4**	Accesses all five virtual terminal lines. The prompt changes to Router(config-line)#. Other line options include console and AUX ports.
Router(config)#**router rip** or **router igrp** *number*	Configures a routing protocol. The prompt changes to Router(config-router)# for additional settings.
Router(config-if)#**ip address** *address subnet*	Sets an IP address and subnet for a specific router port. Must be set in interface configuration mode.
Router(config-if)#**desc** *description*	Sets a description for a specific interface.
Router(config-if)#**clock rate** *baud*	Sets the clock rate for a DCE serial interface.
Router(config-if)#**bandwidth** *size*	Sets the bandwidth for a serial interface. Otherwise it will default to a T1 connection or 1.544 Mbps.

Summary of Commands (Continued)

Command Prompt, Syntax, and Options	Description
`Router(config-if)#`**`shutdown`** or **`no shutdown`**	Shutdown – Disables an interface. No shutdown—Enables an interface.
`Router(config)#`**`enable secret`** *`word`*	Sets an encrypted password to enter privileged EXEC (enable) mode.
`Router(config)#`**`enable password`** *`word`*	Sets a nonencrypted password for privileged EXEC (enable) mode.
`Router(config)#`**`line console 0`** `Router(config-line)#`**`login`** `Router(config-line)#`**`password`** *`word`*	Sets a password for the directly connected console. The command can also set Telnet (line VTY 0-4) or AUX ports (line aux 0).
`Router#`**`show interface`** or **`sh int e0`**	Displays the interface configuration and statistics.
`Router#`**`show running-config`** or **`sh run`**	Displays the current router configuration stored in DRAM. This is not saved in the event of power loss.
`Router#`**`show startup-config`** or **`sh start`**	Displays the contents of NVRAM. This area is saved during a power loss.

Module 8 Quiz

1. Which of the following commands is used to obtain information about a router's current configuration?

   a. **show running-config**

   b. **show startup-config**

   c. **show cdp neighbors**

   d. **show flash**

2. Which command is used to enter global configuration terminal mode?

   a. **configure**

   b. **config t**

   c. **config m**

   d. **config n**

3. Which command prompt indicates you are currently in global configuration mode?

   a. Router#

   b. Router>

   c. Router(config)#

   d. Router(config-if)#

4. Which edit key combination is used to go back to the very beginning of a command?

   a. **CTRL+B**

   b. **CTRL+A**

   c. **CTRL+F**

   d. **CTRL+E**

5. Which of the following commands enables you to get a listing of the commands last entered?

   a. **show terminal**

   b. **show running-config**

   c. **show memory**

   d. **show history**

6. The prompt `Router>` indicates a router is currently in which mode?
   a. Privileged EXEC mode
   b. User EXEC mode
   c. Global configuration mode
   d. Interface configuration mode
7. Which of the following commands would you use to enable an interface?
   a. **enable**
   b. **no shut**
   c. **activate**
   d. **on**
8. The command `Router(config)#`**`enable secret cisco`** is used for which purpose?
   a. To configure a Telnet password of Cisco
   b. To configure an encrypted password of Cisco
   c. To configure a clear text password of Cisco
   d. To configure a console password of Cisco
9. The prompt `Router(config-line)#` is used for which purpose?
   a. Configuring the VTY, console, or auxiliary connections
   b. Configuring the serial interfaces
   c. Configuring the WAN interfaces
   d. Configuring the router line protocol
10. Which piece of information is not found in the running-config?
    a. Host name
    b. Enable passwords
    c. IP addresses of interfaces
    d. The IOS version

11. Which two methods allow you to move from global configuration mode to privileged EXEC mode?
    a. **Exit** and **disable**
    b. **Exit** and press **CTRL+Z**
    c. Press **CTRL+Z** and **disable**
    d. **Logout** and **disable**
12. Which of the following allows you to get help at any location in the CLI?
    a. **?**
    b. **help**
    c. **exit**
    d. **enable**
13. An important setting on some routers is the clock rate used for synchronization. What type of interface requires that this setting be configured to work properly?
    a. Serial CSU/DSU
    b. Serial DCE connection
    c. Serial DTE connection
    d. Any WAN connection
14. A special banner message used to display information for a particular day is called what?
    a. **banner line**
    b. **banner exec**
    c. **banner login**
    d. **banner motd**
15. What is the configuration setting required to define the 10-Mbps Ethernet media type for an RJ-45 connector on a UTP cable?
    a. Router(config-if)#**media-type AUI**
    b. Router(config-if)#**media-type 100baset**
    c. Router(config-if)#**media-type 10baset**
    d. Router(config-if)#**media-type mii**

16. Which command could be used on the console line to prevent the session from timing out after 10 minutes?

    a. `Router(config)#`**`logging synchronous`**

    b. `Router(config-line)#`**`no logout`**

    c. `Router(config-line)#`**`no timeout`**

    d. `Router(config-line)#`**`exec-timeout 0 0`**

17. Which of the following settings could be configured at the following prompt: `Router(config)#`. (Choose two.)

    a. IP address for the interface

    b. hostname

    c. username and password

    d. interface description

18. If you type in a command and the device replies with the response "`%incomplete command`," what is the problem?

    a. One of the words is misspelled.

    b. There are not enough letters in the command to match the syntax.

    c. A keyword or value is missing.

    d. The command is being confused with another command.

19. What is the purpose of assigning a hostname?

    a. To provide an easy-to-identify name for the device prompt

    b. To access a device

    c. To call the device to act as a network host

    d. To use common names instead of network names

20. How can you abort the initial setup process if you make a mistake and want to start over?

    a. Press the **CTRL+Z** keys together

    b. Type **`exit`**

    c. Type **`end`**

    d. Press the **CTRL+C** keys together

21. Which key allows you to see an entire page of text after `---MORE---` is displayed?
    a. Enter
    b. Return
    c. Spacebar
    d. Esc
22. Which mode allows you to view the bandwidth being used on a switch by means of the LEDs?
    a. System LED
    b. Port LED
    c. Util LED
    d. RPS LED
23. Which configuration prompt is used to access the component that could configure a serial interface for T1 or E1 WAN connectivity?
    a. `Router(config-if)#`
    b. `Router(config-controller)#`
    c. `Router(config-t1)#`
    d. `Router(config-wan)#`
24. What is used to access the CLI on a Catalyst switch?
    a. K
    b. Enable
    c. Enter
    d. Access
25. Which connection methods require an IP address to be assigned? (Choose two.)
    a. Telnet
    b. Console
    c. Auxiliary
    d. TFTP

Module 9
Managing the Network Environment

This module provides the tools an administrator needs to manage a network and its devices. It begins with an introduction to the Cisco Discovery Protocol (CDP). As its name implies, CDP can discover any directly connected network device. It is network protocol- and topology-independent, which allows it to be transmitted across any network environment, even if misconfigured. CDP uses a broadcast for transmissions and sends updates every 60 seconds.

Lesson 2 discusses Telnet, a service that originated with the "telephone network." This tool provides a means to remotely configure and monitor devices instead of requiring a directly connected administrative terminal. It is frequently used for connections to routers, switches, telephone switch equipment, and mainframes. It provides a command line interface (CLI) into a remote device.

Lesson 3 provides an overview of router components, including memory, the Internetwork Operating System (IOS), and configuration files. It discusses the steps taken when a router starts up: performing a power-on self test (POST), finding and loading the IOS, and finding and loading the configuration file. For this process to work, the configuration register stored in a router's nonvolatile random access memory (NVRAM) is accessed. The configuration register has a boot field that tells the router where to look for and load the IOS and startup-configuration file.

Lesson 4 describes the steps involved in backing up or restoring the IOS and configuration files. Backups are necessary before performing an IOS upgrade or to prevent significant downtime if the operating system (OS) becomes corrupt. The startup configuration file of each router should also be backed up to prevent extensive reconfiguration or when replacing the router.

Finally, Lesson 5 presents the administrative tasks of adds, moves, and changes. It also discusses a few administrator tools used for faster device access and troubleshooting. These tools include host-name tables that provide name-to-Internet Protocol (IP) address resolution, ping to test connectivity, and traceroute to determine the path a packet takes through a network to its destination. We also discuss debug commands that can help an administrator by displaying traffic and processes as they are happening.

Lessons

1. Discovering Network Neighbors
2. Connecting to Remote Devices
3. Router Startup and the Configuration Register
4. Cisco Device Management
5. Network Administration

Lesson 1—Discovering Network Neighbors

CDP is a very useful tool that is enabled by default on all Cisco routers and switch devices, and even devices such as Cisco IP telephones. It is network protocol- and topology-independent. It exchanges information with directly connected devices running CDP. This is helpful to an administrator, who often does not have the luxury of installing and configuring the devices initially. Using CDP, an administrator can learn the physical connections and document the network environment. The only requirement for CDP to work is a physical connection and an active interface. This lesson reviews CDP and presents a number of show commands that can be used to gather network information. It also reviews some configuration commands used to adapt CDP for a specific network environment.

Objectives

At the end of this lesson you will be able to:

- Discuss the key components of CDP
- Identify information obtained with CDP
- Use the show CDP neighbors command
- Monitor and configure CDP settings
- Document a network using CDP information

Key Point

CDP is independent of Network Layer protocols. This allows it to display important information about network connectivity without depending on other configurations. All that is necessary for CDP to work is an active interface; it will "discover" its neighboring devices automatically.

Key Components of CDP

CDP is a Cisco proprietary protocol that is helpful in gathering information about directly connected devices. It runs on Cisco routers using IOS version 10.3 or later, as well as Cisco switches and hubs. CDP can be used to help troubleshoot a physical connection, as well as document a network.

CDP works at the Data Link Layer of the Open Systems Interconnection (OSI) model, connecting physical media with upper-layer protocols. This concept is illustrated on the CDP at the Data Link Layer Diagram. Therefore, CDP is considered network protocol-independent, meaning it does not require IP, Internet Packet Exchange (IPX), or a routing protocol to communicate with another device. The advantage of this architecture is that CDP can detect other Cisco devices, even if their Network Layer addresses or routing protocols are misconfigured. In addition, CDP provides connections between devices running different Network Layer protocols.

Network Layer	IP, Novell's IPX, Appletalk, Others
Data Link Layer	CDP works in conjunction with Ethernet, Token Ring, Frame relay, ATM, PPP
Physical Layer	LAN - Coax, UTP, STP, Fiber, Wireless WAN - Serial point-to-point, dialup, wireless

CDP at the Data Link Layer

It is topology-independent, meaning it can also be used over Ethernet, Token Ring, Fiber Distributed Data Interface (FDDI), and serial connections. It uses Subnetwork Access Protocol (SNAP) to communicate. Therefore, all network environments that support SNAP can use CDP. In addition to the local area network (LAN) environments, this also includes frame relay and Asynchronous Transfer Mode (ATM), and wide area network (WAN) connections. Although CDP is automatically enabled on all Cisco devices, it can be turned off on a port-by-port basis.

A router or switch maintains a table of information gathered using CDP. This table is updated with new information on an ongoing basis using two main CDP components:

- **CDP timer**—The CDP timer determines how often CDP packets are sent out all active interfaces. By default, CDP packets are sent as a broadcast every 60 seconds. This number can be increased or decreased to balance network traffic.
- **CDP hold time**—The hold time is the amount of time an entry stays in the CDP table. The default is 180 seconds, which means if the device does not communicate in that period of time, the entry is dropped from the table.

The CDP configuration options (presented later) allow you to change these settings and turn off CDP in traffic-intensive networks.

The most recent release of this protocol, CDP version-2 (CDPv2), provides several advanced features. It has a built-in reporting function, as well as faster error detection and tracking. Error messages can be logged to a console or, to reduce the impact on a device, to an error tracking server. Two major differences from the earlier CDP version include identification of mismatched Institute of Electrical and Electronics Engineers (IEEE) 802.1Q native virtual local area network (VLAN) IDs, and detection of different duplex settings on connecting ports.

Information Obtained With CDP

You can use a number of show commands to gather information about a network using CDP. Each command displays specific information and several commands are often used together to provide a more complete picture of the network.

Show CDP

The **show cdp** command provides the timer and hold time configuration information. The default time of 60 seconds and hold time of 180 seconds are shown on the top half of the Show CDP and Show CDP Neighbors Commands Screen Capture.

```
RouterB#show cdp
Global CDP information:
        Sending CDP packets every 60 seconds
        Sending a holdtime value of 180 seconds

RouterB#show cdp neighbors
Capability Codes: R - Router, T - Trans Bridge, B - Source Route Bridge
                  S - Switch, H - Host, I - IGMP, r - Repeater

Device ID        Local Intrfce     Holdtme    Capability  Platform  Port ID
RouterC             Ser 1          158            R        2500     Ser 0
RouterA             Ser 0          150            R        2500     Ser 0

RouterB#
```

Show CDP and Show CDP Neighbors Commands

Show CDP Neighbors

The **show cdp neighbors** and **show cdp entry** commands gather basic information about connected devices. They include the following information, as the Show CDP Command Screen Diagram displays:

- **Device ID**—Provides the hostname of the device directly connected to the interface.
- **Local interface (Local Intrfce)**—Identifies the outgoing interface used to connect to the network; also referred to as the local port.
- **Hold time (Holdtme)**—Specifies the amount of time information about a device is maintained. If new information is not received and the hold time expires, the entry is dropped.
- **Capability**—Identifies the device functionality (for example, R = router, S = switch, H = host, r =repeater, and B = bridge).
- **Platform**—Identifies the model of the connected device.
- **Port ID**—Identifies the incoming interface used to connect the remote device.

To gather more detailed information about a particular device, specifically the IP address (Network Layer) and IOS version information, use either of the following commands:

Router#**show cdp neighbors detail** or
Router#**show cdp entry ***

Note that the `show cdp entry *` command does not work on the Catalyst 1900 switch. Use `show cdp neighbors detail` instead.

The information and format that these two commands provide is shown on the Show CDP Neighbors Detail Command Screen Capture.

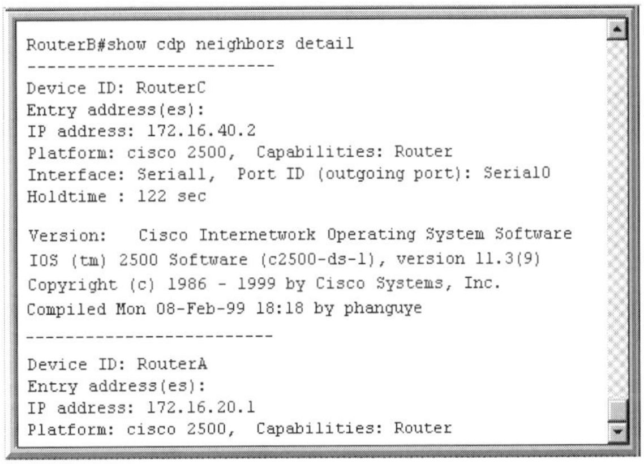

```
RouterB#show cdp neighbors detail
-------------------------
Device ID: RouterC
Entry address(es):
IP address: 172.16.40.2
Platform: cisco 2500,  Capabilities: Router
Interface: Serial1,  Port ID (outgoing port): Serial0
Holdtime : 122 sec

Version:   Cisco Internetwork Operating System Software
IOS (tm) 2500 Software (c2500-ds-1), version 11.3(9)
Copyright (c) 1986 - 1999 by Cisco Systems, Inc.
Compiled Mon 08-Feb-99 18:18 by phanguye
-------------------------
Device ID: RouterA
Entry address(es):
IP address: 172.16.20.1
Platform: cisco 2500,  Capabilities: Router
```

Show CDP Neighbors Detail Command

Notice that this command includes the hostname of the device, platform, capabilities, and interface information. The main difference between this command and the **show cdp neighbors** command is that this command also provides the Network Layer address of the connected device (in this case, the IP address). This can be particularly helpful when documenting a large network environment. After you have identified the IP address of the next device, you can access it using Telnet, and use the **show cdp** command again to determine the next set of directly connected devices. Cisco uses this technique in their CiscoWorks 2000 network management software to discover the network topology.

Monitoring and Configuring CDP

You can use several commands to monitor and configure CDP, as presented in this section.

Show CDP Interface

The **show cdp interface** command shows the current configuration and encapsulation type of each interface. It displays information about the CDP timer and hold time setting, as well as the port status (enabled or disabled). Information available from this command is displayed on the Show CDP Interface and Show CDP Traffic Commands Screen Capture.

```
RouterB#show cdp interface
Ethernet0 is up, line protocol is up
   Encapsulation ARPA
   Sending CDP packets every 60 seconds
   Holdtime is 180 seconds
Serial0 is up, line protocol is up
   Encapsulation HDLC
   Sending CDP packets every 60 seconds
   Holdtime is 180 seconds
Serial1 is up, line protocol is up
   Encapsulation HDLC
   Sending CDP packets every 60 seconds
   Holdtime is 180 seconds

RouterB#show cdp traffic
   CDP couters:
        Packets output: 534,     Input:38
        Hdr syntax: 0,    Chksum error: 0,    Encaps failed: 2
        No Memory: 0,  Invalid Packet: 0,    Fragmented: 0
```

Show CDP Interface and Show CDP Traffic Commands

Show CDP Traffic

The **show cdp traffic** command gathers information about the number of inbound and outbound CDP packets sent and received by a device. It also includes statistical information about bad packets and other network errors. The error statistics reported with this command include fragmented or invalid packets, syntax or checksum errors, failed encapsulations, and buffer overflow (out of memory) errors. The **show cdp traffic** command is not available on the Catalyst 1900 series switch.

Other CDP Configuration Options

CDP can create a lot of traffic on a network because each device sends a CDP packet out all active interfaces every 60 seconds by default. This may be unnecessary across some links. The following configuration settings allow you to control CDP and maintain its functionality:

- `Router(config)#`**`no cdp run`**—The command **`no cdp run`** is executed from global configuration mode on any Cisco device and disables CDP for the entire device. The device will no longer send CDP updates, and thus, other devices on the network will not learn about this device. The **`cdp run`** command is not available on the Catalyst 1900 switch. Instead, use **`cdp enable`** or **`no cdp enable`** at the interface level.
- `Router(config)#`**`cdp timer`** *`number`*—The **`cdp timer`** command changes the amount of time between CDP updates. The default is 60 seconds. To change this value, provide a number (in seconds) after the **`cdp timer`** command.
- `Router(config)#`**`cdp hold time`** *`number`*—The **`cdp hold time`** command is used to change the amount of time an entry is maintained in the CDP table of information. The longer the hold time, the longer the entry will be maintained without receiving updates.
- `Router(config-if)#`**`no cdp enable`**—The **`no cdp enable`** command shuts off CDP on a particular interface. No CDP updates will be sent or received on this port; no other interfaces will be affected.
- `Router(config-if)#`**`cdp enable`**—The **`cdp enable`** command activates CDP updates for a particular interface if they have previously been disabled. This only affects the specific interface.

Documenting a Network Using CDP Information

As this lesson has explained, CDP information is automatically distributed to all directly connected devices, unless it has been disabled for the device or a specific interface. Therefore, using the commands listed in this lesson, an administrator can get a better understanding of the network topology and use that information to build a logical and physical map of the network. It is important to remember that the administrator can only get information from one device at a time. The CDP Directly Connected Devices Diagram shows several Cisco network devices connected to Router 2. The accompanying `show cdp neighbors` screen capture shows the CDP neighbors of which Router 2 is aware. Although there are other devices are on the network, Router 2 can only "see" those that are directly connected and running CDP.

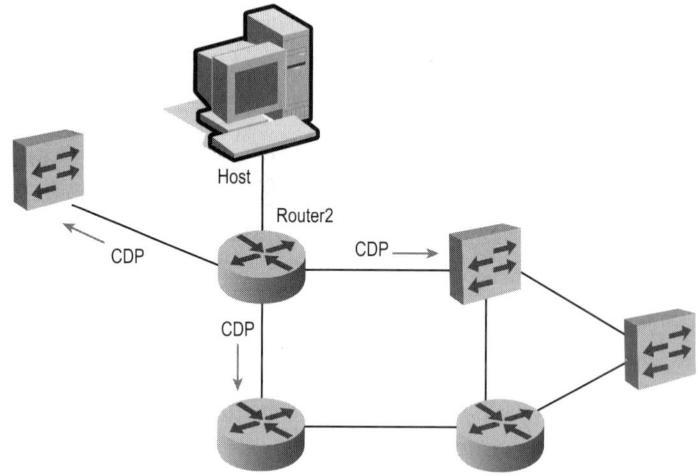


```
Router2#show cdp neighbors
Capability Codes: R - Router, T - Trans Bridge, B - Source Route Bridge
                  S - Switch, H - Host, I - IGMP, r - Repeater

Device ID        Local Intrfce     Holdtme    Capability  Platform  Port ID
Router1             Ser 1          158            R         2600     Ser 0
Switch_2900         Eth 0          150            S         2900     Eth 0/1
Switch_2950         Eth 1          128            S         2900     Eth 0/1
Router2#
```

CDP Directly Connected Devices

This is the information an administrator needs to begin the process of documenting a network. Starting with this, the administrator would probably use the **`show cdp neighbors detail`** command next to determine the IP addresses of each directly connected device. Then the administrator could Telnet into each device one by one and use the same commands to get their neighbor's information. During the process, the administrator can write down or print out the display from each CDP command and gather documentation on network components. When the administrator feels he or she has a good list of all possible devices, the administrator can map the physical layout of cable connections, as well as local and remote interface(s). The administrator can also document the IP address(es), hostname, device model, capability, and IOS version for each network component. The end result of all this work is shown on the Network Map Diagram.

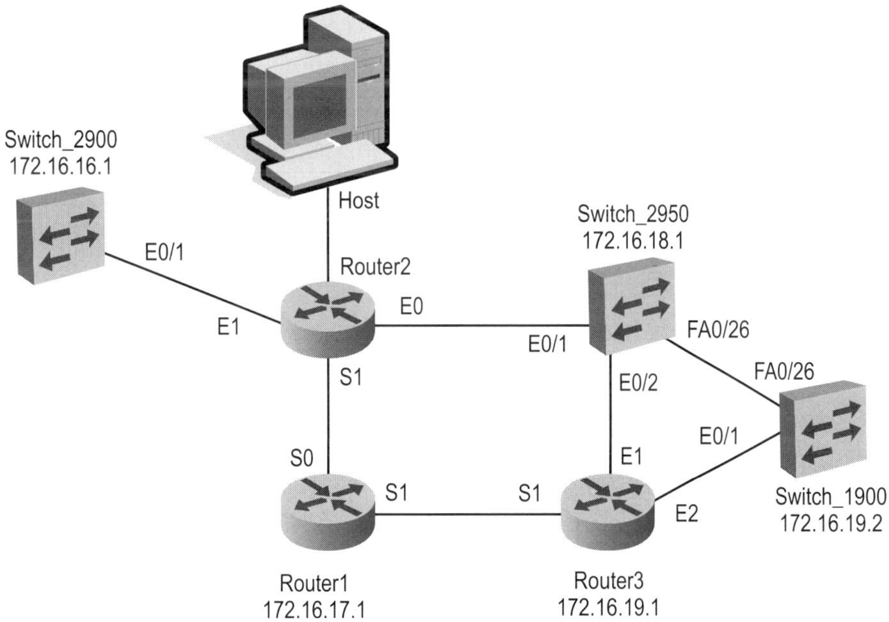

Network Map

Although we were able to see the layout of the devices in the last diagram, in this case the network administrator had to build this map from the information obtained using CDP. Then the administrator had to fill in the hostname, interface, and IP addresses of each device. Using the CDP commands saved this administrator a lot of walking around. Without CDP and Telnet, the administrator would have had to dig through cable closets and make a physical, console connection to each device. The administrator probably would have tried to trace cables as well. Using these two utilities to document a network helps you avoid a lot of legwork.

Review Questions

1. Which of the following best describe CDP? (Choose two.)
   a. Requires a Network Layer protocol
   b. Works only on routers
   c. Is protocol-independent
   d. Is topology-independent
2. What command would you use to disable CDP communications for an entire device?
   a. **`no cdp`**
   b. **`shut cdp`**
   c. **`cdp disable`**
   d. **`no cdp run`**
3. What protocol is necessary for CDP packets to transmit in a network?
   a. IP
   b. IPX
   c. SNAP
   d. Appletalk
4. Which pieces of information are displayed when using the command **`show cdp neighbors`**? (Choose two.)
   a. MAC address of remote device
   b. Capability of remote device
   c. Hostname of remote device
   d. IP address of remote device
5. Given the following information, what type of device is NA2?

   NA2 S0 130 R 2600 Ser 0

   a. Router
   b. Switch
   c. Source route bridge
   d. Repeater

6. CDP operates at which layer of the OSI model?
   a. Network
   b. Data Link
   c. Physical
   d. Application
7. Which statement is true regarding the CDP discovery process?
   a. CDP will discover all directly attached devices from any vendor.
   b. CDP will discover only directly attached Cisco products.
   c. CDP will discover only directly attached Cisco devices running CDP.
   d. CDP will discover PCs, servers, routers, switches, repeaters, and IP phones.
8. Which statements describe a network running CDP? (Choose two.)
   a. CDP runs in a network configured with different Network Layer protocols.
   b. CDP runs in a network where routing protocols are misconfigured.
   c. CDP runs only in networks using IP.
   d. CDP runs only in LANs.
9. When using the **`show cdp neighbors`** command, the capability column displays R, S, and B. What do these characters represent?
   a. Router, switch, and brouter
   b. Repeater, switch, and bridge
   c. Router, switch, and source route bridge
   d. Repeater, server, and bridge

Extended Activities

To obtain hands-on experience using the commands outlined in this lesson, visit the Student Resources section of WestNet Learning's Web site at **http://www.westnetlearning.com**.

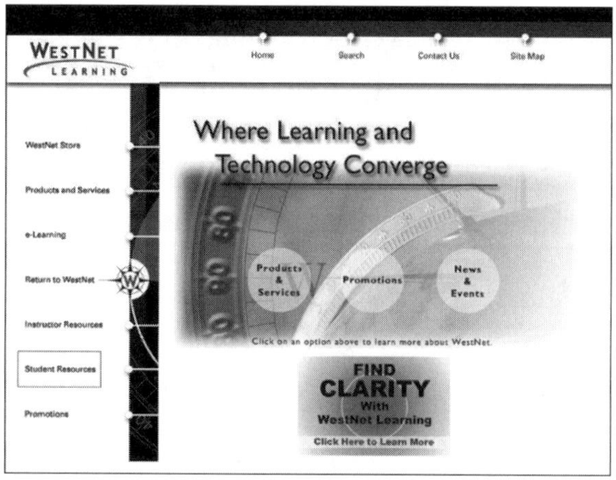

To enter the site, use your e-mail address to login and then type in this course's ISBN number. After you're in the Resources pages, look for the Suggested lab options associated with this module and lesson. Then answer the following questions.

Review the Show CDP Neighbors Command Screen Capture and answer the following questions.

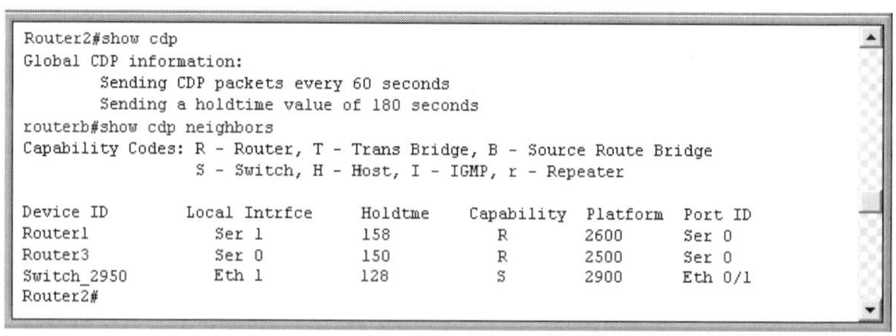

```
Router2#show cdp
Global CDP information:
        Sending CDP packets every 60 seconds
        Sending a holdtime value of 180 seconds
routerb#show cdp neighbors
Capability Codes: R - Router, T - Trans Bridge, B - Source Route Bridge
                  S - Switch, H - Host, I - IGMP, r - Repeater

Device ID        Local Intrfce     Holdtme    Capability  Platform  Port ID
Router1             Ser 1           158           R        2600      Ser 0
Router3             Ser 0           150           R        2500      Ser 0
Switch_2950         Eth 1           128           S        2900      Eth 0/1
Router2#
```

Show CDP Neighbors Command

1. What device is connected to Router2 through the Serial 0 interface?

   ____

2. What is the model number of Router1?

   ____

3. What does the capability of S indicate?

   ____

4. How often are CDP packets being sent between these devices?

   ____

5. What interface is Switch_2950 using to connect to Router2?

   ____

6. Draw a simple diagram of the device connectivity identified using this **`show cdp neighbors`** command on Router2. Label the device hostname, capability, Router2 interface, remote interface, and model type.

Lesson 2—Connecting to Remote Devices

Telnet is often used for troubleshooting connectivity all the way to the Application Layer of a device. Telnet is more specific than Ping, which can only verify connectivity through the Network Layer. However, Telnet provides other capabilities. Telnet is a configuration and administration tool that provides a CLI. It allows access to a device as if it were a direct console connection. Telnet emulates a virtual terminal session, which allows remote connectivity through the LAN, a WAN, over a modem, or the Internet. It is an important part of the IP suite, and is also available as a software package, offering connectivity and testing capabilities. An administrator must configure a device for Telnet access using the console port. This is usually done during the initial configuration. Future connections will most likely be performed with a Telnet session through the network.

In a production environment, software packages such as HyperTerminal, TerraNova, and many others are available to make these connections. A handy feature of Telnet is the ability to make a connection to several devices simultaneously. In fact, you can establish a Telnet connection, and then Telnet within that connection to another device.

Note: Do not Telnet into a device, then open a Telnet session back to the source. This could create a connection loop, cause problems with the session, and has been known to crash a device.

Objectives

At the end of this lesson you will be able to:

- Configure Telnet capabilities
- Make a Telnet connection
- Suspend and resume a Telnet session
- End a Telnet session

Key Point

Telnet is used to provide a remote console connection into a device. An administrator uses Telnet to configure and manage network devices without making a physical connection.

Configuring Telnet

Before a Telnet session can be started, several configuration steps are necessary:

1. Access the virtual terminal line configuration mode in the device.
2. Configure the login authentication for Telnet. This allows only authorized users access to the device.
3. Configure a Telnet password so that secure login can take place.

The Telnet Configuration Screen Capture shows the three steps necessary to set up Telnet access. Keep in mind that this must be done on every Cisco device where Telnet access is required.

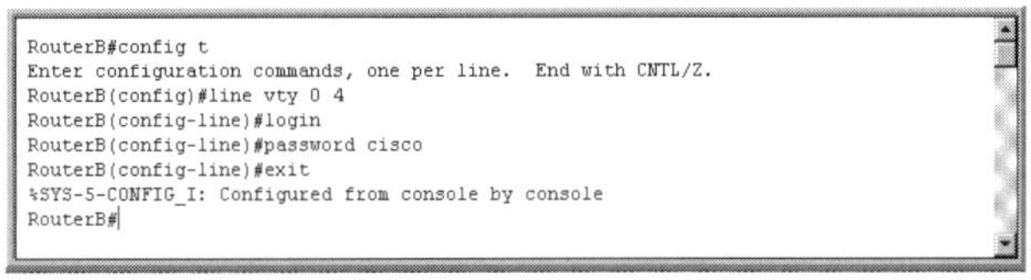

```
RouterB#config t
Enter configuration commands, one per line.  End with CNTL/Z.
RouterB(config)#line vty 0 4
RouterB(config-line)#login
RouterB(config-line)#password cisco
RouterB(config-line)#exit
%SYS-5-CONFIG_I: Configured from console by console
RouterB#
```

Telnet Configuration

The diagram begins by accessing global configuration mode. The command to access all virtual line connections is `Router(Config)#`**`line vty 0 4`**. If only one or a few virtual lines are being configured, these numbers can be changed. Remember that 0 represents the first line, and 4, in this case, is the last connection. A total of five simultaneous Telnet connections are possible on this device.

Notice that after the line command is entered, the prompt changes to `Router(config-line)#`. The login command is entered to activate login authentication. This is a critical step and must not be overlooked. Even after setting a password, Telnet access will not be granted if login authentication was not configured first. Finally, a Telnet password is assigned. Although possible, this password should not be the same password used to access enable mode (privileged EXEC mode) on the router. The following list shows the Telnet configuration commands in the order they are executed:

```
Router#config t
Router(config)#line vty 0 4
Router(config-line)#login
Router(config-line)#password word
```

If these steps are not performed, Telnet access to the device will not be possible. One of the following error messages will result when attempting to make a Telnet connection without configuration:

```
RouterB#telnet 172.16.20.1
Trying 172.16.20.1 .... Opening
Password Required, but none set
[Connection to 172.16.20.1 closed by foreign host]
```

or

```
RouterB#telnet 172.16.20.1
% Connection timed out; remote host not responding
```

The first connection to the router must be performed through Telnet with a physical connection through the console port on a router. After the VTY lines are configured, Telnet can be used across the LAN/WAN or via the Internet with the appropriate connections. To use Telnet through a modem, the auxiliary (AUX) line must be configured.

Making a Telnet Connection

Once configured, it is very easy to make a Telnet connection. In fact, from a Cisco router or switch, you only need to type the IP address or hostname of the device. The command is automatically assumed to be a Telnet request, and, if possible, a connection is made. At that point, a Telnet password will be requested. The Telnet Connection Screen Capture shows the process of establishing a Telnet session from one device to another. Notice that no characters are shown after the password. This is for security purposes so that no one tries to guess the password based on the number of asterisks.

Telnet Connection

Note: Although you can Telnet in to a Catalyst 1900 switch, you cannot use this connection to Telnet in to another network device.

After authentication takes place, the prompt changes from the original device to the Telnet device. For example, notice on the screen capture how the prompt changes from `RouterB#` to `RouterC#`. All commands that are issued will now be executed on RouterC. The original connection to RouterB is temporarily suspended in the background.

Suspending and Resuming Telnet Sessions

Knowing the way to "toggle" between different Telnet sessions may be important if you are trying to compare key configurations or cut and paste settings from one device to another. First use a special series of keystrokes. It is worth remembering this for ease of use, and, as always, it is good test material. Press the **CTRL+SHIFT+6** keys simultaneously, then release and press **X**. Although this may seem a bit strange, you will become accustomed to this procedure. It then becomes second nature. This key combination takes you back to the router from which you initiated the Telnet session.

From that router, use the **`show sessions`** command. This command displays all of the active Telnet sessions. The first one is the original session, and all other sessions after that are numbered consecutively. This can get somewhat confusing if you have started more than one Telnet session. Thus, to make it a bit simpler, an asterisk is placed next to the current session. Using this method, you can "toggle" or resume previous sessions by selecting a number from the session list. At that point, the prompt will change to reflect access to a different device. This is when hostnames are useful, not only to make the connection, but also to differentiate between devices.

When toggling between sessions, you can use the **`resume`** or **`resume`** *`session-number`* command. The other option is to use the **ENTER** key.

Ending a Telnet Session

You can use three methods to end a Telnet session. The first is from the device that initiated the Telnet connection. To end the session completely, type **`exit`** while at the remote prompt. This terminates the session with the response `[connection 172.16.40.2 closed by foreign host]`. If all sessions are closed, you can no longer toggle between them. To confirm that all sessions are closed, type **show sessions**. If all connections are terminated, the device should respond with `%No connections open`. These commands can be seen on the Exiting a Telnet Session Screen Capture.

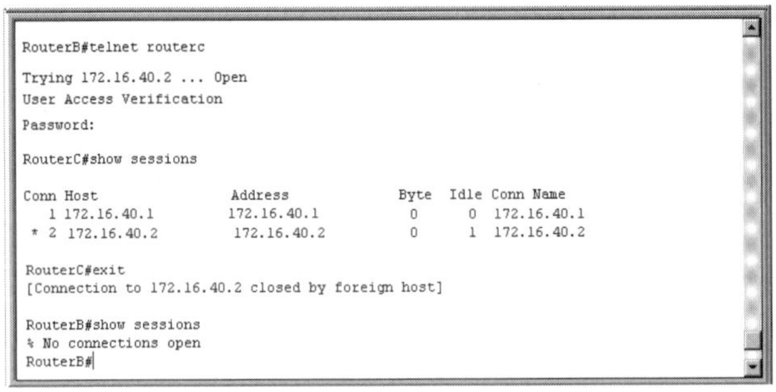

```
RouterB#telnet routerc
Trying 172.16.40.2 ... Open
User Access Verification
Password:
RouterC#show sessions

Conn Host              Address          Byte  Idle Conn Name
   1 172.16.40.1       172.16.40.1       0      0  172.16.40.1
 * 2 172.16.40.2       172.16.40.2       0      1  172.16.40.2

RouterC#exit
[Connection to 172.16.40.2 closed by foreign host]

RouterB#show sessions
% No connections open
RouterB#
```

Exiting a Telnet Session

Notice from the screen capture that the initial Telnet session is from RouterB. A Telnet session is established to RouterC, and the prompt changes to indicate this. To verify a Telnet session is active, use the **show sessions** command. From the secondary device, the **exit** or **logout** command will terminate the connection. Note that the prompt returns to `RouterB#`, and **show sessions** indicates no connections are open.

Another possible option after using **show sessions** is to use the **disconnect** command. After you get back to the originating router by pressing **CTRL-SHIFT-6+X** and a session number is determined by typing **show sessions**, an administrator can use the command `RouterB#`**disconnect** *session-number*, which terminates the appropriate Telnet connection. If only one Telnet session is active, just use the **disconnect** command alone; no session number is needed.

From the device that receives Telnet sessions, another method is available for session termination. One reason to use this method is to clear a connection that has "hung" or locked up for some reason. Another, and more important reason to clear a Telnet connection is in the event of unauthorized access or suspicious activity. From the device in which the Telnet session has been connected, use the following command:

```
RouterC#show users
```

This command shows all the connections that have been made using a console or auxiliary connection, as well as Telnet access. Your current connection will have an asterisk next to it, as shown on the Show Users Command Screen Capture. Using the **ENTER** key returns you to the prompt for the connection displayed with an asterisk.

```
RouterC#show users
    Line       User       Host(s)              Idle Location
*  0 con 0                idle                  00:00:00
   1 vty 0                172.16.40.1           00:01:43

RouterC#
```

Show Users Command

Notice that the other information available using the **`show users`** command includes the line type, user name (if available), host address, and how long the session has been active. To terminate access for the Telnet session, use the following command:

`RouterC#`**`clear line`** *`number`*

The Telnet session will end with the message `[Connection closed by foreign host]`.

Review Questions

1. Which command cannot be used to terminate a Telnet connection?
   a. **`exit`**
   b. **`clear line 2`**
   c. **`disconnection 1`**
   d. **`kill session 2`**
2. Which of the following is not part of the key sequence to toggle between Telnet sessions?
   a. **CTRL**
   b. **SHIFT**
   c. **ENTER**
   d. **6**
   e. **X**
3. Which command is used to display all the current Telnet connections?
   a. **`show users`**
   b. **`show lines`**
   c. **`show sessions`**
   d. **`show telnet`**
4. Which character indicates the active Telnet session when using the command **`show sessions`**?
   a. !
   b. *
   c. x
   d. #

Extended Activities

To obtain hands-on experience using the commands outlined in this lesson, visit the Student Resources section of WestNet Learning's Web site at **http://www.westnetlearning.com**.

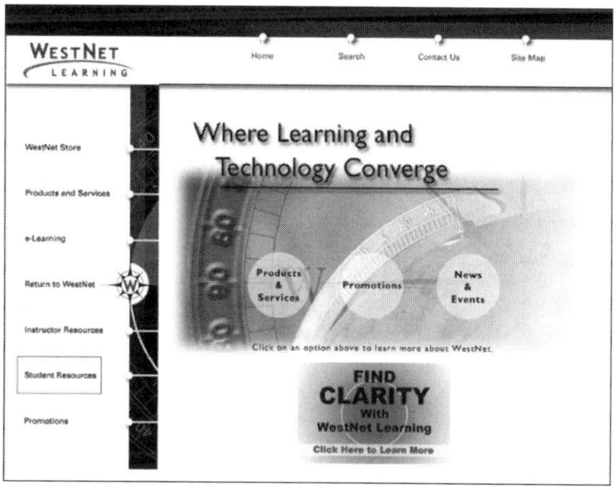

To enter the site, use your e-mail address to login and then type in this course's ISBN number. After you're in the Resources pages, look for the Suggested lab options associated with this module and lesson. Then answer the following questions.

1. Write the steps necessary to initially set up Telnet capabilities on a device.

   ____

   ____

   ____

2. What information can you enter at the prompt to make a Telnet connection to a remote device?

   ____

3. Does the word "Telnet" have to be included in the command to access another device?

   ____

4. What error is received when attempting to make a Telnet connection and the receiving device is not configured?

   ____

5. How can you tell if you are connected to a different device using Telnet?

   ____

6. What key combination can be used to toggle between sessions?

   ____

7. What commands can be used to terminate a Telnet session?

   ____

Lesson 3—Router Startup and the Configuration Register

When a router is powered on it performs a POST. This process is designed to test the key components of the device to prevent future issues or failures. After the POST successfully completes, the router reads the contents of the configuration register boot field. The boot field is the last four bits of the hexadecimal register value, and tells the router where to find and load its OS and startup configuration file. The Cisco IOS is typically found in flash memory. The startup configuration file is stored and most often loaded from NVRAM. This lesson defines all the components found in a router. It also lists the contents of each storage component and how they are accessed.

Objectives

At the end of this lesson you will be able to:

- Identify the key components of a router, including its internal components
- Make a router console connection
- Identify steps in the router boot sequence
- Identify the process to find and load the IOS
- Identify the configuration register and its boot field

Key Point

A router is made up of different memory components that are used to store the IOS, configuration files, configuration register, routing tables, and other important routing information.

Router Connections and the Startup Process

Similar to Catalyst switches, the first connection to a Cisco router is performed through the console port. The console port on a Cisco router is an RJ-45. This port is located on the back of the device and is connected to a computer using a rollover cable. The pin configuration of a rollover cable has the opposite pinouts on either end. Cisco ships this cable with a device, along with one or more connectors to attach it to the serial port of a computer. The router can then be configured over a Telnet session using the directly connected communications (COM) port. No password is initially set for the console connection. Other router models have different physical connections. Review the product literature for the correct method to connect and access your router through the console interface.

In addition to cabling a console connection, all other serial and Ethernet network connections should be made. After these connections are complete, the router can be plugged in and turned on. From a computer directly connected to the router, open a terminal emulation program (for example, Hyperterm using 9600 baud, 8 bits, no parity, and 1 stop bit [9600-8N1]), and select the appropriate COM port. After the communication is established, the information shown on the Router Boot Process Screen Capture is displayed. This screen indicates the router's boot process is taking place, including running the POST, loading the IOS, and identifying the device interfaces.

```
System Bootstrap, Version 11.0(10c), SOFTWARE
Copyright © 1986-1996 by Cisco Systems
7500 processor with 2048 bytes of main memory

F3: 5270536+64224+261748 at 0x3000060

                        Restricted Rights Legend
Text omitted

Cisco Internetwork Operating System Software
IOS (tm) 2500 Software (c500-D-L) Version 11.2(9). RELEASE SOFTWARE (fc1)
Copyright (c) 1986-1997 by Cisco Systems, Inc.
Compiled Mon 22-Sep-97 21:41 by ckralik
Image text base: 0x0302b1c4, data base: 0x00001000

Cisco 2500 (68030) processor (revision N) with 2048/2048K bytes of memory
Processor board ID 06164510, with hardware revision 00000000
Bridging software
X.25 software, version 2.0, NET2, BFE and GOSIP compliant
1 Ethernet/IEEE 802.3 Interface(s)
2 Serial Network Interfaces
32K bytes of non-volatile configuration memory
8192K bytes of process board System flash (Read Only)
```

Router Boot Process

After configuration is complete, remote connections can be made to the device using the AUX port and a modem. You can also configure Telnet connections across the network. However, these options are not available until a console connection is made and the appropriate settings are configured.

Router Boot Sequence

Three main functions take place during the router boot process. The three steps are virtually the same for a router as they are for a personal computer (PC). The first step is a hardware check, or POST, to verify the physical components of the device. The second step involves finding and loading the IOS. Finally, the device finds and loads a configuration file to provide its basic settings. A detailed description of the three steps follows:

1. **Run POST.** This diagnostic process verifies that the internal components, such as the memory, central processing unit (CPU), and ports, are all working properly. The microcode used during POST is stored in read-only memory (ROM), and activated every time a router is turned on. The POST process ensures that problems will not be encountered later due to faulty hardware.
2. **Find and load the IOS.** A special code, the bootstrap code, is used to locate, load, and run the Cisco IOS software. After loading, the bootstrap is not used until the router is powered off/on or reloaded.

   The bootstrap code reads the configuration register to find and load the IOS. As stated earlier, the IOS is normally loaded from flash memory by default. It is stored in a compressed format, and must be uncompressed before being moved into random access memory (RAM) for faster access. Some router models, including the Cisco 2500 series used in the classroom, do not have enough RAM to store the entire IOS image. Those devices simply run the IOS directly from flash memory.
3. **Find and load the configuration.** Like the special settings on your computer, a router also has a configuration that provides important settings, such as a hostname, IP addresses, routing protocol configurations, and much more. Some of these settings can be created during the initial setup process discussed later in this section. Manual configuration commands are also necessary to set up a router; many of these commands are presented in the next section.

   After the router is configured, the settings must be saved in the startup-config file and stored in NVRAM. Each time the device is restarted, it will find and execute the contents of the startup-config file to provide the router's functionality. If the startup-config file is not found in the designated location (NVRAM by default), the router will begin an autoinstallation process to set up an initial configuration. Auto Install will first look for a preconfirmed Trivial File Transfer Protocol (TFTP) server for downloading a configuration file.

The process of locating the IOS goes through a very specific sequence, since there are times when the configuration register may point to a location, but the image file cannot be found. The bootstrap code looks for the IOS image in several locations in the following order:

- **Location specified in the general configuration register**—The last four bits of this hexadecimal value define where the bootstrap should find the IOS image. It can point to flash memory, an alternate configuration file, or a network (TFTP) server, or it can load without a full image, and therefore resort to ROM monitor mode.
- **Location specified in NVRAM configuration file**—Commands can be typed into global configuration mode to define and save the desired location for the IOS to be loaded. The commands used to define a specific boot location include:

```
Router(config)#boot system flash filename
Router(config)#boot system tftp filename ip_address
Router(config)#boot system rom
```

- **First file in flash memory**—If neither the configuration register nor the boot system commands in NVRAM provide an IOS image, the bootstrap code will review the contents of flash memory. If an IOS image is found, it is loaded.
- **A TFTP server**—Although rarely used, a network device can locate the IOS image and download it from a TFTP server. In most cases this would have already been performed from the boot system command earlier. The router will make five attempts to communicate with the TFTP server. If this connection fails, it reverts to the next location.
- **A mini-IOS (boot helper)**—Some routers have a subset of commands that can be loaded if the full IOS image is missing or corrupt. This mini-IOS is stored in ROM and does not have routing capabilities. It can function as an IP host to download or upgrade an image.
- **ROM monitor**—If the router does not include a mini-IOS or if the router's mini-IOS is corrupted, the device will attempt to load into ROM monitor (ROMMON) mode. Not all routers have a mini-IOS or ROMMON capabilities, therefore, these last two steps would not be performed in that situation.

Components of a Cisco Router

A number of physical components exist in a router. These components allow the device to store an OS and configuration file, process commands, make routing decisions, and connect network segments. The Physical Components of a Router Diagram presents the key components and the functions they serve.

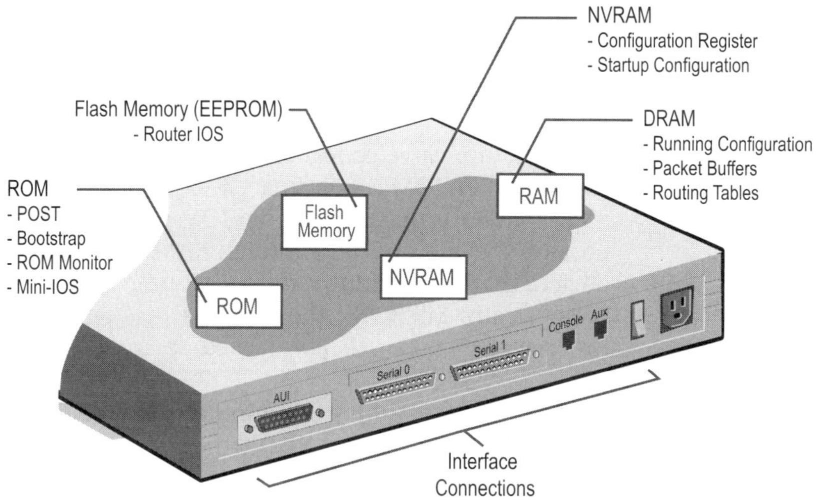

Physical Components of a Router

ROM

ROM stores microcode that is essential in the bootup process and other basic functionality. It is programmed into a chipset and is not overwritten or lost when a device is powered off or rebooted. The contents of ROM include:

- **POST**—POST consists of a diagnostic microcode that checks and verifies the physical hardware of a device.
- **Bootstrap program**—The bootstrap program consists of code used to execute and load other components. The bootstrap reads the configuration register to determine the proper boot process. As instructed, it will locate and load the IOS and configuration file.

- **ROM monitor**—This boot mode provides a low-level OS that is normally only used for testing by the manufacturer or during a troubleshooting process. Once started, the ROM-MON mode displays the `rommon>` prompt.
- **Mini-IOS (RXBOOT or Bootloader)**—The mini-IOS provides only a small subset of the functionality found in the full IOS. However, it is sometimes necessary to use when loading a new software image or performing maintenance operations. In mini-IOS mode, the router behaves like an IP host. It has no routing capabilities, but it can retrieve a file from a TFTP server. If the mini-IOS has been loaded, the router prompt changes to `router(boot)>`.

Flash Memory

Flash memory is electronically erasable, programmable read-only memory (EEPROM). Its primary function is to store the IOS image. Some router models run the IOS directly from flash memory because they do not have enough RAM to load the entire OS. These devices are called "run-from-flash routers." Because flash memory is physically EEPROM, the IOS can be upgraded to provide new functionality. It can also be backed up and restored as necessary.

NVRAM

NVRAM stores the router configuration register and the startup-config file. Anything saved into NVRAM is maintained and not erased or cleared when a router is restarted. NVRAM contains:

- **Configuration register**—This 16-bit software register tells a router how it should boot up and where to look for the IOS and configuration file.
- **Startup-config file**—The startup-config file is a compilation of all the settings configured and saved on a router. It holds information about IP addresses, interface settings, hostnames, routing protocols, and many other important components. Without this configuration information, a router could run an OS, but would provide no additional functionality.

RAM

RAM provides long- and short-term routing capabilities, such as packet buffering, storing routing tables, and executing the running configuration. Many of the newer router devices have enough memory to also load and run the entire IOS image. These devices are aptly named "run-from-RAM routers." All configuration settings take effect as soon as they are entered. However, because they are stored as the running-config file in dynamic RAM (DRAM), they are not saved when a router is restarted. It is very important to save the running-config file settings to the startup-config file, which is stored permanently in NVRAM.

Interfaces

The most visible parts of a router are the interfaces, because they make up the backplane of the device. The interfaces on a router vary greatly from device to device. Some routers have only a few "fixed" interfaces or ports that cannot be changed. If you need different port types, you must get a different router. Many Cisco routers come with a modular physical configuration. In this case, a router can easily be reconfigured or expanded using WAN interface cards. Possible interface types include:

- **LAN interfaces**—These interfaces include Ethernet, Fast Ethernet, Gigabit Ethernet, Token Ring, and FDDI. They are identified by their type and respective number, starting with Port 0 (for example, E0, E1, FA0, FA1, and To0). Notice that the entire name is not necessary because the IOS recognizes the first few unique characters of a command. On modular routers, interfaces are identified by name, slot, and instance (for example, Ethernet 0/1).
- **Management interfaces**—These are console and AUX ports, and virtual terminal connections used to access, monitor, and manage a router device. The console port allows a terminal to be directly connected to the device. The AUX port allows a remote console connection using a modem. Finally, a virtual terminal port allows console connections through a network using terminal emulation software and an IP address. This type of connection is not a physical interface on the router, but rather a virtual session. The management interfaces are identified as lines: line console, line aux, and line VTY, respectively.
- **WAN interfaces**—These are asynchronous and synchronous serial ports and Integrated Services Digital Network (ISDN) interfaces (Basic Rate Interface [BRI] or Primary Rate Interface [PRI]). These interfaces are identified with a corresponding letter and number similar to a LAN port (for example, S0 for a serial interface and BRI0 for an ISDN port).

The Configuration Register and Boot Field

The configuration register is a software component stored in NVRAM that tells a router where it should look for boot information. Remember that a router first performs a POST before finding and loading the IOS, and then finds and loads the startup config.

The configuration register is a 16-bit software register, with the lowest 4 bits (numbered 3 to 0) representing the boot field. This 16-bit number is displayed in hexadecimal format. The current configuration register setting can be verified using the **`show version`** command, as seen on the Show Version Command Screen Capture.

```
RouterB#show version
ROM: System Bootstrap, Version 5.2(8a), RELEASE SOFTWARE
BOOTFLASH: 3000 Bootstrap Software (IGS-RXBOOT), Version 10.2(8a),
RELEASE SOFTWARE (fc1)

RouterB uptime is 11 minutes
System restarted by power-on
System image file is c5000-d-1_113-5.bin, booted via flash

Bridging software.
X.25 software, Version 3.0.0.
1 Ethernet/IEEE 802.3 interface(s)
2 Serial network interface(s)
32K bytes of non-volatile configuration memory.
8192K bytes of processor board System flash (Read ONLY)

Configuration register is 0x2102

RouterB#
```

Show Version Command

Notice that in addition to showing the configuration register value at the very bottom of the screen, the command also provides the IOS file name, router interfaces, and memory information. At this point, we are most interested in the last line of the **`show version`** command, which displays the number 0x2102. This is the default value for the configuration register and is factory-set. Each number in the register value provides specific information as follows:

- **0x**—The 0 and the letter "x" indicate that this number is being displayed in hexadecimal format.
- **2**—The 2 in the first position (after 0x) indicates the router will "Boot default ROM software if network boot fails." This means the router will run the mini-IOS or RXBOOT from ROM if it cannot find an IOS image in flash memory or on a TFTP server.
- **1**—The 1 in the second position tells the device that Break is disabled. This is used for security purposes, preventing someone from breaking out of the boot process, thus bypassing password prompts.

- **0**—The 0 in the third position indicates nothing is set for this section. If set to 4, the router will ignore its startup configuration. This is useful for password recovery. See **http://www.cisco.com/warp/public/474/pswdrec_2500.html** for more information.
- **2**—The 2 in the last position is the factory default and indicates the router will use the boot commands specified in NVRAM (startup-config file).

In most cases, the first few digits of the configuration register number will never change, and will therefore be 0x210X. The last number, which represents the boot field, has a few possible options, as shown in the following scenarios:

- **0x2100**—A 0 in the last position (boot field) tells the router to enter ROMMON mode. The router must then be manually booted with the **`b`** command, and, once reloaded, the router will display `rommon>` as the prompt. This configuration is used for very specific troubleshooting and maintenance purposes.
- **0x2101**—A 1 in the boot field tells the router to load the IOS image stored in ROM (RXBOOT). This is a limited IOS image and is usually used for troubleshooting and some maintenance purposes. The prompt will be `router (boot)>` in this mode.
- **0x2102**—A 2 in the boot field is the default setting, telling the router to load the IOS from the location specified in NVRAM. Any hexadecimal value of 2 through F in the boot field will have the same effect.

To change the configuration register, enter global configuration mode and use the **`config-register`** command shown below:

```
Router(config)#config-register 0x2101
```

Notice that the entire configuration register number must be entered, including the hexadecimal indicator, even though only one number is being changed. The changed value takes effect upon reload or power cycle.

Note: When performing password recovery, it is often necessary to view or change the configuration register in ROMMON mode. Depending upon the prompt, choose the command that is appropriate:

```
>o or
rommon>conf-register
```

Review Questions

1. ROM is used to store which of the following components? (Choose all that apply.)
   a. Configuration file
   b. Mini-IOS
   c. Bootstrap program
   d. All packet buffers
2. To save a configuration file so that it is available after a router is restarted, it should be saved to which of the following?
   a. ROM
   b. RAM
   c. Flash memory
   d. NVRAM
3. Which of the following is the default location where the IOS is stored?
   a. NVRAM
   b. ROM
   c. RAM
   d. Flash memory
4. Why is it possible to upgrade the IOS?
   a. It is written to a hard drive that can easily be changed.
   b. It is written to an EEPROM that can be upgraded.
   c. It is stored in RAM, which changes constantly.
   d. It is changed with configuration options.
5. Which of the following is the first step in the bootup process of a router?
   a. Find and load the IOS.
   b. Run POST.
   c. Find and load the configuration.
   d. Run the setup routine.

6. Which of the following is the correct order for the boot process?
   a. POST, find and load the configuration, find and load the IOS
   b. Find and load the IOS, find and load the configuration, POST
   c. POST, find and load the IOS, find and load the configuration
   d. Find and load the configuration, POST, find and load the IOS
7. NVRAM holds which important router components? (Choose two.)
   a. Configuration file and IOS
   b. Configuration register and startup-config file
   c. Configuration register and IOS
   d. IOS and startup-config file

Extended Activities

1. Match the following descriptions with the correct corresponding terms:

   a. The electronically erasable, programmable memory chip that stores the IOS

   b. The default configuration register value

   c. The memory area that is not erased when a router is restarted; holds startup-config file

   d. The diagnostic self-test performed when a router is started to check hardware

   e. The configuration register value used for password recovery

   f. The memory area that stores the running-config file, routing tables, and packet buffers

   g. The component that contains the boot field

   h. The default location where the IOS is stored

   i. The location for microcode programs such as POST, bootstrap, and the mini-IOS

   j. The router components that provide physical network connectivity

   NVRAM __________

   RAM __________

   ROM __________

   0x2102 __________

   POST __________

   EEPROM __________

   0x2142 __________

   Flash memory __________

   Configuration register __________

   interfaces __________

Lesson 4—Cisco Device Management

A very important job performed by a network administrator is backing up the IOS and configuration files for a router or switch. The IOS is the OS of the device that provides its network communication capabilities, security, scalability, and functionality. Without an IOS, a device cannot perform any functions. The configuration file(s) on a router or switch define parameters associated with physical and logical addressing, interface configurations, activated ports, security features, and many other settings. A device without a configuration file can function as a device, but it will not be able to provide the specific services a network requires. Unfortunately, instances occur when the IOS may be corrupt or problematic. There may be times when a new configuration causes problems, or is maliciously changed and no longer works as originally intended. On occasion it is even necessary to upgrade the IOS of a device.

For all these reasons, an administrator needs to know how to back up and restore the IOS and configuration files. To do that, the administrator needs to be able to locate the necessary configuration and IOS image files. It is therefore important to recognize the IOS image file naming conventions, and use this information to perform the backup and/or restore process. This lesson highlights these functions and more.

Objectives

At the end of this lesson you will be able to:

- Identify the components of the Cisco IOS file system (IFS)
- Verify and save a configuration
- Back up and restore a configuration file
- Back up and restore the IOS
- Reload and restart a router

Key Point

To help prevent a major outage in the event the router IOS becomes corrupt or the configuration is lost or changed, it is a good idea to back up these components on a regular basis.

The Cisco IFS

The Cisco IOS file system (IFS) is composed of a number of different short- and long-term storage locations. All of these are accessed through the CLI using a specific naming convention. The naming varies depending upon the IOS version in use. Before we introduce the different syntax used to access these areas, let us first review the file storage locations. As we do this, note the Universal Resource Locator (URL) syntax for each area. This will help in recognizing them when using commands with IOS version 12.0, discussed in the next section. The file storage locations are as follows:

- **Flash memory**—Long-term storage area for holding the IOS image file. The URL for flash memory is **`flash:`**. It may also be necessary to log flash updates; the URL for this is **`flh:`** (flash load helper log files). Other flash options include **`bootflash:`**, **`slot0:`**, and **`slot1:`**. The slot references are used on devices that have Personal Computer Memory Card International Association (PCMCIA) functionality for backup and storage purposes.
- **ROM**—Storage for POST, bootstrap code, mini-IOS, and ROMMON code. These are usually not changed except by the manufacturer.
- **RAM**—Short-term memory used to hold the running-configuration file of all current configurations. You can access RAM using the **`configure terminal (config t)`** command. It also holds other short-term information such as routing tables. The URL for this area is **`system:`**.
- **NVRAM**—Storage used to hold startup-configuration file and configuration register. The startup-config can be changed using copy commands either from running-config or a TFTP server. The configuration register can be changed in global configuration or ROMMON mode. The URL for this storage area is **`nvram:`**.
- **Network file storage**—TFTP or FTP server locations that can be accessed to backup or restore the IOS image and configuration files. The Remote Copy Protocol (RCP) can be used for this process. The URLs for these memory areas are **`tftp:`**, **`ftp:`**, and **`rcp:`**, respectively.

Version 12.0 Copy Commands

The IOS Version 12.0 Copy Commands Table defines the newest syntax used with version 12.0 and the commands that it replaced. In some instances, special commands are noted for syntax used prior to version 10.3. Keep in mind that many of the commands may be reduced to **sys**, **run**, or **start**, and the **TAB** key can always be used to finish off a partially typed command. In addition, the Help key **?** can always be used to identify the expected syntax or command structure.

IOS Version 12.0 Copy Commands

Version 12.0 and Newer Commands	Pre-12.0 Commands
copy ftp:system:running-config **copy rcp:system:running-config** **copy tftp:system:running-config**	**configure network** (pre-IOS 10.3) **copy rcp running-config** **copy tftp running-config**
copy ftp:nvram:startup-config **copy rcp:nvram:startup-config** **copy tftp:nvram:startup-config**	**configure overwrite-network** (pre-IOS 10.3) **copy rcp startup-config** **copy tftp startup-config**
more nvram:startup-config	**show configuration** (pre-IOS 10.3) **show startup-config**
erase nvram:	**write erase** (pre-IOS 10.3) **erase startup-config**
copy system:running-config nvram:startup-config	**write memory** (pre-IOS 10.3) **copy running-config startup-config**
copy system:running-config ftp: **copy system:running-config rcp:** **copy system:running-config tftp:**	**write network** (pre-IOS 10.3) **copy running-config rcp** **copy running-config tftp**
more system:running-config	**write terminal** (pre-IOS 10.3) **show running-config**

Regardless of the syntax used, in addition to the **copy** command, the first variable is the source (where the file is being sent from), and the second variable is the destination (where the file is being sent to). Remember also that the word **system:** is associated with DRAM, and **nvram:** is just as it says, nonvolatile RAM.

Verifying and Saving the Configuration

Like a switch, you can use `show` commands to verify the configuration. Unlike a switch, however, the current running-configuration is not automatically saved. Therefore, it is important for an administrator to save the configuration so that it is available even if a router is turned off. In addition, it is a good idea to back up the IOS and configuration files to another location for recovery purposes.

The **`show run`** command is used to display the contents of the configuration currently running on a router from DRAM. The running-config file is volatile, meaning that if a router is powered off, the settings in DRAM will be lost. This could be a big problem. Over time many settings may be configured on a router, and the router runs them as soon as they are entered. However, they must be saved manually into NVRAM to make sure they are not lost after a restart.

Fortunately, the process of verifying a configuration is very simple. The running-config file is stored in DRAM and is volatile. The startup-config file is stored in NVRAM and is maintained even after a restart. To view the contents and verify whether the two configurations are the same, you can use one of several commands.

To access the configuration in DRAM (volatile), use:

```
Router#show run or
Router#show running-config
```

To access the configuration in NVRAM (permanent), use:

```
Router#show start or
Router#show startup-config
```

To access the startup configuration in NVRAM in IOS versions 10.3 and earlier, use:

```
Router#show config
```

To save a new configuration, or make sure an existing configuration is saved, use the **`copy`** command. Copy can be used for several functions, including copying the saved configuration to current, copying the current configuration to saved, and backing up or restoring the IOS and configuration files from a TFTP server.

The **copy run start** command saves the current configuration for future use. All settings currently running on the device will now be available upon future restarts. The **copy run start** command completely overwrites the contents of the NVRAM startup-config file. When this command is issued, a router responds with `Building Configuration...... [OK]`. The proper syntax for the command is:

Router#**copy run start** or

Router#**copy running-config startup-config**

`Building Configuration ??? [OK]`

The **copy start run** command, reverts the current configuration back to the saved settings. This may roll back a change that has not yet been saved but is causing problems. This command overwrites or overlays DRAM, and therefore the router must activate any differences from the startup configuration to the current running-config file. When this command is executed, a router responds by changing the interface shutdown status as appropriate. It indicates the copy is complete with the message `%SYS-5-CONFIG_I: Configured from memory by console`. The syntax for the **copy start run** command is as follows:

Router#**copy start run** or

Router#**copy startup-config running-config**

`Sys-J-Config-I: Configured from Memory by Console`

The Copy Commands Screen Capture shows the **copy run start** and **copy start run** commands and the results of using each one.

```
RouterA#copy run start
Building configuration...

[OK]

RouterA#copy start run
%LINEPROTO-5-UPDOWN: Line protocol on Interface TokenRing0, changed state to down
%LINK-5-CHANGED: Interface TokenRing0, changed state to initializing
%LINEPROTO-5-UPDOWN: Line protocol on Interface TokenRing0, changed state to up
%LINK-3-UPDOWN: Interface TokenRing0, changed state to up
%SYS-5-CONFIG_I: Configured from memory by console
RouterA#
```

Copy Commands

Backing Up and Restoring the Startup Configuration

All settings saved in the startup-config file stored in NVRAM are permanent until overwritten with another save command. However, if something is saved that causes network communication problems, it is not easily fixed. Therefore, it is a good idea to have a backup of the startup-config file for just this type of incident. It is also a good practice in case the configuration becomes corrupt or is tampered with. Some administrators have a common configuration that they load on all routers and then modify as necessary.

The startup-config file can be backed up to any device that provides TFTP services. TFTP is an IP application, and requires IP addresses and protocol configuration for communication. TFTP was selected because it does not require login authentication and has a very limited set of transfer options. It is perfect for the simple process of backing up and restoring a router configuration file.

Before backing up to a TFTP server, the following steps should be performed:

1. Verify communication with the TFTP server using Ping.
2. Verify the file system naming standards, which are dependent upon the TFTP server type.
3. Verify that the TFTP server has adequate disk space.

To verify communication before getting started, it is a good idea to "ping" the device you will be backing up to. Ping tests IP connectivity between two IP hosts on an internetwork. Copy commands are then used to perform both the backup and restore processes. When the **copy start tftp** command is issued, the router requests additional information about where to send the backup, including the IP address of the TFTP server and the name of the backup file. The following lines display this process:

```
Router#copy start tftp
Remote host [   ]?  172.16.30.2
Name of configuration file to write [Router-config]?
ENTER
Write file router-config on host 172.16.30.2 [confirm]
ENTER
Writing router-config !!!
452 bytes copied in 10.45 seconds
```

A default configuration file name is automatically created from the hostname-config file. This is important to note if you have more than one device with the same name, or the routers still display the factory hostname of Router. If this file name is not changed when prompted and more than one router is backed up, the file will be overwritten. After the information has been entered, the router will attempt to communicate with the TFTP server and transfer the file. Exclamation points, as observed in the above syntax, indicate the TFTP server is receiving successful User Datagram Protocol (UDP) segments. If the writing status shows periods (.......), this indicates communication with the TFTP server is not successful. The router will eventually display a message indicating the backup failed. The last line provides the size of the configuration file.

The restore process is just as easy as backing up a router, and consists of using the copy command in reverse and providing the requested information. To force the settings to take place immediately, restore the backup to the running-config file. Just make sure that network functionality is not adversely affected with the restored configuration. The following lines show the process used to restore the configuration to RAM:

```
Router#copy tftp run
Host or network configuration file [host]? ENTER
Address of remote host [255.255.255.255]? 172.16.30.2
Source file name [ ] ? Router-config
Destination file name [running-config] ? ENTER


Accessing tftp://172.16.30.2/router-config...
Loading router-config from 172.16.30.2 (via ethernet0):
!!!
[OK - 452/4096 bytes]
452 bytes copied in 11.21 seconds
%SYS-5-CONFIG_I: Configured from tftp://172.16.30.2/
router-config
Router#
```

Notice that the destination defaults to the running-config file, which means the restore process will take effect immediately. When copying the configuration file from a TFTP server into running-config, it merges the two and does not overwrite the contents of RAM. In some cases (for example, if access lists are being applied or IP addresses are being changed), loading the new file will change an important parameter. This could prevent the router from communicating with the TFTP server, and the remainder of the transfer may fail. In that case, you may need to copy from the TFTP server to the startup-config file (**copy tftp start** command) and reread the startup-config file (**reload** or **copy start run** command).

If the router cannot communicate with the TFTP server, you will be notified after entering all information that access to the server has failed. If the connection is made successfully, the file must be located and retrieved. UDP segments are transmitted, as indicated by exclamation points. Upon completion, the router will respond with the `OK` message and display the size of the transfer. The router will then finish with the `%SYS-5-CONFIG_I:` message indicating DRAM was written to by a TFTP server.

Backing Up and Restoring the IOS

Remember that the IOS is stored in the flash memory of a router. The IOS provides all the functionality of the device. If the IOS becomes corrupted or an upgrade fails, the device will be unusable. Therefore, it is very important to have a backup of a router's IOS file.

The **`show flash`** command views information about the contents of flash memory and the file name and file size of the IOS image. The command **`show flash`** is typed at the privileged EXEC mode and displays the information presented on the Show Flash Command Screen Capture.

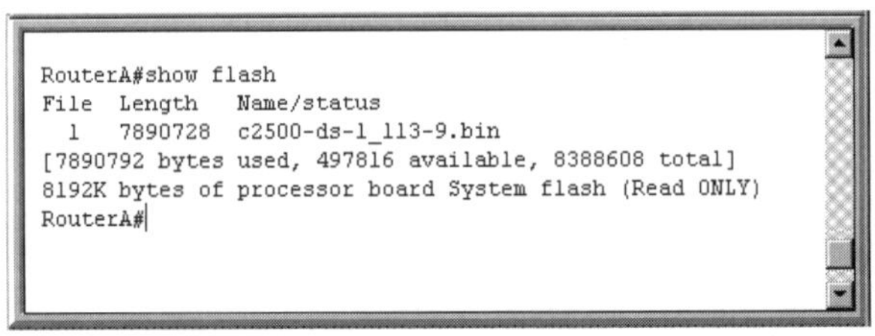

```
RouterA#show flash
File  Length   Name/status
  1   7890728  c2500-ds-1_113-9.bin
[7890792 bytes used, 497816 available, 8388608 total]
8192K bytes of processor board System flash (Read ONLY)
RouterA#
```

Show Flash Command

In this example, c2500-ds-1_113-9.bin is the file name of the IOS image. The file name can be deciphered by looking at each piece as follows:

- **c2500**—The first portion of the file name indicates the router is a Cisco 2500 series model.
- **ds**—This portion of the name provides the special capabilities of the file. The letter "d" indicates this is a desktop feature setup (instead of an enterprise setup, which uses the letter "j"). The letter "s" indicates extended capabilities.

- **l**—The next portion specifies where the image is run from and any compression settings. The letter "l" indicates the file is not compressed and can be relocated.
- **113-9**—These numbers represent the version number (11.3) and revision number (9) of the IOS image.
- **bin**—This file extension tells an administrator that the file is stored in binary format.

The last two lines displayed with the **`show flash`** command provide information on the size of the IOS image, which is approximately 7 megabytes (Mb) in this example. It also shows the total amount of memory (8 Mb) and space available.

The **`show flash`** command is used when backing up the IOS to determine the IOS file name. For the backup and restore processes, remember the copy command from the last section? The same command copies the IOS to a TFTP server. Some router models allow backups to be sent to a flashcard as a convenient and flexible way to back up and exchange IOS versions. This class focuses on using the copy command and a TFTP server. The Backing Up the IOS Screen Capture shows the commands and associated requests made by a router to perform this operation. (Note that this screen was taken from a different router than the one used for the Show Flash Command Screen Capture.)

```
RouterB#copy flash tftp
System flash directory:
File  Length   Name/status
  1   6078548  c2500-d-l_113-5.bin

[6078612 bytes used, 2309996 available, 8388608 total]
Address or name of remote host [255.255.255.255]?172.16.30.2
Source file name? c2500-d-l_113-5.bin
Destination file name [c2500-d-l_113-5.bin]?
Verifying checksum for 'c2500-d-l_113-5.bin' (file # 1)...  OK
Copy 'c2500-d-l_113-5.bin' from Flash to server
as 'c2500-d-l_113-5.bin'? [yes/no]y
!!!!!!!!!!!!!!!!!!!!!!!!!!!!!!!!!!!!!!!!!!!!!!!!!!!!!!
!!!!!!!!!!!!!!!!!!!!!!!!!!!!!!!!!!!!!!!!!!!!!!!!!!!!!!
!!!!!!!!!!!!!!!!!!!!!!!!!!!!!!!!!!!!!!!!!!!!!!!!!!!!!!
!!!!!!!!!!!!!!!!!!!!!!!!!!!!!!!!!!!!!!!!!!!!!!!!!!!!!!
!!!!!!!!!!!!!!!!!!!!!!!!!!!!!!!!!!!!!!!!!!!!!!!!!!!!!!
!!!!!!!!!!!!!!!!!!!!!!!!!!!!!!!!!!!!!!!!!!!!!!!!!!!!!!

Upload to server done
Flash copy took 0:00:40 [hh:mm:ss]
RouterB#
```

Backing Up the IOS

Before you begin, it is a good idea to verify connectivity to the TFTP server using the `ping` command. Then, to start the backup process, use the `Router#`**`copy flash tftp`** command. This tells a router that the contents of flash memory are being backed up. The router responds with the file name of the router IOS.

The router will prompt for the IP address of the TFTP server. You are then prompted for the source file name, which is the IOS file name observed with the **`show flash`** command or directly after the **`copy flash tftp`** command. The destination file name is automatically the same unless you specify a new name. A word of caution: make sure that each device backup uses a unique name for the IOS file. The file name could be the same for a number of routers with the same model number, IOS settings, and versions, and you will not be prompted if an existing file will be overwritten. To keep the names separate, you may consider adding the hostname to the destination file name. These file names should also be documented, because it would be a waste to have a backup but not be able to locate it.

The router performs the next few steps as it packages the flash file and begins the process of copying to the TFTP server. The exclamation points verify that the UDP segments were sent and received successfully. Upon completion, the message `Upload to the server done`, and the amount of time that it took, is displayed. The IOS is now backed up for safekeeping.

If a router has experienced a bad upgrade, or otherwise has problems with the IOS, and a restore is required, the following steps can be used. Again, the copy command restores the IOS with the same requests as the backup process. If performing an IOS upgrade, the same commands are used; however, the file name would be different than the one specified during the backup. The Restoring the IOS Screen Capture shows the commands and restoration process.

```
RouterB#copy tftp flash
Proceed? [confirm]
System flash directory:
File  Length   Name/status
  1   6078548  c2500-d-l_113-5.bin

[6078612 bytes used, 2309996 available, 8388608 total]
Address or name of remote host [255.255.255.255]?172.16.30.2
Source file name? c2500-d-l_113-5.bin
Destination file name [c2500-d-l_113-5.bin]?
Accessing file 'c2500-d-l_113-5.bin' on 172.16.30.2...

Erase flash device before writing? [confirm]
Flash contains files. Are you sure you want to erase? [confirm]

Copy 'c5000-d-l_113-5.bin' from server
as 'c5000-d-l_113-5.bin' into Flash WITH erase? [yes/no]
Erasing device... eeeeeeeeeeeeeeeeeeeeeeeeee ... erased
Loading 'c2500-d-l_113-5.bin' from 172.16.30.2 (via Ethernet0): ! [OK]
!!!!!!!!!!!!!!!!!!!!!!!!!!!!!!!!!!!!!!!!!!!!!!
!!!!!!!!!!!!!!!!!!!!!!!!!!!!!!!!!!!!!!!!!!!!!!
[OK - 7890792/8388608 bytes]
```

Restoring the IOS

Although not shown on the screen capture, the flash load helper displays the following notice before the copy commences:

```
****** NOTICE ******
Flash load helper v1.0

This process will accept the copy options and then
terminate the current system image to use the ROM based
image for the copy. Routing functionality will not be
available during that time. If you are logged in via
telnet, this connection will terminate. Users with
console access can see the results of the copy
operation.

-----************-------
```

This notice informs you that the router will be reloaded when the restoration is complete and, if you are accessing the device through a Telnet session, it will be terminated. Restoring the IOS should not be performed during production hours, because all router functionality will cease during the process. Notice that after you are prompted for the TFTP server and file information, you are notified that flash will be erased and that it contains files. To proceed with erasing and restoring the IOS, you must confirm this process. The router erases the contents of flash memory, which is indicated with the letter "e." It then begins loading the IOS image from the TFTP server, again using the exclamation point to indicate successful progress. After it is completely finished, the router reloads and is ready for network functionality.

Erasing the Configuration and Reloading a Router

If it is ever necessary to completely remove all settings in the startup configuration file and restore a router to factory defaults, this can be done with two simple steps. This process should not be taken lightly, however, and should only be performed on a device that is not being used in a production environment. The following commands completely erase the startup-config file stored in NVRAM, including the hostname, passwords, interface configurations, IP addresses, and routing protocols. Everything configured on the device will be removed. To erase the startup-config file and reload a router with factory defaults, use the following command:

```
Router#erase start
```

For IOS version 12.0 or later, the command is as follows:

```
Router#erase nvram
```

If the **show startup-config** command is used at this point, the router will return the message:

```
%% Non-volatile configuration memory has not been set up
or has bad checksum
```

The router configuration can still be salvaged if necessary by copying the running-config file stored in DRAM to the startup-config file, using the command **copy run start**. If the device is to be restarted with no configuration information, use the reload command as follows:

```
Router#reload
Proceed with reload [confirm]?ENTER
```

After the device is reloaded, it will display the following message:

```
NOTICE: NVRAM invalid, possibly due to write erase.
```

After the router completes the boot process and loads the IOS, it will attempt to find a startup-config file. Because the **erase start** command removed this file, the device will activate the setup process to automate basic device configuration. This is the same setup routine that would be executed on an unconfigured router.

Review Questions

1. What command is used to back up the startup-config file to a TFTP server?

   ____

2. What command is used to save the running-config file to NVRAM?

   ____

3. What command is used to identify the IOS file name?

   ____

4. What command is used to restore a configuration from a TFTP server?

   ____

5. What command is used to back up the IOS to a TFTP server?

   ____

6. What command is used to restore the IOS from a TFTP server?

   ____

7. What is the character that indicates flash memory is being erased?

   ____

8. What is the character that indicates UDP segments were successfully transferred?

   ____

9. What happens to a router after the IOS image is restored?

   ____

10. What happens to a router if you use the command **`erase start`**?

    ____

Extended Activity

To obtain hands-on experience using the commands outlined in this lesson, visit the Student Resources section of WestNet Learning's Web site at **http://www.westnetlearning.com**.

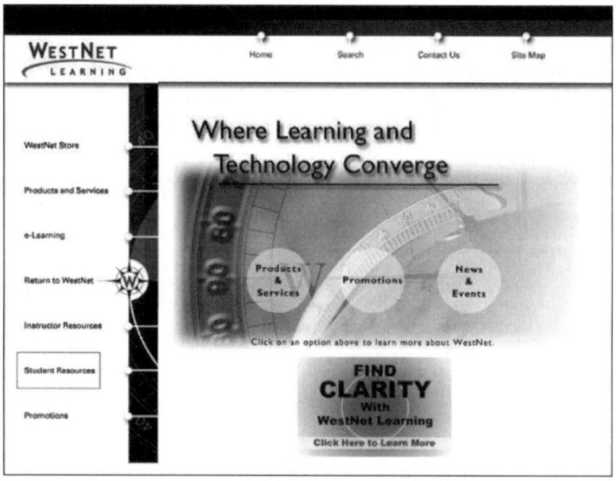

To enter the site, use your e-mail address to login and then type in this course's ISBN number. After you're in the Resources pages, look for the Suggested lab options associated with this module and lesson.

Lesson 5—Network Administration

Some of the major tasks an administrator has to perform are adds, moves, and changes of network devices. When adding equipment, the administrator must perform the setups necessary to properly configure and integrate the device(s). Moving equipment happens because of building changes, distance limitations, or possibly unforeseen problems such as flooding or fires. The network administrator may have to change out components of existing equipment, or upgrade the IOS to get new functionality. In any case, the administrator must make sure that, regardless of the change, he or she properly configures and tests the equipment for the least amount of impact on the production network. More often, these network modifications are done after hours. Regardless of the time frame, its important for the administrator to have extensive knowledge about the necessary steps, a plan of action, and a contingency plan in case the modification does not work.

Administrators have a few tools that help them locate devices, as well as provide some high-level troubleshooting. Host names assign identifiable, human-readable names to commonly accessed systems. For example, it is much easier to remember Router2floor than it is to remember 172.16.45.68. There are two ways that hostnames can be associated with an IP address. One of them is to use a hostname table that is manually entered into each device. The other way is to send name resolution requests to a name server, also called a Domain Name Server/Service (DNS). This lesson discusses how to configure and view both methods for name resolution.

A hostname is also helpful when accessing a device by means of Telnet, or for troubleshooting purposes such as using ping or trace to test connectivity. This lesson provides an overview of the ping utility, which is used to test communications between two devices up to the Network Layer. Traceroute is another Network Layer communication test that shows the actual path selected for a transmission.

This lesson ends with an overview of debug commands. Debug is a way for an administrator to view how the IOS is processing and responding to traffic. It is helpful when troubleshooting difficult problems because it can report the minute details of exactly how everything is being processed. Debug displays this information to the console, or it can log it to a file.

Objectives

At the end of this lesson you will be able to:

- Describe the items involved when performing adds, moves, and changes
- Describe and configure hostnames and name resolution services
- Use the ping command to test connectivity
- Use the traceroute command to view a transmission path
- Identify the use of debug commands when troubleshooting

Key Point

One of the important jobs of an administrator is adding, moving, and changing equipment. Administrators depend on tools such as hostname resolution, ping, traceroute, and debug commands to access and test network communication capabilities.

Performing Adds, Moves, and Changes

The job of an administrator is to set up and maintain network hardware, software, and configurations. Networks are not stagnant places. They often go through changes as new equipment is added, old equipment is removed, equipment is moved around, and existing equipment is modified. These types of network changes happen for a number of reasons. For example, new technologies, a topology change, or obsolete equipment may warrant that new devices are added to a network. This requires the administrator to know the proper way to configure and integrate the new device with the existing infrastructure.

There are also times when it is necessary to move equipment to another location. This may be when a building is remodeled, or because of space, heating and ventilation, or convenience issues. The administrator's job is to ensure network continuity and verify connectivity is maintained. Finally, there are times when the equipment itself is changed. This could be an IOS upgrade, a major reconfiguration, or when adding or removing components in modular devices. Each type of modification requires a number of decision-making, planning, and implementation steps that are worth reviewing. The components suggested here are just the basics. Each project will have its own special characteristics and often things that do not go as planned.

The basics of adding new equipment include assigning the device an IP address, and providing the proper configuration. Much of this work can be done during production hours, because it should not have any impact on network traffic. The following steps are appropriate when adding new equipment:

1. Unpack and verify the device interfaces and IOS version using the packing documentation.
2. Make a console connection to the device using a rollover cable, serial interface on a workstation, and Telnet application.
3. If the router is totally new, meaning it has not been configured with a startup-configuration file, it will begin the setup autoinstall routine. Use the setup to configure basic password, interface, and protocol settings. If the setup routine is not desired, you can exit it by pressing the **CTRL+C** keys together. The remaining steps are either already done during the setup process, or are in addition to the basic level of configuration available with the setup routine.
4. Assign an appropriate IP local loopback address. This address is used for administrative purposes and is helpful because it is always available and cannot be shut down like an interface.
5. Configure console, VTY, and AUX login authentication and passwords as appropriate. The console connection does not have a password by default; it can be set for future security. As discussed earlier, VTY lines allow Telnet access across the network; they should be configured for ease of administration. The AUX line may or may not be configured based on the corporate security policy for external device access. The AUX interface allows modem connectivity to the device. Not all routers have AUX ports
6. Configure privileged EXEC mode passwords using the **`enable`** and **`enable secret`** password settings.
7. Configure a hostname for the device, as well as informational banner messages and name resolution services as appropriate.
8. Configure each interface with the appropriate settings, such as description, Network Layer addresses, and, for serial DCE interfaces, `clock rate` and `bandwidth` parameters. Make sure the interfaces are enabled using the **`no shut`** command.

9. Determine the correct IP address and subnet mask for each interface. Typically, each router interface represents a different subnetwork. Therefore, it is very important for network communications that these addresses be set correctly.
10. Configure a routing protocol (Routing Information Protocol [RIP], Interior Gateway Routing Protocol [IGRP or EIGRP], or Open Shortest Path First [OSPF]) as appropriate. Make any necessary configuration settings for the specific protocol used.
11. Configure network management support using Simple Network Management Protocol (SNMP) if the network device will be monitored with that protocol.
12. Configure appropriate security methods such as access-list test statements.
13. Change network documentation to reflect the new device and its addressing, connectivity, hostname, and security components.

It is often necessary to move equipment to a different location. This could happen for a number of reasons, such as a company or department move to a new building or new part of a building. The move may be temporary such as during construction, or some sort of problem such as a flooded network closet or a heating or air conditioning unit breaking down. Regardless of the event and whether it is long- or short-term, moving equipment has its own considerations to keep in mind. It is always important to communicate with the network users if the move will impact the production network for any significant amount of time. The following steps help ensure the successful moving of equipment:

1. Identify the new location for the equipment. Verify the temperature and humidity variations in the room. Verify the available power and whether appropriate battery backup is available. Determine whether the device will be rack-mounted, or shelved, or will sit on a desktop. Too many data closets exist where the location was never planned for, and the device literally "hangs" by its network cables until something better is constructed. Make sure that the location is physically secure, so that no one can tamper with the equipment.

2. Make sure that the running configuration file has been copied to the startup configuration file. You do not want to move a device only to find out that the running configuration was never saved to NVRAM, and, upon startup, that the router has fewer settings than expected. If it has not been done recently, back up the startup-configuration file and IOS to a TFTP server, just in case an unforeseen event requires a reload. It is always better to be safe than sorry.
3. Validate the change from the existing location. Make sure that the components connected to the device as it is currently installed will not be impacted by the change. Moving the device may have to be performed after hours to prevent a network outage. Check for specialized components such as modem lines or WAN connections that would be difficult to move away from the demarcation (demarc) location.
4. Make any configuration changes as necessary to accommodate the network location and network connectivity.
5. Check security components such as access lists, that may have to be created, changed, or removed to allow or deny traffic from newly connected subnets.
6. Create a contingency plan before moving the equipment. Define the time frame and resources necessary to make the move successful. Define what steps will be necessary if the move does not work in a timely fashion, and have a backup plan ready for action.
7. Once moved, verify all network communications. Use show commands to verify the router is passing traffic and that routing protocols are functioning properly. Test the connectivity to and from each and every subnet.
8. Change the network documentation to reflect the new location, as well as changes to addressing, connectivity, hostname, and security components.

Two major types of equipment changes take place in a network environment: hardware and software. Configuration changes are an ongoing process performed on an as-needed basis. Some of these configuration changes are planned for, such as changing routing protocols. Other changes happen for security reasons, such as enabling or disabling an interface, changing passwords, or adding test statements to an access list.

Some configuration changes are reactionary, and are necessary to respond to failed equipment or a network communication problem. Finally, a lot of changes are initiated because of new technologies that require new hardware components in modular devices, or an upgrade to the IOS to gain new features and functionality. Just like during a move, communication is essential with network users because the change could impact network communications. The following list includes things to keep in mind when changing existing network equipment:

1. If the equipment is being replaced, check all existing connections and special configurations to make sure that they can be duplicated as necessary with the new replacement device. Document all physical connections and configuration settings.
2. Back up the IOS and configuration files of the old equipment in case they are needed and the device is no longer available. Leave the old equipment in place, or stored securely nearby in case it is needed for a fallback plan. After the new device is verified, erase all configurations for security purposes before storing, selling, or disposing of it.

For hardware changes

1. Check that the existing hardware will be able to physically support the new component(s). Also verify that the current version of the IOS supports the new modules; some require a certain release to function. If both changes are required, it may be a better idea to upgrade the IOS and verify its functionality before changing the hardware. Hardware and IOS upgrades should not be performed at the same time because it may make troubleshooting and administration difficult.
2. Make sure all equipment is available and that the appropriate tools are handy. Have antistatic mats and grounding straps available for the installers. Electrostatic discharge can easily damage or ruin circuit boards even if it cannot be felt. Hold the new components by the leads or face plate. Avoid touching the circuitry of the board.
3. Unpack the new component(s), and read the documentation and installation instructions before manipulating the existing hardware.

4. Determine whether the equipment must be powered down before installation. Some Cisco routers include a hardware hot-swap capability, called "Online Insertion and Removal" (OIR), that allows administrators to replace certain faulty modules, one at a time, without powering off the router. The router can then remain online while some maintenance procedures are performed.
5. Install the module, power on, and validate that the component is recognized. Then configure the new component as appropriate. Test network communication capabilities.
6. Document the physical hardware changes and configuration settings as appropriate.

For software changes

1. Read all documentation for the new version of the IOS. Verify that the physical hardware can support the new version. That is, verify that it has the appropriate flash storage capacity, as well as RAM for running the IOS, providing features, and performing network operations.
2. Verify that the new IOS will provide the existing features in use, as well as meet future demands.
3. Read all instructions for performing the upgrade.
4. Back up the existing IOS onto a TFTP server, for the just-in-case fallback plan.
5. Upgrade to the new version of the IOS from a TFTP server, CD-ROM, World Wide Web (Web) interface, or other method as appropriate.
6. Reload the router and modify the configuration settings as necessary for the new version. Test network communication capabilities and router functionality.
7. Document the IOS version information and changes to the configuration settings as appropriate.

Hostnames

A hostname is a human-provided name for a network resource such as a computer, server, or printer; an application such as a database; or a network device such as a switch or router. The hostname is usually a descriptive unique identifier. Many companies determine naming standards that define how hostnames will be established. However, administrators sometimes choose hostnames that are completely unrelated. For example, they may choose cartoon characters, mountain ranges, exotic travel destinations, animals, sports teams, star constellations, astrology signs, and many others. Although these are not as helpful for identification or location purposes, a hostname can be anything that is easily remembered.

Hostnames in this format have been used for many, many years. So much so that servers are often called by name. Where do you think HAL came from? Note that more than one name can be assigned to a single device. This is helpful to provide "alias" or alternate names to systems that are known by more than one name. They can also be used for naming by different people or for long names that could easily be shortened when trying to access them.

Regardless of the purpose or location of the component that requires a hostname, it must have a unique IP address. The hostname is only used temporarily until the proper IP address can be determined. Thus, the system needs to be able to associate the human-assigned hostname with an IP address. This can be done using either a host table or a name server.

Host Tables

The earliest method for associating a hostname with an IP address is a host table. This requires that the hostname and IP address be entered manually line by line and stored in a file. Computers, routers, and switches can all use these names to make address associations. The commands to build a host table for address resolution are discussed shortly. This manual configuration process is simple if only a few entries are necessary. However, if a network has many devices that require name resolution, a name server is a must.

Regardless of the method used for address resolution, a hostname makes tasks such as Telnet, ping, and traceroute easier because only the hostname needs to be known. Administrators do not have to remember every IP address to be able to access or test another device. Hostnames also provide easier access to devices for configuration purposes. For example, in a large network, an administrator can Telnet into the Router5flr (hostname of the router on the fifth floor), instead of remembering its IP address (161.145.100.245).

The process used to build host tables is not terribly difficult. It involves setting a hostname and IP address for every device that must be resolved. It also requires that a host table, if being created manually, is built on every device that needs to perform address resolution. For example, if 15 routers exist in a network, each router will need a table with entries for all other devices. That equals 15 tables that need to be created, with 14 entries per table. Because the routers never exchange this information, it is up to an administrator to keep it current.

If you are using manual hostname tables, try to keep them very simple. The commands shown on the IP Host Table Configuration Screen Capture create hostname tables on a Cisco router.

```
RouterB#config t
Enter configuration commands, one per line.  End with CNTL/Z.
RouterB(config)#
RouterB(config)#ip host RouterA 172.16.20.1 172.16.10.1
RouterB(config)#ip host RouterC 172.16.40.2
RouterB(config)#ip host Switch1 172.16.10.3
RouterB(config)#ip host TFTPsrv 172.16.30.2
RouterB(config)#exit
%SYS-5-CONFIG_I: Configured from console by console
RouterB#
```

IP Host Table Configuration

Notice from the first line that you must be in global configuration mode to create a host table entry. From there, the simple command is as follows:

Router(config)#**ip host** *hostname* [*port*] *ip-address* [*additional-ip-address(es)*]

To remove an entry that was previously added to a hostname table, use the command exactly as it was entered with a **no** in front of it as follows:

Router(config)#**no ip host** *hostname* *ip-address*

On the IP Host Table Configuration Screen Capture, four hostnames have been created in a hostname table on RouterB. They represent the devices RouterA, RouterC, Switch1, and the TFTP server. To access these devices using Telnet or test their connectivity using Ping, only the hostname is necessary.

Keep in mind the following considerations when creating a host table:

- Every hostname and IP address must be manually entered into every device for name resolution.
- Each item entered into the system is appended to the bottom of the table as a permanent entry.

- Up to six different IP addresses can be associated with any given hostname. Notice that two IP addresses were associated with RouterA in the IP Host Table Configuration Screen Capture. This is particularly helpful for identifying a router that has multiple IP addresses based on the physical ports, but a single hostname. Only one entry is necessary to make this association. Simply string the IP addresses out, separating them with a space. Alternately, several name entries can also be made to the host table to represent each IP address.
- More than one hostname can be associated with an IP address to represent a device that is called different things by different people. For this option, simply type the different hostnames, separating them with spaces before the IP address(es).
- The hostname table is read from top to bottom during the resolution process. If a name is encountered that matches the request, but the associated IP address does not resolve correctly, it will continue reading through the list to attempt to locate a usable address.
- Notice from the command that a Transmission Control Protocol (TCP) port number can also be provided in addition to an IP address. The TCP port can identify a specific application.
- Hostnames and IP addresses that are manually configured remain permanent entries until removed by an administrator.

Name Servers

The other possibility for resolving IP addresses is to reference a server that holds this information. This is far more efficient, because the server can be updated dynamically and is centralized. Consider the previous example of 15 routers. In this case, a separate host table is built on each one, with an entry for the other routers. If one entry changes, all 15 routers must be reconfigured to reflect the change. On the other hand, if a name server is used, only one change is necessary.

The Internet and most organizations use DNS to provide automatic, centralized hostname-to-IP address resolution capabilities. Instead of looking for a host table with the right configuration, the device "points" to a name server designed to maintain the host table. Because all devices point to the same name server, it greatly reduces administrative overhead, typing requirements, errors, and maintenance issues. The assumption here is that the name server has been configured with the appropriate information.

DNS resolution services have become a basic component in almost all network operating systems (NOSs), and are relatively easy to configure and access. By default, all Cisco devices are configured to broadcast name resolution requests to 255.255.255.255. This broadcast address searches for any name server on a network. To reduce broadcast traffic, configure a specific name server as follows:

```
Router(config)#ip name-server [server-ip-address1]
[server-ip-address2]...
```

Up to six IP addresses can be configured, which provide for redundancy in case a server goes down or is otherwise unreachable. A name resolution attempt will be made starting with the first address. If that one does not respond, the next one will be contacted and so forth, through each address. If none of the servers respond, or the name cannot be resolved, the following error will be returned:

```
% Unknown command or computer name, or unable to find
computer address
```

Names resolved by a name server are temporarily cached into the router memory. This helps reduce the number of resolution requests for commonly accessed devices. These addresses are dynamic because they are learned by the device instead of manually entered. If not requested during a specific period of time, the hostname and IP address will eventually expire from the host table to make room for other entries.

Disabling Name Resolution

A router and switch assume that every typed command is valid. If the command is not within the standard CLI syntax, the device will attempt to resolve the command to an IP address using either the host table or a name server. This can get really annoying if you have forgotten a command or had a typographical error. You must wait for the resolution process to take place before you have access to the command prompt again. To prevent this from happening, you can explicitly turn DNS lookup capabilities off using the following command:

```
Router(config)#no ip domain-lookup
```

This disables all name resolution capabilities. This means the device will not attempt to broadcast name resolution requests; thus, erroneous commands will simply return to a command prompt. A host table must be configured on the device if name resolution is still desired.

Viewing a Host Table

All entries either entered manually or learned from a name server are cached in router memory. To view these hostnames and associated IP addresses, use the **show hosts** command. The Show Hosts Command Screen Capture displays all the hostnames that have been added to the host table.

```
RouterB#show hosts

Default domain is not set
Name/address lookup uses domain service
Name servers are 255.255.255.255

Host                     Flags        Age Type   Address(es)
tftpsrv                  (perm, OK)    0  IP     172.16.30.2
switch1                  (perm, OK)    0  IP     172.16.10.3
routerc                  (perm, OK)    0  IP     172.16.40.2
routera                  (perm, OK)    0  IP     172.16.20.1
RouterB#
```

Show Hosts Command

After the **show hosts** command is entered, a list of the name servers is displayed, assuming any are configured. In this case, no name servers are configured; thus, the device will make a broadcast request if a name cannot be resolved in the host table. From there, the actual cached host entries are displayed. The fields displayed are as follows:

- **Host**—Presents the human-assigned name of the host device used for access instead of the IP address.
- **Flags**—Defines how the name and address were learned. The first part is either `perm` or `temp`. `Perm` is a permanent entry that was manually configured using the **ip host** command. `Temp` is an entry learned using a name server. The last part is either `OK` or `EX`. `OK` indicates the entry is current, either a permanent entry or just learned from a name server. `EX` indicates the entry has aged out or expired.
- **Age**—Indicates the amount of time (in hours) since the entry was last referenced. After a certain period of time, temporary entries from a name server expire.
- **Type**—Identifies the associated protocol (in this case, IP).
- **Address(es)**—Lists the associated IP address(es) that relate to a particular hostname.

Ping Command

Ping is the command used to test end-to-end protocol and physical connectivity between two devices. It is actually part of the Internet Control Message Protocol (ICMP) suite. Ping is an ICMP echo request and echo reply process. You may recall that ICMP is located at the Network Layer (layer 3) of the OSI model. When using Ping to test connectivity, it tests successful communications capabilities from layer 3 of the sending device to layer 3 of the receiving device.

Ping is a great tool and is used frequently to test connectivity; just keep in mind that it has a limitation. Although Ping can test for successful connection, it cannot check application access capabilities. This means that because it only goes to the Network Layer, it cannot test Transport Layer or other upper-layer connectivity capabilities. Although you may be able to ping a device, you may not be able to Telnet, send files, login, or otherwise use the remote system.

Another problem now prevents Ping from being as useful as it once was. Hackers realized that Ping is a simple protocol component found in all network environments. Because it is used for test purposes, it is not considered a potential threat to network devices. However, when used en masse (that is, when thousands of Ping packets are being transmitted to a single device in a short time), it can disrupt the normal capabilities of the device. The device would spend all its processing power responding to the Ping requests, and could not process any other traffic. This is often called "the ping of death" and is considered a denial of service attack. To help prevent this, Ping (ICMP echo request/echo reply) capabilities are often disabled by Internet service providers (ISPs) when entering or leaving a network.

Within a network, Ping is frequently used and plays an important role in an administrator's toolkit. Two versions of Ping are available on Cisco devices: basic Ping and extended Ping. Basic Ping allows you to test the connectivity between two devices using the IP address or hostname. Basic Ping sends five echo requests and should receive five echo replies. This allows time for a slow connection or a delay in response from the receiving device. Extended Ping allows the administrator to configure a number of other parameters to provide more advanced testing.

To perform a basic ping on a router device, from privileged EXEC mode using the following command:

```
Router#ping {ip-address|hostname}
```

The Ping Command Screen Capture shows three different ping attempts. The first ping echoes RouterC. The hostname is resolved to an IP address from the host table and is successful. The second ping is sent to the IP address of RouterA. A successful ping is indicated by the five exclamation points (!!!!!). The last ping is sent to Switch1, which resolves properly, but does not send back an echo reply. An unsuccessful ping is distinguished using five periods (. . . . .), as shown toward the bottom of the screen capture.

```
RouterB#ping RouterC
Type escape sequence to abort.
Sending 5, 100-byte ICMP Echos to 172.16.40.2, timeout is 2 seconds:
!!!!!
Success rate is 100 percent (5/5), round-trip min/avg/max = 4/4/4 ms

RouterB#ping 172.16.10.1
Type escape sequence to abort.
Sending 5, 100-byte ICMP Echos to 172.16.10.1, timeout is 2 seconds:
!!!!!
Success rate is 100 percent (5/5), round-trip min/avg/max = 4/4/4 ms

RouterB#ping switch1
Type escape sequence to abort.
Sending 5, 100-byte ICMP Echos to 172.16.10.3, timeout is 2 seconds:
.....
Success rate is 0 percent (0/5)
RouterB#
```

Ping Command

The following list presents characteristics of the ping command, as displayed in the screen capture:

- By default, five echo requests are sent, and five echo replies should be received. This allows for the possibility of a slow link or other delay. In some instances, the first one or two replies fail, and the rest reply successfully.
- The size of the ICMP echo packet is 100 bytes.
- If a hostname is resolved, the IP address is displayed.
- The timeout of two seconds is displayed, which is the amount of time before the echo request is no longer valid.

- The next line has either five exclamation points that indicate success, or five periods that indicate failure. This line may have a combination of exclamation points and periods based on the response. Other responses include:
  - U = Destination unreachable
  - Q = Source quench or destination busy
  - ? = Unknown packet type
  - & = Time-to-live (TTL) exceeded
- The success rate shows the percentage and number of successful replies out of the default five attempts.
- If the ping is successful, the round-trip time is also displayed, with a minimum, average, and maximum time frame. Each of the successful examples took four milliseconds round trip.

To provide more specific control or determine connectivity using another network protocol, an administrator can use the extended Ping option. To access extended Ping features, type **`ping`** without an address or hostname. The system responds with a series of questions that include protocol options, target address, source address, and number of echo requests. Extended Ping is helpful for a number of reasons. First, it can show connectivity through a particular device. It can also be set up to echo any number of times, which is very useful when troubleshooting a physical connection. To do this, activate an extended Ping, then take the necessary troubleshooting actions. When the connection is made, Ping changes from a period (failure) to an exclamation point (success). Make sure to terminate an extended Ping when you no longer need it. Network bandwidth is used for the echo request and reply.

Ping capabilities are also available on all workstation and server platforms that support the IP protocol suite. Different syntax is used to achieve extended Ping capabilities.

Traceroute Command

The tool traceroute or trace, also has an ICMP component based on TTL-exceeded messages. Traceroute is a utility that determines all routing devices (handoff points or hops) from a source to a final destination. It does this by setting a very low TTL on each packet. As the next-hop device receives a packet, ICMP responds to the sending device that the TTL has expired and throws away the packet. The sender subsequently increases the TTL by one and sends the packet back on the network, where the next-hop router does the same thing. This continues until the packet reaches the destination or the path reaches 30 hops. Each hop in the path is tracked and reported.

Traceroute is a helpful tool because it shows the network infrastructure and may be able to pinpoint a failed connection. Whereas Ping indicates whether connectivity is possible, traceroute identifies the path that makes the connection possible. Traceroute also tests to the Network Layer of the OSI model because it is an ICMP component. It is not very helpful within a network segment because it requires that the transmission pass through a router to achieve a response.

The command used to execute a trace is as follows:

```
Router#trace {ip-address|hostname}
```

The **trace** command is similar in operation to the Microsoft Windows tracert and Unix/Linux traceroute commands. Each, when issued from their respective operating systems, can be used to trace a packet's path. Either an IP address or hostname can be used.

When the **trace** command is used, the screen displays each hop (handoff point/router) that the packet encounters from the device that initiated the trace to the specified destination. The Trace Command Screen Capture shows an example of the content displayed when directing this command to a Web location.

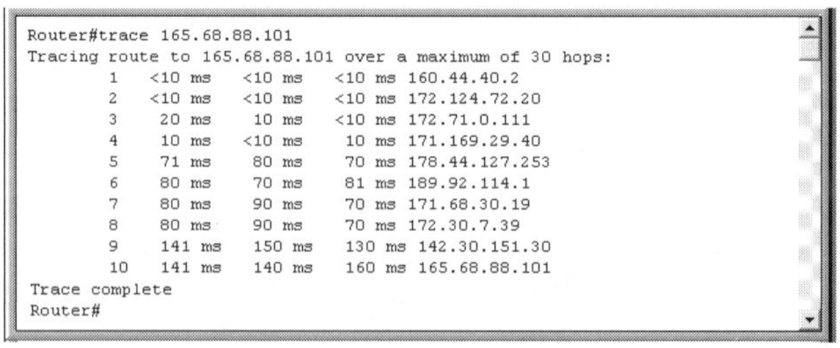

Trace Command

Notice from the screen capture that it took 10 hops to get to the destination address. Also notice that the trace was completed. Some trace communications will time out or end in * signs, indicating a network communication problem, or possibly a firewall or other security mechanism in place that is preventing the request from being returned.

On a Cisco router or switch, performing a trace may provide different information than the typical traceroute on a workstation. Other information that may be returned includes:

- A = Administrator prevention (access-list or firewall)
- Q = Source quench
- I = User interrupt test
- T = Timeout
- ? = Unknown packet type
- P = Protocol unreachable
- N = Network unreachable
- H = Host unreachable
- U = Port unreachable

Using Debug Commands for Troubleshooting

Debug is a more advanced and involved troubleshooting method. It goes beyond show commands and other communication tests like Ping and traceroute. Debug provides play-by-play action on how a router is processing and the traffic it is transmitting. This allows an administrator to see everything as it is happening.

Debug is not a tool that is used on a daily basis. The information it provides is only helpful for the exact time frame when it is being displayed. After the displayed information rolls off the screen the transmission is over or the process is complete. Network administrators use debug commands to view very specific events in an attempt to determine where transmissions are bottlenecking (slowing down) or being dropped or where a process is not functioning as expected or failing altogether.

Show vs. Debug Commands

Some of the information obtained when using debug commands can be viewed in a different way using show commands. The differences between these two tools are as follows:

- Show commands are a snapshot of time, recording exact statistics at the point the display is generated. They are very helpful for documenting a device and network connectivity. They can also be used to detect and troubleshoot a problem. Show commands require little if any overhead to generate information and display it to the screen. They are static in the information they provide.
- Debug commands display dynamic information as it is happening. They are helpful for troubleshooting potential problem areas, including the flow of traffic, routing protocols that are not updating properly, physical or logical connectivity issues, and processor functions. They require a lot of overhead for processing and displaying all information as it happens.

The term debug is something of a contradiction. It can provide extensive troubleshooting information while turned on, which is helpful to determine a problem. However, due to its high overhead, it is not usually turned on until needed. Therefore, an event that happened before debug was used would not be seen. This, unfortunately, makes debug useless for trying to determine the cause of a problem that already happened. A better way to monitor and track information of this sort is to use SNMP, which can monitor and report event statistics to a management component. The benefit of debug is in solving an ongoing problem. Administrators turn debug on for short periods of time to view very specific events.

The other contradiction about debug is that it should be used when traffic is lowest and the fewest number of users will be impacted. However, that is never when problems surface. Debug is an excellent tool to obtain specific information, and then disable to prevent unnecessary resource use. The following list presents a few characteristics of debug:

- All debug commands are typed in privileged EXEC mode.
- Debug is very processor- and memory-intensive. It is given high priority by the processor, and therefore other essential device functionality may be severely impacted while debug is running. It should only be used for a short period of time, preferably with the lowest traffic and user access.

- Each debug command handles the display of information differently. Some fill the screen in an instant and overwhelm even the fastest reader. Others display a single line of text at longer intervals. Knowing the format and time frame for display will prevent unnecessary concern and additional troubleshooting. Only use those debug commands appropriate to a specific problem.
- The information provided by debug may be too high-level or detailed for the troubleshooting process.
- Be ready to turn off some or all of the debug commands quickly. This is necessary to reduce the impact on device performance.

To determine the available debug commands and decide which one(s) may be appropriate to troubleshoot a particular problem, use the **`debug ?`** command in privileged EXEC mode.

The **`debug all`** command is used to turn on all debug options. This command should NEVER be used because it will overtake the processor and the device will be useless until disabled. **`Debug all`** has even been known to crash a device that is heavily used. It is very common to use the command **`no debug all`**. This command is helpful to ensure that all debug screens and associated background processes have been turned off.

Before initiating any debug command, it is a good idea to determine the processor resources in use. This will help an administrator determine whether the device is too busy to run debug commands. To get process statistics, use the command **`show processes`**. The first line of output from this command is probably the most telling, because it provides statistics information for the last five seconds, one minute, and five minutes. The numbers are given in percentage from 0 through 100%. If utilization is currently high, repeat this show command to find a more appropriate time frame when processing is lower. The first line of the **`show processes`** command is displayed as follows:

```
Router#show processes
  CPU utilization for five seconds:  2%/5%, one minute:
10%, five minutes: 10%
```

More information will be displayed that details the exact processes that are using device resources. Keep in mind the trade-off. It may be necessary to view debug information and impact performance in order to solve a problem and get things working correctly.

Debug Configuration

The `logging` command provides additional options for controlling which types of messages the system sends to the logging device. By replacing the word `debugging`, which displays everything to the specified logging device, with one of eight message severity levels, you control which messages types are sent to which device. Cisco assigns system messages severity levels from 0 (the highest) to 7 (the lowest). The System Message Table lists the system message types and their associated severity levels.

System Message

Message Type	Severity Level
Emergencies	0
Alerts	1
Critical	2
Errors	3
Warnings	4
Informational	5
Notifications	6
Debugging	7

In an instance where you wouldn't want to send all message types to a logging device, such as when using `debug all` to troubleshoot, you can set a device's logging severity level to tell the system to send to it only certain message types. The system sends the remaining messages to another location, such as to the log buffer or a virtual terminal. All messages from the highest severity level (alerts) down to the level designated will go to the specified device. The following example sends messages from severity level 0 to 6 to the console and all messages to a virtual terminal:

```
Router (config)#logging console informational
Router (config)#logging monitor debugging
```

The system will only log debugging messages on the virtual terminal device. All other severity levels are logged to both locations.

Finally, as a last reminder, it is critical to make sure that debug commands are turned off. As stated, the command to do this for all debug screens is **`no debug all`**. Using debug wisely can provide rapid knowledge access, and hopefully lead to a trouble-free network.

Review Questions

1. Which of the following can a name server resolve? (Choose all that apply.)
   a. Host name
   b. MAC address
   c. Domain name
   d. Application name
2. Where is name resolution configuration performed?
   a. User EXEC mode
   b. Privileged EXEC mode
   c. Global configuration mode
   d. Interface configuration mode
3. What happens when a command is typed that is not recognized by the CLI?
   a. The router tries to resolve it to a hostname and Telnet to the device.
   b. The router ignores the command.
   c. The router parses the command into the most closely recognizable command.
   d. The router exits privileged EXEC mode.
4. How many IP addresses can be associated with a single hostname?
   a. 2
   b. 3
   c. 4
   d. 6
5. When can a router use a hostname instead of an IP address? (Choose two.)
   a. When trying to Telnet to another device
   b. When trying to e-mail another device
   c. When trying to ping another device
   d. When sending a packet to another device

6. Which of the following best describes the address resolution process using DNS?
   a. The addresses must all be manually entered and maintained.
   b. The addresses are stored in a central database, which is accessed for name resolution services.
   c. Each device must be accessed if an IP address is changed.
   d. A public DNS server works well for locating commonly accessed LAN devices.
7. What does the flag `OK` indicate when using the command **`show hosts`**?
   a. That the entry is current and valid
   b. That the entry has expired
   c. That the entry was learned using a public DNS server
   d. That the entry is permanent and will never expire
8. To prevent name resolution services from being performed, which command should be used?
   a. `Router(config)#`**`no ip resolve`**
   b. `Router(config)#`**`no ip domain-lookup`**
   c. `Router(config)#`**`no ip names`**
   d. `Router(config)#`**`no host resolution`**
9. Which layer of the OSI model does Ping test up to?
   a. Network
   b. Data Link
   c. Transport
   d. Application
10. A ping is performed using which protocol?
    a. TCP
    b. UDP
    c. ICMP
    d. IPX

11. When a ping is transmitted to another device, what is actually begin transmitted?
    a. An echo reply
    b. An echo request
    c. A trace command
    d. A TTL expired response
12. Which types of ping commands that can be performed? (Choose two.)
    a. Basic
    b. Extensive
    c. Diagnostic
    d. Extended
13. Which things can a device use in a ping command? (Choose two.)
    a. A NetBios name
    b. An IP address
    c. A hostname
    d. A MAC address
14. What information is shown in a traceroute?
    a. The number of echo replies
    b. The name that was resolved to an IP address
    c. The hops or routers between source and destination
    d. The protocols being used on the network
15. What characters indicate a successful ping?
    a. . . . . .
    b. !!!!!
    c. #####
    d. sssss
16. A company must have a DNS server to perform name resolution processes. True or False?
17. Host names manually entered into a host table will be exchanged with other routers. True or False?

18. If a ping is successful in testing connectivity to a device, this guarantees other communications. True or False?
19. Trace can be used to show the number of switches and routers that handled a packet. True or False?
20. Trace can show an unlimited number of hops between source and destination. True or False?

Extended Activities

To obtain hands-on experience using the commands outlined in this lesson, visit the Student Resources section of WestNet Learning's Web site at **http://www.westnetlearning.com**.

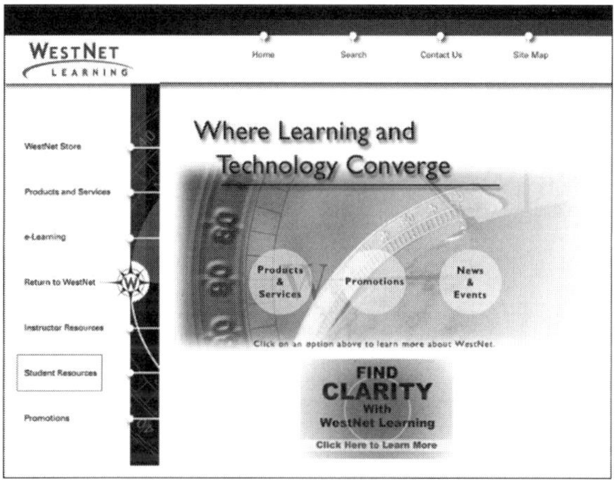

To enter the site, use your e-mail address to login and then type in this course's ISBN number. After you're in the Resources pages, look for the Suggested lab options associated with this module and lesson. Then answer the following questions.

1. What command is used to add entries into a host table?

 ____

2. What command is used to display the contents of the host table?

 ____

3. What entries are shown when this command is used?

 ____

4. Are these entries permanent or temporary?

____

- From a DOS prompt on any Windows workstation with Internet connectivity, use the commands:

  ```
  Click Start | Run
  ```

  In the window, type **command** or **cmd** if it is not already there. At the DOS prompt, type:

  ```
  ping www.westnetlearning.com
  ```

1. Did the domain name resolve to an IP address? Write the IP address here.

   ____

2. Was the ping successful?

   ____

3. If not, why do you think it failed?

   ____

4. How many hops did it take to get to the final destination?

   ____

5. Did the request time out (give an *) before it finished?

   ____

6. What could you tell from the names of the routers that were handling the tracert?

   ____

Summary

Lesson 1 began this module with a focus on Cisco's proprietary CDP, which is network protocol- and topology-independent. CDP gathers information about directly connected devices running CDP and can help document a network. Several show commands were reviewed to gather neighbor information.

Lesson 2 reviewed Telnet and virtual terminal capabilities. Telnet is an IP application that has the ability to make remote console connections for configuration and monitoring purposes. This is useful instead of having to go to the device location and making a connection. It is possible to make five virtual connections to a router (using the enterprise edition IOS). These connections are labeled line vty 0 4 and must be initially configured using the console port. This lesson reviewed how to configure Telnet capabilities, toggle between sessions, show Telnet information, and terminate sessions.

Lesson 3 presented many of the important components of a Cisco router, including physical components such as memory areas and interfaces, as well as software components such as the boot microcode, the IOS, and configuration files. A router reads the configuration register to determine the proper boot process. To boot up, the router runs a POST, finds and loads the IOS, and then finds and loads a configuration.

The process of backing up and restoring configuration files and the IOS to a TFTP server was covered in Lesson 4. This process is very important to protect the router and network environment.

The final lesson discussed network administration functions and tools. An administrator is often tasked with adding new equipment to a network, moving devices, and changing existing hardware and software components. Lesson 5 discussed the steps necessary to make these tasks successful. Several administration tools were also reviewed in this lesson. These tools include name resolution services, Ping to test connectivity, traceroute to verify transmission path, and debug commands to view dynamic network statistics.

The Summary of Commands Table summarizes the syntax of the various commands introduced in this module.

Summary of Commands

Command Prompt, Syntax, and Options	Description
Router#**show cdp**	Displays the CDP configuration.
Router#**show cdp neighbors** Router#**show cdp entry**	Displays a list of the directly connected neighbors discovered with CDP. Ports must be enabled to work.
Router#**show cdp neighbors detail** or **show cdp entry ***	Provides specifics such as IP address and IOS version.
Router#**show cdp interface**	Displays how an interface is configured for CDP.
Router#**show cdp traffic**	Displays real-time CDP communications.
Router(config)#**no cdp run**	Disables CDP for the entire router.
Router(config-if)#**no cdp enable** or **cdp enable**	Disables or enables CDP for a particular interface.
Router#**telnet** *ip-address* or **telnet** *hostname* Note: Only the IP address or hostname is necessary.	Attempts a virtual terminal connection with another device. The device must have VTY password and login set.
Router#**CTRL+SHIFT+6** then the **X** key	Used to toggle between two active Telnet sessions.
Router#**show sessions**	Displays the Telnet, console, and AUX connections.
Router#**disconnect** *session-number*	Ends a Telnet session from the connected device.
Router#**show users**	Displays the user's current connections.
Router#**clear line** *line-number*	Ends a Telnet session from the host device.
Router#**show version**	Displays the IOS file name, memory, hardware statistics, and contents of the configuration register.
Router#**show flash**	Displays the model info, IOS version, and file name.
Router#**copy run start**	Saves the current configuration to NVRAM.

Summary of Commands (Continued)

Command Prompt, Syntax, and Options	Description
Router#**copy start run**	Saves the NVRAM contents over the current configuration.
Router#**copy run tftp** or **copy start tftp**	Backs up the configuration file to a TFTP server. A number of questions must be answered for success.
Router#**copy tftp run** or **copy tftp start**	Restores a copy of the configuration file from a TFTP server. The administrator is then prompted for the file name, IP address, and so forth.
Router#**copy flash tftp**	Backs up the IOS to a TFTP server.
Router#**copy tftp flash**	Restores or upgrades the IOS from a TFTP server.
Router#**erase start**	Removes the contents of NVRAM to factory default.
Router#**reload**	Reloads the router and prompts for configuration.
Router(config)#**ip host** *hostname* *ip_address*	Manually configures a hostname and IP address in the host table for address resolution.
Router(config)#**ip name-server** [*server-ip-address1*] [*server-ip-address2*]...	Configures the IP address of known name servers used for address resolution without a host table.
Router(config)#**no ip domain-lookup**	Prevents the router from attempting to resolve any command not recognized as typed.
Router#**show hosts**	Displays the contents of the host table both manually entered and learned from a name server.
Router#**ping** *ip-address* or **ping** *hostname*	Sends an ICMP echo request to check connectivity.
Router#**trace** *ip-address* or **trace** *hostname*	Displays the hops from sender to destination device.
Router(config)#**boot system flash** *filename* Router(config)#**boot system tftp** *filename ip_address* Router(config)#**boot system rom**	Defines the boot location for the IOS image; options include flash memory, TFTP server, or ROMMON mode.

Summary of Commands (Continued)

Command Prompt, Syntax, and Options	Description
Router#**debug all** Router#**no debug all**	Turns on all debug commands. Should never be used because it will have detrimental impact on any device. The **no debug all** command will turn off all debug displays.
Router#**show processes**	Displays the processor utilization. Helpful when deciding if it is appropriate to use a debug command based on processor usage.
Router(config)#**service timestamps debug datetime msec**	Configures timestamps when displaying debug information.
Router(config)#**logging console debugging** Router(config)#**no logging console**	Displays the contents of all debug information to the console screen. Use the privileged EXEC command **show debugging** to view the displayed information.
Router(config)#**logging monitor debugging** Router(config)#**no logging monitor**	Displays the contents of debug information to a virtual terminal. Use the privileged EXEC command **terminal monitor** to see the debug screen.
Router(config)#**logging** *ip_address* Router(config)#**no logging** *ip_address*	Sends debug information to a UNIX SYSlog server that maintains the log information. The output can be displayed using the appropriate UNIX commands.
Router(config)#**logging buffered** Router(config)#**no logging buffered**	Sends the debug information into the internal device buffer. This method has the lowest resource usage. To view the output, use the privileged EXEC command **show logging**.

Module 9 Quiz

1. In a router, flash memory is used to store which of the following?
   a. Startup-config file
   b. Running-config file
   c. Boot image
   d. The IOS
2. The configuration register is a 16-bit software register. Reading from left to right, which bits represent the boot field?
   a. The first four (15 to 12)
   b. The second four (11 to 8)
   c. The third four (7 to 4)
   d. The last four (3 to 0)
3. What is the default configuration register value set to?
   a. 0x2100
   b. 0x2102
   c. 0x2101
   d. 0x2142
4. Which commands are used to identify the IOS file name? (Choose two.)
   a. **`show version`**
   b. **`show flash`**
   c. **`show run`**
   d. **`show config`**
5. By default, what is the CDP timer set to when exchanging information between devices?
   a. Every 180 seconds
   b. Every 60 seconds
   c. Every 30 seconds
   d. Every 45 seconds

6. Which of the following commands is used to back up the IOS to a TFTP server?
   a. **copy tftp flash**
   b. **copy run flash**
   c. **copy run start**
   d. **copy flash tftp**
7. Which of the following components is not required when creating a backup to a TFTP server?
   a. IP address of the TFTP server
   b. Login and password for the TFTP server
   c. Source file name
   d. Destination file name
8. During a restore of the IOS from a TFTP server, the lowercase letter "e" represents what?
   a. Successful transfer of UDP segments
   b. Successful copy of the IOS images
   c. Current contents of flash memory being erased
   d. Startup-config being erased
9. After the IOS is restored to a router, what is the next step?
   a. The router is fully functional.
   b. The router automatically reloads itself.
   c. The router is shut down and must be manually restarted.
   d. The router sends out updates letting other devices know it is available.
10. Which memory component is used to store packet buffers, routing tables, and the current running configuration?
    a. NVRAM
    b. DRAM
    c. Flash memory
    d. ROM

11. Which components are stored in NVRAM on a router? (Choose two.)

    a. Flash memory and the IOS

    b. The IOS and startup-config file

    c. Startup-config file and configuration register

    d. Startup-config file and running-config file

12. To configure a Telnet password for all five sessions, which command would you execute?

    a. **login**

    b. **line VTY 0 4**

    c. **line telnet 0 4**

    d. **telnet session 5**

13. Which **show cdp** command allows you to view IP address information?

    a. **show cdp timers**

    b. **show cdp neighbors**

    c. **show cdp neighbors detail**

    d. **show cdp traffic**

14. The command **show cdp neighbor details** is the same as which other command?

    a. **show cdp entries ***

    b. **show cdp neighbors**

    c. **show cdp traffic**

    d. **show cdp interface**

15. When a router boot sequence is first initiated, from where does it load the IOS by default?

    a. ROM

    b. Flash memory

    c. NVRAM

    d. TFTP server

16. Which command is used to back up the current configuration so it is available after a restart?
    a. **copy run start**
    b. **copy start run**
    c. **copy start tftp**
    d. **copy tftp start**
17. Which command is used to clear the contents of NVRAM?
    a. **erase run**
    b. **erase memory**
    c. **erase nvram**
    d. **erase start**
18. Which command is used to perform a "warm boot" of a router?
    a. **restart**
    b. **shut down**
    c. **no shut**
    d. **reload**
19. When a router is booted up, what is the first process that takes place?
    a. The router performs a POST.
    b. The router reads the configuration register.
    c. The router finds and loads the IOS.
    d. The router finds and loads the startup-config file.
20. If a configuration file is not located, how will a router respond?
    a. Reboot again and try and find the config file
    b. Look in another location for the configuration
    c. Enter setup mode, and prompt with basic configuration questions
    d. Shut down because it cannot function without a configuration

21. Which tool is used to test connectivity only up to the Network Layer of the OSI model?
    a. Ping
    b. Telnet
    c. Track
    d. RIP
22. Which command line includes the first command that must be used to configure Telnet access?
    a. `Router(config)#`**`password`**
    b. `Router(config)#`**`login`**
    c. `Router(config)#`**`line aux`**
    d. `Router(config)#`**`line console`**
23. When a ping is performed to test connectivity, what is really taking place?
    a. An ICMP echo request and echo reply are being used.
    b. An ICMP TTL has expired.
    c. An ICMP source quench message is sent.
    d. A data packet is acknowledged to indicate connection.
24. The systems used to resolve IP addresses associated with hostnames could be all of the following except which?
    a. Host name table
    b. DNS server
    c. Name server
    d. ARP
25. Which method cannot be used to terminate a Telnet session?
    a. **`disconnect 1`**
    b. **`exit`**
    c. **`end`**
    d. **`clear line 2`**

26. What is the key sequence used to toggle between active Telnet sessions?
    a. **CTRL+ENTER**, then **Z**
    b. **CTRL+Z**
    c. **CTRL+SHIFT+6**, then **X**
    d. **CTRL+ALT+DELETE**
27. Which command correctly configures a Telnet password?
    a. **`login password telnet`**
    b. **`line vty 0 4 password`**
    c. **`password telnet`**
    d. **`password vty 0 4`**
28. The **`trace`** command shows transmissions through which type of device?
    a. Hubs
    b. Switches
    c. Routers
    d. Repeaters
29. If a hacker is suspected of getting access to a router through a Telnet connection, and the **`show users`** command has been used to verify it, how could the connection in question be terminated?
    a. clear user 1
    b. disconnection user 1
    c. clear line 1
    d. kill session 1
30. Which command correctly configures a device by the name of "stargate" to the IP address 172.16.37.44?
    a. `Router(config)#`**`ip host 172.16.37.44 stargate`**
    b. `Router(config)#`**`ip host stargate 172.16.37.44`**
    c. `Router#`**`ip hostname stargate 172.16.37.44`**
    d. `Router#`**`ip name stargate ip 172.16.37.44`**

31. Which command could be used to determine which Telnet connection is currently active on screen?
    a. `Router#`**`show users`**
    b. `Router#`**`show vty`**
    c. `Router#`**`show sessions`**
    d. `Router#`**`show telnet`**
32. In what order will a device look for the IOS image to load during the bootup process?
    a. Flash memory, location specified in configuration register, location in NVRAM
    b. TFTP server, flash memory, location specified in configuration register
    c. Location specified in NVRAM, location specified in configuration register, the first file found in flash memory
    d. Location specified in configuration register, location specified in NVRAM, the first file found in flash memory
33. If the configuration command **`boot system rom`** is entered, how will the IOS image load?
    a. In ROMMON mode
    b. With the full IOS image in flash memory
    c. From a TFTP server location
    d. Using the mini-IOS image
34. What is the URL syntax used to identify RAM in IOS version 12.0 and later?
    a. **`nvram:`**
    b. **`ram:`**
    c. **`dram:`**
    d. **`system:`**

35. Using the URL syntax, what is the proper command to replace **copy run start** in IOS version 12.0 and later?

    a. **copy system:running-config nvram:startup-config**

    b. **copy nvram:startup-config system:running-config**

    c. **copy dram:running-config nvram:startup-config**

    d. **copy ram:run config:start**

36. Which configuration steps should be performed when installing/adding a new device to a network? (Choose two.)

    a. Configure a MAC address on all router interfaces.

    b. Configure an IP address on all router interfaces.

    c. Use the debug command to see network traffic.

    d. Configure a routing protocol.

37. Which of the following is not a consideration when upgrading the IOS image?

    a. Whether there is enough flash memory storage

    b. Whether the IOS version is compatible with the hardware

    c. Whether there is an expansion slot for the IOS module to fit into

    d. Whether there is enough RAM to run the IOS feature set

38. Which command is used to disable debug information?

    a. **no logging debug**

    b. **no debug all**

    c. **no show debug**

    d. **debug off**

39. Which characteristics of using debug commands for troubleshooting? (Choose two.)

    a. Debug commands can show activity on a remote device.

    b. Debug is resource-intensive because it gets priority processing.

    c. Debug shows dynamic network traffic as it is being transmitted.

    d. Debug shows specific statistics information in a snapshot format.

Course Quiz

1. What are the layers of the OSI reference model, in order?
   a. Application, Transport, Network, Physical, Data Link, Presentation
   b. Application, Presentation, Session, Network, Transport, Data Link, Physical
   c. Application, Presentation, Session, Transport, Network, Data Link, Physical
   d. Application, Session, Transport, Physical, Network, Internet, Presentation
2. What is the function of CSMA/CD?
   a. It passes a token around a star topology.
   b. Nodes listen to access the network and retransmit if they detect a collision.
   c. Nodes connect to a dual ring of fiber-optics and use a token-passing scheme.
   d. Nodes break the frames into tiny cells and forward them through a cell-switching network.
3. What does the hierarchical Network Layer address represent?
   a. A hardware address of the machine
   b. A unique address with node portion and a hardware portion
   c. A unique address with network portion and a node/host portion
   d. A network address associated to a hardware address

4. Which of the following statements describes a broadcast domain?
   a. Only a few nodes on the network see the data addressed for those nodes.
   b. All nodes in a network segment see all the broadcast messages.
   c. The network informs all the nodes of a network failure.
   d. All the devices must contend for the same bandwidth.
5. To access the global configuration mode of a switch, you would use which two commands?
   a. `Switch>Config t`
   b. `Switch#Enable`
   c. `Switch#Config t`
   d. `Switch>Enable`
6. You can confirm that you are in the privileged EXEC mode by which prompt?
   a. `Switch>`
   b. `Switch(config)#`
   c. `Switch#`
   d. `Switch(config-if)#`
7. To determine the operational status of an interface, which command do you use?
   a. `display interface status`
   b. `show interface`
   c. `show status interface`
   d. `display interface`
8. Which of the following can be used to move from a configuration mode to the privileged exec mode?
   a. Ctrl+Z or `exit`
   b. `Enable` or `exit`
   c. Ctrl + Break or `close`
   d. `Exit` or `logout`

9. What is the term for wrapping a data unit with a header and passing it to the next protocol?
   a. Windowing
   b. Encapsulation
   c. Wrapping
   d. Buffering
10. What command can be used to see the router's neighbors from your local router if no Network Layer protocols are configured?
    a. `show cdp`
    b. `show cdp neighbor`
    c. `show neighbor`
    d. `show network`
11. By default, how many commands are stored in the command history buffer?
    a. 5
    b. 10
    c. 15
    d. 20
12. In what is the IOS image normally stored?
    a. RAM
    b. NVRAM
    c. Shared RAM
    d. Flash
13. The boot field consists of ______________________________.
    a. The lowest four bits of the configuration register
    b. The entire configuration register
    c. The highest four bits of the configuration register
    d. Bits 4 through 7 of the configuration register

14. What is the default configuration register number?
    a. 0x2101
    b. 0x2100
    c. 0x2102
    d. 0x2142
15. To view the configuration register settings, which command do you enter?
    a. `show running-configuration`
    b. `show startup-configuration`
    c. `show version`
    d. `show config`
16. Which two commands are used to determine the release of route IOS?
    a. `show flash`
    b. `show running-config`
    c. `show startup-config`
    d. `show version`
    e. `show IOS`
17. What is the command to backup the saved configuration to a TFTP server?
    a. `copy startup-config tftp`
    b. `copy flash tftp`
    c. `copy tftp running-config`
    d. `copy tftp startup-config`
18. After typing the command **`int e0`** from global configuration mode, the router prompt will change to:
    a. `router(config)#`
    b. `router(config-line)#`
    c. `router(config-if)#`
    d. `router(config-int)#`

19. What command will access the prompt used to set a password for all telnet sessions?
    a. `Line vty 0 4`
    b. `Line telnet`
    c. `Line console`
    d. `Line aux`
20. What is the sequence of events that occurs when you power up your router?
    a. Find configuration file, load IOS image, test hardware
    b. Load IOS image, test hardware, find configuration file
    c. Test hardware, find configuration file, load IOS image
    d. Test hardware, load IOS image, find configuration file
21. How do you temporarily suspend (toggle between) a Telnet session and the original host prompt?
    a. Use the command SUSPEND SESSION.
    b. Use the show sessions, then type exit.
    c. Use the keystrokes Ctrl-Shift-6 + X.
    d. A Telnet session cannot be suspended. You must quit the session and initiate it again if you want to go back to it.
22. Which characters indicate a successful PING?
    a. !!!!!
    b. .....
    c. XXXXX
    d. ******
23. What class of address is 190.233.27.13?
    a. Class A
    b. Class B
    c. Class C
    d. Class D

24. To view name-to-IP address mappings cached on the router, what command would you issue?
    a. `Router#show hosts`
    b. `Router(config)#show hosts`
    c. `Router#ip name-server`
    d. `Router(config)#ip name-server`
25. What is the purpose of subnetting?
    a. To create smaller broadcast domains
    b. To divide a network between servers and workstations
    c. To allow bridging between network segments
    d. To isolate groups of hosts so they can't communicate
    e. To get more IP host addresses
26. What is UDP?
    a. A protocol that makes the Transport Layer independent
    b. A connectionless, unreliable transport protocol
    c. A protocol that allows multiple applications to share a network connection
    d. A function that makes remote procedures appear to be local
27. What is the purpose of a routing table?
    a. It is the physical support for the router to sit on.
    b. It contains a list of all the timers used to prevent routing loops.
    c. It is used to select the best route using a metric.
    d. It manages the periodic update algorithm.
28. What qualities match TCP?
    a. Connectionless, reliable
    b. Connection-oriented, reliable
    c. Connectionless, unreliable
    d. Connection-oriented, unreliable

29. What class of address is 100.233.27.13?
    a. Class A
    b. Class B
    c. Class C
    d. Class D
30. What is ARP (Address Resolution Protocol) used for?
    a. Finding workstations on the network by name
    b. Identifying a MAC address when the IP address is known
    c. Identify an IP address when the MAC address is known
    d. Resolving IP to a hostname
31. What is the default mask for a Class C network?
    a. 255.0.0.0
    b. 255.255.255.0
    c. 255.255.0.0
    d. 255.225.0.0
32. What is the decimal value of the binary number 11001011?
    a. 203
    b. 171
    c. 207
    d. 193
33. Given a subnet mask of 255.255.240.0, which of these addresses is not a valid host address?
    a. 150.150.37.2
    b. 150.150.16.2
    c. 150.150.32.0
    d. 150.150.49.15
34. If you were issued a Class C address and needed to divide the network into five subnets, with up to 15 hosts in each subnet, what subnet mask would you use?
    a. 255.255.255.224
    b. 255.255.224 .0
    c. 255.255.255.240
    d. None of the Above

35. Three of the addresses below are in the same network using the subnet mask 255.255.248.0. Which address is not?

    a. 172.16.8.16

    b. 172.16.15.250

    c. 172.16.16.11

    d. 172.16.12.200

36. Which type of interface consists of a set of text-based commands that the user types in to perform functions?

    a. Command and Control Interface

    b. Graphical User Interface

    c. Command Line Interface

    d. Text Entry Interface

37. Which IEEE standard is the specification for Gigabit Ethernet over fiber optic cable?

    a. 802.3u

    b. 802.3

    c. 802.3z

    d. 802.5

38. The router that is the single access point from a LAN to the outside network is known as the border router, or ____________________.

    a. Boundary router

    b. LAN guard

    c. Default gateway

    d. Application server

39. ________________ communication occurs when signals are sent and received with a clocking signal to coordinate serial transmission.

    a. Asynchronous

    b. Simultaneous

    c. Full duplex

    d. Synchronous

40. How much bandwidth does a digital service level 0, or DS0, connection provide?

    a. 256 Kbps
    b. 128 Kbps
    c. 64 Kbps
    d. 56 Kbps
    e. None of the above

41. ____________ connect storage media so they are accessible by any number of end systems.

    a. MANs
    b. WANs
    c. SANs
    d. DANs
    e. CLANs

42. Wireless transmission uses portions of the ______________ to carry signals through open space.

    a. Bandwidth frequency
    b. Electromagnetic spectrum
    c. Internet protocol
    d. Frequency spectrum

43. A UTP cable contains eight wires, of which four are used for data transmissions. Identify the wires used:

    a. 1, 2, 3, and 6
    b. 1, 4, 5, and 7
    c. 5, 6, 7, and 8
    d. 2, 4, 6, and 8

44. What is used in the first step in setting up a console connection to a router to make a physical connection?

    a. LAN connection
    b. Straight-through cable
    c. Rollover cable
    d. Wireless uplink

45. xDSL service is provided over what type of connection?
    a. T1
    b. T3
    c. POTS line
    d. Coaxial cable
46. If you connect two routers in a back-to-back serial link to extend your network, you will need to configure one of them to do which of the following?
    a. receive transmissions from the other router only
    b. transmit a clocking signal to synchronize transmissions
    c. read from the other router's addressing table
    d. send "keep-alive" packets over the network
47. Routers that support cable modem connections, such as Cisco's uBR905, provide a(n) ____________ on the backplane to enable connection to a coaxial cable.
    a. F-connector
    b. BRU interface
    c. Modular interface
    d. RJ-48 connector
48. Because broadcast traffic can slow down network performance, it is often useful to divide a network into smaller broadcast domains using routers, layer 3 switches, or ________________.
    a. Hubs
    b. Bridges
    c. VLANs
    d. Cubicles
49. What is the maximum segment length specified by both Ethernet 10BaseT and 100BaseT standards?
    a. 50 meters
    b. 100 meters
    c. 185 meters
    d. 500 meters

50. If a switch cannot locate the MAC address specified by a frame in its address table, what does the switch do?
    a. Broadcasts the frame to all nodes
    b. Floods the frame out to all ports, except the one by which it entered the switch
    c. Drops the frame and sends an error notification
    d. Filters the frame from all ports, except the one by which it entered the switch
51. Which switch method reads an entire frame and performs a CRC before forwarding it?
    a. Cut through
    b. Modified cut through
    c. Store and forward
    d. CRC check and forward
52. What type of device do you need to enable communication between two VLANs?
    a. Router
    b. Layer 3 switch
    c. Router Switch module
    d. Layer 2 switch
    e. Any of the above
    f. Only A, B, or C
53. The two encapsulation options that identify and maintain VLAN separation are Cisco's InterSwitch Link and IEEE ________________.
    a. 802.11b
    b. 802.1D
    c. 802.1Q
    d. 802.6G

54. Which IP function ensures that packets conform to the maximum transmission units (MTUs) of other network segments?
    a. Hierarchical Addressing
    b. Connectionless Best Effort Delivery
    c. Fragmentation
    d. None of the above
55. Which field helps identify and prioritize traffic when the packet passes through a router?
    a. Protocol field
    b. Type of Service field
    c. Source IP Address field
    d. Destination IP Address field
56. What are the two most common protocols and protocol numbers used in the Protocol field?
    a. 6 = TCP and 1 = ICMP
    b. 17 = UDP and 9 = IGRP
    c. 6 = TCP and 41 = IPv6
    d. 17 = UDP and 6 = TCP
57. What term describes a data can flow process that adapts to congestion or packet loss?
    a. Hand-off point
    b. Three way handshake
    c. Wink and a nod
    d. Sliding windows
58. Which of the following Upper Layer protocols are associated with e-mail transmissions? (Choose two)
    a. POP3
    b. SNMP
    c. SMTP
    d. MAIL2
    e. EMAP

59. Which two components are found in a UDP header? (Choose two.)
    a. Segment number
    b. Acknowledgement
    c. Source Port
    d. Destination Port
    e. IP address
60. Besides Network and Broadcast, what is another reserved IP address?
    a. Host
    b. MAC
    c. Destination
    d. Local loopback
61. A network is being designed with a requirement for 200 subnets. What is the subnet mask necessary to fulfill this requirement when using a Class B address?
    a. 255.255.255.0
    b. 255.255.248.0
    c. 255.255.240.0
    d. 255.255.255.192
62. You are reconfiguring a network for future growth. The current IP address is 172.16.0.0, and the subnet mask is 255.255.224.0. The network needs to expand by 40 additional subnets. What subnet mask must be used to accommodate this requirement?
    a. 255.255.248.0
    b. 255.255.255.0
    c. 255.255.252.0
    d. 255.255.240.0

63. Using logical ANDing, on which subnet is the address 192.168.40.123 255.255.255.248 located?
    a. 192.168.40.112
    b. 192.168.40.120
    c. 192.168.40.122
    d. 192.168.40.116
64. Which of the following provides a total bandwidth of 1.536 (1.544) Mbps?
    a. DS0
    b. T1 line
    c. T3/DS3 line
    d. All of the above
65. Which of the following are techniques to carry multiple conversations or data communications channels over a single facility? (Choose two.)
    a. Time division multiplexing
    b. Frequency division multiplexing
    c. Data division multiplexing
    d. Packet modulation
66. What does the phone company need to install to make DSL service available?
    a. Modem Bank
    b. Cable modem head end
    c. Network Control Link Protocol (NCLP)
    d. Digital Subscriber Line Access Multiplexer (DSLAM)
67. What distinguishes ADSL from SDSL?
    a. Asymmetric is analog; symmetric is digital.
    b. Asymmetric is digital; symmetric is analog.
    c. Asymmetric has more bandwidth for download than upload; symmetric is the same bandwidth for both upload and download.
    d. Asymmetric is high bandwidth; symmetric is low bandwidth.

68. What does ATM transmit?
    a. 1500 byte frames
    b. 1.544 Mbps
    c. 53 byte cells
    d. 64 Kbps B channels
69. Which groups of commands are commonly used on a router for troubleshooting purposes? (Choose two.)
    a. `Debug`
    b. `Show`
    c. `Shutdown`
    d. `Routing`
    e. `Config`
70. Which of the following are Cisco IOS functions on a Router? (Choose three.)
    a. Connectivity
    b. Administrator interface
    c. Scalability
    d. Reliability
    e. VLAN configuration
71. Which method is used for in-band administrative access to a router?
    a. Telnet over the LAN
    b. Console port
    c. AUX port
    d. Router configuration module
72. Which key sequence allows you to break out of setup mode on a router?
    a. CTRL + BREAK
    b. CTRL + C
    c. Shift + Enter
    d. Exit

73. Which item cannot be setup when configuring a router for the first time using the menu driven setup utility?
    a. IP address
    b. Enable password
    c. Routing protocol
    d. MAC address
    e. Telnet password
74. What is the very first process that takes place when a switch or router is started?
    a. Run the setup program
    b. POST process
    c. Load the IOS
    d. Load the configuration
    e. Access the CLI
75. Which error message would indicate not enough characters were typed to distinguish the command from another?
    a. Unknown device
    b. Ambiguous command
    c. Invalid input detected
    d. Incomplete command
    e. Unknown command or computer name
76. What will happen when the command `Router(config-if)#`**`ip address 192.168.14.4`** is typed?
    a. The serial port will be assigned the IP address 192.168.14.4.
    b. The router will be assigned the IP address 192.168.14.4.
    c. An incomplete command error will be returned.
    d. An unknown command error will be returned.
77. When the router prompt is displayed as `Router(config-controller)#`, what is being configured?
    a. An ISDN line
    b. A PPP encapsulation
    c. A T1 or E1
    d. An auxiliary line

78. The prompt `Router(config-line)#` is configured with which three configuration modes?

    a. Interface

    b. ISDN

    c. Auxiliary

    d. Console

    e. Telnet/VTY

79. Which command would be necessary to set up a synchronization signal for a serial DCE connection?

    a. `Router(config-if)#`**`serial clockrate on`**

    b. `Router(config-if)#`**`clock rate 56000`**

    c. `Router(config-if)#`**`serial synch clock`**

    d. `Router(config-if)#`**`synchronization on`**

80. What is the default bandwidth of a serial interface on a router?

    a. 56 Kbps

    b. 64 Kbps

    c. 10 Mbps

    d. 1.544 Mbps

81. What command is used to activate an interface for transmission?

    a. `Router(config)#interface on`

    b. `Router(config)#active`

    c. `Router(config-if)#no shut`

    d. `Router(config-if)#activate`

    e. `Router(config-if)#enable`

82. Which command properly configures an encrypted enable password of "Monday" on a router?

    a. `Router(config)#password encrypt monday`

    b. `Router(config)#enable password monday`

    c. `Router(config)#enable encrypted password monday`

    d. `Router(config)#enable secret monday`

83. What items can be seen when using the command **`show cdp neighbors detail`**? (Choose three.)
    a. The MAC address of the neighbor device
    b. The IP address of the neighbor device
    c. The capability of the neighbor device
    d. The routing protocol of the neighbor device
    e. The interface connected to the neighbor device
84. Which items are stored in NVRAM on a router? (Choose two.)
    a. running-config file
    b. startup-config file
    c. IOS
    d. TFTP services
    e. Configuration register
85. What minimum components are necessary to create a peer-to-peer network between two PCs?
    a. A server
    b. A crossover cable
    c. A straight-through cable
    d. A router
    e. A common protocol
86. A network administrator suspects a hacker has logged into a router using a telnet session. What command could be used to terminate the connection?
    a. `kill user`
    b. `disable telnet`
    c. `clear line`
    d. `shutdown`
87. What does **`c2500-d-1_113-5.bin`** represent?
    a. The running-config file for a Cisco 2500 router
    b. An 11.3 version of an IOS file
    c. The name of a TFTP backup server
    d. A binary router flash-bios file

88. When you perform an IOS restore from a TFTP server, you are prompted for ________________________.
    a. IP address of the remote host
    b. The source file name
    c. The destination file name
    d. All of the above
    e. A and C
89. To restore a router's configuration to the factory-default settings, use the ________________ command.
    a. `erase eeprom`
    b. `erase start`
    c. `delete config`
    d. `delete IOS`
90. When troubleshooting a physical network issue which items should be checked first? (Choose two.)
    a. Telnet access into the router
    b. Routing protocols
    c. Cable connections
    d. Interface configurations
    e. IP addresses
91. When adding a new switch to the network, what step will never be performed?
    a. Assigning a hostname
    b. Making all cabled connections
    c. Configuring IP addresses for the serial ports
    d. Assigning passwords
92. A reload of the router is required to get a configuration change to take place. True or False?
93. On a router, the running-configuration file is stored in NVRAM. True or False?
94. Each independently controlled network environment is called an "autonomous system (AS)" and is managed under a common administrative entity. True or False?

95. Border Gateway Protocol (BGP) is an exterior routing protocol that communicates between autonomous systems.
    True or False?

96. What is the command to view the stored configuration in NVRAM on a router?

    ____

97. What command is necessary to type to enter Privileged EXEC mode?

    ____

98. At what layer of the OSI model is ICMP, IP, ARP, and RARP located?

    ____

99. What is the port number used for DNS that includes both a TCP and UDP portion?

    ____

100. What is the broadcast address for the given network address 192.168.45.16 and the subnet mask 255.255.255.240?

    ____

GLOSSARY

For additional terms and definitions, visit WestNet's IT Multimedia Glossary—complete with animations and graphics—at **http://glossary.westnetinc.com**

10Base2—10Base2, also called Thinnet, is one of several physical cabling standards for 802.3 Ethernet networks. It transmits Ethernet frames at a maximum of 10 Mbps, using a baseband signal over thin coaxial cabling, in a bus topology for a distance of 185 meters.

10Base5—10Base5, also called Thicknet, is one of several physical cabling standards for 802.3 Ethernet networks. It transmits Ethernet frames at a maximum of 10 Mbps, using a baseband signal over thick coaxial cabling, in a bus topology for a distance of 500 meters.

10BaseT—10BaseT is the IEEE standard for Ethernet transmission, using unshielded twisted pair (UTP) cable. It transmits Ethernet frames at a maximum of 10 Mbps, using a Baseband signal over a minimum Category 3 (CAT3) cable, (T for twisted pair). The maximum cable segment is 100 meters, using a star topology.

10GBASE-E—10GBASE-E is 10 Gbps 9.0 single-mode fiber with a 1550-nm laser light source and serial transmission for a minimum distance of 40,000 meters.

10GBASE-L—10GBASE-L is 10 Gbps 9.0 single-mode fiber with a 1310-nm laser light source and serial transmissions for a minimum distance of 10,000 meters.

10GBASE-LX4—10GBASE-LX4 is a standard that has two specifications: 10 Gbps 62.5 multimode fiber with a 1310-nm laser light source, using Coarse Wave Division Multiplexing (CWDM) technology for a minimum distance of 300 meters and 10 Gbps 9.0 single-mode fiber with a 1310-nm laser light source, using CWDM for a minimum distance of 10,000 meters.

10GBASE-S—10GBASE-S is 10 Gbps 50.0 multimode fiber with an 850-nm laser light source. The S at the end of the standard stands for serial transmission over a minimum of 65 meters.

10-Gigabit Ethernet—Formerly ratified in June 2002, the IEEE 802.3ae standard for 10-Gigabit Ethernet outlines the cable types and technologies used to achieve this high level of bandwidth.

80/20 Rule—The 80/20 rule states that 80 percent of network traffic should stay in local subnets, and only 20 percent should cross the backbone to reach a remote subnet.

100BaseT (or TX)—100BaseT (or TX) is the group of proposed IEEE 802.3 Physical Layer specifications for 100-Mbps Ethernet (Fast Ethernet) over various unshielded twisted pair (UTP) wiring specifications.

802.11—802.11 is the IEEE standard that specifies medium access and Physical Layer specifications for 1 Mbps and 2 Mbps wireless connectivity, using the 915 Mhz unlicensed frequency and frequency hopping spread spectrum.

802.11a—802.11a was ratified by the IEEE to provide very high rate transmissions up to 54 Mbps. It uses the 5 Ghz frequency and a process called "orthogonal frequency division multiplexing." The 5 Ghz frequency is not unlicensed throughout the world, which causes conflicts with equipment in some areas. Therefore, 802.11g was created to address this issue.

802.11b—802.11b was ratified as the IEEE as the "High Rate" amendment in September 1999; it added two higher speeds (5.5 Mbps and 11 Mbps) to 802.11. The basic architecture, features, and services of 802.11b are defined by the original 802.11 standard, changing only the Physical Layer to add higher data rates and more robust connectivity. 802.11b is also referred to as 802.11 High Rate or Wi-Fi. It uses the 2.4 Ghz unlicensed frequency and direct sequence spread spectrum.

802.11g—IEEE 802.1g is a proposed wireless network standard designed to provide the bandwidth of 802.11a networks (54Mbps) while maintaining backward compatibility with 802.11b networks using the 2.4 GHz unlicensed frequency.

802.1D—802.1D is the IEEE standard that covers the process of preventing active loops in bridged and switched networks using the spanning tree algorithm.

802.1p—802.1p is the IEEE Data Link Layer standard that allows for the prioritization of frames based on MAC layer header information. 802.1p uses a portion of the 802.1Q VLAN tag to represent priority values that define eight different queue levels.

802.1Q—802.1Q is the IEEE vendor neutral standard for VLAN implementation. The standard specifies a 2-byte VLAN tag that includes a 12-bit VLAN identifier, used by network switches to decide which network segment they should forward a frame.

802.2—802.2 is the IEEE standard for the Upper Data Link Layer sublayer, also known as the Logical Link Control (LLC). It is independent of the 802.3 (Ethernet), 802.4 (Token Bus), and 802.5 (Token Ring) standards at the Data Link MAC sublayer.

802.3—802.3 is the IEEE standard that covers carrier sense, multiple access with collision detection (CSMA/CD). This LAN technology is more commonly known as Ethernet. 802.3 offers Physical Layer cabling specifications as well as MAC sublayer encapsulation and frame handling methodologies.

802.3ab—802.3ab is the IEEE standard that defines the fiber optic cable types and technologies used to run Gigabit Ethernet (1000 Mb).

802.3ae—802.3ae is the IEEE standard for 10-Gigabit Ethernet cable types and technologies.

802.3u—Fast Ethernet specifies 100-Mb transmission over UTP Category 5 or fiber optic cable.

802.3z—802.3z is the IEEE standard that defines the unshielded twisted pair (UTP) cable types and technologies used to run Gigabit Ethernet (1000 Mb).

802.5—802.5 is the IEEE standard for the token-passing (Token Ring) access method of LAN protocols. It encompasses standards both at the Data Link and Physical layers.

1000BaseCX—1000BaseCX is 1 Gigabit Ethernet over shielded twisted pair (STP) copper media.

1000BaseLX—Also called LH, 1000BaseLX ("L" for long wavelength) is the 802.3z technology that defines optical transceivers or Physical Layer devices for laser fiber cabling. The wavelength of LX lasers is 1,270 to 1,355 nm, and is commonly referred to as 1,350 nm. 1000BaseLX is also based on the Fibre Channel physical signaling specification. 1000BaseLX is specified for use on either multimode or single-mode fiber.

1000BaseSX—1000BaseSX ("S" for short wavelength) defines optical transceivers or Physical Layer devices for laser fiber cabling. The wavelength of SX lasers is 770 to 860 nanometers (nm), and is commonly referred to as 850 nm. 1000BaseSX is based on the Fibre Channel physical signaling specification. Targeted for multimode fiber only, 1000BaseSX transceivers are less costly than those found in products implementing the long wave-length specification, such as the 1000BaseLX (long wavelength) specification.

1000BaseT (or TX)—1000BaseTX ("T" for twisted pair) is the developing specification for Gigabit Ethernet over four-pair Category 5/5e/6 UTP copper cabling for distances up to 100 m.

1000BaseZX—1000BaseZX is the shorthand name for a 1,000 Mbps Gigabit Ethernet Physical Layer specification defined in the IEEE 802.3z document, which runs over 9/12.5 single mode fiber optic cable with a maximum segment length of 100,000 meters.

access list—An access list is a set of commands designed to filter traffic through a network. An access list is composed of one or more test statements and is categorized by the complexity of the test process as either standard or extended.

acknowledgment (ACK)—An acknowledgment is the connection-oriented service provided by TCP that lets a sending device know a segment was received by the destination and more data can be sent. If an acknowledgment is not received for a specific segment or within a specified amount of time, the sender host will retransmit.

active loop—An active loop is found in a bridge or switch environment that has redundant routes that may be misconfigured. Active loops can cause a number of issues that can dramatically impact network performance. Active loops are addressed using the IEEE 802.1D Spanning Tree Algorithm.

address—An address is a unique identifier that can be physical (MAC address), logical (a hierarchical IP address), a specific application or software process (port number), or a fully qualified domain name (universal resource locator URL). Addresses are necessary at many layers of the OSI model to send transmissions from source to destination.

Address Resolution Protocol (ARP)—ARP is an Internet Control Message Protocol (ICMP)/Network Layer protocol used to identify a MAC address when the IP address is known. An ARP request is transmitted as a broadcast and cached into memory.

address range—The address range is the range of IP addresses available for host assignment. It begins one address greater than the network number and one less than the broadcast address for the network segment.

adjacency—Adjacency is a relationship formed between selected neighboring routers and end nodes for the purpose of exchanging routing information. Adjacency is based upon the use of a common media segment.

administrative distance (AD)—AD is the number assigned to each routing protocol that provides the "believability" of a path. The number ranges from 0 to 255. The higher the number, the less trustworthy the path; the lower the number, the more believable the path. A router uses this number to determine which routing protocol to select if more than one is configured.

aging—Aging is the process of removing an entry from a MAC address table when it has not communicated in a specified period of time.

American National Standards Institute (ANSI)—ANSI is a national voluntary organization that develops and publishes standards for data communications, programming languages, magnetic storage media, office systems, and encryption.

analog—An analog signal is transmitted as a pattern of continually changing electromagnetic waves.

American Registry for Internet Numbers (ARIN)—ARIN handles registration of western-hemisphere domain names in the following top-level domains: com, org, net, and edu. (The U.S. government manages mil and gov domain names.)

American Standard Code for Information Interchange (ASCII)—The ASCII format is a coding standard that uses 8 bits for the representation of alphanumeric characters.

amplitude—Amplitude is the height of a wave or how far from the center it reaches.

analog—Analog is a term that describes a signal that is transmitted as a pattern of continually changing electromagnetic waves.

ANSI/EIA/TIA-568A and -568B—ANSI/EIA/TIA-568A and -568B are the ANSI/EIA/TIA-568 designations for 100-ohm unshielded twisted-pair cables and associated connecting hardware whose characteristics are specified for data transmission up to 100 Mbps. These designations are equivalent to AT&T standard 258A.

Application Layer—The Application Layer is the highest layer in the OSI protocol stack; it contains the software code that provides program functionality and provide a user interface. Examples of applications include Web browsers, Web servers, word processing software and database applications.

application-specific integrated circuit (ASIC)—ASIC is an electronics technology that hard-wires a device to switch a specific Layer 2 protocol, such as Ethernet, or a Layer 3 protocol, such as IP. Switches that use ASIC hardware are much faster than switches that rely on slower software.

Asia Pacific Network Information Center (APNIC)—APNIC manages IP addresses in the Asia Pacific area.

Asymmetric Digital Subscriber Line (ADSL)—ADSL is a technology used to delivery high-speed Internet transmissions across the analog local loop. See Digital Subscriber Line.

asynchronous—Asynchronous is a term that describes operation that involves bits that are not transmitted on any strict timetable. Transmitting a start bit indicates the start of each character. After the final bit of the character is transmitted, a stop bit is sent, indicating the end of the character. The sending and receiving modems must stay in synchronization only for the length of time it takes to transmit the eight bits. If their clocks are slightly out of synch, data transfer will still be successful.

Asynchronous Transfer Mode (ATM)—ATM is a connection-oriented cell relay technology based on small (53-byte) cells. An ATM network consists of ATM switches that form multiple virtual circuits to carry groups of cells from source to destination. ATM can provide high-speed transport services for voice, data, and video.

Attachment Unit Interface (AUI)—An AUI is a connector used to attach end devices to coax or shielded twisted pair cable.

attenuation—Attenuation is the weakening of a signal over distance.

authentication—Authentication is the process of confirming a user's identity to gain access to network resources. This is usually performed using a password or some other method of identification

authorization—Authorization is the method for assigning rights and all use or network resources after successful authentication.

autonomous system (AS)—An AS is a collection of routers and networks administered by a single organization that connects to the Internet.

auxiliary (AUX) port—The AUX port on a router is used to make an out-of-band connection via a modem for configuring or monitoring a device. The AUX port must first be set up using a standard console connection.

B (bearer) channel—A B channel is a 64 K channel used in ISDN BRI or PRI service for circuit switched voice, video or data service.

backbone—A backbone is the portion of a network that carries the most significant traffic. It is also the part of a network that connects many smaller networks to form a larger network.

bandwidth—Bandwidth is a measure of the information-carrying capacity of a channel. Analog networks measure bandwidth in cycles per second (Hz). Digital networks measure bandwidth in Kbps, Mbps, and Gbps.

base 2—See Binary.

base 16—See Hexadecimal.

baseband—Baseband is a form of digital modulation in which one signal takes up the entire available bandwidth of the communication channel.

Basic Rate Interface Integrated Services Digital Network (ISDN-BRI)—ISDN-BRI provides two "bearer" channels (B channels) of 64 Kbps each, plus one control channel (D channel) of 16 Kbps for a total of 144Kbps. (ISDN is a digital multiplexing technology that can transmit voice, data, and video single local loop.)

baud—Baud is the number of electrical or signal state changes that take place in one second. Baud and bits per second are not equivalent in the higher speed transmissions used today.

bearer (B) channel—See B channel.

best effort—Best effort refers to a transmission method that does not guarantee any particular level of speed, throughput, delay, or reliability. IP and IPX are considered best effort delivery.

binary—Binary refers to the base 2 numbering system used by computers to represent digital information. Binary numbers consist of only two values: 1 and 0.

biometrics—Biometrics are login methods that use characteristics unique to an individual, such as voice recognition, fingerprint, hand shape, face characteristics, and retinal scan.

BIOS—BIOS, which stands for basic input/output system, is a set of programs, usually in firmware, that enables each computer's central processing unit to communicate with printers, disks, keyboards, consoles, and other attached input and output devices.

bit—A bit is a "binary digit," that is, a single value that makes up a binary number. A bit can be either 1 or 0. See binary.

bits per second (bps)—Bps is a measure of the number of binary bits transmitted per second. This can also be represented in kilobits (1000 bits per second), megabits (1000000 bits per second), and gigabits (1000000000 bits per second).

bootstrap—Bootstrap is a term that refers to the microcode that executes the boot process in a router and finds and loads the IOS and configuration file.

Bootstrap Protocol (BOOTP)—BOOTP, described in RFC 951, is a method in which a diskless workstation or terminal can obtain configuration information, such as a base operating system, configuration file, and IP address from a server. BOOTP can also be used by a client to make a DHCP request for IP address and configuration information.

Border Gateway Protocol (BGP)—BGP is an interautonomous system routing protocol. The primary function of a BGP-speaking system is to exchange network reachability information with other BGP systems.

border router—A border router is a router at the edge of a network that is responsible for exchanging reachability information with the border routers of other networks.

bounded media—Bounded media denotes all physically cabled network transmissions.

bridge—A bridge is a device that operates at the Data Link Layer of the OSI model. Bridges build MAC address tables and read MAC addresses to perform filter and forward decisions.

British Naval Connector or Barrel Node Connector (BNC)—BNC are used to connect end devices to a Thinnet or Thicknet coaxial cable. BNC terminators are used on either end of an bus cable segment to prevent signal reflection.

broadcast—The term broadcast is used in several different ways in communications and networking. A broadcast is a frame addressed to all devices on a network that uses a special destination MAC address of all 1s. A broadcast at the Network Layer has all binary's 1s in the host position of the logical address. Routers generally do not forward broadcasts.

broadcast containment—Broadcast containment is the practice of creating separate broadcast domains by physically or logically segmenting a network at Layer 2 or 3.

broadcast domain—A broadcast domain is the area of a network through which broadcast packets are forwarded. Routers, Layer 3 switches, and VLANs create network segments that are separate broadcast domains, because they do not forward broadcast packets from one segment to another.

broadcast frame—See Broadcast.

broadcast storm—A broadcast storm occurs because faulty network components or active network loops can create a situation where a single broadcast is transmitted indefinitely. The result is a "storm" of broadcast frames that can severely impact network performance, which, if not corrected, could bring down a network.

broadcast traffic—See Broadcast.

brouter—A brouter is an internetworking device that combines the functions of both a bridge and a router. It is designed to route when a routable protocol is available and designed to bridge when a non-routable protocol is present.

buffer—A buffer is a holding area where incoming data is temporarily stored until the transmission is complete or it can be processed. When a buffer is full, newly received data will be dropped. Flow control methods are used to prevent a buffer overflow issue.

burned-in access (BIA)—See Media Access Control address.

bus—A bus is a single electrical circuit to which all devices in the network are connected (although the bus might be made up of many individual pieces of wire). A bus topology is a broadcast network. When a node transmits data, the signal travels down the bus in both directions. Each node connected to the bus receives the signal as it passes that connection point. A bus network is created using coaxial cable that is terminated on each end to prevent signal reflection.

Business to Business (B2B)—B2B is a business that sells to other businesses, not directly to consumers.

Business to Consumer (B2C)—A B2C is a retail business that sells directly to consumers.

byte—One byte is equal to 8 binary bits. It is used to represent information, such as alphanumeric characters and digital transmissions.

cable modem—A cable modem is a device located in a cable television subscriber's home that provides broadband Internet access over a Hybrid Fiber Cable (HFC) network.

campus area network (CAN)—CANs consist of LANs connected across multiple buildings within a short distance of each other, usually on the same property or possibly across the street.

capacity—Capacity is the maximum transfer rate of a communications media.

carrier—A carrier has several definitions. A carrier is a company that provides communications circuits. The term carrier can also be used to describe a digital communication channel, such as a T1 or T3.

carrier sense multiple access/collision detection (CSMA/CD)—CSMA/CD is the technique used by Ethernet to control access to the shared medium. Any node may attempt to transmit when it senses the medium is silent. If two nodes transmit simultaneously, a collision occurs, both nodes stop transmitting and then wait a random amount of time before attempting to retransmit.

Category 3 (CAT3) cable—CAT3 cable is the ANSI/EIA/TIA-568 designation for 100-ohm unshielded twisted-pair cables and associated connecting hardware whose characteristics are specified for data transmission up to 16 Mhz.

Category 4 (CAT4) cable—CAT4 cable is the ANSI/EIA/TIA-568 designation for 100-ohm unshielded twisted-pair cables and associated connecting hardware whose characteristics are specified for data transmission up to 20 Mhz.

Category 5 (CAT5) UTP—CAT5 UTP is the ANSI/EIA/TIA-568 designation for 100-ohm unshielded twisted-pair cables and associated connecting hardware whose characteristics are specified for data transmission up to 100 Mhz.

Category 5E (enhanced) (CAT5e) cable—CAT5e cable provides data rates up to 200 Mhz through more precise manufacturing techniques.

CD-ROM—CD-ROM is an abbreviation for compact disk read-only memory. An optical digital storage device, of high capacity, capable of being read from but not written to.

CD-RW—A CD-RW is a CD drive that has both read and write capabilities. Using the right media, the CD can be written to more than once. Capacity is generally around 800 Mb.

cell—A cell is a unit of transmission that is fixed in length. Cells associated with ATM technology are typically 53-bytes.

central office—A central office (CO) is a telephone company facility where local loops are terminated. A CO connects individual telephones through a series of switches. It is also called a local exchange, wiring center, or public exchange.

central processing unit (CPU)—Also called a microprocessor, the CPU is the main computer processor that interprets and executes most instructions and calculations.

Centralized administration—Centralized administration allows control over resource and file access and prevents unauthorized use of network services.

Challenge Handshake Application Protocol (CHAP)—CHAP is described by RFC2484 as a security protocol used to authenticate remote network access over point to point connections, such as those between an ISP and its dial-in customers. CHAP initiates a three-way handshake between the authenticator and the client. The authenticator challenges the client with a challenge message, to which the client responds with a client-calculated, one-way hash. The authenticator then verifies the client response against what it calculates it should receive. If the values match, the connection proceeds. Randomly, during the course of the communication session, the channel/response process repeats.

channel—A channel is a communications path between two or more communicating devices. Channels are also referred to as links, lines, circuits, and paths.

channel service unit (CSU)—A CSU is a device that connects customer equipment to digital transmission facilities, such as a T1 circuit. The CSU is the device that actually generates the transmission signals on the local loop, that is, the telephone channel. CSUs are often coupled with DSUs in a device called a "CSU/ DSU." See data service unit.

circuit switching—Circuit-switching describes networks that establish a logical connection between two nodes and in which all transmissions in one session are passed between the same nodes by "switching" them through intermediate points. Circuit switching guarantees that all packets in the same transmission will sequentially travel over the established circuit path. Each transmission is limited to one path, and cannot achieve greater transfer speed by using multiple parallel paths.

Cisco Discovery Protocol (CDP)—CDP is a Cisco proprietary protocol and topology-independent communication method that reports hardware and software information to directly connected neighbor devices. CDP works on routers, switches, and other Cisco equipment.

cladding—Cladding is the clear plastic or glass layer that encloses the light-transmitting core of a fiber optic cable. The cladding has a lower refractive index than the core, and reflects the light signal back into the core as the light propagates down the fiber.

Class A Address—The Class A address range starts with binary 0, and is from 1.0.0.0 through 126.255.255.255. Although 127 is included as part of the addressable area for a Class A network, this address is reserved for local loopback and is not assigned. The default subnet mask for a Class A network is 255.0.0.0. There are 126 possible networks and 16,777,214 possible unique hosts per network. Class A addresses have been reserved for very large organizations and Internet service providers.

Class B Address—The Class B address range starts with the binary numbers 10, and is from 128.0.0.0 through 191.255.255.255. There are 16,384 possible networks and 65,534 possible unique hosts per network. The default subnet mask is 255.255.0.0.

Class C Address—The Class C address range starts with the binary numbers 110, and is from 192.0.0.0 through 223.255.255.255. There are 2,097,152 possible networks and 254 possible unique hosts per network. The default subnet mask is 255.255.255.0.

Class D Address—The Class D address range is used for multicast groups rather than network and host address assignment. This address range starts with the binary numbers 1110 and includes 224.0.0.0 through 239.255.255.255. There is no defined subnet mask because Class D addresses are not used for host assignment.

Class E Address—Used for research and experimental purposes, the Class E address range begins with 240.0.0.0 and is never assigned in production environments.

class of service (CoS)—In general, CoS measures different characteristics of a transmission service. In the context of the OSI reference model, applications can specify QoS parameters as part of a request for a communication channel. These parameters define different levels of service based on the requirements of an application; for example, bandwidth, reliability, delay, throughput, or cost value.

classful protocol—A classful routing protocol assumes that the default subnet mask has been used and that all subnet masks are the same throughout the network. A classful routing protocol does not send subnet mask information along with routing updates, so it cannot recognize various subnet addresses if route summarization or variable length subnet masks have been used.

Classless Interdomain Routing (CIDR)—CIDR is also known as supernetting, route summarization, or aggregation. CIDR is a technique used to reduce the number of routing table entries a router must maintain and advertise for internal IP networks. CIDR aggregates multiple consecutive Class C network addresses into a single routing table entry.

classless protocol—A classless protocol is a routing protocol that does not assume the default subnet mask, but instead uses a bit mask to define address hierarchy. Classless protocols pass subnet mask information with routing updates so that variable length subnet masks and classless interdomain routing can be performed.

client—A client is any program that requests a service or resource from a server. See client/server.

client/server—Client/server is a model in computer networking where individual PCs (clients) can access data or services from a common high-performance computer (server).

clock speed—Clock speed is the rate at which a CPU executes computer instructions. Serial transmission devices, such as modems and CSU/DSUs, use clock signals for synchronization purposes.

cloud—A cloud is any switched service provider network that provides MAN and WAN services. A customer connects to the edge of the cloud and trusts the network to handle the details of moving a transmission to its destination. The public switched telephone network (PSTN) and frame relay are two well-known examples of cloud networks.

Coarse Wave Division Multiplexing (CWDM)—CWDM is a type of wave division multiplexing in which uncooled lasers are used to overlay optical light channels in a pipe. The use of uncooled lasers reduces cost, compared with dense wavelength division multiplexing, which uses cooled lasers.

coating—Coating is a reinforced plastic outer jacket that protects the fiber optic cable from damage.

coaxial (coax) cable—Coaxial cable is a type of copper wiring typically used for cable television transmission and high-speed Internet connectivity. Coaxial cable typically consists of a central copper conductor surrounded by flexible insulation, a shield of wire mesh, and an outer plastic jacket. Older installations of Ethernet LANs also used coax cable.

coder/decoder (codec)—A codec is a hardware/software device that takes an analog signal and converts (codes) it to digital format for compression and transmission. On the receiving end, the digital signal is put back (decoded) into the original analog signal.

collision—A collision occurs in an Ethernet network when two transmissions are put onto the physical medium at the same time and overlap fully or partially. When a collision occurs, it is sensed as a voltage spike, and the data on the physical segment is no longer valid.

collision detection—Collision detection is the ability of a node to identify that a collision has occurred on the physical link. The device handles the collision by sending a jamming signal, clearing the line, and retransmitting at a specific interval.

collision domain—Collision domain is the portion of a network where all nodes receive every frame transmitted. It is a part of a network in which nodes compete for access to the same physical medium.

command line interface (CLI)—The CLI is the user interface to a router, accessed through a terminal emulation program. The CLI is used to view the device configuration, monitor network statistics, and administer new settings.

committed information rate (CIR)—CIR is the guaranteed average data rate for a frame relay service.

Communication (COM) port—Also called serial port, a COM port is used for mouse devices, keyboards, console connections to routers or switches, serial printers, and many other external peripherals. Bits are transmitted one at a time over a serial port.

compression—Compression is the process of reducing the number of bits required to represent data without altering the meaning of the data. The primary reason for using compression techniques is to optimize the use of the communication channel.

configuration register—The configuration register is the 16-bit software register stored in NVRAM that provides a router with important boot parameters.

connectionless—Connectionless service means that each packet or datagram is delivered using a best effort method without an initial setup process between sending and receiving devices. Connectionless protocols may drop or deliver packets out of sequence.

connection-oriented—A connection-oriented data communication service is one in which the sending system initiates a connection before transmissions begin. The two devices maintain the connection for the duration of transmission.

console connection—A console connection is made to a switch or router using the console port and an RS-232 serial cable from a terminal device, such as a PC. Terminal emulation software then establishes out-of-band communication to configure or monitor the device.

console port—The physical console port on a router is used to make an out-of-band terminal connections.

content networking—Content networking is a function performed by a group of integrated services to get a real-time, multimedia, or bandwidth intensive request filled and a response returned as quickly as possible, providing the highest level of service to each user's request.

content-addressable memory (CAM)—CAM is a memory area which is used to store information like the MAC address table in a switch. The memory is dynamic and is not stored if the device is power cycled.

contention—A contention is a condition that arises when two or more end devices attempt to transmit at the same time over shared media. Contention is the process a device must use to access the network media in an Ethernet network. Each device must wait for all other devices on the wire to cease transmission before the device can begin transmitting.

convergence—Convergence is the process used to update network path information on routers and switches to produce a stable end-to-end path. Large networks converge more slowly than small networks, because of the number of devices that must be updated after a configuration change.

cost—Cost is a routing metric that can be based on one or more network characteristics or designated by an administrator. In most cases, cost does not refer to the financial cost of a link, but rather an arbitrary number chosen to meet specific criteria.

crossover cable—A crossover cable is a UTP cable used to connect similar devices (switch with switch and PC with PC, for example). The pin configuration applies the EIA/TIA-568A standard to one end and the EIA/TIA-568B standard to the other.

Crosstalk—Crosstalk is a specific type of noise, caused by an electrical signal in one cable that induces a voltage fluctuation in an adjacent cable. In telephone lines, crosstalk allows you to hear someone else's faint conversation in the background. In data lines, it is detectable as errors.

customer premises equipment (CPE)—CPE, which also stands for customer provided equipment, refers to telecommunications equipment that resides at a customer site.

cut-through switching—Also called fast forward, this frame switching method reads only the destination address of a frame before identifying the appropriate port and forwarding the frame to the receiving station. It provides no error checking, and transmits at a continuous rate regardless of the frame size. In relatively error-free networks, this speeds up the transmission time for a frame traveling across a switch.

cyclic redundancy check (CRC)—CRC is an error-checking mechanism that calculates the frame content with a binary divisor.

D channel—D channel is the channel used to transmit signal information to perform call setup, maintain the circuit, and tear down the call path. A separate channel for signaling is called "clear channel signaling (CCS)" or "out-of-band," because it is separated from the information being sent. The D channel is used for ISDN services at 16-Kb for BRI or 64-Kb for PRI.

data circuit equipment (DCE)—DCE is the device or devices in a DEC network that transmits and receives the DTE data. DCE uses a clocking signal for a synchronized transmission.

data link connection identifier (DLCI)—A DLCI is frame relay header field that is has a 10-bit address that identifies the virtual circuit of the connection between the customer premise equipment and the service provider's frame relay switch. The DLCI is only locally significant.

Data Link Layer—The Data Link Layer is the second layer of the OSI model. It is divided into two sublayers, the logical link control (LLC) and media access control (MAC). The Data Link Layer is responsible for transmitting frames.

data service unit (DSU)—A DSU is a device that takes data from the LAN and translates it into digital information suitable for public transmission facilities such as a T1 circuit. It is normally used in conjunction with a CSU in a device called a DSU/CSU or CSU/DSU.

data terminal equipment (DTE)—DTE is the end device in a network that is dependent on the DCE to connect to the network that transmit sand receive data.

debug tools—Debug tools are coded into the IOS to monitor and troubleshoot updates and software processes in real-time. They should only be used for short periods of time, because displaying many entries to the screen can be very resource-intensive.

decapsulation—Decapsulation is the process that occurs as a data transmission is passed up through the protocol stack of a receiving computer. Each protocol layer removes the appropriate header added by the sending computer and then passes the remaining data to the protocol layer above.

decimal—Decimal refers to the base 10 numbers represented by the digits 0-9, which are commonly used for counting.

default gateway—A default gateway is a router that provides access to remote networks and the Internet. Each host is assigned a default gateway to send packets that are not addressed within their local network segment.

default routing—Default routing defines how to exit a stub network when there is only one way in and one way out. Also, it is a route of last resort to be used when dynamically learned routes are unavailable or incomplete.

Defense Advanced Research Projects Agency (DARPA)—DARPA is the government agency that sponsored the development of ARPANET and what eventually became the Internet.

delay—Also called "latency," delay can be caused by many different processes and components in the transmission from source to destination. Low delay is the most desirable for transmissions.

demarcation point (Demarc)—Demarc is the connection between a private telephone system and the PSTN. It is the physical point at which the telephone company's responsibility ends and the customer's begins. The demarc is also called the "Minimum Point of Entry" (MPOE).

demodulation—Demodulation is the process a modem performs to change a modulated analog signal back into digital information.

demultiplexing—Demultiplexing is the process of separating a multiplexed signal into its original multiple transmissions.

denial of service attack—A denial of service attack is a hacking attempt that is designed to prevent a device or software process from performing its intended function. One example of a denial of service attack is the "ping of death."

Dense Wavelength-Division Multiplexing (DWDM)—DWDM uses multiple light wavelengths to transmit signals over a single optical fiber. Each wavelength, or channel, carries a stream of data at rates as high as 2.5 Gbps and higher. It can use over fifty channels.

destination address—The destination address is the unique identifier of the host intended to receive a transmission. A destination address can be physical (the MAC address of the NIC) or logical (an IP address or a port number).

differentiation services (DiffServ)—DiffServ is specified by RFC2475 as a QoS architecture for providing preferential treatment to IP packet transmissions. Applications or devices classify traffic based on specific criteria of priority, bandwidth, delay, reliability, and throughput and tag the packet with a diffserv code point (DSCP). Routers that can read the DSCP will use the information to provide special handling methods. Although identified, this value in itself does not guarantee quality.

digital signal—A digital signal is transmitted as a pattern of binary bits (1s and 0s) as high or low electrical voltages, or the absence or presence of light.

Digital Data Service (DDS)—DDS, also known as "Dataphone Digital Service," is a digital facility offered by a telecommunications company. DDS comes in several speeds, including 2400 bps, 4800 bps, 9600 bps, and 56 Kbps.

Digital Signal Level 0 (DS0)—DS0 is a 64 Kbps channel that provides the bandwidth required for one digital telephone call. The DS0 signal is the fundamental building block of the North American digital signal hierarchy.

Digital Signal 1 (DS1)—DS1 is a digital signaling rate that combines 24 DS0s to create the total bandwidth, including overhead of 1.544 Mbps. A DS1 is equivalent to the North American T1 and Japanese J1 designation.

Digital Signal 3 (DS3)—DS3 is a digital signal rate that combines 672 DS0s to create the total bandwidth, including overhead of 44.736 Mbps, corresponding to the North American T3 designation.

Digital Subscriber Line (DSL)—DSL is a modem technology that converts existing twisted pair telephone lines into high-speed data lines that can also carry separate telephone communications. Variants of DSL include: ADSL, RADSL, ADSL Lite, and SDSL.

distance vector algorithm (DVA) or distance vector routing protocol—Distance vector routing protocols exchange network path information on a constant basis, every 30 to 90 seconds. Distance vector routing protocols are easy to configure and work well in small to medium networks. Drawbacks to these types of protocols include constant network traffic and the potential for routing loops. RIP and IGRP are examples of distance vector routing protocols.

Domain Name System (DNS)—DNS is the online distributed database system used to map human-readable computer names (URLs) to IP addresses.

dotted decimal notation—Dotted decimal notation is the format for writing a 32-bit Internet address as four octets separated by decimal points. The value of each octet is expressed independently as a decimal number between 0 and 255.

DSL Access Multiplexer (DSLAM)—A DSLAM is an interface point between DSL subscriber lines and the carrier's network. ISPs and network carriers use DSLAMs to remove high frequency DSL upload and download information from the telephone service on the same local loop.

duplex—Duplex is the process of transmitting data in two directions. There are two modes of transmission: half-duplex and full-duplex. In half-duplex, a device can either send or receive, but not at the same time. Full-duplex transmission allows signals to travel in both directions simultaneously.

Dynamic Host Configuration Protocol (DHCP)—DHCP is a client/server architecture that provides configuration settings and IP information to network hosts.

Dynamic Random Access Memory (DRAM)—DRAM is the memory of a computer that can be read from or written to by hardware components, such as a processor. DRAM is volatile memory and is erased if the device is shut down.

dynamic routing—Dynamic routing is a technique in which each router automatically builds and maintains its own routing table. Dynamic routing algorithms respond automatically to changes in the network topology.

E1—E1 is the European equivalent of the North American T carriers. E1 is also known as "CEPT1,"and can transmit 2.048 Mbps with 30 64 Kbps digital channels for voice or data transmissions, plus a 64 Kbps signaling channel and a 64 Kbps channel for framing, timing, and maintenance.

echo—An echo is an ICMP message used to indicate connectivity up to the Network Layer. A ping command executes an echo request and echo reply.

EEPROM (electrically erasable programmable read-only memory)—EEPROM is a type of PROM that can be erased and reprogrammed by an electrical signal, without having to remove the chip from its device.

egress interface or exit interface (INT)—The egress interface is used by a router when sending packets destined for another network.

Electronic Industries Association/Telecommunications Industry Association (EIA/TIA)—EIA is a national trade organization that publishes hardware-oriented standards for data communications. TIA is an organization based in Great Britain that develops and promotes telecommunications standards.

EIA/TIA-232—Formerly known as RS-232, EIA/TIA-232 is a DB-25 pin or DB-9 connection standard. It is a common connector from a DCE to a DTE, or a serial port to a modem and supports 64-Kbps transmissions over fairly short runs.

EIA/TIA-449—EIA/TIA-449 is a DB-37 pin serial connection used for both DCE and DTE connections. It can support up to 2 Mb transmission with longer distance runs than the EIA/TIA-232.

EIA/TIA-612/613 High-Speed Serial Interface (HSSI)—HSSI is a 50-pin SCSI-II-type connector that provides DTE connection to T3 (45 Mbps), E3 (34 Mbps), and SONET STS-1 (51.82Mbps). The bandwidth depends on the service and connection equipment.

EIA-530—EIA-530 is a DB-25 pin connection that can only be used for DTE connections (it is not DCE compatible).

electromagnetic interference (EMI)—EMI is the leakage of electromagnetic field from a device that can cause problems with electronic circuitry and communication systems. EMI can be reduced in networks by using shielding on copper wiring. Fiber optic cable is immune to EMI because it uses light instead of electrical signals.

electromagnetic spectrum—The electromagnetic spectrum is the range of electromagnetic frequencies from zero to infinity. (The electromagnetic spectrum was formerly divided into 26 alphabetically designated bands. This usage still prevails to some degree. However, the ITU formally recognizes 12 bands, from 30 Hz to 3000 GHz. New bands, from 3 THz to 3000 THz, are under active consideration for recognition.)

electronic mail (e-mail)—E-mail is a widely used application for transferring messages and files between communication devices. Simple Mail Transfer Protocol (SMTP) is the TCP/IP Application Layer protocol used to transfer e-mail between servers. Post Office Protocol (POP3) is used to move e-mail from a server to a destination client computer.

encapsulation—Encapsulation is the process that occurs as a data transmission is passed down through the protocol stack of the sending computer; each protocol layer adds its own header to the data it receives from the layer above. When a message is physically transmitted from a sending computer, it includes a header for each of the protocols that processed it.

Enhanced Interior Gateway Routing Protocol (EIGRP)—EIGRP is a Cisco proprietary hybrid routing protocol that enhances IGRP to address large-scale, complex networks. EIGRP stores both the primary route and a feasible successor in case the primary route should become unavailable. It provides very rapid convergence during an outage.

EPROM (erasable programmable read-only memory)—EPROM is a special type of PROM that is erased by exposing it to ultraviolet light. An EPROM can be reprogrammed and reused after it has been erased. If a computer's BIOS program is stored in EPROM, the BIOS can be upgraded when necessary.

Ethernet—Ethernet technology, originally developed in the 1970s by Xerox Corporation in conjunction with Intel and DEC, is now the primary medium for LANs. Original Ethernet provides 10-Mbps throughput and uses the CSMA/CD method to access the physical media. Fast Ethernet (100-Mbps Ethernet) and Gigabit Ethernet (1,000-Mbps Ethernet) are also newer Ethernet options.

Ethernet frame header—The Ethernet frame header provides the information that computers need to successfully transmit data from the source computer to the destination computer using the physical MAC address of each device.

exit interface—See egress interface.

expansion bus—An expansion bus connects expansion boards to the processor (CPU) and memory.

expansion card—An expansion card is a manufactured circuit board that plugs into an expansion slot in the motherboard. Each card provides a specific function, such as high-resolution video and graphics, audio and music input or output, game ports, NIC, modem capabilities, and many other functions.

Exterior Gateway Protocol (EGP)—RFC904 describes EGP, a routing protocol used to exchange routing information between one or more autonomous systems. All AS gateway routers must run the same EGP to exchange reachability information. Border Gateway Protocol (BGPv4) is the standard EGP currently in use.

extranet—An extranet is a broader form of a private intranet. Extranets are private TCP/IP networks that are shared between closely aligned organizations and are unavailable to the general public. See B2B and B2C.

F-Connector—An F-connector is used to connect a router to a cable TV service for Internet access.

Fast Ethernet—Fast Ethernet is Ethernet that runs at 100 Mbps over CAT 5/5e UTP or fiber optic cable. Fast Ethernet is specified under the IEEE standard 802.3u.

Fiber channel—Fiber Channel (or fibre channel) is a very high-speed fiber optic data transfer interface that can carry multiple protocols, such as IP and SCSI.

Fiber Distributed Data Interface (FDDI)—FDDI is a token-passing network architecture that uses dual counter-rotating optical rings to provide 100 Mbps transmissions.

fiber optic cable—Fiber optic cable is a transmission medium typically used for high-speed digital transmission. It consists of a flexible clear glass or plastic core surrounded by a reflective plastic cladding layer and protected by a thin jacket or sheath. A signal is transmitted by focusing a light source into the core, and then switching the source on and off. Light is reflected off the cladding layer, so that nearly all of the light radiated into one end of the cable reaches the other end.

File Transfer Protocol (FTP)—FTP is a TCP/IP Application Layer protocol used to transfer files between two systems. FTP uses well known TCP ports 20 and 21.

filtering—Filtering is the process a switch uses to block frames from non-addressed ports, when forwarding the frame to the proper destination. This reduces network traffic and increases available bandwidth.

firewall—A firewall is a controlled access point between sections of the same network, which is designed to confine problems to one section. A firewall is also a controlled access between a private network and a public network (the Internet, for example), usually implemented with a router and special firewall software.

flash memory—Also called flash ROM, flash memory consists of an EEPROM chip that stores the IOS on a router. Because of the storage device, the IOS can be upgraded, backed up, and restored to flash memory.

flooding—Flooding is the process of transmitting the same signal out all ports of a bridge or switch when the destination address in not found in the MAC address table.

Floppy disk drive—A floppy disk drive is a disk used to read and write data to high-density, 3.5-inch diskettes for 1.5 Mb of storage capacity.

flow control—Flow control is a method of controlling the quantity of transmissions sent between two systems. Practically every data communication protocol contains some form of flow control to keep the sending system from transmitting more than the receiving system can process.

forwarding—Forwarding is the process a switch uses to transmit a frame directly to the port associated with the destination address. In STP, this is the final stage a bridge or switch port enters when passing traffic.

Fractional T1 (FT1)—FT1 is a leased-line service that provides data rates from 64 Kbps to 1.544 Mbps by allowing a user to purchase one or more channels of a T1 link. If a customer needs less bandwidth than 1.544 Mbps, FT1 is a low-cost alternative to purchasing a full T1.

fragment-free switching—Also known as modified cut-through or runt-free switching, fragment-free switching reads the first 64 bytes of data to verify that it has not been involved in a collision or otherwise smaller than 64 bytes (considered a runt). The switch then determines the destination address to forward the frame if there are no problems or to drop it if corruption is detected. The transmission rate is the same regardless of the frame size.

fragmentation—Fragmentation is the IP process of dividing a datagram into smaller pieces to accommodate various maximum transmission units (MTUs).

frame—A frame is a unit of information transmitted at the Data Link Layer. In a LAN, each frame contains the hardware MAC address (NIC address) of the source and destination devices.

frame check sequence (FCS)—FCS is a 4-byte CRC value used to check for errors in a frame.

frame relay—Frame relay is a telecommunications switching technology developed to transport data efficiently across a service provider network while minimizing the number of dedicated circuits required. Although it was developed for data, in recent years, advancements have made frame relay suitable for voice. Frame relay is a Data Link Layer connection-oriented protocol. It is unreliable because transmission errors are detected but not corrected, and transmissions that exceed the specified committed information rate (CIR) are discarded. Frame relay is a wide-area data transmission technology that normally operates at speeds of 56 Kbps to 1.5 Mbps. (Some service provider's now offer up to 45 Mbps).

frame relay access device (FRAD)—FRAD is a device, typically a router, that connects a business to a frame relay network.

frequency—Frequency is the number of times per second that a wave changes state from the beginning point to its ending point. It is the number of wave crests or cycles that pass a fixed point during a particular period of time.

Frequency Division Multiplexing (FDM)—FDM is a method of multiplexing that assigns each signal to a different frequency. See multiplexing.

full-duplex—See duplex.

fully qualified domain name (FQDN)—An FQDN is the combination of a hostname and domain name that uniquely identifies a network resource, device, Web location, e-mail user, and so forth.

G.703—G.703 is a BNC-style connector for Hybrid Fiber Coaxial (HFC) Cable, for CPE connections to the CO, with bandwidth capabilities up to E1 (2.048Mbps) rate.

gateway—The term "gateway" can have two definitions in the context of networking. A gateway can be a protocol converter/translator, and a gateway can also be a router used to connect different networks together, like a private network connection to the Internet.

giant frame—A giant frame is an Ethernet frame that is larger than the maximum frame size.

Gigabit Ethernet—See 802.3ab, 802.3z, 1000BaseCX, 1000BaseLX, 1000BaseSX, 1000BaseTX

gigabit interface connector (GBIC)—A GBIC is a component that allows for easy installation and reconfiguration of Gigabit Ethernet for various media types. The GBIC fits into a slot on a switch or router and is responsible for providing the correct signal, media access, and physical wired connectivity.

gigabits per second (Gbps)—See bits per second.

gigahertz (GHz)—See hertz.

global configuration mode—Global configuration mode is a router configuration mode used to establish settings associated with the device itself (for example, IP address, host name, Domain Name Server [DNS] name server, default gateway, and so forth).

graded-index multimode fiber—A graded-index multimode fiber is the core of a graded-index fiber cable, which has several transparent layers, each with a different refractive index. This planned inconsistency allows light modes to travel at different speeds through the core. Thus, all modes reach the far end of the fiber more uniformly.

graphical user interface (GUI)—A GUI is a user interface based on graphics (icons, pictures, and menus), instead of text; a GUI uses a mouse and a keyboard as input devices.

guard band—A guard band is a band of unused frequencies that prevents overlap between adjacent transmissions. The frequency bands assigned to two adjacent radio stations, for example, are separated by a transmission-free guard band.

half-duplex—See duplex.

handshake—A handshake is an exchange of instructional signals that prepares two devices to communicate with each other.

Hard drive—Also called a "hark disk," a hard drive is used for high-capacity, long-term storage.

hardware—Hardware is the physical equipment used to provide specific services.

head end—A head end is a cable television central control system that provides aggregation, multiplexing and remodulation functions.

header—A header is instructional and addressing information added to data during the encapsulation process before transmission. Intermediary devices read header information to select a transmission path and can provide flow control services, as well as error detection. Headers are removed by the receiving device during decapsulation.

hertz (Hz)—Hz represent the cycles per second in which radio signals are measured. One Hz is 1 cycle per second; 1,000 cycles per second is 1 KHz; one million cycles per second is 1 MHz and one billion cycles per second is 1 GHz.

hexadecimal—Hexadecimal is the base 16 numbering system used to represent binary information in a condensed format. Hexadecimal numbers use 4 bits, which represent 16 values: 0 through 9, plus A through F.

Hierarchical addressing—Hierarchical addressing is a scheme of addressing that uses a logical hierarchy to determine location. For example, IP addresses consist of a network portion, a subnetwork portion, and a unique host portion. IP routing algorithms use the hierarchal address to route the packet to the appropriate location.

High-Level Data Link Control (HDLC)—HDLC is a wide area Data Link Layer protocol standard developed by ISO. The HDLC protocol suite represents a wide variety of Data Link Layer protocols, such as SDLC, LAPB, and LAPD.

hop (handoff point)—A hop is the next routing device used to forward a packet through a network. A hop count is the metric used by RIP to make best path selection.

hop count—Hop count is the number of intermediate routers that a packet must traverse to travel from source to destination in a multi-router environment.

host—A host is a computer system that contains the hardware and software to connect and operate in a network environment. A host is any device that is assigned an IP address.

host address—A host address is a unique IP address assigned to an end node. This address cannot contain all binary 0s (network) or all binary 1s (broadcast).

host table—A host table consists of a list of hostnames and their associated IP addresses. These can be manually entered or dynamically learned. If manually entered, the hostnames are considered permanent; if learned, they will expire.

hostname—A hostname is a unique name assigned to a device for easier access and administration. Hostnames can be associated with IP addresses for name resolution purposes. See fully qualified domain name (FQDN).

hot-swapping—Hot-swapping is the ability to remove and replace a component while a device is active.

hub—Also referred to as a wiring concentrator, a hub is a repeater with multiple ports. A signal coming into one port is repeated out the other ports; therefore, a hub represents a physical star and logical bus. All devices connected to a hub are in the same collision domain and broadcast domain.

Hybrid Fiber-Coax (HFC)—HFC is a network design method, common in the cable television industry, that combines optical fiber and coaxial cable into a single network. Fiber optic cables run from a central site to neighborhood head ends. From the head end, coaxial cable serves individual homes.

Hypertext Markup Language (HTML)—HTML is a text-based formatting language used to generically format text for Web pages. A Web browser reads an HTML document and displays it as indicated by the HTML formatting tags and the browser's default settings.

Hypertext Transfer Protocol (HTTP)—HTTP is the Application Layer protocol used to request and transmit HTML documents. HTTP is the underlying protocol of the Web.

in-band management—In-band management is the process of controlling a network device by sending network management commands over the network itself.

Industrial Scientific Medical (ISM) band—The ISM band is the FCC-authorized unlicensed frequency bands used for wireless networks, telephones, and other devices. The ISM frequency bands are 902-928Mhz, 2.4-2.5Ghz, and 5.725- 5.875Ghz.

inbound interface (ingress)—The inbound interface is used to enter a router from a sending device.

input/output (I/O)—I/O is the process of moving data to and from a computer CPU to a peripheral device. Input devices include keyboards and mouse devices. Output devices include monitors and printers. Some devices are used for both input and output, such as a disk drive or NIC.

Institute of Electrical and Electronic Engineers (IEEE)—IEEE is a professional organization composed of engineers, scientists, and students. Founded in 1984, IEEE publishes computer and electronics standards, such as the 802 series that defines shared-media networks, such as Ethernet and Token Ring.

Integrated Services Digital Network (ISDN)—ISDN is a digital multiplexing technology that can simultaneously transmit voice, video, and data over a single local loop. See Basic Rate Interface (BRI) and Primary Rate Interface (PRI).

Interior Gateway Protocol (IGP)—IGP is the generic term applied to any protocol used to propagate network reachability and routing information within an AS. Although there is no single standard IGP, RIP and OSPF are popular vendor-neutral IGPs.

Interior Gateway Routing Protocol (IGRP)—IGRP is a Cisco-proprietary distance-vector routing protocol used to update routers with network information. IGRP uses a composite metric of bandwidth and delay to make route selection decisions.

Intermediate System to Intermediate System (IS-IS)—IS-IS is an OSI link-state hierarchical routing protocol based on DECnet Phase V routing, in which routers exchange routing information based on a single metric to determine the network topology.

International Telecommunication Union-Telecommunications Standardization Sector (ITU-T)—Formerly the CCITT, the ITU is an international telecommunication standards-setting body based in Geneva, Switzerland. ITU is the United Nations agency responsible for adopting international treaties, regulations, and standards governing telecommunications.

Internet Assigned Numbers Authority (IANA)—IANA was the original organization responsible for assigning public Internet IP addresses. IANA was superseded by ICANN.

Internet Control Message Protocol (ICMP)—ICMP is an integral part of the IP suite that handles error and control messages. Routers, gateways, and hosts use ICMP to report problems about datagrams back to the original source. The ping command is an example of an ICMP echo request and echo reply message that can be used for troubleshooting purposes.

Internet Corporation for Assigned Names and Numbers (ICANN)—ICANN is the non-profit corporation that was formed to assume responsibility for IP address allocation, protocol parameter assignment, domain name system management, and root server system management functions now performed under U.S. Government contract by IANA and other entities.

Internet Engineering Task Force (IETF)—IETF is a large, open, international community of network designers, operators, vendors, and researchers concerned with the evolution of the Internet architecture and smooth operation of the Internet.

Internet Message Access Protocol version 4 (IMAP4)—IMAP4 is a protocol used for retrieving e-mail messages from a mail server. IMAP4 is a version of IMAP similar to POP3; however, it supports additional features, such as searching for keywords in e-mail messages while the messages are still on the mail server.

Internet Protocol (IP)—IP is a Network Layer protocol responsible for getting a packet (datagram) through a network. IP provides a hierarchical address, as well as connectionless, best-effort packet delivery service.

Internet Protocol Security (IPSec)—IPSec was proposed by the IETF as a set of protocols and procedures for securing IP packet traffic on publicly accessible IP networks. IPSec supports several cipher algorithms and enables both payload authentication and encryption.

Internet service provider (ISP)—ISPs are companies that provide Internet access to individuals and businesses. ISPs typically provide a range of services necessary to provide corporate networks and other users with dedicated or dial-up access to the Internet.

Internet Society (ISOC)—ISOC is a professional membership society with more than 150 organizational and 6,000 individual members in over 100 countries. ISOC provides leadership in addressing issues that confront the future of the Internet, and is the organization's home for groups responsible for Internet infrastructure standards, including IETF and IAB.

Internet—The term "Internet," capitalized, refers to the global internetwork of IP-based autonomous systems that make up the World Wide Web.

internet—The term "internet," noncapitalized, refers to a IP internetwork without reference to the scope of the connection. This term is often used to describe two or more networks using a common protocol.

Internetwork Operating System (IOS)—The IOS is Cisco's underlying software code that provides device functionality, reliability, administration, and other key features.

internetwork—A internetwork is a complex network that may combine smaller networks in different physical locations, based on different types of network architectures.

Interoperability—Interoperability is the ability of different types of computers, networks, OSs, and applications to work together effectively.

Inter-Switch Link (ISL)—ISL is a Cisco Systems proprietary VLAN tagging protocol. ISL adds an ISL header and FCS field to the Layer 2 frame. These fields are incompatible with non-ISL aware devices.

intranet—An intranet is a local, or private, Internet. An intranet is generally only accessible by corporate network users, but it runs all the same protocols and services as an Internet site.

invalid frame—An invalid frame is one in which the CRC and the FCS do not match.

IP address—An IP address is the logical or hierarchical address made up of a network portion and host portion, as defined by the subnet mask. IP addresses allow communication between computers with different operating systems, as well as with the Internet.

IP Telephony—IP telephony refers to voice telephone service provided over an IP network, instead of the public- switched telephone service.

IP Version 6 (IPv6)—Also known as IP next generation (IPng), IPv6 is designed to expand the now limited 32-bit IPv4 address space, while providing support for per-packet authentication and encryption, address autoconfiguration, flow control, and other capabilities not built into IPv4. An IPv6 address is 128-bits in length.

Internet Packet Exchange (IPX)—IPX is Novell's Network Layer protocol that is a derivative of the Xerox Network Systems protocol. IPX provides a hierarchical address. It is connectionless, and offers best effort delivery. IPX uses SPX at the Transport Layer to provide end-to-end connectivity and reliability.

iSCSI—iSCSI is Internet SCSI (small computer system interface), an IP-based storage networking standard for linking data storage facilities, developed by the IETF. By carrying SCSI commands over IP networks, iSCSI is used to facilitate data transfers over intranets and to manage storage over long distances.

Java—Java is an interpreted, platform-independent, high-level programming language developed by Sun Microsystems. Java is a powerful language with many features that make it attractive for the Web.

JavaScript—JavaScript is an interpreted, client-side scripting language developed by Netscape. All major browsers offer built-in support for JavaScript, and can interpret blocks of JavaScript code embedded in an HTML page.

Jazz and zip drives—Jazz and zip drives are removable media that allow for high density storage. The only drawback with these drives is that, unlike a floppy drive or CD-ROM, their disk drives are not commonly installed on PC systems.

keepalive—A keepalive is a message sent by one network device to inform another network device that the virtual circuit between the two is still active.

kilobits per second (Kbps)—See bits per second.

Kilohertz (Khz)—See hertz.

laptop—Also called a notebook, a laptop is a smaller, more compact version of a full-sized computer.

latency—Latency is the transmission delay created as a device processes a frame or packet.

Layer 2 switch—A switch is a device that operates at the Data Link Layer of the OSI reference model. A switch can connect LANs or segments of the same media. Because each switch port is considered its own collision domain, a switch dedicates its entire bandwidth to each frame it switches. Switches are also found in Wide Area Networks (WANs): devices such as Frame Relay switches and ATM switches are used to move information from one network to another.

Layer 3 switch—A Layer 3 switch is a high-speed routing device that switches packets. Layer 3 switches provide more efficient processing because they are built with application-specific integrated circuits (ASICs) and offer fewer features than routers.

Layer 2 Tunneling Protocol (L2TP)—L2TP is an extension of the Point-to-Point Tunneling Protocol (PPTP) used by an Internet service provider (ISP) to enable the operation of a virtual private network (VPN) over the Internet. L2TP merges the best features of two other tunneling protocols: PPTP from Microsoft® and Layer 2 Forwarding protocol (L2F) from Cisco Systems®.

leased line—A leased line is a transmission line reserved by a communications carrier for the private use of a customer. It is also called a "dedicated line" or "physical circuit."

least-cost routing (LCR)—In data networks, least-cost routing describes the methods routers use to determine the lowest cost link between networks. Least cost routing makes these determinations based on cost factors such as bandwidth, delay, and cash costs. In voice networks, LCR is a PBX feature that automatically selects the least costly path over which to route a particular call.

light-emitting diode (LED)—An LED is a device that converts electrical signals into light pulses. LEDs are used to generate light for signalling in multimode fiber optic cabling systems.

line—A line is a logical transmission path carried over a physical local loop.

Link Access Procedure Balanced (LAPB or LAP-B)—LAPB is an HDLC protocol subset used primarily in X.25 communications. LAPB is a Data Link Layer protocol that defines how devices access a network using in-band signal and control.

Link Access Procedure for D Channel (LAPD) (or LAP-D)—LAPD is part of the ISDN layered protocol. It is very similar to LAPB. LAPD defines the protocol used on the D channel to interface with the telecommunication's Signal System 7 (SS7) network for setting up calls and other signaling functions.

Link Access Procedure, Frame mode bearer (LAPF)—LAPF is a link access procedure that has characteristics similar to LAPD, but is designed for frame relay services. See frame relay.

Link Aggregation Group (LAG)—LAG refers to multiple lines that are aggregated together to form a link aggregation group, in such a way that the bandwidth can be treated as a single, higher-bandwidth link.

Link Control Protocol (LCP)—LCP is a transmission protocol used by Point-to-Point Protocol (PPP) to set up and test a serial connection.

Link (or line)—A link is a communications path between two or more networked devices. Links are also called "channels," "lines," "circuits," and "paths."

link-state advertisement (LSA)—Link-state advertisements are sent between routers running link-state routing protocols. These are usually in the form of multicast packets, containing neighbor router information, path costs, and informational network updates.

link-state algorithm—Also known as a Dijkstra algorithm, a link-state algorithm allows each router to broadcast or multicast network route cost information concerning its neighbors to every node in the internetwork. Networks using a link-state routing protocol build a topology map that details the status of each link. This dynamic routing method is well suited to large, complex networks that require scalability and more advanced path selection.

load—Load is the amount of traffic found on a particular link or using a router resource.

load balancing—Load balancing is the process used to send data over more than one equal (or nonequal) path through a network. This can greatly increase throughput, as well as provide redundant connections in case of failure.

local area network (LAN)—A LAN is a group of computers networked to share common resources. A LAN is made up of all the end-devices, media, protocols, operating systems, software, and network devices managed within a single area.

local bus—Local bus is a term that usually refers to a fast internal bus that connects devices directly to the CPU.

local exchange carrier (LEC)—A LEC is a company that makes telephone connections to subscribers' homes and businesses, provides telephone services, and collects fees for those services. The terms Central Office (CO), incumbent local exchange carrier (ILEC), and Regional Bell Operations Center (RBOC) are similar terms.

local loop—A local loop is the pair of copper or fiber optic wires that connects a customer's premise to the LEC's switching system.

local loopback address—A local loopback address is an IP address of 127.0.0.1 that is reserved for testing the internal networking components of a device. This address cannot be assigned to a network or host.

Local Management Interface (LMI)—An LMI is a signal process used to manage a connection by identifying the status of the frame relay link. It is also used to maintain the permanent virtual circuit (PVC) using keep-alives sent out on a constant basis. LMI activities were originally included in the CCITT (now the ITU-T) frame relay standards. The "gang of four," including Cisco, DEC, Northern Telecom, and StrataCom, enhanced and added significant components to make LMI interoperable and support various protocols.

logical address—A logical address is a software-assigned or administratively assigned address used to uniquely identify a device or application.

logical circuit—A logical circuit defines the use of the physical media. Using special encoding, signaling, and multiplexing techniques allows the physical circuit to be used for a number of different communication channels. For example, with the right components, a T1 can transmit 24 DS0s. This means that over a two-wire or four-wire physical circuit, 24 separate communication channels are available.

Logical Link Control (LLC)—See 802.2.

logical topology—A logical topology shows the signal transmission path. They eliminate some details to make the important relationships easier to see.

loopback—A loopback is a test to check network access capabilities of the IP protocol and local networking components (NIC and media). See local loopback address.

mainframe—A mainframe is a powerful, large-scale computer system. Mainframes often attach to networks and peripheral devices, such as tape drives, disk drives, and printers.

Management Information Base (MIB)—An MIB is an SNMP database that lists managed objects and all relevant information that can be tracked for each object.

Maximum Transmission Unit (MTU)—An MTU is the maximum amount of data that can be carried by a packet or frame. For example, the MTU of Ethernet is 1,500 bytes.

Media—Media is the Physical Layer, wired or wireless connection used to transmit bits.

Media Access Control (MAC)—MAC is one of the media-specific IEEE 802 standards (802.3, 802.4, and 802.5) that defines the protocol and frame formats. It is the lower sublayer of the Data Link Layer of the OSI model used to transmit frames between NICs.

Media Access Control (MAC) address—A MAC address is used by the Data Link Layer to deliver a frame to the destination node. A MAC address is the 48-bit address burned into a NIC or network device. The MAC address has two parts: 24 bits assigned to the product vendor, and 24 bits to uniquely identify the component itself. Other names include NIC address, hardware address, physical address, Data Link Layer address and burned-in address.

Media Access Control (MAC) address table—A MAC address table is the same as a filter table. It is stored in the CAM of a switch, which holds all learned, permanent, and statically assigned MAC addresses for end nodes, as well as their associated port number.

megabits per second (Mbps)—See bits per second.

megahertz (MHz)—See hertz.

memory—Memory is the internal temporary storage area within a system or device used to hold information for faster access. See DRAM, CAM and NVRAM.

mesh network—A mesh network is a network that consists of multiple physical paths between endpoints. In a fully meshed network, every node is directly connected to every other node. Mesh topology can be found in a WAN.

message—In data communications, a message is the complete unit of information being transmitted from one node to another associated with the upper four layers of the OSI model.

Message Digest 5 (MD5)—MD5 is a one-way hash algorithm that converts a message into a fixed string of digits called a "message digest." It is used to create digital signatures for authentication.

Metric—Metric identifies the value used to measure the distance to another network. This helps the router select the best path to send traffic through, based on the lowest metric. Each protocol has its own metric—for example, hops (the number of routers to pass through), bandwidth (the size or speed of the channel), or tick (the time in one-eighteenths of a second).

metropolitan area networks (MANs)—MANs are formed by connecting LANs in several locations across a city or small region.

microsegmentation—Microsegmentation is the practice of increasing usable bandwidth by subdividing networks into smaller segments and isolating broadcast traffic on shared bandwidth. Switches microsegment a network because every switch port is a separate collision domain.

microwave—A microwave is a high-frequency radio wave. Microwaves are commonly used for wireless transmissions. While broadcast radio stations usually transmit between 535 and 1,605 kHz, cellular phone systems operate in bands of 824 to 849 MHz and 869 to 894 MHz. See hertz.

mini-IOS—Also called "RXBOOT" or "bootloader," a mini-IOS provides only a small subset of the functionality found in the full IOS. It is sometimes necessary, however, to use a mini-IOS when loading a new software image or performing maintenance operations. If the mini-IOS has been loaded, the router prompt changes to Router(boot)>.

modal dispersion—Modal dispersion is an effect that occurs in a fiber optic cable with modes traveling different distances but at the same speed. The spread of the signal increases over time and can cause data errors due to the overlapping of light pulses.

mode—A mode is an independent light signal traveling through an optical fiber.

modem—The term modem is a contraction for modulator/demodulator. Modems are used to convert binary data into analog signals suitable for transmission across an analog local loop.

modem-on-hold (MoH)—MoH is a term that describes software that pops up with a box that lets you place your Internet connection on hold, and take the incoming call, ignore it, or disconnect.

modulation—Modulation is the process of modifying the form of a carrier wave (electrical signal) to enable it to carry intelligent information on a communications medium.

motherboard—Sometimes called the system board or main board, the motherboard is the main circuit board of a system. The motherboard typically contains the processor (or CPU), BIOS (basic input/output system), memory, mass storage interfaces, serial and parallel ports, expansion slots, and all the controllers required to communicate with standard peripheral devices, such as the display screen, mouse, keyboard, and disk drive.

multicast—A multicast is a frame addressed to a specific group of nodes. See Class D address.

multilayer switch—A multilayer switch is a switch that works on more than one layer of the OSI model. A multilayer switch filters and forwards transmissions based on one or more addresses, such as a MAC address or an IP address and/or port number.

multimedia—Multimedia refers to multiple types of media, namely voice (telephony), data (computer files), fax, and video. Some protocols, such as ISDN and ATM, were developed to support multimedia transfer of information. Special handling methods are often used to meet the demands of these different transmission types.

multimode fiber—Multimode fiber is a fiber optic cable thick enough to simultaneously transmit several different optical signals by being reflected at different angles. Multimode fiber is best suited for distances under 2 km. See single-mode fiber.

multiplexer (MUX)—A MUX is a processing technique or electronic equipment that allows multiple signals to travel over a single channel. See frequency division multiplexing, time division multiplexing, and statistical time-division multiplexing.

Multipurpose Internet Mail Extension (MIME)—MIME is an extension of SMTP that supports the exchange of a wide variety of document files by means of an e-mail system.

Multistation Access Unit (MAU)—A MAU is a device used in Token Ring networks to provide connectivity between individual workstations. It is also called a "Token Ring hub."

name resolution—The process used to associate a human-assigned hostname to an IP address used by a computer. It can be performed using a host table or name server.

name server—A name server is a server or software program designed to dynamically associate and return an IP address when a hostname is specified.

NetBIOS Extended User Interface (NetBEUI)—NetBEUI is a Network and Transport Layer protocol designed to work within a single physical LAN to provide recognizable names for hosts and network resources. NetBEUI works in conjunction with NetBIOS and is not routable because it does not have a hierarchically addressing structure.

Network Basic Input/Output System (NetBIOS)—NetBIOS is a software system developed by Sytek and IBM that has become the de facto standard for application interface to LANs. It operates at the Session Layer of the OSI protocol stack. Applications can call NetBIOS routines to carry out functions such as data transfer across a LAN.

NetWare Link Services Protocol (NLSP)—NLSP is a Network Layer protocol with upper-layer components. This Novell proprietary link-state routing protocol uses firsthand information about a network topology to make efficient routing decisions.

network address—A network address identifies the logical address of network segments known to the router. An entry must be kept for each protocol used on the network because the different addresses cannot be used interchangeably.

Network Address Translation (NAT)—NAT is a system that allows an administrator to use private IP addresses within a LAN and a few globally unique IP addresses for Internet connectivity. NAT allows more efficient use of the limited supply of IPv4 addresses.

Network Control Protocol (NCP)—NCP is used by PPP to configure Network Layer protocols that operate over a link. PPP allows multiplexing of more than one protocol onto the same link.

Network File System (NFS)—NFS is a file management system used with TCP/IP and UNIX systems originally developed by SUN Microsystems. NFS can be found on various systems and platforms, especially PC-based platforms that utilize the TCP/IP protocol.

network interface card (NIC)—A NIC is an expansion board inserted into a computer for network connectivity.

network interface unit (NIU)—A NIU is a component that offers connectivity to an ISDN service provider. An NIU is also used to provide connectivity for cable modem Internet connections.

Network Layer—The Network Layer (Layer 3) is the OSI layer that is responsible for providing a hierarchical address, routing packets across a network, and fragmenting different maximum transmission unit (MTU) sizes.

Network Management System (NMS)—An NMS consists of the servers, workstations, and software that enable network monitoring, management, and configuration.

network mask—The network mask is the number of mask bits that correspond to an IP address and define address hierarchy. The mask bits set to binary 1s define the network, while the mask bits set to a binary 0 define the host. See subnet mask.

network operating system (NOS)—NOS is the software that manages server operations and provides services to clients. The NOS manages the interface between the network's underlying transport capabilities and the applications resident on the server.

network termination type 1 (NT1)—An NT1 is an ISDN component that is used to provide connectivity from the customer premise to the ISDN service provider.

node—A node is any device connected to a network. Typically, nodes are thought of as workstations or PCs that have network communication capabilities.

non-routable protocol—A non-routable protocol does not have a hierarchical address or Network Layer implementation. Examples of non-routable protocols include Digital Equipment Corporation's Local Area Transport (DEC-LAT), IBM's Systems Network Architecture (SNA), NetBIOS, and NetBEUI. The router has to bridge these protocols.

nonvolatile random access memory (NVRAM)—NVRAM is the area of memory that maintains its contents even when power is removed from a device. NVRAM stores the running configuration and configuration register used to provide the specific router settings and boot parameters.

octet—See byte.

one-armed-router—Also called a "router on a stick," a one-armed router is a router that routes between VLANs. Traffic enters and leaves the device over the same physical trunk link.

online insertion and removal (OIR)—OIR is a feature that permits the addition, replacement, or removal of cards without interrupting the system power, entering console commands, or causing other software or interfaces to shutdown. See hot-swapping.

Open Shortest Path First (OSPF)—OSPF is an intra-autonomous system routing protocol. OSPF is based on link-state technology and scales well with large, complex networks. Its features include least-cost routing, multipath routing, and load balancing in a vendor-neutral environment.

Open Systems Interconnection (OSI) reference model—The OSI model is a refer ence model standard, developed by the ISO, that includes seven layers. This model is used extensively throughout the industry for vendor interoperability, software development, and an easy way to break a complicated network infrastructure into more understandable pieces.

operating system (OS)—An OS is the basic system software of a computer that provides low-level services to applications.

orthogonal frequency-division multiplexing (OFDM)—OFDM is an FDM modulation technique for transmitting large amounts of digital data over a radio wave. OFDM works by splitting the radio signal into multiple smaller sub-signals that are then transmitted simultaneously at different frequencies to the receiver. OFDM reduces the amount of crosstalk in signal transmissions. 802.11a and 802.11g are wireless LAN technologies that use OFDM.

out-of-band management—Out-of-band management is a network management feature that allows a network device to be accessed "outside" of the network through a terminal directly attached to the device using an RS-232 and console port, or through a modem and an auxiliary port.

out-of-band signaling—Out-of-band signaling is control signaling that takes place over a transmission path separate from the information. Out-of-band signaling can occur simultaneously with a voice conversation or data transmission. An ISDN D channel is a good example of out-of-band signaling.

packet—A packet is a unit of information processed by the Network Layer of the OSI reference model. The packet header contains the logical, Network Layer address of the source and destination nodes.

packet switching—Packet switching occurs at the intermediate nodes as a packet is traveling between the source and destination nodes. When the packet travels through the intermediate node (a packet switch), that node must "switch" the packet to the next node in sequence.

packetization delay—Packetization delay occurs as real-time information (voice, audio, and video) are accumulated in a NIC until there is enough to fill a packet. It is important to balance delay with efficient use of bandwidth.

parallel bus—A parallel bus is an I/O bus that carries multiple bits simultaneously. See bus and serial bus.

parallel port—Also called an LPT port, a parallel port is used mainly to connect printers. Parallel ports are also used to provide a security lock (called a "dongle") for certain software packages. Parallel ports send eight bits simultaneously.

Password Authentication Protocol (PAP)—PAP is a method used to identify and authenticate Point-to-Point Protocol (PPP) peers.

patch cable—Also called a patch cord, a patch cable is a UTP cable with RJ-45 connectors at both ends, designed to connect a computer's NIC to a port of a hub or switch. See crossover cable and straight-through cable.

path—A path is a route between any two transmission points.

PCI—See Peripheral Component Interconnect.

peer—In networking terms, a peer is a device or process in one computer that has the same intelligence and functionality as a device or process in another computer.

peer-to-peer—Peer-to-peer is a term that describes two programs or processes that use the same protocol to communicate and perform approximately the same function for their respective nodes. Ten or fewer PCs can create a peer-to-peer network for file and resource sharing.

peripheral—A peripheral is an internal or external component that offers a specific functionality. Peripherals can include various storage media, modems, printers, scanners, fax capabilities, and so forth.

Peripheral Component Interconnect (PCI)—PCI is a local bus that provides a high-speed connection between peripherals and a CPU. It includes buffers that allow relatively slow peripherals to operate asynchronously and can be used with other buses such as ISA or EISA.

permanent virtual circuit (PVC)—A PVC is a connection across a frame relay network, or cell-switching network such as ATM. A PVC behaves like a dedicated line between source and destination end-points and is always available for transmissions.

Personal Computer Memory Card International Association (PCMCIA)—The PCMCIA slot in a laptop was designed for PC memory expansion. NICs and modems can also attach to a laptop through the PCMCIA slot.

photodiode—A photodiode is a semiconductor device that converts light into electrical signals.

physical circuit—A physical circuit is the hardware and cabling used to connect devices together.

Physical Layer—The Physical Layer is the lowest layer in the OSI reference model and is responsible for transmitting bits across the communications media.

physical topology—Physical topologies show more details about a network's connectors, cabling, and wide area links.

PING (Packet Internet Groper)—PING is a command that determines connectivity up to the Network Layer. It uses ICMP echo request and echo reply messages to determine whether communication is possible.

ping of death—A ping of death is a denial of service attack that sends numerous packets exceeding the IP maximum packet size, causing the receiving system to crash, reboot, or otherwise shut down.

plain old telephone service (POTS)—POTS is a term used to describe the analog telephone network.

Plug-and-Play (PnP)—PnP is a standard that gives computers the ability to automatically recognize a newly installed device without a complex process of user configuration.

point of presence (POP)—The POP is a location where a service provider makes a connection to the PSTN or an ISP makes a connection to the Internet backbone. It may be co-located, meaning that it is a shared connection of equipment at the subscriber's location.

Point-to-Point Protocol (PPP)—PPP allows a computer to transmit one or more Network Layer protocols over a point-to-point link. It supersedes SLIP for dial-up Internet connections. PPP is a vendor-neutral encapsulation method that operates at the Data Link Layer of the OSI model and offers mutiprotocol support and authentication (PAP or CHAP).

Point-to-Point Tunneling Protocol (PPTP)—PPTP was developed by Microsoft for virtual private networks (VPNs) using Microsoft Windows and Linux/Unix based systems. PPTP can support tunneling of IP,

IPX, and NetBios/NetBEUI protocols inside IP packets.

port—A port is a physical interface in a device, such as a port on a switch or router. A port is also a software number used to identify a software process or application function.

port address translation (PAT)—PAT is a network address translation method that reuses or "overloads" a single or a few public IP addresses for access to the Internet. The original source IP address, as well as the TCP or UDP source ports, are used to identify a transmission.

portability—Portability is the ability of software to run on more than one type of computer or operating system.

Post Office Protocol version 3 (POP3)—POP3 is the latest iteration of the POP protocol. POP is an e-mail service implemented on TCP Port 110 that provides clients access to a mail drop or post office in which their messages are stored.

Power supply—Power supply provides proper power voltages to all internal components. It does not shield power or protect the system from power surges or drops.

power-on self test (POST)—A POST is the process a device initiates upon startup to check physical components.

preamble—A preamble is the information that is used to synchronize computers attached to a communications network. For example, each Ethernet frame transmitted in an Ethernet LAN contains a preamble 56 bits long (7 bytes) that is used to synchronize NIC cards so that information is received correctly.

Presentation Layer—The Presentation Layer is the sixth layer of the OSI model and handles the representation, encryption, and compression of transmissions.

Primary Rate Interface Integrated Services Digital Network (ISDN-PRI)—ISDN-PRI is a version of ISDN that is associated with a T1 service. ISDN is a digital multiplexing technology that can transmit voice, data, and video simultaneously over a single local loop. See ISDN.

private address—A private address is an address set aside for internal use only (it cannot be used on the Internet). Private addresses defined in RFC 1918 include 10.X.X.X, 172.16.X.X - 172.31.X.X and 192.168.X.X.

private branch exchange (PBX)—A PBX or network branch exchange (NBX) is a sophisticated business telephone system. Today, PBXs are being updated to open-standards voice, communication, or media servers that offer traditional, as well as IP-based telephony services.

privileged EXEC mode—Privileged EXEC mode is the command line interface (CLI) execution mode that allows an administrator to perform many key functions, such as viewing the existing device settings, and providing access to the full range of configuration options on a switch or router.

processing latency—Processing latency is the processing time of a packet through a switch.

Programmable read-only memory (PROM)—A PROM is a memory chip on which you can store a program. After the PROM has been programmed, you cannot wipe it clean and reprogram it.

propagation—Also known as propagation delay, propagation is the amount of time it takes a signal or packet to travel across a circuit from the transmitter to the receiver. Propagation is most often used to measure the transmission delay found in wireless transmissions, such as satellite.

protocol—A protocol is a defined method of communicating between computers or computer applications.

protocol converter—See gateway.

protocol data unit (PDU)—PDU is the name give to a unit of information at each layer of the OSI model as headers and a trailer are added during the encapsulation process and removed in decapsulation.

protocol number—A protocol number identifies the correct Transport Layer protocol requested. For example, the number 6 is used for TCP, whereas the number 17 is used for UDP.

protocol stack—A protocol stack contains a suite of dependent components used to provide specific functions and transmit information between communication devices. A number of protocol stacks are defined from layer 3 to 7; IP and IPX are two examples.

Proxy Address Resolution Protocol (ARP)—Proxy ARP is a variation of the ARP protocol, where an intermediate device, such as a router, sends an ARP response to the requesting host on behalf of the end node.

proxy server—A proxy server is a "middleman" process, often used as a firewall, that does not permit direct packet communication between an external and internal network. A proxy server reads the content of the upper three layers to make filtering and forwarding decisions.

public-key encryption—Public-key encryption is a cryptographic system that uses two mathematically related keys: one key is used to encrypt a message, and the other to decrypt it. Systems that need to receive encrypted messages distribute their public keys, but keep their private keys secret.

public-switched telephone network (PSTN)—The PSTN is the worldwide voice telephone network.

Pulse Code Modulation (PCM)—PCM is a method of converting an analog voice signal to a digital signal that can be translated accurately back into a voice signal after transmission. A codec samples the voice signal 8,000 times per second, then converts each sample to a binary number that expresses the amplitude and frequency in a digital form. The receiving codec reverses the process, using the stream of binary digits to re-create the original analog voice waveform.

quality of service (QoS)—QoS defines the type of service a communications link can provide to a specific information type. QoS often specifies factors such as priority, delay, throughput, and reliability. QoS is the ability to identify and provide specialized handling to various traffic types.

radio frequency (RF)—RF is any frequency within the electromagnetic spectrum normally associated with radio wave propagation. These frequencies fall into a spectrum range from 3 KHz to over 300 GHz.

radio frequency interference (RFI)—A decrease in signal strength or quality caused by two or more devices using the same electromagnetic radio frequency.

radio frequency spectrum—The radio frequency spectrum is composed of wavelengths that are longer than visible light used for wireless transmissions like infrared, microwaves, and radio.

Random Access Memory (RAM)—RAM is a systems's main working memory used to hold instructions and data during processing. This type of memory is both changeable and volatile. Applications can repeatedly write new data to the same RAM; however, all data is erased from RAM when a system loses power or shuts down. See DRAM, NVRAM, and memory.

read-only memory (ROM)—ROM is memory that is not written to or reconfigured in any way. A router uses ROM to store the microcode necessary for programs, such as POST, bootstrap loader, the mini-IOS, and ROMMON.

redundancy—Redundancy is the equipment and/or actions necessary to restore information, connections, or device functionality during or shortly after a failure.

Remote Monitoring (RMON)—RMON is a protocol that gathers network information at a central workstation. RMON defines additional MIBs with more detailed information about network usage and status than MIBs defined by SNMP.

remote procedure call (RPC)—RPC is a call made by a software program for services across a network connection, usually to a server.

repeater—A repeater is a Physical Layer device that connects one cable segment of a LAN to another, possibly connecting two different media types. The repeater regenerates and boosts electrical signals, to extend the distance of a network cable segment.

Request for Comment (RFC)—An RFC is one of the working documents of the Internet Engineering Task Force research and development community. A document in this series may be on essentially any topic related to computer communication, from a meeting report to the specification of a standard.

Reverse Address Resolution Protocol (RARP)—RARP is an IP-based Network Layer function that is used to obtain an IP address when a MAC address is known.

ring—A ring is the physical network topology that connects all end devices to a signal wire attached at both ends to form a ring. See Token Ring.

RJ-11—Also called "silver strand," RJ-11 is the typical cable used for connecting a telephone to a wall jack. It has a smaller clip than an RJ-45 and uses pins 3 and 4. This cable and connector type are typically used for voice communications and xDSL connections.

RJ-45—An RJ-45 connector is a snap-in connector for UTP cable, which allows eight wires and four pairs to be terminated. RJ-45 connectors are commonly used for most LAN implementations.

RJ-48—An RJ-48 uses a clear plastic clip similar to an RJ-45. However, the cable is shielded twisted pair, heavier gauge wire, and uses pins 1, 2, 7, and 8 for transmission. It can be used with some T1, Fractional T1, BRI, and subrate facilities.

rollover cable—A rollover cable is used to make a console connect a terminal or computer with a switch or router for configuration. This is a special cable with RJ-45 connectors on both ends. The pinout is the complete reverse on each side using the following pins: 1-8, 2-7, 3-6, 4-5, 5-4, 6-3, 7-2, and 8-1.

routable protocol (routed protocol)—Also called a routed protocol, a routable protocol supports Network Layer routing. To be routable, a protocol must have a hierarchical address. IP and IPX are both routable protocols found in a LAN.

route once, switch many—A Layer 3 switch is more sophisticated in its method for sending packets through the network. When the first packet is received, the layer 3 switch determines the best path for transmission (route once), for all additional segments going to the same destination, the switch predicts that the original path should remain the same. Therefore instead of make a path selection for each packet, it simply switches them to the destination. This route once (for the first transmission) and switch many (all additional transmissions to the same destination) greatly reduces processing requirements and improves performance.

router—A router is a Layer 3 device that reads the hierarchical address in a packet header, reviews its routing table, and makes best path selections based on a specific metric value. A router is designed to segment broadcast domains, provide security, and isolate traffic. A router can also function as a gateway for providing access to another network, or it can perform protocol translation services. Routers are used when connecting to the Internet or other WAN links.

router-on-a-stick—See one-armed-router.

Routing Information Protocol (RIP)—RIP is a distance-vector routing protocol supported by TCP/IP and Novell networks, designed for use within small networks. IP RIP uses a hop count for a metric, and tick/hop for IPX RIP. RIP allows a maximum of 15 hops.

routing loop—A routing loop is a problem created by a real or perceived circular reference within a network. Routers are susceptible to routing loops when using a distance-vector routing protocol, such as RIP. Fortunately, several mechanisms have been put in place to prevent routing loops.

routing protocol—A routing protocol is used by Network Layer devices to exchange network addresses, path, metric, or reachability information. They are necessary for routers to dynamically learn routes and make best path selections.

routing table—A routing table is information stored in router memory. At a minimum, the information includes the network address, egress interface, next hop address, and metric value for all reachable networks.

runt frame—A runt frame is an Ethernet frame that is smaller than the minimum frame size of 64 bytes.

RXBOOT—See mini-IOS.

satellite communications systems—Satellite communications systems transmit signals from earth stations to satellites located in space. Antennas located on earth (ground stations) are pointed at a satellite to transmit and/or receive information.

SC connector—An SC connector is a standard connector that clicks into place to connection fiber optic cable. The two-fiber connectors are also called "FDDI connectors." See ST connector.

Secure Multipurpose Internet Mail Extension (S/MIME)—S/MIME is a MIME version that supports message and attachment encryption using public-key encryption technology. This ensures that e-mail is sent and received in a manner that is secure from interception and tampering.

segment—A segment is broken from a larger transmission by TCP to allow data transmissions within the maximum transmission unit (MTU). The term segment can also be used to define a broadcast domain that has been separated from the rest of the network to form a section or subnet. The term segment also describes a length of cable that is less than or equal to the cable's distance limitation.

sequence number—Sequence number is the number assigned to each data segment by TCP to make sure that the segments are properly acknowledged and reassembled in the correct order.

Sequenced Packet Exchange (SPX)—SPX is the Transport Layer protocol concerned with connection-oriented services, such as sequencing packets and guaranteeing their delivery. SPX provides reliability for IPX communications.

serial—The term serial describes the transmission of bits one at a time, which allows the transmission to be sent greater distances. WAN communications typically use serial transmissions.

serial bus—A serial bus is an I/O bus that carries one bit at a time. See bus and parallel bus.

serial converter—A serial converter is a connector that converts an RJ-45 UTP cable connector to a DB-9 or DB-15 connector that plugs into a COM port.

Serial Line Internet Protocol (SLIP)—SLIP is not an official Internet standard, but a de facto standard included in many implementations of TCP/IP for dial-up connections to the Internet. It does not provide a high-level authentication method and can only transit IP. PPP has replaced SLIP.

Serial port—See communication (COM) port.

server—A server is any program that provides a service to a client program. This term is often used to refer to the computer that hosts the server program. See client/server.

server farm—A server farm is a collection of departmental servers placed in a data center, where they can be provided with consolidated backup, uninterrupted power supply, and a proper operating environment.

service access point (SAP)—SAP is the LLC header field that identifies the Network Layer Protocol stack.

Session Layer—The Session Layer is the fifth layer of the OSI model; it provides the higher layers with services to keep multiple transmissions separate, including establishing a session (separately from a connection), conducting dialogs (prevent both parties from transmitting data at the same time), managing activities (divide the session into parts), and ending the session gracefully (terminating the session).

shielded twisted pair (STP)—STP is a type of copper wiring used for some computer network transmissions. A twisted pair consists of copper wires, twisted around each other to cancel crosstalk. A flexible metal sheath encloses the wires to provide additional protection from EMI and RFI.

Signaling System 7 (SS7)—SS7 is an out-of-band system that exchanges control signals and call routing information between CO switches.

Simple Mail Transfer Protocol (SMTP)—SMTP is an Application Layer protocol used to send e-mail from a client to a mail server, and for transferring e-mail between mail servers across a TCP/IP network.

Simple Network Management Protocol (SNMP)—SNMP is a TCP/IP Application Layer protocol used to send and receive information about the status of network resources. Network management, by means of SNMP, consists of several elements that work together, including a management console, management information base (MIBs) and agents.

simplex—Simplex transmission refers to the process of transmitting data in only one direction. See duplex.

single-mode fiber—Single-mode fiber is a thin fiber optic cable that can transmit only one optical signal. Single-mode fiber can typically transmit farther than multimode because there is less refraction, a laser light source, and only one signal that eliminates interference. See multimode fiber.

sliding window—The term windowing is also referred to as a sliding window. Windowing provides a method for protocols such as TCP to control the flow of data.

software—Software is a set of computer programs, procedures, and associated documentation concerned with the operation of a data processing system—for example, compilers, library routines, manuals, and circuit diagrams. Software is also information (generally copyrightable) that may provide instructions for computers; data for documentation; and voice, video, and music for entertainment or education.

source address—A source address ia a physical or logical address that identifies the sending device or process. See destination address.

source quench—An ICMP source quench message tells a sending host that the buffers of the receiving host are full, and that it should temporarily suspend transmission. This flow-control process helps eliminate dropped packets.

Spanning Tree Algorithm (STA)—Also called Spanning Tree Protocol (STP), STA is a bridging algorithm that avoids active loops (multiple paths between nodes that could create infinite loop transmission patterns). If multiple paths exist between a bridge and a destination, the algorithm requires the bridge to use only one connection. If the connection fails, the algorithm activates an alternate or backup connection. See 802.1D and active loop.

Spread Spectrum—Spread spectrum is a technique that scatters a signal over a broad range of frequencies, using a low level of power for each individual frequency. Frequency hopping spread spectrum and direct sequence spread spectrum are two varieties of wireless transmission methods.

SQL—Structured Query Language. SQL is a standardized language used to retrieve data from a database.

ST connector—An ST—or straight tip—connector is a bayonet-style connector that uses a push-and-twist motion to attach one multimode or single mode fiber. See SC connector.

star—Star is the most common physical network topology. In a star topology, end devices are connected to a central device, such as a hub or switch. When a computer sends information to another computer, it is transmitted through the central device.

star ring—A star ring topology combines a physical star configuration with a logical ring for information flow. In a star ring topology, wires run from each node to a central ring wiring concentrator, also called a "multistation access unit (MAU)."

static route—A static route is a path defined by an administrator using commands in a router's global configuration mode. The network number and next-hop router are manually defined. Updates or changes require additional configuration and are not dynamic.

Statistical Time-Division Multiplexing (STDM)—STDM is a more flexible method of TDM. A statistical multiplexer analyzes transmission patterns to predict "gaps" in a channel's traffic that can be temporarily filled with part of the traffic from another channel.

step-index multimode fiber—Fiber optic step-index fiber consists of only two transparent layers (core and cladding) and cannot compensate for the multimode signal dispersion effect.

storage area network (SAN)—SANs connect storage devices (machines that contain large disk media) to all servers and clients that need access to files and applications. The storage devices can be accessed from a LAN, CAN, MAN, WAN, or VPN.

store-and-forward switching—The store-and-forward switching method involves receiving an entire frame into a switch, performing a CRC, and, upon successful completion, forwarding the frame toward its destination. Although it is slower than other switching methods, it is the most reliable because it blocks the propagation of errors onto a network.

straight-through cable—A straight-through cable is used to connect two dissimilar devices (for example, a PC with a switch) or two similar devices when an X port is being used on one device.

stub network—A stub network is a network that provides only one way in or out. A default route identifies the neighboring device used to leave the stub network.

subinterface—A subinterface is one of a number of virtual interfaces on a single physical interface. The command prompt is displayed as (config-subif)#.

subnet—A subnet is a subdivision of a network, in which users are grouped logically based on their workgroup location, resource requirements, network connectivity, and network address. Subnets are formed by routers, layer 3 switches or logically with VLANs; therefore, each subnet is a separate broadcast domain.

subnet address—A subnet address is an IP address that represents a network and subnetwork. The host portion of the address is represented with binary 0s.

subnet mask—A subnet mask is an address mask or bit mask used to define the hierarchy by masking bits from an IP address to subdivide a network. The mask is 32 bits long, and defines the network and subnet portion using all binary 1s. The host portion is represented with all binary 0s.

subnetting—Subnetting is the process of creating subdivisions of a network by connecting network segments to routers, layer 3 switches, or VLANs, and assigning the appropriate subnet mask and IP address(es). The process of calculating a subnet mask is also called subnetting.

subnetwork—See subnet.

Subnetwork Access Protocol (SNAP)—SNAP is an LLC header extension. It consists of 5 bytes of data: the first 3 bytes refer to the protocol, and the last 2 bytes refer to the Ethertype.

switch—A switch is a device that operates at the Data Link Layer of the OSI reference model. A switch can connect LANs or segments of the same media type. A switch dedicates its entire bandwidth to each frame it switches. Switches are also found in Wide Area Networks (WANs), as devices such as frame relay switches and ATM switches are used to move information from one network to another.

Switched Multimegabit Data Service (SMDS)—SMDS is a cell-oriented connectionless service found most often in MAN environments with rates up to 45 Mbps. SMDS is referenced in the IEEE 802.6 specification.

Switched Virtual Circuit (SVC)—An SVC is a temporary connection established through a switched network. During data transmission, an SVC behaves like a wire between the sender and receiver. ATM VCs and telephone connections are both examples of SVCs.

Symmetric Digital Subscriber Line (SDSL)—SDSL is DSL technology that supports symmetric upstream and downstream data rates over standard POTS lines.

synchronous transmissions—Synchronous transmissions are controlled by a microprocessor clock, so that signals are permitted to start and stop at particular times. To use synchronous communication, the clock settings of the sending and receiving systems must match.

Synchronous Data Link Control (SDLC)—SDLC is the foundation of the HDLC standard. It is the Data Link Layer protocol most often found in SNA networks.

Synchronous Digital Hierarchy (SDH)—SDH is an international standard for synchronous data transmission over fiber optic cables; SONET is the U.S. implementation. The standard SDH transmission rate, called STM-1, is 155.52 Mbps. This is equivalent to SONET's OC-3.

Synchronous Optical Network (SONET)—SONET is an optical transmission standard that defines a signal hierarchy. The basic building block is the STS-1 51.84-Mbps signal, chosen to accommodate a T3 signal. The STS designation refers to the interface for electrical signals. The optical signal standards are correspondingly designated OC-1, OC-2, and so forth.

Synchronous Transport Signal level 1 (STS-1)—See SONET.

Systems Network Architecture (SNA)—SNA is IBM's architecture for computer networking between terminals, mainframes, and peripherals.

T1—T1 is one of the T-carrier telecommunication standards for multiplexing digitized voice signals. The total bandwidth of a T1 with timing overhead is 1.544 Mbps. A T1 has 24 - 64 Kbps channels that are used for transmitting digital voice, video, or data.

Tape drives—Tape drives are used as backup media or off-line storage because they are not particularly fast access methods. Tape capacity is variable.

tap—Tap is the point at which a device connects to the bus.

T-carrier—The T-carrier system is a hierarchical system for multiplexing digitized voice signals. The first T-carrier was installed in 1962 by the Bell System. The T-carrier family of systems now includes T1, T1C, T1D, T2, T3, and T4 (and their European counterparts E1, E2, etc.). The letter "T" in the name stands for terrestrial since they are land-based connections, as opposed to microwave or otherwise wireless.

Telnet—Telnet is an upper-layer application component of IP that provides terminal emulation capabilities. Telnet is used to make a connection to a router or switch for access and configuration purposes.

terminal emulation—A terminal emulation program allows a local computer to connect to a remote computer and appear to be logged on to the remote computer locally using a command line interface. Terminal emulation programs are often used to access mainframe computers. See Telnet.

terminator—A terminator is an electrical resistor that absorbs an electrical pulse when it reaches the end of a coaxial bus cable segment. If a terminator is not installed, a signal will reflect back down the bus cable, causing a network outage.

three-way handshake—A three-way handshake is the synchronize request, connection negotiation, and acknowledgment process that occurs in a connection-oriented protocol.

throughput—Throughput describes the overall capacity of a network to perform useful work. While bandwidth measurements focus on the raw number of bits a network can carry, throughput measurements express the actual or effective data rates of a network. Throughput is most often used to describe the overall performance of a network; it is measured in packets per second (PPS) or bits per second (bps).

tick—Tick is transmission time calculated to 1/18th of a second. It is combined with hop count for IPX RIP.

Time-Division Multiplexing (TDM)—TDM is a multiplexing technology that guarantees each transmission a fixed amount of bandwidth on a rotating basis. TDM is suited to constant-bit-rate traffic. It is a way for many slow communications channels to "timeshare" a very fast channel.

time-to-live (TTL)—A TTL is a number assigned to each IP packet that indicates how long it can travel on a network. If the TTL has expired, an ICMP time expired message will be returned to the sender and the packet will be dropped. This prevents packets from circling a network indefinitely if they cannot be delivered.

tip and ring circuit—A tip and ring circuit is an analog voice line, or POTS.

Token Ring—Token Ring is the IEEE 802.5 specified, ring-based, token-passing LAN topology. Each node on the ring acts as a repeater, passing the token from node to node as the token travels around the entire ring. Each node must wait its turn to transmit data and may only transmit when it controls the token.

toll network—The toll network or public switched network is a series of toll offices that house high-end switches tied together with trunk lines. The toll network provides an end-to-end connection from source to destination. A cloud represents the toll network in most WAN diagrams.

topology—Topology refers to the specific physical configuration of a network or a portion of a network. Ring and star are examples of different physical network topologies.

trace—A trace is information captured by a protocol analysis tool to display network activity.

traceroute—Traceroute is a process that uses ICMP Time expired (TTL) error messages to return every routing device in a path from a sender to a receiver. This tool can be very helpful to identify the entire path through a network.

tracert—Tracert is the command used to perform a traceroute process.

traffic—Traffic refers to the amount of information traveling across a network. It includes both user data and network-related information.

traffic isolation—Traffic isolation is the process of dividing a network into smaller sections to improve overall network performance. Devices such as bridges and switches provide separate collision domains. Routers, Layer 3 switches, and VLANs on a Layer 2 switch provide separate broadcast domains.

trailer—A trailer is the last part of a data frame that carries the error control information. The error control information usually comes in the form of a cyclical redundancy check (CRC) or frame check sequence (FCS).

transceiver—A transceiver is a device that transmits and receives signals from one media type to another. It is considered a Physical Layer gateway because it is converting the physical cable type.

Transmission Control Protocol (TCP)—TCP is the Transport Layer protocol that provides reliable, connection-oriented transmission services.

Transport Layer—The Transport Layer is the fourth layer in the OSI model and is concerned with controlling the end-to-end transport of messages in a network.

Trivial File Transfer Protocol (TFTP)—TFTP is a stripped-down version of FTP that simply allows files to be sent and received without authenticating. It is often used to update firmware and to backup and restore configuration files and operating systems.

trunk—A trunk is a high-speed cabled connection that connects two switches together.

tunneling—Tunneling is the process of encapsulating one network protocol within the packets of another. For example, tunneling can be used to encapsulate various network protocols within IP packets for transmission across the Internet. Tunneling is also used to describe the process of creating a virtual private network (VPN) connection through the Internet from a client into another network. See VPN.

twisted pair—See UTP.

Type of Service (ToS)—ToS is a field in the IP header used to identify and define priority for packets. Additional bits can be combined with the ToS field to provide quality of service (QoS) routing.

unbounded media—Unbounded media denotes all wireless network transmissions.

unicast—A unicast is a transmission sent to a single network address. See broadcast and multicast.

Universal Access Server—A Universal Access Server is a Cisco server that handles voice, fax, data, security, routing, gateway, and wireless communications.

Universal Resource Locator (URL)—A URL is an Internet address used to locate resources from within a Web browser. The naming convention can also be used to identify many network resources.

Universal Serial Bus (USB)—USB is an external bus that can transfer up to 12 Mbps and connect various peripheral devices.

unshielded twisted pair (UTP)—UTP is the most common type of cabling and is used extensively in telephone networks and data communication networks. UTP is categorized to define frequency, and maximum transmission rate. UTP cables can transmit a signal up to 100 m.

User Datagram Protocol (UDP)—UDP is a Transport Layer protocol that provides a connectionless, unreliable datagram delivery.

user EXEC mode—User EXEC mode is the execution mode that allows only basic commands for displaying information about a device. No configuration or high-level access is available in this mode. See Privileged EXEC mode.

V.22bis—V.22bis is the original international modem standard that provided for simultaneous transmit and receive capabilities (full-duplex). This standard provides 2,400 bps at 600 baud.

V.24—V.24 is the ITU standard for DTE to DCE cable connections.

V.32—V.32 is the ITU-T standard serial line protocol for bidirectional data transmissions at speeds of 4.8 or 9.6 Kbps.

V.32bis—V.32bis is the ITU-T standard that extends V.32 to speeds up to 14.4 Kbps. See V.32.

V.34—V.34 is the ITU-T standard that specifies a serial line protocol. V.34 offers improvements to the V.32 standard, including higher transmission rates (28.8 Kbps) and enhanced data compression.

V.35—V.35 is the DB-34 pin serial connection created by the ITU and often used with T1 lines.

V.42bis—V.42bis is the ITU-T standard that is a group of protocols that provide error correction by allowing the receiving device to request retransmission of corrupted data.

V.90—V.90 is the standard for full-duplex modems for data communication across telephone lines at up to 56 Kbps downstream. The V.90 standard specifies that there may only be one analog-to-digital conversion in the path between a carrier and modem. The upstream data transmission is limited to approximately 35 Kbps.

V.92 with V.44—ITU has introduced a new modem standard that offers 56 Kbps downstream and 48 Kbps upstream. It allows for both asynchronous and synchronous communications.

variable bit rate (VBR)—VBR is the opposite of constant bit rate. In other words, the amount of information varies over time. ATM networks, for example, were designed to accommodate VBRs based on the needs of the application.

variable-length subnet mask (VLSM)—VLSMs are a mechanism for providing subnets of different sizes within a single network. A routing protocol must exchange subnet mask information in addition to the network address to support VSLM.

video display—Video display is a monitor's image, the type and quality of which are determined both by the monitor itself and by a circuit board called a "video adapter," "video card," or "graphics adapter." The monitor plugs into the video adapter or video port, which generates the signals that produce visible images.

virtual channel (VC)—A VC refers to all ATM cells that form a single transmission from a source to a destination.

virtual channel identifier (VCI)—A VCI is a value in an ATM cell header that uniquely identifies one ATM VC. Each VC is one data transmission from a source node to a destination node.

virtual circuit—A virtual circuit is a communication path that appears to be a single circuit to the sending and receiving devices, even though the data may take varying routes between the source and destination nodes. See permanent virtual circuit and switched virtual circuit.

virtual local area network (VLAN)—A VLAN is a switching technology that allows Layer 2 switches to break broadcast domains in subnets, provide security, and allow for a more flexible and scalable network configuration. Traffic for devices within a VLAN are separate from other traffic on the switch. Network changes are performed through software configurations instead of physically recabling a connection.

virtual path identifier (VPI)—A VPI is a value in an ATM cell header that identifies the ATM virtual path from the source to the destination network.

virtual private network (VPN)—A VPN is a connection over a shared network that behaves like a dedicated link. VPNs are created using a technique called "tunneling," which transmits data packets across a public network, such as the Internet, another commercially available network, or in a private "tunnel" that simulates a point-to-point connection. The tunnels of a VPN can be encrypted for additional security.

virtual terminal—See terminal emulation and telnet.

VLAN Membership Policy Server (VMPS)—A VMPS is a high-end Catalyst switch or an external server that holds a database that contains a map matching MAC addresses to VLAN membership. Switches can use this mapping to make dynamic VLAN assignments.

Voice over IP (VoIP)—VoIP is a technology that consists of telephone signals transmitted as IP packets.

WAN interface card (WIC)—A WIC connects the system to the WAN link service provider.

wavelength—Wavelength is the distance between one crest of a wave and the next. Light wavelengths are measured in nanometers (nm), or billionths of a meter. Each nanometer is 10-9 meter.

wavelength-division multiplexing (WDM)—WDM is the bandwidth available within a standard single-mode optical fiber is 25000 GHz. WDM systems get around this limitation by using multiple frequency or wavelength channels in this bandwidth. The channels are spaced typically 1 nm apart in wavelength (120 GHz apart in frequency). Each channel can be used to transmit data at the few Gb/s afforded by electronic speeds, allowing realization of networks with extremely large capacities.

Web server—A Web server is a software application (or suite of applications) that allows an Internet host computer to respond to requests for Web pages, forward e-mail, and perform other HTTP services.

well-known ports—Well-known ports are the preassigned logical addresses assigned for specific use by Transport Layer protocols to identify the upper layer applications or services. There are 1024 well-known port numbers assigned. Some applications do not use well-known port numbers, but instead select from a number above 1024.

wide area network (WAN)—WANs essentially interconnect LANs or MANs. A WAN connection uses point-to-point, leased lines, service provider links, dial-up or tunneled connections across a wide geographic area.

window—A window is the number of transmissions in bytes that a sending host may transmit before an acknowledgment is expected from the destination device. A window mechanism provides for efficient transmission by allowing TCP to send multiple segments without individually acknowledging each one.

Windows Internet Naming Service (WINS)—WINS is a Microsoft client/server application that resolves network computer host names (NETBios names) to IP addresses.

wire speed—The term wire speed refers to transmission that is not slowed down by the processing of an internetworking device. Switches are considered wire-speed devices.

wireless NIC—A wireless NIC is a network interface card that allows devices such as laptops, mobile phones, and PDAs access to a wireless network.

wiring closet—A wiring closet is a centralized (often secure) location where cable segments are terminated in patch panels, and then connected to networking devices.

workgroup—A workgroup is a group of users sharing common files and network resources.

World Wide Web (Web)—The Web is the global collection of servers that store and respond to requests for hypertext documents (Web pages) made available for public access by means of the Internet. To retrieve Web pages, a user must have a browser application.

X.21—X.21 is a DB-37 pin serial connection used for both DCE and DTE connections. This connector is mainly found in Europe and Japan.

X.25—X.25 is a connection-oriented packet-switching network, typically built upon leased lines from public telephone networks. In the United States, X.25 is offered by most carriers. The X.25 interface lies at OSI Layer 3, rather than Layer 1. X.25 defines its own three-layer protocol stack, and provides data rates only up to 56 Kbps.

xDSL—xDSL is a group term used to refer to the various types of DSL service. See DSL, ADSL and SDSL.

INDEX

Numerics

A

B

C

D

E

G

H

I

J

K

L

M

N

O

P

R

S

T

W

X

Z

Notes

Overall Course Evaluation Survey

Congratulations on completing this course! We hope you enjoyed your learning journey.

This survey will help us identify where we can focus our strengths and improve our weaknesses. As a token of our appreciation for your time in completing this survey, we will send you a Certificate of Appreciation (if you tell us who you are!).

CCNA, Introduction to Cisco Networking Technologies

Course # (see book cover): ____________________

Location of course: ____________________

Instructor-led ☐ Self-paced ☐

Did you use the CD? Yes ☐ No ☐ Comments: ____________________

Did you access the online course? Yes ☐ No ☐ Comments: ____________________

Did you use the Web board for support? Yes ☐ No ☐ Comments: ____________________

Did you visit the student Web site? Yes ☐ No ☐ Comments: ____________________

What are this course's strengths?

What did you like best? ____________________

What are this course's weaknesses? ____________________

What did you like least? ____________________

Would you be interested in other titles from this publisher? ____________________

If so, what specific topics would you like to see addressed? ____________________

Optional (must provide this information if you would like a Certificate of Appreciation):

Name: ____________________

Occupation/Title: ____________________

Company: ____________________

Address: ____________________

City/State/ZIP: ____________________

Country (if outside USA): ____________________

E-mail address: ____________________

Gender: Male ☐ Female ☐

Age: Under 25 ☐ 26-40 ☐ 41-60 ☐ 61+ ☐

Please return this survey to: WestNet Learning Technologies, Attn: Executive Vice President, 5420 Ward Rd., Suite 150, Arvada, CO 80002 USA

Or fax to: 303-432-2565

NO POSTAGE
NECESSARY
IF MAILED
IN THE
UNITED STATES

BUSINESS REPLY MAIL

BULK RATE MAIL PERMIT NO. 83 ARVADA CO

POSTAGE WILL BE PAID BY ADDRESSEE

WESTNET
LEARNING TECHNOLOGIES

5420 WARD ROAD STE 150
ARVADA CO 80002-9929